Even More Excellent

HTML with XML, XHTML and JavaScript

Timothy T. Gottleber

North Lake College

Irving, Texas

Timothy N. Trainor

Muskegon Community College

Muskegon, Michigan

 McGraw-Hill
Irwin

Boston   Burr Ridge, IL   Dubuque, IA   Madison, WI   New York   San Francisco   St. Louis
Bangkok   Bogotá   Caracas   Kuala Lumpur   Lisbon   London   Madrid   Mexico City
Milan   Montreal   New Delhi   Santiago   Seoul   Singapore   Sydney   Taipei   Toronto

McGraw-Hill Higher Education

A Division of The **McGraw-Hill** *Companies*

EVEN MORE EXCELLENT HTML WITH XML, XHTML, AND JAVASCRIPT

Published by McGraw-Hill/Irwin, a business unit of The McGraw-Hill Companies, Inc., 1221 Avenue of the Americas, New York, NY, 10020. Copyright © 2003, by The McGraw-Hill Companies, Inc. All rights reserved. No part of this publication may be reproduced or distributed in any form or by any means, or stored in a database or retrieval system, without the prior written consent of The McGraw-Hill Companies, Inc., including, but not limited to, in any network or other electronic storage or transmission, or roadcast for distance learning. Some ancillaries, including electronic and print components, may not be available to customers outside the United States.

This book is printed on acid-free paper.

domestic   2 3 4 5 6 7 8 9 0 QPD/QPD 0 9 8 7 6 5 4 3
international 1 2 3 4 5 6 7 8 9 0 QPD/QPD 0 9 8 7 6 5 4 3 2

ISBN 0-07-250916-3e

Publisher: *George Werthman*
Sponsoring editor: *Dan Silverburg*
Developmental editor I: *Sarah Wood*
Manager, Marketing and Sales: *Paul Murphy*
Senior producer, Media technology: *David Barrick*
Senior project manager: *Christine A. Vaughan*
Production supervisor: *Gina Hangos*
Design manager: *Laurie J. Entringer*
Senior supplement producer: *Rose M. Range*
Senior digital content specialist: *Brian Nacik*
Cover design: *Asylum Studios*
Interior design: *Asylum Studios*
Typeface: *10/12 Times New Roman*
Compositor: *Shepherd Incorporated*
Printer: *Quebecor World Dubuque Inc.*

Library of Congress Cataloging-in Publication Data
Gottleber, Timothy T.
     Even more excellent HTML with XML, XHTML, and Javascript / Timothy T.
Gottleber, Timothy N. Trainor.
       p. cm.
     ISBN 0-07-250916-3 (alk. paper)—ISBN 0-07-119522-X (international : alk. paper) 1. HTML (Document markup language) 2. XML (Document markup language) 3. XHTML (Document markup language) 4. JavaScript (Computer program language) I. Trainor, Timothy N., 1953– II. Title.

     QA76.76.H94 G678 2003
     005.7'2—dc21

                                                                                2002026555

INTERNATIONAL EDITION ISBN 0-07-119522-X
Copyright © 2003. Exclusive rights by The McGraw-Hill Companies, Inc. for manufacture and export. This book cannot be re-exported from the country to which it is sold by McGraw-Hill. The International Edition is not available in North America.

http://www.mhhe.com

*This book, and all that went into it,
are dedicated to our parents:*

*Dick and Lenore Gottleber
Tom and Val Trainor*

Table of Contents

PREFACE

▸▸CHAPTER One: An HTML Overview   **1**

What Is HTML?   **2**

What's in a Name?   **2**

Browsers   **5**
Graphical Browsers   7
Text-Only Browsers   8
Nonvisual Browsers   9

What Is a URL?   **9**
Protocol   10
Domain   11
Path and Filename   12

HTML Terminology   **12**
Tags and Containers   12
Attributes   13

HTML Code Format   **14**

World Wide Web Consortium (W³C)   **14**

Necessary Tools   **16**
ASCII Editor   16
Browser   16
Internet Service Provider (ISP)   17

Nice-to-Have Tools   **18**
HTML Editor   18
Text-to-HTML Converter   20

HTML Validator   21
JavaScript Editor   21
XML Editor   22

Places to Get Neat Stuff on the Net   **22**
Where to Get Browsers   22
Where to Get HTML Editors   23
Where to Get Text-to-HTML Converters   23
Where to Get HTML Validators   24
Where to Get XML Editors   24
Shareware Sites   24
Search Sites   24

Organizations Promoting Internet Usage   **25**

▸CHAPTER Two: Your First Web Page   **27**

Elements of a Web Page   **28**
Creating an HTML Template   28
<html>HTML Document</html>   29
dir   29
lang   29
version   31
<!DOCTYPE>   31
<head>Header Data</head>   32
profile   32
<title>Descriptive Title</title>   32
<body>Majority of Document</body>   34
Styles   34
Intrinsic Events   35

XHTML Structure Module   **36**

Common Coding Errors   **36**

More Web Page Elements   **37**
<!--Comment-->   38
<h1>Heading</h1><h2></h2><h3></h3><h4></h4><h5></h5><h6></h6>   39
<p> Paragraph</p>   40

Editing an HTML Document   **42**

Commonly Used Empty Tags   **42**

    43
<hr />   43

Body Tag Attributes   **44**
bgcolor   44
background   45
text   48
alink, link, and vlink   48

A Few Considerations   **49**

⮞ CHAPTER Three: Linking: Let's Get Hyper — 55

Why Is Hypertext Hyper? — 56

Storyboarding Page Links — 56
Sequential and Indexed-Sequential Designs — 56
Hierarchical Design — 57
Custom Design — 57
Source Anchors — 59
href — 61
rel and rev — 61
Targets — 62

Paths to Files — 63
Absolute Path Names — 63
Relative Path Names — 64
Absolute versus Relative Path Names — 65

Intersystem Source Anchors — 66
Linking Considerations — 66
Domain Name or IP Address? — 66
Sample Intersystem URLs — 67

Intrapage Targets — 68
name — 68
id — 68
name or id? — 70

Intrapage Source Anchors — 70

URLs with Intrapage Targets — 71

Anchor Placement — 71

Intrasystem Source Anchors — 72

One-Way Streets — 72
Links Back Using Intrapage Target — 73
Links Back Using Intrasystem Target — 73

The "Click Here" Faux Pas — 74

Mailto: Protocol — 75

Page Footers — 75

Server-Side Includes — 77

⮞ CHAPTER Four: Lists: Bringing Order out of Chaos — 81

Plain-Text Lists — 82

List-Making Tags — 82

Ordered and Unordered Lists — 82
<ol>Ordered List</ol> — 83

start   84
type   85
style   86
<li>List Item</li>   88
Blocked and Inline Elements   88
type   88
style   89
value   89

HTML-Compliant Code   **91**
<ul>Unordered List</ul>   92
type or style   93
list-style-position: outside/inside   94

Lists of Lists: Nesting   **97**
Combining Ordered and Unordered Lists   97
Nesting Unordered Lists   97
Nesting Ordered Lists   97

Readability   **100**

Lists of Definitions   **100**
<dl>Definition List</dl>   101
<dt>Definition Term</dt>   102
<dd>Definition Definition </dd>   102

XHTML List Module   **103**

Deprecated List Forms: Menus and Directories   **103**
<menu>Menu List</menu>   103
<dir>Directory List</dir>   104

▸▸CHAPTER Five: Formatting: Is What You See What You Get?   **109**

Glyphs and Fonts   **110**

Document-Wide Style Changes   **111**
<style>Document Style Changes</style>   111
type   113
Formatting List Items   113
Formatting Different Tags Simultaneously   114
<--Comment Lines-->   115
Font Changes   116

Inline Styles   **120**
Physical Styles   120
XHTML Presentation Module   122
Logical Styles   122
<address>Address</address>   123
Strongly Emphasized Text   123
Emphasized Text   124
<abbr>Abbreviation</abbr>   124
<acronym>Acronym</acronym>   124
<dfn>Definition</dfn>   124
<var>Variable Values</var>   124
<samp>Output</samp>   124

<cite>Citation</cite>   125
<blockquote>Block Quote</blockquote>   125
<q>Quote</q>   126
<ins>Insert</ins> and <del>Delete</del>   126
XHTML Text Module   127
Special Characters   128

Turning Off Formatting   **130**
<pre>Preformatted Text</pre>   130

Deprecated Font-Handling Techniques   **132**
<font>Font of Text</font>   132
color   132
size   132
face   133

Final Comment   **133**

» CHAPTER Six: Images: A Picture Is Worth a Thousand Words   **137**

Images and Multimedia   **138**

Image Formats   **138**
GIF   138
JPEG   139
PNG   139
SVG   139
PDF   140
TIFF   140
BMP   140

Choosing an Image Format   **140**

Image Sizes   **140**

Bits per Bixel (BPP)   **141**

Graphics Tips   **142**

<img>   **144**
src   144
alt   146
longdesc   147
height and width   148
Horizontal Alignment   150
Vertical Alignment   152

Line Breaks   **153**
clear   153

Centering Images   **154**
Centering Objects   154
Centering a Paragraph   155

Image Borders   **156**
border-style: dotted | dashed | solid | double | groove | ridge | inset | outset |
hidden | none   156

border-width: thin | medium | thick | absolute | inherit   156
border-color: color# | transparent | inherit   157

Image Margins   **158**
margin: margin-width | insert   158
vspace and hspace   158

Images as Bullets   **160**
list-style-image: url | none | inherit   161
Definition List   161

Image Links   **161**

Two HTML Coding Tricks   **163**
lowsrc   163
<nobr>No Line Break</nobr>   164

To Image or Not to Image   **164**

»CHAPTER Seven: Tables: Data in Rows and Columns   **169**

What's in a Table?   **170**

Table Containers   **171**
<table>Table</table>   171
border   172
rules   173
frame   174
width   176
Table Background Color   177
summary   178

Changing Standards   **178**
style   178

Controlling White Space   **181**
Table Margins   182
Cell Spacing   182
Cell Padding   182

Table Text Alignment   **183**
<tr>Table Row</tr>   184
align   184
valign   184
char   185
charoff   186

Table Data and Headers   **186**
<td>Table Data</td>   186
<th>Table Header</th>   186
align   187
bgcolor   188
valign   188
colspan   188
rowspan   188
abbr   190
headers   190

scope   191
axis   191
style   191

Table Captions   **193**
<caption>Caption</caption>   193
Caption Alignment   195

Table Columns   **195**
<colgroup>Column Group</colgroup>   195
span   196
<col />   197
width   198
valign   199

Scrolling Big Tables   **199**
<thead>Table Header</thead>   199
<tfoot>Table Footer</tfoot>   200
<tbody>Table Body</tbody>   201

XHTML Table Module   **201**

▸CHAPTER Eight: STYLE: Some Have It and Some Don't   **207**

What Is a Cascading Style Sheet?   **208**

Why Use External Style Sheets?   **208**

Applying External Style Sheets   **209**
<link>   210
rel, href, and type   212

Classes of Styles   **212**
class   213
Inheritance   214
Generic and Tag-Level Classes   214

Style-Sheet Elements to Divide and Span   **215**
Divide Document   215
Span Area   218

Common Style Properties   **219**
Text Manipulation and Alignment   219
background: color | image repeat | attachment | position   221

Changing Link Colors   **224**

Box Definitions   **224**
width: [absolute] | [percentage] | auto | inherit   225
height: [absolute] | [percentage] | auto | inherit   226
visibility: visible | hidden | collapse | inherit   226
margin: top | right | bottom | left   226
white-space: normal | pre | nowrap | inherit   227
border: width | style | color   228
padding: top | right | bottom | left   230
float: left | right | none | inherit   232
clear: none | left | right | both | inherit   232

Media Types 233

Paged Media 233
page-break-before: auto | always | avoid | left | right | inherit 233
page-break-after: auto | always | avoid | left | right | inherit 234
page-break-inside: auto | avoid | inherit 234
size: [length-width] | [length-height] | auto | portrait | landscape | inherit 235
Orphans and Widows 235
Crop and Cross Marks 236

Printer-Friendly Web Pages 236

Conclusions 237

▶CHAPTER Nine: Multimedia: Watch Your Inclusions 241

Using Multimedia 242
Inserting Object with href 242
<applet>Java Applet</applet> 243
<object>Insert Object</object> 245
classid and data 245
codetype and type 245
Embedding Other HTML Documents 246
standby and declare 247
Nesting Objects 247
<param> 249
name and value 250
value type 251
code base 251

XHTML Object Module 252

When to Use Code Augmentation 252

Adding Sound 253

Types of Sound Files 253
μ-Law (Mu-Law) Files 254
RIFF WAVE Files 255
AIFF and AIFC Files 256
MPEG Audio 256
MIDI Files 256
Other Formats 256

Choosing Formats 257

Aural Style Sheets 257
Aural Properties 258
speak: normal | non | spell-out | inherit 258
volume: [number] | [percentage] | silent | x-soft through x-loud | inherit 258
cue: cue-before | cue-after | inherit 260
pause: [time] | [percentage] | inherit 260
Sound Orientation 261

Ethical Questions 261

Adding Video **261**
MPEG Video 262
QuickTime 262
AVI 263

Streaming Audio/Video **263**

To Link or to Copy? **264**

▸ CHAPTER Ten: Frames: Divide and Conquer **267**

Considerations When Using Frames **268**

Frame Navigation **269**

Formatting Frames **271**
Frameset Document Type Definition 271
<frameset>Frame Setting</frameset> 271
rows and cols 272
onload and onunload 272
Nested <frameset> Containers 272
<frame / > 276
src 276
name 276
id 279
scrolling 279
noresize 280
marginheight and marginwidth 280
title and longdesc 280
frameborder 281
<noframes>No Frames</noframes> 282
target 283
<base/> 285
Special Targets 285
<iframe>Inline Frame</iframe> 287

Alternatives to Frames **289**

Final Comments **291**

▸ CHAPTER Eleven: Forms and Forms Processing **297**

Form and Function **298**

Handling Electronic Mail **299**

Designing Forms **301**
<form>Contents of the Form</form> 301
action 301
method 302
enctype 305
target 305
style 306
name (for <form>) 307
title 307
Intrinsic Events 307

<input />   307
name (for <input />)   308
type   309
type="text"   309
size   310
maxlength   311
value   311
type="password"   312
type="file"   312
type="checkbox"   313
checked (for checkbox)   315
type = "radio"   315
checked (for radio button)   317
type="reset"   319
type="submit"   320
Multiple Submit Controls   321
type="button"   321

Graphical Buttons   **322**
type="image"   323
Hidden Data Fields   324
type="hidden"   324
<button>Button Text and/or Images</button>   324
disabled   325
tabindex   325
Intrinsic Events   325
<textarea>Optional Text String</textarea>   325
rows and columns   326
wrap   327
wrap="virtual"   327
wrap="physical"   327
wrap="off"   327

Drop-Down List Boxes   **328**
<select>Set of <option> Elements </option> </select>   328
size   330
multiple   330
disabled   331
<option>Option Text</option>   332
value   332
selected   333
<optgroup>Collection of <option></option>s</optgroup>   333
label   334
<fieldset>[<legend>]<input>[s]</fieldset>   334
<legend>Text</legend>   334
accesskey   335
<label>Text</label>   336
for   336

XHTML Form Module   **336**

Processing Data Automagically (CGI)   **336**

How CGI Works   **338**

▸▸CHAPTER Twelve: CGI, Metatags, and Other Tricks of the Trade   345

Processing Data Automagically	**345**
How CGI Works	**345**
Updating Database with CGI	347
Searchable Documents	349
<isindex/>	349
Data Entry Using <input> Element	349
Calling Document	350
Search Request Page	350
Success Page	351
Miss Page	352
The Data File	353
<base/>	**354**
href	355
target	355
Creating New Tags	**355**
<meta />	356
http-equiv	356
Guidelines for Using Refresh	361
name	362
Other Common Name Values	363
scheme	363
Multicolumn Pages	**363**
Headlines	**365**
Sidebars	**366**
Pseudo-Elements and Pseudo-Class	**366**

▸▸CHAPTER Thirteen: JavaScript Programs for Your Pages   373

What Is JavaScripit?	**374**
Misconceptions About JavaScript	**374**
JavaScript Is Not Java "Lite"	374
JavaScript Is Not a Wimpy Little Pseudo-Language	374
What JavaScript Can't Do	374
What JavaScript Can Do	375
Introducing JavaScript	**376**
<script>Script(s)</script>	377
src	377
type	377
<meta />	377
defer	378
language	378

The Hello( ) Function 378

Invoking Functions 379

Basic Programming Structures 380
Sequence of Statements 381
Selection of Code 381
Testing for JavaScript 381
Iteration of Statements 383

Object-Oriented Concepts in JavaScript 383

Date Object 386

Intrinsic Events 388

Document Object 389

Window Object 391
Status Bar 391
Dialog Boxes 392
New Windows 395
onload and onunload 398
Navigator Object 398

Another Interesting Bit 403

Things JavaScript Should Not Be Forced to Do 405

▸CHAPTER Fourteen: Dynamic HTML: Charismatic Pages 409

Image Maps 410
Server-Side Image Maps 410
Client-Side Image Maps 411
Image Coordinates for Hot Spots 411
usemap 411
<map>Contents of Image Map</map> 413
title 414
alt versus title 414
<area /> 414
alt 414
shape 415
coords 415
href 415
nohref 416
HTML 4 Considerations 416
Making It Easy 416
Other Considerations 416
Simple Rollovers 417

Professional Rollovers 420

Color-Changing on the Fly 421
Color Preferences 421
Keeping Forms HTML-Compliant 421
Invoking the Script 423

A Little Fancier Color-Changing 424

How the Cookie Crumbles 426
Deleting Cookies 426
A Note on Testing 427
Checking for Cookies 427
Prompt Box to Input Name 428
Global Variables 430
Setting Cookie's Value 430
Checking to See If Cookie Exists 431
Leftover Legacy Code 431
Checking Cookie's Identity 431
Using Cookie Data 432
Using Cookies Appropriately 433

▸CHAPTER Fifteen: XML: The Next Best Thing **437**

What Is XML, Anyway? 438

The Language of XML 438

DTD Up Close and Personal 439

The Reason for XML 440

DTD Models 441
XML/EDI Model 441
OFX Model 441
GedML Model 441
Database Models 441
DocBook Model 441

Relationship between XML and XHTML 442

XML Is More Than a Markup Language 443

Building HTML from XML 445

Creating PDF Output from XML 448

What's Next? 449

XML and Databases 450

▸CHAPTER Sixteen: Pragmatic Hypertext: It Ain't All Pictures! 455

Common Misconceptions 456

Text 456

Literature 457
Basic Text 457
Text and Illustrations 458
Hyperlinked Text 459

Corporate/Government Documentation 459

Electronic Books (Ebooks) **460**

Web-Based Reference Manuals **461**

Online Help **463**

Online Education (Distance Learning) **464**

The Wireless Web **465**
WAP (Wireless Application Protocol) 466
Wireless Internet 467

Knowledge Is Power **467**
Wireless Data 467
Aural Data 468

Web Site versus Web Page **468**

Migrating from Text to Hypertext **469**
Optical Scanning 470
Text Converters 470
Aural Browsing 470
International Considerations 471

Online Text Sites **472**

Appendix A: A Style Manual **475**

Appendix B: File Transfer Protocol **485**

Appendix C: History of the Internet **497**

Glossary **503**

Index **527**

⋛Preface⋚

TO THE STUDENT

This book was written for you. You want to learn how to build and maintain Web pages. You have the tool to help you do that in your hands. This book originated as *Excellent HTML* when Tim G. began to design the HTML course he teaches, He couldn't find a book that would work well as a text for the class. There were many technical books and reference manuals available, but none of them written for students, and none were designed to be an aid in learning how to build Web pages. They were, and remain, excellent references once you know what you are doing, but they are not textbooks. This book, along with the associated *Reference Guide,* is designed to do both. It is a result of talking to our students about what they wanted in a text. Even *More Excellent HTML with XML, XHTML, and JavaScript* is a result of all those discussions and our experience with previous editions.

After Tim G. finished the first edition, the W³C (World Wide Web Consortium) revised the HTML standard for the last time and released HTML 4.0. In addition, the world moved away from considering Java applets as the ideal "dynamic" inclusion into Web pages, and JavaScript has come into favor. As the new book began to take shape, Dr. Tim Trainor came on board as coauthor, providing new ideas and vision. The result was a very dynamic team that was responsible for the second iteration of the text, *More Excellent HTML with an introduction to JavaScript.* We also had the opportunity to talk to students about what they wanted or needed to learn in order to create their personal and/or commercial Web pages.

The world of the Web continued to evolve, and XHTML is now the cutting edge. We have completely rewritten the previous book, incorporating XHTML throughout. *Even More Excellent HTML* also has a new chapter on XML to give you a taste of that new paradigm. In addition, we have expanded our coverage of alternate media to include the growing wireless Web.

There are two ways to approach learning how to code the HyperText Markup Language (HTML) used to create Web pages. **The first way is to just jump in and see what you can hack together through trial and error.** HTML isn't that complex, and it isn't that difficult to create some, well at least fair, pages that way. However, there are three distinct disadvantages to that approach:

- You can learn some awful habits.
- You miss out on some great techniques.
- You can easily create pages that are difficult if not impossible to maintain and update

The second way to learn HTML is to follow a more structured approach:

- First, learning how to use simple tags.
- Then moving on to the more complex ones.
- All the while having the support and guidance of a couple of guys who have been there.

It is very useful and productive to see what you can do with just a handful of selected tags before you start using the really "slick" ones like frames or tables.

This book uses the second approach. You will begin building Web pages in Chapter 2, and keep building more and more complex pages as you work through the text. If you have a special need, feel free to look ahead. Remember, however, we created the explorations, and the exercises at the end of each chapter, to give you a chance to gain experience with the new tags you learned in that chapter and refresh your memory on the tags you have already learned. In addition, if you want to be compliant with the very latest XHTML techniques, you can reference the XHTML sections with many of the commands to see how to make your code XHTML-compliant as well.

Welcome to the wonderful world of HTML; it is an exciting place that is changing even as you read this. And one final note: You will read this many times throughout the text, but we would like to focus your attention upon it at the very beginning of your study of HTML. Your job is to provide new and exciting content to the community we call the World Wide Web. Concentrate on the content, and let the browsers that load your pages worry about the formatting. Go play on the Web, and if you want to see what our students are doing, come visit us at **http://phred.dcccd.edu** and **http://student. muskegon.cc.mi.us** and take a look at the student pages hosted there. They have done and are doing some wonderful things.

TO THE INSTRUCTOR

Teaching HTML is challenging and exciting. In part, the first book was developed because Tim G. was frustrated with the texts currently being used to teach HTML. There were reference books and technical manuals available, but nothing designed to be used in the classroom. Our students come to the class with a wide range of computer expertise, from the absolute novice to the professional programmer. The first edition of this text proved to be an easier way to teach HTML and give students what they needed to succeed.

Then the World Wide Web Consortium (W³C) revised the HTML standard and released HTML 4.0. In addition, students and instructors around the country began expressing a stronger interest in JavaScript than in Java applets. Here was a chance for Tim G. to take a fresh look at Web-page creation. Dr. Tim Trainor joined the project, bringing his years of HTML teaching experience, his wit, and his wonderful ideas.

The book you hold in your hands has been polished and refined in the crucible of the classroom. It is designed to take the student from an overview of the history and origins of HTML through the design and development of clean, easy-to-maintain Web pages using style sheets, JavaScript, and other dynamic HTML features while enabling the students to create XHTML-compliant code. We have woven the new specifications throughout the text. Unlike many of the texts on the market that address Dynamic HTML and the 4.0 standard and XHTML in just a chapter or two, we have built them into this text from the beginning. The first seven chapters have very few examples of styles and style sheets, because we want the student to learn how to use the inline tags first. Starting in Chapter 8, where we introduce styles, and continuing throughout the rest of the book, the examples use style elements. The chapters about JavaScript and the other features of Dynamic HTML provide the students with a solid grounding in those techniques as well. Finally, we provide a taste of XML in a new chapter, and expand the last chapter to include new features like the wireless Web and producing pages for handheld devices such as PDAs and cell phones.

In writing this book we have not assumed the reader, your student, has an in-depth background with computers, but we have assumed a minimal level of computer literacy. Still, we ourselves have had a couple of students who were completely new to computing and they succeeded, albeit by putting in some serious work.

The text is laid out in the order we teach our own classes. It starts with some simple tags and progresses into the more sophisticated tags as the students become comfortable with the format and syntax of HTML. Although you don't have to follow any particular order (since most chapters can pretty much stand alone), there are a few back references that give the students grounding and refresh concepts. As each new tag is introduced, there are both examples of the HTML code and screen captures showing what that code generates. This allows the students to play with HTML and compare their results to those shown in the text. Throughout each chapter we have included "Explorations" to allow your student to practice what they have learned. At the end of the chapter, exercises enable the student to create pages using the tags they have learned. The design process (and some of the exercises) build from chapter to chapter. In our experience, this is the best way to teach HTML. Give the students a tag, tell them how it works, and then let them use it. That way they can have actual hands-on experience with the tags and thus tend to learn more quickly.

The physical layout of the content is geared to serve the student as a reference but also to provide an advanced organizer for your lecture. Each new tag is enclosed within a graphical element showing the tag name, type of tag, a list of its attributes, and special notes on the use of that tag. Attributes shown in italic have been deprecated and those in bold are discussed in detail in the following section. You don't have to have several texts open at the same time as you lecture; all the information is right there for you.

A wealth of ancillary tools come with the text as well:

1. A *Reference Guide* that provides complete list of every HTML

elements with a list of related attributes, properties with associated values, common character codes, four-color chart of browser-safe colors and more. Each of the textbook's graphical elements is cross-referenced in the *Reference Guide* when more detailed explanations or additional examples are needed.

2. A Web site that contains the JavaScript and most of the HTML examples from the book as well as instructor notes, suggestions, and a sample syllabus.

3. A CD included with the book that contains

   • Most of the HTML examples from the text.

   • All the JavaScripts used in the book, with a simple HTML page to drive each.

   • A selection of buttons, backgrounds, and lines for use on Web pages.

   • CuteFTP, a handy file transfer protocol tool to move data across the Web.

   • WinZip, a useful tool for compressing HTML and images before shipping them across the Web.

   • CSE HTML Validator, a really powerful HTML validation and editing program that will check for both required and recommended HTML syntax.

You and your students can access the HTML examples by pointing your browser at D:/html/index.html—this assumes that D: is your CD-ROM drive. The HTML index gives access to the different chapter indices, each of which provides the HTML examples for the figures in that chapter. In some cases, two or more HTML examples are very similar. They are included for completeness and to keep in step with the text. You can run the HTML code from any browser that supports the HTML 4.0 standard. Actually, you can use a browser that supports the 3.2 standard, but some of the new, dynamic features won't appear unless you use one of the more recent incarnations of the browsers like Navigator 6+, Internet Explorer 6+, or Opera 6+.

Some of the software on the CD is made up of demo versions of the products. *They are full-featured software, but they expire after 30 days.* For that reason, you may wish to wait to have the students install them until a couple of weeks into the semester. We don't let our students use the features of the page-development tools until the final project. Up to that point, they use only CSE HTML Validator or the Unix editors (Tim G.) or Notepad (Tim T.) as an ASCII editor. That requires them to learn how the HTML code is actually built. It also requires them to learn the syntax and order of the various tags. If they begin by using all the features of an HTML development tool, they become dependent upon that tool and then encounter difficulty if they need to modify their code on the server. (The first time Tim G. taught HTML, he allowed the students to use all the features of the HTML editors, and his students had many problems later, because they didn't learn the codes, but only how to invoke the tools to create the codes.) We both restrict how much our students are allowed to do with the HTML editors, and things have gone much more smoothly. For example, creating the correct path to an image can be tricky. If the students have to hand-build the path, they learn how HTML renders the address. If all they have to do is click on the target icon and then browse for the correct filename; they won't necessarily learn how to create the correct path. There are other editing tools available for download from the Web. Explore—You might find others that you really like.

The most important thing about this or any text is that it should free you to focus on your teaching. Enjoy it, enjoy your students, and have fun!

ACKNOWLEDGEMENTS

Creating a book is a time-consuming process. First and foremost, I want to thank Patti and Richard for working around a husband and father who seemed chained to his computer, and for the support they provided throughout the whole process. Thanks, you two: I owe you, once again!

Next, I thank my students; they suffered through this process, too, working the exercises, listening to the lectures, and most importantly for this book, commenting on the content. Working with Tim Trainor was and is an absolute delight. His insights, ideas, friendship, and general harassment made this project great fun. (Besides, he always removed my parenthetical notes.) Thanks Tim!

A word of thanks to Buddy Mondlock, Patty Larkin, Mannheim Steamroller, Richard Wagner, Edvard Grieg, LVB, and J. S. Bach for the music that kept me sane.

Finally, thanks to Wendy the Pooh who kept reminding me of the important things in life like playing tug, wrestling with the puppy, and especially playing chase-the-laser.

Tim Gottleber—

I'd like to thank Tim Gottleber again for inviting me onto the team. The time and effort spent in writing this book was a labor of love. Luckily, my soulmate, Diane, understands this and not only puts up with my long hours in front of the word processor, she provided many valuable suggestions that make the final product better. I'd also like to thank fellow Jayhawk Mike Merrill for the invaluable suggestions of Blues musicians he thought I should use in my Hall of Frames list. Finally, my students need to be acknowledged for the extra work they put in when reading rough drafts of this text.

Tim Trainor—

We both want to thank the folks at McGraw-Hill Higher Education who were instrumental in making this book happen: Dan Silverburg, Sarah Wood, and Christine Vaughan, who provided the professional support to bring this project to fruition. This book would not have been possible without them. A special thanks to Maggie Jarpey, way up North, who again did yeoman's duty, making grammatical and logical sense out of our scribblings. The English language is safe as long as we have people like Maggie keeping watch and fixing mistakes.

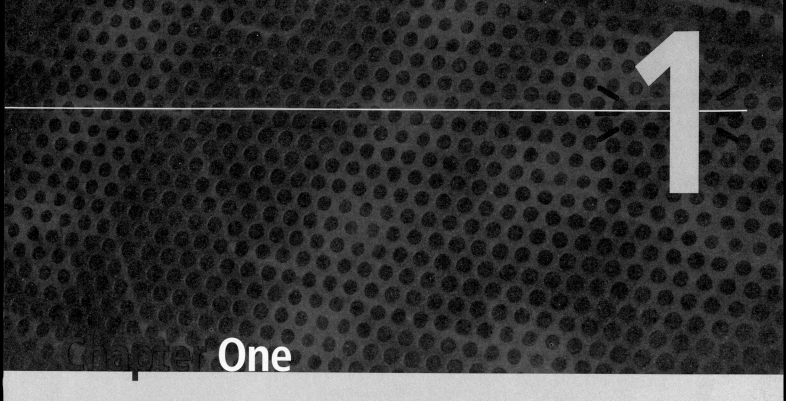

## Chapter One

An HTML Overview

This chapter gives an overview of *hyper text markup language (HTML)*, the set of codes used to build Web pages. You need to be able to use HTML in order to build, change, and maintain your own pages on the Internet's World Wide Web, also called the Web. As in almost any aspect of the world of computing, HTML authors use some special vocabulary. If you find a word that you don't understand, please check in the glossary at the end of this book. Knowing the meaning of the special terms used with HTML is very important. Often half the battle in learning a new skill is learning the vocabulary of that skill.

CHAPTER OBJECTIVES

After reading this chapter you should be able to do the following:

- Use terminology associated with the creation and use of hypertext documents.
- Talk intelligently about the role HTML, SGML, XML, and XHTML play in the development of Web pages.
- Name three popular graphical browsers, a text-based browser, and common features of graphical browsers.
- Explain the parts of the uniform resource locator (URL).
- Employ a URL to display a Web page and identify the protocol, domain name, path, and filename used to find it.
- Give the steps used by the World Wide Web Consortium to change HTML coding recommendations.
- Tell where to find current HTML, XML, and XHTML recommendations.
- Identify the essential and nonessential tools for creating and maintaining a Web site.

▸▸WHAT IS HTML?

Before we look at what HTML is, it is important to make sure you understand what HTML is not. First, HTML is not hard to learn or use! Just like anything new, it looks a little strange when you first see it, but in a short time you can be reading and writing HTML like a pro. Second, HTML is not a true programming language. In other words, it is not a language used to write Web programs. We will get into programming when we explore JavaScript in Chapter Thirteen. HTML also is not a page-description language, or a WYSIWYG (What You See Is What You Get) word processor, or a desktop publishing tool. HTML is used primarily to define the content of a document (what it says) and secondarily to describe the page layout (how it looks). You can determine exactly what the document says with HTML but not precisely how it will look when displayed.

The terms *document* and *page* are often used interchangeably when talking about the World Wide Web. They do not mean exactly the same thing. HTML is used to create electronic documents that can be read on many different systems using software called a **browser**. The browser translates the HTML codes into a presentation on the screen. Technically, the **document** is the actual HTML codes and text you write and the **page** is how it looks when viewed (Figure 1.1). Most Net cruisers do not make that distinction, so you may see the terms used interchangeably.

One fundamental fact of HTML is that although the author controls the content, the browser controls the layout of a document (with one exception that we will look at later). You can spend lots of time hand-editing (inserting extra spaces, tabs, blank lines, and such) to make your page look great, but most browsers will remove all those spaces, and all your careful work will be lost. The HTML term for one or more spaces, tabs, or carriage returns is **white space**. HTML browsers usually compress all the white space into a single space.

▸▸WHAT'S IN A NAME?

Let's look at how HTML got its name. The H stands for "hyper." A **hyper document** is one that contains links to other "things" or places either within or outside the document. A **link** is the general term for a specially marked place on the screen that will cause something to happen when you activate it. Activating (clicking with a mouse button or pressing the Enter key) a link can open another HTML document, move you to another place in the current document, display a picture, play a sound, or run a video clip. One of the earliest uses of hyper documents and links was by Apple's Macintosh computer with its HyperCard, which linked hyper documents together with hyper links. Its release in 1987 was a forerunner to hyper document applications on the World Wide Web.

As you move from hyper document to hyper document, the browser builds a chain of the pages you have visited so that you can easily go back and revisit one. Since the browser builds a chain, each page you have visited could be called a link in that chain. As an HTML author, or Web weaver, you will code links from your documents to other documents, both on your computer and across the world. For example, if this text were a hyper document, and if the author had built in a link that defined the word *Internet,* that word might appear in a different font from the rest of the document. It could be underlined and/or in a different color, like this: <u>Internet</u>. By moving your screen pointer to that spot on the page and clicking the mouse button or touching Enter, you would cause the link to open a small page that defined the word *Internet.*

Here is another example: Suppose you go to the University of Virginia's Electronic Text Center, where many books are online. At that site you see the screen presented at the

Figure 1.1

Example of HTML document and
resulting Web page

```
<html>
<head>
<title>Sample HTML Document</title>
</head>

<body>
<h1>Level-1 Heading</h1>
<p>The elements of an HTML document
and the resulting Web page are the
same as those found in any written document.
For example, a paragraph like this one is a
common design element.
</p>

<h2>Level-2 Heading</h2>
<p>There are ordered lists:</p>
<ol>
   <li>This</li>
   <li>That</li>
   <li>Another thing</li>
</ol>

<h3>Level-3 Heading</h3>
<p>There are unordered (bulleted) lists:</p>
<ul>
   <li>This</li>
   <li>That</li>
   <li>Another thing</li>
</ul>
</body>
</html>
```

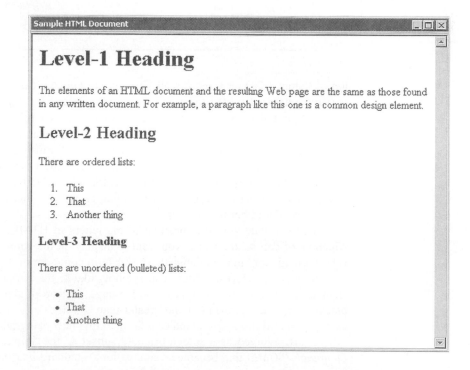

Figure 1.2

University of Virginia's online library and first page of the electronic version of *Through the Looking Glass* by Lewis Carroll

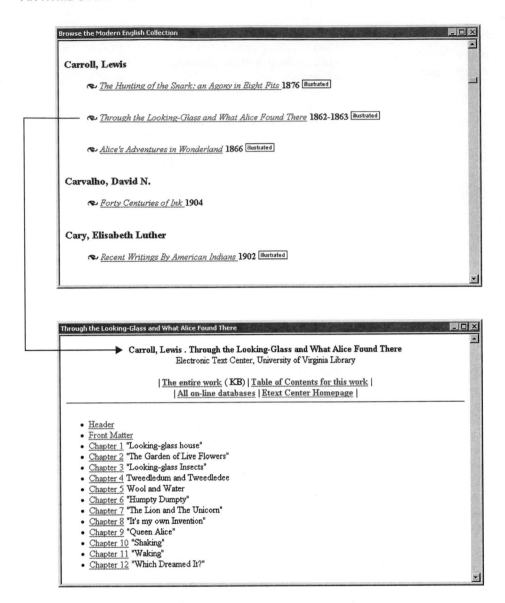

top of Figure 1.2. You want to read *Through the Looking-Glass . . . ,* so you move your screen pointer to that title (the second entry on the screen) and press the left mouse button. The next thing that appears on your screen is the first page of the electronic text, as shown at the bottom of the figure. The title on the previous page was a link to the actual document.

Hyper documents are often considered more useful than standard text documents because by activating the links the author provides, the user can explore relationships among the ideas presented or get definitions for selected terms. Some people predict that in the future almost everyone will be reading books like this one over the World Wide Web as *ebooks,* rather than on paper.

Let's continue with the meaning of the letters in HTML. The T stands for "text," which is, of course, the words you want to display on the computer's screen. The ML in HTML stands for "markup language." This term comes from the publishing industry and its proofreaders' marks. Editors use symbols like ¶, the paragraph mark, to indicate a change in the way the text appears on the page. Instead of symbols, HTML uses letters bracketed in the less-than (<) and greater-than (>) signs, also called *angle brackets.* For example, HTML uses <p> to indicate the start of a new paragraph.

HTML evolved as a screen-oriented subset of the *Standard Generalized Markup Language (SGML)* that became an international standard in 1986. More recently the *Ex-*

tensible Markup Language (XML) has been evolving to complement the text-oriented HTML. This markup language is used to identify data, like a person's name or an order number, that needs to be handled in a special way by a browser. Since XML has many features in common with HTML, this book will include information about it as well.

All of these markup languages are "portable across platforms," meaning they allow all sorts of computers, anywhere in the world, to view documents containing HTML or XML codes. The term *platform* refers to the combination of the type of computer and its operating system, browser, and so on. For example, an Intel-based personal computer (PC) running Microsoft's Windows operating system and using Internet Explorer or the Opera browser is one type of platform. A Macintosh running the System X operating system and using Netscape's Navigator browser is a different type of platform.

We can use HTML to change the general way the text is laid out, but we are always at the mercy of the browser used to view our HTML document for the exact format. Some browsers recognize only a subset of the HTML codes and ignore the others. There is little consistency among the various browsers. Some display headings like this:

This is a heading

Others will display the same heading like this:

This is a heading

Any one browser will, however, be consistent within itself in the way it displays text marked up in a particular way.

One central concept of HTML development is that *you are responsible for the content, but the browser handles the layout.* In other words, you have limited control of the format, so you should focus on the content—the information you are making available—and leave the formatting to the browser.

▸▸ BROWSERS

A browser is the computer program (interface) you use to explore the Web. The browser program translates documents containing the HTML language into words and images on the screen. Most browsers

1. Respond to the following navigation buttons or keys (Figure 1.3):

   • Back

   • Forward

   • Home (the Web page your computer system looks for first)

   • Refresh or Reload (to retrieve page from Web server again)

2. Print pages (Figure 1.3, page 6)

3. Provide a navigation line for entering a new Web address (Figure 1.4, page 6)

4. Display images (Figure 1.5, page 7)

5. Display translated HTML documents as pages (Figure 1.6, page 7)

6. Display the HTML codes in a document (Figure 1.14, page 19)

7. Play video and sound clips with the help of a *plug-in*, an independent program module that can be added to the browser.

Navigator, Opera, Internet Explorer, and Lynx (pronounced "links") are four examples of browser programs. Browsers can be text-only, like Lynx, or graphical, like Navigator and Internet Explorer. Once a browser is installed, people often start their Web cruising at a *search site*. These specialized Web pages are designed to help people find

Figure 1.3

Navigation buttons, File menu options, and View menu options for popular graphical browsers

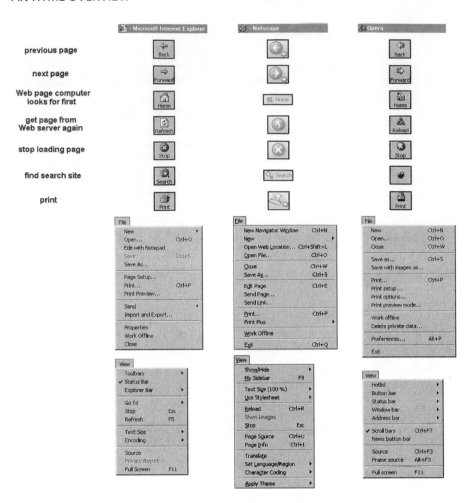

other pages by means of one or more *keywords* (words contained in what you are looking for). The search site in Figure 1.4 is set to look for any Web pages that refer to Lewis Carroll. A list of popular search sites is presented at the end of this chapter.

Figure 1.4

Graphical browser display with search-site address in navigation line

Navigation Line

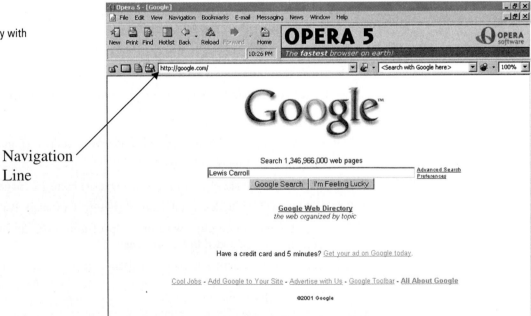

GRAPHICAL BROWSERS

Graphical browsers like Opera (Figure 1.4), Navigator (Figure 1.5), and Internet Explorer (Figure 1.6) display pictures, play sounds, and show animations. Thus, they are *multimedia* presentation tools, meaning they make use of multiple media instead of just text and graphics. To take full advantage of HTML's multimedia capabilities your computer needs to have a color monitor and sound card to support speakers or headphones. Some people would say a microphone is mandatory input hardware.

Multimedia features place high demands on data transmission and storage hardware. It takes a lot of transmission time as well as disk space to utilize video and high fidelity sound. Figure 1.5 shows "phred the Underground Web Server" as seen with Netscape's Navigator browser.

Navigator Netscape's Navigator browser (Figure 1.5) is one of the two most widely used graphical browsers on the Web. The Netscape Communications Corporation, a subsidiary of America Online (AOL), also distributes Navigator as part of its Communicator package of desktop software. You will find that Navigator is always being upgraded to keep current with new HTML specifications. It is free to students and faculty.

In addition to the current release of Navigator, Netscape offers interested users access to beta releases, which are experimental versions that test new features before they become part of the current release. You can download Navigator from Netscape's home page at http://home.netscape.com. To **download** is to copy a file from another computer to your computer. A Web site's **home page** is its first page. The **Web site** itself is a series of related Web pages.

The founding members of Netscape gained much of their expertise working on the Mosaic browser, the first popular graphical browser. Developed by the National Center for Supercomputing Applications (NCSA) at the University of Illinois, Urbana-Champaign, Mosaic is no longer being revised, but it can be downloaded using the university's Web site at http://archive.ncsa.uiuc.edu/SDG/Software/Mosaic/

Figure 1.5

Display by Netscape's Navigator graphical browser

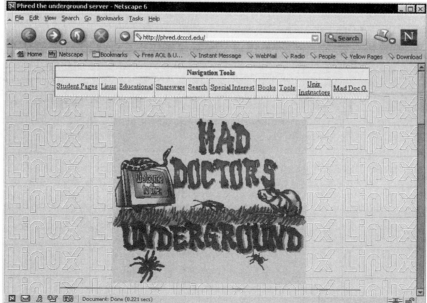

Internet Explorer The other common graphical browser is Microsoft's Internet Explorer (refer again to Figure 1.6). These two browsers, Netscape's Navigator and Microsoft's Internet Explorer, are major players in the current "browser wars" being fought on the Web. Microsoft is also tangling with the U.S. Justice Department as to whether a browser is independent of a computer's operating system. Microsoft claims that browsing the Internet is just another task performed by a computer's operating system. Since Microsoft sells the most popular operating system in the world, Windows, it hopes to gain an edge over Netscape by integrating Internet Explorer into the Windows package of desktop software.

You may find it interesting that the browser used by America Online (AOL) has historically used Internet Explorer as the underlying program code. Since AOL now owns Netscape Navigator, many Web users have speculated that the AOL browser will eventually switch over and use Navigator's program code in the future.

Internet Explorer is available through the Web using Microsoft's home page at http://www.microsoft.com. Beta copies of new releases are available from this Web site as well. Both Microsoft and Netscape offer online forums for discussing software problems and solutions. They also provide technical support for troubleshooting.

Figure 1.6

Microsoft's Internet Explorer graphical browser display of the HTML code in Figure 1.1

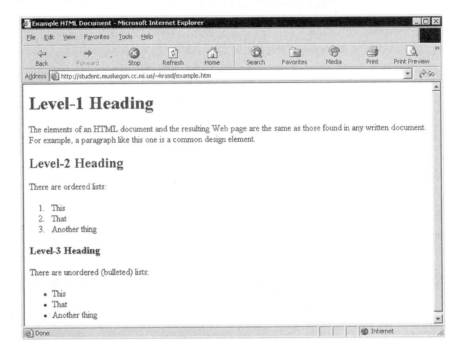

Opera A relatively new graphical browser from Oslo, Norway, entered the browser wars in 1996. Opera's claim to fame is that it is smaller, faster, contains better security, and is more standard-compliant than the others. These characteristics have given it a foothold in the mobile Internet device market. Figure 1.4 shows the Opera browser displaying a search site. This browser was originally created while the founders worked for Telenor, a Norwegian telecommunications company. Opera works across a variety of computer platforms and supports its own email and instant-messaging software to help it compete with the other popular browsers. It can be downloaded from http://www.opera.com. Beta versions are available.

TEXT-ONLY BROWSERS

There is a loyal community of Internet users who support text-only browsers. They maintain that the Web exists to share information and that most information can be more quickly shared if users do not have to wait for large graphic files to cross the Web. They use graphical browsers only for obtaining images or for recreation on the Web. In addition, the increasing popularity of handheld devices with limited text capacity and no resources for displaying images or graphics has increased the use of text-only browsers. Lynx is the most popular.

Lynx Lynx was developed at the University of Kansas (go Jayhawks!) for computer platforms using the Unix operating system. It ignores all HTML references to colors, pictures, sounds, or videos. Figure 1.7 shows "phred the underground server" as it looks

Figure 1.7

Lynx text-only browser display

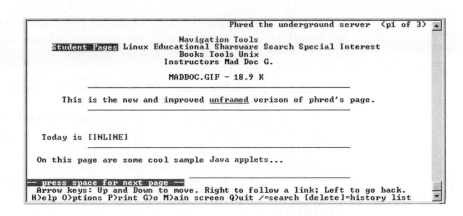

when displayed with the Lynx browser. This is the same home page shown with a graphical browser in Figure 1.5. This screen took less than a second to appear on Tim G's (coauthor Gottleber) computer. Why did it load so fast with the Lynx browser? Because the graphic files were not transferred.

As you write HTML code, it is important to keep in mind the different ways that different browsers handle the documents you create. As a user, you can simply pick the browser you like best. But as a Web weaver, you need to try your pages out with at least two different graphical browsers and a text-only browser to see how they work. Some graphical browsers include a text-only mode.

NONVISUAL BROWSERS

Web weavers must also be aware of nonvisual applications for the Internet. A new generation of PCs will come equipped with speech synthesizers. These systems will be used not only by visually impaired users, but by sighted people working away from their computer screens.

Audio One new area of competition by the popular graphical browsers is that of audio—their ability to translate HTML code into sounds called *voices,* using the computer's speech synthesizer. As a Web weaver, you can control the gender of the voice and even how fast it talks! Applications for this type of browser go beyond the needs of the visually impaired. For example, people could use hands-free audio browsers to look up addresses while they are driving in their cars.

Braille Specialized browsers are also available to convert HTML code into Braille output. Like text-only browsers, these Braille browsers can render only text, not graphics, images, sound, or video.

▸▸WHAT IS A URL?

Throughout our discussion of the Web, we will be using the term ***URL***, which stands for ***Uniform Resource Locator***. It is pronounced as three letters, "you are ell," not as one word, "erl." The URL simply describes the location, or ***Internet address***, of the specific resource we want to use for a document. A URL can point to a different Web page, to another location in the current page, or to a component of a page, like an image. For example, http://home.netscape.com/ is the URL of the Netscape home page, and http://www.yahoo.com/ is Yahoo's home page.

When we study links and anchors, we will be using different kinds of URLs. But every URL must conform to a set of rules. These rules allow browsers and other programs to understand the URL and use it to reliably move the data across the Internet from one location or page to another. When you create your Web page, it will have a URL that is unique to that page. That unique URL, or address, will allow anyone on the World Wide Web to find your page and view the information you place there.

The general form of a full URL is protocol://domain name/path/filename.

For example, the page from the Electronic Text Library at the University of Virginia (Figure 1.2) that lets you browse for authors with a last name that starts with C is

http://etext.lib.virginia.edu/modeng/modengC.browse.html.

Here the protocol is http://, the domain name is extext.lib.virginia.edu/, the path is modeng/, and the filename is modengC.browse.html.

In some cases you need to specify only part of a URL. For example, to go to the Electronic Text Library at the University of Virginia, you would need to specify only the protocol and the domain name, http://etext.lib.virginia.edu/

When the filename is missing, most Web servers use a filename of index.htm or index.html. Let's look at each of the parts of the URL and see what they mean.

PROTOCOL

The *protocol* of a URL identifies the format of the information being accessed from the Internet. The browser must know how to interpret what it finds. To explain this, let's suppose your browser can translate French, German, or Chinese into English. In order to accomplish this task, it must know which of those languages it is translating from. That is what the protocol tells the browser—how the information it is receiving is organized. There are seven common protocols, shown in Table 1.1. As you might expect, we will primarily use the *hypertext transfer protocol (http)* with your browser to display the hyper documents created throughout this book.

Table 1.1   Types of Internet protocols

Protocol	Example	Description
file:	file:///c|foobar.htm	Used for a file you want the browser to read. Usually the file is located on the same computer as the document that points to it. Notice that the address has three slashes, not two, and the drive letter "C" is followed by a vertical bar, not a colon.
ftp:	ftp://ftp.fancyfoo.stuff/foobar.txt	Used for a resource you want to bring back to the current computer. Usually this is used if you want your users to be able to download or copy a file to their computers.
gopher:	gopher://deep.gopher.hole/	Used to transfer control to a gopher site and allow you to display the files available there.
http:	http://unreal.place.com/	Used for links that point to other Web pages. The link is specified as an http link so the browser knows it is looking for another Web page.
mailto:	mailto:someone@somewhere.net	Used to start a mail program if the browser supports mailto URLs. Often used to request feedback about a Web page. Notice that there are no slashes.
news:	news:alt.some.cool.newsgroup news:C6491Rt@netplace.net	Used if the browser supports Usenet news URL. The first example opens the news reader for a specific newsgroup. The second example opens a specific article from a specific newsgroup. Each article is given a number to identify it. Notice that there are no slashes.
telnet:	telnet://user:password@server:port telnet://server:port	The first example will login remotely at the computer specified, using the username and password supplied. This is a dangerous practice, because your username and password are visible in the HTML code. In the second example, the browser will prompt for a username and password before making the connection. It is a safer alternative. Always remember to tell your users what username and password to use if you don't supply one.

DOMAIN

The **domain name** is the second part of the URL. It specifies the physical location of the file or information resource. A *domain* is the computer that runs the Web server software handling the protocol specified in the first part of the URL. The domain portion of the URL starts immediately after the colon or the two slashes (//) ending the protocol. The domain name ends with a single slash. You can specify the domain either by its IP address (discussed next) or by using a domain name that stands for the site's IP address.

Internet Protocol (IP) addresses are four sets of one, two, or three digits separated by periods. No three-digit number is ever greater than 255. An example of an IP address is 198.95.251.5. IP addresses identify specific computers on the Internet, including the Web. If you choose to use a domain name instead of an IP address, a special program called a *Domain Name Server (DNS)* will try to translate the domain name into the IP address. If it cannot translate the domain name, you will see the annoying "DNS unable to translate domain name" message.

Since most people find numbers harder to remember than names, it is a better practice to tell someone to download software from www.mycompany.com than from 198.95.251.53, the IP address. Domain names can be very long. They usually end in a two- or three-character extension. Some extensions indicate the country of the domain. For example, a domain name that ends in .au indicates an Australian site, and one that ends in .fr indicates a location in France.

In addition to country domain name extensions, other common extensions supported by the Internet Corporation for Assigned Names and Numbers (ICANN) are shown in Table 1.2. Included in this table are new extensions that were approved for international use by ICANN in November 2000. This list of new extensions was shorter than many Web users had expected in view of the increased use of the Internet worldwide. As an alternative to ICANN's closed selection process, the OpenNIC group is promoting the democratic selection of new domain name extensions.

Table 1.2   Common domain name extensions

Original Extensions	Meaning
.edu	Educational site, usually a college or university
.com	Commercial site or business
.gov	Government sites like the White House or Senate
.org	Nonprofit organizations
.net	Usually an ISP (Internet Service Provider)
New Extensions	**Meaning**
.aero	Air transport industry
.biz	Business
.coop	Cooperatives
.info	Unrestricted
.museum	Museums
.name	Personal applications
.pro	Professionals such as accountants, doctors, and lawyers

If you want to look at the main page for a domain, you can usually just give the protocol and domain without specifying a path or filename. For example, to see Netscape's home page, just type the following into the navigation line for your browser: http://home.netscape.com / To see Yahoo's home page, use http://www.yahoo.com.

PATH AND FILENAME

If the resource you are connecting to is a file (HTML document), then the URL will end in a filename. In the example for Figure 1.2, the URL of http://etext.lib.virgina.edu/modeng/modengC.browse.html was used. The path and filename appear after the forward slash that follows edu. The HTML document's filename is modengC.browse.html, and its path is modeng, which is the name of the folder directory in which the file is located. URLs are the heart of navigation across the World Wide Web, and we will use them throughout our exploration of HTML.

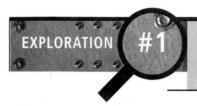

EXPLORATION #1 Use a search site to find a Web site that registers domain names. Find an available domain name that uses one of the extensions found in Table 1.2. How much would it cost to register this domain name for one year?

▸▸HTML TERMINOLOGY

Like any other specialized skill, using HTML requires that you learn some specific terms. Some of the terms are logical, and some are, well, a little odd. If you're going to read books about HTML, talk with people about HTML, or cruise the Net to find out more about HTML, you will need to learn a handful of specialized terms.

TAGS AND CONTAINERS

One of the first terms you will run across is ***tag***. Tags are HTML codes enclosed in angle brackets (<and>). These tags are used to lay out the Web page. For example, the <br> tag adds a line break into the text. Other tags format text, insert graphics, or change the screen color. You will learn more about specific HTML tags in the chapters that follow.

Tags come in two general types: containers and empty tags. The tag <br> is an *empty tag;* it does not hold, or surround, any text. *Containers,* on the other hand, do hold text. They have both a starting tag and an ending tag. Between the starting and ending tags is information that is controlled by the container. For example, the **bold** container tag is very useful when formatting text. It looks like this in HTML:

This text is bold

This container would produce the following when viewed by most browsers:

This text is ***bold***

The bold container makes the text it holds, or contains, appear in a bold font. If a bold font is not available, the browser may make the text appear in reverse video (white text on a black background) or underlined. Notice that the bold tag starts with what looks like an empty tag () and ends with a slightly different form of that tag. The ending tag has a right, or forward, slash before the tag character (). It is very important to place the ending tag immediately behind the text it contains. In this case, if we left off the ending tag, the browser would bold the rest of the text in the document.

ATTRIBUTES

Empty or starting container tags can contain other HTML elements called *attributes*, which are special codes that modify the related tag. For example, the <p>paragraph</p> container identifies a paragraph of text. One of its attributes, **align,** allows you to have the contents of the paragraph left justified, right justified, or centered in the line like this:

Place this line in the middle of the page.

Ending container tags cannot have attributes.

The browser will usually choose to align the text on the left margin unless you specify otherwise. In other words, left alignment is the default value. A *default value* is the option or feature a program uses when the user does not specify a particular one.

The **align** attribute is part of the starting tag. Let's look at the examples of this container in Figure 1.8 so that you can see how tags and attributes look in actual HTML code. If we put the code at the top of Figure 1.8 into an HTML document, it will look like the screen shown at the bottom of Figure 1.8 when displayed by a browser.

Don't worry if some of the code you see appears a little odd right now. You are just beginning your exploration of HTML. As with learning any new language, it will take a little time to figure it out.

Good HTML authors always close every container. We realize that popular browsers no longer require the ending tag for several commonly used tags. However, new standards, like XML, require that all containers be closed. Actually, the XML extensions to HTML don't even support empty tags.

HTML specifications are constantly changing; new tags are added, older tags are *deprecated*, meaning they are listed as nearing *obsolete* status, when they can no longer be used. The way tags are used evolves. Regardless, professionals follow the rules until a tag is declared obsolete. The organization that oversees these changes is discussed in the next section.

One of the more interesting and yet confusing features of most HTML browsers is their ability to infer, or guess, when to close a container. For example the code in Figure 1.9 will

Figure 1.8 The HTML code is used by the browser to create the screen display below

```
<html>
<head>
<title>Paragraph Using align Attribute</title>
</head>
<body>
<p align="right">
Right is Right
</p>

<p align="center">
Center is Middle
</p>

<p align="left">
Left is Left
</p>

<p>
Left is also the Default
</p>

</body>
</html>
```

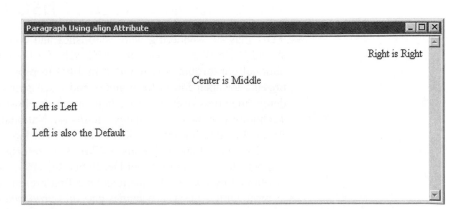

Figure 1.9

This HTML code is poorly written because the ending tags are missing

```
<p align="right">
Right is Right

<p align="center">
Center is Middle

<p align="left">
Left is Left

<p>
Left is also the Default
```

produce exactly the same results shown in Figure 1.8. Compare this poorly written HTML code in Figure 1.9 with the code in Figure 1.8.

Notice that there are no closing paragraph tags in Figure 1.9. Most browsers will properly infer when you want to end one paragraph and start another, so you might be able to "get away" with using the code in Figure 1.9. But good Web weavers do not leave things to chance. One of the coding rules to live by is to close every container, even those at the end of a document. Otherwise, you could produce some very strange-looking pages. If you are coding in XML, every tag *must* have an ending tag.

▸▸HTML CODE FORMAT

The <p> container provides a good example of the general format of HTML coding. It is used to contain the paragraphs within an HTML document. You will see exactly how to use this container when you build your first Web page in Chapter Two. For now we will use it to examine the code's format.

You can see from Figure 1.10 that there are three parts to an HTML container. The beginning tag, which may have attributes, is the first part. The text held by the container is the second part. The ending tag is the third part. If you choose not to use a particular attribute, the browser reading the document will choose a value, the default, for you. The general format of an empty tag is just like the starting tag of the container. We will explore both types of tags in more detail in Chapter Two.

Figure 1.10

HTML code format

```
<p align="RIGHT">Right is Right</p>
   |—— attribute ——|
|—— beginning tag ——|—— content of container ——|– ending tag –|
```

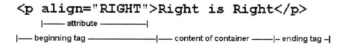

▸▸WORLD WIDE WEB CONSORTIUM (W^{3}C)

You may be wondering who establishes and controls HTML protocols and tags. The World Wide Web Consortium (W^{3}C) sets, for the most part, these standards. This international consortium was founded in 1994 to promote the evolution of the Web and to provide an open forum to organize and discuss changes. Over 200 commercial or academic members oversee W^{3}C. It is physically hosted by the Massachusetts Institute of Technology in the United States, the Institut National de Recherche en Informatique et en Automatique in Europe, and Keio University in Japan.

The current specifications, HTML 4, were originally published by the W^{3}C on December 18, 1997, and revised December 24, 1999, as HTML 4.01. HTML specifications developed by consortium members are first presented as a *working draft.* If the new tag or protocol has merit, it becomes part of a *proposed recommendation.* When W^{3}C members reach consensus on a proposed recommendation, it is elevated to a *recommendation.*

Figure 1.11

The World Wide Web consortium specifications for HTML 4.01

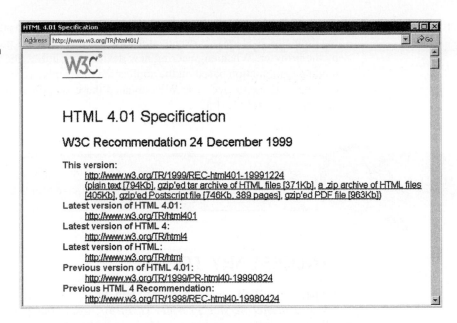

Software developers are then supposed to design new browsers and other Internet tools using these recommendations. In some cases developers push the W³C by incorporating proposed recommendations into beta releases of their software. Once a recommendation is published, periodic updates follow to correct minor problems. Figure 1.11 is from the December 24, 1999, revision.

Sometimes recommendations offer a new method to achieve a given result. For example, the <style> tag that changes font attributes has replaced the <basefont> and <font> tags. The W³C takes a two-step approach to eliminating older tags. The first step is to list deprecated HTML tags. As explained earlier, these tags are still supported by software but are designated as "on their way out." Eventually W³C members agree on when tags have become *obsolete,* meaning that they should no longer be used because the updated versions of the browsers will not recognize them.

When reading W³C recommendations you will encounter some terminology that is a little different from what you read in this book. For instance, browsers are referred to as *user agents.* The W³C also uses the term *URI (Uniform Resource Identifier)* instead of URL. The term URI has broader implications then URL, as the following quote from the W³C's reference on this issue indicates:

> The term "Uniform Resource Locator" (URL) refers to the subset of URI that identify resources via a representation of their primary access mechanism (e.g., their network "location"), rather than identifying the resource by name or by some other attribute(s) of that resource. (Berners-Lee, T., Fielding, R., Masinter, L., "Uniform Resource Identifiers (URI): Generic Syntax, August 1998)

We will continue to use the term URL in this text to mean a specific Internet location because this term is universally understood in this context.

The W³C released specifications for the *Extensible HyperText Markup Language (XHTML)* in December 1999 as an advancement of its HTML 4 recommendation. XHTML is seen as a set of specifications that bridge the development of Internet browsers from HTML to XML. While using structures and tags popularized by HTML, XHTML organizes these tags into modules. Browsers working in wireless devices, cellular phones, or handheld computers can then be designed to recognize selected XHTML modules.

The W³C realizes that users' information needs vary depending on how they are accessing the Internet. A cellular telephone displaying the departure time of someone's flight to Chicago has one set of requirements, usually quite limited. The student using her desktop computer to display a video from the school's Web site has a more robust set of requirements. XHTML is designed to provide flexibility in the amount of memory used by the browser. When engineering new devices that utilize the Internet, designers select a module combination based on the application (text-only, voice-only, graphical) and memory needs of the device. The W^3C updated these specifications in April 2001 when recommending XHTML 1.1.

EXPLORATION #2   Use your favorite browser to display the World Wide Web consortium's home page found at www.w3c.org. Bookmark or save this Web page as a favorite.

▸▸ NECESSARY TOOLS

To become a Web weaver, you need only three tools: a simple ASCII editor, a browser, and an ***Internet Service Provider (ISP)*** to "host" your page. An ISP is a company or school that will put your document on a Web server so other people can browse your page from across the Internet. Making your page available on a known domain is called ***hosting*** your page. The ***Web administrator*** is the person who maintains the Web server, operating system, security, backup, and other basic computer "housekeeping." This person is not to be confused with a ***Web master***, who is responsible for a collection of Web pages on a Web site.

Let's look at the three tools every Web author must have: an ASCII editor, a browser, and an ISP.

ASCII EDITOR

The first requirement for building Web pages is a tool that produces plain ASCII files as output. ASCII stands for *American Standard Code for Information Interchange*. An ***ASCII editor*** produces a standard ASCII file, meaning a file with just the text and no embedded word-processing codes. Most word-processing software will add formatting, font, and other types of codes to the document. Browsers don't know what to do with those extra characters. Figure 1.12 shows an ASCII editor (Windows' Notepad) displaying the HTML codes for the page shown in Figure 1.6.

To produce HTML code, you need a simple editor. If you are using a Unix system, the vi editor is an excellent choice. The Notepad editor in Windows or Simple Text editor for the Macs will also work. Most of the word processors can save a file as plain ASCII. You need to select the "Save as" option and ask for "DOS text." Remember to save your document with an extension of .htm in Windows or .html in Unix so that browser software will recognize it as an HTML document. For example, an HTML document called compare.htm on a computer running Windows would be called compare.html on a Unix or Macintosh platform.

Almost any word-processing or editing package can be used, but it is sometimes easier to produce HTML code with a simple HTML editor. Add-ons are available for some of the more popular word processors that enable them to act as HTML editors. Later in this chapter we will discuss specialized HTML editors.

BROWSER

An ASCII editor initially saves the HTML document on the Web weaver's personal computer. Once it is saved on one of the computer's disks (hard or floppy), any browser can open and display it. Before this file is ever posted on the Internet, you will open and close it many times as you fine-tune the content and test it on different browsers. There are a couple of ways you can view your document to see how it will appear on the World Wide Web.

Figure 1.12

ASCII editor displaying codes for
Web page shown in Figure 1.6

```
example.htm - Notepad                                    _ □ ×
File  Edit  Format  Help
<html>
<head>
<title>Example HTML Document</title>
</head>
<body>

<h1>Level-1 Heading</h1>
<p>The elements of an HTML document
and the resulting Web page are the
same as those found in any written document.
For example, a paragraph like this one is a
common design element.
</p>

<h2>Level-2 Heading</h2>
<p>There are ordered lists: </p>
<ol>
  <li>This </li>
  <li>That </li>
  <li>Another thing </li>
</ol>

<h3>Level-3 Heading</h3>
<p>There are unordered (bulleted) lists: </p>
<ul>
  <li>This </li>
  <li>That </li>
  <li>Another thing </li>
</ul>

</body>
</html>
```

The recommended way to preview your documents is with your browser. Most browsers allow you to specify the source of the HTML documents you are browsing, which can be the hard disk of your personal computer. For example, with Internet Explorer and Opera, you simply click on the File menu, click on Open, identify the disk storing the file, and type in the name of the file you just created. Navigator uses the Open File menu option.

The latest versions of most word-processing software can open HTML documents. If you are using an older word processor, check to see if you can download an HTML viewer add-on for it. With such a viewer, you see what your new document will look like as a Web page, at least in regard to your choice of colors, fonts, and local images. Be aware, however, that word-processing software often formats the Web page differently than a browser. Therefore, you might find the placement of images or the spacing of text different in the browser than it was in your word processor.

Remember that you want your Web page to be useful in text-only browsers so always view it in a text-only browser like Lynx as well as in a graphical browser. Responsible Web weavers ensure that users with nongraphical browsers will be able to gain information from their pages.

INTERNET SERVICE PROVIDER (ISP)

Most people don't maintain a full-time, high-speed connection to the Internet. As a result, they need an organization to store your Web pages and make them available on the Internet. As mentioned earlier, companies that host Web sites are called ISPs (Internet Service Providers). Your college may act as an ISP and host student Web sites. Or it may provide Internet access and email but not the storage space or personal Internet address needed to maintain a Web site. Colleges usually ask students to pay additional fees to support these ISP capabilities. If you don't know what Internet services your college supports, ask your instructor or someone in student services.

As you might expect, services and the related fees vary among ISPs. Some charge a monthly fee for the storage space you use. Others include a fixed amount of space in their pricing but charge you for any space you use above the limit. For example, one ISP charges users $49.95 per year for Internet access. This ISP will host up to 2 megabytes of Web pages as part of the yearly fee. If the user needs more storage space, the cost is $1.95 per megabyte per month. There is no additional fee for connect time, email messages sent or received, or any other services. However, technical support is available only during office hours, Monday through Friday.

Another ISP charges $19.95 a month. For this charge the user gets access to the Internet, an email account with unlimited send and receive capabilities, a customized graphical browser, special services (like online stock portfolio management) and technical support 24 hours a day, seven days a week. If you want this ISP to host your Web site, you are charged an additional $2.50 per megabyte per month.

These two different ISPs illustrate some of the significant difference in services and price. Consider a budget-priced ISP if you are able to download your own browser and install it on your computer and don't need much technical support. If you want more support, or want to be able to just type "install" to load the customized browser the ISP sent you on the CD, you may wish to subscribe to a more expensive "value-added" ISP, like AOL. As always, you get what you pay for.

▸▸NICE-TO-HAVE TOOLS

You can get by with just the tools mentioned in the previous section, but there are other HTML tools that will make your job of building and maintaining Web pages much easier.

1. Although you can build Web pages with a simple ASCII editor, it is much easier and faster to use an ***HTML editor*** that automatically embeds tags into your document.

2. For a "quick and dirty" Web page design you can use your *word-processing program* to create an HTML document from formatted text using a text-to-HTML converter, which comes with most recent releases.

3. To ensure that your Web page works correctly, we would suggest using an ***HTML validator*** to verify that your hyperlinks are valid and your HTML syntax and structure are correct.

4. You can use your Web pages to execute programs of your own creation through the use of a *JavaScript editor* or other scripting tools.

5. Those of you who are looking ahead to future technologies would benefit from having an *XML editor*. The W^{3}C has told Web authors to look at these recommendations for further developments in Web page design.

These tools are found in a variety of software packages. Software developers often combine them into a single product. Let's look at each tool individually.

HTML EDITOR

An HTML editor adds tags at the click of a button to create an HTML document. Many HTML editors are available for downloading from the Internet. Some are free (*freeware*), some are commercial products, and some are ***shareware***. While you can legally give copies of either freeware or shareware to a friend, installing and using shareware *obligates* you to register the software and pay any registration fees.

There is quite a bit of variability in the way HTML editors work. Some show the HTML tags in their own window area. The user then switches to a viewing area to preview the Web page just as you do with a browser. This type of editor often allows the Web weaver to split the view between the two areas as shown in Figure 1.13. Being able to see the tags and attributes, not simply the results is an advantage in editing, or modifying, the document. A disadvantage is that you can edit only in the code area and therefore have to switch back and forth between HTML code view and Web design view. Another

Figure 1.13

HTML code as it appears in
Dreamweaver HTML editor

Code Area

Preview Area

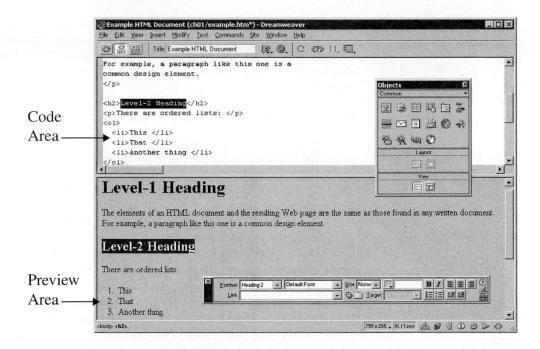

disadvantage of this type of editor is that the way it displays a page may be vastly different than the way the browsers will display it.

Other HTML editors take a *WYSIWYG (What You See Is What You Get)* approach to displaying the code. Compare the way the editor in Figure 1.13 displays code with the way the WYSIWYG-type editor displays the same code in Figure 1.14. This type of HTML editor acts like a browser, but allows the Web author to edit the document and insert HTML tags. One disadvantage to the WYSIWYG approach is that the user must often infer which attributes, like bold or single spacing, are being used. Furthermore, you are never guaranteed that any independent HTML editor or viewer will handle the codes the same as your favorite browser.

Figure 1.14 shows Netscape's Composer, which is the HTML editor that comes with Netscape's Communicator software package. It shows you the HTML tags and provides a set of menus and buttons that assist you in editing the document. Buttons are used to insert new tags. Authors select attributes from pop-up menus.

Figure 1.14

Example HTML code as it
appears in Netscape's Composer
HTML editor

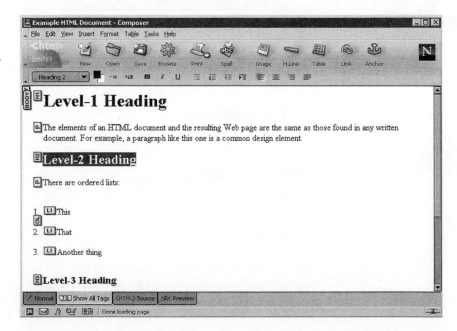

The editing style you choose is a personal decision. Almost any editor will get the job done for you. However, as teachers, we prefer editors that let the student see as much of the code as possible. By working with HTML code at this level students get a better understanding of the relationships between the code and what ends up on the browser's screen.

TEXT-TO-HTML CONVERTER

Text-to-HTML converters can be used to embed codes within an existing text file to make it an HTML document. Popular word processors can convert word-processed documents into HTML documents. For example, the latest versions of Word come with a text-to-HTML converter as shown in Figure 1.15. Depending on the software, you convert a file by using the File menu's "Save as HTML" or "Save as Web Page" option. Other word processors, like StarWriter, part of the Star Office suite, use the File menu's "Save As" option and have you set the file type to "HTML."

Compare the HTML code in Figure 1.15 with the code in Figure 1.12. While the code results in the same screen display, many text-to-HTML converters are notorious for adding unnecessary tags and using complicated coding when simple alternatives would suffice. Figure 1.12 contains 28 lines of code. This is the bare bones minimum HTML code necessary to produce the desired results, but it is missing comments and other optional tags we are going to recommend using. The HTML code generated by Word in Figure 1.15 contains 191 lines of HTML code to get essentially the same screen display.

Figure 1.15 Word processor displaying HTML source code

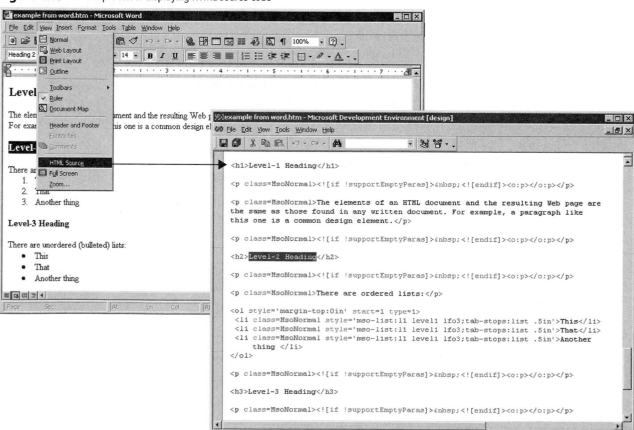

HTML VALIDATOR

Before publishing your page on the Web, you must make sure that it works. If you have some links that don't connect, or some containers that are left unclosed, your users may end up with results you didn't intend. To solve these problems, you can personally test each link and exercise each part of your page to ensure that it performs as expected. However, if you have a large set of pages with hundreds of links, it would take a lot of time to do the testing. HTML validators (Figure 1.16) check your pages for errors, testing each link and making sure the syntax is correct.

The URLs for obtaining the CSE validator by AI Internet Solutions and the Weblint validator are listed at the end of this chapter. You can also visit the W³C's Web site and use its validator to have your pages evaluated. If you are building a large Web site or for some other reason cannot take the time to evaluate all your links and syntax, you should use one of these validation resources.

Many of the full-feature HTML editors, like Macromedia's Dreamweaver or Microsoft's FrontPage, incorporate a *site manager* to test links used within the code for accuracy. If the site manager finds a link that does not connect to a Web page, it flags it as a "broken link."

JAVASCRIPT EDITOR

Just as an HTML editor makes writing and testing HTML somewhat easier, a JavaScript editor can simplify the task of building and testing JavaScript code. We will provide you with an overview of JavaScript in Chapter Thirteen. For now let's just say that the JavaScript editor helps you write your own computer programs that become part of the Web page. Figure 1.17 shows the opening screen for a popular JavaScript editor called ScriptBuilder. It shows some of the library tools available in the left frame, and the source code for an HTML page that has a JavaScript on the right. Notice how the different parts of the script look different. They are also colored differently to help the author distinguish them. If you are going to use JavaScript, investing in a good JavaScript editor can significantly lighten your load.

Figure 1.16   HTML validator checks for syntax errors in the coding

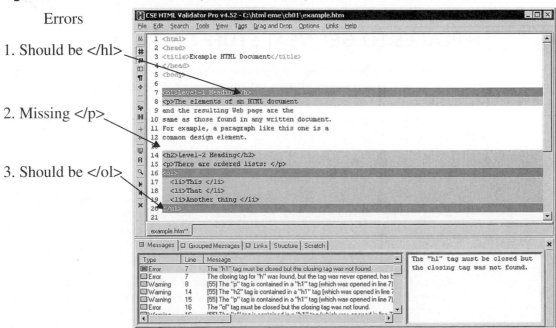

Figure 1.17

JavaScript editor

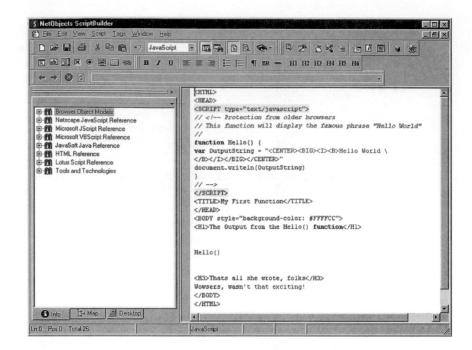

XML EDITOR

Good Web authors have a variety of software tools available so as to handle different Web page designs appropriately. If Web authors embrace W³C's XML recommendations, then an XML editor will eventually be one of these tools, if for no other reason than the fact that HTML editors will evolve into XML editors. One additional function of an XML editor is to create and maintain *document type definitions (DTD),* which define the tags and attributes that describe data sets used by the Web page. For example, your school might have a DTD that describes the data about classes for Web-based enrollment. This DTD might define the <course></course> tag, which contains <section></section>, <description></description>, <maxsize></maxsize>, and <semester></semester> tags. Not every Web page needs the flexibility provided by XML coding. We will introduce you to XML coding in Chapter Fifteen.

▸▸PLACES TO GET NEAT STUFF ON THE NET

An astounding number of Web sites provide software that works with HTML. What follows is only a partial listing of the available software. Since URLs may change from day to day, some of these sites may be no longer be available, in which case you can use a search site to find other sites that are more current. This list is a place to start, not an exhaustive one.

WHERE TO GET BROWSERS

1. **Netscape** (http://www.netscape.com)**.** This is one of the favorite browsers for the Web. You can download the most recent version of this browser, and if you are associated with a school, you can register your copy for free. From this site you can download the Navigator browser for several platforms including both Macintosh and Windows platforms.

2. **Opera** (http://www.opera.com)**.** This new guy is faster and sleeker than the others and is gaining quite a following, especially from those in the know within cyber space.

3. **Internet Explorer** (http://www.microsoft.com). This is the other "big" browser in the browser wars. You can download the most recent version free from Microsoft.

4. **Lynx** (http://www.cc.ukans.edu/about_lynx/about_lynx.html and ftp://www.cc.ukans.edu/pub/lynx). This is one of the most often used non-graphical, or text-only, browsers. You should always test your pages with a non-graphical browser so you know you are addressing the needs of those users who don't believe that a picture is worth a thousand words. The first URL given here tells you about Lynx, and you can download it from the second URL.

WHERE TO GET HTML EDITORS

A wide selection of HTML editors exists. Many are shareware or freeware, and some are commercial packages. These editors are often designed for the nonprofessional to build what we call "one-shot" Web pages for situations where updating won't be needed. For example, your neighbor could use one of these tools to build a page to display her quilt patterns if she knew she would not be adding any more patterns and therefore would never need to change the page. The following list is just a small sample of the available products.

1. **Dreamweaver** (http://www.macromedia.com). This is a full-feature HTML editor that includes code validation and site management features. Developed by Macromedia, which is famous for Web plug-ins like Flash and development software like ColdFusion, this editor links with a variety of home-grown software tools.

2. **FrontPage** (http://www.microsoft.com). FrontPage is bundled with Microsoft Office's Developer edition or may be purchased as an independent package. Due to the popularity of the Office suite of application software, FrontPage is one of the more frequently used HTML editors.

3. **HotDog** (http://www.sausage.com). This is one of the better HTML editors if you want to see HTML presented as the language rather than as the outcome. If you purchase the professional version, it includes a page viewer, so you don't need a browser as you initially code your pages. However, the page viewer is limited in the attributes it accepts. Therefore, it is best to have a browser available to view the page.

4. **NoteTab** (http://www.notepad.com). This highly respected HTML editor can be purchased for under $20 and a "lite" version is offered for free.

WHERE TO GET TEXT-TO-HTML CONVERTERS

If you need to convert an existing electronic file into an HTML document, you can use an HTML editor or one of the following word processors.

1. **Star Office** (http://www.sun.com). Sun Microsystems's inexpensive, multiplatform suite of application software, including word processing, is rapidly gaining popularity with people who seek a very powerful and functional alternative to expensive, proprietary office tools.

2. **Word** (http://www.microsoft.com). The word-processing component of Microsoft's popular Office suite of application software is currently the most used word processor on the market.

3. **WordPerfect** (http://www.corel.com). Once the most widely used word-processing package, WordPerfect has evolved to become the centerpiece of Corel's WordPerfect suite of application software.

WHERE TO GET HTML VALIDATORS

It is important to ensure that your Web page contains valid links and correct syntax. You can use these HTML verifiers at the URLs listed.

1. **CSE** (http://www.htmlvalidator.com). The latest version of this full-power validator is found at the Web site for AI Internet Solutions. A demonstration version is included on the CD that comes with this book.

2. **Weblint** (http://www.sai.msu.su/admin/). This HTML validator is now being hosted by Moscow University's Sternberg Astronomical Institute.

3. **W³C** (http://validator.w3c.org). This is the validation service of the W³C.

WHERE TO GET XML EDITORS

As editors go, XML editors are relatively new and still trying to find their market niche. We would recommend using your favorite search site to find the latest XML editor reviews before downloading any demonstration packages.

1. **XmetaL** (http://www.sq.com). This product from SoftQuad (now owned by the Corel Corporation) is an example of the evolution of a respected HTML editor (HoTMetaL) into an XML editor.

2. **XML Pro** (http://www.vervet.com). This product gets good reviews and has an easy-to-use editing window.

3. **XML Spy** (http://www.xmlspy.com). This product is considered to have one of the more intuitive interfaces and gets high marks as an XML editor.

SHAREWARE SITES

Many of the software tools used by Web weavers are shareware packages that can be downloaded for free from the Internet. You can read product reviews and download related software from these Web sites:

1. **Tucows—The Ultimate Collection of Windows Software** (http://www.tucows.com). This popular Web site for access to the latest shareware rates programs from one to five cows, with a five-cow rating being the best.

2. **Ziff Davis Shareware Download** (http://www.zdnet.com/downloads). The Ziff Davis publishing group has a strong presence on the Internet through its ZDNet and CNET Web sites. The ZDNet site provides links to shareware downloads and electronic publications that tie into the company's television programming and magazines.

3. **CNET Shareware** (http://shareware.cnet.com and http://www.download.com). The CNET Web site provides access to shareware along with reviews of new software and hardware.

SEARCH SITES

Many new and better HTML tools will become available as more and more people begin to use the Web to transfer information. Following are some of the more popular search tools for exploring the Web to find additional resources.

1. **Alta Vista** (http://www.altavista.com)

2. **Ask Jeeves** (http://www.aj.com)

3. **Dogpile** (http://www.dogpile.com)

4. **Excite** (http://www.excite.com)

5. **Google** (http://www.google.com)

6. **Hotbot** (http://www.hotbot.com)

7. **Momma** (http://momma.com)

8. **Northern Light** (http://www.northernlight.com)

9. **Teoma** (http://www.teoma.com)

10. **Yahoo** (http://www.yahoo.com)

▸▸ORGANIZATIONS PROMOTING INTERNET USAGE

Following are the URLs for the Internet organizations mentioned in this chapter.

1. **ICANN** (http://www.icann.org). This organization assigns domain names and extensions for the Internet.

2. **OpenNic** (http://www.openic.unrated.net). This Internet group advocates a democratic voting process for the assignment of new domain name extensions.

3. **W³C** (http://www.w3.org). The latest HTML, XML, and XHTML recommendations can be obtained here.

▸▸KEY TERMS

ASCII editor	Internet Protocol (IP) address
Attribute	Internet Service Provider (ISP)
Browser	Link
Default value	Page
Deprecated	Platform
Document	Plug-in
Domain name	Protocol
Download	Search site
Home page	Shareware
Hosting	Tag
HTML editor	Uniform Resource Locator (URL)
HTML validator	Web administrator
Hyper document	Web master
Hypertext markup language (HTML)	Web site
Internet address	White space

▸▸REVIEW QUESTIONS

1. Define each of the key terms.
2. With respect to the Internet, what is the difference between a document and a page?
3. Who or what controls a Web page's content and layout?
4. Why is a hyper document considered more useful than a standard text document?
5. How is XML different from HTML?
6. What seven features are common to most graphical browsers?
7. What are the names of three graphical browsers and one text-only browser?
8. How many browsers should a Web weaver use to test a newly designed Web page?
9. Identify and describe seven protocols used on the Internet.

10. List 12 domain name extensions approved by ICANN and describe the orientation of sites using each extension.

11. What special characters enclose HTML tags?

12. In HTML container tags, what distinguishes the ending tag from the beginning tag?

13. What does the World Wide Web Consortium do?

14. Describe the five-step life cycle of an HTML tag.

15. How do the XHTML recommendations advance HTML?

16. Describe three tools every Web weaver uses.

17. What are three situations that might require additional fees from ISPs?

▸▸EXERCISES

1.1. Use an ASCII editor to describe the computer platform you are using for this class.

1.2. Find and print two Web site designs, one you like and one you don't like. Use an ASCII editor to type and print a brief narrative about each page explaining what made you pick it as an example.

1.3. Find and print the latest revision to the HTML specifications. Your instructor might want to limit the number of pages you output.

1.4. Use the Internet to find a page where you can get a legal copy of your favorite browser, then employ an ASCII editor to explain how you would do it.

1.5. Print the HTML code for the home page of a Web site you like to use.

1.6. Visit the ICANN and OpenNIC Web sites. Use an ASCII editor to summarize the different approaches to establishing new domain name extensions.

## Chapter Two

Your First Web Page

Now that you know some of the terminology used in HTML, it's time to build a simple page. The purpose of the World Wide Web is to share information. Your page should provide unique information to your users in a way that is easy to understand and pleasant to view. Remember that not all the users will have graphical browsers, so build your page in a way that is usable in both graphical and text-only modes. Let's look at the basic tags used in every HTML document.

CHAPTER OBJECTIVES

After reading this chapter you should be able to do the following:

- Identify the SGML and HTML elements required in every HTML document.
- Use an HTML template to create a new Web page.
- Write internationalized HTML code that is language specific.
- Incorporate specific W3C-supported DTDs into a Web page's coding.
- Identify the HTML elements that make up the XHTML Structure module.
- Integrate into HTML documents meaningful titles and comments.
- List common HTML coding errors.
- Use a browser to view Web pages saved on a local disk drive.
- Employ heading and paragraph elements within a well-written HTML document.
- Explain how empty tags are coded differently when using the HTML versus the XML specifications.
- Appropriately use line breaks and horizontal rules within a Web page.
- Use browser-safe RGB hexadecimal numbers or color names to change a Web page's background or text color.
- Identify the pitfalls in using background images and changing the default link colors.

▸▸ELEMENTS OF A WEB PAGE

As mentioned in Chapter One, in HTML there are two major types of markup labels: empty elements (tags) and containers. ***Empty elements*** are used for page formatting. An empty element has no closing tag and so does not enclose any text. It starts with a left angle bracket (<) followed immediately by the tag identifier, or name. Next come any ***attributes***—special words that modify the way the tag works—separated by spaces. The tag ends with a right angle bracket (>). For example, <hr width="50%"> is an empty tag that puts a line across the screen. The attribute, width="50%", determines how long the line is, in this case 50 percent of the screen width.

Container elements are used to manipulate, or control, the contents placed within them. Containers begin with a starting tag, which is enclosed within angle brackets like an empty tag. They also have an ending tag that marks the end of the text they contain, or surround. The ending tag starts with a left angle bracket, has a slash (/) preceding the tag identifier, and ends with a right angle bracket: </html> is an example of an ending tag. There can be no attributes on an ending tag, and the tag identifier (name) must be preceded by a slash (/).

CREATING AN HTML TEMPLATE

The starting container element that surrounds the whole Web page is <html>. It is closed by the </html> tag. All the HTML contents of a Web page or document must be enclosed by the <html> *contents of page* </html> container. This is the beginning of your first HTML document.

A handful of other HTML elements are used in almost every *HTML document* along with the <html></html> container shown in Figure 2.1. We recommend that you type them into your computer using an ASCII editor and save them as html-tmp.htm or html-tmp.html. Use this file as a template whenever you create a new HTML document. Remember that you need to save a copy of this template file as a new file under a different name, so that you won't overwrite the template by mistake.

All the elements used in Figure 2.1, except DOCTYPE, are containers. Notice that a container element can contain other container elements. When this happens, wise Web weavers always double-check that they do not accidentally reverse the order of the ending tags. In Figure 2.1 the <title> tag is inside the <head> tag. Therefore, the </title> ending tag must precede the </head> ending tag.

What follows is an overview of how these tags work and some of the common attributes associated with each tag.

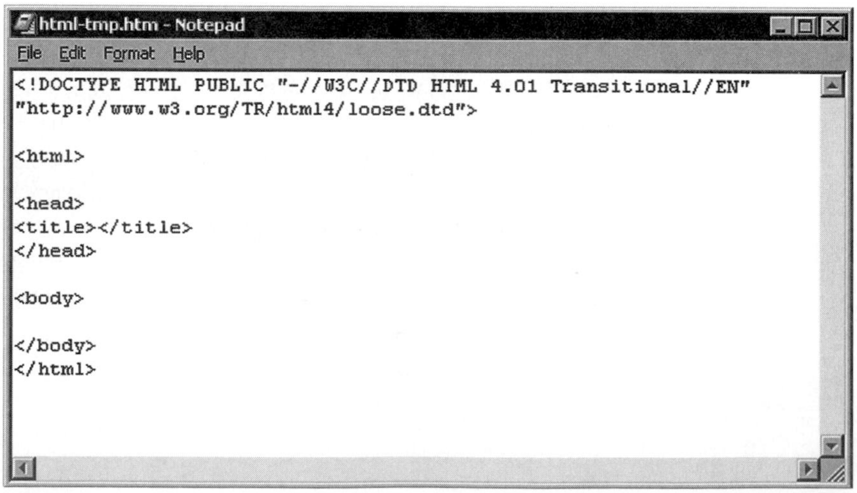

Figure 2.1

HTML template of commonly used codes

```
html-tmp.htm - Notepad
File  Edit  Format  Help

<!DOCTYPE HTML PUBLIC "-//W3C//DTD HTML 4.01 Transitional//EN"
"http://www.w3.org/TR/html4/loose.dtd">

<html>

<head>
<title></title>
</head>

<body>

</body>
</html>
```

EXPLORATION #1 Open an ASCII editor and type the code shown in Figure 2.1. Save the file as html-tmp.html on your class disk.

HTML `<html>html document</html>`

Description: first and last line in every HTML document.
Type: container.
Attributes: dir, lang, *version.*
Special note: should be preceded by SGML <!DOCTYPE> tag.

The <html> tag identifies the type of document we are creating, as well as marking the beginning and ending of our Web page. If you look at Figure 2.2, you will see the <html></html> container tags surround all the other tags and text that make up an HTML document. Browsers recognize HTML tags in either uppercase or lowercase; however, the latest XHTML specifications describe them as lowercase only, so you should code them in lowercase. In this text, we will show the HTML tags in lowercase to follow the newest standard. Be aware, though, that many older Web pages contain code that uses uppercase HTML tags.

dir

The HTML 4 specifications brought with them additional emphasis on the internationalization of the Internet. Both the **dir** and **lang** attributes (discussed next) address this issue and are recognized by almost every HTML container. The **dir** attribute sets the base direction for displaying and printing text. You can set this attribute to one of two values: LTR for left-to-right and RTL for right-to-left. For example, if you are using English, Spanish, or some other Indo-European language, the following HTML code would set the directionality of a Web page to left-to-right: <html dir="ltr">. This left-to-right text direction places the scroll bar on the right side of the screen. Languages like Hebrew that are read and written from right to left would utilize code that looks like this: <HTML dir="rtl">. In this case, the scroll bar is placed on the left side of the screen.

lang

The **lang** attribute specifies the base language of an element's attribute values and text content, as seen in Figure 2.2. The HTML 4 specifications have this to say about the **lang** attribute:

> The intent of the **lang** attribute is to allow user agents [browsers] to render content more meaningfully based on accepted cultural practice for a given language. This does not imply that user agents should render characters that are atypical for a particular language in less meaningful ways; user agents must make a best attempt to render all characters, regardless of the value specified by lang (section 8.1).

While the popular browsers often default to English ("en" is the language code for English), the **lang** attribute allows the Web weaver to create language-dependent content. Using the **lang** attribute will help the browser to properly render quotation marks, spacing, hyphenation, and ligatures. On a broader level, spell checkers and grammar checkers can benefit from having the language identified. Furthermore, using the **lang** attribute will help search sites document a page's content and help speech synthesizers pronounce words.

The **lang** attribute is set equal to a language code. For example, the following HTML code sets the page's language to Spanish: <html lang="es">. The language codes can be divided into a primary code and subcode. Two-letter primary codes are reserved for the

Figure 2.2

HTML document including SGML DOCTYPE tag, comments, heading, and paragraph tags

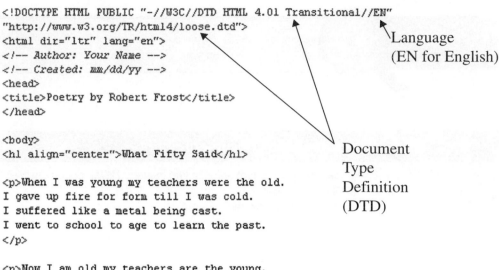

```
<!DOCTYPE HTML PUBLIC "-//W3C//DTD HTML 4.01 Transitional//EN"
"http://www.w3.org/TR/html4/loose.dtd">
<html dir="ltr" lang="en">
<!-- Author: Your Name -->
<!-- Created: mm/dd/yy -->
<head>
<title>Poetry by Robert Frost</title>
</head>

<body>
<hl align="center">What Fifty Said</hl>

<p>When I was young my teachers were the old.
I gave up fire for form till I was cold.
I suffered like a metal being cast.
I went to school to age to learn the past.
</p>

<p>Now I am old my teachers are the young.
What can't be molded must be cracked and sprung.
I strain at lessons fit to start a suture.
I go to school to youth to learn the future.
</p>

</body>
</html>
```

Language
(EN for English)

Document
Type
Definition
(DTD)

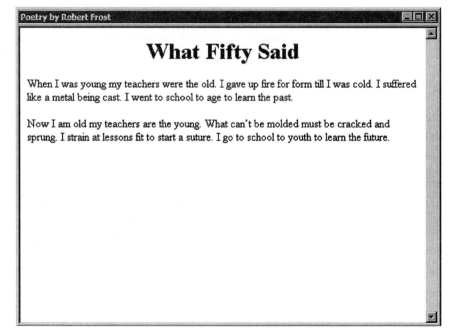

ISO 639 standard for language abbreviations. Here are some common two-letter primary codes:

Arabic—ar	Hindi—hi
Chinese—zh	Italian—it
Dutch—nl	Japanese—ja
French—fr	Norwegian—no
German—de	Portuguese—pt
Greek—el	Russian—ru
Hebrew—he	Spanish—es

The subcode identifies a dialect of the primary language, such as the English spoken in the United States versus the English spoken in Great Britain. In this case the primary code is "en" for both, but the subcode is different and is separated from the primary code by a hyphen. For U.S. English, the code is `<html lang="en-US">`. For the British cockney version of English, the code is `<html lang="en-cockney">`. Some of the subcodes identify unique languages like Navajo (lang="i-navajo"), spoken by some Native Americans, or even Klingon (lang="x-klingon"), which is spoken by very few folks on Earth.

If you have need of them, please use both the **lang** and **dir** attributes; however, other than in Figure 2.2, we will forgo the use of them in order to keep our examples as simple as possible. Our intent is not to underplay the importance of these elements, but to focus attention on the new elements being discussed and demonstrated by the related screen captures of the browser's display.

version

The <html> tag has three attributes you can use: **dir, lang,** and **version.** However, the **version** attribute was deprecated in the HTML 4 specifications. Interestingly, it was deprecated in favor of the *SGML* tag <!DOCTYPE> (discussed next). Both of these tags tell the browser which HTML specifications were used to create the document. For example, version="-//W3C//DTD HTML 4.01 Final//EN" indicates the document was created using the HTML 4.01 specifications for English. Including the **version** attribute can cause problems with some browsers, so most experts advise against its use.

<!DOCTYPE>

HTML validators require that authors identify which DTD and version of the HTML specifications they used when writing the Web page. This information is also beneficial when a company employs teams of Web weavers to maintain huge corporate Web sites. Doing so lets Web weavers new to the project know which syntax rules and elements they can expect to encounter when modifying the HTML code.

The W³C now recommends that authors use the SGML <!DOCTYPE> tag instead of the deprecated **version** attribute when they identify which HTML specifications were used. As mentioned in Chapter One, HTML is actually a subset of the universally recognized *Standard Generalized Markup Language (SGML)*. These tags were adopted by the International Standards Organization (ISO) in 1986 to describe an electronic document. The <!DOCTYPE> is an empty tag that precedes the <html></html> container. In other words, this is the first tag in the document, as shown in Figure 2.2. The <!DOCTYPE> tag is the only tag name that should be coded in uppercase characters.

The <!DOCTYPE> tag identifies which DTD is in use by the HTML document. The **Document Type Definition (DTD)** states rules governing HTML coding syntax and structure. HTML validators use one of three HTML 4.01 DTD files supported by the W³C: strict, transitional, or frameset. Deprecated coding is flagged as an error when using the strict DTD. We suggest using the *transitional DTD* while learning HTML because it allows you to use deprecated code without causing validators to generate errors. The *frameset DTD* should be used only when the Web page design breaks the screen display into multiple frames. The appropriate DOCTYPE syntax for each DTD follows:

- **Strict**

  <!DOCTYPE HTML PUBLIC "-//W3C//DTD HTML 4.01//EN"

  "http://www.w3.org/TR/html4/strict.dtd">

- **Transitional**

  <!DOCTYPE HTML PUBLIC "-//W3C//DTD HTML 4.01 Transitional//EN"

  "http://www.w3.org/TR/html4/loose.dtd">

- **Frameset**

  <!DOCTYPE HTML PUBLIC "-//W3C//DTD html 4.01 Frameset//EN"

  "http://www.w3.org/TR/html4/frameset.dtd">

Notice that these tags reference the W³C Web site with the HTML 4 specifications. The DOCTYPE element also identifies the language to be used by the DTD. The HTML template in Figure 2.2 is designed to use the transitional DTD written in English. Like

HTML tags, this tag can be placed on one or more lines. Where the author breaks the line does not matter. Usually authors break long lines to make the code easier to read. Even though every HTML document should start with the DOCTYPE tag, the remaining examples used in this book will not include this element so as to keep the screen captures as short as possible.

 **<head>header data</head>**

Description: provides descriptive information about a document as part of the header.
Type: container.
Attributes: dir, lang, **profile.**

The <head> container primarily serves to identify the other tags that make up the header. It can include the **dir** and **lang** attributes just discussed. However, the W^3C now strongly encourages the use of the SGML DOCTYPE tag, which always specifies a language. It appears that the **lang** attribute will probably become deprecated since the DOCTYPE tag serves this function, so it is safe to omit the **lang** attribute.

The complete <head> container is always placed between the <html> tag and the <body> tag (discussed later). Because it is always located in this area of the document, the <head> and </head> tags can be inferred (guessed at) by some browsers. Unfortunately, you may find Web pages without a <head> container because the Web weaver hoped the browser would infer that there should be one. You should not depend on the browser to infer the location of a tag, because it may not guess the way you want it to.

The <head> container can include a variety of tags that define and manage the content of the document, as shown in Table 2.1. The only required element used within the <head> container is the <title> tag (discussed shortly). The other tags found in Table 2.1 will be discussed in later chapters.

profile

The **profile** attribute is set to a URL that identifies information the browser should use when rendering or indexing the contents of the related Web page. The attribute is used in conjunction with the <meta> tag that is discussed in detail in Chapter Twelve. The contents of the <meta> element usually identify information about a document rather than document content. One application could be for search sites to use a common profile to identify the author, copyright information, and publication date of a collection of Web pages. The HTML code would look like this:

<head profile="http://www.bugsbeewee. com/profiles/catalog">

Applications for the **profile** attribute are evolving as we write this book.

 **<title>descriptive title</title>**

Description: provides descriptive information about the document for display at the top of the screen, not in the body of the document.
Type: container.
Attributes: dir, lang.
Special note: every HTML document must have a <title> element.

The <title> element can include the **dir** and **lang** attributes. It is used to identify the title of the document you are building and must be coded inside the <head> container. If you

Table 2.1

Tags used within <head>
container

Tag	Function
<base>	Sets the base URL for the document; used if the URL of the document is not the base for the other URL references.
<isindex>	Indicates that the page can be searched.
<link>	Defines the relationship between the current document and another document on the Web, including external style sheets.
<meta>	Specifies additional information about the Web page, including keywords, content type, and other Web server name-value pairs.
<style>	Identifies document-level style sheets that control text formatting.
<script>	Contains one or more functions written in one of the scripting languages like JavaScript or Visual Basic.
<title>	The only tag that is required in the <head> of the document. Very important because it should accurately describe your page.

enclose other tags in the <title> element, they are ignored. See Figure 2.2 for a sample <title> in the HTML code and its appearance in a browser.

Notice that the browser displays the title along the top of the screen or window in the title bar. Many people confuse headings with the title and look for the title to be displayed in the body of the page. Most browsers, if they display the title at all, display it outside the actual text area of the page. The title is a required part of a Web page, and it is important for three reasons:

1. People who visit your page may use the title in a *Bookmark, Favorite,* or *Hot List* (entries marking Web sites for future revisiting). The title should help them define the contents of the page so they can easily recall why they want to return to it.

2. An Internet search site or cataloging program may return only the title as a description of your page. People will then make the decision whether to visit your page or not based on this information.

3. People who are surfing the Net and come upon your page should have some idea of the contents as soon as they arrive.

For all these reasons, it is important to have a descriptive title. However, your title should also be brief, because many graphical browsers place the title in the bar across the top of the screen, and long titles may be cut off. Examples of some good titles follow:

<title> Basic HTML commands </title>

<title> TNT's Ten Terrific Time Tested Tenting Tenets </title>

<title> Pictures of Green Sea Turtles </title>

The next group of titles are not good, either because they do not give enough information to Web cruisers or because they are so long that they will be cut off by the browser:

<title>Stuff</title>

<title>My Home Page</title>

<title>Really Cool Pictures of Turtles I Have Taken While On Vacation </title>

The title must be plain text. Do not use any tags within it, because they will be ignored. Choose a title that will draw interest to your page and that accurately reflects the contents.

Save the HTML template as chapter2.html. In this new HTML document use your ASCII editor to type *your name's Home Page* (for example, Patti's Home Page) between the <title> and </title> tags. Save the file again.

HTML   <body>majority of document</body>

Description: identifies the contents of the Web page.
Type: container.
Attributes: *alink, background,* **bgcolor,** class, dir, id, lang, *link,* onclick, ondblclick, onkeydown, onkeypress, onkeyup, onload, onmousedown, onmousemove, onmouseout, onmouseover, onmouseup, onunload, **style,** *text,* title, *vlink.*

The <body> container holds the majority of your page. Before version 3 of HTML was released, the <body> tag had no attributes. Anything within the <body></body> container was called the "body content." HTML version 3.0 introduced a series of attributes to give the author greater control over the appearance of the document. Later in this chapter we will discuss the most commonly used <body> attributes.

The remainder of this chapter will concentrate on the HTML tags used within the <body></body> container. These are the tags you use to render your Web page. You need to learn how to use these tags at two different levels:

1. In creating eye-catching pages that communicate the desired information to the reader.

2. In creating easy-to-read HTML documents that other Web weavers can readily understand and, if necessary, easily modify.

The mystery of both levels is what separates the amateurs from the professionals. Two types of attributes have taken on elevated importance with the HTML 4 specifications: *styles* and *events*. The reason these attributes have become more important is the increased use of mouse-controlled graphical browsers. While these attributes are discussed in detail later in the book, you need to be aware of the design issues they bring to Web page layout.

STYLES

A *style* is a set of formatting rules that indicates to a browser how the author would like to display the contents of all or part of a page. The style can identify alignment, size, color, font characteristics, and so on. The HTML 4 specifications have introduced the *cascading style sheet (CSS),* with which the Web weaver may create several different types of style sheets that apply to the same document. A CSS can be an independent document linked to the Web page, document-specific and defined within the page itself, or coded as an attribute to an individual tag. In each case the style sheet overrides the default attributes assigned to a tag. This may seem like a trivial matter to casual Web page designers. However, the proper use of the CSS can save Web masters hundreds of hours of work when modifying HTML documents.

The simplest way to change an attribute's default value is with an *inline style,* meaning one that is changed while it is being rendered by the browser. This is accomplished with the **style** attribute, which sets different formatting options. For example, the level-1 heading in Figure 2.3 that defaults to a bold black font at the top of the document can be changed to a blue italic font using the color and font features of the **style** attribute. The HTML code (as shown in the figure) would look like this:

```
<h1 style="color: blue; font-style: italic">Fancy Heading 1</h1>
```

Because an inline style overrides document-level and linked style sheets, its spurious use can cause havoc on pages that need to follow the sitewide formatting standard re-

Figure 2.3

HTML code showing heading tags with and without inline styles

```html
<html>
<head>
<title>Heading Tag (H1-H6) Demonstration</title>
</head>

<body>
<h1>Heading 1</h1>
<h2>Heading 2</h2>
<h3>Heading 3</h3>
<h4>Heading 4</h4>
<h5>Heading 5</h5>
<h6>Heading 6</h6>

<h1 style="color: blue; font-style: italic">Fancy Heading 1</h1>

</body>
</html>
```

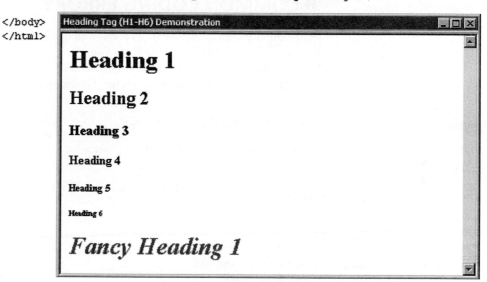

quired by many businesses. This is not to say that inline styles ought not be used. Quite the contrary, they are used to add emphasis by changing the standard presentation format. Furthermore, learning the different formatting attributes and inline style helps you explore the design options that are available with different elements. In Chapters Five and Eight we will address how style sheets are used in professional Web site development and management.

INTRINSIC EVENTS

Mouse activities, like click and double-click, and document changes, like loading or unloading a page, are called *intrinsic events.* Moving the mouse pointer over an element on the screen, loading a picture, or performing any computer activity initiated by using a Web page are all considered intrinsic events. For example, have you ever moved your mouse over an icon on the screen and had the icon change shape or a list of menu options appear? This is accomplished using the **onmouseover** attribute, an intrinsic event that activates a script that displays the menu or changes the icon's shape. This particular feature is called a *rollover* because a script is executed when the mouse "rolls over" the icon.

Sophisticated Web page designs can use JavaScript scripts that intercept various intrinsic events and act upon them. JavaScript event-handling code is discussed in Chapter Thirteen. You will see attributes like **onclick** or **onload** listed for several tags used within the <body> container.

▸▸XHTML STRUCTURE MODULE

As mentioned in Chapter One, the W³C has established XHTML as an extension of HTML that addresses the need for a markup language for wireless devices, handheld computers, and other Internet-capable devices. Part of the XHTML recommendations modularizes the code by grouping HTML tags into 20 modules. The <html>, <head>, <title>, and <body> containers make up the XHTML Structure module. It is one of the four minimum modules needed to create a working Web page. This shouldn't be a surprise, since every HTML document uses these elements. The other required modules, Text, Hypertext, and List, are discussed in detail in future chapters.

▸▸COMMON CODING ERRORS

A common computer cliché is, "To err is human, but to really mess things up takes a computer." Writing HTML code gives you plenty of opportunities to make errors that result in wild screen displays or no display at all! Sometimes the erroneous display gives you many clues as to what went wrong. For example, in Figure 2.4 the expected title is

Figure 2.4   A missing <title> tag results in the title not appearing in the title bar

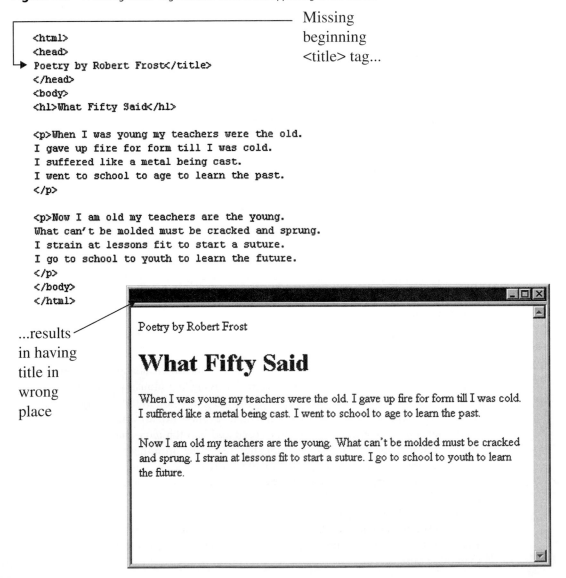

Figure 2.5

Result of missing </h1> ending tag

```
<html>
<head>
<title>Poetry by Robert Frost</title>
</head>
<body>
<h1>What Fifty Said

<p>When I was young my teachers were the old.
I gave up fire for form till I was cold.
I suffered like a metal being cast.
I went to school to age to learn the past.
</p>

<p>Now I am old my teachers are the young.
What can't be molded must be cracked and sprung.
I strain at lessons fit to start a suture.
I go to school to youth to learn the future.
</p>
</body>
</html>
```

> **Poetry by Robert Frost**
>
> **What Fifty Said**
>
> **When I was young my teachers were the old. I gave up fire for form till I was cold. I suffered like a metal being cast. I went to school to age to learn the past.**
>
> **Now I am old my teachers are the young. What can't be molded must be cracked and sprung. I strain at lessons fit to start a suture. I go to school to youth to learn the future.**

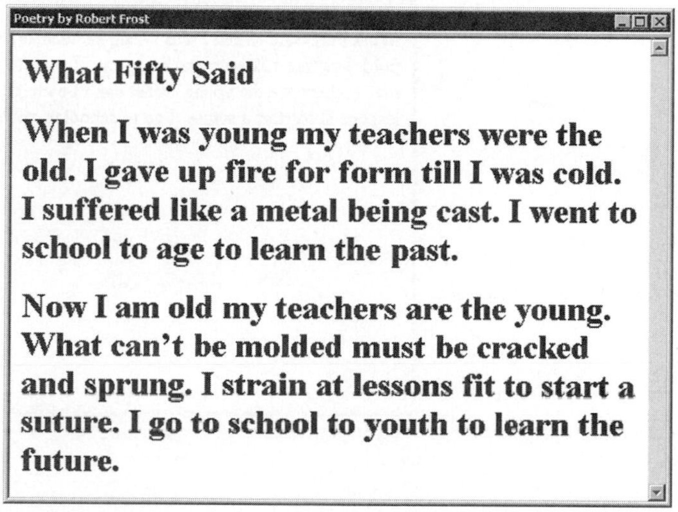

missing from the screen's title bar and appears somewhere else. This is the only clue an experienced Web weaver would need to know to look for the problem in the <head> container that holds the title.

Sometimes the error does not cause a problem in the line with the mistake, but farther down in the code. In Figure 2.5, the missing ending for the level-1 heading causes a problem with the rest of the page, not the heading. Some common coding errors follow:

- Forgetting the ending tag.
- Reversing the order of ending tags (i.e., closing the <head> container before the <title> container).
- Placing the slash in the ending tag in the wrong place.
- Forgetting to place attribute values within quotes.
- Forgetting one of the quotes around an attribute value.
- Forgetting to include an octothorp in front of an RGB hexadecimal number.
- Using less than or more than six digits in an RGB hexadecimal number.

▸▸ MORE WEB PAGE ELEMENTS

As you can see from the browser view of Figure 2.6, there is a lot more to HTML than placing <body> tags around text. We need to introduce to you two more commonly used HTML tags that will make your Web page more readable. You should have open an ASCII

Figure 2.6

Example of how white space in HTML <body> code is ignored when poem is displayed in browser

```
<html>
<head>
<title>Poetry by Robert Frost</title>
</head>
<body>
What Fifty Said

When I was young my teachers were the old.
I gave up fire for form till I was cold.
I suffered like a metal being cast.
I went to school to age to learn the past.

Now I am old my teachers are the young.
What can't be molded must be cracked and sprung.
I strain at lessons fit to start a suture.
I go to school to youth to learn the future.
</body>
</html>
```

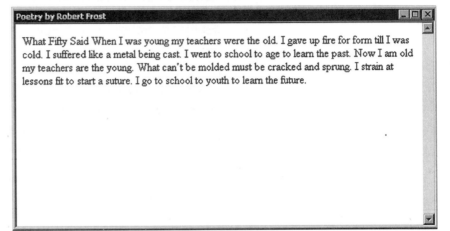

editor and your favorite graphical browser as you read the following about tags for inserting paragraphs and headings. But first let's look at a tag that has nothing to do with the appearance of your page, yet is very important in the construction of your page: the comment tag.

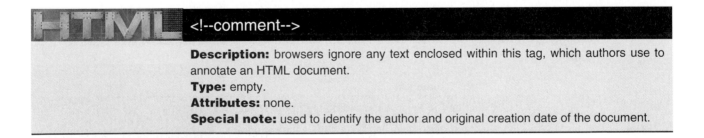

<!--comment-->

Description: browsers ignore any text enclosed within this tag, which authors use to annotate an HTML document.
Type: empty.
Attributes: none.
Special note: used to identify the author and original creation date of the document.

Before we go on with building your first page, it is time to discuss the need to annotate your work, which involves use of the comment tag. As you write your Web page, it is important to add *comments* that identify who created it, when it was created, and, where appropriate, brief explanations of why you have done what you have done. Document your page as you build it, *not* after it is complete. If you wait until you are finished, you will most likely never do the necessary documentation.

Text enclosed in the <!--comment-->container will not appear when your page is browsed (see Figure 2.2), but it will appear when the source document is viewed (again, see Figure 2.2). Many authors make the mistake of putting in comments that tell what they did but not why:

```
<body link="#FFOOFF" vlink="#OOFFOO">
```

```
<!– Make the Link colors FFOOFF and the vlink OOFFOO –>
```

This comment tells what has been done, but the same information can be read from the HTML. A much better set of comments would be as follows:

```
<body link="#FFOOFF" vlink="#OOFFOO">
```

```
<!– Set link to Magenta and vlink to Green –>
```

```
<!– Use these colors to match the school's colors –>
```

Now we know not only what colors were chosen but why they were chosen instead of the default colors.

Your comments are designed as much as for you as for other Web weavers. It is very frustrating to come back to modify your page at some later date and have no earthly idea why you have built some particular elements the way you did. Well-written comments can guide you back through your logic and remind you of why you did what you did.

It is also handy to include comments that document where you found the images and backgrounds you used. That way, should you lose them from your local disk, you can easily obtain them again. Moreover, it is courteous to give credit to the Web authors who have allowed you to use their artwork.

Comments should be only one line long and should not contain any other HTML tags. Following is an example of a comment that might follow a <head> tag:

```
<!– Author: Your Name –>
```

```
<!– Created: mm/dd/yy –>
```

These comments will be seen only if the user elects to view the source code of the page (see Figure 2.2). Careful, consistent use of comments will help you maintain your page. Comments will also help other Web weavers who want to understand how you achieved your results or who might someday work with your page.

Be especially careful to always close your comment containers. While we strongly recommend that you make your comments only one line long, the standard allows for multiple-line comments. If you open a comment, and forget to close it, the rest of the document becomes part of the comment, and the browser ignores it! That is called a Bad Thing.

EXPLORATION #3 In chapter2.htm after the <head> tag add two comment lines: one with your name and the other with today's date. Save the file again.

HTML <h1>heading</h1><h2></h2><h3></h3><h4></h4><h5></h5><h6><\h6>

Description: identifies one of six levels of headings
Type: container
Attributes: *align,* class, dir, id, lang, onclick, ondblclick, onkeydown, onkeypress, onkeyup, onmousedown, onmousemove, onmouseout, onmouseover, onmouseup, style, title.

A document that contains page after page of unbroken text can be very difficult to read. Web pages should be broken up with appropriate headings to divide the text into manageable pieces. HTML allows six different levels of heading elements (<h1> </h1> .... <h6> </h6>).

The way the headings are displayed depends on the browser used to read the document. Some browsers will display the headings in different sizes of fonts. Others may indicate them by bolding, underlining, moving them to a different position on the page than the regular text, or changing their color. In addition, users can define how a browser will display headings as part of a *style sheet.* The code in Figure 2.3 specifies six different headings, which are shown the way one graphical browser would display them.

The headings each start a new line and provide some formatting. However, you can't rely on this feature to make your page look a certain way. If the browser used to view your page shows the different headers only by color, then your formatting will be lost. Do not attempt to use headings to control how the text looks on the page but only to break up the text flow. Remember our rule: the browser controls the format; the author controls the content.

A level-1 heading (<h1>) is often used at the start of the body of the page or document. It should restate the title. Other headings are used to divide the text into manageable sections and to help users scan through the page to find the information they are seeking.

Remember that you must always use the closing heading tag to end your heading. The browser cannot guess where you want your heading to end, so it cannot supply the ending tag for you. If you forget to close a header, you might be unpleasantly surprised with the result. Look at Figure 2.5 again to see what happens when a header is added without the ending tag. Without the tag that would have closed the first heading after the poem's title, the browser views the rest of the document as part of the heading. You will run across this problem from time to time as you cruise the Net.

Headings can be aligned left, center, or right using the **align** attribute as shown in Figure 2.7. The **class** and **style** attributes are discussed later in this text. In addition, headings can contain a wide variety of other HTML tags. For example, a heading may contain images <img>, line breaks <br>, format changes like <strong>, and font modifiers like <b>, <i> or a style. It is sometimes appropriate to add small images to headings. Some of the more effective ones are logos, bullets, or small icons. A document divided by easy-to-read headings helps the user identify salient points. Remember that the main reason to put a page on the Web is to provide information as quickly and efficiently as possible. Good headings help users find what they want.

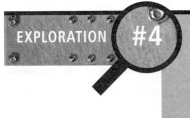

EXPLORATION #4

In chapter2.html after the <body> tag add a level-1 heading by typing <h1>your name's First Web Page</h1>. Save the file again. Next, open your favorite browser and use the File menu to open chapter2.html. You should see your name in the browser's title bar and the level-1 heading you just typed in the browser's main display area. If nothing is displayed on your screen, reread the section on "Common Coding Errors" in this text, and check to see if you made one of these mistakes.

HTML

<p>Paragraph</p>

Description: identifies a continuous string of text within the page.
Type: container.
Attributes: *align,* class, dir, id, lang, onclick, ondblclick, onkeydown, onkeypress, onkeyup, onmousedown, onmousemove, onmouseout, onmouseover, onmouseup, style, title.

When writing a report or term paper, you divide the text into sections called paragraphs. To do that, you end the line and start the next with a tab or perhaps insert a blank line on your page. That blank line is called a *white space.* So is the space created by your tab key. In computer jargon, white space includes *any* spaces or tabs. And Web browsers treat all

Figure 2.7 HTML code showing applications for center alignment, line breaks <br>, and horizontal rules <hr>

```
<html>
<head>
<title>Poetry by Robert Frost</title>
</head>
<body>
<h1 align="center">What Fifty Said</h1>
<hr align="center" noshade size="4" width="50%">

<p align="center">When I was young my teachers were the old.<br>
I gave up fire for form till I was cold.<br>
I suffered like a metal being cast.<br>
I went to school to age to learn the past.<br>
</p>

<p align="center">Now I am old my teachers are the young.<br />
What can't be molded must be cracked and sprung.<br />
I strain at lessons fit to start a suture.<br />
I go to school to youth to learn the future.<br />
</p>

<hr align="center" size="2" width="50" />
</body>
</html>
```

XML compliant

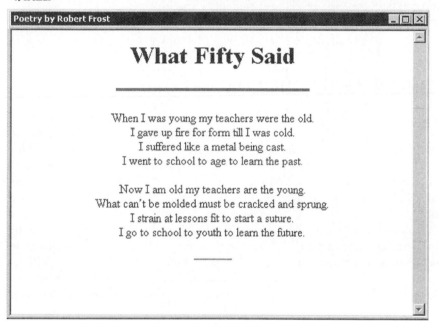

Poetry by Robert Frost

What Fifty Said

When I was young my teachers were the old.
I gave up fire for form till I was cold.
I suffered like a metal being cast.
I went to school to age to learn the past.

Now I am old my teachers are the young.
What can't be molded must be cracked and sprung.
I strain at lessons fit to start a suture.
I go to school to youth to learn the future.

---

white space the same; they compress it into a single space. Therefore, you cannot use tabs or blank lines to create paragraphs in HTML documents. A browser will close them all up and make your lines of text flow into each other. For this reason, the HTML document with text on separate lines and a blank line between them that you studied in Figure 2.6 is displayed as a continuous line of text.

Since you can't insert tabs or blank lines to create paragraphs, you need some other tool to do this. We have seen that headings can divide the text, but headings are intended to break the page into larger units than is the case for paragraphs. One way to divide text into smaller logical blocks is to use the ***paragraph*** (<p>) container as shown in Figure 2.7. The <p> container can be said to identify a continuous string of text within the page. Notice that the first paragraph is closed by the ending tag, </p>. A blank line between the two paragraphs would be ignored by the browser, but it automatically puts an extra line between the two paragraphs in response to the <p> container.

As we saw in Chapter One, many browsers can infer the ending paragraph tag. You will find some older documents on the Web that, unfortunately, were built relying on this browser ability. Therefore, it is good practice to close all your paragraph containers just in case a browser might not infer the closing tag.

Furthermore, we recommend placing the ending tag on a separate line whenever text fills more than one line. It is easy to lose an ending tag in long strings of text. Placing the ending tag on a new line helps you find the ending tag and visually match it with the beginning tag.

The <p> tag recognizes the **align** attribute. Like headings, a paragraph can be aligned left, center, or right. Left alignment is the default; it is what the browser uses if you don't specify which type of alignment you want. Figure 2.7 illustrates center alignment of both paragraphs.

Paragraph containers often include other tags. For example, they may contain links (<a>), images (<img>), font changes (like <b> or <i>), line breaks (<br>), and style changes (like <cite> or <strong>). However, if the browser encounters any other tag in a paragraph, like a heading tag, that causes a break in the text flow, it assumes that the closing paragraph tag is missing and ends the paragraph for you—whether you wanted the paragraph closed there or not.

EXPLORATION **#5** In chapter2.html after the heading tag add a brief biographical paragraph. Save the file and refresh/reload the page on your browser.

▸▸ EDITING AN HTML DOCUMENT

Once the text and tags are entered into the ASCII editor, you need to save the file (document) on disk with either an .htm or .html filename extension. You will notice that to keep things consistent throughout this textbook, we are using the .htm extension in the examples and .html for all the files created in the "Exploration" Web pages. After the HTML document is saved on disk, you can view it by using the browser's File menu Open option. The browser will display the contents of any .htm or .html file you load from a disk.

After the document is loaded into the ASCII editor and the page is displayed in the browser, you can start editing the HTML tags in the editor. When you make a change to the document, you should immediately save the new version to disk. The browser will not display the changes until you click the Refresh or Reload button on the toolbar. An HTML editor lets you do the same jumping between the document view of HTML tags and the page view, but it may not display the rendered page exactly as a browser will.

Just a note on safety and sensibility: before you can change an HTML page, you should make a backup copy of it just in case you want to go back to the way the page was before you made your changes. One easy way to do that is to simply name the copy of the page identically to the original page, but with an extension of .001 for the first backup, and so on. That way, if you decide your changes weren't all that wonderful, you can simply rename the backup page with a .htm extension and be back where you started.

▸▸ COMMONLY USED EMPTY TAGS

The Robert Frost poem we have been using was actually written as two four-line stanzas as shown in Figure 2.7. We are sure Frost would agree that the way the poem is displayed affects how it is read and internalized. Good Web weavers have an eye for page layout that helps the reader get the point.

Our poem needs a *line break* (<br>) (discussed next in this chapter) at the end of each line. It would also help to visually separate the title from the body of the poem. This is best handled by a *horizontal rule* (<hr>) (discussed after the line break) as shown in Figure 2.7. Both of these design elements are coded as HTML empty tags. The structure of an empty tag is different in HTML versus XML specifications. XML and XHTML require that every tag, even empty tags, have an ending tag. The W[3]C suggests that Web weavers writing XML/XHTML code place a space and a forward slash (/) behind the tag identifier in the beginning tag. For example, the <br> tag should be written as <br /> as shown in the second paragraph of the HTML code in Figure 2.7.

Another way to handle empty tags with XML/XHTML coding is to close empty tags the way you close container tags, with a forward slash (/) at the start of an ending tag. However, the W[3]C reports that using the alternative syntax of
</br> allowed by XML gives uncertain results in some browsers, especially older browsers. As we examine usage of both the line break <br> and horizontal rule <hr> tags, we will note this handling of empty tags by XML.

HTML **
**

Description: creates a line break.
Type: empty.
Attributes: class, clear, id, style, title.
XML: requires closing tag using

The *line break* tag (<br />) causes the browser to stop the current line and move the cursor to the first position on the next line. It functions like a carriage return on a typewriter or the Enter key on your keyboard when you are typing. It is often used for formatting text or inserting blank lines. For example, our poem is broken into two four-line stanzas by placing a <br /> after each period. Figure 2.7 shows the result on a browser.

HTML **<hr />**

Description: creates a horizontal line on page.
Type: empty.
Attributes: *align,* class, id, *noshade,* onclick, ondblclick, onkeydown, onkeypress, onkeyup, onmousedown, onmousemove, onmouseout, onmouseover, onmouseup, *size,* style, title, *width.*
XML: requires closing tag using <hr />, for example, <hr width="50%"/>
Special note: The Opera browser does not recognize the noshade attribute.

The *horizontal rule* element (<hr />) puts a horizontal line, or rule, across the screen. This is an empty tag. It has four attributes you can use to modify the way the line appears on the screen. The horizontal rule at the top of Figure 2.7 uses all four. Even though the tag contains attributes, it is called an empty tag because it has no closing, or ending, tag unless you are building XML-compliant pages. The horizontal rule at the bottom of Figure 2.7 was generated by XML- and XHTML-compliant code.

The **align** attribute defines the horizontal placement, left, center, or right, of the line on the page. The **size** attribute determines how thick the line is. The default line is the width of the screen, side to side, 2 pixels (Internet Explorer and Opera) or 3 pixels (Navigator) thick. The term *pixel* stands for picture element. It is one of the many tiny dots that make up the display on your computer screen. Usually a pixel is about the size of one point of type on a standard 75 dot-per-inch display. Typical typefaces are about 12 points, or 12 pixels tall. The pixel is the smallest addressable unit of space on a screen. In Figure 2.7, the first line is 4 pixels thick, and the second line is 2 pixels thick.

The **width** attribute sets the length of the line. In Figure 2.7, the first rule is one-half, or 50 percent, of the screen width. The second rule is 50 pixels wide. As you can see, the **width** attribute can be expressed in either the exact number of pixels or as a percentage of the actual screen size. It is better to use the percentage measure because then the rule will look the same regardless of the screen size. If you use an absolute width, setting width to a fixed number of pixels, the browser will use that length regardless of screen size, and it will look different on computers with various screen sizes (15-inch, 17-inch, 19-inch, etc.) or with different browsers.

Many browsers shade a horizontal rule using some combination of black, white, dark gray, or light gray pixels to make it look like it has been chiseled into the screen. This shading is easier to see on the thick (size 5 or 6) lines. The rule is displayed as a solid color when the **noshade** attribute is present (see Figure 2.7). Notice that this attribute does not need an equal sign to change the default value. Its presence within the tag turns the shading off. Attributes like **noshade** that turn on or off a preset feature are referred to as *toggles* or *switches.*

EXPLORATION #6   In chapter2.html between the heading and the paragraph place a horizontal rule that is 5 pixels tall. Save the file, and refresh/reload the page on your browser.

▸▸BODY TAG ATTRIBUTES

You have now been introduced to a set of HTML elements that will enable you to create a wide variety of professional-looking Web pages. Before concluding this chapter we would like to expand upon some of the attributes associated with the <body> tag. We will also cover some of these features as part of the introduction to style sheets in Chapters Five and Eight.

bgcolor

The **bgcolor** attribute controls the background color of the page. Like everything else that appears on your screen, it is expressed as a mixture of *red, green, and blue (RGB).* Each of these colors has an intensity range of 0–255, with zero representing no color and 255 representing the most intense value for that color. Actually, there are three color "guns" in a CRT monitor, and three LEDs in a flat screen at each pixel location. The value 0 for a color tells that gun or LED to emit no color. The value 255 tells the gun or LED to emit maximum intensity for that color. Each value between 0 and 255 changes the intensity of that color.

There is a little twist with HTML, though: these color numbers must be expressed as two-digit hexadecimal (base-16) numbers, as shown in Figure 2.8. The digits in the hexadecimal numbering system are 0123456789ABCDEF.

Two easy ways of converting the decimal *RGB number* to a hexadecimal are

1. Using a calculator that supports hexadecimals.

2. Using a table like the one found in the Reference Guide.

You will find that some of the numbers are simple: 255 decimal = FF in hex, and 0 decimal = 00 in hex. Here are some of the colors you can use:

| White | FFFFFF | Green | 00FF00 | Yellow | FFFF00 | Aqua (Cyan) | 00FFFF |
| Red | FF0000 | Blue | 0000FF | Magenta | FF00FF | Black | 000000 |

To make life a little easier, the popular graphical browsers support standard color names rather than just the hexadecimal numbers. A list of some of those names is in-

Figure 2.8 Background colors are designated using three two-digit hexadecimal numbers for red, green, and blue

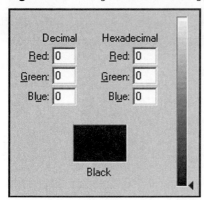 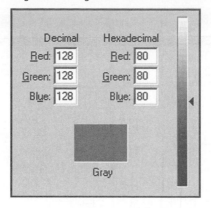 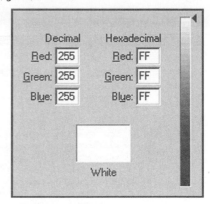

cluded on the color insert in the back of this text. But the use of color names is not consistent from version to version of the browsers or even across different computers. Earlier versions of the Internet Explorer use a small subset of the names. For these reasons, we recommend that you always code colors in hexadecimals or in the browser-safe standard color names. For example,

```
<body bgcolor="yellow">
```

or

```
<body bgcolor="#FFFF00">
```

You can see from the chart presented earlier that FFFF00 is the code for yellow. Notice in the code above the octothorp, #, that is part of the color code. The octothorp tells the browser that the value following is a hexadecimal number representing the color, not a color name. Always code the octothorp as the first character of your color designators for **bgcolor.**

When you decide to add colors to your page, you can spend a significant amount of time trying to get them just the way you want them—and you can create some absolutely horrible combinations. For example, bright red letters on a bright blue background are very distracting. A background color that does not contrast well with your text color can make your page hard or even impossible to read. See Figure 2.9, "e" and "f" for an example of a lack of contrast and Figure 2.10 for a good contrast in color. You also need to remember that the readers of your page can configure their browsers to automatically set different colors and override all your hard work. The default background color for most browsers used to be light gray but now is white.

background

The **background** attribute allows you to place a picture, or image, in the background of your page. Graphical browsers will display the image you select and will *tile,* or repeat, the image both vertically and horizontally to fill the whole background. The effect is similar to the wallpaper in Windows. You should select a dim, subtle image for your background. If the background is too intense, too bright, or too busy, it will distract from or interfere with the text and other images you have on your page.

If you choose a background image, your choice of background color **(bgcolor)** will be hidden unless your background image has transparent areas. We will discuss transparent images when we look at using images in Chapter Six. The value specified in the background attribute is the path, or URL, for the background image you have selected. It should be a small image because it will need to be moved across the Internet to your viewer's location. Figure 2.9 illustrates how the poem looks with different backgrounds in place. As you can see any background image will, to some extent, interfere with readability.

Figure 2.9

Examples showing how a simple background that contrasts with the text color is easiest to read

a.

b.

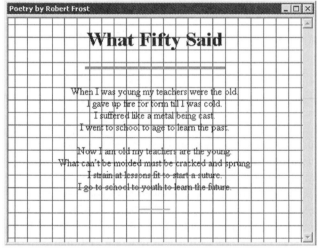

c.

d.

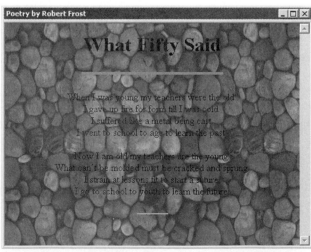

e.

f.

Figure 2.10

Light text needs a consistently dark background to be easily read

```
<html>
<head>
<title>Poetry by Robert Frost</title>
</head>

<body background="wood.jpg" text="#FFFF00">
<!-- text = yellow -->
<h1 align="center">What Fifty Said</h1>
<hr align="center" noshade size="4" width="50%" />

<p align="center">When I was young my teachers were the old.<br />
I gave up fire for form till I was cold.<br />
I suffered like a metal being cast.<br />
I went to school to age to learn the past.<br />
</p>

<p align="center">Now I am old my teachers are the young.<br />
What can't be molded must be cracked and sprung.<br />
I strain at lessons fit to start a suture.<br />
I go to school to youth to learn the future.<br />
</p>

<hr align="center" size="2" width="50" />
</body>
</html>
```

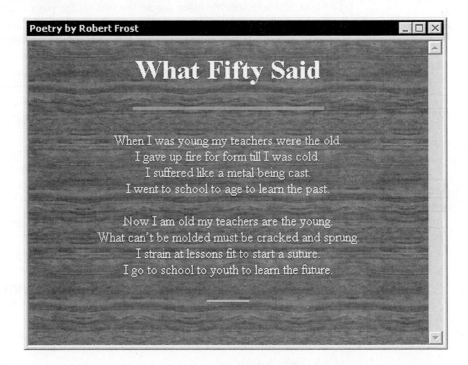

Avoid building large, full-screen images, because they are slow to load and will increase the congestion on the Internet. Your URL for an image should point to the Web server that hosts the page. Never use a URL that points to a file on a different Web server, because that can greatly increase the time it takes to load your page.

For example, the HTML code in Figure 2.10 for the background wood.jpg, resides on the author's computer. When the browser starts to build the page, it needs to look only at this file to create the background. If instead this file were located on another Web server, the URL would look like this:

http://an.othersystem.net/pub/bground/wood.jpg

The browser would have to establish communication with the an.othersystem.net computer, look in the /pub/bground directory, and copy the image in the file wood.jpg back to the current computer before it could build the background for the page. This procedure greatly increases the traffic on the Internet and slows the browser down as it build the page.

One of the best ways to get nice backgrounds is to find them on the Net. Many sites offer *public-domain* background files, usually in *GIF (Graphic Interchange Format), JPEG (Joint Photographic Experts Group),* or *PNG (Portable Network Graphics)* format (all of which are discussed later in this book).

You can use your browser to collect these backgrounds and save them on your own computer. Popular graphical browsers allow you to right-click on a background to access the "Save Background" feature. With some versions of Navigator you have to view the background image before you can save it. If you choose to use another Web weaver's work this way, always ask permission. Usually the page will contain a way to email the person who built the page. Ask the owner of the work if you can use the background on your page. Most of the time, authors are pleased that you want to use their work.

Remember the cardinal rule about background images: any background image will interfere with the readability of your text, as shown earlier in Figure 2.9. Make sure your background image is worth even a slight degradation of the readability of your page.

text

The **text** attribute sets the color for all the text on the page except the text enclosed in an anchor, <a>, container and text that is under the influence of a style that specifies color. We will explore creating links using anchors in the next chapter. For now, we want to emphasize that you need to ensure that your text color works with your selected background color or background image. Refer again to Figure 2.9 to see how the dark wood.jpg choice provides a terrible background for the default black text. A light text color, like white, yellow, or aqua (cyan), is necessary to provide a contrast with this background that allows for readability. Figure 2.10 shows how the choice of yellow works for the text.

Text color is selected just as background color is, using a hexadecimal value like "#FFFF00" or a color name like "yellow" if you are targeting the popular graphical browsers. The following <body> tag establishes the text color as yellow:

<body background="wood.jpg" text="#FFFF00">

As you cruise the Net, you will come across some pages that are very difficult to read because the author of the page made a poor text-color selection. The **background, bgcolor,** and **text** all have to be chosen carefully. To help you in your choice of background and text colors, we have included a little hint on the color table found in the Reference Guide. If the printing on the color is in black, that means the color is suitable for a background for default black text. If, on the other hand, we have coded the text on that color block in white, that means the color is too dark to make a good background for default black text. Generally the lighter the color for backgrounds, the better.

alink, link, and vlink

The following three attributes allow you to control the color of links:

- **alink**—specifies the color of the active link, or the link that is being targeted by the mouse.

- **link**—specifies the color of all the hyperlinks the user has not yet followed.

- **vlink**—specifies the color of all the links the user has already followed or visited at one time or another and that are kept in the browser's history.

Keep in mind that changing these colors can confuse and frustrate your users. Most browsers keep the link colors constant, and users have come to depend on those colors.

As mentioned earlier, on most browsers, the links not yet chosen are blue and the links that have been visited are dark purple. Using the attributes **link** and **vlink,** you could reverse those values, making the followed links blue and those not yet visited dark purple. That would be very confusing for your users. Furthermore, the popular graphical browsers are inconsistent in their recognition of these deprecated attributes.

If you have a special need to change these colors, remember to make them different from the text color and from each other. You can specify the colors just as you did with the text and background colors, using either a hexadecimal value, the preferred method, or a color name. The following code sets the color of the unvisited links to red and of those that have been visited to bright green.

```
<body link="#FF0000" vlink="#00FF00">
```

But remember, you should change the default colors only if you have an absolutely compelling reason to do so.

EXPLORATION #7   In chapter2.htm change the background color to light yellow, FFFFCC, and the text color to dark blue, 0033FF. Save the file, and refresh/reload the page on your browser.

▸▸ A FEW CONSIDERATIONS

Using lots of colors and fancy images, you can produce a Web page that is a work of art. But there are some things that can go wrong with that approach:

1.   Using a background image will increase the time it takes to load your page. The delay may not only frustrate your users, but will also increase congestion on the Internet. If you use a large image as the background, that will substantially increase load time. Remember, not all your users are tied directly to the Internet. Some depend on 28,800-baud modems or pay for each minute of connect time. They may not appreciate a beautiful background image that takes 10 minutes to download.

2.   Your page may look wonderful on a computer with a high-resolution screen and 16 million available colors. But if your user has a machine with fewer available colors (like a 16-color VGA Windows machine), your pretty screen may become unusable. In the process of replacing your colors with those available for that machine, the browser might set the background color and the text color to the same value, making it impossible to read! When you use colors in your page that the local computer does not have available, the local browser is forced to *dither* the image. Dithering is the process of replacing one uniform color with repeating patterns of other colors that approximate the original color. This can make your text very difficult or impossible to read, or just plain ugly. Dithering is discussed in more detail in regard to images in Chapter Six, and you can see several examples in Figure 6.3.

3.   Even though you are using a wonderful image as your background, you might want to reconsider using an image at all. Putting text on top of an image always makes the text harder to read.

4.   If you use a background image, the browser must fill in that image as the user scrolls through the page. This forced processing by the browser can lead to slower scrolling.

5.   Pages with very light text on dark backgrounds may prove difficult (if not impossible) to print.

A careful selection of colors and images can create a wonderful Web page. As you cruise the Net, you will find many examples of beautifully crafted pages. The careful use of colors and images allows you to express yourself artistically and enables you to create unique HTML documents. Playing with color and form is great fun. However, as you play, keep in mind that the real purpose for most Web pages is to transmit information. If colors and images get in the way of the transferal of information, then perhaps you need to rethink your layout.

At this point it is important to address the idea of Web page design. Usually the minds that are capable of excellent coding and HTML development aren't the same kinds of minds that are capable of excellent layout and page design. It is tempting to use all the "bells and whistles" possible when developing a page, often to the detriment of the actual content. If you are developing a professional Web page, it is almost a necessity to consult with a graphics designer. The designer can tell you which colors go together well, how much "white space" you should have on your page, where to place images for greatest effect, and so on. Your users will appreciate the result.

EXPLORATION **#8**   Validate the HTML code in chapter2.htm using the CSE validator on the CD that accompanies this book or the W³C's validator at http://validator.w3.org

▸▸ KEY TERMS

Attributes	Line break
Comments	Paragraph
Container element	Pixel
Document Type Definition (DTD)	Rollover
Empty element	Style
Horizontal rule	Toggle
Intrinsic event	

▸▸ NEW TAGS

\<html> \</html>	\<h1> \</h1>
\ 	\<h2> \</h2>
\<hr />	\<h3> \</h3>
\<p> \</p>	\<h4> \</h4>
\<head> \</head>	\<h5> \</h5>
\<title> \</title>	\<h6> \</h6>
\<body> \</body>	

▸▸ REVIEW QUESTIONS

1. Define each of the key terms.
2. How are each of the tags introduced in this chapter used? (Provide examples.)
3. Which HTML tags should be included in a minimal HTML template?
4. When is the SGML \<!DOCTYPE> tag used?
5. What tag must be included in every \<head> container element?
6. Give three reasons why the contents of the \<title> element should be short and descriptive.
7. Name seven common HTML coding errors.
8. How do you update a browser's screen after changing the content or tags in the related HTML document?
9. How are comments used within an HTML document?
10. From a design point of view, what are headings used for?

11. What does a browser automatically insert between two paragraphs?

12. When and why should ending tags be placed on a new line?

13. How are empty tags handled differently to be XML/XHTML-compliant?

14. If the **bgcolor** and **background** attributes both appear in a <body> tag, which tag takes precedence?

15. In what two ways are color attributes designated? Which is preferred?

16. Why should a background image file reside on the hosting computer instead of being referenced at another URL?

17. When using a graphical browser, how do you save background images you like?

18. Describe a situation that would require you to change the text color.

19. Give four reasons why you might choose not to use a background image.

▸▸EXERCISES

2.1. Ruby Garnet wants to take her business online. She just bought Gwen's Glorious Gemstone Gallery in Emporia, VA. Ruby needs a Web page to bring customers to her store at 231 Lee Street. Since the store is in her house, she doesn't get much walk-in traffic, and she thought a Web site would help her business grow. Here is what she would like you to create for her:

   a. A Web page explaining her very selective inventory. The page should have a soft jade green background, #CCFFCC, and amethyst text, #9933FF.

   b. The title should simply be her company name.

   c. There should be a first-level heading that includes the company name.

   d. The page should have four paragraphs laid out exactly as shown here, including the horizontal rules that are half a page wide.

Welcome to Gwen's Glorious Gemstone Gallery. We are the largest genuine gemstone shop in all of Emporia, Virginia. Our commitment to you is that we will offer you only natural gems. Our gems have not been "cooked," "tweeked," "adulterated," or modified in any way. What you see is just exactly what Mother Nature created. All human hands have done is to our gems is to bring out their inner fire by cutting and polishing them. You will not be disappointed with our stones, they are a wonderful investment.

Gemstones are generally divided into two categories: those with color, and clear stones. Our stock is mostly made up of colored stones. We have a very few diamonds or other clear stones, as many shops carry those. We specialize in the wonderful colored stones that are so very rare and precious. Stop by and check out our stock, it changes very often as we have buyers around the world looking for the best quality gems.

For the very discerning collector, we have a very small stock of natural pearls along with our colored stones. These are true natural pearls, not the more common and easily found cultured pearls. We have a supplier in the Pacific region that will find specialty pearls for that special someone. Please remember that our buyers need at least 3 months, and more frequently 6 months or more to find exactly the gem you require. Please allow sufficient lead time in your quest for true beauty.

Stop in and visit us, and prepare yourself for a wondrous adventure. We are just down the block from the entrance to the Greensville Ruritan Club Grounds. Stop by on your way to or from the Pork Festival, and be amazed at the beauty nature can create. Our address is:

Gwen's Glorious Gemstone Gallery
231 Lee Street
Emporia, VA 23847
733-436-7829

  e. Ruby wants to have her page used internationally, across all browsers, and may want to expand the role the Net plays in her business, so your page should be XML-compliant.

  f. You should ensure that the page will validate with the W^{3}C validation engine, or with the CSE HTML validator. (Don't worry about deprecated attributes just yet.)

  g. Document your page so Ruby knows who wrote it and why you chose particular colors for the page.

  h. Save the file under the name `ruby1.html`.

2.2. Create a Web page to sell used goods that is similar to the want ads in your local paper. The HTML document should include a background color or image, comments with your name and the assignment due date, and the following information for at least five items you want to sell:

  a. Item name

  b. Description of the product (include dimensions when appropriate)

  c. Condition: mint-in-box, excellent, good, poor, handyman's special

  d. Approximate age

  e. Asking price

2.3. As a follow-up to Exercise 1.3, create a Web page that describes the computer platform you are using for this class. The HTML document should include a background color or image, comments with your name and the assignment due date, and the following information:

  a. Your name

  b. Computer's brand name

  c. Processor type and speed

  d. Screen size and resolution

  e. Audio hardware

  f. Hard disk capacity

  g. Type of removable disk or tape and associated storage capacity

  h. Hardware used to access the Internet

2.4. Create a personal Homework home page. Your instructor will use this page to link to homework assignments from this class. The HTML document should include a background color or image, comments with your name and the assignment due date, and the following information:

  a. Your name

  b. Class identifier (like "CIS 257")

  c. Class name (like "Introduction to HTML")

  d. Section number

  e. Instructor's name

  f. Instructor's office number

  g. Instructor's office telephone number

  h. Your school's name

  i. Other information specified by your instructor

To protect your privacy, do not include personal information like your address or telephone number.

2.5. Create a home page for your school. The HTML document should include a background color or image, comments with your name and the assignment due date, and the following information:
   a. School's name
   b. Address
   c. Main telephone number
   d. Top administrator's name and position
   e. School colors
   f. School mascot
   g. Words to the school's fight song

2.6. Create a Web page that provides an overview of your favorite movie. The HTML document should include a background color or image, comments with your name and the assignment due date, and the following information:
   a. Movie's name
   b. Release date
   c. Studio that released the film
   d. Rating
   e. Minutes the movie runs
   f. Actors and actresses
   g. Paragraph on why you like the movie
   h. A recommendation of the appropriate snacks to eat while watching this film

2.7. Create a page to match the following poem by Eugene Fitch Ware. The HTML document should include a background color or image along with comments containing your name and the assignment due date. The poem's title is "He and She." It was written as two four-line stanzas:

When I am dead you'll find it hard,
Said he,
To ever find another man
Like me.

What makes you think, as I suppose
You do,
I'd ever want another man
Like you?

3

Chapter Three

Linking: Let's Get Hyper

Lots of books pontificate on the subject of designing Web pages, so there is much information available on the use of fonts, color coordination, and other visual design rules. However, the experts all agree that the use of links is the most important design decision you can make when creating Web pages. In the last chapter we built a simple, *static* Web page. A static Web page contains no links—no way for the user to move within the document other than simply scrolling up and down and no way to go to other documents or to graphics, or to interact in any way with the page. Now it is time to learn how to incorporate links into a document, those specially marked places on the screen that perform certain actions when activated by a mouse click—and add the "hyper" to the term *hypertext.*

CHAPTER OBJECTIVES

After reading this chapter you should be able to do the following:

- Explain how storyboards are used to develop professional-looking Web pages.
- Create storyboards that outline hierarchical, sequential, and indexed-sequential Web page designs.
- Use anchor tags to create intrasystem and intersystem hyperlinks.
- Identify the HTML element found in the XHTML Hypertext module.
- Properly employ relative and absolute paths in source-anchor coding.

- Establish intrapage target names in HTML code, and use these names as hyperlink references.
- Give some ways to avoid the "click here" faux pas.
- Create a hyperlink that opens the user's email client.
- List potential design elements for page footers.
- Talk intelligently about server-side includes.

⏩WHY IS HYPERTEXT HYPER?

A hypertext document is one that contains the elements called *links* that allow users to activate a particular part of the screen to perform some action. The actions can include

1. Moving to another part of the document.
2. Opening another document on the same Web site.
3. Opening a document on a Web site somewhere else in the world.

In this chapter we will deal with all three actions. In later chapters we will add links to sounds, images, and videos.

Documents having dynamic links to other documents or to places within the same document date back to the 1980s. At that time the Apple Macintosh supported Hyper-Card, which allowed users to create buttons within a document that would, when clicked, load an image, play a sound, or open and display another text file. The documents were called *stacks,* and each page or screen was a card in that stack. Different cards could be linked together. The main stack containing cards with links to related stacks, the table of contents, was called the *home stack.* The Hypertalk programming language used to create these buttons was a true programming language that was interpreted into the computer's machine language—unlike HTML, which is simply a markup language dependent upon the browser to execute.

Like Hypertalk, however, HTML enables you to build documents with dynamic links. These links should create a logical path to related information, whether within the same document or on another Web page. A professional Web weaver provides intuitive (logical) links that help the user pick up definitions, play sounds, view pictures and video, or move about through a collection of documents with a simple click of a mouse button. To do this properly, and avoid the rookie mistake of weaving a maze for the user, you need a good Web page design. Storyboards, our next subject, can help.

⏩STORYBOARDING PAGE LINKS

A storyboard is a diagram that illustrates how two or more Web pages, or sections of a Web page, relate to one another. The term comes from the film industry, where such diagrams have long been used to lay out the action sequences in a film. Figure 3.1 shows four simple storyboards for Web pages. The links from one page to another create the "story." In real life these storyboards might originate on coffee-stained napkins, but eventually the Web weaver will create a more formal diagram like one of those shown in the figure. The three basic designs shown here—sequential, indexed-sequential, and hierarchical—can spawn quite a few depending on the amount and nature of the information being presented. Plus, there is the option of creating a custom-tailored design.

Storyboards are especially important for larger projects or when several Web weavers are writing documents for the same Web site.

The subject matter and target audience usually dictate how you link pages together. You can count on the browser to provide basic navigational options like back, forward, and home.

SEQUENTIAL AND INDEXED-SEQUENTIAL DESIGNS

Large amounts of related text lend themselves to a *sequential* design. Two variations on this theme are available to the Web weaver: sequential, link one page to another (see Figure 3.1 again) and *indexed-sequential* designs (also in Figure 3.1), link sections of text within one page.

The page-to-page sequence is appropriate for larger bodies of text, like this book, that can be read from beginning to end and often have logical subsets that stand alone. These subsets are called sections, chapters, lessons, and so on. The designer might write each chapter or lesson or whatever as a separate Web page and sequentially link Chapter 1 to

Figure 3.1

Storyboards showing four
different Web site designs

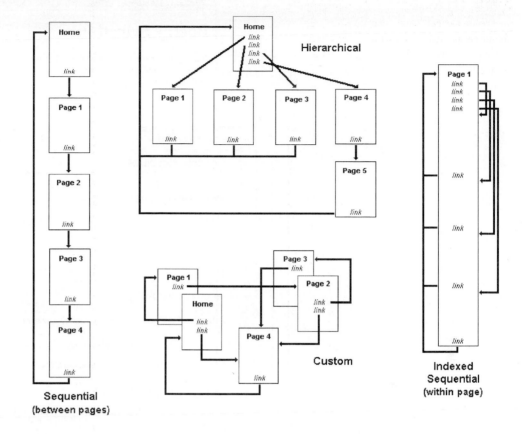

Chapter 2 (or Lesson 1 to Lesson 2) and Chapter 2 to Chapter 3, and so forth. In this design, the associated links identify pages that are independently stored on the same computer or stored at other Web sites.

When, on the other hand, the text is limited in length and can easily be broken into
headings associated with a few paragraphs, then all the text can reside in a single document (the indexed-sequential design in Figure 3.1). The links will jump the user from one
heading or another. For example, Figure 3.2 shows a simple HTML document that contains four poems and links to each poem at the beginning of the document. This is an
indexed-sequential layout within a single Web page. The advantage of this design is that
users don't have to scroll down the page to read Ms. Bruner's poem; they can activate a
link and see that part of the page immediately.

HIERARCHICAL DESIGN

A *hierarchical* design can be used when related text does not need to be read in any particular order. Figure 3.3 (p. 60) shows our favorite poems as separate pages linked hierarchically by author. A storyboard with this design is presented in Figure 3.1. An operations manual for your favorite word-processing program is a good example of material
suitable for the hierarchical design. If each chapter of the manual describes different
menu options offered by the program, then users can read about features when they need
to use them, which would not necessarily be in any particular order.

CUSTOM DESIGN

Sometimes a subject requires a unique set of links, or a *custom* design (Figure 3.1). It is
especially important to make a storyboard for this type of Web site. Often the process of
creating the storyboard reveals associations you had not considered. Hence, better designs sometimes become apparent as the storyboard progresses.

Figure 3.2

Indexed sequential design using intrapage links that jump user to different areas within the same document

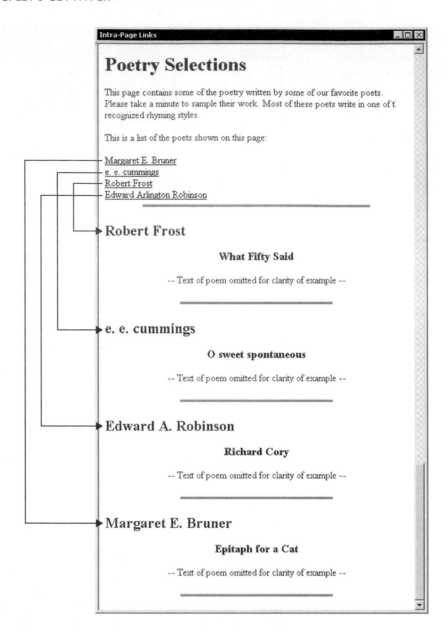

Use your ASCII editor and the HTML template from Chapter Two to create an HTML document that displays Matthew Prior's poem, "*A Reply.*" Save it as **prior.html.** Add your name as a comment, and type Poetry by Matthew Prior between the <title> and </title> tags. In the body of this document do the following:

1. Create a centered level-1 heading for "*A Reply.*"

2. Insert a centered, **noshade** horizontal rule that is 4 pixels tall and uses 50 percent of the window's width.

3. Within a single, centered paragraph, enter the following four-line poem with a line break at the end of each line:

   Sir, I admit your general rule
   That every poet is a fool;
   But you yourself may serve to show it,
   That every fool is not a poet.

Save the file again. Next, use your favorite browser to display **prior.html.**

<a>anchor</a>

Description: provides data to link images, sounds, another area within the page, or to another Web page.
Type: container.
Attributes: accesskey, charset, class, **coords,** dir, **href, hreflang,** lang, **id, name,** onblur, onclick, ondbblclick, onfocus, onkeydown, onkeypress, onkeyup, onmousedown, onmousemove, onmouseout, onmouseover, onmouseup, **rel, rev, shape,** style, **tabindex,** target, title, type.

The anchor container (<a></a>) serves as the basis for all the links we are going to create in this chapter, and it is the only element in the XHTML Hypertext module. It is a very powerful HTML element that recognizes a variety of attributes. Since this chapter's focus is on creating links, we are deferring discussion of many of the common attributes to other chapters. Table 3.1 presents some esoteric attributes recognized by the anchor tag with a brief description of how they are used.

There are several ways to refer to the relationship between the document housing the link and the document pointed to by the link. In some texts you will find the term *head* used for the place where the link starts and *tail* for the place the link points to. In others you may find the terms *start* and *destination* for these two locations. In this book we will use ***source*** to indicate the origin of a link and ***target*** to indicate the end of the link.

SOURCE ANCHORS

A source anchor container is used to create the area on the page where a link will be activated, either by the click of a mouse or some other method. The following source anchor identifies a link to the target HTML document **frost.html:**

```
<a href="frost.html">Robert Frost</a>
```

Graphical browsers underline the link and display related text in a different color. As mentioned in Chapter Two, this color is controlled by the **link** attribute of the <body> container. The anchor element in the previous example would underline "Robert Frost" to indicate that it is link text ("hot" words) that when activated will bring the user additional information. Your graphical browser would most likely display the code as follows: Robert Frost. This is an example of a link to an HTML document stored on the same Web server and in the same directory (file folder) as the Web page containing the code.

Table 3.1 Common attributes recognized by anchor tag

Attribute	Description
accesskey	Assigns a single-character access key to the link. Pressing this access key can initiate the link just as clicking on the link text would. For example, F could be assigned as the access key to the Robert Frost poem.
charset	Identifies the character encoding of the resource designated by the link. The **charset** attribute might include special math or chemistry symbols.
hreflang	Identifies the base language of the link (similar to the **lang** attribute) designated by the hyper reference (**href**) attribute and should be used only when **href** attribute is specified.
tabindex	Identifies the position of the current element in the document's tabbing order. The **tabindex** can be set to any number from 0 to 32,767.

Figure 3.3 Intrasystem links that open new document on the common Web server

```
<html>
<head>
<title>Intra-System Links</title>
</head>
<body>

<h1>Poetry Selections</h1>
<p>This page contains some of the poetry written by some of our
favorite poets. Please take a minute to sample their work.
Most of these poets write in one of the recognized rhyming styles.
</p>

<p>This is a list of the poets shown on this Web site: </p>
<a href="bruner.html">Margaret E. Bruner</a><br />
<a href="cummings.html">e. e. cummings</a><br />
<a href="frost.html">Robert Frost</a><br />
<a href="robinson.html">Edward Arlington Robinson</a><br />

</body>
</html>
```
Source

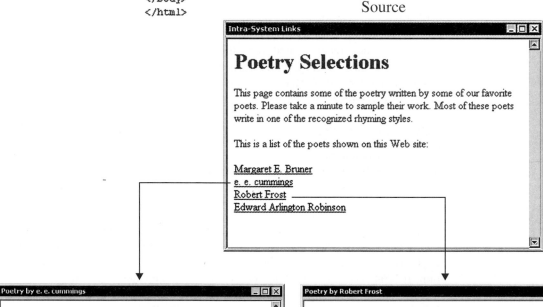

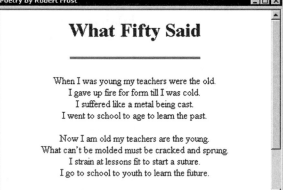

Targets

href

Every source anchor contains the special attribute **href,** which stand for Hypertext REFerence. The **href** attribute identifies the pointer, or pathway, to the target of the link. An example would be

```
<a href="poetry.html#RF">Robert Frost</a>
```

The target of a link is a URL. In this case the URL is local to, or within, the document we have created. This reference directs the browser to begin loading at a section of the **poetry.html** Web page labeled "RF." In other words, the source anchor's **href** attribute allows the user to jump to a selected poet by activating a link on the page.

Figure 3.3 shows the home page for a hierarchical site. This design employs separate HTML documents for each poet. In our earlier example, Robert Frost's poems are saved in **frost.html.** The anchor container, `<a href="frost.html">Robert Frost</a>`, creates a link to this Web page using the name "Robert Frost" as the link text.

Many computer systems are ***case-sensitive,*** meaning they recognize the difference between uppercase and lowercase letters. The target **Frost.html** and the target **frost.html** are different on a case-sensitive system. On a case-insensitive system, like Windows, both targets are considered the same. To be safe, make sure your hypertext reference exactly matches the target.

Always enclose the value associated with the hypertext reference in quotation marks. There are some special cases when this is unnecessary, but most of the time the quotation marks are required, and using them is a good habit to develop. The text between the end of the opening tag and the beginning of the ending tag is the text the user will see that indicates a link exists. Always use the closing `</a>` anchor tag, as it cannot be inferred by the browser. Be sure not to include leading or trailing blanks in your text. They will appear as underlined spaces and look bad.

As you remember from the last chapter, the link text will be a different color and may be specified by the **link** attribute of the `<body>` container. The fact that the link text may be displayed in a different color and/or be underlined tells the user that it is a link. Also, when the user moves the cursor of a graphical browser over the link, it becomes a pointing finger rather than the normal arrowhead. This change in the pointer is another indication that the text under it is a link.

rel and rev

Next we will look at the two anchor attributes that will someday define document relationships: **rel** and **rev.** Both specify the relationship between the source document and the target of the link. These attributes are not widely used as yet, but they are expected to gain importance with new releases of the standard browsers.

The **rel** attribute points forward, from source to target. The **rev** attribute points backward, from target to source. Both describe the relationship between the URL and the **href** attribute. The set of possible valid values is open-ended. More are being defined, and as the browsers begin to support them, some standardization should evolve. Here are four of the more common values for **rel** and **rev:**

- *next*—indicates that the URL referenced in the **href** is the next in the series. This is usually used only with the **rel** attribute. Here is a sample of a link to the next page in a series: `<a rel="next" href="http://mysite.com/p2.html">More Info</a>`

- *index*—shows that the document pointed to by the **href** is the index or table of contents for the series. Here is how an index looks when coded:

```
<a rel="index" href-"http://mysite.com/index.html">Index</a>
```

- *previous*—shows that the document pointed to by the **href** is the previous element in a series. That is, the element is the one that precedes the URL in the **href**. Normally this is used with the **rev** attribute. The anchor shown here illustrates the use of this value:

```
<a rev="previous" href="http://mysite.com/p1.html">Page One</a>
```

• *start*—indicates that the document listed as the URL for the **href** is the original source, or home page, of the file that points to it. It is used as follows:

<a rev="start" href="http://mysite.com/index.html">Home Page</a>

TARGETS

Figure 3.4 illustrates two types of targets: intrapage and intrasystem. A link that directs the browser to load data from a different location within the same HTML document is called an ***intrapage link.*** Indexed-sequential page designs call for intrapage links. This type of target is discussed later in the chapter.

Intrasystem links (shown in Figure 3.3) identify other Web pages stored on the same Web server as the source document. They include the HTML document's filename (and if necessary, the path that describes the disk directories) where the file is stored.

When the hypertext reference includes a URL for another Web server, the anchor is creating an ***intersystem link.*** For example, if the poems in Figure 3.3 were maintained on other Web servers, then intersystem instead of intrasystem links would be employed. The following anchor container includes a hypertext reference for an HTML document found in the stu01 directory the student Web site:

<a href="http://student.college.edu/~stu01/frost.htm">Robert Frost</a>.

As you can see, the hypertext reference for an intersystem link contains the Web page's complete URL. As we learned in Chapter One, URL contains the protocol (http), domain name (student.college.edu), path (/~stu01/), and filename (frost.htm) for the targeted Web page.

The third part of a URL, the path, is often the most misunderstood part of an intersystem (or intrasystem) link. Usually the ***path*** is a set of directory names allowing the browser to find the specific HTML document referenced by the link.

Figure 3.4

Intrapage versus intrasystem links

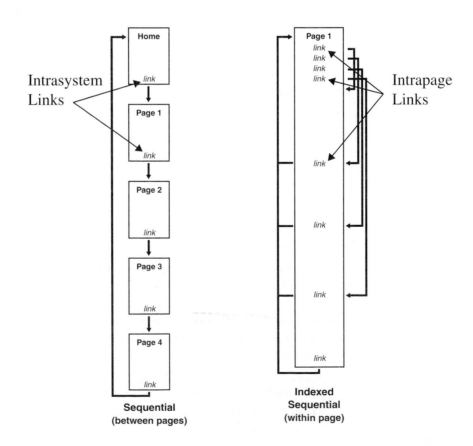

Sequential
(between pages)

Indexed
Sequential
(within page)

EXPLORATION   **#2**

Copy the file select.html from the student CD to the same disk directory where you previously saved prior.html. Use an ASCII editor to make the following changes to select.html.

1. Incorporate your name as a comment after the <html> tag.

2. Add an intrasystem link to prior.html using <u>Matthew Prior</u> as the link text. This source anchor should be placed under the <u>Edward Arlington Robinson</u> hyperlink.

Save the file. Next, use your favorite browser to display and test the new link in select.html.

▸▸ PATHS TO FILES

There are a few important considerations when using a path name. First, since the vast majority of the computers that run Web servers use the Unix operating system, and Unix is case-sensitive, you need to be careful with the case of your path names. If the file you want is in the path wilbur.pages.stuff, and you code Wilbur.pages.stuff as part of your link address, the link will fail. <u>W</u>ilbur and <u>w</u>ilbur are two different directories on a Unix computer.

Second, if there is no path, or if the path is simply a forward slash (/), the document you retrieve will be the highest-level HTML index document on that server. This is called the *home page*. Sometimes it is named public_html or public.htm. On Unix computers it is usually named index.html. This document normally provides the doorway into the rest of the HTML files on that site. Actually, the name of the default home page is set by the system administrator when the server software is set up.

Third, the shorthand use of the tilde (~) symbol is used to specify a path name to a personal HTML directory in the home directory of the individual specified. For example, the URL of http://somecompany.com/~clyde/ would bring up the highest-level HTML document in Clyde's subdirectory structure. Usually this would be Clyde's index.html file, which is Clyde's home page.

This raises an interesting point. Usually a well-constructed home page will provide links to all the other pages, or at least the index to each set of pages on that server. The exact location of that index.html depends on the following:

1. The actual server software.

2. The system administrator or Web weaver who set up the site.

The main index page for the whole server is obviously a home page. However, in the parlance of the Web, the index into Clyde's collection of HTML pages is also considered to be a home page. Generally, you should avoid coding the filename **index.html** in a URL when linking to a home page; let the browser pick the name.

When you specify the path that the browser should take to find a document, you can use either an absolute or relative path name. Both have a purpose and use, so let's discuss each of them.

ABSOLUTE PATH NAMES

Absolute path names always start with a slash (/) and contain the full path to the document you are referencing. The browser knows that you are using an absolute path when the path name starts with the slash. Since the majority of the servers on the Internet run on the Unix operating system, the way we specify paths is more Unix-like than Windows-like. In Unix, the right, or forward, slash (/) is used to divide the parts of a path name. You will need to use this convention when coding absolute path names. In addition, when you specify a

Table 3.2   Samples of absolute path names

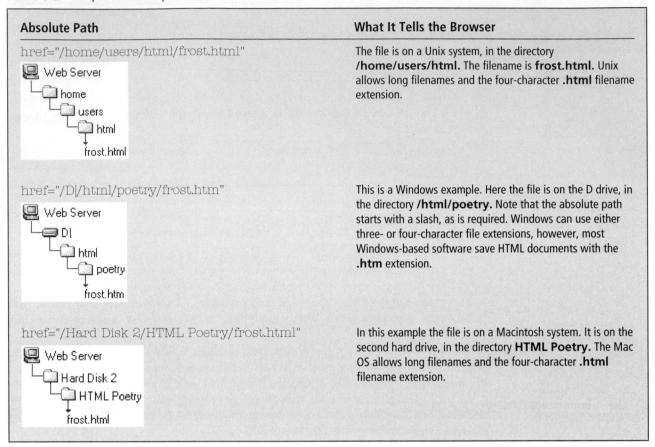

Absolute Path	What It Tells the Browser
href="/home/users/html/frost.html"	The file is on a Unix system, in the directory **/home/users/html.** The filename is **frost.html.** Unix allows long filenames and the four-character **.html** filename extension.
href="/D|/html/poetry/frost.htm"	This is a Windows example. Here the file is on the D drive, in the directory **/html/poetry.** Note that the absolute path starts with a slash, as is required. Windows can use either three- or four-character file extensions, however, most Windows-based software save HTML documents with the **.htm** extension.
href="/Hard Disk 2/HTML Poetry/frost.html"	In this example the file is on a Macintosh system. It is on the second hard drive, in the directory **HTML Poetry.** The Mac OS allows long filenames and the four-character **.html** filename extension.

drive letter, you should follow it with the vertical bar (|) rather than the colon the way you have to in Windows. Table 3.2 provides examples of code for absolute path names on three different operating systems.

As you can see in the table, the same path name looks a little different on different operating systems. In each case, though, an absolute path tells the browser exactly where to find the file by specifying the complete path name.

RELATIVE PATH NAMES

Although initially it may seem a good idea to always specify a full path name, sometimes a better way to tell the browser how to find the files it needs is by means of *relative path* names. Relative paths do not need to give the current position because they start from the directory in which the browser is currently working, the directory that contains the active document. They must not start with a right (forward) slash, because the right slash is the first character of an absolute path. Thus, the difference between an absolute and a relative path is that the relative path name does not include the current position in the file structure, whereas the absolute path gives every directory leading to the target.

The simplest relative path names point to target files contained in the same directory as the source document. This is the ideal path because it is the default. Table 3.3 presents examples. Note that in the first example we direct the browser to look in the same directory where it found the menu page to find frost.html.

Table 3.3 Samples of relative path names

Relative Path	What It Tells the Browser
href="poem.html" 	This file is in the active directory. This is the simplest relative path–naming scheme.
href="poetry/poem.html" 	In this case the target is in the directory or folder called **poems,** which is a subdirectory of the active directory.
href="lit/poetry/poem.html" 	Here the target is in the subdirectory or folder called **poetry,** which is in the subdirectory or folder called **lit,** which is in the active subdirectory or folder.
href="../poem.html" 	This is the way we direct the browser to move back or up one directory or folder. Here we are saying that the file we want is in the parent directory for the active directory. The .. notation says to move up or back one level.
href="../../poetry/poem.html" 	Here the target is located up two levels and is in the subdirectory or folder called **poems** at that level.
href="../D|/lit/poetry/poem.htm" 	Here the source document was in the C drive root directory, and the target is on the D drive on the system. In this case the absolute path would be shorter.

ABSOLUTE VERSUS RELATIVE PATH NAMES

Most experts agree that relative path names should be used instead of absolute path names whenever possible. As you can see by comparing Table 3.2 with Table 3.3, in most cases the relative path is shorter than the absolute path. Relative path names are usually faster for the browser to use as well. Of course, in order to use relative path names efficiently, you should have all the files you are referencing in the same directory or in subdirectories of that directory. That way the browser doesn't have far to look to find related files. Also, you can easily move the files as a group if you are moving your site from one server to another. Another advantage of relative path names is that they make it easier to maintain your Web page because you don't need to keep changing your path names when you move your files from directory to directory.

▶▶INTERSYSTEM SOURCE ANCHORS

Now let's take a closer look at the intersystem links that bring data from distant machines. Linking across the World Wide Web requires a path description and the Web server's domain name as part of the hypertext reference. The HTML coding is as easy as linking to a document on the same Web server, but it consumes Net resources and can lead to problems that are outside the control of the Web weaver. For example, if we link to a site to bring in an audio file, that site may be down, preventing our users from hearing the audio clip. Or perhaps the site that has the clip is working just fine, but between our site and the Net, a problem occurs, preventing our users from getting onto that path. Still another possibility is that the site we are linking to may change its address.

The technical term for this inevitable loss of links is *link rot,* and wise Web weavers will regularly check to ensure that the links from their pages are valid. Some software packages will do this for you, but to be absolutely sure they are working, you should check your links yourself at regular intervals.

LINKING CONSIDERATIONS

When you create a link to a page on another machine, you are giving the user's browser a different Internet address from which to download data. Often this process is referred to as "sending the user across the Net." Naturally, this is only a figure of speech, as your user stays exactly where she was but simply begins to use data from a different Web server. In most cases, when the user finishes accessing the distant server, she can return to accessing data on your server using the Back button.

DOMAIN NAME OR IP ADDRESS?

You can specify a hypertext reference or URL (the value of the **href** attribute to the <a> container), by either the IP or the domain name. As explained earlier, an *IP address* is a set of four numbers separated by periods or dots. For example, 204.151.55.44 is an IP address. Each device connected to the Internet has a unique IP address. The domain name describes the path to the server by giving the server's actual name and the other names of the computers that constitute the domain of the server. For example, www.McGraw-Hill.com is a domain name. Some domain names are short, and others can be quite long. The parts of domain names were discussed earlier.

If you choose to use a domain name, the browser must access a *Domain Name Service (DNS)* to translate the domain name into an IP address. Some Web weavers think that this extra step is best avoided, so they code the domain as an IP address. Although that procedure does save a little time when the browser takes the link, it is not a good practice, because the code is harder to maintain.

For example, we know of a company that decided it needed a *firewall,* a program that protects the security of networked computers. This company had an extensive Web site and used IP addressing throughout, even to link to other pages on its own site. When it implemented the firewall computer, it had to change the IP address of its Web server. This meant going into hundreds of pages and finding and changing all the addresses. After making the laborious change, the company started using a domain name instead of an IP address.

In addition to being more stable, domain names can give the user, as well as the Web weaver, an idea of where the link will go. When the user moves the mouse pointer over a link, most browsers indicate the address to which the link points. If the user sees http://204.151.55.44/, he has little idea where the link will take him, unless he memorizes IP addresses! However, if the user sees http://www.McGraw-Hill.com/, he has some idea of the kind of information he will be seeing.

In addition, the Web weaver herself, in maintaining her page, will be more likely to remember where the domain name www.McGraw-Hill.com points to than she would the IP address 204.151.55.44. All things considered, it is best to use domain names rather than IP addresses as targets for links.

SAMPLE INTERSYSTEM URLS

Following are examples of URLs for intersystem links that point to different Web pages. The comments after each URL explain the particular features being referenced.

- http://www.yahoo.com/. This link assumes that there is a home page, or index page, on the root directory of the www.yahoo.com Web server. (This is actually the Yahoo search engine's home page.) Notice that there is no index.html coded, as the Web server software supplies it automagically.

- http://www.mcgraw-hill.com/books.html. In this case, the link points to an actual page on the McGraw-Hill Web server. Rather than retrieving the default home page (index.html), this link will cause the browser to retrieve the particular page specified. You need to be careful with this sort of link, as it can lose the user. In this case, for example, if the user doesn't know that she can just change the address (location) of the link to www.mcgraw-hill.com, she may not know how to get to the main page, and the Back button will send her back to your page, not the main page of McGraw-Hill.

- http://www.server.com/subpage.html#frag. This is a fictitious site used here to show how a particular **id** (discussed later under "Intrapage Targets") or target anchor within a page may appear as part of the URL. In this case, the browser will retrieve the subpage.html from the server.com site. When it begins displaying the document, it will start at the intrapage target, frag. This address allows direct access into a longer document, allowing the user to go directly to information of interest deep within the page rather than having to jump again, to the intrapage target, or scroll down through the document to the information wanted. To establish this sort of linkage, the Web weaver must know the target document and how it is constructed.

- http://www.otherserver.com:80/subpage.html#frag. This fictitious site demonstrates the use of a *port number*. Port numbers are necessary only if the server is set up to receive http traffic on a network port other than the default port, 21. In this example, the server, otherserver, expects WWW requests to come into port 80. If you need to code a port number, it must follow the actual server name and be preceded by a colon, as shown in the example.

We have already examined the considerations involved in creating good links in your documents. When you create links across the Web, you should apply the same rules of good structure that you use for internal links. In addition, you should ensure that the links you create actually work! Think how frustrating it is for your user to take a link to a site you recommend, only to see "Unable to locate the server" or "The server does not have a DNS entry"—or the even more deadly message, "404 Not Found the requested URL. . . was not found on this server."

EXPLORATION **#3** The HTML document select.html that was modified in Exploration #2 uses intrasystem links to files, like frost.html. Change this hypertext reference to http://www.mhhe.com/it/eme/frost.html to create an intersystem link. Save the file, and use your browser to test the new intersystem link in select.html.

▸▸INTRAPAGE TARGETS

Let's now turn our attention to intrapage targets, targets within the same document. If we want to allow the user to examine particular points within a document, or to begin retrieving data from a specific point in another document, we must have an element that identifies the link's ***intrapage target name***. The <a> (anchor) container with the **name** attribute provides an intrapage target name that will serve to identify specific locations within an HTML document.

name

The **name** attribute is used to identify a location within an HTML document. The HTML code in Figure 3.5 uses RF and ee as intrapage target names. RF is the name for the target poem by Robert Frost. The text that is contained within the anchor container, in this case Robert Frost, will be displayed on the screen in a format governed by any other containers that enclose it. When used as a <h1> element, each author's name is formatted as a level-1 heading. The HTML code that identifies the start of the Robert Frost poem in this intrapage example looks like this:

```
<a name="RF">Robert Frost</a>
```

Each intrapage target name must be unique and begin with a letter of the alphabet. In other words, the name RF cannot be used again in this document. After the first letter you can use any combination of letters, digits (0–9), hyphens (-), underscores (_), colons (:), and periods (.). You must not use spaces as part of the intrapage target name. Furthermore, with uppercase RF already used, lowercase rf is unacceptable as an intrapage target name within this document. Later we will explain how the intrapage target name becomes part of the URL.

This type of intrapage link is common when you are presenting a large volume of related information, such as a large document in which the table of contents contains the intrapage links. These links will allow users to select the sections they wish to view, activate them, and immediately see their selections without having to scroll down through the document. If you are building a menu for your page, you can also use this indexed-sequential design. Remember that the user can always scroll through the whole document using the scroll bar on the right side of the page. What you are doing with this type of internal link is providing an easy way for the user to navigate around the page.

id

The HTML 4.0 specifications added the **id** attribute, which, like the **name** attribute, can identify intrapage target names. Either **name** or **id** can be used, but the target name must be unique within the document. For example, the following HTML codes create the intrapage target named RF:

```
<a id="RF">Randal, Felix</a>
```

or

```
<h2 id="RF">Randal, Felix</h2>
```

Figure 3.5 Intrapage target names with **name** anchors and **id** attributes

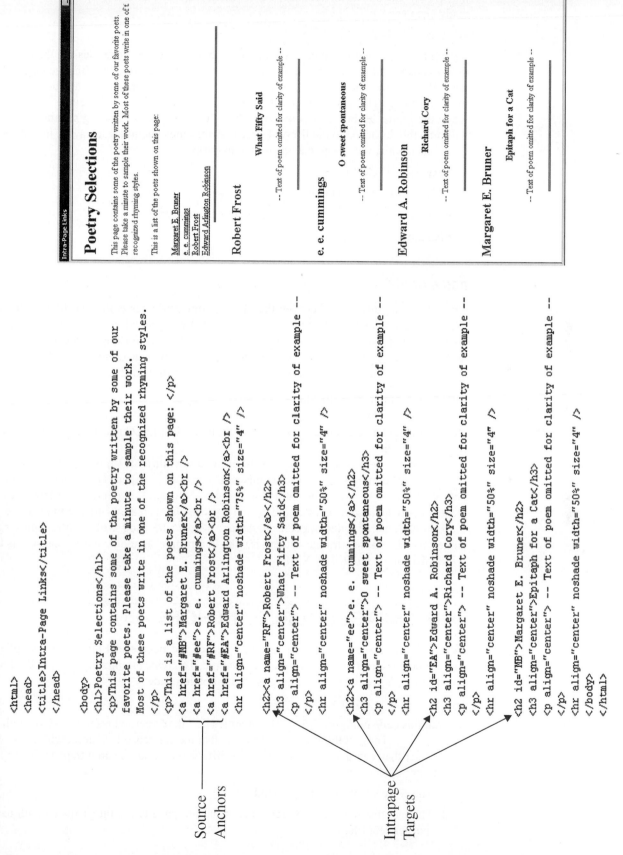

```
<html>
<head>
<title>Intra-Page Links</title>
</head>

<body>
<h1>Poetry Selections</h1>
<p>This page contains some of the poetry written by some of our
favorite poets. Please take a minute to sample their work.
Most of these poets write in one of the recognized rhyming styles.
</p>
<p>This is a list of the poets shown on this page: </p>
<a href="#MB">Margaret E. Bruner</a><br />
<a href="#ee">e. e. cummings</a><br />
<a href="#RF">Robert Frost</a><br />
<a href="#EA">Edward Arlington Robinson</a><br />
<hr align="center" noshade width="75%" size="4" />

<h2><a name="RF">Robert Frost</a></h2>
<h3 align="center">What Fifty Said</h3>
<p align="center"> -- Text of poem omitted for clarity of example --
</p>
<hr align="center" noshade width="50%" size="4" />

<h2><a name="ee">e. e. cummings</a></h2>
<h3 align="center">O sweet spontaneous</h3>
<p align="center"> -- Text of poem omitted for clarity of example --
</p>
<hr align="center" noshade width="50%" size="4" />

<h2 id="EA">Edward A. Robinson</h2>
<h3 align="center">Richard Cory</h3>
<p align="center"> -- Text of poem omitted for clarity of example --
</p>
<hr align="center" noshade width="50%" size="4" />

<h2 id="MB">Margaret E. Bruner</h2>
<h3 align="center">Epitaph for a Cat</h3>
<p align="center"> -- Text of poem omitted for clarity of example --
</p>
<hr align="center" noshade width="50%" size="4" />
</body>
</html>
```

Source Anchors

Intrapage Targets

RF is the same intrapage target name you see used in Figure 3.5, but it cannot be used in that HTML document for "Randal, Felix" because of the following code, which has already been used.

```
<a name="RF">Robert Frost</a>
```

Each intrapage target name must be unique within a document regardless of the attribute used to create it. In Figure 3.5, the **id** attribute is used to identify the intrapage targets EA and MB. You may be asking yourself why the W³C would create two attributes that do the same thing. The answer is that the **id** attribute is associated with every HTML tag, while the **name** attribute is limited to anchor <a> tags. The anchor tag's **name** attribute will probably be added to the list of deprecated attributes one of these days. The 4.0 specifications identify these applications for the **id** attribute:

- Style sheet selector
- Target anchor for hypertext links
- Reference to a specific script (programming) element
- Naming <object> elements

name or id?

One interesting difference between the **id** and **name** attributes is that the **name** attribute may contain character references that use an ISO-recognized code to identify special characters. For example, Ü is the character reference for the uppercase U with an umlaut appearing over it—Ü. If we want to create the intrapage target name of ÜN, the **id** attribute cannot be used. Only HTML code using the **name** attribute will work in this situation. It would look like this:

```
<a name="&Uuml;N">Brünnhilde, Valkyrie</a>
```

Other special character codes are discussed in more detail in Chapter Five and shown in the Reference Guide.

So which one should you use—the **id** or the **name** attribute? It is a question you will be asking several times while reading this text. The answer depends on when you want to go with the new specifications and stop using the old ones. Anyone using Internet Explorer or Navigator versions 4 or older cannot use anchors created with the **id** attribute. In these situations, or when special characters need to be used within intrapage target names, use the **name** attribute. Otherwise, the **id** attribute should be used because it is the standard attribute utilized by XML.

▸▸INTRAPAGE SOURCE ANCHORS

With the intrapage targets in place for each of the poems in Figure 3.5, use of the source anchor's **href** attribute is relatively simple. To create an intrapage link to the Frost poem farther down in the Web page, use the following code:

```
<a href="#RF">Robert Frost</a>
```

Look at this code in Figure 3.5. You will notice that the hypertext reference starts with an octothorp (#). The octothorp tells the browser that the reference is a target within a document rather than a target to another file. The differences in coding an intrapage link rather than an intrasystem link are:

1. The presence of the leading octothrop.
2. The fact that the hypertext reference is an intrapage target rather than a path to an independent file.

Notice in Figure 3.5 that the links are still underlined. You cannot tell just by looking at the link whether it points within the document, across documents on the same system, or across the Internet. From the browser's point of view, a link is a link.

▸▸URLS WITH INTRAPAGE TARGETS

As mentioned earlier, intrapage targets can be used within intrasystem and intersystem links. For example, if the HTML document in Figure 3.5 is named poems.html, then the following intrasystem link targets the Robert Frost poem found within the Web page:

```
<a href-"poems.html#RF">Robert Frost</a>
```

If this Web page is stored in the us-poets directory maintained by the poetry.org Web server, then the intersystem link to the same poem looks like this:

```
<a href="http://poetry.org/us-poets/poems.html#RF">Robert Frost</a>
```

Don't forget that many Web servers are case-sensitive. If you used a target of Rf in your **name** or **id** attribute, you should also have an **href** or Rf. We would recommend always using lowercase characters in intrapage targets, directory names, and filenames in order to be consistent and to avoid making hard-to-find typographical errors.

We will revisit this idea when we talk about Back links that send users back to the page they started on. In this case, your Back link should send users to the place within the page that contains the original link. To do that you will use intrapage links on the pages you link to.

▸▸ANCHOR PLACEMENT

It is also important to remember that an anchor can be used within another container. Thus, we could put an anchor within a heading element if we wanted the header to be the target of a link. It is bad HTML style, though, to put a heading element within an anchor. Proper style would be as follows:

```
<h2 align="right"><a href="phred.html">Phred's Page</a></h2>
```

Here the anchor is contained within the heading, and Phred's Page will appear the way the browser presents a level-2 heading. If users select a link to Phred's Page, they will be transferred to the related Web page.

Consider the following HTML code:

```
<a href="phred.html"><h2 align="right">Phred's Page</h2></a>
```

This code is an example of bad syntax; because the anchor contains another container, in this case a level-2 heading. Some browsers will try to close the anchor container before opening the heading container. That action could cause unpredictable results.

If you want to have working links that appear as you design them, you must maintain the integrity of your containers. In the following example, it would be easy to make the mistake of closing the heading before closing the anchor, like this:

```
<h2 align="right"><a href="phred.html">Phred's Page</h2></a>
```

Notice that the heading container is closed before the anchor container. Some browsers could get confused and miss the closing anchor tag, thus keeping the anchor open. Other browsers will detect this crossed container as an error and not set up the anchor at all. Some browsers will even see the close anchor tag as an auxillary close tag and stop the display of style data. In any case, the results will not be what you expect. Close your containers in the reverse order from the order you opened them, with inner containers closed before outer containers.

EXPLORATION #4

Copy the file poems.html from the student's CD to a disk directory on your computer. You are going to insert Matthew Prior's poem, "*A Reply,*" into this Web page along with adding a new intrapage link and target name.

First, to insert the poem with a target name before </body> tag, follow this procedure:

- Create a left-aligned level-2 heading for Matthew Prior.

- Incorporate into the new level-2 heading the intrapage target name mp.

- Under this heading create a new, centered level-3 heading of A Reply.

- Next, within a single, centered paragraph, enter this four-line poem with a line break at the end of each line:

  Sir, I admit your general rule
  That every poet is a fool;
  But you yourself may serve to show it,
  That every fool is not a poet.

- Under the poem, insert a centered, **noshade** horizontal rule that is 4 pixels tall and uses 50 percent of the window's width.

At the top of the document, below the <u>Edward Arlington Robinson</u> hyperlink, insert a source anchor to the intrapage target name of mp using <u>Matthew Prior</u> as the link text. Save the file, and use your browser to display and test the new links in poems.html.

▶▶INTRASYSTEM SOURCE ANCHORS

If you choose to write a long hypertext document with many intrapage links, you may be causing these unnecessary problems for users:

1. A long document is slower to download than a short one.

2. A set of short documents may be easier for users to navigate among because they can easily return to the home page or table of contents from any other other documents.

3. One of the rules of HTML design says you should have each document focus on a single topic and do *one* thing well.

A large hypertext document providing information on 14 different topics is not doing one thing well. A more structured format for the information would be 14 smaller hypertext documents, each presenting one of the facets of the information in a well-organized fashion, with one document serving as a table of contents and providing a menu of links to the others. In addition to being easier for the user to use, smaller documents are easier for you to maintain.

One of the most important functions you will perform for your users is to ensure that the links you provide are valid links. This means you will need to check them at regular intervals. Some software packages will check your links for you, but, as mentioned earlier, to make absolutely sure that they are working properly, you should check them yourself from time to time. Always make an effort to root out link rot.

▶▶ONE-WAY STREETS

One of the common problems you will discover as you cruise the Web is the lack of backward pointers linking long pages back to the top or multiple pages back to a home page. The first of these two problems exists with our sequentially designed poetry selections. The menu at the top of the document helps the user link to different poems within the page. However, once the user has finished reading the poem, he must scroll back to the top. Sometimes clicking on the Back button will return the user to the top of a page, but this option is not reliable across browsers.

LINKS BACK USING INTRAPAGE TARGET

Our solution to the "one-way street" problem is shown in Figure 3.6. The first-level heading at the beginning of the document is assigned the intrapage target top using the following code:

```
<h1 id="top">Poetry Selections</h1>
```

We could have also used an intrapage target name like this:

```
<h1><a name="top">Poetry Selections</a></h1>
```

An anchor container linking Top of Page to the top intrapage target would then be placed at the end of each poem (see Figure 3.6). The source anchor container looks like this:

```
<a href="#top">Top of Page</a>
```

EXPLORATION #5

As part of the Matthew Prior poem added to poems.html in Exploration #4, you need to create a link back to the top of the page. Do so under the poem by inserting a source anchor with a hypertext reference to the intrapage target name top using Top of Page as the link text. Save the file, and use your browser to display and test the new link.

LINKS BACK USING INTRASYSTEM TARGET

The hierarchically designed intrasystem poetry pages shown in Figure 3.3 need links back to the home page we called select.html. Relying on the Back button can get you in trouble in this situation as well. When testing a set of pages like this, many Web weavers use the Back button in their browser to move from a subpage back to the home page. This works just fine if all the users always start at the home page of the series. But this approach has a flaw if users place the URL of a target page in their Bookmarks/Favorites file. When these users come back to that page in a different browsing session, they will be unable to return to the main page. Why? Because their browser no longer holds the Back pages in memory. It is very frustrating to be on a subpage of the page you want, with no way to return to the home page except to either search for it again or, if you remember the URL, retype it all in again.

You should never create such one-way traps for your users. Always include a "Back to the home page" link in each of your documents. That way you provide linkage in both directions for your users. They may choose the Back feature of their browser, but they also have the opportunity to return to the main page through a designated link. The HTML code for our poetry pages looks like this:

```
<a href="select.html">Return to Poetry Selections</a>
```

If you want to follow the guideline of sending users back to the exact place they left, the HTML code would look like

```
<a href="select.html#top">Return to Poetry Selections</a>
```

providing that the wise Web weaver coded a target of top near the link to this page. Figure 3.7 illustrates how a browser handles this code.

Figure 3.6

HTML code linking users to top of page using **id** attribute

```
<html>
<head>
<title>Intra-Page Links</title>
</head>

<body>
<h1 id="top">Poetry Selections</h1>
<p>This page contains some of the poetry written by some of our
favorite poets. Please take a minute to sample their work. Most of
these poets write in one of the recognized rhyming styles.
</p>
<p>This is a list of the poets shown on this page: </p>
<a href="#MB">Margaret E. Bruner</a><br />
<a href="#ee">e. e. cummings</a><br />
<a href="#RF">Robert Frost</a><br />
<a href="#EA">Edward Arlington Robinson</a><br />
<hr align="center" noshade width="75%" size="4" />

<h2><a name="RF">Robert Frost</a></h2>
<h3 align="center">What Fifty Said</h3>
<p align="center"> -- Text of poem omitted for clarity of example --
</p>
<p align="center"><a href="#top">Top of Page</a>
</p>
<hr align="center" noshade width="50%" size="4" />
```

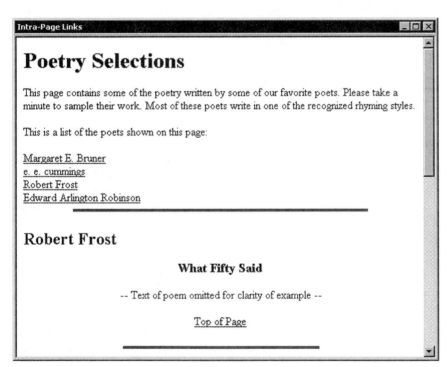

▸▸THE "CLICK HERE" FAUX PAS

Many new Web weavers fall victim to the "click here" faux pas, a classic error of link design in which sentences like, Click here to go to the next page," or, Click here to send me email," are used to let the user know that there are links available on the current page. When you understand how the browser displays links, you won't feel compelled to explicitly tell the user that there are links available. It looks far more professional to say, "You can go to the next page," or, "See pictures of my dog," or even, "Send me some email." Be subtle with your links. The users understand how their browsers display links—give them some credit.

Figure 3.7

Two links, one back to home page and one that opens email client

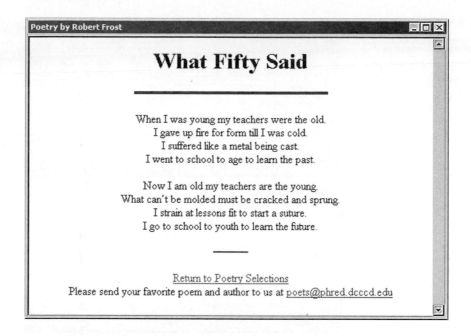

▸▸MAILTO: PROTOCOL

This is a good time to show you how to insert a link to your email system using the mailto protocol. The anchor container is also used to link the user to the computer's email software. Back in Table 1.1, we listed mailto: as one type of Internet protocol. Since it is an Internet protocol, it can be used as **href** just like http: to link to an Internet-supported service. For example, if you were using Navigator and clicked on the poets email address (Figure 3.7), an email composition window similar to Figure 3.8 would open.

The email address must be preceded by mailto: and be enclosed in quotes just like the other **href** attributes. However, the email address does not have to be used as text as shown in Figure 3.7. The following code would open the same email composition window:

```
<a href="mailto:poets@phred.dcccd.edu">Email Our Poetry Aficionado</a>
```

▸▸PAGE FOOTERS

We are starting to accumulate an interesting list of links that must appear at the end of every HTML document. For lack of a better name, we call this accumulated information the *page footer*. Page footers usually provide, in addition to a list of the navigation links used, basic information about the creator of the page. All page footers within the same hierarchical layout share a common design. Besides a Back link and email address, a page footer could have all or none of the following information:

- Organization's name
- Logo
- Street address
- Telephone number
- Fax number
- Web weaver's name
- Date page was last updated
- Links to related pages

Many organizations and individual Web weavers make the page footer their signature code. Figure 3.9 shows the code for a page footer.

Figure 3.8

Using the mailto protocol as hypertext reference to open an email composition window

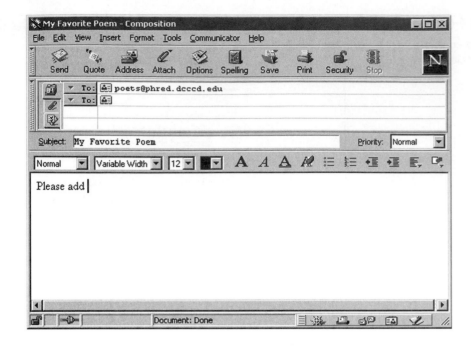

Figure 3.9

HTML code for page footer

```
21  <hr align="center" noshade size="2" width="50" />
22
23  <p align="center">
24  <a href="select.html">Return to Poetry Selections</a><br />
25  Please send your favorite poem and author to us at
26  <a href="mailto:poets@phred.dcccd.edu">poets@phred.dcccd.edu</a>
27  </p>
```

Return to Poetry Selections
Please send your favorite poem and author to us at poets@phred.dcccd.edu

EXPLORATION #6

The HTML document prior.html created in Exploration #1 needs a footer that does the following:

1. Displays a center-aligned horizontal rule with noshade, 2 pixels tall and 50 pixels wide.

2. Provides a centered intrasystem link back to **select.html** using Return to Poetry Selections as the text link.

3. Provides a centered email link to poets@phred.dcccd.ed using Email Our Poetry Aficionado as the link text.

Save the file, and use your browser to display and test the new links.

▶▶ SERVER-SIDE INCLUDES

Designing a common page footer to be used for every Web page within a Web site creates a unifying look. However, any change to this footer means every page in the site needs to be updated. One interesting way to handle this situation is to use ***server-side includes***, code within an HTML document that asks the Web server software to perform some special task while the page is being sent to the browser. Exactly how it is done depends on the Web administrator and the server software. The server could be asked to display the date and time a file was last modified or insert some additional HTML code found in an independent document. This last situation could be used to insert the same footer into the bottom of every page in a site. Instead of using the HTML code found in Figure 3.9 at the bottom of every HTML document, a Web weaver could save the code as an independent document named footer.html. Placing the following comment where the footer usually goes establishes a server-side include:

```
<!- #include file="footer.html" ->
```

While different Web servers handle server-side includes in various ways, one popular method is to use a .shtml filename extension on any HTML document containing one. When the server sees this filename extension, it looks for the server-side include and executes the code. The appeal of this approach is obvious. A Web weaver can design and update a single HTML document and have it incorporated into any number of Web pages.

Now, having introduced the idea of server-side includes, which Web weavers should know about, we must caution against their use within any of your HTML documents for several reasons:

1. They increase network traffic.

2. They slow page loading.

3. They increase the exposure to hostile interventions, like someone adding destructive code to the insertion.

4. They create another file the Web weaver must maintain.

Furthermore, professional Web authors have other tools available that allow them to automate the updating of multiple files.

▶▶ KEY TERMS

Absolute path	Path
Case-sensitive	Relative path
Intersystem link	Server-side include
Intrapage link	Source
Intrapage target name	Static
Intrasystem link	Storyboarding
Page footer	Target

▶▶ NEW TAGS

`<a></a>`

▸▸REVIEW QUESTIONS

1. Define each of the key terms.
2. In what two situations are storyboards especially useful?
3. What is the most important reason to use storyboards?
4. What is the basic code for a source anchor container that creates a hyperlink?
5. Which anchor tag attributes control the HTML document that is assigned to the next or previous Web page displayed by a browser?
6. What are three different types of links found in a HTML document?
7. Identify four parts of a URL.
8. What identifies an absolute path?
9. Why is it usually better to use a relative path?
10. What are four potential problems associated with intersystem links?
11. Why is it recommended to use a domain name instead of the IP address?
12. Identify two ways to establish an intrapage target name, and give an advantage and disadvantage of each way.
13. What identifies an intrapage target name in a source anchor?
14. Why is it considered bad style to place heading tags within an anchor container?
15. Why would a Web author break a long HTML document down into several short, single-topic documents?
16. What is the "click here" faux pas?
17. What is the basic code for an anchor container that opens the computer's email composition window?
18. What type of information is found in a page footer?

▸▸EXERCISES

3.1 This exercise is a continuation of Exercise 2.1 from Chapter Two. Ruby now wants to add an education page to her collection. She needs you to create a second page for her shop. Here is what she wants you to do:

a. Use the same colors for this page, a soft jade green background, #CCFFCC, and amethyst text, #9933FF.

b. This page (Ruby's second page) should be entitled "Ruby's Links."

c. There should be a first-level heading with the company name. In addition, there should be a level-2 heading of "Links."

d. This page should contain the following paragraph, set off from the first and second level headings by two horizontal rules of 50 percent width:

Here at Gwen's Glorious Gemstone Gallery we feel an educated customer is a happy customer. Many of the delightful folks who come to visit us don't know quartz from citrine and that is fine. However, if you would like to know a little more about the gems you will see in our shop, please visit the following links and begin, or expand, your education.

The best place to start your education is the American Gem Trade Association (http://www.agta.org).

If you want to learn about pearls, check out the Pearling Industry homepage (http://www.atlaspacific.com.au/html/Overview/Pearl%20Industry.htm).

If you are looking to diamonds, you should check out the Gemological Institute of America (http://www.gia.org).

Note: The underlined strings should be the links to the URLs shown in parentheses; don't put the URLs on the actual page.

e. In addition to these links, Ruby would like to have links from the words "citrine" and "quartz" to the two pages, **eme03gems-citrine.html** and

eme03gems-quartz.html, which are included on your student disk. Copy those two pages from the data CD, and place them in your working directory. Then create links from this new page to those pages.

f. There should be good navigation, so the return link from the quartz and citrine pages should take users right back to where they left the "links" page. You will need to modify the quartz and citrine pages to have return links. This return link should look this way:

Back to the <u>links</u> page.

and should appear between two 25-percent wide horizontal rules, just above the address, which is the same as the first page and repeated on every page. Again, the underlined text should be the link.

Gwen's Glorious Gemstone Gallery
231 Lee Street
Emporia, VA
23847
733-436-7829

g. Save your page under the name eme03-links.html.

h. All pages should be XML-compliant, well-documented, and pass validation with only messages about deprecated tags.

3.2. Create a genealogy site that tracks at least five families. All the families must be related by blood. Every page should contain comments with your name and the assignment due date after the <html> tag.

i. Draw a storyboard of the links used in this exercise.

j. Create a home page with the family name, a general overview of the family, and links to one or more of the family pages.

k. Each family page should contain the names of the two parents and any children. Besides the date the couple were married, provide every birthday, death day, and the town and state in which each person resides. Provide Back and Forward links to pages with related people.

l. Create a common page footer and place it at the end of each family page. The page footer should include a horizontal rule, the family name, a link back to the home page, the date the page was last updated, your name, and a link to your email address if you have one.

3.3. Create an interactive glossary. Every page in the glossary should contain comments with your name and the assignment due date after the <html> tag.

a. The home page should provide a topic name and a heading that states "Everything You Ever Wanted To Know About__". How many glossary pages between 5 and 26 you want to make is up to you. At a minimum, there should be five links on the home page to HTML documents with terms and their definitions in the following ranges: A–E, F–J, K–O, P–T, U–Z.

b. At least 40 definitions need to appear in the glossary.

c. Each glossary page should have a page footer that contains a horizontal rule, a Back link to the home page, a Forward link to the next alphabetical page (the page with Zs should link to the page with As), the date the page was last updated, your name, and a link to your email address if you have one.

d. Draw a storyboard of the links used in this exercise.

3.4. Retrieve the Homework home page you created in Exercise 2.4. Every page should contain comments with your name and the assignment due date after the <html> tag.

a. Draw a storyboard of the links used in this exercise.

b. Use your school's name as the text for a link to the school's home page. If your school does not have a Web site, complete Exercise 2.5, and create a link to this page.

c. Create three documents, and use HTML Assignment #1, HTML Assignment #2, HTML Assignment #3 as the titles. Add to your Homework home page a new "Homework Assignments" heading, and place links to the three new documents under the heading.

d. Create a page footer you can use in the new documents. The footer should contain a horizontal rule, the class identifier, a link back to the Homework home page, the date the page was last updated, your name, and a link to your email address if you have one.

e. If you completed Exercise 2.3, link the resulting page to the Homework home page, and add the new page footer to it.

3.5. Retrieve your school's home page created in Exercise 2.5. Every page you create should contain comments with your name and the assignment due date after the <html> tag.

a. Draw a storyboard of the links used in this exercise.

b. Replace the words to the school's fight song with a link to a separate page that contains the words.

c. Create a new Telephone Directory page that lists the main telephone number and at least 10 other important telephone numbers related to school. Replace the main telephone number in the home page with a link to this new page.

d. Create three new HTML documents that provide information about the school. Add links to these new pages onto the school's home page. These pages could provide biographical information about teachers, coaches, or administrators. Other pages could provide schedules for sports teams, concerts, or club activities.

e. Create a page footer you can use in the new documents. The footer should contain a horizontal rule, the school's name, the date the page was last updated, your name, and a link to your email address if you have one.

3.6. Retrieve the Web page you created about your favorite movie in Exercise 2.6.

a. Add a new "What Others Think" heading to the page. Under the heading place two links to Web sites that provide information about the movie and about one of the principal actors or actresses or the director.

b. Create at least two new HTML documents that contain biographical information about someone associated with the movie. Create links in the original page to these new pages.

c. Create a page footer you can use in the new documents. The footer should contain a horizontal rule, the movie's name, a link back to the home page, the date the page was last updated, your name, and a link to your email address if you have one.

d. Every page should contain comments with your name and the assignment due date after the <html> tag.

e. Draw a storyboard of the links used in this exercise.

3.7. Create your own "Poetry Corner" HTML document that uses intrapage links to connect to at least four poems. This document should contain comments with your name and the assignment due date after the <html> tag. If you completed Exercise 2.7, use the HTML code for one of the poems.

a. Draw a storyboard of the links used in this exercise.

b. The beginning of the document should contain a list of the poems by title and author. Each title should be an intrapage link to the related poem.

c. Start each poem with a horizontal rule, the poem's title, and the author's name.

d. After each poem there should be a Back link to the top of the page.

e. Create a page footer that contains a horizontal rule, your name, a link to your email address if you have one, the date the page was last updated, and a link to another Web site that displays a poem.

3.8. Create two storyboards. One should employ a simple sequential design and the other a hierarchical design.

## Chapter Four

Lists: Bringing Order out of Chaos

The reason we build Web pages is to bring unique, easily accessed information to the world. Lists are one way to organize information for easy access. People use lists to organize information in their day-to-day lives, and we can organize data in that comfortable format for the users of our Web pages.

CHAPTER OBJECTIVES

After reading this chapter you should be able to do the following:

- Create HTML-compliant ordered, unordered, and definition lists.
- Use alternative sequencing schemes to organize ordered list items.
- Start an ordered list's sequencing at another value.
- Change the default bullet used in an unordered list.

- Reposition a list item in a line.
- Code HTML-compliant nested lists.
- Use spaces and blank lines to create easy-to-read code.
- Identify the HTML elements that make up the XHTML List module.

▸▸PLAIN-TEXT LISTS

We can build what appear to be lists of information by using the <br /> element to force a line break after each item in the list. This is a *plain-text list,* in which no list-making tags are used. To use this "brute force" method to create a list of three items, we could use the code shown in Figure 4.1. As you can see, the Web weaver must put in the numbers in the layout to make the page look like a list. There is a better way to create a list, as we shall see.

Figure 4.1

HTML code showing "brute force" (plain-text) method of building list with line breaks (<br />)

```
<html>
<head>
<title>Plain Text List</title>
</head>

<body>
The following shows a brute force way to build a Christmas list:<br />
1.  Partridge in pear tree<br />
2.  French Hens<br />
3.  Calling Birds<br />
</body>
</html>
```

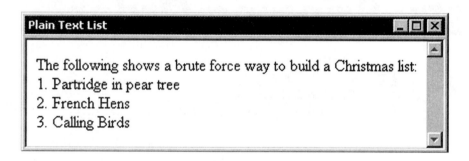

▸▸LIST-MAKING TAGS

HTML has special list-making tags that provide a much better way to make a list than the plain-text method. In fact, five different kinds of lists can be created:

1. Ordered lists
2. Unordered lists
3. Definitions
4. Menus
5. Directories

The first three are the most commonly used.

▸▸ORDERED AND UNORDERED LISTS

Your material will determine whether you should use an ordered or unordered list. When your list items have no particular priority or chronological order, you should use an unordered list. Ordered lists are appropriate for instructions, chronological material, items presented in order of importance, and so forth.

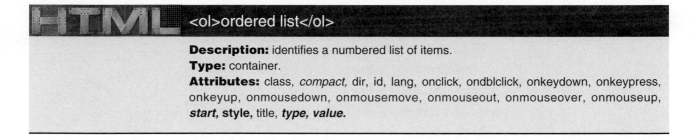

Description: identifies a numbered list of items.
Type: container.
Attributes: class, *compact,* dir, id, lang, onclick, ondblclick, onkeydown, onkeypress, onkeyup, onmousedown, onmousemove, onmouseout, onmouseover, onmouseup, *start,* style, title, *type, value.*

A simple *ordered list* (<ol>) numbers each item as shown in Figure 4.2. Two tags are used: the ordered-list container, <ol>. . .</ol>, which encloses the list, and the list-item container, <li>. . .</li>, used to start each new list element.

Figure 4.2

HTML code for ordered list

```
<html>
<head>
<title>Ordered List</title>
</head>

<body>
The following ordered list is a more efficient way to build the Christmas list:
<ol>
  <li> Partridge in pear tree</li>
  <li>French Hens</li>
  <li> Calling Birds</li>
</ol>
</body>
</html>
```

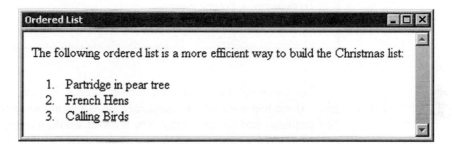

The <ol> container is a rather sophisticated one, with some interesting attributes. The easiest way to code it is to simply enter the <ol> tag and then the individual list items, each enclosed with an <li> (list item) container (discussed later on). Some people treat the <li> element as an empty tag because all the current browsers infer a closing list-element tag </li> when they find another <li> or the end of the list. Nevertheless, we recommend closing all list items with an </li> tag, as is required in all XML/XHTML coding. It takes just a second longer to add the ending tag, and it ensures maximum compatibility.

The simple form of the ordered list causes most browsers to put a number at the beginning of each list item. The default is for Arabic numerals, starting with number 1. Figure 4.2 shows how this list would look using a graphical browser. Notice that a space is automatically placed between the item number and the item. In the code shown in this figure, French Hens immediately follows the starting tag of <li>, but the browser inserts a space after the numeral.

One advantage of using the list container instead of coding plain-text lists using line breaks (<br />) becomes obvious when you try to insert an element into the middle of the list. For example, in our Christmas list in Figure 4.1, we were missing the turtledoves!

There need to be two turtledoves before the three French hens. Using the plain-text method, we would have to perform the following steps to modify the list:

1. Type in the new line between lines 1 and 2.

2. Renumber line 2 as line 3.

3. Renumber line 3 as line 4.

These corrections would result in the HTML code shown in Figure 4.3.

Figure 4.3

HTML code for plain-text list that requires renumbering when new items are inserted

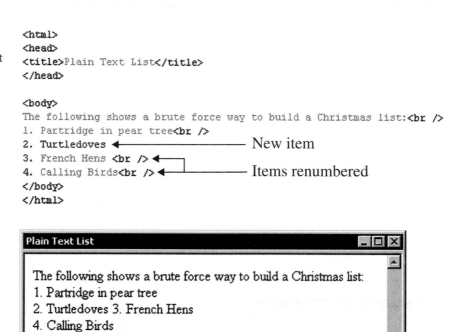

Bah, humbug! We forgot to put the <br /> after the new entry. Now we have to edit it again. If we had used an <ol> container, all we would have had to do was insert a new <li> container and the new entry. The browser would have updated the numbers for us, and we would not have needed to remember the <br />, either.

Because it is easy to use the <ol> container, and because people order their worlds in lists, most Web weavers use this container a lot. Three attributes that make it even more useful for specific tasks are **start, type,** and **style.**

start

It is sometimes handy to have a list start at some number other than 1. The **start** attribute lets you do this. For example, you may wish to list the steps in a task, with some discussion interspersed among the steps. You can code the first list container that describes the first three steps to close the list, type your discussion, and then continue your list by starting a second list container that begins with the number 4. Figure 4.4 shows an example. The list is restarted at item 4 using the following code:

<ol start="4">.

Notice how the **start** attribute allows the browser to build the lists, but lets the author control the ordering of the numbers (the list is restarted again at item 8). This attribute is a very handy tool. Unfortunately, although it has been deprecated for use within the <ol> container, related formatting capabilities have not been incorporated into other attribute properties with the current HTML 4 specifications.

Figure 4.4   HTML code using the **start** attribute

```
<html>
<head>
<title>Ordered List Using the Start Attribute</title>
</head>

<body>
There are 8 steps to change the oil in your car:
<ol>
  <li>Find a comfy place to park the car, in the shade in summer,
      in the sun in winter.</li>
  <li>Get the waste oil pan, filter wrench, and 14mm box end wrench ready.</li>
  <li>Find 4 quarts of 5W-30 oil and a good oil filter.</li>
</ol>

It is really important, or so the folks tell us, to use 5W-30 oil and good oil
filters.
<ol start="4">
  <li>Remove the oil drain plug, and drain the old oil into the waste oil pan.</li>
  <li>Remove the old filter...then clean up the mess you made.</li>
  <li>Replace the oil drain plug after the oil stops dripping.</li>
  <li>Put the new oil filter on, 1/4 turn past finger tight.</li>
</ol>

Always remember to put just a bit of  oil on the rubber gasket before you put the
oil filter back on.  This will make a better seal, and help you get the filter
tightened correctly.
<ol start="8">
  <li>Put 4 quarts of 5W-30 oil into the engine.</li>
</ol>
</body>
</html>
```

```
Ordered List Using the Start Attribute                              _ □ ×

There are 8 steps to change the oil in your car:

    1.  Find a comfy place to park the car, in the shade in summer, in the sun in winter.
    2.  Get the waste oil pan, filter wrench, and 14mm box end wrench ready.
    3.  Find 4 quarts of 5W-30 oil and a good oil filter.

It is really important, or so the folks tell us, to use 5W-30 oil and good oil filters.

    4.  Remove the oil drain plug, and drain the old oil into the waste oil pan.
    5.  Remove the old filter...then clean up the mess you made.
    6.  Replace the oil drain plug after the oil stops dripping.
    7.  Put the new oil filter on, 1/4 turn past finger tight.

Always remember to put just a bit of oil on the rubber gasket before you put the oil filter back on.
This will make a better seal, and help you get the filter tightened correctly.

    8.  Put 4 quarts of 5W-30 oil into the engine.
```

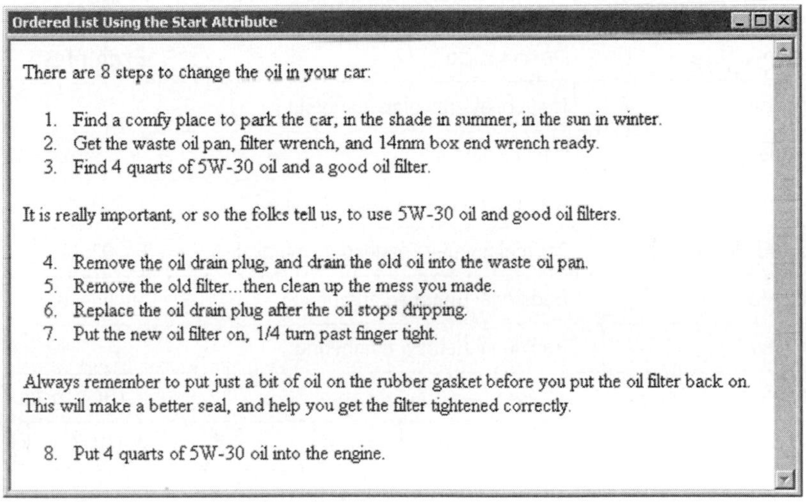

type

Besides letting you choose the starting number for your list, HTML also provides a way for you to change the style of the numbers or letters of the list elements. Table 4.1 presents the different number and letter styles provided by the **type** attribute. Figure 4.5 shows some coded examples.

This attribute is handy for making outlines, as we will see later in the chapter, when we put lists inside lists. However, the **type** attribute, like the **start** attribute, has been deprecated in favor of the **style** attribute.

Table 4.1 List Options for Labeling Items in Ordered List

Type	Style Value	Description	Examples
A	upper-alpha	Uppercase letters	A. B. C. D.
a	lower-alpha	Lowercase letters	a. b. c. d.
I	upper-roman	Uppercase Roman numerals	I. II. III. IV.
i	lower-roman	Lowercase roman numerals	i. ii. iii. iv.
1	decimal	Arabic numerals (default)	1. 2. 3. 4.

style

As mentioned in Chapter Two, the **style** attribute is used with a variety of HTML tags to control the appearance of the page layout. Figure 4.5 shows how to use this attribute to set the list-style-type property equal to **upper-alpha**, producing the same results as setting the **type** attribute equal to "A". The HTML code looks like this:

```
<ol style="list-style-type: upper-alpha">
```

The syntax associated with the **style** attribute was introduced for the first time in the HTML 4 specifications. It requires assigning one or more **property: value** pairs to the **style** attribute. The preceding example uses the list-style-type property and upper-alpha as the value. Not only does the **style** attribute, through the list-style-type property, support the style values listed in Table 4.1, it also supports the <ol> values shown in Table 4.2. The values in Table 4.2 are in keeping with the W^{3}C's intent, along with the

Table 4.2 Additional List-Style-Type Values for Ordering List Using **style** Attribute

Style Value	Description	Examples
armenian	Traditional Armenian numbering	
cjk-ideographic	Plain ideographic numbers	
decimal	Arabic numerals (default)	1. 2. 3. 4.
decimal-leading-zero	Decimal numbers padded by initial zeros	01. 02. 03.
georgian	Traditional Georgian numbering	an. ban. gan.
hebrew	Traditional Hebrew numbering	
hiragana		a. i. u. e. o. ka. ki.
katakana		A. I. U. E. O. KA. KI.
hiragana-iroha		i. ro. ha. ni. ho. he. to.
katakana-iroha		I. RO. HA. NI. HO. HE. TO.
lower-alpha	Lowercase letters	a. b. c. d.
lower-greek	Lowercase classical Greek letters	α. β. χ.
lower-latin	Lowercase ASCII letters	a. b. c. d.
lower-roman	Lowercase Roman numerals	i. ii. iii. iv.
upper-alpha	Uppercase letters	A. B. C. D.
upper-latin	Uppercase ASCII letters	A. B. C. D.
upper-roman	Uppercase Roman numerals	I. II. III. IV.

Figure 4.5 HTML code for list options using **type** and **style** attributes to label items in an ordered list

```
Ordered list using UPPERCASE letters:
<ol type="A">
  <li>for excellent students</li>
  <li>for those above average</li>
  <li>for the average</li>
</ol>

Ordered list using lowercase letters:
<ol type="a">
  <li>is for apple</li>
  <li>is for banana</li>
  <li>is for cantaloupe</li>
</ol>

Ordered list using UPPERCASE roman numerals:
<ol type="I">
  <li>is for first place</li>
  <li>is for second place</li>
  <li>is for third place</li>
</ol>

Ordered list using lowercase roman numerals:
<ol type="i">
  <li>is for the money</li>
  <li>is for the show</li>
  <li>is to get ready</li>
</ol>
```

```
Ordered list using UPPERCASE letters:
<ol style="list-style-type: upper-alpha">
  <li>for excellent students</li>
  <li>for those above average</li>
  <li>for the average</li>
</ol>

Ordered list using lowercase letters:
<ol style="list-style-type: lower-alpha">
  <li>is for apple</li>
  <li>is for banana</li>
  <li>is for cantaloupe</li>
</ol>

Ordered list using UPPERCASE roman numerals:
<ol style="list-style-type: upper-roman">
  <li>is for first place</li>
  <li>is for second place</li>
  <li>is for third place</li>
</ol>

Ordered list using lowercase roman numerals:
<ol style="list-style-type: lower-roman">
  <li>is for the money</li>
  <li>is for the show</li>
  <li>is to get ready</li>
</ol>
```

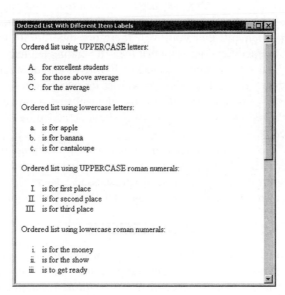

HTML 4 specifications, to support internationalism by accounting for different languages besides English.

Style versus Deprecated Attributes An old sixties song by Bob Dylan bemoans that "the times, they are a'changin'." This could also be said about the handling of lists with the HTML 4 specifications. The introduction of *cascading style sheets* and the *inline* **style** attribute (inline elements are discussed later) is changing the way Web weavers format a list. As we write these words, though, only the latest versions of the popular browsers recognize some of the new **style** attributes recommended by W[3]C. Read that last sentence carefully; the key word is "some." At this time, none of the commonly available browsers recognize all of the new **style** attributes. For this reason, we also explain deprecated attributes in this text, because you need to know both kinds of attributes in order to maintain backward compatibility with older browsers.

As we look ahead to new trends in coding, the property: **value** pairs (like list-style-type: **lower-roman**) used by the **style** attribute are central to the style-sheet–based formatting of XML and XHTML documents. These ideas are explored in more detail in chapters Five and Eight.

 **<li>list item</li>**

Description: identifies a specific item in an ordered, unordered, menu, or directory list.
Type: container.
Attributes: class, dir, id, lang, onclick, ondblclick, onkeydown, onkeypress, onkeyup, onmousedown, onmousemove, onmouseout, onmouseover, onmouseup, **style**, title, *type, value.*
XML: requires the closing tag </li>.

You have already seen the way the list-item container (<li>) is used to indicate elements of a list. Although the <li> tag is really a container, browsers can always infer the end of this container by what follows. Nevertheless, we once again recommend using the closing tag, in this case </li>, because we believe that good page design leaves the browser little to infer, or guess. Furthermore, the XML/XHTML specifications require ending tags for every element. Our code will therefore incorporate the ending tags even though the HTML specifications state that the </li> ending tag may be omitted.

The <li> container is used with ordered and unordered lists. What the <li> container generates depends on the type of list for which it defines an element. In an ordered list, the <li> container specifies a list element that is preceded by a number or letter. In an unordered list, it specifies a list element preceded by one of the different types of bullets or icons.

The <li> container can contain almost anything if it is used in an ordered or unordered list. It can contain text, images, or even other lists. However, if the list item is within a directory or menu list (discussed later in this chapter), it cannot contain other lists or *blocked elements* (discussed next) like paragraphs or forms.

BLOCKED AND INLINE ELEMENTS

A ***blocked element*** has a clearly defined beginning and end, for example, a paragraph, quote, heading, or list. It generally begins a new line and can include line breaks. It also can contain other blocked elements or ***inline elements***, like bold or italics, which are so named because they usually appear within a line of text and do not initiate line breaks. An inline element can contain other inline elements, for instance, an italic container inside a bold container. But an inline element should not contain a blocked element, like an ordered list inside a bold container. Blocked elements are generally larger structures than inline elements. Commonly used inline formatting elements are discussed in Chapter Five.

type

The **type** attribute of the <li> container is very much like the **type** attribute of the <ol> container. The difference is that the <ol> type specifies the style of the numbers for the whole list, whereas the **type** attribute on a single <li> changes the style of the numbering beginning with that list item and continuing through the rest of the list items, or until it is changed. Figure 4.6 shows the different values for the **type** attribute, with each list item having its own label style. This <li> **type** attribute was deprecated in the HTML 4 specifications in favor of the style attribute's list-style-type property.

Figure 4.6

HTML code showing variations of the <li> **type** and **style** attributes

```
<html>
<head>
<title>Ordered List With Line Item Options</title>
</head>

<body>
This list shows item options offered by type attribute:
<ol>
  <li type="A">This element is of type A.</li>
  <li type="a">This element is of type a.</li>
  <li type="i">This element is of type I.</li>
  <li type="i">And this element has a type i.</li>
</ol>

This list shows item options offered by the style attribute:
<ol>
  <li style="list-style-type: upper-alpha">This element is upper-alpha.</li>
  <li style="list-style-type: lower-alpha">This element is lower-alpha.</li>
  <li style="list-style-type: upper-roman">This element is upper-roman.</li>
  <li style="list-style-type: lower-roman">And this element is lower-roman.</li>
</ol>
</body>
</html>
```

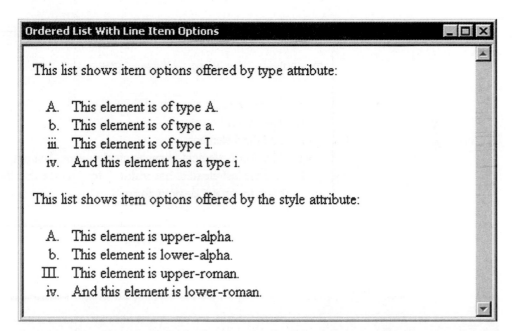

style

Both the **type** and **style** attributes can produce the same results, as shown in Figure 4.6, but the **style** attribute has a wider range of item labels available (see Table 4.2).

value

Like the start attribute of the <ol> tag, the value attribute of the <li> tag can specify a particular starting value that will serve as the new base number for the rest of the items in the list—unless a subsequent item specifies another value.

Misusing the **value** attribute can cause confusing results, as shown in Figure 4.7. In this figure, you can see that each time the value was changed, the change was propagated from that point down the list until there was another change. You need to be very careful when changing the **style** or **value** for list elements. It is rare that you will need to change either.

Figure 4.7

HTML code showing misuse of the <li> **value** and **style** attributes

```
<html>
<head>
<title>Misuse of List Item value and style Attributes</title>
</head>

<body>
The following list shows each type of list item:
<ol>
<li value="5">This is the first element of the list.</li>
<li value="1"> The second element</li>
<li value="11"> The third element</li>
<li style="list-style-type: lower-roman">The fourth element changes number type,
    but not <b>value</b></li>
<li value="1"> and the last element has <b>value</b> 1 too,
    notice that the list-style-type back to default decimal format!</li>
</ol>
</body>
</html>
```

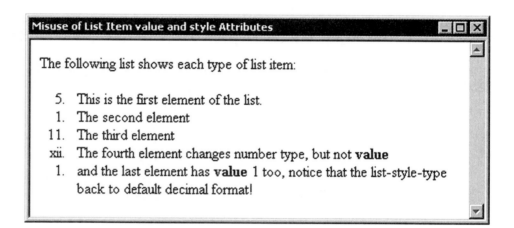

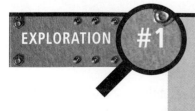

EXPLORATION #1

Use your ASCII editor to save the HTML template as chapter4.html. In this new HTML document use "*your name's* Restaurant" in the <title> container. Start the document using a level-1 heading with a made-up restaurant name. Under the name create an ordered list for the restaurant's menu. Use upper-roman numbers and the following three items:

   I.Appetizers
  II.Entrées
 III.Desserts

Save the file, and display it using your favorite browser.

▸▸HTML-COMPLIANT CODE

If you are trying to build clean, fully HTML-compliant code, you should never embed any text or other items within a list outside a list-item container. For example, Figure 4.8 shows how we could code the oil-change example that appeared earlier in Figure 4.4 without changing lists. We have included two descriptive paragraphs within the list, yet

Figure 4.8 Noncompliant HTML code with paragraphs inside the ordered list—an example of what not to do

```
<html>
<head>
<title>Poorly Written HTML Code </title>
</head>

<body>
There are 8 steps to change the oil in your car:
<ol>
  <li>Find a comfy place to park the car, in the shade in summer, in the sun in winter.</li>
  <li>Get the waste oil pan, filter wrench, and 14mm box end wrench ready.</li>
  <li>Find 4 quarts of 5W-30 oil and a good oil filter.</li>

<p>It is really important, or so the folks tell us, to use 5W-30 oil and good oil filters.
</p>

  <li>Remove the oil drain plug, and drain the old oil into the waste oil pan.</li>
  <li>Remove the old filter...then clean up the mess you made.</li>
  <li>Replace the oil drain plug after the oil stops dripping.</li>
  <li>Put the new oil filter on, 1/4 turn past finger tight.</li>

<p>Always remember to put just a bit of oil on the rubber gasket before you put the oil filter
back on.  This will make a better seal, and help you get the filter tightened correctly.
</p>

  <li>Put 4 quarts of 5W-30 oil into the engine.</li>
</ol>

</body>
</html>
```

Poorly Written HTML Code

There are 8 steps to change the oil in your car:

1. Find a comfy place to park the car, in the shade in summer, in the sun in winter.
2. Get the waste oil pan, filter wrench, and 14mm box end wrench ready.
3. Find 4 quarts of 5W-30 oil and a good oil filter.

   It is really important, or so the folks tell us, to use 5W-30 oil and good oil filters.

4. Remove the oil drain plug, and drain the old oil into the waste oil pan.
5. Remove the old filter...then clean up the mess you made.
6. Replace the oil drain plug after the oil stops dripping.
7. Put the new oil filter on, 1/4 turn past finger tight.

   Always remember to put just a bit of oil on the rubber gasket before you put the oil filter back on. This will make a better seal, and help you get the filter tightened correctly.

8. Put 4 quarts of 5W-30 oil into the engine.

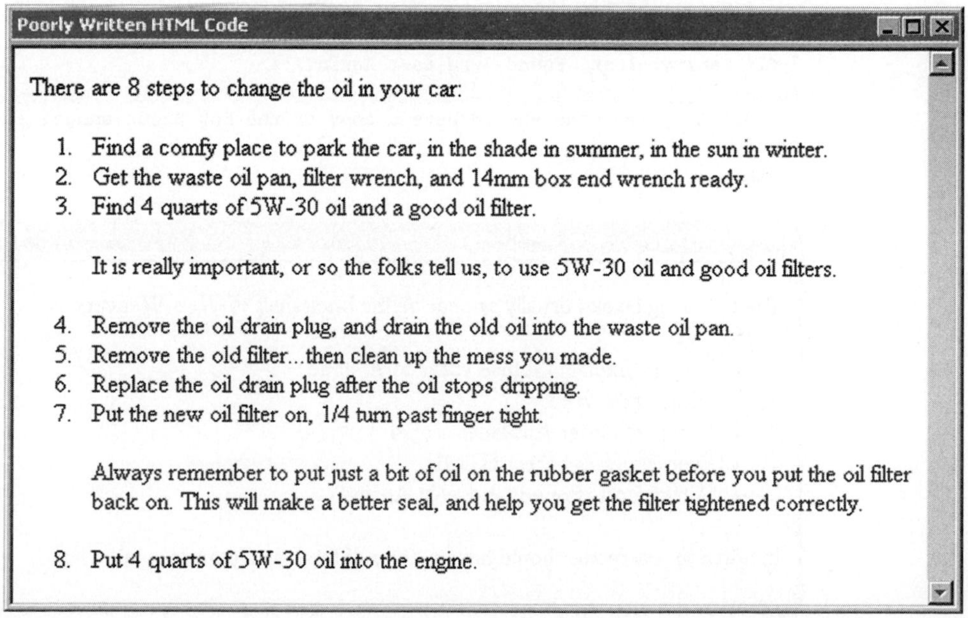

we keep them outside the actual list elements. With this noncompliant design, the browser does not need to restart the numbering on successive lists. However, unlike the first line of text, the embedded paragraphs are indented with the list items when displayed by the browser. This display is a subtle difference from the oil-changing steps created by the HTML-compliant code in Figure 4.4. Figure 4.8 is shown to illustrate a bad example! In other words, don't try this at home.

HTML <ul>unordered list</ul>

Description: identifies a list of items with no specific order implied.
Type: container.
Attributes: class, *compact,* dir, id, lang, onclick, ondblclick, onkeydown, onkeypress, onkeyup, onmousedown, onmousemove, onmouseout, onmouseover, onmouseup, **style,** title, **type.**

The ***unordered list*** (<ul>) is used when you want to make a list of items that have no necessary order. These lists use ***bullets***, decorative labels assigned to each list item. The W^3C uses the term ***marker*** instead of bullets. A five-item unordered list is shown in Figure 4.9. Except for the fact that bullets rather than numbers or letters precede the list elements, the format of this list is very similar to that of the ordered list. Each list item is contained within an <li>list item</li> container.

Figure 4.9

HTML code for an unordered list with five list items

```
<html>
<head>
<title>Unordered List</title>
</head>

<body>
The following books usually appear on the bookshelf of Web Weavers:
<ul>
  <li>How to Explain Obtuse Ideas to Anyone</li>
  <li>Charlotte's Web</li>
  <li>Excellent Paper Airplanes Vol. 4</li>
  <li>Even More Excellent HTML</li>
  <li>Sanity: Lost, Found, and Lost Again</li>
</ul>
In addition, everyone should have a copy of the Boy Scout manual at hand.
</body>
</html>
```

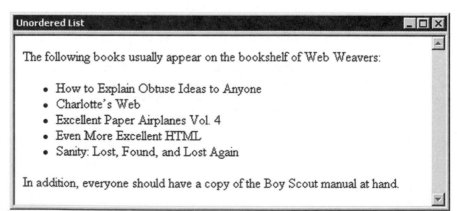

Unordered List

The following books usually appear on the bookshelf of Web Weavers:

- How to Explain Obtuse Ideas to Anyone
- Charlotte's Web
- Excellent Paper Airplanes Vol. 4
- Even More Excellent HTML
- Sanity: Lost, Found, and Lost Again

In addition, everyone should have a copy of the Boy Scout manual at hand.

type or style

It is possible to change the shape of the bullets in an unordered list by using the **type** or **style** attributes. Three different marker styles are recognized by the HTML 4 specifications: disc, circle, or square. Disc is the default format, as shown in Figure 4.9.

In the following HTML code, the **type** attribute would establish an unordered list that uses a square as the preceding bullet for each list item:

```
<ul type="square">
```

As mentioned earlier in this chapter, the **type** attribute was deprecated in the most recent W3C specifications in favor of the **style** attribute. Both options are shown in Figure 4.10. The HTML code for changing the bullet to a circle using the **style** attribute is as follows:

```
<ul style="list-style-type: circle">
```

Figure 4.10

HTML code using the **type** and **style** attributes to change the bullets in an unordered list

```
<html>
<head>
<title>Unordered List With Line Item Options</title>
</head>

<body>
The marker style was originally changed using the <b>type</b> attribute.<br>
This list uses the square bullet:
<ul type="square">
  <li>How to Explain Obtuse Ideas to Anyone</li>
  <li>Charlotte's Web</li>
  <li>Excellent Paper Airplanes Vol. 4</li>
  <li>Even More Excellent HTML</li>
  <li>Sanity: Lost, Found, and Lost Again</li>
</ul>

The <b>style</b> attribute provides a new way to change the marker's look.<br>
This list uses the circle bullet:
<ul style="list-style-type: circle">
  <li>How to Explain Obtuse Ideas to Anyone</li>
  <li>Charlotte's Web</li>
  <li>Excellent Paper Airplanes Vol. 4</li>
  <li>Even More Excellent HTML</li>
  <li>Sanity: Lost, Found, and Lost Again</li>
</ul>
Unordered lists use the disc marker as a default bullet.
</body>
</html>
```

Unordered List With Line Item Options

The marker style was originally changed using the **type** attribute.
This list uses the square bullet:

- How to Explain Obtuse Ideas to Anyone
- Charlotte's Web
- Excellent Paper Airplanes Vol. 4
- Even More Excellent HTML
- Sanity: Lost, Found, and Lost Again

The **style** attribute provides a new way to change the marker's look.
This list uses the circle bullet:

o How to Explain Obtuse Ideas to Anyone
o Charlotte's Web
o Excellent Paper Airplanes Vol. 4
o Even More Excellent HTML
o Sanity: Lost, Found, and Lost Again

Unordered lists use the disc marker as a default bullet.

The **style** attribute's list style-type property is utilized in both ordered and unordered lists to change the look of the item label.

Note that some browsers don't recognize the **type** attribute used within the <li> tag. For example, although Navigator will recognize the disc property within the <li> tag, earlier versions of Internet Explorer would not. Of course, none of the earlier versions recognize the **style** attribute. Consequently, it is best to avoid using the **type** attribute within the <li> tag.

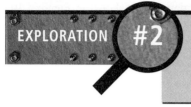

EXPLORATION #2

Modify chapter4.html by adding the level-2 heading "Wine List" under the dinner options. Next, add an unordered list using square bullets and the following three items: "Reds," "Whites," and "Champagnes." Save the file, and refresh/reload the browser's screen display.

list-style-position: outside | inside

The **style** attribute's list-style-position property changes the location of the list items within the line. Two values are available: **outside** and **inside**. The first list in Figure 4.11 demonstrates how the default position is *outside*. In this case a single list item is positioned inside the others using the list-style-position property set to **inside** as part of <*li*> beginning tag. This code is:

```
<li style="list-style-position: inside">

Superseded by Even More Excellent HTML

</li>
```

As you can see, this code offsets the list item from the others, which visually daws attention to it.

The lower list in Figure 4.11 is designed to achieve the opposite effect. The list items in this list are positioned inside by setting the list-style-position property to **inside** as part of the beginning <ul> tag. It is also important to note in this example that when the style attribute is used to make several changes using the same tag, semicolons are used to separate each property: value pair. For example, the following code (from Figure 4.11) sets the bullets in the unordered list of squares and positions them inside:

```
<ul style="list-style-type: square; list-style-position: inside">
```

Most often you will leave list items in their default outside position. However, changing the position of all or one of the list items can have a good visual impact for special occasions.

Another alternative for combining list property: value pairs in a single **style** attribute is to use the W[3]C approved shorthand property of list-style. This property can be set equal to values associated with the list-style-type and list-style-position properties. Only one value for each property is allowed. The following code accomplishes the same results as the preceding code. Both codes list items inside and set the bullets to square:

```
<ul style="list-style: square inside">
```

If you incorrectly set list-style to **square** and **circle** some browsers will use the last value listed. Others will ignore the **style** attribute altogether when unacceptable values like that are used. Another common error some Web weavers make is to use commas or other punctuation to separate the elements of the value of this property. The browsers are *very* picky about the syntax of cascading style sheets. They must be coded exactly right.

Figure 4.11   HTML code that changes line location of list item using list-style-position property

```html
<html>
<head>
<title>Unordered List Using list-style-position Property</title>
</head>

<body>
The <b>style</b> attribute also provides a way to change the marker's position on the line.
The following list items default to an outside position, with one item set to an inside
position:
<ul>
  <li>How to Explain Obtuse Ideas to Anyone</li>
  <li>Charlotte's Web</li>
  <li>Excellent Paper Airplanes Vol. 4</li>
  <li>More Excellent HTML</li>
  <li style="list-style-position: inside">
    Superseded by Even More Excellent HTML
  </li>
  <li>Sanity: Lost, Found, and Lost Again</li>
</ul>

This list below is set to an inside position with one item positioned outside:
<ul style="list-style-type: square; list-style-position: inside">
  <li>How to Explain Obtuse Ideas to Anyone</li>
  <li>Charlotte's Web</li>
  <li>Excellent Paper Airplanes Vol. 4</li>
  <li>More Excellent HTML</li>
  <li style="list-style-position: outside">
    Superseded by Even More Excellent HTML
  </li>
  <li>Sanity: Lost, Found, and Lost Again</li>
</ul>
</body>
</html>
```

Unordered List Using list-style-position Property	_ □ ☒

The **style** attribute also provides a way to change the marker's position on the line.
The following list items default to an outside position, with one item set to an inside
position:

- How to Explain Obtuse Ideas to Anyone
- Charlotte's Web
- Excellent Paper Airplanes Vol. 4
- More Excellent HTML
  - Superseded by Even More Excellent HTML
- Sanity: Lost, Found, and Lost Again

This list below in set to an inside position with one item positioned outside:

- How to Explain Obtuse Ideas to Anyone
- Charlotte's Web
- Excellent Paper Airplanes Vol. 4
- More Excellent HTML
- Superseded by Even More Excellent HTML
  - Sanity: Lost, Found, and Lost Again

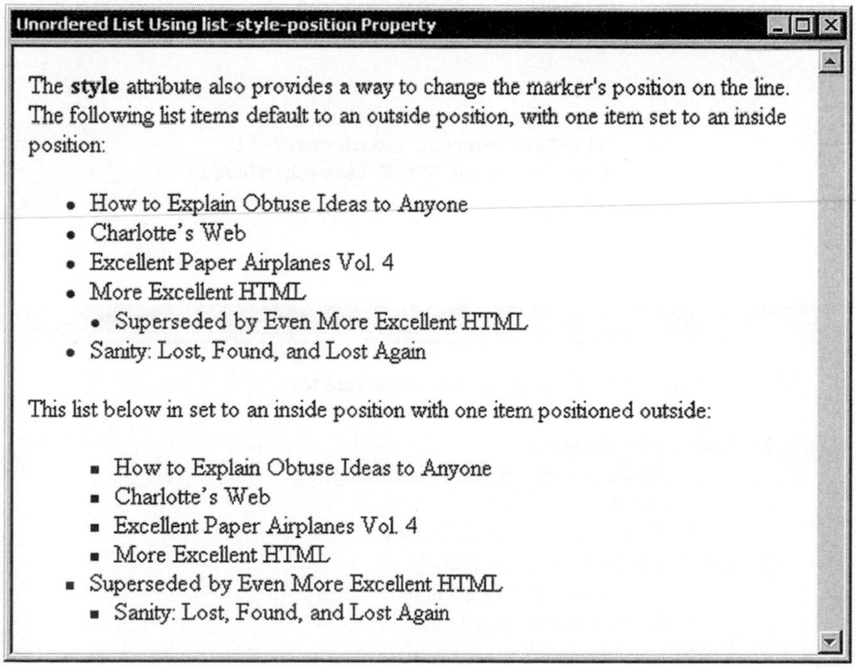

The list-style property can be used with a single value. The following code sequences an order list using lowercase alphabetic characters:

```
<ol style="list-style: lower-alpha">
```

In most cases we will avoid using shorthand properties like list-style in favor of the specific property: value pairings like list-style-type: **lower-alpha**, because we want you to understand how to use the various style properties. However, if you feel especially bold and patient, feel free to play with shorthand assignments.

EXPLORATION #3 Change chapter4.html by placing the list item "Champagnes" at the line's inside position. Save the file, and refresh/reload the browser's screen display.

Figure 4.12

HTML code for unordered lists contained within ordered list

```
<html>
<head>
<title>Nested Lists</title>
</head>

<body>
When packing a briefcase to go to school, be sure to:
<ol>
<li>Pack Yoda, the laptop.
  <ul>
  <li>Get the power cord and transformer.</li>
  <li>Find the box of disks.</li>
  <li>Check on the PCMCIA cards.</li>
  </ul>
</li>

<li>Check that the Day-Timer is there.
  <ul>
  <li>Check that it is the right month.</li>
  <li>Check that it is the right year.</li>
  </ul>
</li>

<li>Take correct textbooks.</li>
<li>Make sure LUNCH is packed!</li>
</ol>
</body>
</html>
```

Beginning tag → `<li>Pack Yoda, the laptop.`
Nested list → (the `<ul>...</ul>` block)
Ending tag → `</li>`

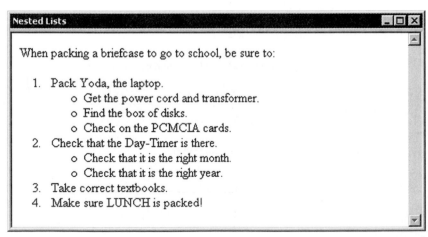

Nested Lists

When packing a briefcase to go to school, be sure to:

1. Pack Yoda, the laptop.
    o Get the power cord and transformer.
    o Find the box of disks.
    o Check on the PCMCIA cards.
2. Check that the Day-Timer is there.
    o Check that it is the right month.
    o Check that it is the right year.
3. Take correct textbooks.
4. Make sure LUNCH is packed!

▸▸LISTS OF LISTS (NESTING)

Sometimes it is necessary to build lists of lists. In both ordered and unordered lists, it is possible to put another list (a sublist) inside a list element. This procedure of *nesting lists* allows you to build structures that convey complex relationships.

COMBINING ORDERED AND UNORDERED LISTS

Figure 4.12 shows an ordered list that has two small unordered lists within it. As you can see from this example, the browser indents the list within a list to increase readability and show the subordinate relationship. The fact that the subordinate lists are indented in the HTML code has no bearing on how the browser displays them. This indention is only to make the code easier to read, understand, and debug.

Figure 4.12 also illustrates how a nested list falls within a list item of the first list. To create compliant code, the nested list must be contained within another list item container, as shown in the figure. We recommend using a couple of spaces to indent the code for the nested list and vertically aligning the open and close list tags. Although indenting and aligning the code has no effect on how it is displayed, this practice will help you check the code to make sure you haven't forgotten the ending list-item tag, </li>.

NESTING UNORDERED LISTS

In nested unordered lists, most browsers use different bullet types to show that some elements are subordinate to others. The code at the top of Figure 4.13 has three levels of nested unordered lists. In Navigator and newer versions of Internet Explorer this code would generate the display as shown, with different bullets on each of the different levels generated. The Opera browser, however, is one exception to this rule.

NESTING ORDERED LISTS

Nesting ordered lists allows the creation of outlines. For example, if we change the HTML code in Figure 4.13 to use ordered lists, the result would be as shown in Figure 4.14.

Hmmmm. Figure 4.14 is not quite what we had in mind. Although it does indeed show a nested list of ordered lists, it isn't all that readable. What we need to do is change the **style** attribute's list-style-type property to different list types to show subordination. It is best to use the standard outline order (I., A., 1., a.).

Figure 4.15 presents the HTML code that will make the list more understandable. Notice that we specify the **style** attribute only for the opening tag of each list, not for each element. Using ordered or unordered lists can make your page more understandable to your users. In later examples you will see why lists are a standard feature of many of the pages on the Web. As you cruise the Net, look for examples of lists, both good and bad.

EXPLORATION #4

Time to fill out the menu items in chapter4.html by nesting three unordered lists, one under each ordered list item as follows:

I. Appetizers	II. Entrées	III. Desserts
• *Soup*	• *Beef*	• *Ice cream*
• *Salad*	• *Chicken*	• *Pie*
• *Cheese Spreads*	• *Fish*	• *Cake*

Use a solid disc as the bullet. Save the file, and refresh/reload the browser's screen display.

Figure 4.13 HTML code for nested unordered lists

```html
<html>
<head>
<title>Nested Unordered Lists</title>
</head>

<body>
When packing a briefcase to go to school, be sure to:
<ul>
<li>Pack Yoda, the laptop.
  <ul>
  <li>Get the power cord and transformer.</li>
  <li>Find the box of disks.
    <ul>
    <li>Get this semester's homework disk</li>
    <li>Get the grading software disk</li>
    <li>Make sure the games disk is packed!</li>
    </ul>
  </li>
  <li>Check on the PCMCIA cards.</li>
  </ul>
</li>

<li>Check that the Day-Timer is there.
  <ul>
  <li>Check that it is the right month.</li>
  <li>Check that it is the right year.</li>
  </ul>
</li>

<li>Take correct textbooks.</li>
<li>Make sure LUNCH is packed!</li>
</ul>
</body>
</html>
```

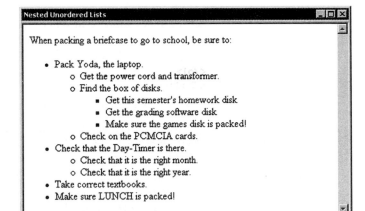

Figure 4.14

Display of nested ordered lists in which the same list style was used for each list

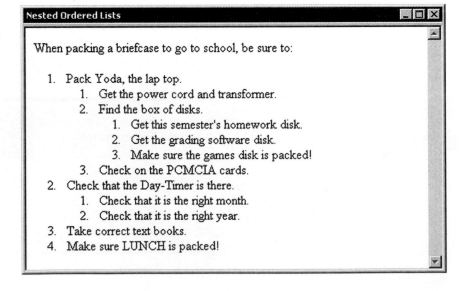

Figure 4.15

HTML code for nested ordered
lists using different list styles

```
<html>
<head>
<title>Nested Ordered Lists</title>
</head>

<body>
When packing a briefcase to go to school, be sure to:
<ol style="list-style-type: upper-roman">
<li>Pack Yoda, the lap top.
  <ol style="list-style-type: upper-alpha">
  <li>Get the power cord and transformer.</li>
  <li>Find the box of disks.
    <ol style="list-style-type: decimal">
    <li>Get this semester's homework disk.</li>
    <li>Get the grading software disk.</li>
    <li>Make sure the games disk is packed!</li>
    </ol>
  </li>
  <li>Check on the PCMCIA cards.</li>
  </ol>
</li>

<li>Check that the Day-Timer is there.
  <ol style="list-style-type: upper-alpha">
  <li>Check that it is the right month.</li>
  <li>Check that it is the right year.</li>
  </ol>
</li>

<li>Take correct text books.</li>
<li>Make sure LUNCH is packed!</li>
</ol>
</body>
</html>
```

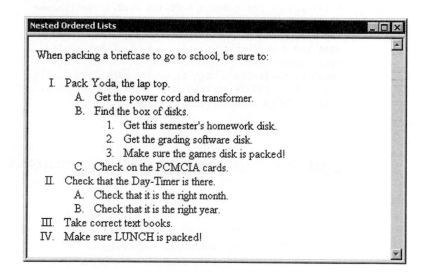

▸▸READABILITY

This is a good time to bring up the issue of *readability*, which refers to how easily the HTML code you write can be read, understood, and debugged. As the HTML code you craft gets longer and more complex, you will find that it saves you both time and effort if you take readability into account as you build the page.

A document with good readability uses white space to separate the page's design elements. These elements could be lists, paragraphs, tables, and so forth. Inserting a couple of blank lines around a particular structure, like a list, requires little time and effort yet makes it just a little easier to find. Likewise, it is simple to insert a tab or a couple of spaces in front of subordinate items to show their relative relationship. Another good practice is to put each logical part of the HTML code on a separate line, making it easier to understand.

The code in Figure 4.16 violates all of these readability rules. Although it is very short, you can see how much more difficult it is to read and maintain than the previous examples of HTML code. If you look closely, you will find that this is the same HTML code that generated the ordered lists within lists of Figure 4.15. All the blank lines, spaces, and extra carriage returns from the code in Figure 4.15 have been removed in Figure 4.16. Both codes will generate exactly the same nested lists, but the code in Figure 4.16 is not only harder to read and understand but would be much more difficult to maintain than the code in Figure 4.15.

Figure 4.16

HTML code with poor readability—an example of what *not* to do

```
<html><head><title>Nested Ordered Lists</title></head>
<body>When packing a briefcase to go to school, be
sure to:<ol style="list-style-type: upper-roman"><li>
Pack Yoda, the lap top.<ol style="list-style-type:
upper-alpha"><li>Get the power cord and transformer.
</li><li>Find the box of disks.<ol style="list-style-
type: decimal"><li>Get this semester's homework disk.
</li><li>Get the grading software disk.</li><li>Make
sure the games disk is packed!</li></ol></li><li>
Check on the PCMCIA cards.</li></ol></li><li>Check
that the Day-Timer is there.<ol style="list-style-
type: upper-alpha"><li>Check that it is the right
month.</li><li>Check that it is the right year.</li>
</ol></li><li>Take correct text books.</li><li>Make
sure LUNCH is packed!</li></ol></body></html>
```

Good formatting will make it easier for you to find your way around your own HTML code as well as making it easier for other people to see what you have done. Readability will become ever more important as you begin to modify longer and more complex pages you have written. You can puzzle out the code shown in Figure 4.16, but what if you were faced with 20 pages of code all jammed together like that? While this is an extreme example, some Web weavers (and many of the popular HTML editors) build whole sites of pages like this, and they are for all intents and purposes unreadable. This example also brings home the point that while the Web weaver controls the content, the browser controls the format, because, remember, the jammed-together HTML code will generate exactly the same page in your browser as the more readable code.

▸▸LISTS OF DEFINITIONS

A special kind of list is needed for a glossary, or any time you want to define more than a couple of terms. In a list of definitions you need to distinguish the term from its definition. HTML provides tags for that purpose.

HTML `<dl>definition list</dl>`

Description: identifies a term and its definition as part of a glossary-like list.
Type: container.
Attributes: class, dir, id, lang, onclick, ondblclick, onkeydown, onkeypress, onkeyup, onmousedown, onmousemove, onmouseout, onmouseover, onmouseup, style, title, type.

Most browsers support this form of list, called a ***definition list***, which presents a term and its definition formatted like a glossary or a dictionary. It is the ideal format to present lists of words or phrases with their meanings. Figure 4.17 presents the code for a definition list describing the various types of lists. As you can see, the browser does some nice text formatting. Notice that the code for the definition list uses different elements (terms and definitions) than the list items employed by the other two types of lists we have studied. Our use of white space in the Figure 4.17 code is just to improve readability and has no bearing on the way the browser presents the lists.

Figure 4.17

HTML code for a definition list

```
<html>
<head>
<title>Definition List</title>
</head>

<body>
<h2>The Three Common Types of HTML Lists:</h2>
<dl>
  <dt>Ordered Lists</dt>
  <dd>An ordered list contains several elements, each of them preceded
      by a number, letter, Roman numeral, or special symbol.
  </dd>

  <dt>Unordered Lists</dt>
  <dd>Unordered lists show a series of elements, preceded by some form
      of marker (bullet) character.  Most browsers show subordinate
      lists indented and preceded by a different marker.
  </dd>

  <dt>Definition Lists</dt>
  <dd>A definition list is used to display a word or phrase, followed by
      the definition or explanation of that word or phrase.  They are
      commonly used in dictionary or glossary lists.
  </dd>
</dl>
</body>
</html>
```

Definition List `_ □ X`

The Three Common Types of HTML Lists:

Ordered Lists
  An ordered list contains several elements, each of them preceded by a number, letter, Roman numeral, or special symbol.
Unordered Lists
  Unordered lists show a series of elements, preceded by some form of marker (bullet) character. Most browsers show subordinate lists indented and preceded by a different marker.
Definition Lists
  A definition list is used to display a word or phrase, followed by the definition or explanation of that word or phrase. They are commonly used in dictionary or glossary lists.

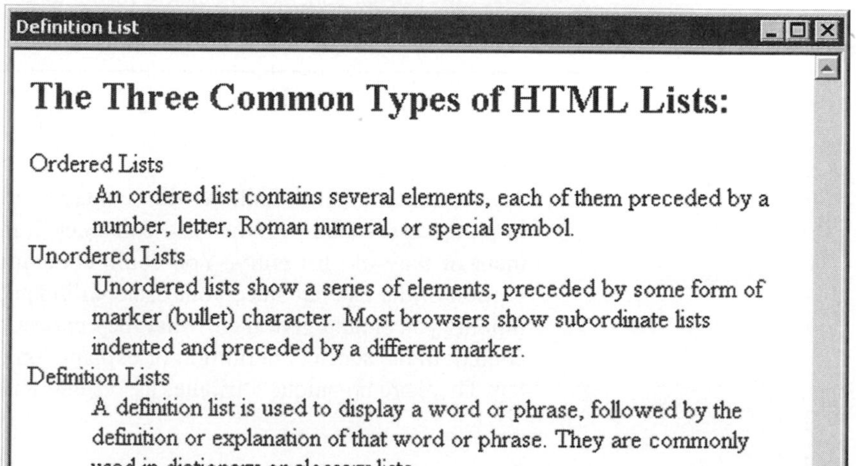

Definition lists are enclosed with the <dl>definition list</dl> container. The </dl> ending tag is *never* omitted. Each element of a definition list is composed of two different parts, the word or phrase to be defined, followed by the definition. Each of the parts of an element has a particular HTML tag to define it. A definition list does not use the <li>list element</li> container unless the definition itself contains an ordered or unordered list.

 **<dt>definition term</dt>**

Description: identifies term in a definition list.
Type: container.
Attributes: class, dir, id, lang, onclick, ondblclick, onkeydown, onkeypress, onkeyup, onmousedown, onmousemove, onmouseout, onmouseover, onmouseup, style, title.
Special Note: considered inline content.
XML: requires ending tag.

The <dt>definition term</dt> container indicates the term that is to be defined, as shown in Figure 4.17. It is valid only within a <dl> element. The <dt> element is a container and must include an ending </dt> tag when used within XML and XHTML code. Even though HTML 4 specifications allow it to be used as an empty tag, like <li>, we recommend against using <dt> in this way. It is technically possible to follow the <dt> tag with a long expression, but traditionally a single word or short phrase is used. There are no new attributes associated with the<dt> element.

 **<dd>definition definition</dd>**

Description: identifies definition in a definition list.
Type: container.
Attributes: class, dir, id, lang, onclick, ondblclick, onkeydown, onkeypress, onkeyup, onmousedown, onmousemove, onmouseout, onmouseover, onmouseup, style, title.
Special Note: considered block-level content.
XML: requires ending tag.

The <dd>definition definition</dd> container is coded immediately following the word or phrase associated with the <dt> container. It marks the beginning of the definition segment of the <dl> list entry. You could code any HTML construct within the definition portion of the list, but since your users will expect this type of format to be used for definitions, you should give them what they expect. In other words, it is best to restrict your content to the succinct definition or explanation of the word or phrase shown by the <dt> tag. There are no unique attributes associated with the <dd> element.

EXPLORATION #5

Update `chapter4.html` by adding the level-3 heading "Special Wine Notes:" under the wine-list options. Next, add a definition list under the new heading using the following term-definition pairs:

White Wine—often served with chicken, turkey, or fish dinners.
Red Wine—often served with beef or pork dinners.
Champagne Wine—often served for toasting special occasions and with light meals or breakfasts and to impress your date.

Save the file, and refresh/reload the browser's screen display.

▸▸XHTML LIST MODULE

The list elements introduced thus far, <dl>, <dt>, <dd>, <ol>, <ul>, and <li>, have been bundled together in the XHTML specifications to form the List module. This module is one of the four modules that are required for formatting an XHTML document. The other required modules include the Structure module (Chapter Two), Hypertext module (Chapter Three), and Text module (Chapter Five).

▸▸DEPRECATED LIST FORMS: MENUS AND DIRECTORIES

As you cruise the Web and look at code, you will see a couple of other types of lists: menus and directories. These lists were used with older versions of HTML and are generally handled like unordered lists, so they have been deprecated. As with other lists that use the <li> element, the **type** or **style** attribute, if recognized, specifies the marker design for the list.

<menu>menu list</menu>

Description: identifies a single column list of no implied order.
Type: container.
Attributes: class, dir, id, lang, onclick, ondblclick, onkeydown, onkeypress, onkeyup, onmousedown, onmousemove, onmouseout, onmouseover, onmouseup, style, title.
Special Note: deprecated in favor of an unordered list.

The <menu> element was designed to present single-column menu lists (Figure 4.18). In the past, the <menu> element was used to represent items in a pull-down menu format rather than in an unordered list. Some browsers eliminate the leading bullet when formatting this element. Each item is indicated by the <li> tag, as in both ordered and unordered lists. Most browsers present this list just like an unordered list with some slight formatting differences. For example, in the Opera browser the menu list elements are slightly indented from the margin.

Figure 4.18

HTML code to create <menu>
and <dir> lists

```
<html>
<head>
<title>Deprecated Lists </title>
</head>

<body>
<h3>A MENU type list</h3>
<menu>
   <li>Breakfast Burrito</li>
   <li>Green Eggs and Ham</li>
   <li>Hash and Grits</li>
</menu>

<h3>A DIRECTORY type list</h3>
<dir>
   <li>HOMEPAGE.HTM</li>
   <li>INDEX.HTM</li>
   <li>README.TXT</li>
</dir>
</body>
</html>
```

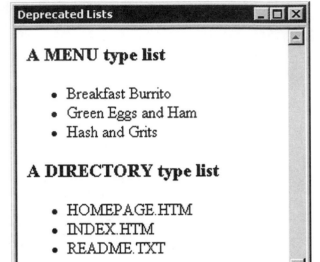

HTML   <dir>directory list</dir>

Description: identifies a multicolumn directory list of no implied order.
Type: container.
Attributes: class, dir, id, lang, onclick, ondblclick, onkeydown, onkeypress, onkeyup, onmousedown, onmousemove, onmouseout, onmouseover, onmouseup, style, title.
Special Note: deprecated in favor of an unordered list.

The <dir> element was designed to be used for creating multicolumn directory lists. Most browsers now treat it as an unordered list, but if they don't, the browser expects very short (20 characters or less) entries for each <li> element in the list. In some of the older versions of the browsers, elements in a <dir> list could be displayed in multiple columns. The graphical browser in Figure 4.18 presents this list the same way as an unordered list.

▶▶KEY TERMS

Blocked element	**Menu list**
Bullet	**Nesting lists**
Definition list	**Ordered list**
Directory list	**Readability**
Inline element	**Unordered list**
Marker	

▸▸NEW TAGS

<dd> </dd>   <li> </li>
<menu> </menu>
<dl> </dl>   <ol> </ol>
<dt> </dt>   <ul> </ul>

▸▸REVIEW QUESTIONS

1. Define each of the key terms.

2. How is each of the tags introduced in this chapter used?

3. What is an advantage to creating an ordered list using the <ol> element instead of manually numbering each item?

4. What are two ways you change the sequencing of an ordered list?

5. What are two ways you can change the style of the numbers or letters used in an ordered list?

6. Explain the rule for handling non-list items in HTML-compliant code for lists.

7. What is the difference between an ordered and unordered list?

8. How do you change the shape of the marker used in an unordered list?

9. What **style** property changes the line location of a list item?

10. Explain the HTML syntax for using two or more property: value pairs in the same **style** attribute.

11. What is the proper way to code a nested list?

12. What can you do to make nested ordered lists easier to read?

13. Identify three ways you can make all your HTML code more readable.

14. When would you use a definition list?

15. What are the two parts of a definition list?

16. What HTML element does the W³C recommend using in place of a <menu> or <dir> list?

▸▸EXERCISES

4.1. This exercise is a continuation of Exercise 3.1 from Chapter Three. Ruby now wants to add another page to her collection. She needs you to create a second education page for her shop. Here is what she wants you to do:

a. Ruby wants to change colors on this page; now she wants a faint citrine, #FFFFCC, background, and a gray quartz, #666666, text.

b. Ruby's second education page should be entitled "Gemological Facts 1."

c. There should be, as usual, a first-level heading with the company name on this page. In addition, there should be a level-2 heading of "Gemology Concepts and Terms." In the body of the page, the words "Elements" and "Terms" should also be second-level headings.

d. This page should contain the following lists, set off from the first- and second-level headings by two horizontal rules of 50-percent width each. The lists should also be set off from each other with full-width horizontal rules. Copy the page c04raw.html from the student CD. It has the text for this page without the associated HTML code. You will need to add the tags to the code to make it look the way it should. You may need to "tweak" the words a bit to match what is shown here, but it should save you some typing. You must not use the <pre></pre> container! The page's content follows:

Many of our customers are not familiar with the concepts and terms used in the gemology and jewelry business. We have included this page to help you better understand us when we discuss your purchases.

Elements

The following elements either make up or provide color to gemstones. Notice that the chemical symbol is followed by the common name. You should be aware of these elements:

- Al—aluminum
- B—boron
- Be—beryllium
- C—carbon
- Ca—calcium
- Cr—chromium
- F—fluorine
- Fe—iron
- K—potassium
- Mg—magnesium
- Mn—manganese
- Na—sodium
- O—oxygen
- Si—silicon
- Ti—titanium

Terms

There are a handful of terms with which the savvy gem stone buyer must become familiar. Here are some of those terms:

Carat

The basic unit of measure for gemstones. 1 carat = 200 milligrams. Therefore 5 carats = 1 gram. The abbreviation for carat is ct.

Clarity

The term used to describe the clearness of the stone. Many gemstones have "stuff" in them, called inclusions, which decrease the clarity. Perfect stones have no inclusions, or the inclusions are too tiny to be noticeable.

Color

The color of a stone determines its value. Diamonds should be clear, or have no color. Rubies should be deep, rich red. The type of stone determines the best color. Citrine, for example, should have no red tints as that indicates that the stone has been "cooked" or altered.

Cut

The cut of a stone is actually a misnomer. Stones are not usually cut, rather they are polished into planes called facets. There are five specific terms for the areas of facets of a stone:

1. Crown—that part of the stone above the girdle, terminated by the table.
2. Girdle—the narrow band that divides the stone horizontally. It separates the crown from the pavilion.
3. Pavilion—the lower part of the stone, below the girdle, longer than the crown, terminated by the culet.
4. Table—the flat surface forming the top of the crown.
5. Culet—the small flat or pointed region at the bottom of the pavilion.

e. Use the **style** attribute on the bulleted list container to change the bullet from a disc to a square.

f. To aid in navigation, there should be a link from the top of the page to the bottom, and from the bottom to the top. Label the link to the bottom "go to the <u>bottom</u>." The link to the top should appear below a 50-percent horizontal rule and just above the address (which follows) and should be labeled "link to the <u>top</u>."

Gwen's Glorious Gemstone Gallery
231 Lee Street
Emporia, VA
23847
733-436-7829

    g. Save your page under the name ch04gems-lists.html.

    h. All pages should be XML-compliant, well-documented, and able to pass validation with only messages about deprecated tags if any.

4.2. Create a numbered list of four of your favorite CDs. Then create an alphabetic list underneath each numbered entry that lists the tracks on each CD.

4.3. Using multiple list containers, create an HTML document that displays the following outline. This document should contain comments, with your name and the assignment due date after the <html> tag. Remember that nothing but <li> items should occur within the <ol> and <ul> containers.

    I. Lists
        A. Ordered
            1. Type
                a. Alpha
                    i. Uppercase
                    ii. Lowercase
                b. Arabic numbers
                c. Roman numerals
                    i. Uppercase
                    ii. Lowercase
            2. Start
        B. Unordered
            1. Type
                a. Square
                b. Disk
                c. Circle
    II. Examples.

4.4. Retrieve the Homework home page you updated in Exercise 3.4. Every document should contain comments, with your name and the assignment due date after the <html> tag.

    a. Place the links to your homework assignments in an ordered list.

    b. Create a new HTML document with the title of "My Favorite Teachers." Somewhere within the content of this document should be an ordered list that contains the names of at least four teachers you would recommend to others.

    c. Under each teacher's name place an unordered list that shows the school the teacher works in (or retired from) and the subject taught. This page should be linked to and from your Homework home page and contain a copy of the page footer.

4.5. Retrieve your school's home page that you updated in Exercise 3.5.

    a. Place the links to school information in an unordered list.

    b. Convert the list of names and telephone numbers to a definition list. Use the names as terms and the telephone numbers as definitions. Add 10 new names and numbers to the list.

4.6. Retrieve the Web page about your favorite movie that you updated in Exercise 3.6.

    a. Place the "What Others Think" links in an unordered list.

    b. Place the links to the biographical information in an unordered list. If possible, the markers in this list should be different from those used in part "a."

   c. Add a new "Quick Quiz" heading. Under the heading create a five-item ordered list. Each list item should be a trivia question about the movie.

   d. After each question, add the word "ANSWER" to activate a link to an HTML document with the answer.

   e. Create five new HTML documents that contain the following:

- The answer to one of the preceding questions in parts "a" through "e"
- A repeat of the question
- The name of the movie
- A link back to the next question under the "Quick Quiz" heading
- A copy of the footer used in the home page
- Comments with your name and the assignment due date

4.7. Perform each step in order. Neither skip nor combine steps as you create an HTML document. This document should contain comments giving your name and the assignment due date after the <HTML> tag.

   a. List three of your favorite books. Use only the <br> tag, and number the items from 1 to 3. Print this code.

   b. Add an entry between items 2 and 3, then renumber the list.

   c. Change the list from Arabic numbers to lowercase letters (a–g). Print this code.

4.8. Duplicate the three steps from Exercise 4.7, but this time use the ordered list <ol> container. Perform all three steps in the same order.

4.9. Cruise the Net to find and capture at least two examples of excellent uses for lists. Document where you captured them, and create a separate page for those two lists. They should WOW your classmates and your instructor! Be sure to leave a note telling the Web weavers of those sites that you are borrowing their lists for this purpose.

## Chapter Five

Formatting: Is What You See What You Get?

Although the cardinal rule of HTML is that the author controls the content and the browser controls the format, there are some things you can do to affect the way your text appears on the screen. In this chapter you will learn how to ask the browser to do those things that give you, if not complete control, at least partial control over some of the format.

CHAPTER OBJECTIVES

After reading this chapter you should be able to do the following:

- Effectively use font properties in Web page designs.
- Create document-level style sheets.
- Utilize physical and logical HTML elements in Web page designs.
- Establish language rules for quotations.
- Identify the HTML elements that make up the XHTML Text, Presentation, and Edit modules.

- Incorporate special character codes into HTML documents.
- Identify the languages associated with the Latin-1 and Unicode character sets.
- Know how to override text formatting within an HTML document.

▸▸ GLYPHS AND FONTS

Every browser recognizes a variety of symbols, letters, and numbers generically referred to as **glyphs**. Arabic numbers (1, 2, 3, 4, . . .) and lowercase letters (a, b, c, . . .) are popular glyphs. Thus, your text is made up of glyphs. When formatting different glyphs, you will change their **font** properties, which consist of the specific typeface and its size, style, weight, and other features. *Typeface* describes the design of the characters in a font. The *font-family* is the name given to different typefaces, either generic, like "serif" (discussed in detail later) or specific, like Arial or Times New Roman. In addition to specifying the size of the type *(font-size),* you can specify a change in its appearance, such as italic (the *font-style*) or bold (the *font-weight*). Text defaults to a normal (standard) weight in a browser with bold considered a "heavy" weight. HTML lets you manipulate the following font properties when formatting text:

- font-family: serif | sans-serif | cursive | fantasy | monospace | others
- font-size: pt | 1–100% | larger | smaller | xx-small through xx-large
- font-size-adjust: <number> | none
- font-stretch: normal | wider | narrower | ultra-condensed through ultra-expanded
- font-style: normal | italic | oblique
- font-variant: normal | small-caps
- font-weight: normal | bold | bolder | lighter | 100–900.

Professional printers measure type size in *points.* The term originated in France in 1737 as a way to standardize the size of type measurement. In 1886 English printers adopted the point system that was standardized in America as .01384, or 1/72, of an inch for one point. The abbreviation "pt" is used in writing HTML Code. Twelve points equals one pica, and six picas equals one inch.

Figure 5.1 illustrates how different font sizes appear on popular graphical browsers. The default font size is usually 12 points; on an absolute scale of 1 to 7, the default would be 3, or on a scale from xx-small to xx-large, the default would be medium. But don't forget that each browser ultimately controls these default values.

As you would expect, type size affects the number of characters displayed per inch. The smaller the type size, the more words fit on a line. Beware of reducing your type size to the point where it is difficult to read. For example, this type size is too small for comfortable reading. Another way of increasing the number of characters on a line is through **proportional spacing**, which is a way of naturally fitting letters together so that they only take up the

Figure 5.1

Examples of different typefaces and point sizes

Fonts

Serif 8 point

Serif 10 point

Serif 12 point

Serif 14 point

Serif 28 point

Serif 48 point

Sans-Serif 9 point

Sans-Serif 11 point

Sans-Serif 13 point

Sans-Serif 15 point

Sans-Serif 36 point

requisite amount of space on the line. In a proportionally spaced font, letters and symbols take up different amounts of space on the line depending on their widths instead of equal space for each character as on a typewriter. For example, the letters M and W require more space than the letters i and l. In contrast to proportionally spaced fonts, when each letter in a font is given equal space, it is known as a ***monospace font***. The majority of the text in this book is proportionally spaced, but a `monospace font is used for computer code. See how much more space lines take in this font?`

The terms *serif* and *sans serif* originated with Roman stone carvers who created two different forms for carving letters, one in which the letters had short line segments or extensions projecting from their upper or lower ends (serif form), as with the leg of an uppercase L or R, and the other in which the letters did not include these short lines (sans serif). You can compare the two in Figure 5.1. Another font family consist of cursive typefaces. A *cursive* typeface looks like the perfect handwritten script of the elementary schoolteacher who taught you handwriting. Some browsers also recognize *fantasy* typefaces, which vary between browsers, but usually have exotic designs. You can see examples of these font families later in this chapter in Figure 5.3.

It is generally acknowledged that serif fonts are easier to read because the serifs draw the reader's eye across a line of text. These typefaces are also more traditional since they date back to the Romans. Reports and books written in the United States often use serif fonts for standard text, reserving sans serif type for titles, headings, and captions. Screen designs for Web pages are more liberal in their application of sans serif fonts, using them in a wider range of situations. Be cautious in using cursive fonts, because they are hard to read unless displayed in larger font sizes. By the same token, beware of the fantasy font, because its display varies greatly among browers.

▸▸ DOCUMENT-WIDE STYLE CHANGES

The need of Web weavers to have more control over the formatting of their Web pages and the W^3C's desire to promote international and handicap-sensitive designs has led to an increased emphasis on style sheets. A ***style sheet*** is a set of design rules that apply to one or more HTML documents.

Style sheets are not a new idea. Word-processing programs often make style sheets available to users to support the uniform development of related documents. Newsletters and books, for instance, use style sheets to maintain the same design elements, like the color of the headings or the font used as paragraph text, throughout the document.

There are basically two types of style sheets: document-level and external. A ***document-level style sheet*** establishes formatting rules that affect from one to all of the elements found within the related document's <body> container. The <style> container found as part of the <head> element identifies these formatting rules, or style changes.

External style sheets, which are independently written ASCII files, can be used by more than one HTML document to provide continuity between document designs. Style sheets, especially external style sheets, take on additional importance when you are coding in XML and XHTML. These markup languages focus on standardizing designs using style sheets and have deprecated some of the inline formatting elements. External style sheets will be discussed in more detail in Chapter Eight.

HTML   <style>Document Style Changes</style>

Description: identifies formatting changes to elements that appear in the document's <body> container.
Type: container.
Attributes: dir, lang, media, title, and **type.**

The <style> container can be placed only within the <head> element. To see how this container works, compare Figure 5.2 with Figure 5.3. Figure 5.2 shows an HTML document with no inline formatting of page content. Figure 5.3 shows how the page could be coded using a style sheet. The idea is to identify all of the document-wide formatting specifications within the <style> container. Tags that have properties specified are listed on separate lines. Style sheets are composed of property: value pairs. Use the following rules when using the <style> element to change tag properties:

1. Place each tag for which you are going to define properties on a separate line.

2. Put a left curly brace ({) after the tag name. Usually it is best to place this curly brace on the line following the tag name so you can line all the braces up; this alignment helps the readability of your code.

Figure 5.2 Original HTML code and browser display before style sheet in Figure 5.3 is added

```
<html>
<head>
<title>Document-Level Style Sheets</title>
<!-- No style sheet -->
</head>

<body>
<h1 id="pagetop">Week 1</h1>
<h2>Class Topics</h2>
<ol>
  <li>Syllabus and class format</li>
  <li>Lab login procedures</li>
  <li>Discussion of browsers</li>
</ol>

<h2>Homework (due next week)</h2>
<h3>Read</h3>
<p>Chapter 1</p>

<h3>Turn In</h3>
<ol>
  <li>Turn in the URL for a favorite Web site and be prepared to
     say a few words about what you like about this site in class.
    <ul>
      <li>Navigation</li>
      <li>Design
      <ol>
        <li>Text/Background contrast</li>
        <li>Easy to read text</li>
        <li>Desirable content</li>
      </ol>
      </li>
    </ul>
  </li>
  <li>Turn in the URL for a Web site you think is poorly designed.
  </li>
</ol>

<h3>Key Terms</h3>
<ul>
  <li>ASCII editor</li>
  <li>Uniform Resource Locator (URL)</li>
</ul>

<hr />
<p align="center">
<a href="#pagetop">Top of Page</a><br />
<a href="../index.htm">Back to Homework Home Page</a><br />
Please send comments regarding this web page to:
<a href="mailto:trainort@muskegon.cc.mi.us">trainort@muskegon.cc.mi.us</a>
</p>
<h4>MUSKEGON COMMUNITY COLLEGE<br />
221 South Quarterline Road<br />
Muskegon, MI 49442<br />
231.773.9131<br />
</h4>
</body>
</html>
```

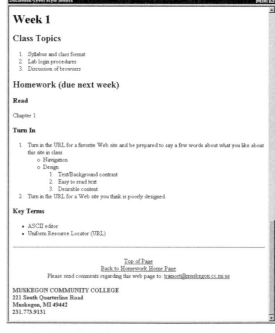

3. List each property name, like font-family or font-weight, followed by a colon. The colon tells the browser that a value for that property comes next.

4. Type in the property value, like **sans-serif** or **bold**.

5. Place a semicolon to mark the end of the value. (This is required syntax when you are listing more than one property: value pair, so make it a habit to always include the semicolon.)

6. Close the property list with a right curly brace, again on a line by itself.

Look at the following example, then study Figure 5.3. You will notice how nicely the tags and their properties line up. This makes the code easier to read and maintain.

```
h1
    {
    font-family: sans-serif;
    font-size: 30pt;
    font-weight: bold;
    }
```

However, all of this information could be presented on a single line like this if you don't care about readability and maintainability:

```
h1 {font-family: sans-serif; font-size: 30pt; font-weight: bold;}
```

type

The style tag's **type** attribute is needed to identify the style-sheet rules used to create the document-level style sheet. The examples in this chapter follow the W[3]C's *cascading style sheet (CSS)* specifications. As a result, the style tag in Figure 5.3 uses a **type** attribute set to text/css. This code is as follows:

```
<style type="text/css">
```

The HTML 4 recommendations now require every style tag to identify the style sheet rules with the **type** attribute. CSS and other types of style-sheet specifications are explored in more detail as part of the discussion of external style sheets in Chapter Eight.

FORMATTING LIST ITEMS

It is not by accident that the syntax for formatting list items is the same as that used by the **style** attribute. The properties you previously used with inline **styles** are identical to those used within the <style> container. In Chapter Four we introduced you to the list-style-type style property that changed the sequencing scheme of an ordered list and the marker in an unordered list. These tags are formatted by identifying the main and subordinate elements. In the following code the first-level items in an ordered list are sequenced using uppercase letters of the alphabet (A, B, C, etc.):

```
ol li {list-style-type: upper-alpha;}.
```

In Figure 5.3, the third-level list items are sequenced using lower-alpha with this syntax:

```
ol li li li
    {
    color:#0000FF;
    list-style-type: lower-alpha;
    }
```

If you want the second-level items of an unordered list to use square markers, the code would look like this:

```
ul li li {list-style-type: square; }
```

To set all the unordered list bullets to use square makers, simply code

```
ul {list-style-type: square;}
```

FORMATTING DIFFERENT TAGS SIMULTANEOUSLY

More than one tag can be assigned new properties at the same time. List them together, and separate each tag from the other by commas. For example, all of the heading tags in Figure 5.3 are set to a gray color using this code:

```
h1, h2, h3, h4, h5, h6
    {
    color: #666666;
    }
```

Figure 5.3 HTML code from Figure 5.2 with style sheet added

```
<html>
<head>
<title>Document-Level Style Sheets</title>
<style type="text/css">
<!--
h1, h2, h3, h4, h5, h6
    {
    color: #666666;
    }
h1
    {
    font-size: 28pt;
    text-align: center;
    font-family: sans-serif;
    }
h2
    {
    font-style: italic;
    font-size: 16pt;
    font-family: cursive;
    }
h3
    {
    font-size: 14pt;
    font-family: fantasy;
    }
h4
    {
    font-size: x-small;
    text-align: center;
    font-family: serif;
    }
ol
    {
    font-family: serif;
    font-size: 12pt;
    list-style-type: upper-roman;
    }
ol li li li
    {
    color: #0000FF;
    list-style-type: lower-alpha;
    }
ul
    {
    font-family: sans-serif;
    font-size: 12pt;
    list-style-type: square;
    }
hr {width: 50%;}
-->
</style>
</head>
```

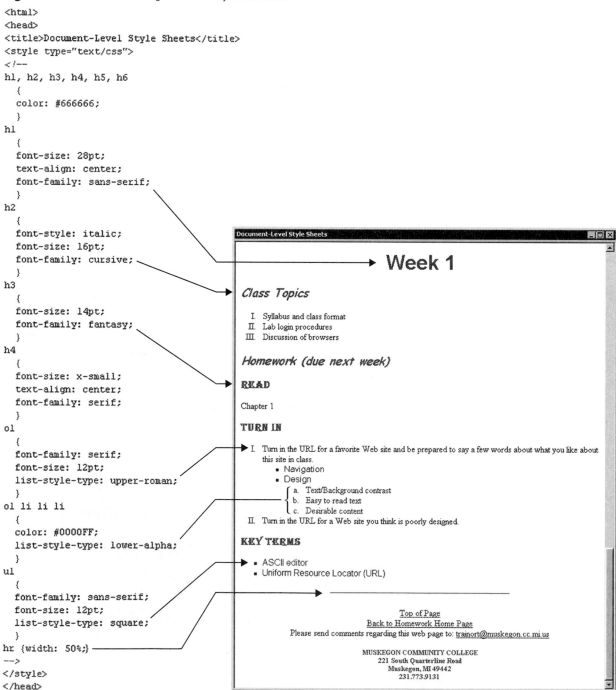

The Web weaver can then fine-tune each heading by making specific, individual changes. In Figure 5.3, the level-1 heading is set to gray with the code just shown. When displayed by the browser, it is also centered and is shown in a 28-point sans serif font because of the following code, which follows the preceding code in the <style></style> container:

```
h1
    {
    font-size: 28pt;
    text-align: center;
    font-family: sans-serif;
    }
```

text-align: left | center | right | justify

Several of the values assigned the text-align property should be familiar: left, center, and right. The fourth, justify, means the text is aligned at both the left and right margins. This is done by inserting additional spaces between words within the line. The default value is dependent on whether the writing direction, as set with the **dir** attribute, is set to left-to-right (default = left) or right-to-left (default = right).

The idea behind using document-level style sheets is to take the time to establish your design before beginning to code, or to choose a standard design for your page. Then HTML coding within the <body> container becomes straightforward and easy, because you just use the tags without any attributes. The <style> element has already established the attributes you want to use.

<!-- COMMENT LINES -->

In Figure 5.3 a comment line follows the beginning <style> tag and precedes the ending </style> tag; thus the style changes are enclosed within a comment container. This is done to prevent older browsers from accidentally displaying the format changes as text. See Figure 5.4 for an example of what can happen with an older browser. Here the Mosaic (version 3.0) browser displays the contents of the uncommented <style> container instead of using this code for document-level formatting. Since these browsers are not equipped to utilize document-level style changes, handling the related code in this way enables them to treat this code as comments. You will see comment containers used this way later in the book when we are handling JavaScripts.

Figure 5.4

Results of code in Figure 5.3 when the Mosaic (version 3.0) browser is used

Missing comment tag

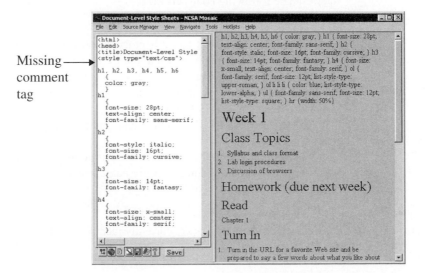

▸▸ FONT CHANGES

Before going crazy with the various font options provided by style sheets, remember that too many fonts within the same page will distract the reader. If the objective is to provide easy-to-read information to your readers, then you would be wise to follow the age-old KISS principle (Keep It Simple, Sweetie). Usually three typefaces per document are sufficient. Assign one typeface to the headings, another to the principal text used in paragraphs and list items, and a third to emphasize specific words. For example, in this text we have been using a different typeface for style properties like font family.

Bold and italics, when used for emphasis, must follow similar constraints. One or two bold words in a page adds emphasis to a point. *A page or even a sentence full of bold and italic text neutralizes the impact these font values have for adding emphasis.* (See?) Following is an overview of the more commonly used font properties available in HTML. We strongly suggest that you look over the current HTML and CSS recommendations for a comprehensive review of all the font properties at, respectively, http://www.w3.org/MarkUp/ and http://www.w3.org/Style/.

font-family: serif | sans-serif | cursive | fantasy | monospace | [Arial, Courier, . . .]

The font-family property requests that the browser use a particular typeface, providing it is available. You can use a specific family name (Arial or Times New Roman) or a generic name (serif or sans serif). Family names that contain spaces must be enclosed in quotes. The following code sets the font-family for all paragraphs to Times New Roman:

```
p {font-family: "Times New Roman";}
```

Using a specific font name is practical only when the Web weaver knows that the font specified is available on each and every one of the computers accessing the page. But the only time you can be sure that a specific font is available on every computer is when the page is being designed for use on an *intranet* within a company, where all of the machines are set up the same way. Otherwise, if the font name you specify is not available to the browser, it will substitute one, and that may make your page look far different than you expected.

Because the browser assigns representative typefaces to each generic family, it is always best to include a generic family name, rather than just specific fonts, in the list of typefaces. An example would be

```
p {font-family: "Times New Roman", serif,}
```

Five generic family names are currently identified in the W³C recommendations:

- Cursive

- Fantasy

- Monospace

- Sans-serif
- Serif

Generic family names are keywords in HTML and therefore must not be enclosed in quotes.

font-size: pt │ 1–100% │ larger │ smaller │ xx-small through xx-large

As you saw in Figure 5.1, the size of the font is measured and referenced in points (1/72 inch). However, there are other ways to specify the size of the font, either absolutely or relatively. Popular browsers maintain a table of absolute font sizes that correspond to the following values:

- xx-small
- x-small
- small
- medium
- large
- x-large
- xx-large

These absolute sizes are shown in a typical graphical browser in Figure 5.5. Take note that older browsers do not recognize these font properties. Notice that the heading in the figures is in a serif font (Times New Roman), but the paragraphs are in the Arial font as a result of the document-level style coded in the heading!

Figure 5.5 Examples of common font size and style properties

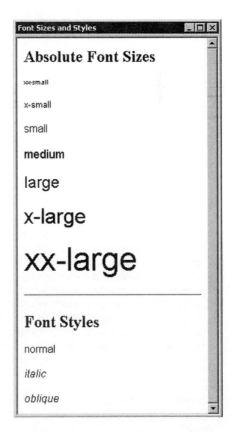

```
<html>
<head>
<title>Font Sizes and Styles</title>
<style type="text/css">
  p {font-family: Arial;}
</style>
</head>

<body>
<h2>Absolute Font Sizes</h2>
<p style="font-size: xx-small">xx-small</p>
<p style="font-size: x-small">x-small</p>
<p style="font-size: small">small</p>
<p style="font-size: medium">medium</p>
<p style="font-size: large">large</p>
<p style="font-size: x-large">x-large</p>
<p style="font-size: xx-large">xx-large</p>

<hr />
<h2>Font Styles</h2>
<p style="font-style: normal">normal</p>
<p style="font-style: italic">italic</p>
<p style="font-style: oblique">oblique</p>
</body>
</html>
```

You can also change the font size relative to the current setting. A relative size change can take place using the property value of larger or smaller. This would indicate a 20 percent relative change in size one way or the other. For example, if the default paragraph font size is 12 pt, the following code would set the point size to approximately 20 percent larger, or 14.4 pt:

```
p {font-size: larger;}
```

Another way to change the relative size is to indicate a percentage increase or decrease in size. This code would set the font size of the paragraph to 40 percent of the current size, making the text very small.

```
p {font-size: 40%;}
```

font-style: normal | italic | oblique

The font-style can be normal, italic, or oblique. The difference between italic and oblique is a bit esoteric (see Figure 5.5). Generally any text that is slanted when printed is considered oblique. Sometimes the family name will contain the word "slanted" or "incline" when it is considered oblique. Whereas the italic style is also considered slanted, it is a matter of degree that separates it from oblique. For all intents and purposes, both fonts have the same visual impact. The following code will set the paragraph to oblique if the browser supports this property:

```
p {font-style: oblique;}
```

font-weight: normal | bold | bolder | lighter | 100–900

The font-weight is what makes text look lighter or darker, as shown in Figure 5.6. If you use a word processor, you know that bold is a popular way to emphasize text. The font-weight property actually provides the Web weaver with the tools to change the weight on an absolute or relative basis. The *second cascading style sheet (CSS2)* recommendations have assigned absolute values from 100 to 900 for quantifying the "boldness"

Figure 5.6 Examples of common font weight and variant properties

```
<html>
<head>
<title>Font Weight and Variant Properties</title>
<style type="text/css">
  p {font-family: Arial;}
</style>
</head>

<body>
<h2>Font Weights</h2>
<p style="font-weight: bold">bold</p>
<p style="font-weight: 100">weight = 100</p>
<p style="font-weight: 200">weight = 200</p>
<p style="font-weight: 300">weight = 300</p>
<p style="font-weight: 400">weight = 400 (normal)</p>
<p style="font-weight: 500">weight = 500</p>
<p style="font-weight: 600">weight = 600</p>
<p style="font-weight: 700">weight = 700 (bold)</p>
<p style="font-weight: 800">weight = 800</p>
<p style="font-weight: 900">weight = 900</p>
<p>This is the traditional inline <b>bold</b> text format.</p>

<hr />
<h2>Font Variant</h2>
<p style="font-variant: small-caps">small-caps</p>
</body>
</html>
```

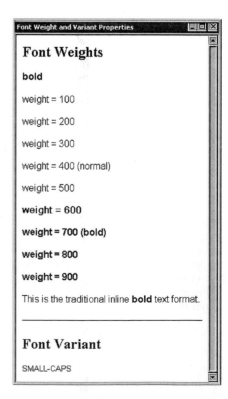

of text. These numbers are incremented by hundreds, with 100 being the lightest and 900 being the darkest. Normal text has a bold value of 400, while bold text has a value of 700.

To make the text of an unordered list item as dark as the browser will make it, use this code:

```
ul li {font-weight: 900;}
```

To change the relative boldness of that list item, you can reassign the weight value to 800 and thus make the text somewhat lighter:

```
ul li {font-weight: lighter;}
```

font-variant: normal | small-caps

The font-variant property is used to format text in small capital letters, called **small-caps** (see Figure 5.6). The May 12, 1998, CSS2 specifications have this to say about small caps:

> If a genuine small-caps font is not available, user agents (browsers) should simulate a small-caps font, for example by taking a normal font and replacing the lowercase letters by scaled uppercase characters. As a last resort, unscaled uppercase letter glyphs in a normal font may replace glyphs in a small-caps font so that the text appears in all uppercase letters. (Section 15.2.3)

The HTML code to change the level-4 heading to small capital letters looks like this:

```
h4 {font-variant: small-caps;}
```

font-stretch: normal | wider | narrower | ultra-condensed through ultra-expanded

For a special effect, text can be squashed or stretched horizontally. The font-stretch property can be set to make this change absolutely or relatively. The absolute options are as follows, from narrowest to widest:

- ultra-condensed
- extra-condensed
- condensed
- semi-condensed
- normal
- semi-expanded
- expanded
- extra-expanded
- ultra-expanded

To stretch a level-2 heading as far across a line as the browser permits, you would use this code:

```
h2 {font-stretch: ultra-expanded;}
```

The keywords *wider* and *narrower* are used to change the relative length of the text. We should also remind you that these font-stretch properties are new and not yet recognized by the popular browsers.

All of the example style changes we have shown you up until now have been delineated property by property as shown in Figure 5.3. The CSS2 specifications also allow for a shorthand notation to change a font's style, variant, weight, size, and family properties using the keyword font. You could, for example, set the level-1 heading to a 30-point, bold, italic, sans serif typeface using this code:

```
h1 {font: italic bold 30pt sans-serif;}
```

Notice that you would use a blank space (no commas) to separate the list of properties. While it is indeed possible to use shorthand code like this, we recommend that you don't, because these shorthand methods have limited utility when writing XML code. It is far, far better to code each style property on its own line with the full property name. That way, everybody knows exactly what the document-level style sheet does, and none of the readers, regardless of their experience, are confused.

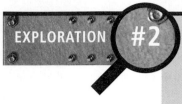

EXPLORATION #2

Update the document-level style sheet in chapter5.html in the following ways:
- Level-1 heading changed to sans serif font family.
- Level-2 heading changed to cursive font family.
- Level-3 heading changed to fantasy font family.
- Level-4 heading changed to serif font family.
- Level-5 heading changed to Arial font family.
- Paragraph changed to Comic Sans MS font family.
- Ordered lists changed to Book Antiqua font family.

Use the **style** attribute to make the following changes in the second (#2) version of each tag:
- Level-1 heading changed to xx-small, italic font.
- Level-2 heading changed to 12-point font of 100 weight.
- Level-3 heading changed to large, small caps font.
- Level-4 heading changed to 20-point, italic font.
- Level-5 heading changed to x-large, small caps font.
- Paragraph changed to 10-point font.
- Ordered lists changed to medium font.
- Unorder lists changed to x-small, italic, small caps font.

Notice how the changes made using the item level **style** attribute override formatting specified by the document-level style sheet. Save the file, and refresh/reload the browser display.

▶▶ INLINE STYLES

The use of style sheets helps a Web author maintain related Web site pages and keep them consistent. This does not mean that inline style changes are unnecessary or undesirable. They are used for special emphasis and for one-time style changes. There are two general forms on inline styles: physical and logical. For the purposes of this book, we will define them like this: *physical styles* describe the way the text is to look in a browser; *logical styles* describe the way the text within the container is used.

PHYSICAL STYLES

All the style-sheet properties we have been discussing, like font-family and list-style-type, are physical styles. Some of these physical styles relate back to a Teletype era when output was printed on paper by dumb terminals. These machines used a monospace font few oldtimers will ever forget. The bold and <i>italic</i> containers date back to the HTML 2 recommendations. These inline elements represent some of the earliest attempts by Web weavers to wrest control of the display from the browser.

Physical styles can play off each other, and it is acceptable to nest inline style containers: bold italics is popular. You nest the <big> or <small> containers to increase or decrease the font size. For example, `<big><big>real big</big></big>` is bigger than `<big>big</big>`. Table 5.1 shows the complete list of physical styles. The related HTML code and browser renditions are shown in Figure 5.7.

Table 5.1 Common physical styles

Tag	Description	Special Note
`<b>bold</b>`	Darker typeface	
`<i>italic</i>`	Slanted typeface	
`<sup>superscript</sup>`	Half line above text bottom	Used in scientific and mathematical notations.
`<sub>subscript</sub>`	Half line below text bottom	Used in scientific and mathematical notations.
`<tt>teletype</tt>`	Monospaced typeface	
`<code>computer code</code>`	Monospaced typeface	
`<kbd>keyboard</kbd>`	Monospaced typeface	
`<big>big text</big>`	Default is 3; ranges from 1 to 7	Small is 1; 7 is large.
`<small>small text</small>`	Default is 3; ranges from 1 to 7	Small is 1, 7 is large.
`<u>underline text</u>`	Line drawn under text	Deprecated.
`<s>strikethrough</s>`	Line drawn through text	Deprecated.
`<strike>strikethrough</strike>`	Line drawn through text	Deprecated.

Description: physical inline tags.

Type: container.

Attributes: class, dir, id, lang, onclick, ondblclick, onkeydown, onkeypress, onkeyup, onmousedown, onmousemove, onmouseout, onmouseover, onmouseup, style, title.

Figure 5.7 Common physical tags

```
<html>
<head>
<title>Common Physical Styles</title>
</head>

<body>
<b>bold</b><br />
<i>italic</i><br />
super<sup>script</sup><br />
sub<sub>script</sub><br />
<tt>teletype</tt><br />
<code>computer code</code><br />
<kbd>keyboard</kbd><br />
<big>big</big><br />
<small>small</small><br />
<u>underline</u><br />
<strike>strike</strike><br />

<br />
Inline styles can be nested,<br />
for example, <b><i>bold italic</i></b>.
</body>
</html>
```

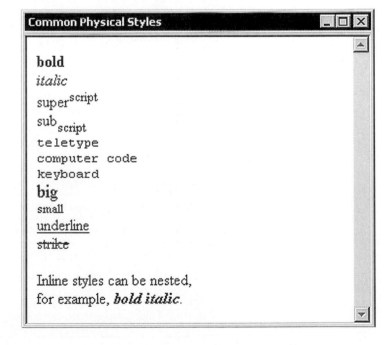

XHTML PRESENTATION MODULE

Several of these physical tags, along with the horizontal rule tag, have been organized into the XHTML Presentation module. Although this module is considered optional, you can assume it will be incorporated into every full-featured graphical browser. The Presentation module includes the following HTML elements:

<b>

<big>

<hr>

<i>

<small>

<sub>

<sup>

<tt>

A wise Web weaver will use only these physical styles, since all of us will most likely need to be XML-compliant in the very near future, and it is a pain to have to go back and record pages that use unrecognized code.

LOGICAL STYLES

Logical styles, also called *content-based styles,* require the Web weaver to consider not what the page should look like, but rather how the particular text sequence is supposed to be used as part of the information provided to the user. The logical styles shown in Table 5.2 can convey more information than the physical tags in Table 5.1, because they

Table 5.2   Common logical styles

Tag	Type of Data	Special Attribute
<abbr>abbreviation</abbr>	WWW, URL, or W3C	
<acronym>acronym</acronym>	NASA, BASIC, or FBI	Adds at end
<address>address</address>	4604 Briarwood Ave.	Adds at end
<blockquote>long quote</blockquote>	Longer than 40 words	**cite**
<cite>citation</cite>	1937 by Robert Frost	
<del>deleted text</del>	Removed from page	**cite** and **datetime**
<dfn>definition</dfn>	Large black object	
emphasized text	Enroll by June 30th	
<ins>inserted text</ins>	Added to page	**cite** and **datetime**
<q>quote</q>	Less than 40 words	**cite**
<samp>sample output</samp>	Printer output	
strongly emphasized text	Warning!	
<var>variable values</var>	last_name = "Smith"	

Description: logical inline tags.

Type: container.

Attributes: class, dir, id, lang, onclick, ondblclick, onkeydown, onkeypress, onkeyup, onmousedown, onmousemove, onmouseout, onmouseover, onmouseup, style, title.

not only change the appearance of the text, but also explain *why* the text was set off from the body of the page. Use logical styles whenever you can, marking text according to how it is to be used rather than how you expect it to look. Figure 5.8 shows the display for some common logical tags.

The fact that a particular group of characters is enclosed within a specific logical container is what is important, not how the browser chooses to display those contents. For example, a scholar may search through many Web pages, pulling out the examples of character strings that are enclosed within <cite></cite> containers. That the Web weaver chose to enclose the text within that particular tag conveys the information that the text in the container is a citation. That information is far more important than how the text appears on the page. With this idea of conveying information in mind, you need to choose your logical styles carefully and consistently.

Figure 5.8 Common logical tags

```
<html>
<head>
<title>Common Logical Styles</title>
</head>

<body>
<abbr>abbreviation</abbr><br />
<acronym>acronym</acronym>
<address>address</address>
<blockquote>blockquote</blockquote>
<cite>citation</cite><br />
<del>delete</del><br />
<dfn>definitions</dfn><br />
<em>emphasis</em><br />
<ins>insert</ins><br />
<q>quote</q><br />
<samp>sample</samp><br />
<strong>strong</strong><br />
<var>variable</var><br />
</body>
</html>
```

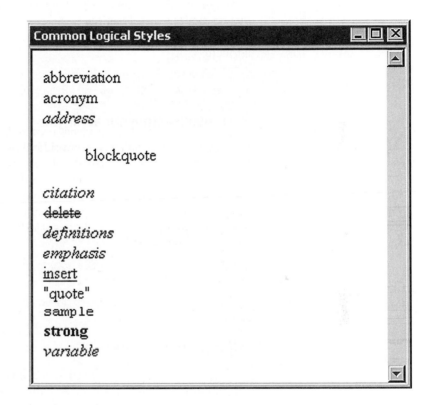

<address>Address</address>

Any Web document you create should have your address, or at least the address of a responsible party, located somewhere on the page, usually in a footer. You may wish to use the <address>. . .</address> container to put your own name and address into a page so people can use both the regular postal service and email to contact you. Figure 5.8 presents the code and typical display format for the <address> container (third item on display). Please be careful about putting your home address or phone number on a page, however. You are making those data available to the whole world, and you may not want the whole world to have your personal data. This is a fine place for your business address, but think twice about putting your home address here.

<strong>Strongly Emphasized Text</strong>

The <strong> . . . </strong> container is used to bring strong emphasis to the enclosed text. Many browsers will bold the contents (see Figure 5.8 again), but that is not the required change. If a speech synthesizer is used, the sound rendition may change in pitch, volume, or speech rate to strongly emphasize the word or words. This tag calls for more emphasis than the <em> tag, discussed next.

<em>Emphasized Text</em>

The <em> . . . </em> container indicates a milder form of emphasis than the <strong> container. Currently most browsers will render this text in italics. Figure 5.8 presents code for both the <strong> and <em> containers. You can also nest one logical container inside another to achieve combined effects. Remember that all combinations are not necessarily supported, so you may not see (or hear) exactly what you expect.

<abbr>Abbreviation</abbr>

Our world is so full of abbreviations for words that the HTML 4 specifications added the <abbr></abbr> container to identify them. The W^{3}C points out that abbreviations are not an Indo-European phenomenon—both the Chinese and the Japanese use analogous abbreviation mechanisms. Identifying abbreviations can assist spell checkers, speech synthesizers, translation systems, and search-site indexing. What follows is code using the **title** attribute:

The <abbr title="World Wide Web Consortium">W3C</abbr> recommends using the <b>titile</b> attribute to identify the complete spelling of the abbreviation.

<acronym>Acronym</acronym>

In addition to abbreviations, our world is also full of acronyms, like RADAR (RAdio Detecting And Ranging) and BASIC (Beginners All-Purpose Symbolic Code). As you can see, an acronym is a word formed by the first (or first few) letters of several words. The HTML 4 specifications added the <acronym> element to identify these words. This feature can help spell checkers, speech synthesizers, translation systems, and search-site indexes. The following code identifies BASIC as an acronym and uses the **title** attribute to identify the root words:

The programming language <acronym title="Beginners All-Purpose Symbolic Code">BASIC</acronym> was developed in the early 1960s.

Currently, the popular browsers do not recognize either the <acronym> or the <abbr> elements.

<dfn>Definition</dfn>

The <dfn> . . . </dfn> container sets apart a definition. Figure 5.8 illustrates how the popular browsers italicize text in the <dfn> container.

<var>Variable Values</var>

The <var> . . . </var> container is most frequently used with a tag like <pre> (discussed later in this chapter) to identify a program variable or to show something that the user is supposed to input. Like the physical-style <code></code> container, the <var> container is usually used when showing computer input or a computer program. Figure 5.8 presents the code for the <var> container and the display by a popular browser.

<samp>Output</samp>

The <samp></samp> element also dates back to a time and place when the Internet was used to display computer programs and the resulting output. In those situations the <samp> . . . </samp> container was used to highlight sample computer output. Figure 5.8 illustrates the code and resulting screen display. This element is not used much anymore. The <code> container is generally used to represent input, output, and code generated by or used with a computer.

<cite>Citation</cite>

When you put a bibliographical citation in your document, you can enclose it in the <cite> . . . </cite> container. This will help your user find the documents you are referencing. Figure 5.8 presents the code for a citation. As you can see, citation tags usually display text in an italic font. But the importance of the citation is to identify your references, not to change text to italics. The <cite> container can be used in conjunction with the inline quote container <q></q> (discussed later in this section) as follows:

```
<cite>Yogi Berra</cite> is often quoted as having said <q lang = "en"> It ain't
over till it's over.</q>
```

<blockquote>Block Quote</blockquote>

In a formal paper or article, a long quotation, usually more than 40 words, is set off in a separate paragraph that is usually indented on both sides. Sometimes it also appears in a different font from the rest of the text. You can create a similar effect with some of the browsers using the <blockquote> . . . </blockquote> container. Although the exact rendering will vary among the different browsers, the <blockquote> container indicates that the text contained within it is a long quotation. Figure 5.9 presents the code for a block

Figure 5.9

Applications for <blockquote> and <q> container tags

```
<html>
<head>
<title>Long and Short Quotes</title>
</head>

<body>
<h3>Block Quote</h3>
<blockquote cite="Trainor, Timothy N., Computer Literacy:
Concepts and Applications, Mitchell Publishing, 1984, p. 14">
The impact computers are having on these and other occupations
are not fiction. The world is going through a transition. The
industrial revolution has created the computer age. We can ride
this new wave of technology into the future or be drowned by it.
As always, the choice is ours.
</blockquote>

<h3>Inline Quote</h3>
Tim responded, <q lang="en">I asked Diane for directions to the
Eiffel Tower, and she said,
<q lang="fr">Tu es marteau! Nous sommes à Marseille.</q>
I just wanted to crawl into a hole and cover myself up after
that.</q>
</body>
</html>
```

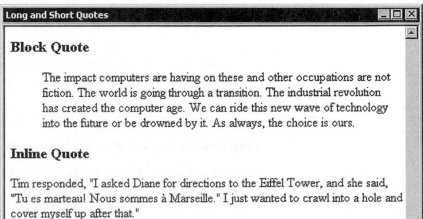

quote and shows how popular browsers will render this coding. Notice that the quote is indeed indented on both margins, and line breaks have been inserted before and after the text. Block quotes are treated as block-level elements and so break the flow of styles.

Both the <blockquote></blockquote> and <q></q> containers recognize the **cite** attribute. As shown in Figure 5.9, the **cite** attribute could contain text that provides a traditional citation for the quotation. However, the cite attribute also allows the Web author to reference the Web site the quotation comes from by including the URL. The following example fittingly provides the quote and URL for the special note about block quotes in the HTML 4 recommendations:

<blockquote cite="http://www.w3.org/TR/1998/REC-html40-19980424">

We recommend that style sheet implementations provide a mechanism for inserting quotation marks before and after a quotation delimited by BLOCKQUOTE in a manner appropriate to the current language context and the degree of nesting of quotations.

However, as some authors have used BLOCKQUOTE merely as a mechanism to indent text, in order to preserve the intention of the authors, user agents (browsers) should not insert quotation marks in the default style.

The usage of BLOCKQUOTE to indent text is deprecated in favor of style sheets.

</blockquote>

<q>Quote</q>

The <q></q> element was added to the list of logical styles as part of the HTML 4 specifications. Its addition reinforces our position that even with the trend toward style-sheet formatting, it is appropriate for Web weavers to build their pages using logical styles. This element was added to provide support for short, inline quotations, leaving the <blockquote> </blockquote> container for long quotes that need to be visually separated from the body of the document.

Figure 5.9 demonstrates how the <q> container can be nested inside another <q> container. The handling of embedded quotes is language-dependent, and the W³C recommends using the **lang** attribute to identify how the quote should be displayed. For instance, the inner quote found in Figure 5.9 indicates that the quote should be rendered using French rules of sentence structure:

<q lang="fr">Tu es marteau! Nous sommes á Marseille.</q>

English-oriented text should enclose the embedded quotation in single quotes (') and enclose the outside quotation in double quotes ("). However, the example in Figure 5.9 does not make the distinction between the inner and outer set of quotes. At the time of this writing Internet Explorer does not recognize this element, and Navigator and Opera use double quotes for all quotes, no matter how they are nested inside one another.

<ins>Insert</ins> and <del>Delete</del>

We must not forget that HTML is a markup language. In keeping with this fact, the HTML 4 specifications added the <ins>insert</ins> and <del>delete</del> containers to help Web weavers maintain and update documents. For example, let's say that an online public safety document needs to be updated to take into account a speed limit change. Currently the online document reads, "A speed limit of 45 miles per hour has been posted for Woodward Avenue." To mark up this change we want to delete "45" and replace it with "55." With these new insert and delete tags, the HTML code would look like this:

```
<p>A speed limit of <del>45</del><ins>55</ins> miles per hour has been
posted for Woodward Avenue.</p>
```

As you know by now, how the changes are displayed is dependent on the browser. The popular graphical browsers strike through text contained within the <del> element and underline text within the <ins> element (see Figure 5.8). The <del> and <ins> elements form the XHTML Edit module.

Both of these elements can be used for either inline changes or block-level (blocked) changes that incorporate text in several tags—like paragraphs, lists, and tables. Both the <del> and <ins> beginning tags recognize the **cite** and **datetime** attributes. As mentioned earlier in regard to quotations, the **cite** attribute can contain a URL that references comments about the change or a traditional text citation for an article or book that provides more information. The **datetime** attribute lets you document the date and time that the change takes place. Using our earlier example of the speed limit change, we could use these attributes to document that the change occurs on January 1, 2004, and to inform the user that more information is available in the comments.html page at the highway Web site under limits:

```
<ins datetime="2004-01-01T00:00Z"
cite="http://www.highway/limits/comments.html">55</ins>
```

The date and time for the **datetime** attribute in this example must follow a specific format. The generic format looks like this: YYYY-MM-DDThh:mm:ssTZD. The *YYYY* stands for the four-digit year. *MM* represents a two-digit number that stands for the month (01 = January, 02 = February, etc). The day, *DD,* is a two-digit number from 01 to 31. An uppercase *T* separates the date from the time. Time is always listed in a 24-hour format, with *hh* representing the 24 hours in the day (00 through 23) and *mm* and *ss* representing the minutes and seconds, respectively. Acceptable values for minutes and seconds are the two-digit numbers 00 through 59. Zero (00) is assigned to the seconds, minutes, and hours if the related part of the time format is left out.

The last part of the time format is the *time zone designator (TZD).* An uppercase Z at the end of the date indicates that *coordinated universal time (UTC)* is being used. UTC is now used instead of Greenwich Mean Time to represent the 0, or starting point of the day. It still covers England, Iceland, Liberia, Morocco, Senegal, Ghana, and several other countries at the longitude associated with Greenwich Mean Time. Local times are represented by adding or subtracting hours from UTC. For example, *Eastern Standard Time (EST),* used by the East Coast of the United States is five hours behind UTC and is coded like this: -05:00. The date format for March 21, 2003, at 11:00 PM EST follows:

```
2003-03-21T23:00-05:00
```

EXPLORATION #3   Copy the file inline.html from the student CD to a disk directory on your personal computer. Open inline.html using an ASCII editor, and change the <title></title> container to *Inline Formatting by your name.* Use the physical and logical style tags found in Tables 5.1 and 5.2 to format the related uppercase words in this document. For example, the word BOLD should be placed in a bold font using the <b> container: <b>BOLD</b>. Save the file as chapter5-3.html, and display it using your favorite browser.

XHTML TEXT MODULE

As mentioned in earlier chapters, XHTML's modular design centers on a series of HTML containers grouped into modules, four of which are required: Structure, Hypertext, List, and Text. The Text module is the last of the required modules to be covered here and incorporates the following HTML elements:

<abbr>	<div>	<kbd>
<acronym>	<em>	<p>
<address>	<h1>	<pre>
<blockquote>	<h2>	<q>
 	<h3>	<samp>
<cite>	<h4>	<span>
<code>	<h5>	<strong>
<dfn>	<h6>	<var>

Each of these elements, except for <div> and <span>, which are covered in Chapter Eight, have been discussed in this and earlier chapters. These elements are considered to be the basic design elements, along with lists, of a Web page, and it is not by accident that many of them are logical tags.

SPECIAL CHARACTERS

One drawback with powerful browsing agents like Opera, Netscape, and Internet Explorer is that they try to interpret every recognizable character sequence as if it were a set of tags. For example, were we to convert this document into HTML and try to show it on a browser, a line that said, "The format of standard tag is <tag> with the < starting the tag and the > closing it," wouldn't look like that when displayed, because the browser would try to resolve the <s and the >s. Being unable to do so, it would ignore them. Let's see how that would actually look. Figure 5.10 shows the HTML code and browser display for the previous several lines of text. All that is changed in the code is the addition of several line breaks to set the quoted statement off from the rest of the text and a closing </s> so that the rest of the page won't have a line through the text.

This is even more interesting than we might have expected. Not surprisingly, "<tag>" is not shown because the browser can't figure it out and so ignores it. But the string "<s and the >" has been interpreted as an <s> (strikethrough) tag, with some unknown attributes, so the rest of the text is shown in a strike-through font. Obviously, we shouldn't use spurious special characters.

There are times when special characters like > < are needed. For instance, we wanted to refer to the greater than (>) and less than (<) symbols in Figure 5.10. In that case the browsers mistakenly tried to interpret < as the start of an HTML container. In other situations we might want to use special characters like © (copyright), ™ (Trade Mark), ® (Registered Trade Mark), & (ampersand), or even ð (the Icelandic eth). The designers of HTML anticipated this need and created a whole set of glyphs ranging from currency symbols like ¥ (the yen) to simple typographical symbols like . . . (the ellipsis).

Most of the common symbols can be coded two ways—either as a named entity or as that character's numeric position in the Latin-1 standard character set (Figure 5.11). The *Latin-1 character set*, designed by the International Standards Organization (ISO), is a list of common letters, numbers, symbols, and punctuation marks used in Western languages. Each symbol has a numeric value, and some also have names. The common ASCII character set is a subset of Latin-1. For example, the ampersand (&) has a numeric value of 38 and the standard name of &. The Reference Guide contains a list of commonly used special characters currently recognized by the standard browsers. As the international flavor of HTML permeates the browsers, more and more characters will be added. Check the specifications at regular intervals to see if any new glyphs are available.

Figure 5.10

Can you figure out what
happened to <tag> in the
second sentence and why a line
runs through part of the third
paragraph?

```
<html>
<head>
<title>Special Characters I</title>
</head>

<body>
<b>Without Special Characters</b><br />
For example, were we to convert this document into HTML and try
to show it on a browser, a line that said:<br />
<br />
"The format of a standard tag is <tag> with the < starting the
tag and the > closing it."<br />
<br />
wouldn't look like that when displayed, because the browser
would try to resolve the <s and the >s. Being unable to do so,
it would ignore them. Let's see how that would actually look.
</s>◄────────────────────────────────────────────── Hint!
<br />
<br />
<b>With Special Characters</b><br />
"The format of a standard tag is &lt;tag&gt; with the &lt;
starting the tag and the &gt; closing it."<br />
<br />
</body>
</html>
```

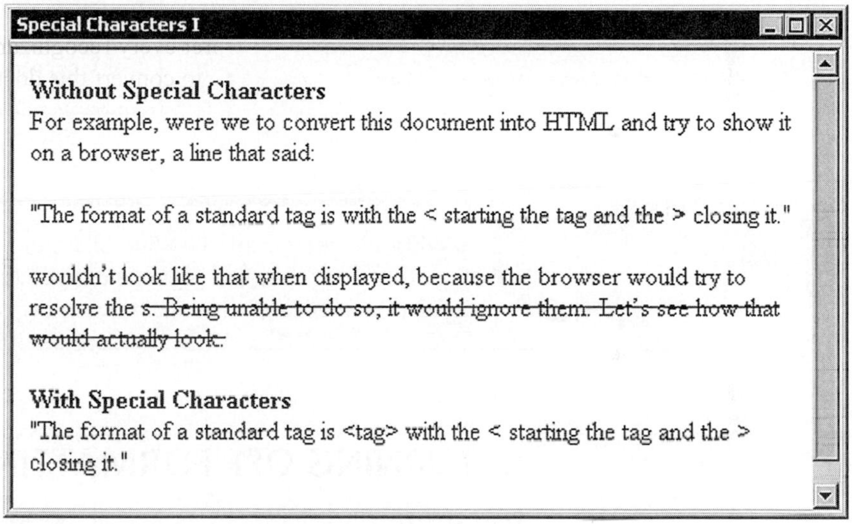

Special Characters I

Without Special Characters
For example, were we to convert this document into HTML and try to show it
on a browser, a line that said:

"The format of a standard tag is with the < starting the tag and the > closing it."

wouldn't look like that when displayed, because the browser would try to
resolve the ~~s. Being unable to do so, it would ignore them. Let's see how that
would actually look.~~

With Special Characters
"The format of a standard tag is <tag> with the < starting the tag and the >
closing it."

The Latin-1 character set is traditionally used in English, French, German, and other
Indo-European languages; however, it does not take into consideration other languages,
such as Chinese and Japanese, that employ thousands of characters. A new coding system
called *Unicode* supports 65,536 different possible binary combinations. According to the
W[3]C, Unicode is a coded character set that assigns unique numbers to (currently) about
30,000 of the possible characters in the world's languages. It is a superset of all standard
character repertoires, including Latin-1. Unicode is designed as a way for computers to
process and store text in every known written language. The Reference Guide includes a
few commonly used Unicode codes.

When you code special symbols, called *entities* in XML, you start with an ampersand
(&) and end with a semicolon (;). After the ampersand, you put either the standard name
or an octothorp (#), followed by the numeric positional value for that character. That
sounds confusing, but it is simple when you look at some examples. The bottom of Figure 5.10 shows how that earlier problem sentence would look using the < and >
characters instead of < > in the HTML code. Figure 5.11 shows how the characters could
be coded using their names and their numeric designations.

Figure 5.11 HTML code showing how special characters begin with an ampersand (&) and end with a semicolon (;)

```
<html>
<head>
<title>Special Characters II</title>
</head>

<body>
<h3>Special Characters</h3>
&#38; or &amp; - ampersand<br />
&#169; or &copy; - copyright<br />
&#60; or &lt; - less than<br />
&#62; or &gt; - greater than<br />
&#174; or &reg; - registration<br />
&#34; or &quot; - double-quote<br />

<h3>Foreign Language</h3>
&#192; or &Agrave; - uppercase A + grave accent<br />
&#193; or &Aacute; - uppercase A + acute accent<br />
&#194; or &Acirc; - uppercase A + circumflex accent<br />
&#195; or &Atilde; - uppercase A + tilde<br />
&#196; or &Auml; - uppercase A + umlaut<br />
&#197; or &Aring; - uppercase A + ring<br />
&#198; or &AElig; - uppercase A + dipthong<br />
&#199; or &Ccedil; - uppercase C + cedilla<br />
&#208; or &ETH; - uppercase Eth (Icelandic)<br />
&#216; or &Oslash; - uppercase O + slash<br />
&#222; or &THORN; - uppercase THORN (Icelandic)<br />
</body>
</html>
```

EXPLORATION #4 Modify the code in the last line of chapter5-3.html using the special character codes for copyright and registration (see Figure 5.11) to replace the words. Save the file, and refresh/reload the browser display.

⯈⯈ TURNING OFF FORMATTING

Sometimes it is necessary to prevent the browser from taking control of the way a portion of the screen looks. In the past, one way to achieve this outcome was to use the <plaintext> tag, which converted everything into plain text. Inexperienced Web weavers would get into trouble coding it, because after it was used in a document, no other HTML tags were recognized. It turned its own ending tag into text! The <plaintext> became obsolete with the HTML 4 specifications, which recommend the use of the <pre> container instead.

HTML **<pre>Preformatted Text</pre>**

Description: identifies preformatted text that the browser is instructed not to alter.
Type: container.
Attributes: class, dir, id, lang, onclick, ondblclick, onkeydown, onkeypress, onkeyup, onmousedown, onmousemove, onmouseout, onmouseover, onmouseup, style, title, **width.**

Special Note: replaces obsolete <plaintext>, <listing>, and <xmp> containers.

The `<pre>pre-formatted text</pre>` container is designed to present a block of text without enforcing additional formatting by the browser. In a `<pre>` container, *supernumerary* (extra) blanks are not removed. The **width** attribute, now deprecated, determines how many characters fit on a single line. Using the **width** attribute is a request to the browser, not an absolute demand, and not recognized by many browsers. Lines that are longer than the width of the browser pane will extend outside it, requiring the user to scroll right in order to read all of the text. The ***browser pane*** is the part of the screen that displays the Web page and is normally visible to the user without scrolling. The common browsers will support lines longer than their normal pane if they are required to by the HTML code. Usually it is a bad idea to force text beyond the screen display, because the user may overlook it. Also, it places an additional burden on users because they have to scroll to access all the information you are providing.

You should not use tags that cause a paragraph break, like `<blockquote>`, within the `<pre>` container, because they may cause inconsistent behavior across browsers. Some browsers interpret these tags as simple line breaks, whereas others infer a `</pre>` tag before the break and thus end the container. Style tags are allowed within a `<pre>` block, so if the text within the block contains characters like the ampersand (&) or the greater-than (>) and lesser-than (<) signs, you will need to use the special symbols we just discussed to avoid having the browser simply ignore them (Figure 5.12).

Figure 5.12   HTML code showing how the `<pre>` tag is used to display screen lines exactly as originally formatted

```
<html>
<head>
<title>Using Pre-Formatted Text</title>
</head>

<body>
<big><big><tt><b>DOS DIR Command</b></tt></big></big><br />
After the DOS prompt type: <tt>dir a:</tt><br />
The computer will display: <br />
<pre>
 Volume in drive A has no label.
 Volume Serial Number is 0000-0000

 Directory of A:\

08/24/99  01:33p                67,584 Case Study Prospectus.doc
08/18/99  02:34p                37,888 hwk102f.doc
08/18/99  02:20p                59,904 PSY102f.DOC
08/24/98  10:29a                78,848 100SYL.DOC
08/10/99  12:23p                 7,061 hwk110df.htm
08/10/99  12:31p                 6,891 hwk110nf.htm
08/10/99  11:15a                 4,317 cis110sy.htm
08/19/99  01:55p                72,727 cis110sg.jpg
08/19/99  01:59p                73,144 cis110tx.jpg
08/19/99  02:03p                71,025 cis110lb.jpg
08/19/99  02:06p                65,909 cis100tx.jpg
08/24/99  07:36p                29,184 CIS100HW.DOC
08/30/99  12:52p        &lt;DIR&gt;        work
09/28/99  12:33a                   808 nletter.css
09/28/99  12:33a                 3,327 newsletter.htm
10/05/99  12:39a                   962 e05-11.htm
10/05/99  12:39a                   491 e05-10.htm
10/04/99  09:59p                 2,351 e05-05.htm
09/09/99  05:57p               623,392 css2.txt
            19 File(s)        1,205,813 bytes
                                75,776 bytes free
</pre>
<br />
To clear the screen type: <tt>cls</tt>
</body>
</html>
```

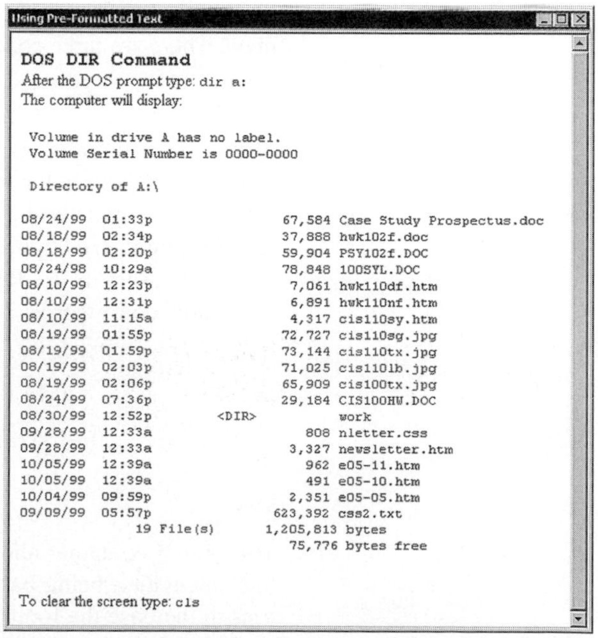

Usually a <pre> element is used to protect and illustrate tabs or other formatting for computer programs and the like. Don't use the <pre> container simply to avoid having the browser format your text—and especially don't use it in place of the list containers.

Figure 5.12 presents the code for a <pre> block. This text was created to show how the DIR command of DOS displays a disk directory. Sometimes you can get unexpected results, because the browser will use a much larger tab value than the HTML editor did. If you are going to use the <pre> container, it is a good idea to use spaces rather than tabs to perform your alignment.

▸▸ DEPRECATED FONT-HANDLING TECHNIQUES

In the past, document-level font changes were handled by the <basefont></basefont> and <font></font> containers. These elements were deprecated in the HTML 4 specifications, in favor of the *style* attribute and the popular graphical browsers no longer recognize the <basefont> element. Instead of using points to set the size of the font, the <font></font> element recognizes a set of font sizes that start at size 1 and run all the way through size 7. Font size 3 is the default size. These seven values correspond to the absolute font sizes shown in Figure 5.5, where 1 is equal to xx-small and 7 is equal to xx-large.

You can both increase and decrease the size of the glyph displayed by using the <font> tag. According to the W^{3}C specifications, the relationship between the different virtual font sizes is about 20 percent for each change. For example, font size 4 is supposed to be 20 percent larger than font size 3 (the default size), and font size 1 is supposed to be 40 percent smaller than font size 3.

HTML <font>Font of Text</font>

Description: changes the color, typeface, or size of the font.
Type: container.
Attributes: class, **color, face,** id, lang, **size,** and title.

Special Note: deprecated in favor of **style** attribute.

In the past if you wanted to change the size or color or typeface of the font for a small part of the page, perhaps even just a character or two, you used the <font></font> element. There are three common attributes for this tag: **color, size,** and **face.**

color

The color of the text enclosed in the container is set by the color attribute, just as you learned to set text color in the <body> tag. The recommended way is to use an octothorp (#) followed by a six-digit (hexadecimal) number, with each successive pair of numbers representing the *red, green, and blue (RGB)* components of the desired color as shown on the color insert in the Reference Guide. While we discourage it, you can also use the "standard" color words. The HTML code to change the font color to blue looks like this:

```
<font color="#0000FF">This code changes the text to blue.</font>
```

or

```
<font color="blue">This code changes the text to blue.</font>
```

size

The <font> container allows you to change the size of the contained text, with each relative calculation being based on the default. Figure 5.13 illustrates this method. The code tries to increase the font size two times, using two <font></font> containers, intending to move it from size 3 to size 5. The code then tries to decrease the font size two times. As you can see, the size increases from the base size of 3 to a size 4 the first time the code tries to increase it, but subsequent +1 size increases have no further impact. Attempts to decrease the font size meet with the same results; that is, the increase occurs only the first time. The reason this happens is that each time the <font></font> element is closed, it resets the size of the text to the default. If you don't explicitly close the <font></font> container, it will infer a closing tag before the next <font></font> container is opened. Because of the confusion generated, Web weavers should specify the <font> size value as an absolute number rather than a relative one.

Figure 5.13

HTML code in which the deprecated <font></font> container changes font size, typeface, and color

```
<html>
<head>
<title>Font Changes</title>
</head>

<body>
<font size="3">This line is shown in the normal font.</font><br />
<font size="+1">Up 1 to change the basefont size to 4.</font><br />
<font size="+1">Up another size does not work.</font><br />
<font size="-1">Down a size works the first time.</font><br />
<font size="-1">Down another size does not work.</font><br />
<font size="3" face="sans-serif">Generic family names like sans-serif work.</font><br />
<font face="Forte">Family names like Forte are recognized if found.</font><br />
<font color="#999999">Text color changes to gray.</font><br />
Line of text outside of the &lt;font&gt; container.<br />
</body>
</html>
```

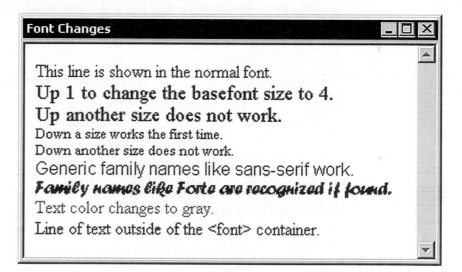

face

The face attribute of the <font></font> container allows for the specification of a series of different typefaces for the text contained within the container. Usually the Web weaver will specify a series of different typeface, hoping that the target machine contains one of them. If none of the specified typefaces are available on the target machine, the browser will use the default typeface. A browser using the following code would first try to use the Arial typeface; if Arial is not recognized, the default sans serif typeface will be used:

<font face="Arial, sans-serif">This text is a sans-serif face.</font>

▸▸ FINAL COMMENT

Formatting the text in your pages has become in one way much easier and in another way much more complex since the release of the HTML 4 specifications. Formatting is easier because by using document-level formatting with style sheets, you can, in one place, create the styles for all of the elements you wish to control. It is more complex because there are so many more features you can consider when making decisions on how the text should look. Be careful not to lose your message among the formatting codes! In Chapter Eight you will learn how to incorporate all of these refinements into cascading style sheets and external style sheets.

▶▶ KEY TERMS

Browser pane
Document-level style sheet
Font
Glyph
Latin-1 character set

Logical style
Monospace font
Physical style
Proportional spacing
Style sheet

▶▶ NEW TAGS

<abbr></abbr>
<address></address>
<b></b>
<big></big>
<blockquote></blockquote>
<cite></cite>
<code></code>
<del></del>
<dfn></dfn>
<em></em>
<font></font>
<i></i>
<ins></ins>

<kbd></kbd>
<pre></pre>
<q></q>
<s></s>
<samp></samp>
<small></small>
<strike></strike>
<strong></strong>
<style></style>

<tt></tt>
<u></u>
<var></var>

▶▶ REVIEW QUESTIONS

1. Define each of the key terms.
2. How is each of the tags introduced in this chapter used?
3. What are four font properties?
4. What are two ways you can increase the number of characters per line of text?
5. In what situations is a sans serif typeface used?
6. How can several tags be assigned new properties at the same time?
7. What does the default value for the text-align property depend on?
8. Why should style changes within the <style> element be embedded within a comment?
9. How does the KISS principle apply to style-sheet design?
10. What five properties can the font shorthand notation change?
11. What HTML tags are associated with the XHTML Text, Presentation, and Edit modules?
12. How do logical tags convey more information than physical tags?
13. Identify three ways a speech synthesizer might emphasize text.
14. How are the situations using the <blockquote> and <q> elements different?
15. What special syntax identifies a special character within HTML code?
16. Identify two different ways you can code a special character for the greater-than symbol (>).
17. How does the <font> element set relative character sizes like small or larger?

▸▸ EXERCISES

5.1. This exercise is a continuation of Exercise 4.1 from Chapter 4. Ruby is getting a good response from her Web site. Now she wants to add yet another set of pages. The main page should link to the other pages, and there should be back links as well. The pages should all have document-level style sheets. You can use inline styles only where indicated and must not use deprecated style information from this point on. Remember, Ruby is having her pages validated, and you need to be careful to keep the pages up to the W^{3}C standard.

a. She wants to change colors on this page. Now she wants a soft amethyst background, #FFCCFF, with ruby red, #990000, text.

b. The page should be entitled "The Sapphire Story."

c. There should be a first-level heading with the company name on this page, as always. In addition, there should be a level-2 heading of "The Sapphire Story." In the body of the page, the words "History," "Inclusions," and "Uses" should also be second-level headings.

d. First-level headings should be dark amethyst, #660099. Second-level headings should be beautiful sapphire blue, #0099CC. All headings should be in a sans serif font and centered.

e. The first-level heading should be set off from the rest of the page by two 50-percent horizontal rules.

f. The majority of the text can be found on your student CD in the file called ch05-raw.html. You will need to clean it up, add the necessary HTML code, and add links to make this a small site. No lines in the HTML file should extend more than 50 characters.

g. You will need to modify the code in the colors and corundum files as well as the raw file. There should be a link to the file ch05gems-corundum.html from the word *"corundum"* in the first paragraph. There should be a link to the page ch05gems-colors.html from the word *"colors"* in the second paragraph. You will need to create these pages from the raw source found on the student CD.

h. There should be a link back to the main page from each of the extra pages.

i. The word "Rolex" is a registered trademark; annotate it in that manner.

j. The format of the corundum page should be as follows:

1. The title of the page should simply be "Corundum."
2. The corundum page should have a gray background, #CCCCCC, with dark gray text, #333333.
3. The corundum page should have a link back to the styles page, and all three link colors should be lighter gray, #666666.
4. There should be the standard "Gwen's" level-1 heading.
5. The page should have a level-2 heading that says "Corundum."
6. All headings on the corundum page should be sans serif, 18 pt, and green, #339966.
7. The background color for heading level-2 should be white, #FFFFFF.
8. The formula for corundum is AL^2O^3; note the superscripts.
9. The company name, "RealRuff," is a registered trademark; indicate that on the page.
10. There should be a link from this page back to the styles page.
11. The rough source for this page is on your data CD, ch05-corundum.html.
12. Save the finished page as ch05gems-corundum.html.

k. The format of the colors page should be as follows:

1. The title of this page should be "Colors of Sapphire."
2. The background should be soft blue, #CCFFFF. The regular color should be a rich blue, #0066CC.
3. There should be the standard "Gwen's" level-1 heading.
4. The page should have a level-2 heading that says "Sapphire Colors."
5. Each color mentioned in a heading should be in that color (use inline styles), according to the following codes:
   • Emerald—#009900
   • Sapphire—#66CCFF

- Topaz—#FFCC00
- Padparadschah—#CC3300

6. Headings should be in 22 pt monospaced font and a beautiful blue-gray, #336666.
7. All the text within paragraphs should be bold and in a sans serif font.
8. The text in all the paragraphs except the first one should also be set back from the left margin by 3 ems. The first paragraph is the exception; it should not be indented.
9. There should be a link from this page back to the styles page.
10. The background color for the link should be blue-gray, #99CCFF.
11. The rough source for the page is on your student CD, ch05-colors.html.
12. Save the finished page as ch05gems-colors.html.

l. The shop address should be on the bottom of every page, separated from the rest of the page by a 50-percent rule, as always.

Gwen's Glorious Gemstone Gallery
231 Lee Street
Emporia, VA
23847
733-436-7829

m. Save the main page under the name ch05-styles.html.

n. All pages should be XML-compliant, well-documented, and able to pass validation. Since you know how to use styles now, you should have *no* compliance error messages.

5.2. Create a page that demonstrates ten physical-style tags. The title bar should display "Physical Style Demonstration," with your name and the assignment due date included within comment lines.

5.3. Create a separate page that demonstrates and explains the 13 logical-style tags. The title bar should display "Logical Style Demonstration," with your name and the assignment due date included within comment lines.

5.4. Create a document-level style sheet for the Homework home page used in earlier exercises, including Exercise 4.4. Establish unique properties for all heading levels, paragraphs, and list items used within the document.

5.5. Create a document-level style sheet for your school's home page or another page you created in earlier exercises, including Exercise 4.5. Establish unique properties for all heading levels, paragraphs, and list items used within the document.

5.6. Create a document-level style sheet for one of the Web pages created as part of the movies Web site for Exercise 4.6. Establish unique properties for all heading levels, paragraphs, and list items used within the document.

5.7. Create a new HTML document with a short list, eight to ten items long, set off above and below by a nice pair of centered horizontal rules. The list should show special characters (different from those in Figure 5.12) and should show how they are coded. Your list should demonstrate how to code both special characters that have names and those that must be coded by number. The title bar should display "Special Character Demonstration," with your name and the assignment due date included within comment lines.

5.8. Use the <style> container in a new HTML document to create a document-level style sheet that outlines the formatting rules shown here and establishes unique properties for all six heading levels. Provide copies of the HTML code and sample screen display using data of your own choosing. The title bar should display "Internal Style Sheet Demonstration," with your name and the assignment due date included within comment lines.

5.9. Create a table of 10 rows and three columns, with tabs separating each column, using your ASCII editor. The data could be a list of teams and their respective win-and-lose records or an inventory of items with quantity and unit cost. Copy the table into a new HTML document, and enclose it using the <pre> container. The title bar should display "<pre> Tag Demonstration," with your name and the assignment due date included within comment lines.

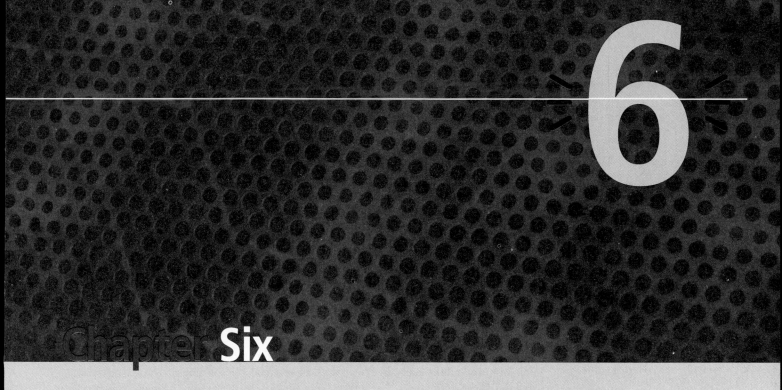

## Chapter Six

Images: A Picture Is Worth a Thousand Words

"A picture is worth a thousand words" is certainly an understatement in the world of the Web, where a picture is worth many thousands of words, at least in terms of how much space a picture takes. It is not unusual for a picture to take up thousands and thousands of bytes. For example, the parrot on the left side of Figure 6.1 has a 4,982-byte file size. A text file takes up one byte per character. If we were to pick an arbitrary size for the "average" word—let's say, a word of five characters—then any image that is larger than 5,000 bytes (5 kilobytes) would be bigger than a thousand words!

CHAPTER OBJECTIVES

After reading this chapter you should be able to do the following:

- Recognize applications for common image formats.
- Insert an image into an HTML document and control its height and width.
- Identify the only HTML element associated with the XHTML Image module.
- Create a text-based alternative to an inline image.

- Float an image within a Web page in such a way that text flows around it.
- Place a border around an image.
- Center an image within a screen display.
- Use an image as a hyperlink.
- Create unordered lists that use image bullets.

▸▸ IMAGES AND MULTIMEDIA

Images and multimedia are what some people believe the Web is all about. They say that without pictures, a Web site becomes just a collection of text files. Indeed, properly used, pictures, charts, maps, drawings, logos, and art will enhance your Web pages, make them look more professional, draw users into the page, and make it easier for them to navigate through the information you provide. Of course, if the media you choose are overly large, or if you use too many, they can clutter up your page and significantly increase the download time for your users.

Images and other multimedia elements are a critical part of the Web, and it is important for you to learn how to use them, when to use them, and when to avoid them. In this chapter we will concentrate on two-dimensional *pictures* which could be photographic images, drawings, charts, or some type of graphic art. Chapter Nine covers multimedia that includes sound recordings and videos.

▸▸ IMAGE FORMATS

When HTML authors speak of *images,* they are referring to a whole range of picture-like elements, including such diverse things as scanned photographs, icons, illustrations, drawings, and animations. Let's take a closer look at the common image formats you encounter when cruising the Web.

GIF

Created by CompuServe, *GIF* stands for *Graphics Interchange Format.* It supports 8-bit color and is the most common image format. All graphical Web browsers recognize the .gif filename extension. There are three forms of GIF:

1. *Plain GIF,* in which the picture looks like a snapshot.

2. *Transparent GIF,* in which the background is invisible, so the image seems to be painted directly on the Web page.

3. ***Animated GIF***, in which a series of still GIF images are quickly changed to create simple animation.

Figure 6.1 shows the difference between a plain GIF and a GIF with a transparent background. The page's background color shows through a transparent GIF file, whereas a plain GIF file supplies its own background color.

Figure 6.1

GIF image with transparent versus normal background

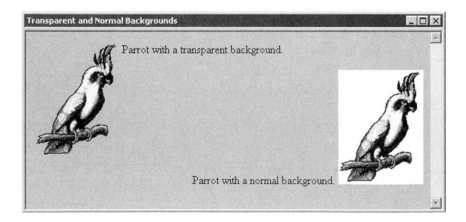

GIF compression is considered "lossless" because the quality of the image does not change (or suffer a "loss") through many conversions to GIF format. ***Lossless compression*** accounts for all the data bits in the image when the image is compressed. This results in a somewhat larger file, but the image quality does not degrade when it is compressed and then uncompressed many times. This type of compression is best suited for line art that contains large areas of the same color.

JPEG

JPEG stands for *Joint Photographics Experts Group* and is a better choice for photographic-quality color than GIF, because it can support either 8-bit or 24-bit color. A JPEG file is also smaller than a GIF file of the same image, because JPEG uses a higher compression ratio. However, you must be careful when repeatedly saving a JPEG file because of the ***lossy compression*** used to store the image. Each time an image is compressed into the JPEG format, some of the pixels are discarded. The first few times this happens, it doesn't really detract from the image, because the human eye cannot distinguish such a small loss of data. But when an image is repeatedly compressed into JPEG format, the image quality will discernibly degrade. Generally by the third or fourth compression, the image starts to take on a "blocky" look. All the graphical browsers support JPEG and recognize these files by the .jpeg or .jpg filename extensions.

When saving an image as a JPEG file, many image editors offer to save it in a "progressive" format. A ***progressive image*** file is saved as layers. You usually have a choice of saving three to seven layers. Graphical browsers will load and display the JPEG image one layer at a time, which has the visual effect of building the image. This is considered by some authors to be a visually appealing effect that catches the eye of interested users. Unfortunately, a progressive image file is slower to load.

PNG

PNG stands for *Portable Network Graphics* and is a newer format that supports both 8-bit and 24-bit color. It uses a lossless compression algorithm. PNG is currently an ***open standard***, which means that anyone is free to use it, and no single body or organization has fixed all the parameters of the standard. In other words, an open standard is a standard that is still developing. PNG is supported by some of the most up-to-date browsers but not by all, the way GIF and JPEG are. A PNG file is recognized by the .png filename extension. There is a large and growing group that is trying to establish PNG as the Web standard.

SVG

In October 2001 the W³C released specifications for a new graphic format: *Scalar Vector Graphic,* or *SVG.* ***Vector graphics*** are based on mathematically determined points, lines, and curves rather than a grid of pixels. As a result, an SVG file is physically small, while the image is easily scaled to be either larger or smaller without losing clarity. This graphic format includes text, and designers can make these images interactive by allowing users to rotate them with a mouse. An SVG can even be animated. SVG images are designed to be XML-compatible and are easily integrated into XML-compliant databases and extracted using XML queries.

The only downside to SVG files is that they require the browser to perform a series of mathematical processes to render the image. On slower machines, (less than 500 MHz), these processes can cause a slight delay in the presentation of the graphic upon the screen. On faster machines, the slower build time is more than offset by the SVG file's much faster download time.

PDF

PDF stands for *Portable Data Format.* These images are created with a special expensive software package from Adobe called Acrobat. PDF images cannot be read by any current browser without an additional software package called Acrobat Reader that must be independently obtained and installed. Any software package that works with a browser this way is called a *plug-in.* Currently the Acrobat Reader plug-in is available for free download. PDF documents can look like a magazine page, with multiple columns. The PDF files support "on page" searching and use the .pdf filename extension. This format is not yet widely used.

TIFF

TIFF stands for *Tagged Image File Format,* which is commonly used to exchange documents between different computer platforms. There are six different "flavors" of TIFF files, so any one TIFF image may not be correctly displayed if the user's viewing software expects one of the other "flavors." TIFF supports 1, 4, 8, and 24 bits per pixel. It is an older formatting scheme, but because of all its variations it is not considered a standard. TIFF files usually have the file extensions of .tif on Windows platforms and .tiff on Apple and Unix systems.

BMP

BMP is a *Bit-Mapped Picture.* It is a standard Windows image format that uses a .bmp filename extension. It can support 1, 4, 8, and 24 bits per pixel. It is not compressed as a rule. These files are usually created using Microsoft's Paint or Paintbrush programs and are used for the wallpaper in Windows. The standard browsers do not currently support this file type without invoking a program like Microsoft Paint.

▸▸ CHOOSING AN IMAGE FORMAT

So what image format should you see? For now it may be best to use only GIF and JPEG image formats for your pages. They are the two standard formats that are supported by all the graphical browsers. Don't shy away from the PNG image format, though, because the popular graphical browsers recognize it. Exotic formats (anything that is not GIF, JPEG, or PNG) may require installing a plug-in before viewing. Try to resist the temptation of using exotic image formats. If your user cannot display them, they have no value.

Image editors and drawing packages allow a file to be saved in any of several formats, so the aspiring artist can usually save a file in GIF, JPEG, or PNG formats. In addition, you can use an image editor to convert exotic image types into something more recognizable. If you are serious about building and maintaining Web pages, it would be a good idea to acquire a good image editor. Commercial editors like Adobe's Photoshop, the shareware Paint Shop Pro, and the freeware StarOffice Image allow you to modify images, add special effects like polarization or texturing, and convert from one form of file format to another. Many of the more interesting images available on the Web were created on paper and then scanned into machine-readable form. The most serious Web weavers have a good color scanner to create images this way.

▸▸ IMAGE SIZES

It is important to understand how quickly an image can become a large, slow, troublesome impediment to your users. Let's do some simple math to see how large an image can become. We will use an image size of 500-by-300, or 150,000, pixels. The image in Figure 6.2, including the 1-pixel black border, is this size. It is a rather large image, but not a full-screen picture. If we were using a file format with 8 bits per pixel, we would have a file of 1,200,000 bits. If the user is using a 56.6-kilobits-per-second modem connection, and if the modem actually connects at 56.6, it would take about 21 seconds to download that one image. That's not too bad if that is the only image we have; most users will wait 21 seconds to see it. But, remember, this is at 56.6 kilobits per second! Many modems actually operate at a speed of only 28.8 kilobits per second (kbps) during the day, regardless of their speed capacity. The same image that took 21 seconds to download at 56.6 kilobits per second will take 42 seconds to download at 28.8 kbps. That is a little long for our user to sit staring at the screen! And this is just one image. If we have 10 or 12 images of the same large size on our page, we need to multiply the wait by the number of images. Then, too, this example is for an 8-bit (8 bits per pixel) image. Suppose instead we were to use a 24-bit image. You can see how images can really add to the download time for pages.

Figure 6.2

An image 500-by-300 pixels in size, stored in a black-and-white format, or 1 bpp

▶▶ BITS PER PIXEL (BPP)

In the preceding discussion of file format types, you saw that each file format supports a specific range of *bits per pixel (bpp)*. This bpp count determines how many colors an image can contain, as follows:

- An image of 1 bpp can have two colors, usually black and white, with no gray scale (see Figure 6.2).

- An image of 4 bpp can have up to 16 colors. This is the old Windows palette. It is good enough for icons but not usually sufficient for pictures.

- An image of 8 bpp can have up to 256 colors. This is the way GIF files are stored. This is an acceptable number of colors for most applications but does not provide the richness necessary for good rendering of photographs or scanned images.

- An image of 16 bpp can have up to 32,768 colors. This is an older ratio and is not often supported, since the next level is so much richer. Many applications skip this level.

- An image of 24 bpp can have more than 16 million colors! Specifically, it allows 16,777,216 different colors. This is sufficient for a good rendering of photographs and other scanned images. The downside of the 24 bpp range is that our example image of 150,000 pixels in Figure 6.2 would take more than 2 minutes to download at 28.8 kilobits per second.

▶▶ GRAPHIC TIPS

Following are some techniques for reducing download time for users while still providing the visually rich environment you wish to create.

1. *Simplify your graphics.* If you are building an image using a graphics package, keep the image simple. Use the fewest colors you can get away with, and save your image in either GIF and JPEG format. Avoid colors on the palette that are created using **dithering** (blending two colors among adjacent pixels to achieve a third color), because that can reduce the compressibility of the image. Another reason not to use dithered colors is that all systems don't dither the same way. Examples of dithering are illustrated in Figure 6.3. Large areas of a single color are best for compression.

Figure 6.3

Examples of dithering, in which new color blends are created by placing different colored pixels next to each other

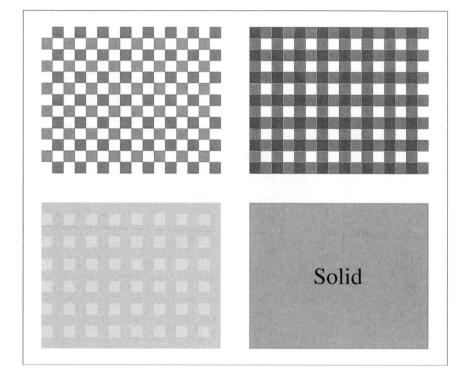

2. *Divide up large pages.* This is a general rule for Web pages, but it is especially important when dealing with pages that have many graphics. Users would rather flip from one quickly loading page to another than wait for one slowly loading, large page. A good rule of thumb is to keep pages under a 50-kilobyte maximum size, including all the graphics. That way the pages will load fairly quickly, even with very slow connection speeds. An absolute rule of thumb is to keep the page, and all the graphics associated with the page, at a size of less than 720 kilobytes. An easy way to accomplish this is to store all the data for one page, both text and the associated graphics, on a single, low-density 3.5-inch floppy disk. If the data won't fit on the disk, the page is too large.

3. *Keep large graphics on their own page.* If you must have a large image, put it on a page by itself and provide a link to it from the current page. This type of image is referred to as an **external image**. We use a familiar tool, the <a>anchor</a> container, to reference external images. The following code displays the image shown in Figure 6.4 as an independent external image:

```
<a href="maddoc.gif">Full size Mad Dr. G's Home Page (110K GIF)</a>
```

You can either use a text link like, "I have enclosed a detailed picture of the part for you to examine; it is a 1.2 Meg image," or you can use a thumbnail image as the link. A ***thumbnail image*** is a very small version of the actual image. Figure 6.4 provides an example of a large graphic used on a home page contrasted with the thumbnail image used as a link. The large image is 110,000 bytes. It is a very large image. The thumbnail is 8,000 bytes. In this example, the thumbnail is much smaller than the full GIF. That is a great savings for the user. You should set up your page so that the user can click on the thumbnail image in order to see the full-size picture. It is also a good idea to tell the user how large that full-size file will be. Then the user can decide if he wants to wait for it. If the "big picture" is an 18-megabit file (1,024 × 768 × 24 bpp), it could take several minutes to download!

Figure 6.4

Home page image and associated thumbnail image used as a link

Thumbnail

4.   *Reuse the images on your page.* This is an especially important rule for icons; however, it is important for other images as well. Most browsers will *cache,* or store, images locally. That way, if you reuse the same image several times, the browser can take it from the local cache and not have to move it over the Net. While it might be nice, visually, to have a different icon for each item in a list, reusing the same icon could provide substantial savings in download time for your user.

5.   *Preload images if you are going to use them in rollovers.* It is becoming common practice to use ***rollovers***, small images that load or change when the mouse pointer moves over (rolls over) a particular part of the screen. If you make the user wait for these rollovers to download you may well spoil the effect for them. When we get to Chapter Nine and then again in Chapter Thirteen, we will teach you different ways to preload images. It is a very useful technique.

6. *Use image-reduction software or Web site to decrease the size of images.* A number of good-quality programs or sites are available that can clean up images by removing unused colors from the palette. The resulting smaller number of colors in the image often allows it to be saved with a lower bpp. One commercial product is GifCruncher (www.spinwave.com).

HTML **<img />**

Description: inserts graphic, photograph, line art, or other image into screen display.
Type: empty.
Attributes: *align, alt, border,* class, dir, **height, hspace,** id, ismap, lang, **longdesc,** onclick, ondblclick, onkeydown, onkeypress, onkeyup, onmousedown, onmouse-move, onmouseout, onmouseover, onmouseup, **src,** style, title, usemap, *vspace,* and **width.**

XML: requires using <img /> or <img></img>; for example, `<img src="chart.gif" />`.

Images are inserted into a document using the <img /> tag. This was originally an empty tag, with the XML and XHTML recommendations making it a container. The <img /> container is the only element in the XHTML Image module. Several attributes are available for this tag, some of them specific to one or the other of the two main graphical browsers, Navigator and Internet Explorer. We will focus on <img /> attributes identified in the W3C HTML specifications. Because the <img /> tag doesn't force a line break, you can insert an image into the text line (inline), and it will simply appear along with the text.

The rendering of images is very browser-dependent. Nongraphical browsers will ignore image tags or just display the **alt** value. Some browsers will force the images into specific size and color limitations. Some users will turn off automatic image loading, causing the browser to omit all the images unless the user specifically asks for one. In light of that, you must ensure that the pages you create make sense even without their images. They must convey the same basic information whether the user uses a graphical browser or not.

Also, the browser will control the colors in the image. The actual hardware at the user site is involved here, too. If you have a wonderful image with 16,000,000 colors, and the user is displaying it on a monochrome monitor, it will appear as a gray-scale image. This is another example of the Web weaver supplying the content while the browser handles the format.

src

The **src** (source) attribute is one of two required attributes of the <img> tag. This attribute tells the browser where to find the image that is to be inserted into your page. There are three schools of thought about where to keep your images:

1. The first school of thought could be called the "minimize the home server's load" approach. The idea here is that all the images should be on remote machines, and the **src** attribute should provide a link across the Net to the remote site. That way the load on the local server that is hosting the page is minimized. Generally, this is the very worst thing a Web weaver can do, because it causes the greatest load on the Net. In this model, each time a new image is requested, the browser must establish a link to another server where the picture is located, retrieve the image, and then send it to the browser requesting the picture before it can be displayed. Many Web sites that have pictures available for use will request that the images be copied rather than having a link pointing to their site. Following is an example of a link across the Net:

`<img src="http://phred.dc3d.edu/images/parrot.gif" />`

2. The second school of thought could be summed up as the "put everything in the same directory" approach. These folks like to be able to minimize the paths coded in the **src** attribute. They want to make it as easy as possible to move a page from one site to another. This approach has some merit for small Web sites or for people who intend to move their pages from site to site. It is very easy to upload and maintain a page when all the links and all the images are local to the home directory. But when the site is large, this may not be practical. Now look at a line of code that shows the minimal <img /> tag (also shown in Figure 6.5):

```
<img src="parrot.gif" />
```

Here all the files, both HTML and images, have been grouped into a single directory.

Figure 6.5

HTML code to display an image

```
<html>
<head>
<title>Images</title>
</head>

<body>
Here is a picture of a nice parrot:<br />
<img src="parrot.gif" /><br />
Actually, this is a Cockatoo from Australia.<br />
</body>
</html>
```

3. The third school could be described as the "a place for everything and everything in its place" approach. Here each type of file is kept in its own directory. Thus, the Web pages will be in a directory called "HTML" or "web-pages," the pictures in a directory called "images," the sound files in a directory called "sounds," and so forth. This approach can be taken to extremes, though, and become cumbersome for everybody involved. At some sites, for example, the "images" subdirectory is divided into "smallgif," "mediumgif," "biggif," "smalljpg," "mediumjpg," and "bigjpg." In the next example, the image is located in the "images" subdirectory, possibly because the site has many images, and several of them are used across many different pages, or possibly because the Web weaver wants to be able to organize files in a useful way:

```
<img scr="images/parrot.gif" />
```

Notice that in all three approaches, the actual filename, or path and filename, is enclosed in quotation marks. Those quotation marks are usually required for the image to work correctly. Sometimes they can be omitted and the image will appear correctly anyway, but at a later time, the image may stop appearing. It is best, therefore, to always code the image, or the image and path, inside quotation marks. Then it will always work as long as the path is correct. This may be the place for a word of caution. In the authors' vast experience helping students learn how to build Web pages, the most common problems with images are path problems and case problems. If you have an image that fails to load, the first thing you should check is that the path to that image is correct. The second thing you need to check is that the image name is spelled and capitalized correctly. Some operating systems shift lowercase filenames to uppercase or initial caps when they are uploaded to another machine. The change can cause all kinds of problems, so you need to be aware of that possibility.

It is usually necessary to create a directory structure when building a commercial site, because that type of site will have hundreds of files, and many times several different pages will use the same images. If images are put in common areas, then everybody can use them. Also, updating them is easy. For example, if 15 different pages all use an image of the corporate logo, and they are stored in 15 different locations, the Web weaver will have to update 15 different files in 15 different directories if a new version of the logo is modified. On the other hand, if a single copy of the logo is kept in a single directory, and all the pages use that one image, then it is easy to update the image.

For new users, it is usually easier to keep all the images, pages, and other files in one directory (the second school of thought in our previous discussion). As you become more sophisticated and as your Web site grows, you will find it easier to collect related files into directories. This will make uploading a little more complex, as you may need to change the paths in the **src** attributes, but it is a small price to pay for organization and easy update. Do not fall into the trap of linking across the Web to an image on a remote machine—that is the worst option available.

Figure 6.5 presented the code for adding parrot.gif to a Web page. Each line ends in a line break, <br />, to force the image onto a line of its own. Later we will see how the **align** attribute allows some control over where the image is placed on the screen, with the float style providing similar positional control. We can see that the default alignment of the image is on the left margin. Figure 6.6 presents the same code, but without the line breaks. In this situation the browser treats the image just like any other text element. Images used this way are called ***inline images***. Since there are no forced line breaks, an inline image appears like any other page elements, in line with the text, and after the word "parrot," as we might expect. The first line of text is pushed down far enough to accommodate the image as well as the text. Notice how the bottom of the image is aligned with the bottom of the actual text. Soon we will see how to modify this vertical alignment as well as the horizontal alignment of an image.

alt

The **alt** attribute is the other required <img /> attribute. It provides a text-based description of the image. You must include the **alt** attribute to allow for text-based browsers and, in the future, aural (sound)-based browsers. This attribute contains a text string that is displayed when graphical browser users move the screen pointer over the image (see Figure 6.6). The text provided by the **alt** attribute is also displayed (as shown in Figure 6.7) when the browser can't display the actual image, either because it is not a graphical browser or because the user has turned off image loading, or because the image is unavailable to the browser for some other reason. This text string must be enclosed in quotation marks if it contains any punctuation or spaces. The string can be up to 1,024 bytes long.

As mentioned earlier in this chapter, the careful Web weaver never places information in an image that is not available somewhere else on the page. The **alt** attribute is one good way to present that information to users who cannot see the images. In addition to providing content support for nongraphical users, the **alt** attribute can serve as a substitute for icons. For example, you could include the following code in your page to indicate a new feature:

```
<h2>See the birdie <img src="hotnew.gif" alt="**NEW**" /></h2>
```

Figure 6.6

HTML code to display inline image, with **alt** attribute describing image

```
<html>
<head>
<title>Images</title>
</head>

<body>
Here is a picture of a nice parrot:
<img src="parrot.gif" alt="Cockatoo woodcut" />
Actually, this is a Cockatoo from Australia.
</body>
</html>
```

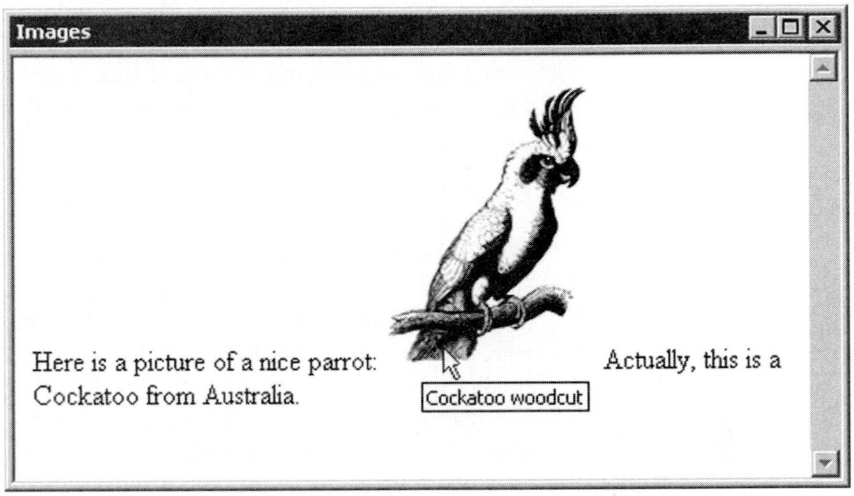

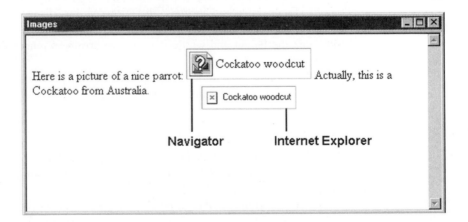

Users with graphical browsers see the "hotnew.gif" image, but those with text-only browsers or those who have turned off automatic image loading will see the string "**NEW**" after the text.

Figure 6.6 presents the code for the parrot page in Figure 6.5 with the **alt** attribute coded. In Figure 6.7 the alternative text is displayed because we temporarily removed the parrot.gif file from the local directory. Using the **alt** attribute must be standard procedure for any image you choose to add to your page.

Figure 6.7

Display of text provided by **alt** attribute when browser cannot find related image

longdesc

The **longdesc** attribute takes the logic behind the **alt** attribute one step further. It specifies a long description of the image that is stored as an independent file. The HTML code would look like this:

```
<img src="parrot.gif" alt="Cockatoo woodcut" longdesc="cockatoo.txt" />
```

This attribute is especially useful when server-side image maps are found on the Web page. Both client-side and server-side image maps are discussed in Chapter Fourteen.

height AND width

One way to reduce the time it takes for the browser to render the page is to tell the browser exactly how much screen real estate to reserve for the image. The **height** and **width** attributes do this. They eliminate the need for the browser to spend time calculating how much space to allow for the image before it continues downloading and presenting the page. In some instances—for example, in JavaScript—image height and width are required. The image dimensions are given in the number of pixels that compose a horizontal line (width) and a vertical line (height). The following code, also shown in Figure 6.8, would create an image 150 pixels high and 200 pixels wide:

```
<img src="bfly.gif" height="150" width="200" />
```

It is a good coding habit to enclose the pixel count in double quotes as shown here.

Since you can control the actual size of the image using **height** and **width,** these attributes provide an easy way to create the appearance of a thumbnail image (Figure 6.8). Be careful with this: even though the image appears small on the screen, the browser must still download the whole image. A true thumbnail image is created by special software and is significantly smaller than the true image. Just displaying an image in a smaller space does *not* create a thumbnail.

It is also important to keep the same proportions when you change the size of an image. If you don't retain the ratio of height to width, you can really distort an image. For example, if the width of the butterfly image was decreased without decreasing the height proportionally, the image would be distorted.

Besides creating pseudo-thumbnail versions of images, you can use this feature to enlarge small images, as shown in Figure 6.8. Usually the larger version doesn't look as good as the original because enlarging it doesn't add data, it just duplicates existing data. But if you enlarge it only a small amount, the image quality doesn't suffer too much.

Another potential problem with coding image sizes is the effect created when the user has disabled the automatic image download. Some browsers, like Internet Explorer and older versions of Navigator, still reserve space for the images, so the screen is filled with nearly empty frames containing only the **alt** text and meaningless place-holder icons. The page looks very unfinished and may be of little use. In Figure 6.8 you can see how such a page would appear. Other browsers just display the text identified by the **alt** attribute (newer versions of Navigator) or nothing at all (Opera). If the Web weaver does not code the height and width, then all the browsers render the place-holders the same small size.

Furthermore, if you don't set the **height** and **width** attributes, and the user has the automatic download option turned off, the browser will also display these small place-holder icons inside the text block instead of reserving the large blocks of empty space shown in Figure 6.8.

Note that you have no choice but to code the **height** and **width** attributes in pixels. Usually it is not a good idea to code anything in pixels, as the number of pixels on your user's screen may differ from the number on your screen, but in this case you have no choice. Just remember that there are variations in users' screens, and take this into account as you set the number of pixels. Suppose you build an image that takes up the right third of your screen, but you have a 1,024-by-1,080 screen whereas your user has a 640-by-480 screen. Your image will be a lot larger on the user's screen. The difference in size can cause problems in presenting information and maintaining a reasonable screen layout.

A final trick you can use with images is called *flood filling*, or extreme image expansion. Here you create a large colored area by using the **height** and **width** attributes to expand a very small image across the screen. For example, the code in Figure 6.9 creates a large line across the screen. The line is 450 pixels wide and 12 pixels tall. This single-

Figure 6.8

HTML code setting the height
and width of an image

```html
<html>
<head>
<title>Image Height and Width Attributes</title>
</head>

<body>
At the <em>Fly Away Home</em> Web site you can experience<br />
many of nature's pretty little creatures<br />
as they frolic about the flowers of the pasture.<br />
<img src="bfly.gif" alt="Painted Lady Butterfly" height="15" width="20" />
<img src="bfly.gif" alt="Painted Lady Butterfly" height="150" width="200" />
<img src="bfly.gif" alt="Painted Lady Butterfly" height="300" width="400" />
</body>
</html>
```

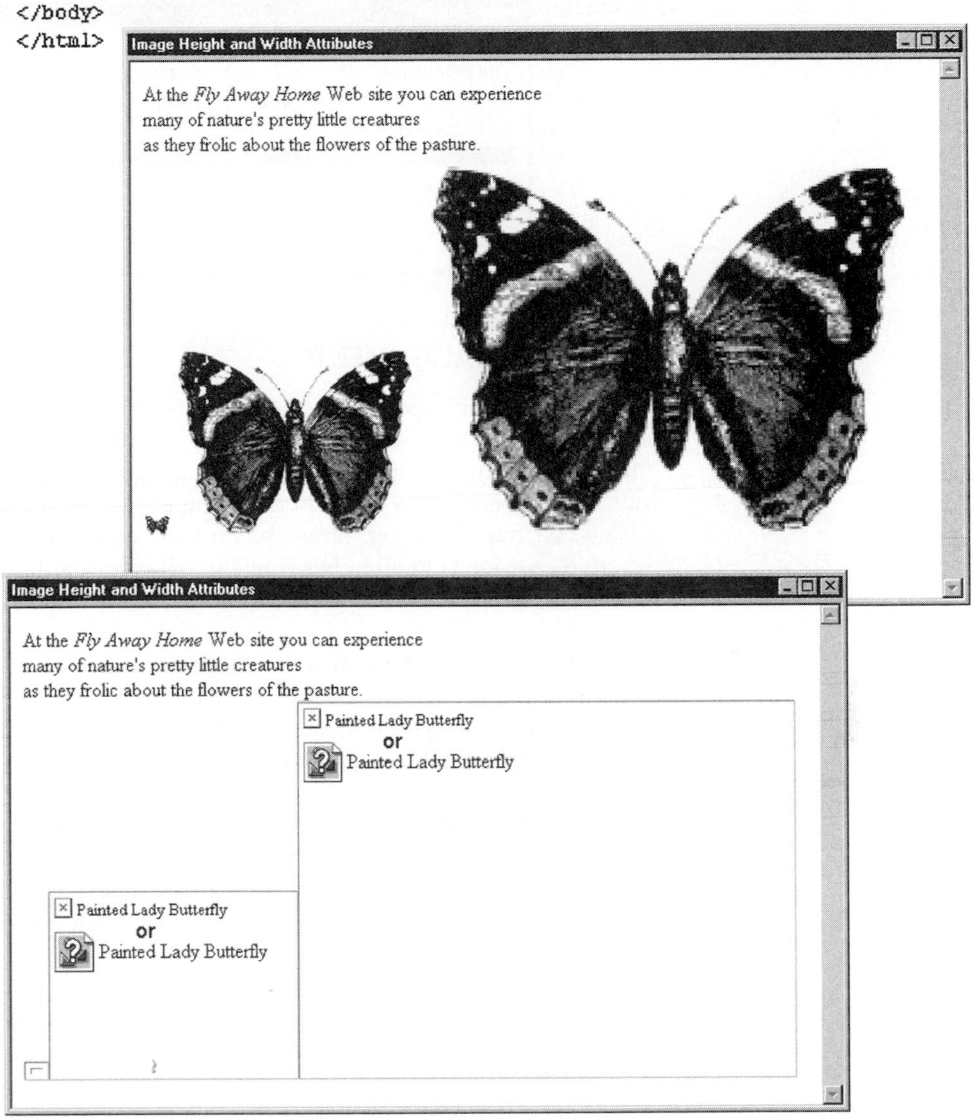

pixel black GIF is used to fill all 5,400 points. Figure 6.9 also shows how the code looks in a graphical browser.

A caveat about flood-fill imaging: As mentioned before, there is always a risk when using absolute pixel counts. Therefore, if the user has a very high-resolution screen, your flood-fill line might extend across only a small part of the screen. On the other hand, if the user has a low-resolution screen, the line might extend nearly the width of the whole screen. The user's browser and hardware will determine how the screen appears.

Figure 6.9

HTML code using the **height** and **width** attributes to flood-fill an image of a single pixel

```
<html>
<head>
<title>Flood Filling</title>
</head>

<body>
The following image is really only one pixel in size,<br />
but by using <b>height</b> and <b>width</b> attributes, you can make it<br />
look like a large bar across the screen!<br />
<img src="onepixel.jpg" height="12" width="450" /><br />
Pretty neat, huh!<br />
</body>
</html>
```

The following image is really only one pixel in size,
but by using **height** and **width** attributes, you can make it
look like a large bar across the screen!

Pretty neat, huh!

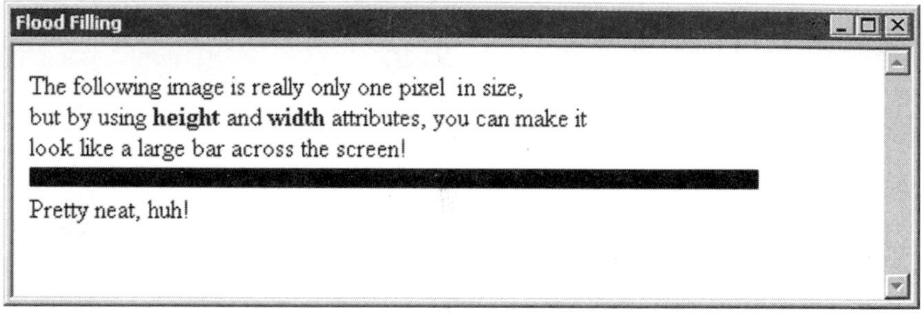

HORIZONTAL ALIGNMENT

The browsers don't specify a default alignment across the page for images, because images are treated like any other text object. As you have seen, if you insert an image in the middle of a text block, it will simply appear there, with the line of text on either side of it. In most cases the browser will align the bottom of the image with the bottom of the text line. However, browsers vary, so a wise Web weaver will always specify where the image is to align horizontally if it makes a difference in the presentation of the information.

style versus align Attributes Although the **align** attribute is a commonly used attribute within paragraphs, headings, and other tags, it has been deprecated for use within <img /> tags. The **style** attribute's float property is now the recommended alternative for horizontal (left or right) image alignment.

left Some Web weavers refer to placing images at either margin as *floating images*. It is often handy to be able to place an image at the margin and then flow the text next to the image rather than imbedding the image in a single line. Figure 6.10 shows how the browser will render a left- (and right-) aligned image. By simply setting the float property equal to left, we have changed the whole look of the screen. Now the text flows along the right side of the image, so the information takes up much less space on the page. This is a nice option for images that are folded into the text stream. The following code would left-align the toad image:

```
<img src="toad.gif" style="float: left" height="70" width="80" />
```

This coding format has replaced the **align** attribute. The preceding code would produce exactly the same results you see in Figure 6.10 if the **align** attribute is used instead of **style,** and is set equal to left with this HTML code:

```
<img src="toad.gif" align="left" height="70" width="80" />
```

right The style="float: right" option and the deprecated align="right" alternative work just like left alignment except that they place the image next to the right margin. The text now flows around the left side of the image, as shown in Figure 6.10. The choice of left or right image placement is determined by the aesthetic taste of the Web weaver.

Figure 6.10

HTML code for horizontal image alignment

```
<html>
<head>
<title>Horizontal Image Alignment</title>
</head>

<body>
Toads are very valuable helpers in most gardens.
<img src="toad.gif" alt="Toad" height="70" width="80" />
They eat many harmful insects including mosquitos, grubs, ants, and flies.
There are at least 11 species of toad that live in North America.
<br /><br />

<img src="toad.gif" alt="Toad" style="float: left" height="70" width="80" />
Here the Float property is set to left when displaying the toad. When enough
text follows the image, it flows to the right and will eventually wrap
underneath the image. The point where the text wraps underneath the image
depends on the browser's screen dimensions.
<br /><br />

<img src="toad.gif" alt="Toad" style="float: right" height="70" width="80" />
Here the Float property is set to right when displaying the toad. When enough
text follows the image it flows to the left and will eventually wrap underneath
the image. The point where the text wraps underneath the image depends on the
browser's screen dimensions and possibly the user's screen size.
</body>
</html>
```

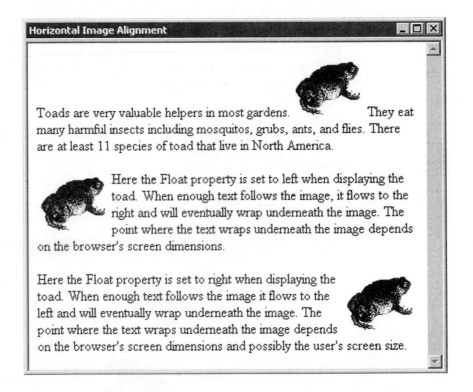

Image placement at the margin is often the best choice for layouts with larger images. However, sometimes it is necessary, especially with small images or icons, to imbed the images inside the line. The use to which the image is put will usually dictate where it should be placed on the page. Unfortunately, there is still no way to have the image centered on the page with the text following on both sides of it. (Actually, you can do something like that if you use tables, but that is several chapters away.)

VERTICAL ALIGNMENT

Of the five different values that control the placement of the image on the page, three values (top, middle, and bottom) control the vertical alignment. These values determine the image's placement up or down within the line as shown in Figure 6.11. Although top, middle, and bottom have been deprecated along with the **align** attribute, there is currently no easy-to-use alternative available. Therefore, despite their deprecated status, we will look at how they work.

top The **align** value of top aligns the top of the image with the top of the tallest item in the current text line. If the tallest item is an image, the top value will align its image with the preceding one. If there are no other images in the current line, it will align its image with the top of the text. Figure 6.11 gives an example of a top alignment when there are no other images in the current text line.

middle The **align** value of middle aligns the middle of the image with the bottom, or baseline, of the text (not the middle of the text). The **baseline** of the text is the imaginary line that runs across the bottom of the letters, like the point of the v and the bottom, or serifs, of the x, not counting the descenders, like the tails of y or g. Figure 6.11 shows an example of a middle alignment.

Figure 6.11

HTML code for deprecated vertical image alignment

```
<html>
<head>
<title>Deprecated Vertical Image Alignment</title>
</head>

<body>
Align equals top
<img src="toad.gif" alt="Toad" align="top" height="70" width="80" />
when displaying the toad.
<br /><br />

Align equals middle
<img src="toad.gif" alt="Toad" align="middle" height="70" width="80" />
when displaying the toad.
<br /><br />

Align equals bottom
<img src="toad.gif" alt="Toad" align="bottom" height="70" width="80" />
when displaying the toad.
</body>
</html>
```

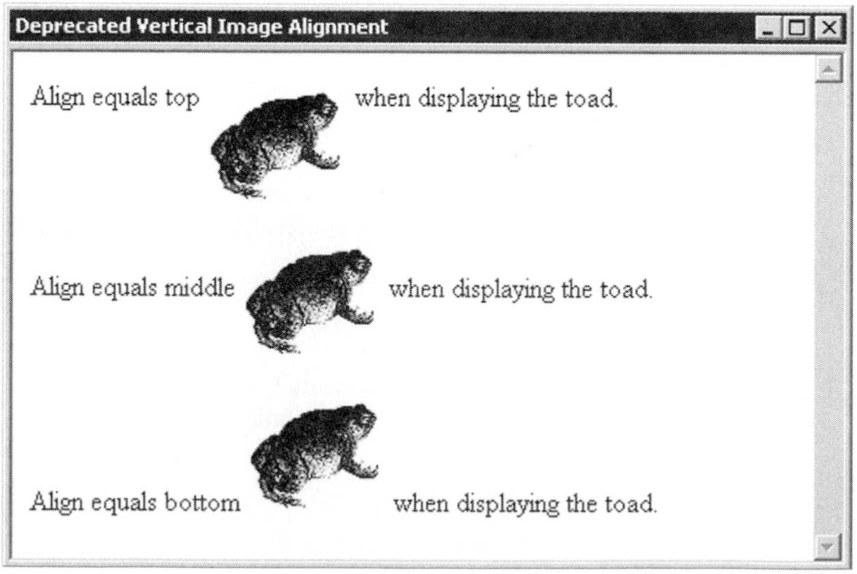

bottom The **align** value of bottom aligns the bottom of the image with the bottom, or baseline, of the text. Although bottom is usually the default value, the wise Web weaver never counts on a browser's default value. It is better to code a value if it is important. This alignment is useful for putting special symbols or small icons into the text line. Figure 6.11 gives an example of bottom alignment.

EXPLORATION #1 Copy the files geyser.html and geyser.jpg from the student CD to the same disk directory on your personal computer. Open geyser.html using an ASCII editor and change the <title> container to *your name's Thoughts on Geysers*. Add the image geyser.jpg immediately under the level-2 heading. The image should float left and be 100 pixels wide and 140 pixels tall. The alternative text should include the word "*geyser.*" Save the file as chapter6.html and display it using your favorite browser.

▸▸ LINE BREAKS

Back in Chapter Two you learned how to insert new-line characters into your document with the <br /> tag. Now we need to explore that tag in a little more detail with respect to image alignment and text flow.

clear

Normally you will use the <br /> tag simply to insert a line break into a Web page. Figure 6.11, for example, contains <br /> tags where we wanted to end a line or create a blank line. However, we can now combine images with our text and need a way to use line breaks to stop the flow of text around an image. The **clear** attribute can be set to left, right, or all in order to do just that. In Figure 6.12 the <br /> tag uses a **clear** attribute set

Figure 6.12

HTML code using the **clear** attribute to stop the left (or right) flow of text around an image

```
<html>
<head>
<title>Clear Image Alignment</title>
</head>

<body>
<img src="toad.gif" alt="Toad" style="float: left" height="70" width="80" />
The toads are very valuable helpers in most gardens. They eat many harmful
insects including mosquitos, grubs, ants, and flies.
<br clear="left" />

There are at least 11 species of toad that live in North America. Almost all
toads are nocturnal, so you will have to wait until late evening or nightfall
to see them out and about.  Although they are usually covered with wart-like
bumps, you cannot catch warts from a toad.
</body>
</html>
```

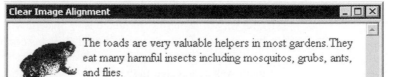

equal to left to cause the browser to force a line break and then resume printing under the toad. This technique can be used to put a short "caption" on an image.

If you want to ensure that your text appears on the line below any image (or table), you can use the following code:

```
<br clear="all" />
```

This will display the text on the next line when both the left and right margins are clear. The **style** attribute can also be used to clear floating text. This HTML code is functionally the same as the preceding code:

```
<br style="clear: both" />
```

In this case the value both is used instead of setting clear to all. Either option is handy to prevent subsequent paragraphs from running up against an image and confusing the reader.

EXPLORATION **#2**   Add to chapter6.html a line break that clears the floating text before the sentence starting with "The following areas . . ." Save the file, and refresh/reload the browser display.

▸▸ CENTERING IMAGES

Right and left image alignments are nice, but what about centering an image? Ideally we should be able to place an image in the center of the screen and flow text on both sides of it. Unfortunately, this option has not yet been created. It no doubt will be in the future. For now, although there are two ways to get an image centered on the page, the text cannot be made to flow around it. The image will be isolated from the text. Let's look at these two ways of centering an image.

HTML   `<center>Centering Objects</center>`

Description: centers object within screen display.
Type: container.
Attributes: none.
Special note: deprecated in HTML 4 specifications.

One way of centering an image is to place it within a <center> container. The image will be separate from the text, but it will be centered on the page. In Figure 6.13 the <center></center> container encloses the first image. To the surprise of some, this element was deprecated in the HTML 4 specifications in favor of setting a tag's **align** attribute equal to center. However, there is no align="center" attribute value for the <img /> element. An alternative way to center images using the <div> container is discussed in Chapter Eight.

Figure 6.13

HTML code for two methods of centering image within page

```
<html>
<head>
<title>Centering Images</title>
</head>

<body>
The toads are very valuable helpers in most gardens.
<center>
<img src="toad.gif" alt="Toad" height="70" width="80" />
</center>

They eat many harmful insects including mosquitos, grubs, ants, and flies.
There are at least 11 species of toad that live in North America.
<p align="center">
<img src="toad.gif" alt="Toad" height="70" width="80" />
</p>

Almost all toads are nocturnal, so you will have to wait until late evening or
nightfall to see them out and about.  Although they are usually covered with
wart-like bumps, you cannot catch warts from a toad.
</body>
</html>
```

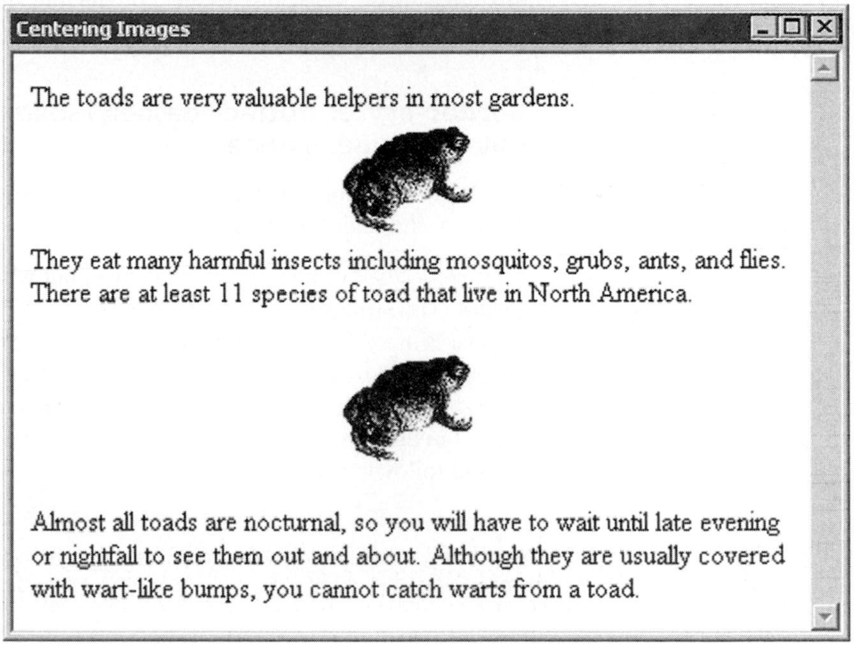

CENTERING A PARAGRAPH

Notice in Figure 6.13 how the text is closer to the top and bottom of the first image than to the second. Although the <center> container was used for the first image, a different method was used for the second. When you want more space above and below the image, you can isolate the image in a <p>paragraph</p> container that has an alignment of center. This technique looks like this:

```
<p align="center">
<img src="toad.gif" alt="toad" height="70" width="80" />
</p>
```

From the code in Figure 6.13, you can see that the two techniques are easy to use. Notice again how the first image is very close to the text above and below it, whereas the second image is separated from the text by a blank line. Although it is not currently possible to imbed an image into a paragraph of text and have the text flow on both sides of the image, these two options for centering an image can be used to achieve something like the desired effect. Along with the two floating options (left and right), they give the Web weaver sufficient control over the placement of images on a page.

As you can see, there is a wealth of image attributes that help a Web designer customize the look and feel of images placed within a Web page. In turn, the HTML 4 specifications have provided **style** properties that accomplish the same thing while deprecating the related attributes. What follow are some additional specific image-related attributes and the **style** properties that should now be used in their place.

▸▸ IMAGE BORDERS

Figure 6.14 presents the code for changing the style, width, and color of the border on three images. Notice that the border can become large enough to be distracting. All three of these images are the same size, and they align on the bottom edge, but the border actually controls the vertical placement on the line. The wide border image is closer to the top of the page than the image with the default solid border.

border-style: dotted | dashed | solid | double | groove | ridge | inset | outset | hidden | none

The basic code for creating a solid black border around an image uses the border-style property and looks like this:

```
<img src="goldfish.gif" alt="Carp" style="border-style: solid; " />
```

Figure 6.14 provides examples of other available border styles. As might be expected, the popular browsers execute these styles in subtly different ways, as shown by the different dotted border styles found in Figure 6.14. Other differences are not documented in this figure.

The **style** attribute's border-style property shown in Figure 6.14 replaces the deprecated **border** attribute. To create a similar border using the **border** attribute you would use the following code:

```
<img src="goldfish.gif" alt="Carp" border="3" />
```

Currently the default border width is 4 pixels in Internet Explorer and 3 pixels in Navigator and Opera.

border-width: thin | medium | thick | absolute | inherit

The style properties to change the border's width and color are also shown in Figure 6.14. The border's thickness is set using the style's border-width property. As pointed out earlier, too large a border around an image can be distracting, so take care when using extremely wide borders. The image border is set to 10 pixels wide with this code:

```
<img src="goldfish.gif" alt="Carp" style="border-style: solid; border-width: 10px; " />
```

The border-width property works only when a border-style property and value are used in the same <img /> tag.

Besides setting the width by specifying the actual pixel count, you can also use thin (2 pixels wide in Internet Explorer and 1 pixel wide in Navigator or Opera), medium (the default setting), or thick (6 pixels wide in Internet Explorer and Opera and 5 pixels wide in Navigator) as border widths. The HTML code looks like this:

```
<img src="goldfish.gif" alt="Carp" style="border-style: solid; border-width: thin; " />
```

border-color: color#| transparent | inherit

The border-color property uses the same six-digit hexadecimal color codes used with background colors or the recognized color names. The browser-safe hexadecimal color codes and color names are found in the color insert in the Reference Guide. The HTML code to create a solid red border around an image follows:

```
<img src="goldfish.gif" alt="Carp" style="border-style: solid; border-color: #FF0000; " />
```

Figure 6.14   HTML code to display borders of different styles, widths, and color around an image

```
<html>
<head>
<title>Image Borders</title>
</head>

<body>
<img src="goldfish.gif" alt="Carp" style="border-style: solid;" />
 
<!-- gray dashed border -->
<img src="goldfish.gif" alt="Carp" style="border-style: dashed; border-color: #CCCCCC;" />
 
<img src="goldfish.gif" alt="Carp" style="border-style: solid; border-width: 10px;" />
</body>
</html>
```

border-style values

border-style: solid;

border-style: dotted;
Internet Explorer

border-style: dotted;
Navigator and Opera

border-style: dashed;
Navigator

border-style: double;

border-style: groove;

border-style: ridge;

border-style: inset;

border-style: outset;

EXPLORATION #3

Update chapter6.html to add a double border around the image that is 10 pixels wide and in the color blue, #336699. Save the file, and refresh/reload the browser display. If the image does not refresh/reload, try the following:

1. Hold down the Ctrl key, and click on the Refresh/Reload button.
2. Click to the right of the URL, and press the Enter key.
3. Flush both disk and memory cache, and refresh/reload page.

▸▸ IMAGE MARGINS

Many Web weavers find that browsers leave too little room between the images and the text, as you can see at the top of Figure 6.15. Such close quarters are even more obvious when the image includes a border around it. The code in Figure 6.15 shows how the space around images can be manipulated by establishing an image margin. The bottom two images in this code have different margins.

margin: margin-width | inherit

We often associate margins with pages, but in HTML any body element can have a margin. This can include paragraphs, headings, and in this example, images. The following code establishes a 15-pixel margin around the image:

```
<img src="grayfish.png" alt="Carp" style="margin: 15px; " />
```

For now we will limit our coding to setting the same value for the top, left, bottom, and right margins, as shown in Figure 6.15. This is called a style *shortcut*. It seems to make coding styles easier, but in Chapter Eight you will learn the preferred method of independently setting each margin side, which gives you more control.

vspace AND hspace

In the past, graphical browsers used two attributes to control the horizontal and vertical space around images: **vspace** and **hspace.** (These attributes were deprecated in the HTML 4 recommendations in favor of the margin **style** property just discussed.) The vertical space represented by the top and bottom margins are set in pixels using the **vspace** attribute. For example, this code sets the vertical space to 20:

```
<img src="grayfish.png" alt="Carp" vspace="20" />
```

The horizontal space associated with the left and right margins is set up using the **hspace** attribute. Adding a 20-pixel horizontal space to the 20-pixel vertical space in this code will create a 20-pixel margin on all four sides of the image like the one shown at the bottom of Figure 6.15. The code looks like this:

```
<img src="grayfish.png" alt="Carp" vspace="20" hspace="20" />
```

The vertical and horizontal spaces that create a margin set the image off from the text. Since monitor resolutions vary from 640 to over 1,600 pixels per line, you need to consider both extremes when establishing image margins. The lower the resolution of the monitor, the greater will be the distance between the image and the text. For that reason, larger margin values usually should be avoided.

Figure 6.15   HTML code that establishes white space around image using margin property

```
<html>
<head>
<title>Image Margins</title>
</head>

<body>
The image below has no margins.
<img src="grayfish.png" alt="Carp" height="70" width="90" style="float: left;" />
Notice how close the text lies to the image. The goldfish has a long and interesting past as
a pet. Ancient Oriental civilizations kept goldfish in ponds, and valued them for their color
and graceful movements. Modern people find that a couple of goldfish add a necessary touch of
life to an otherwise dull and drab existence.
<br /><br />

The image below has the margin set to 10 pixels.
<img src="grayfish.png" alt="Carp" height="70" width="90" style="float: left; margin: 10px;" />
Notice how close the text lies to the image. The goldfish has a long and interesting past as
a pet. Ancient Oriental civilizations kept goldfish in ponds, and valued them for their color
and graceful movements. Modern people find that a couple of goldfish add a necessary touch of
life to an otherwise dull and drab existence.
<br /><br />

The image below has the margin set to 20 pixels.
<img src="grayfish.png" alt="Carp" height="70" width="90" style="float: left; margin: 20px;" />
Notice how close the text lies to the image. The goldfish has a long and interesting past as
a pet. Ancient Oriental civilizations kept goldfish in ponds, and valued them for their color
and graceful movements. Modern people find that a couple of goldfish add a necessary touch of
life to an otherwise dull and drab existence.
</body>
</html>
```

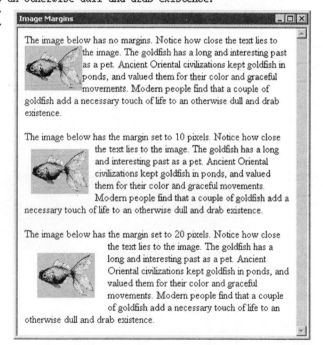

 **EXPLORATION #4**   Modify chapter6.html to include a 15-pixel margin around the image. Save the file, and refresh/reload the browser display.

▸▸ IMAGES AS BULLETS

As we learned long ago—gee, it sure seems a long time ago—there are usually three different bullet types in an unordered list. Sometimes it is necessary, or at least pretty, to have a list that contains special images rather than circles, discs, or squares. Figure 6.16 shows two ways to create unordered lists using image bullets.

Figure 6.16   HTML code to create list with image bullets

```
<html>
<head>
<title>Image Bullets</title>
</head>

<body>
<h1>Some Like It Hot!</h1>
Unordered list using list-style-image property:
<ul style="list-style-image: url(pepper.gif)">
 <li>Habanero</li>
 <li>Jalapeno</li>
 <li>Cayenne</li>
</ul>

Definition list using image as definition term:
<dl>
  <dt><img src="pepper.gif" /></dt>
  <dd>Tabasco</dd>

  <dt><img src="pepper.gif" /></dt>
  <dd>Inca Red</dd>

  <dt><img src="pepper.gif" /></dt>
  <dd>Filius Blue</dd>
</dl>
</body>
</html>
```

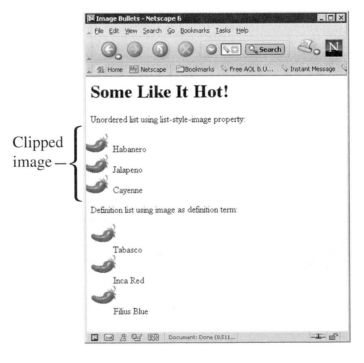

The custom bullets are a nice little addition, as long as the images aren't too big. Remember, pictures take time to download. In this case, however, the little pepper is only a 1.22-KB file, and it needs to be downloaded only once, because the browser will reuse the cached version on each of the five lines of the page. This is a good example of reusing the same image to save download time. If each bullet were a different image, then the browser would have to download all of them. This way, the browser downloads the little pepper one time and then takes the image from cache each time it is used as a bullet.

list-style-image: url | none | inherit

In Chapter Three, you were introduced to the **style** attribute's list-style-type property, which allows the Web weaver to set the bullets used in an unordered list to disc, circle, or square. The list-type-image property assigns an image to the unordered list's bullets, as shown in the top of Figure 6.16. The code looks like this:

```
<ul style="list-style-image: url (pepper.gif)">
```

Also shown in Figure 6.16 is one of the classic pitfalls to any Web page design. In this case one of the popular browsers will clip off the front of the image. Therefore, another way to use this image as a bullet needs to be found—see the discussion of definition lists in the next section. The broader point to be made here is that the Web page designer *must test every page* using all the popular browsers. Not only that, but the wise Web weaver will test with at least the past version of the browser as well as the current version. You can't expect your readers to update to the newer version of the browser just because it is out there. It is foolish to assume that the image bullets worked correctly in all the graphical browsers just because they worked in one!

DEFINITION LIST

Figure 6.16 also presents the code to use the pepper.gif file as an image bullet, but in a different way. As you can see, we used the definition list (<dl></dl>) and inserted the image as the definition term. It isn't a real bulleted (unordered) list, but it looks like one. This alternative technique of creating image bullets is not one to use with impunity, but it will serve as an alternative to the list-style-image property. Used carefully, this technique can provide a consistent look across several pages. Remember, the browser will need to download the image file only once. Later pages will not be affected, as the GIF image will be cached.

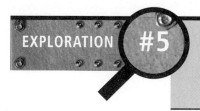

EXPLORATION #5 Copy the file hot.gif from the book's CD to the same disk directory on your personal computer as the other files. Use this image as a bullet for the unordered list at the bottom of chapter6.html. Save the file, and refresh/reload the browser display.

▶▶ IMAGE LINKS

We live in a multicultural, visual world with universal street signs and dashboard buttons. Therefore, it is easy to justify using images as hyperlinks to help users navigate around our Web sites. But be careful not to fall victim to the latest chic of *replacing* textual links with icons or images. Descriptive text should always accompany an image link to support text-only browsers and browsers that use speech synthesis.

Image links are created by including the image's URL, usually the path and filename, within an anchor container. The image becomes a link to the URL specified in the anchor. For example, today it is common to have the link to the home page appear as a little house (see Figure 6.17). The HTML code to make the home.gif file a link to the home page (index.html) looks like this:

```
<a href="index.html"><img src="home.gif" alt="Link to Home Page" /></a>
```

The Web page in Figure 6.17 utilizes seven image links. It is easy to fill a page with images, each a link somewhere, but try to resist the mountain-climber mindset: don't put images on your page just because they can be there. As we discussed at the beginning of the chapter, each image you place on your page should have a definite purpose. Its purpose should justify the space it is taking up on the page and the time it takes to download.

Figure 6.17   HTML code to create image links with and without borders

```
<html>
<head>
<title>Image Links</title>
</head>

<body>
<h2 align="center">Book Reviews</h2>
<a href="cooking.html"><img src="pepper.gif" alt="Cooking" align="middle" /></a> - Cooking
<br /><br />
<a href="ideas.html"><img src="ideas.gif" alt="Ideas" align="middle" /></a> - Great Ideas
<br /><br />
<a href="movies.html"><img src="movies.gif" alt="Movies" align="middle" /></a> - Movie Reviews
<br /><br />
<a href="music.html"><img src="music.gif" alt="Music" align="middle" /></a> - Music Reviews
<br /><br />
<a href="mystery.html"><img src="mystery.gif" alt="Mysteries" align="middle" /></a> - Mysteries
<br /><br />
<a href="travel.html"><img src="travel.gif" alt="Travel" align="middle" /></a> - Travelogues

<hr width="50%" align="center" />
<p align="center">
  <a href="index.html">
    Back to Home Page<br />
    <img src="home.gif" alt="Link to Home Page" style="border-style: none;" />
  </a>
</p>
</body>
</html>
```

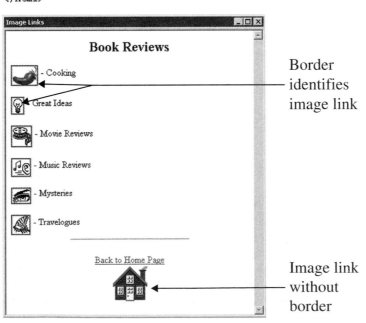

Border identifies image link

Image link without border

Normally a browser will indicate text that is a link by making it a different color and underlining it, as you have seen in previous examples. If an image defines a link, the browsers usually surround the image with a 2-pixel border that is the same color as has been set for link text. The default color is blue for unvisited links and purple for links that have been visited.

Some image links don't look good when surrounded by a border. For instance, a border around the home-page image link of home.gif at the bottom of Figure 6.17 would interfere with the underlined text link above it. The image border was turned off by setting the border-style property to **none** using this code:

```
<img src="home.gif" alt="Link to Home Page" style="border-style: none;" />
```

If you choose to use a borderless image link like this, you must tell the user that the image is a link. At the bottom of the HTML document in Figure 6.17, the text "Back to Home Page," along with the image link of home.gif is included in the anchor container, making both of them hyperlinks.

EXPLORATION #6

Copy the files demo.html, demo.gif, and button.gif from the book's CD to the same disk directory on your personal computer as the other files. Modify chapter6.html to include button.gif as an image link to demo.html at the bottom of the document. The alternative text describing the link should say "*Animated GIF Demonstration.*" Save the file, and refresh/reload the browser display.

▸▸ TWO HTML CODING TRICKS

There are two HTML coding tricks that are not part of the HTML 4 recommendations but are currently recognized by the popular graphical browsers: the **lowsrc** image attribute and the <nobr> tag. We introduce these elements here because Tim G. likes to talk about them in class and because you might encounter them when reading HTML code written by others. Besides, they are truly wonderful little tricks that any wise Web weaver should know and use to fullest advantage.

lowsrc

The **lowsrc** attribute in the <img /> tag specifies that a low-resolution image be loaded before loading the final image. Usually, but not always, this first image is simply a lower-resolution version of the better image that will take its place. The HTML code would look like this:

```
<img src="bflyhi.gif" lowsrc="bflylow.gif" alt="Painted Lady butterfly" />
```

Using the **lowsrc** attribute will speed up the display of the document to the user because the browser will display the lowsrc image the first time it encounters the <img /> tag. Then, after the rest of the page has been displayed, the browser will go back and display the image specified by the **src** attribute. The regular graphic, specified by the **src** attribute, will replace the image first loaded, specified by the **lowsrc** attribute. That way the user doesn't have to wait for the high-resolution image to paint up before she can see the page. One word of warning: be sure that the two images are the same size. If the **lowsrc** image is larger than the final image, parts of it may show "behind" the final image. If the **lowsrc** image is smaller than the final image, the final image might overlay text around the lowsrc image, or only part of the image may display.

HTML   <nobr>No Line Break</nobr>

Description: overrides browser's ability to wrap text to the next line.
Type: container.
Attributes: none.
Special Note: not found in the HTML 4 specifications.

Sometimes it is necessary to display a long line—for example, a line the user should input into the computer. To create a single, unbroken line, you can code the <nobr>text</nobr> container. Text within the container will not be wrapped at the right edge of the browser pane but instead will continue off the right side of the screen, requiring the user to scroll to the right to see the end of the line. The <nobr></nobr> container is most often used to display the following:

1. A line of computer code.

2. A computer input prompt and the associated command as it ought to be typed.

3. Some line of text that would be confusing if it were broken over a line boundary.

4. A long and complex URL.

The <nobr></nobr> also causes a line break before the line if it is longer than the browser window. It is a very intelligent little tag. However, users must use the scroll bar or arrows to see the right side of the line. If they don't notice the scroll bar, they might miss the right end of the line. That is the trade-off you need to make: reducing confusion but possibly pushing data beyond the right margin of the browser pane.

Even though the **lowsrc** attribute and <nobr> tag fall outside the HTML 4 recommendations, the popular browsers recognize them. You won't use them often, but they are handy to know about.

▸▸ TO IMAGE OR NOT TO IMAGE

When you use images on your pages, you must bear in mind that a portion of the Net population will not or cannot use the information contained in images. These are the people who choose to use text-only browsers like Lynx to cruise the Web and those who turn off the automatic image download on graphical browsers. They usually fall into one of three categories:

1. Users with slow modems who don't want to spend lots of time and/or money downloading images.

2. Users with a visual impairment. Many of these users employ text-to-speech software to gather information from the Net. They are candidates for using the aural style sheets discussed in Chapter Eight.

3. Users who want to access lots of information quickly and don't care about "pretty pictures" turn off the automatic image download function of their browser.

To accommodate these users, the wise Web weaver never includes important information that is available only in an image. It is really tempting to scan in a complex table, store the data as an image, and place the image of the table on the page. Unfortunately, the information from that table is available only to those who use graphical browsers.

An additional problem with placing information only in images is that most search engines ignore images. If you want the search engines to find the information you are providing to the world, that information must be presented as text, not as an image.

However, the best argument for a judicious use of images on your pages is the time it takes to download images. Each image you include causes the browser to establish another download session with your page. Users must wait until all the images are downloaded before they have the complete content of your page. Many times the page will not begin to paint up until the majority, or all, of the images are downloaded. Serious users do not want to wait for the pictures to show up. You, too, may have had the experience of waiting and waiting for a page to download, then finally clicking on the "Stop" button and moving on to another page rather than waiting further. Wise Web authors will not force their users to wait to see pictures.

The Opera browser is an excellent tool to demonstrate this since it displays text and image downloading information in the status bar. If you open a page with images in Opera, you will see that the text loads to 100 percent very quickly, while the bulk of the download time is spent loading the images.

▸▸ KEY TERMS

Animated GIF	Inline image
Baseline	Lossless compression
Bits per pixel (bpp)	Lossy compression
Dithering	Open standard
External image	Progressive image
Floating image	Rollover
Flood filling	Thumbnail image
Image editor	Vector graphic

▸▸ NEW TAGS

<img />
<nobr></nobr>

▸▸ REVIEW QUESTIONS

1. Define each of the key terms.
2. How is each of the tags introduced in this chapter used?
3. What filename extension is associated with each of the following image formats?
   a. Bit-Mapped Picture
   b. Graphics Interchange Format
   c. Joint Photographers Experts Group Format
   d. Portable Data Format
   e. Portable Network Graphics
   f. Scalar Vector Graphic
   g. Tagged Image File Format
4. What is the difference between a plain and transparent GIF image?
5. What type of image is best saved as a GIF file and what type is best saved as a JPEG file?
6. Describe a situation where using a lossy compression format could get you into trouble.
7. How many colors are associated with 1 bpp, 4 bpp, 8 bpp, 16 bpp, and 24 bpp?

8. What are six ways you can reduce the download time of an HTML document?

9. What HTML tag is associated with the XHTML Image module?

10. What are the three schools of thought regarding where you should store images?

11. What are two situations where a browser would not display an image?

12. What are five different ways you can align an image? Which of these uses the **style** attribute's float property?

13. How do you break a line of text that is floating next to an image?

14. What are two different ways to center an image within the screen display?

15. How do you establish a border around an image and change the border's width and color?

16. Briefly describe two ways to create unordered lists that use images as bullets.

17. What should always accompany an image link?

18. What is the major consideration when using images?

▶▶ EXERCISES

6.1. Ruby wants pictures! After all, her business is a visual thing, gems are pretty, so she wants to show them off. The images* are on the student CD. They are all labeled as GIF, JPEG, or PNG files. Each filename tells you what gem is in the file. The file gem.gif is the little icon you should use as the list bullet for the list below. The text from the page, without any HTML code is on your student CD in the file ch06rough.html. You should save the final product as ch06-images.html. The page should conform to the following specifications:

    a. The page should have a title of *"Opal, the Fire Stone."* It should have the standard heading for Gwen's shop followed by a centered, level-2 heading that matches the title.

    b. All headings should be in a sans serif font.

    c. The level-1 heading should be 24 pt and dark green, #336600.

    d. The level-2 heading should be 18 pt and deep purple, #330066.

    e. Just below the heading there should be an image of an opal, centered on the page. The image you use is called lopal.gif, and it should be centered under the first level-2 heading. This should be followed by three horizontal rules, 50 percent, 75 percent, and 50 percent wide.

    f. After the first paragraph, there should be a level-2 heading that says, *"Beautiful Opals."*

    g. Then you should have a series of three images of opals in the rough, each one a link to the finished or polished opal associated with that rough stone. Each image should be in its own paragraph, and the descriptive text should flow next to each image. There should also be a single horizontal rule between each pair of paragraphs. The images should alternate sides of the page, with the first and third on the left, and the second on the right side of the page. You should set 10 percent padding between the page boundary and the image. Each image should link to one of the three polished pages described next.

    h. The three polished pages should have the standard headings, with styles that match exactly the images page. That means the same color choices, font choices, and so on. The polished image should be centered on the page, just below three horizontal rules, 50 percent, 75 percent, and 50 percent. Use the following information to create each page:

        1. The first image should be of the Mexican Cherry Opal. The rough image is cherryopalr.jpg and the finished image is cherryopalp.jpg. The finished image should be placed on the page called ch06gems-mexcher.html. You will need to modify your copies of each of these pages to include the images, links back to the calling page, and the other necessary HTML code. The text for the page is found in the file on your CD entitled ch06raw-cherryopal.html.

2. The second image should be the black opal. The rough image is blackopalr.jpg and the finished image is blackopalp.jpg. The raw text is in the file ch06raw-blopal.html. Use these images and text to create ch06gems-blopal.html, which includes links back to the calling page and the other necessary HTML code.

3. The third image is of the Mexican Fire Opal. Rough image is mexfireopalr.jpg, and the finished image is mexfireopalp.jpg. Use these images and the text file ch06raw-mxfireopal.html to create ch06gems-mxfireopal.html, which includes links back to the calling page and the other necessary HTML code.

i. The list of available colors, following the images section, should be preceded by a level-2 heading that reads "*Colors Available.*" That list should use the gem.gif image as a bullet rather than the default bullets.

j. The standard address information at the bottom of each of the pages should be preceded by a 50 percent horizontal rule.

k. All pages should be XML-compliant, well-documented, and able to pass validation. Since you know how to use styles now, you should have no compliance error messages.
   * Our thanks to Hershel Friedman of www.minerals.net and the Gem Hut, www.gemhut.com, for their kind permission to use the images included with this exercise.

6.2. Using a nontransparent image and text of your own choosing, create a Web page that demonstrates each of the possible alignments: top, middle, bottom, left, and right. Make sure the text allows you to demonstrate the alignments correctly. The title bar should display "Image Alignment Options," with your name and the assignment due date included within comment lines.

6.3. Surf the Web to find at least five nice, small (1 to 3 kilobytes), public-domain images. Download them and insert them into a new HTML document. Include **alt** descriptions for each object you insert. The title bar should display "My Favorite Images," with your name and the assignment due date included within comment lines. Turn off auto-loading of images on your browser, or use a text-only browser to verify that your **alt** description works. Print two copies of the page: one with the images turned on and one without the images.

6.4. Retrieve the Homework home page you updated in Exercise 5.4. Use a digital camera, scanner, or free-drawing software to create an image of yourself, and insert it into the page. Make sure you include an **alt** description that your mother would approve of.

6.5. Retrieve your school's home page that you updated in Exercise 5.5. Use a digital camera or scanner to obtain an image of the school that you think reflects positively on you and your fellow classmates, and insert the image into the page. Make sure you have an **alt** description that does the image justice.

6.6. Retrieve the Web page about your favorite movie that you created in Exercise 2.6 (and possibly updated in Exercises 3.6, 4.6, and 5.6). Use the Internet to find at least one related image about the movie and add this image to the Web page. Give your resource credit for the image as part of the related **alt** description.

6.7. Create a new HTML document with an image you have found on the Net. The title bar should display "My Favorite Objects," with your name and the assignment due date included within comment lines. Put text on the page explaining where you found the image. Create an image link to the site where the image was found so that your user can go harvest other images from that site. Demonstrate (a) how the object can be centered by itself with no text around it and (b) how it can be aligned with text on either the right or left.

6.8. Create a personal animated GIF you can use as your signature on Web pages you design. The file should not exceed 15 kilobytes in size. A popular image editor like Corel Draw or shareware like Animagic can be used.

Chapter Seven

Tables: Data in Rows and Columns

We saw in Chapter Four how lists could help our user process information efficiently. Now let's look at the way tables help present information in the most efficient manner possible. Before tables were built into HTML, the only reasonable way to create tabular data (rows and columns) was to use a <pre></pre> container or to capture the data in an image. But the <pre></pre> container could not provide the power or the flexibility gained with the table tags.

CHAPTER OBJECTIVES

After reading this chapter you should be able to do the following:

- Insert a table into an HTML document.
- Manipulate the style, color, and width of a table's border.
- Set the size of a table's margin, cell spacing, and cell padding.
- Change a table's width within the browser pane and cell width within the table.
- Use browser-safe background colors within a table.
- Float text to the left or right of a table.
- Span table data or headers across several rows or columns.
- Place captions above or below a table.
- Independently format individual tables or groups of table rows or columns.
- Identify the HTML elements found in the XHTML Table module.

▸▸ WHAT'S IN A TABLE?

The table is the most concise, direct, and efficient tool for presenting certain types of data. Numeric data, data that show a relationship, any data that are usually displayed in a spreadsheet—all are excellent candidates for an HTML table. In addition, tables are a great way to present related data, like pictures with their descriptions. Because of its utility, the table feature was one of the first features extended into HTML 2.0. It became standard in release 3.0.

Tables are composed of *rows* of data running across the screen and *columns* that run up and down:

C
R O W
L
U
M
N

The intersection of a row and a column is called a *cell.* Most browsers consider each cell a unique entity, and they arrange the data to fit within the space allowed by that cell. Some special formatting provisions and extensions exist that we will discuss later in this

Figure 7.1

HTML code for a 2-by-3 table with caption

```
<html>
<head>
<title>2 by 3 Table</title>
</head>

<body>
The table following is just a simple 2 x 3 table.  It has very few fancy
attributes, but it does show how the parts of the table fit together.
<table border="5">
<caption align="bottom"> This caption is aligned to the bottom.</caption>
<tr>
  <td>Row1/Column1</td>
  <td> R1/C2</td>
  <td> R1/C3</td>
</tr>
<tr>
  <td>R2/C1</td>
  <td>R2/C2</td>
  <td>R2/C3</td>
</tr>
</table>
The table in this example has 6 cells and this text starts below the table.
</body>
</html>
```

2 by 3 Table

The table following is just a simple 2 x 3 table. It has very few fancy attributes, but it does show how the parts of the table fit together.

| Row1/Column1 | R1/C2 | R1/C3 |
| R2/C1 | R2/C2 | R2/C3 |

This caption is aligned to the bottom.

The table in this example has 6 cells and this text starts below the table.

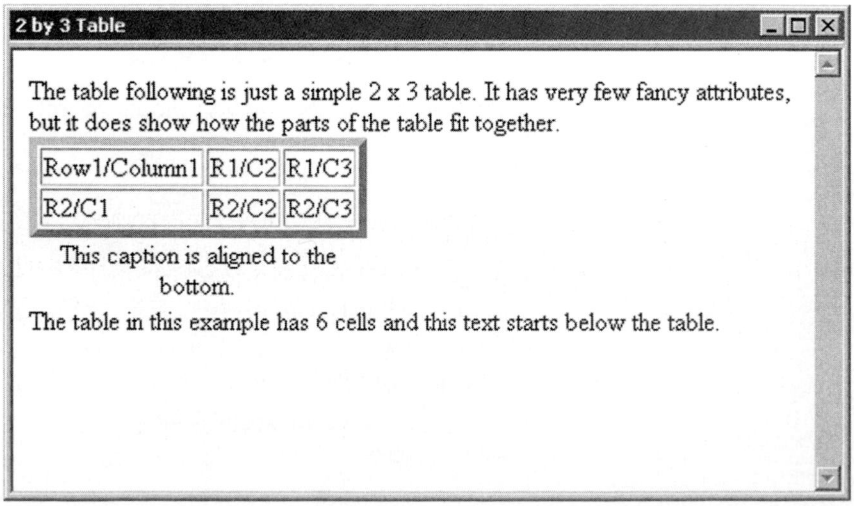

chapter, but for the most part, you can think of each cell as a unique, albeit small, page unto itself. Every table must have at least one row and at least one cell. Everything in a table must be contained within a cell except the caption.

Tables are referred to by row first and by column second. A 2-by-3, or 2 × 3, table has two rows and three columns (Figure 7.1). As you begin to code tables, you will see why this convention is followed. To build a table, you must first declare a row and then declare the elements of each column in that row. Each cell in a table has a row and column address, with the row address preceding the column address.

Nearly anything you can put into an HTML document can be put into the cell of a table, including other tables. You can put in images, rules, headings, lists, and even forms.

▸▸ TABLE CONTAINERS

The original world of tables included five relatively sophisticated tags:

1. <table> . . . </table> encloses the table.

2. <th> . . . </th> defines the table headers.

3. <tr> . . . </tr> defines the table rows.

4. <td> . . . </td> surrounds the actual table data.

5. <caption> . . . </caption> allows you to place a caption either above or below the table.

The latest HTML specifications added five new table tags that let you format table columns and format and scroll portions of long tables.

1. <tbody> . . . </tbody> identifies a scrollable area of a table.

2. <thead> . . . </thead> appears above the scrolling body.

3. <tfoot> . . . </tfoot> appears below the scrolling body.

4. <colgroup> . . . </colgroup> provides means for combining a group of columns in a table.

5. <col /> allows you to control the appearance or attribute specifications for one or more table columns.

Figure 7.1 presents the code for a simple table so that you can see how all the parts fit together. We will discuss each of the table tags in detail, but it's worthwhile to look at a simple table first. As you can see, the coding for a table is just a little more complicated than anything we have considered so far.

It is a good idea to draw your table on paper before you start coding it so that you know how many rows and columns you need and what headings you want to use. As your tables get more complex, this design step will be more and more important. Drawing the table on paper may end up saving you a great deal of time.

The only special attribute used in this example is **border,** which makes the outer frame around the table a little larger. (This attribute will be discussed in detail later.) The caption appears beneath the table as a result of using the **align** attribute set to bottom. Otherwise, this is a plain vanilla table meant to give you the basic idea of how a table is built.

HTML   <table>Table</table>

Description: defines the rows and columns that make up a table.
Type: container.
Attributes: *align,* **bgcolor, border, cellspacing, cellpadding,** class, **frame,** dir, id, lang, onclick, ondblclick, onkeydown, onkeypress, onkeyup, onmousedown, onmousemove, onmouseout, onmouseover, onmouseup, **rules, style, summary,** title, **width.**

The <table> </table> container surrounds the whole table. The browser will stop the current text flow, break the line, insert the table at the beginning of a new line, then restart the text flow on another new line following the table. Normally the table picks up the alignment of the current paragraph, so most tables are aligned left. If the paragraph containing the table is centered, <p style="text-align: center;">, or if the container encloses the table, then the table could be aligned in the center of the page.

Although a *cell* in a table can contain almost any other HTML structure that can appear on a page (obviously tags like <html> or <body> won't work in a table), only the <tr></tr> and the <caption></caption> containers are allowed and recognized within the <table></table> container. A 3-by-2 demonstration table is shown in Figure 7.2. This table has no attributes coded.

Figure 7.2

HTML code for a 3-by-2 table without attributes

```
<html>
<head>
<title>3 by 2 Table</title>
</head>

<body>
<h3>The Team's Home Schedule</h3>

<table>
<tr>
  <td>Dallas</td>
  <td>November 5th</td>
</tr>
<tr>
  <td>Detroit</td>
  <td>November 11th</td>
</tr>
<tr>
  <td>Toronto</td>
  <td>November 17th</td>
</tr>
</table>

</body>
</html>
```

border

The **border** is the line around the table and between each cell. The table in Figure 7.1 has a border defined; the table in Figure 7.2 does not. The border attribute allows you to tell the browser whether or not to put a border around the table and how wide to make the border. A border can be subdivided into frames and rules. The *frame* is the line that surrounds the whole table. A *rule* is the horizontal or vertical line that separates the rows and columns of cells.

The default **border** attribute value is 1, meaning there will be a 1-pixel border around the table and around each of the cells in the table. The table in the top right of Figure 7.3 has a 1-pixel border. If you code a number larger than 1, the browsers will make a wider border around the table, but the division between cells will still be a 1-pixel border (unless you code a **cellspacing** attribute, discussed later). For example, the table in Figure 7.1 has a border of 5 pixels because of this code:

```
<table border="5">
```

If you code a zero or omit the **border** attribute, there will be no border around the table or any of the cells. Even without a border there will still be some space between the cell contents, for example, the space between "Toronto" and "November 17th" in Figure 7.2. This space between the cells is referred to as *padding* and will be further discussed later on.

rules

The **rules** attribute controls the border around individual cells. If you want to maintain continuous lines around the table (the frame), but not within or between the table rows or

Figure 7.3

HTML code for the **rules** attribute, controlling which lines separating table cells are displayed in a table

```
<html>
<head>
<title>3 by 2 Table</title>
</head>

<body>
<h3>The Team's Home Schedule</h3>

<table rules="rows">
<tr>
  <td>Dallas</td>
  <td>November 5th</td>
</tr>
<tr>
  <td>Detroit</td>
  <td>November 11th</td>
</tr>
<tr>
  <td>Toronto</td>
  <td>November 17th</td>
</tr>
</table>

</body>
</html>
```

rules="none"

Dallas	November 5th
Detroit	November 11th
Toronto	November 17th

rules="cols

Dallas	November 5th
Detroit	November 11th
Toronto	November 17th

rules="all"

Dallas	November 5th
Detroit	November 11th
Toronto	November 17th

3 by 2 Table

File Edit View Favorites Tools Help

The Team's Home Schedule

Dallas	November 5th
Detroit	November 11th
Toronto	November 17th

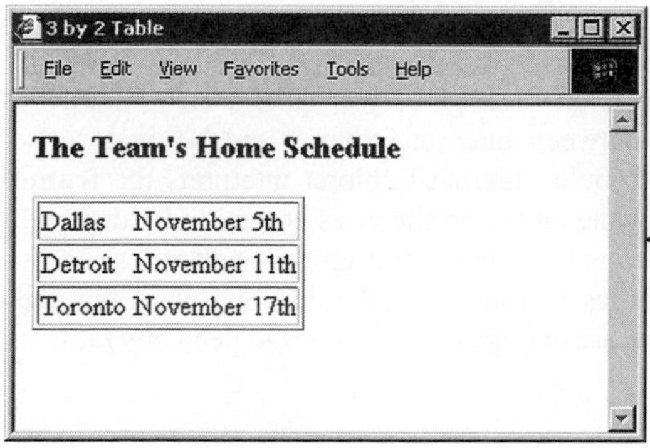

columns, you need to use the **rules** attribute. This attribute specifies which rules appear between cells within a table, as shown in Figure 7.3. The ability to manipulate cell rules was new with the HTML 4 specifications and is currently recognized only by Internet Explorer. The following values are identified by the specifications:

- none: no rules, just the outside frame (default).
- rows: horizontal rules will appear between rows only.
- cols: vertical rules will appear between columns only.
- all: rules will appear between all rows and columns.
- groups: rules will appear between row groups (see <thead>, <tfoot>, and <tbody>) and column groups (see <colgroup> and <col>) only.

The basic code for turning on the horizontal rules for the table's rows looks like this:

```
<table rules="rows">
```

The results are shown in Figure 7.3.

frame

The **frame** attribute specifies which sides of a table's border—that is, the frame—are visible. Whereas the **border** attribute determines a border's thickness (in pixels), the frame attribute turns different border combinations on and off, as shown in Figure 7.4. This attribute is new with the HTML 4 specifications and currently recognized by Internet Explorer and Navigator, but not by Opera. The following values are identified by the specifications:

- border: all four sides.
- box: all four sides.
- void: no sides (default).
- above: top sides only.
- below: bottom sides only.
- hsides: top and bottom sides only—horizontal sides.
- vsides: right and left sides only—vertical sides.
- lhs: left-hand side only.
- rhs: right-hand side only.

Setting frame="void", like setting border ="0", produces the same result as just omitting the attribute. Omitting the attribute is illustrated in Figure 7.2. An example of frame="void" is shown in Figure 7.4.

HTML code to turn on a 1-pixel border could use the **frame** attribute like this:

```
<table frame="border">
```

These results, as shown in Figure 7.4, would also occur by setting the border equal to a width of 1 pixel with this code:

```
<table border="1">
```

The **frame** attribute gives you quite a bit of control of the frame around the table. Differences between Internet Explorer and Navigator also come into sharp focus when using this attribute. Internet Explorer interprets the **frame** attribute by manipulating the frame around the table *and* the rules around individual cells. Navigator manipulates only the frame around the table and ignores cell rules, shown in Figure 7.4. Between the **frame** and **rules** attributes and the differing ways the popular browser handles these attributes, there are enough combinations to keep any table junkie happy.

Figure 7.4 HTML code for the **frame** attribute, controlling which sides of a border are displayed with a table

```html
<html>
<head>
<title>3 by 2 Table</title>
</head>

<body>
<h3>The Team's Home Schedule</h3>

<table frame="above">
<tr>
  <td>Dallas</td>
  <td>November 5th</td>
</tr>
<tr>
  <td>Detroit</td>
  <td>November 11th</td>
</tr>
<tr>
  <td>Toronto</td>
  <td>November 17th</td>
</tr>
</table>

</body>
</html>
```

Internet Explorer

`frame="box"` or `frame="border"`

Dallas	November 5th
Detroit	November 11th
Toronto	November 17th

`frame="hsides"`

Dallas November 5th
Detroit November 11th
Toronto November 17th

`frame="lhs"`

Dallas November 5th
Detroit November 11th
Toronto November 17th

`frame="rhs"`

Dallas November 5th
Detroit November 11th
Toronto November 17th

`frame="vsides"`

Dallas November 5th
Detroit November 11th
Toronto November 17th

`frame="below"`

Dallas November 5th
Detroit November 11th
Toronto November 17th

`frame="void"`

Dallas November 5th
Detroit November 11th
Toronto November 17th

Navigator

`frame="box"` or `frame="border"`

Dallas	November 5th
Detroit	November 11th
Toronto	November 17th

`frame="hsides"`

Dallas November 5th
Detroit November 11th
Toronto November 17th

`frame="lhs"`

Dallas November 5th
Detroit November 11th
Toronto November 17th

`frame="rhs"`

Dallas November 5th
Detroit November 11th
Toronto November 17th

`frame="vsides"`

Dallas November 5th
Detroit November 11th
Toronto November 17th

`frame="below"`

Dallas November 5th
Detroit November 11th
Toronto November 17th

`frame="void"`

Dallas November 5th
Detroit November 11th
Toronto November 17th

---

3 by 2 Table
File Edit View Favorites Tools Help

The Team's Home Schedule

Dallas	November 5th
Detroit	November 11th
Toronto	November 17th

---

3 by 2 Table - Netscape 6

The Team's Home Schedule

Dallas November 5th
Detroit November 11th
Toronto November 17th

width

The **width** attribute controls how wide a table is—that is, how much of the horizontal browser-pane real estate is covered by the table. Normally the browser will make the table wide enough to present the data you have put into the table, with a little padding. You cannot make the table smaller than the minimum size necessary to present the information you have coded. You can, however, make the table wider than necessary.

As with the horizontal rule (<hr />), there are two ways to code the **width** attribute for a table: either as a fixed number of pixels or as a percentage of the screen width (see Figure 7.5). Good practice is to always code in percentages, because different monitors have different resolutions (pixels per inch), so some pixels are bigger than others. Coding a width in pixels can also lead to problems if you are expecting to put a particular amount of text next to a table and have it coded in pixels. On a low-resolution screen (big pixels), there will not be as much room next to the table as on a high-resolution screen. Coding your table width as a percentage of the screen will often eliminate this problem. Figure 7.5 shows a version of our table coded so it will take up roughly 25 percent of the browser pane. The following code is used:

```
<table width="25%">
```

Now compare the table's width to the horizontal rule that is also coded to be 25 percent of the page's width. The browser could not reduce the table's width to exactly

Figure 7.5

HTML code showing that a table's width can never be smaller than the sum of the length of the longest word in each cell in the columns plus the padding and spacing

```
<html>
<head>
<title>3 by 2 Table</title>
</head>

<body>
<h3>The Team's Home Schedule</h3>
<hr width="25%" align="left" />

<table width="25%" border="5">
<tr>
  <td>Dallas</td>
  <td>November 5th</td>
</tr>
<tr>
  <td>Detroit</td>
  <td>November 11th</td>
</tr>
<tr>
  <td>Toronto</td>
  <td>November 17th</td>
</tr>
</table>

</body>
</html>
```

Actual 25% width of screen

25 percent because a table's cell becomes only as small as the largest word in a column. Cells with two words will wrap one word under the other when the table is displayed in a small window, like the dates in Figure 7.5. You cannot use the **width** attribute to make the table smaller than is necessary to display the data. For example, if we coded a width of 10 percent, the table would still be as wide as it is in Figure 7.5. In other words, the browser will not compress the table by hyphenating words or by hiding data.

The HTML 4 recommendations do contain the style property of table-layout, which can override this longstanding limit to a table's width. While we can see few applications for this property: value pair, if table-layout is set to **fixed** value, several browsers will set the table's width at this value even if it means clipping off some of the table data or running it beyond the table's border! Currently none of the popular browsers handle this property: value pair in the same way. Obviously, the possibility of losing data from the table is a very Bad Thing.

TABLE BACKGROUND COLOR

It is possible with the popular graphical browsers to change the color of the background for the text inside the table using the **bgcolor** attribute or the **style** attribute's background-color property. As in other places where you code color, you can use either the standard color names (a practice we discourage) or the hexadecimal codes for the table background (see color insert in the Reference Guide). The following code would set the background to light yellow:

<table style="background-color: "#FFFCC">

As with the background color on your page, you should make sure that the background color of your table will work with the color of the font used for the text. The text should strongly contrast with the background color to be easily readable. The **style** attribute's color property is used to change the color of the text displayed in a table cell. As you can see in Figure 7.6, Internet Explorer and Opera continue the background color throughout the table; Navigator limits the color to the cell itself.

Figure 7.6 shows a simple border; all that was coded here was the **border** attribute, set equal to 5 pixels, and a background color. The border defaults to two different shades of gray, creating a three-dimensional effect, as if the border were raised up from the plane of the document. Another thing to be careful of when choosing a background color is that

Figure 7.6

HTML code for changing background color within cells, showing the two different ways the code is handled by the popular browsers

```
<html>
<head>
<title>3 by 2 Table</title>
</head>

<body>
<!-- table's background color is light blue -->
<table border="5" style="background-color: #CCFFFF;">
<tr>
   <td>Dallas</td>
   <td>November 5th</td>
</tr>
<tr>
   <td>Detroit</td>
   <td>November 11th</td>
</tr>
<tr>
   <td>Toronto</td>
   <td>November 17th</td>
</tr>
</table>
</body>
</html>
```

Dallas	November 5th
Detroit	November 11th
Toronto	November 17th

Navigator

Dallas	November 5th
Detroit	November 11th
Toronto	November 17th

Internet Explorer and Opera

with the wrong color, you can lose part of the border. If your background is too dark, you will lose the bottom and right sides of the border. If your background is too light, you will usually lose the upper and left sides of the border.

summary

The **summary** attribute is specifically intended for users relying on aural presentations of a Web page. It provides a brief description of the table that is heard but not displayed on the screen. The HTML code looks like this:

```
<TABLE summary="This year's Home games include Dallas on November 5th,
Detroit on November 11th and Toronto on November 17th.">
```

It should go without saying that the conscientious Web weaver will always include a brief descriptive summary of the content and structure of each table.

EXPLORATION #1

Copy the file colors.html from the book's CD to a disk drive on your personal computer. Open it using an ASCII editor, and change the <title> container to *your name's Hexadecimal Color Chart.* Make the following changes to the table:

- Add a border that is 7 pixels wide.
- Make the table's width 40 percent of the browser pane.
- Change the table's background color to gray (#CCCCCC).

Save the file as chapter7.html, and display it using your favorite browser.

▸▸ CHANGING STANDARDS

It is important to realize that each new release of the popular graphical browsers incorporates some of the tags and attributes that were formerly unique to some other browser or new to the HTML recommendations. In this way the *standard* is increased even without official sanction. For example, before Release 6 of Navigator, the **frame** attribute was an option recognized only by Internet Explorer. Now both browsers support it. In this way more and more features are available to the Web weaver as the browsers continue to evolve.

style

Table formatting in particular has gone through an evolution that has given Web weavers more control over the look, sizing, and placement of tables on the screen. The use of the **style** attribute has brought the old way of formatting borders into conflict with the new style-sheet terminology and formatting practices. The original use of the **border** attribute created a border that was a frame of a designated width around the table data and 1-pixel rules separating each cell. The code looks like this and is shown in Figure 7.7:

```
<table border="5">
```

border: width | style | color

The border generated by the code of <table border ="5"> is not visually the same as the borders discussed in Chapter Six that were created using the **style** attribute (see Figure 7.7). Rules around the table cells are created only when the **border** attribute is used in the <table> beginning tag. The style properties, border-style, border-width, and border-color, can be used with tables, but no rules are generated within the table. The following code generates a 5-pixel frame around a table but no cell rules:

```
<table style="border-style: solid; border=width: 5px;">
```

This is also true for the shortcut property, border, which allows you to designate the frame's width, style, and color within a single property. The following code produces the same 5-pixel border as the preceding code (see Figure 7.7):

```
<table style="border: 5px solid #000000;">
```

Figure 7.7 HTML code showing how the table is displayed differently depending on whether the **border** or **style** attribute is used to create it

```
<html>
<head>
<title>Traditional Use of Border</title>
</head>

<body>
<h3>The Team's Home Schedule</h3>

<table border="5">
<tr>
  <td>Dallas</td>
  <td>November 5th</td>
</tr>
<tr>
  <td>Detroit</td>
  <td>November 11th</td>
</tr>
<tr>
  <td>Toronto</td>
  <td>November 17th</td>
</tr>
</table>
<br>

</body>
</html>
```

```
<html>
<head>
<title>Border as a Style Property</title>
</head>

<body>
<h3>The Team's Home Schedule</h3>

<table style="border: 5px solid #000000;">
<tr>
  <td>Dallas</td>
  <td>November 5th</td>
</tr>
<tr>
  <td>Detroit</td>
  <td>November 11th</td>
</tr>
<tr>
  <td>Toronto</td>
  <td>November 17th</td>
</tr>
</table>

</body>
</html>
```

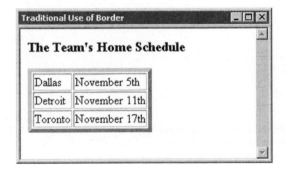

This border application is consistent with borders that are placed around images or other objects. If you want cell rules in a table, we recommend combining the **border** attribute with the **style** attribute. A 5-pixel dashed gray border is created around a table with cell rules using this code:

```
<table border="5" style="border: dashed #CCCCCC;">
```

The introduction of the **style** attribute as part of the HTML 4 specifications has had a broad impact on coding practices for style sheets and inline formatting. The new emphasis on style as part of more dynamic HTML code has given rise to several style properties that affect a table's format. Some, like the border-color, float, and margin properties, have been discussed in earlier chapters. Two new properties control the white space in and around table cells. Together, used in different combinations, these properties give Web weavers new design tools for their Web pages.

border-color: color | transparent

Although Internet Explorer and Navigator still recognize the old **border-color** attribute the "official" way to change the color is with the **style** attribute's border-color property. As mentioned before, you can use either the standard color names or the hexadecimal codes (which is the better way) as property values. We recommend using the hexadecimal codes because older browsers recognize them. For instance, this code sets the border color to red (#FF0000):

```
<table border="5" style ="border-color: #FF0000">
```

If the border-color is set to **transparent**, then the document's background color should be used in the border. However, the border can disappear into the background. Only Navigator recognizes this property value.

float: left | right | none

Tables are objects, like images, that are placed within the browser pane. Yet, unlike images, tables are not part of the normal text flow. Instead, they signal a break in the flow. Normally text flows above or below a table but not next to it. The original way of changing that was with the **align** attribute, which specifies the margin to which the table is jus-

Figure 7.8

HTML code showing how a table is floated to the right of some text using the **style** attribute's float property

```
<html>
<head>
<title>3 by 2 Table Using Style Attribute</title>
</head>

<body>
<h3>The Team's Home Schedule</h3>

<table border="5" style="float: right;">
<tr>
  <td>Dallas</td>
  <td>November 5th</td>
</tr>
<tr>
  <td>Detroit</td>
  <td>November 11th</td>
</tr>
<tr>
  <td>Toronto</td>
  <td>November 17th</td>
</tr>
</table>

Show the home team your support by attending one of the remaining
home games. Our guys need to hear from you as they battle for the
championship. It's a lot of fun, so bring the whole family!
</body>
</html>
```

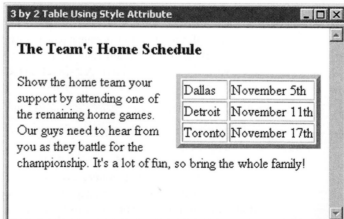

tified, causing the text to flow around the table if there is room. For example, the following code would right-align the table and allow text to flow along the left side of the table:

```
<table border ="5" align="right">
```

This HTML code would produce results similar to those shown in Figure 7.8. Notice how the text now flows to the left of the table.

The **align** attribute recommended in the HTML 3.2 specifications has been deprecated in favor of the **style** attribute's float property, in which a table is floated to the left or right of the text. The following HTML code would align a table along the right margin and float text to the left:

```
<table border="5" style="float: right">
```

When the **style** attribute's float property is set right as shown in Figure 7.8, text is floated to the left of the table. You can also set float to none in which case the text flow is broken above the table and resumed below it.

EXPLORATION #2

Add to the beginning table tag in chapter7.html a **style** attribute that includes properties and values that do the following:

• Use a double border style.

• Change border color to a dark gray (#666666).

• Place the table of the left side of the browser pane with the text floating to the right.

Save the file and refresh/reload the browser display.

▸▸ CONTROLLING WHITE SPACE

The look and placement of a table is controlled to a great degree by the white space around the table, between cells, and within the table cell itself. Figure 7.9 illustrates these three areas that are known as the *margin* (white space around the table), the *cell spacing* (white space between table cells), and the *cell padding* (white space between cell data and the cell rules). This white space is not always white, since you can change the color by using the **bgcolor** attribute or the **style** attribute's background-color property.

Figure 7.9

Table white space

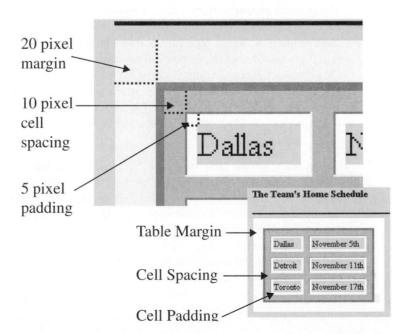

20 pixel margin

10 pixel cell spacing

5 pixel padding

Table Margin

Cell Spacing

Cell Padding

Nevertheless, the size of these spaces (no matter what color) is under the control of knowledgeable Web designers.

Table Margins

Any object within an HTML document can have margins. Image margins were discussed in Chapter Six, and page margins will be discussed in Chapter Eight. By setting a table's margins, you can vertically and/or horizontally offset it from other elements on the page. A margin's size can be set using pixels (px), inches (in), millimeters (mm), centimeters (cm), or ems (the width of the font's uppercase M). The example shown in Figure 7.9 uses a 20-pixel margin. The code to create a margin like this follows:

```
<table style="margin: 20px;">
```

Cell Spacing

Another area you can control within a table is the distance between cells. The **cellspacing** attribute and the **style** attribute's border-spacing property both allow the Web weaver to set the distance between the cell rules as well as between the cell rules and the table's border (see Figure 7.10). The results make each cell in a table stand out. Setting the cell spacing to zero will create the narrowest possible interior cell borders. The code for setting the **cellspacing** attribute looks like this:

```
<table cellspacing="10">
```

All the popular browsers recognize this code. The same results are achieved by setting the border-spacing property to 10 pixels as follows:

```
<table style="border" border-spacing: 10px;">
```

At this time only Navigator and Opera recognize this application of the border-spacing property.

Figure 7.10 shows the result of cell spacing set to 10 pixels. Notice how the white space between the cells has increased in width and definition. Now let's take away the cell spacing altogether by setting it to zero as illustrated at the bottom right corner of the figure. With the border coded, cell rules become a single combined line. This is the smallest cell spacing available. Notice how cramped and uncomfortable the data look.

Cell Padding

The popular browsers allow you to determine the amount of space (padding) between the data in a cell and the cell rule. This value is set using the **cellpadding** attribute. The default padding is 1 pixel. You can set it to a larger number to make the data appear to float in the middle of the cell, or you can set it to zero to make the cells as small as possible. On previous figures showing the demonstration table, notice how the "N" of "November" seems to almost touch the left border of the cell. The space between the "N" and the border is just 1 pixel, the default value for the space around the data. The table in Figure 7.9 displays a cell padding set to 5 pixels. The code to create this cell padding looks like this:

```
<table cellpadding="5">
```

In the top right table in Figure 7.10, notice how the size of the table has increased compared with the table in Figure 7.8 that was created with default settings. As you can imagine, the use of cell spacing and cell padding set to sizes larger than 5 pixels can greatly expand a table's size, especially tables with long rows of cells. Cell padding increases the space on all sides of the data.

Borders, margins, cell spacing, and cell padding all become part of a table's design and deserve careful consideration when laying out your table. When all of these design elements are used within a single table, you can divide the beginning <table> tag over

Figure 7.10   Examples of cell padding and cell spacing

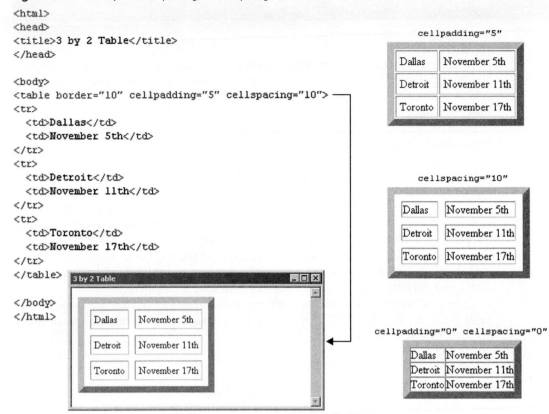

```
<html>
<head>
<title>3 by 2 Table</title>
</head>

<body>
<table border="10" cellpadding="5" cellspacing="10">
<tr>
  <td>Dallas</td>
  <td>November 5th</td>
</tr>
<tr>
  <td>Detroit</td>
  <td>November 11th</td>
</tr>
<tr>
  <td>Toronto</td>
  <td>November 17th</td>
</tr>
</table>

</body>
</html>
```

several lines to make it easier to read, understand, and maintain. For example, the table in Figure 7.9 was created, in part, by the following <table> tag:

```
<table border="5"
    style="border: solid #999999; margin: 20px;"
    cellspacing="10"
    cellpadding="5">
```

This code generates a table with a 5-pixel gray border, 20-pixel margin, 10-pixel cell spacing, and 5-pixel cell padding.

EXPLORATION **#3**   Update the table in chapter7.html to add the following:

- Margin of 12 pixels.
- Cell spacing of 9 pixels.
- Cell padding of 3 pixels.

Save the file and refresh/reload the browser display.

▸▸ TABLE TEXT ALIGNMENT

The <tr>Table Row</tr> container has four attributes that allow you to align the table text in various ways: **align, valign, char,** and **charoff.**

 **\<tr\>Table Row\</tr\>**

Description: defines a table row.
Type: container.
Attributes: align, bgcolor, class, **char, charoff,** dir, id, lang, onclick, ondblclick, onkeydown, onkeypress, onkeyup, onmousedown, onmousemove, onmouseout, onmouseover, onmouseup, style, title, **valign.**
XML: requires using the ending tag.

In HTML, tables are built row first. Each row defines and contains the cells within it that make up the columns. The \<tr\>table row\</tr\> container surrounds the data tags that contain the actual content of a table. Some Web professionals feel you need not code the \</tr\> closing tag, because the browser can infer one when it reaches another \<tr\> or an end-of-table, \</table\>, tag. But skipping the closing tag is not a good idea, because it may cause a compatibility problem with later versions of the browsers. Also, the lack of a closing tag makes finding the end of a particular row just a little harder. Finally, to be XML- and XHTML-compliant every element must have a closing tag.

Some of the attributes for the \<tr\> tag look suspiciously like attributes for the \<table\> tag, but they have different meanings when used with the \<tr\> tag. As an example, let's look at the **align** attribute.

align

When used within the \<table\> tag, the deprecated **align** attribute determines the justification of the table and whether text will flow next to the table. Note that it has not been deprecated for use with the \<tr\> tag. When used within the \<tr\> tag, **align** specifies the horizontal alignment of the data within the cells composing this row. An alignment specified for a particular row affects only the cells in that row, not the cells in other rows. In addition, you can use the **align** attribute to set the common alignment for the row, then change the alignment of one or more particular cells within that row on a cell-by-cell basis.

You will need to set the alignment of the data within cells only if you don't want to use the alignment set by the row, or if that hasn't been set, the defaults. The popular browsers use a default *center* alignment for headers and a *left* alignment for data. So, for example, if you want all the data in a particular row centered rather than left-justified, you can code the align attribute in the \<tr\> tag to set center alignment for all of the cells in that row. Figure 7.11 shows a table with the three different alignments. This table is displayed in a narrow browser pane to show you both horizontal and vertical. It needed to be wide enough to demonstrate how "Align Left" differed from "Align Right," yet narrow enough to make it easy to see the vertical alignment.

You can also align cell values based on a character found in one of the table cells. For example, you might want to align a group of prices on their decimal points or a list of names after a colon. This is accomplished by setting align="char". The character the browser aligns with is specified by the **char** attribute, discussed shortly.

valign

The **valign** attribute is an extension supported by the common browsers. This attribute instructs the browser regarding the vertical placement of the data within the cells in that row. Four different values are available for this attribute. The default is *center*. Then, in addition to *top* and *bottom,* there is a *baseline* value that aligns the data with the bottom of the first row of text in any other cells. This is another example of how the browser

Figure 7.11

HTML code for horizontal and vertical text alignment within table cells

```
<table border="5" width="50%">
<tr align="left">
   <td>Left</td>
   <td>Align Left</td>
</tr>

<tr align="center">
   <td>Center</td>
   <td>Align Center</td>
</tr>

<tr align="right">
   <td>Right</td>
   <td>Align Right</td>
</tr>

<tr valign="top">
   <td>Vertical Alignment Top</td>
   <td>Top</td>
</tr>

<!-- default setting -->
<tr>
   <td>Vertical Alignment Center</td>
   <td>Center</td>
</tr>

<tr valign="bottom">
   <td>Vertical Alignment Bottom</td>
   <td>Bottom</td>
</tr>

<tr valign="baseline">
   <td>Vertical Alignment Baseline</td>
   <td>Baseline</td>
</tr>
</table>
```

Left	Align Left
Center	Align Center
Right	Align Right
Vertical Alignment Top	Top
Vertical Alignment Center	Center
Vertical Alignment Bottom	Bottom
Vertical Alignment Baseline	Baseline

controls the format. In Opera baseline aligns the data with the bottom of the first line of the preceding cell while Navigator aligns with the bottom of the second line in the following cell.

Figure 7.11 shows a table with these different alignments. A different **valign** value was used for *each cell* to illustrate how they all look. Remember, the default for **valign** is centered, so you need to code it only if you want other than centered data.

char

The char attribute allows you to align text based on a specific character, like a period (.) or comma (,). The browser will use the decimal-point character for the current language as set by the **lang** attribute (e.g., the period in English and the comma in French) as the default. To align cell values with a colon, the following code would be used:

```
<tr align="char" char=":">
```

Remember that you will need to code *both* **align** and **char** to align data on a particular character. Interestingly, the W³C does not require browsers to support this attribute.

charoff

Web weavers can offset the alignment of text within a cell by using the **charoff** attribute. When this attribute is employed, it specifies the offset for the first occurrence of the alignment character specified with the **char** attribute. The code to offset text two spaces after a colon looks like this:

```
<tr align="char" char=":" charoff="2">
```

The offset direction is determined by the **dir** attribute. In left-to-right text, like English, offset is from the left margin. In right-to-left text, offset is from the right. If the designated alignment character is missing, the text is shifted horizontally to the end of the alignment position. As with the **char** attribute, the W[3]C does not require browsers to support the **charoff** attribute.

EXPLORATION #4

Use the **style** attribute's background-color property to change the color of each table row in chapter7.html to the associated hexadecimal color. In other words, the background color of the red row should be red, the green row green, and so on. Only in the blue row should you use the **style** attribute's color property to change the text color to white (#FFFFFF). Save the file and refresh/reload the browser display.

▸▸ TABLE DATA AND HEADERS

We have finally reached the containers that hold the actual data in the table. The <td>table data</td> and <th>table header</th> tags surround the information for the table. Each instance of these containers describes one cell in the table. Any content for the table must appear within one of these containers or within the <caption> container. Should you code content that is not enclosed within one of these containers, that will be displayed above, or on top of, the table by the current versions of the popular browsers.

 **<td>Table Data</td>**

Description: defines table data and left-aligns it in cell.
Type: container.
Attributes: abbr, align, axis, bgcolor, class, char, charoff, **colspan,** dir, **headers,** *height,* id, lang, *nowrap,* onclick, ondblclick, onkeydown, onkeypress, onkeyup, onmousedown, onmousemove, onmouseout, onmouseover, onmouseup, **rowspan, scope, style,** title, **valign,** *width.*
XML: requires using the ending tag.

 **<th>Table Header</th>**

Description: defines a table header and centers it in cell. Text is displayed in bold.
Type: container.
Attributes: abbr, align, axis, bgcolor, class, char, charoff, **colspan,** dir, **headers,** *height,* id, lang, *nowrap,* onclick, ondblclick, onkeydown, onkeypress, onkeyup, onmousedown, onmousemove, onmouseout, onmouseover, onmouseup, **rowspan, scope, style,** title, **valign,** *width.*
XML: requires using the ending tag.

The browser renders the <th></th> headers in a bold font and centers them, whereas text within the <td></td> container is left-aligned and displayed in a regular font. In the past some browsers treated data in the <th></th> container the same as data in a <td></td> container. This is no longer the case; all the popular graphical browsers handle data within the two tags as shown in Figure 7.12.

There is an order of precedence for the attributes of a table. Attributes coded at the cell level have precedence over those at the row level. Attributes coded at the row level have precedence over those coded at the table level. Attributes coded at the table level have precedence over attributes coded in a style sheet. Consequently, you have quite a bit of control over the elements of a table. Some of the attributes available for the <td> and <th> tags are identical in name and function to those used with the <tr> tag. Others are unique to the <td> and <th> tags, giving you even more control over the appearance of the table. First let's look at the attributes that are common with other table tags.

Figure 7.12 HTML code using the <td> and <th> tags to identify table data in two different tables

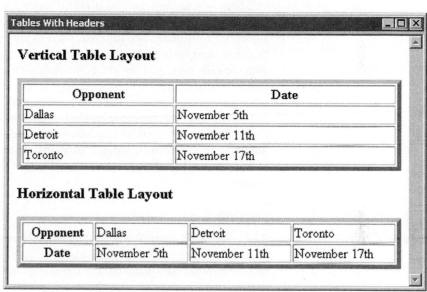

```
<html>
<head>
<title>Tables With Headers</title>
</head>

<body>
<h3>Vertical Table Layout</h3>
<table border="5" width="100%">
<tr>
   <th>Opponent </th>
   <th>Date </th>
</tr>
<tr>
   <td>Dallas </td>
   <td>November 5th </td>
</tr>
<tr>
   <td>Detroit </td>
   <td>November 11th </td>
</tr>
<tr>
   <td>Toronto </td>
   <td>November 17th</td>
</tr>
</table>

<h3>Horizontal Table Layout</h3>
<table border="5" width="100%">
<tr>
   <th>Opponent</th> <td>Dallas</td> <td>Detroit</td> <td>Toronto</td>
</tr>
<tr>
   <th>Date</th> <td>November 5th</td> <td>November 11th</td> <td>November 17th</td>
</tr>
</table>
</body>
</html>
```

align

The **align** attribute for <td> and <th> works exactly like the **align** attribute for <tr>, with the exception that the alignment is set only for the cell for which it is coded. The alignment of the next cell reverts to the alignment specified by the row. If that alignment is not set, it reverts to the alignment set by the table itself. Like the **align** attribute of the

<tr></tr> container, the **align** attribute for a single cell can be set to one of four values: *left, right, center,* or *char.*

bgcolor

Like the **bgcolor** attribute for the <table> tag, the **bgcolor** attribute for <td> and <th> allows you to set the background color for a particular cell. You can set the color with either a color name or a hexadecimal code as shown on the color insert in the Reference Guide. The color you code within this tag applies only to the cell described. The other cells of the row will be the color set in the <table> or <tr> tag. As always when using color, you need to be very careful not to create a visual unpleasantness. Remember that with color, less is more. Be subtle. The **bgcolor** attribute may be of use in creating a table with one or two cells highlighted to bring attention to their contents.

valign

The **valign** attribute is functionally identical to its namesake associated with the <tr> tag. It allows for vertical alignment of the data within a single cell of the table. It is useful for altering the way the data in one specific cell are presented. The alignment of data or headings in subsequent cells is not affected.

How you lay out the actual HTML code for a table makes a big difference in how easy it is to read and understand—and, more importantly, how easy it is to change. Figure 7.12 illustrates two different ways to lay out HTML table code in a readable way. In the vertical table example at the top of the figure, the headings and each piece of the data for each table row are placed on their own lines and indented. At the bottom of the figure is a table with a horizontal layout. The related code is organized to mimic that table's screen appearance, with the heading and data for each row on the same line and indented within the <tr>table row</tr> container. We strongly recommend that you use the vertical arrangement, as it matches the layout of the rest of the page and gives you the ability to easily insert or remove attributes or data without affecting the existing layout. However you lay out your tables, make sure they are easy to read, understand, and change.

colspan

There are times, usually with headings, that some cell information needs *column spanning* capabilities because it applies to more than one column. Use the **colspan** attribute to tell the browser how many columns you want the particular cell to span. Figure 7.13 presents a small table with a header that spans all six columns at the top of the table. The HTML code to have a cell span across six cells looks like this:

```
<th colspan="6">
```

The **colspan** attribute is also used twice in row 3 to span a single price across two different columns. Remember, either <td> or <th> cells can have this attribute. However, if the **colspan** attribute is applied where there are not enough columns in the table to span, it won't add columns to make the **colspan** work. It may cause an alignment problem. When counting columns, count each colspanned column as one. Therefore, if you have a table with six columns and you code a colspan="3", you would need to account for only three more columns in that row. If you added containers for four more columns, your table would be off balance and have one too many columns in one row.

rowspan

Just as you can have one cell span several columns with **colspan,** you can create a cell that has *row spanning* capabilities for use when information is the same for more than one row. The **rowspan** attribute creates a cell that spans two or more rows. This attribute is useful for creating headings and legends for the cells in a table. Set it to an integer

Figure 7.13

HTML code showing how the **colspan** attribute allows cell content to span more than one column

```
<html>
<head>
<title>Column Spanning Cells</title>
</head>

<body>
<table border="5" width="100%">
<tr>
  <th colspan="6">Home Ticket Options</th>
</tr>
<tr>
  <th>Zone</th>
  <td>Red</td>
  <td>Blue</td>
  <td>Green</td>
  <td>Yellow</td>
  <td>Orange</td>
</tr>
<tr>
  <th>Price</th>
  <td>$101.00</td>
  <td colspan="2">$25.50</td>
  <td colspan="2">$9.00</td>
</tr>
</table>
</body>
</html>
```

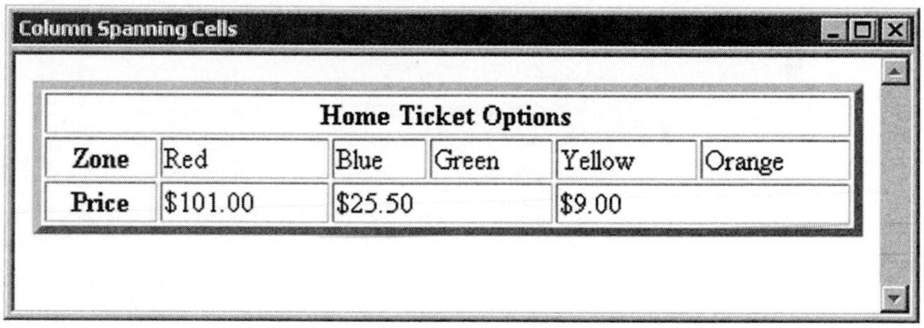

number equal to the number of rows the cell is to span. Figure 7.14 shows a simple table with the **rowspan** attribute set. Notice that these are the same data presented in Figure 7.13, but in a vertical layout instead of a horizontal layout. The first header spans all six rows because of this code:

```
<th rowspan="6">
```

Since the browser renders the table from the top left to the bottom right, the **rowspan** attribute is placed in the <th> or <td> container that incorporates the first of the rows to be spanned. Therefore, when the ticket price of $25.50 needs to span both the Blue and Green rows, the attribute is set in the first <td> definition like this:

```
<tr>
   <td>Blue</td>
   <td rowspan="2">$25.50</td>
</tr>
   <tr>
   <td>Green</td>
</tr>
```

With **rowspan** established for the Blue row, the <td></td> container for the next row contains only the data "Green." The browser then spans the cell with "$25.50" across both rows. Notice that the **rowspan** attribute works equally well with heading or table data.

As with the **colspan** attribute, if we code **rowspan** greater than the number of rows remaining, the browser will not add rows to grant our request.

Figure 7.14

HTML code showing how the **rowspan** attribute allows cell content to span more than one row

```
<html>
<head>
<title>Row Spanning Cells</title>
</head>
<body>
<table border="5" width="100%">
<tr>
  <th rowspan="6">Home Ticket Options</th>
  <th>Zone</th>
  <th>Price</th>
</tr>
<tr>
  <td>Red</td>
  <td>$101.00</td>
</tr>
<tr>
  <td>Blue</td>
  <td rowspan="2">$25.50</td>
</tr>
<tr>
  <td>Green</td>
</tr>
<tr>
  <td>Yellow</td>
  <td rowspan="2">$9.00</td>
</tr>
<tr>
  <td>Orange</td>
</tr>
</table>
</body>
</html>
```

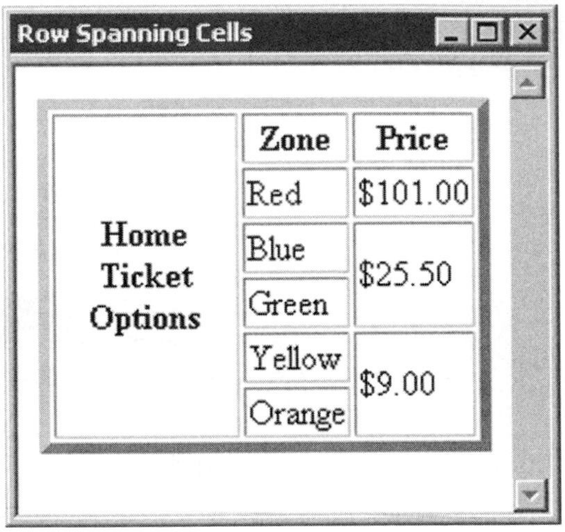

abbr

As we have seen, there are limits to how small a table can be rendered, because the browsers are unable to shrink cells smaller than the longest word. The **abbr** attribute allows Web weavers to assign abbreviations to cell contents that are used only in situations where the table needs to be as small as possible. For example, the following code would provide abbreviations for the cell values displayed in the second row of Figure 7.13:

```
<th abbr="Z">Zone</th>
<th abbr="R">Red</td>
<th abbr="B">Blue</td>
<th abbr="G">Green</td>
<th abbr="Y">Yellow</td>
<th abbr="O">Orange</td>
```

The W[3]C foresees these abbreviations being used by aural-oriented pages where speech synthesizers will output the abbreviated headers before rendering the cell's content. At the time of this writing, none of the major browsers support this attribute.

headers

The **headers** attribute specifies the list of header cells that provide header information for specific table cells. This is another of the new HTML 4 attributes designed to support nonvisual browsers, especially those relying on speech synthesis. Values assigned to this attribute are a space-separated list of cell names that relate to cells with specific identifiers established by the **id** attribute. The W[3]C states that this attribute will most likely be used in conjunction with style sheets.

scope

Because tables are a great way to organize data, they are found on the Web in a variety of sizes and formats. The W³C added the **scope** attribute in the HTML 4 specifications to be used as an alternative to the **headers** attribute when designing simple tables. When specified, this attribute must have one of the following values:

- row: header cell provides header information for the rest of the row.
- col: header cell provides header information for the rest of the column.
- rowgroup: header cell provides header information for the rest of the row group.
- colgroup: header cell provides header information for the rest of the column group.

axis

The **axis** attribute is also new with the HTML 4 specifications. Although none of the popular browsers currently recognize this attribute, the W³C has this to say about its application within HTML documents:

> This attribute may be used to place a cell into conceptual categories that can be considered to form axes in an n-dimensional space. User agents [browsers] may give users access to these categories (e.g., the user may query the user agent for all cells that belong to certain categories, the user agent may present a table in the form of a table of contents, etc.). Please consult the section on categorizing cells for more information. The value of this attribute is a comma-separated list of category names. (HTML 4.01 specifications, section 11.2.6)

style

The HTML 4 specifications provide a number of alternatives for formatting Web pages using the **style** attribute. As you might expect, the Web author can use it to set a table's column width and row height, as shown in Figure 7.15.

width: length | percentage

The **style** attribute's width property is the first we will discuss that is different when used with the <th> and <tr> tags, or the <table> tag. As in the other uses of width, you can code it as an absolute number of pixels, which will change with the varying resolutions of the monitors, or you can code it as a percentage. The code to set a cell's width to 75 pixels looks like this:

```
<td style="width: 75px;">Text</td>
```

When you specify a **width** for the <table> tag, it specifies a width across the browser pane. The **width** coded for <tr> and <th> is different in that when you code it as a percentage, that percentage is of the *width of the table,* not the width of the page. Figure 7.15 shows a three-column table in which the left column is set to a width of 75 pixels with the remaining columns set to be 100 pixels wide. We used absolute cell width in the left column to ensure that "Home Ticket Options" would fall on three lines.

Remember that the width you set for a particular cell also sets the width for that column in the whole of the table. As is true for the table's width, you cannot set a width that is less than what the browser determines to be the minimum necessary for displaying the existing contents of the cells in that column. If you happen to code more than one width in the same column, the browser will take the largest value for the whole column. If you code a width, it is best for maintenance and readability to code it on the first occurrence of that column in the table, as shown in Figure 7.15. That way it won't be buried down in the code for the table as a surprise for someone reading your code.

The introduction of the width property with the HTML 4 recommendations resulted in the deprecation of the **width** attribute. This attribute did essentially the same thing as the width property did. The code to set a cell's width to 75 pixels follows:

```
<td width="75">Text</td>
```

Figure 7.15

HTML code showing how the **style** attribute can set the width and height of cells within a table

```
<html>
<head>
<title>Cell Width and Height Using Styles</title>
</head>
<body>
<table border="5">
<tr>
  <th style="width: 75px" rowspan="6">Home Ticket Options</th>
  <th style="width: 100px; height: 50px">Zone</th>
  <th style="width: 100px">Price</th>
</tr>
<tr style="text-align: center">
  <td style="height: 50px">Red</td>
  <td>$101.00</td>
</tr>
<tr style="text-align: center">
  <td style="height: 30px;">Blue this a long cell to see if nowrap works.</td>
  <td rowspan="2">$25.50</td>
</tr>
<tr style="text-align: center">
  <td style="height: 30px">Green</td>
</tr>
<tr style="text-align: center">
  <td style="height: 30px">Yellow</td>
  <td rowspan="2">$9.00</td>
</tr>
<tr style="text-align: center">
  <td style="height: 30px">Orange</td>
</tr>
</table>
</body>
</html>
```

	Zone	Price
Home Ticket Options	Red	$101.00
	Blue	$25.50
	Green	
	Yellow	$9.00
	Orange	

height: length | percentage

Whereas the width property adjusts the horizontal size of a table column, the **style** attribute's height property adjusts the vertical size of a table row. As shown in Figure 7.15, the height is given in pixels and affects only the row in which the attribute appears. The browser will not let you make the height of a row shorter than is necessary to display the contents. Setting a cell's height to 25 pixels is accomplished with the following code:

```
<td style="height: 25px;">Text</td>
```

In Figure 7.15 the height of the top two rows is set to 50 pixels. Notice that setting the height and width in effect sets the cell padding, since the size of the data font does not change as a result. Setting the height of the remaining cells in the middle column ("Blue," "Green," "Yellow," and "Orange") automatically determines the height of the row-spanning cells in the right column.

As with the **width** attribute, the **height** attribute was deprecated in the HTML 4 specifications in favor of the **style** attribute's height property. This code would set a cell's height to 25 pixels this way:

```
<td height="25">Text</td>
```

Although deprecated attributes like **height** and **width** will be recognized by browsers for some time to come, you would be wise to add the **style** attribute to your HTML vocabulary and to begin converting pages you are maintaining by replacing the deprecated attributes with the new **style**-based controls.

whitespace: nowrap

Generally the browsers will wrap the contents of a cell across multiple lines to make the data fit, visibly, in the requisite cell. Sometimes it is necessary to prevent the browser from wrapping lines this way. As we saw with the <nobr></nobr> container, there are situations in which a broken line could be confusing for the users. Originally this situation was handled in HTML code by adding the **nowrap** attribute to the table definition. The code would look like this:

```
<td nowrap>This text would not be wrapped within the cell.</td>
```

Once again the W³C has decided to deprecate an attribute, in this case the **nowrap** attribute, in favor of the **style** attribute. To prevent the contents of a cell from wrapping using the **style** attribute, you would set the white-space property to **nowrap**. Here is an example of the related HTML code:

```
<td style="white-space: nowrap">This text would not be wrapped within the cell.</td>
```

Other values for the white-space property are covered in Chapter Eight.

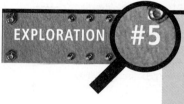

EXPLORATION #5

Modify the table in chapter7.html as follows:

- The red header to 30 pixels tall.
- The green header to 40 pixels tall.
- The blue header to 50 pixels tall.
- The yellow header to 60 pixels tall.
- The magenta header to 70 pixels tall.
- The cyan header to 80 pixels tall.
- The cyan data vertically aligned at the bottom of the cell.

Save the file and refresh/reload the browser display.

▸▸ TABLE CAPTIONS

Most tables need a *caption* to explain their contents. You have a choice about where to place the caption, above or below the body of the table.

HTML   <caption>Caption</caption>

Description: defines a table caption.
Type: container.
Attributes: *align,* class, dir, id, lang, onclick, ondblclick, onkeydown, onkeypress, onkeyup onmousedown, onmousemove, onmouseout, omnouseover, onmouseup, **style**, title.
Special note: permitted only immediately after the <table> start tag.

The popular browsers recognize the <caption></caption> container and by default place the contents above the table. Like any of the cells in the table, the <caption> can contain anything that can be placed in the <body> of an HTML document, but the wise Web weaver will constrain the contents of the <caption></caption> container to a terse description of the table.

Note that the </caption> closing tag is never omitted. Also note that there can only be one <caption></caption> container per table. The popular browsers center the caption with respect to the table edges, as shown in Figure 7.16. While the W^{3}C specifications state that the caption container should immediately follow the starting <table> tag, we have found that the browsers are a little more relaxed about the placement, allowing the Web weaver to place the <caption> element elsewhere in the <table> container. We recommend that you follow the W^{3}C recommendations as closely as possible, though, to ensure compliance with later versions of browsers that will conform more closely to the specifications.

Figure 7.16

HTML code showing how a caption is aligned at the bottom of a table

```
<html>
<head>
<title>Table With Caption</title>
</head>

<body>
<table border="5">
<caption style="caption-side: bottom;">Multiplication Table</caption>
<tr>
   <th> </th> <th>1</th> <th>2</th> <th>3</th> <th>4</th> <th>5</th>
</tr>
<tr>
   <th>1</th> <td>1</td> <td>2</td> <td>3</td> <td>4</td> <td>5</td>
</tr>
<tr>
   <th>2</th> <td>2</td> <td>4</td> <td>6</td> <td>8</td> <td>10</td>
</tr>
<tr>
   <th>3</th> <td>3</td> <td>6</td> <td>9</td> <td>12</td> <td>15</td>
</tr>
<tr>
   <th>4</th> <td>4</td> <td>8</td> <td>12</td> <td>16</td> <td>20</td>
</tr>
<tr>
   <th>5</th> <td>5</td> <td>10</td> <td>15</td> <td>20</td> <td>25</td>
</tr>
</table>
</body>
</html>
```

	1	2	3	4	5
1	1	2	3	4	5
2	2	4	6	8	10
3	3	6	9	12	15
4	4	8	12	16	20
5	5	10	15	20	25

Multiplication
Table

CAPTION ALIGNMENT

All of the browsers support placement of the caption either above or below the table, and they default to placing the caption above *(top)* the table. This is a major improvement over past practices, in which each browser had a different default setting and in some cases used a different attribute! Figure 7.16 illustrates a caption that is aligned at the bottom of a 5-by-5 (six cells across and six cells down) multiplication table.

The most reliable way to place the caption under the table is to use the deprecated **align** attribute as follows:

```
<caption align="bottom">Descriptive text.</caption>
```

The alternative is to use the **style** attribute's caption-side property set to bottom as follows (and shown in Figure 7.16):

```
<caption style="caption-side: bottom;">Descriptive text.</caption>
```

Currently, Internet Explorer does not recognize the caption-side property. The HTML 4 specifications actually do distinguish between alignment values set to **top, bottom, left,** or **right,** but at the time of this writing, none of the browsers recognize **right** or **left** values.

EXPLORATION   #6   Place the table caption in chapter7.html under the table. Then save the file and refresh/reload the browser display.

▸▸ TABLE COLUMNS

Now we come to the columns, to which you can apply a variety of styles to organize your information in the most appropriate way.

HTML   `<colgroup>Column Group</colgroup>`

Description: creates structural divisions within a table that can be independently formatted.
Type: container.
Attributes: align, char, charoff, class, dir, id, lang, onclick, ondblclick, onkeydown, onkeypress, wonkeyup, onmousedown, onmousemove, onmouseout, onmouseover, onmouseup, **span,** style, title, valign, width.

As tables are row-oriented, Web weavers have been limited in their ability to format down columns. Before the <colgroup> element was added to the specifications, Web weavers who wanted to change the background color of selected columns or needed to align a column of numbers on the decimal point could not easily do it. With <colgroup>, they can designate specific columns in a table for special treatment, that is, special formatting. Figure 7.17 shows our multiplication table with the <colgroup> element applied to the first three columns.

A table can contain more than one column group, but if it does, you should be careful to end the first group's definition with a </colgroup> tag before defining the next group. You will find the <colgroup></colgroup> container is a powerful HTML element that offers a variety of alternatives, especially when used with the **span** attribute, discussed next.

span

The **span** attribute allows the Web weaver to apply format changes across several columns in a group. In Figure 7.17 the **span** attribute is set equal to 3, which means that the attributes are applied to three columns. As you can see, the other attributes included in the <colgroup> element, **width** and **style,** are then applied to the first three columns in the table. **Span** must always be an integer greater than 0.

To further explore the <colgroup></colgroup> container, we need to introduce the <col /> tag.

Figure 7.17

HTML code showing how the <colgroup> element formats groups of columns

```
<html>
<head>
<title>Multiplication Table</title>
</head>
<body>
<table border="5">
<caption align="bottom">Multiplication Table</caption>
<colgroup
    span="3"
    width="50"
    align="center"
    style="font-family: sans-serif; font-style: italic; font-size: 16pt;">
</colgroup>
<tr>
   <th> </th> <th>1</th> <th>2</th> <th>3</th> <th>4</th> <th>5</th>
</tr>
<tr>
   <th>1</th> <td>1</td> <td>2</td> <td>3</td> <td>4</td> <td>5</td>
</tr>
<tr>
   <th>2</th> <td>2</td> <td>4</td> <td>6</td> <td>8</td> <td>10</td>
</tr>
<tr>
   <th>3</th> <td>3</td> <td>6</td> <td>9</td> <td>12</td> <td>15</td>
</tr>
<tr>
   <th>4</th> <td>4</td> <td>8</td> <td>12</td> <td>16</td> <td>20</td>
</tr>
<tr>
   <th>5</th> <td>5</td> <td>10</td> <td>15</td> <td>20</td> <td>25</td>
</tr>
</table>
</body>
</html>
```

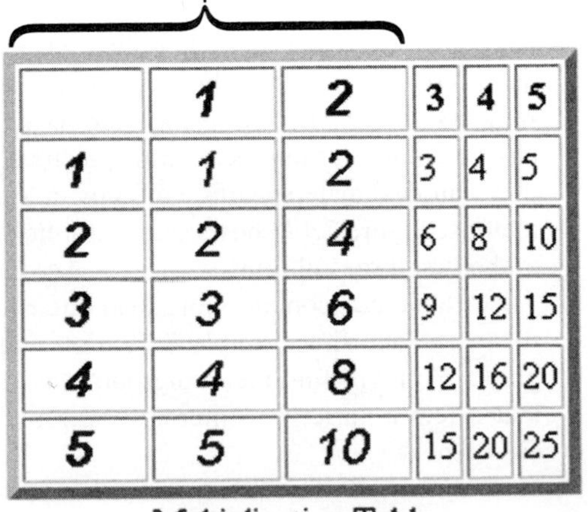

	1	2	3	4	5
1	1	2	3	4	5
2	2	4	6	8	10
3	3	6	9	12	15
4	4	8	12	16	20
5	5	10	15	20	25

Multiplication Table

HTML `<col />`

Description: allows authors to group together attribute specifications for table columns but does not group columns together structurally.
Type: empty.
Attributes: align, char, charoff, class, dir, id, lang, onclick, ondblclick, onkeydown, onkeypress, onkeyup, onmousedown, onmousemove, onmouseout, onmouseover, onmouseup, span, style, title, **valign, width.**
XML: requires closing tag using <col /> or <col></col>, for example, <col width="30" />.

The <col /> element is an interesting addition to the HTML 4 specifications and will probably go through more evolution as an HTML element before all of its capabilities are universally recognized. It is an empty tag that by design works inside the <colgroup> element as an alternative to the **span** attribute. When used as part of XML/XHTML-compliant code a closing tag must be employed as shown in Figure 7.18. However, the W³C tells us that the <col /> element can be used outside a column group (also shown in Figure 7.18).

Figure 7.18

HTML code for selected table columns formatted using <col> element

```
<html>
<head>
<title>Multiplication Table</title>
</head>
<body>
<table border="5">
<caption align="bottom">Multiplication Table</caption>
<col width="10" />
<col width="20" style="font-style: italic;" />
<col width="30" style="font-size: 8pt;" />
<col width="60" span="2" align="center" />
<col width="30" style="font-family: sans-serif;" />
<tr>
   <th> </th> <th>1</th> <th>2</th> <th>3</th> <th>4</th> <th>5</th>
</tr>
<tr>
   <th>1</th> <td>1</td> <td>2</td> <td>3</td> <td>4</td> <td>5</td>
</tr>
<tr>
   <th>2</th> <td>2</td> <td>4</td> <td>6</td> <td>8</td> <td>10</td>
</tr>
<tr>
   <th>3</th> <td>3</td> <td>6</td> <td>9</td> <td>12</td> <td>15</td>
</tr>
<tr>
   <th>4</th> <td>4</td> <td>8</td> <td>12</td> <td>16</td> <td>20</td>
</tr>
<tr>
   <th>5</th> <td>5</td> <td>10</td> <td>15</td> <td>20</td> <td>25</td>
</tr>
</table>
</body>
</html>
```

	1	2	3	4	5
1	1	2	3	4	5
2	2	4	6	8	10
3	3	6	9	12	15
4	4	8	12	16	20
5	5	10	15	20	25

Multiplication Table

Up until now we have used the **span** attribute within a <colgroup> tab to format a group of columns. The <col /> element can also represent one or more columns in a column group. It recognizes the **span** attribute (Figure 7.18). To show you how both of these <colgroup> options work, let's explore the use of the **width** attribute.

width

By this time the **width** attribute has become an old friend. It is particularly powerful when used within the <colgroup> element, because you can set the width of many or all the columns in a table with a single application. For example, the following code would set the width of each of 30 columns, (span="30"), in a table to 60 pixels wide:

```
<colgroup span="30" width="60" />
```

Web weavers can specify column widths in three ways:

1. *Fixed*—based on pixels (width="60")
2. *Percentage*—based on the percentage of the horizontal space available to the table (width="25%"). This is the preferred method.
3. *Proportional*—based on portions of the horizontal space required by a table (width="5*").

The proportional, or relative, specification needs a little more explanation. This **width** option must work in conjunction with a fixed table width provided by the <table> element. For discussion's sake, let's suppose this HTML code was used to set a table's width to 600 pixels:

```
<table border="5" width="600">
```

With this fixed table width established, we could use the <colgroup> element to span six columns of our table and equally distribute the column widths:

```
<colgroup span="6" width="6*" />
```

In this case the math is easy, and you probably figured out that all six columns would be 100 pixels wide. The logic would work just as well if the width were set to 500 pixels. The proportional **width** option also goes beyond this simple application, because you can vary the proportion of horizontal space allocated across columns.

Consider the following HTML code in respect to a three-column table with a fixed width of 600 pixels:

```
<colgroup style="font-style: italic;">
<col width="1*" / >
<col width="3*" / >
<col width="2*" / >
</colgroup>
```

In this situation the proportional widths assigned to each column are as follows:

- Column 1: assigned one-sixth of the horizontal space assigned to the table, i.e., 100 pixels.
- Column 2: assigned one-half of the table's horizontal space, i.e., 300 pixels.
- Column 3: assigned one-third of the table's horizontal space, i.e., 200 pixels.

Notice how the <col /> element is used instead of the **span** attribute to format columns within the column group. The <colgroup> tag can still apply style changes across all three columns, in this case setting the font style to italics, while the <col /> tag specifics the horizontal space assigned to each column. You will find the <col /> element most useful when having to format noncontinuous columns within the column group—for example, when you want to alternate the column widths every other column or every third column.

Just remember our old caveat about the browser always having the final say regarding this type of formatting. The W³C even reminds us of this fact when it writes, "User agents [browsers] may render the table incrementally even with proportional columns" (HTML 4.01 specifications, section 11.2.4).

Just to add a little spice to things, the W³C has thrown in a special form of the proportional width attribute—"0*". The HTML code looks like this:

```
<colgroup width="0*">
```

This code tells the browser to set each column's width to the minimum necessary to render the content. This means the column's content must be known before the width is computed and the table displayed. Using the option means your tables will require a minimum amount of screen real estate but will be slower to load, because the browser cannot render them incrementally.

valign

The **valign** attribute works the same way in the <col> tag as it does within the <tr>, <th>, and <td> tags. It allows for vertical alignment of the data within all the cells in the specified column. You might remember that the popular browsers recognize four different values for this attribute: *center* (the default), *top, bottom,* and *baseline.* Figure 7.11 shows a table with these different alignments.

▸▸ SCROLLING BIG TABLES

In the past, displaying long tables was a problem, because the column headers scrolled off the screen as the table's body did. Users had to scroll back to them when they needed to refresh their memories concerning a column's content, or the Web weaver had to try to guess how many lines of the table would fit on the user's screen and repeat the headings to keep them available to the users. Along the same line, printing these long tables caused a problem in that the column headers appeared only at the beginning of the table, which was often on another page. A running header (or footer) that would always stay on the screen and would appear on each printed page was desirable, but no such tags were identified in the HTML 3.2 specifications. The only way to accomplish this was to use frames; definitely a kluge.

Fortunately, the 4.0 specifications addressed this concern with the <tbody>, <thead>, and <tfoot> containers, although at the time of this writing, none of the browsers have implemented them. What follows is an overview of these elements and a short discussion of how they are supposed to work once they *finally* get implemented.

 **<thead>Table Header</thead>**

Description: defines a table's header.
Type: container.
Attributes: align, char, charoff, class, dir, id, lang, onclick, ondblclick, onkeydown, onkeypress, onkeyup, onmousedown, onmousemove, onmouseout, onmouseover, onmouseup, style, title, valign.

The <thead> element must precede the <tbody> element, as shown in Figure 7.19. It defines a nonscrolling column heading, which is what distinguishes its contents from those used within a <th> tag. In other words, the contents of a <th> tag will scroll off the screen when a long table is displayed, but the contents of the <thead> tag will remain on the screen while the table body scrolls underneath it. The <thead> element must have the same number of columns as the table body.

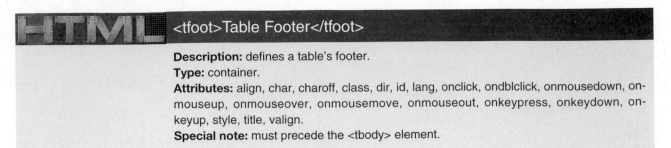

Description: defines a table's footer.
Type: container.
Attributes: align, char, charoff, class, dir, id, lang, onclick, ondblclick, onmousedown, on-mouseup, onmouseover, onmousemove, onmouseout, onkeypress, onkeydown, on-keyup, style, title, valign.
Special note: must precede the <tbody> element.

The <tfoot> element defines nonscrolling column labels that appear below the table body. You need to define the table footer before you define the table body (see Figure 7.19).

Figure 7.19

HTML code for table headers and footers that will not scroll off the screen when the body is scrolled

```
<html>
<head>
<title>Headers and Footers</title>
</head>
<body>
<table border="5" width="100%">
<caption>Common Software Tools</caption>

<thead>
  <tr>
    <th>Icon</th> <th>Description</th>
  </tr>
</thead>

<tfoot>
  <tr>
    <th>Icon</th> <th>Description</th>
  </tr>
</tfoot>

<tbody style="text-align: center">
  <tr>
    <td><img src="save.jpg" alt="Save icon" /></td> <td>Save</td>
  </tr>
  <tr>

    .

    .code was removed here to reduce figure's size

    .
  <tr>
    <td><img src="right.jpg" alt="Right align icon" /></td> <td>Right Align</td>
  </tr>
</tbody>

</table>
</body>
</html>
```

Common Software Tools

Icon	Description
💾	Save
🔍	Print Preview
🖨	Print
✂	Cut
📋	Copy
📋	Paste
≡	Left Align
≡	Center Align
≡	Right Align
Icon	**Description**

◄— Table Header

} —— Table Body

◄—— Table Footer

Though it may seem a little strange to define the footer before the body, it is necessary because the browsers must be able to render both the header and footer before loading all the table rows that make up the table body. The <tfoot> element must have the same number of columns as the <tbody> element.

HTML | <tbody>Table Body</tbody>

Description: defines a table's body.
Type: container.
Attributes: align, char, charoff, class, dir, id, lang, onclick, ondblclick, onkeydown, on-keypress, onkeyup, onmousedown, onmousemove, onmouseout, onmouseover, on-mouseup, style, title, valign.

The <tbody> container identifies the table's contents. The ***table body*** defines which rows in the table will scroll between the <thead> and the <tfoot> when the table is longer than the browser's display area. There can be more than one <tbody> element within the same table if more than one scrollable area is needed. Figure 7.19 illustrates the syntax for defining a table's body.

▸▸ XHTML TABLE MODULE

The table elements introduced in this chapter, <table>, <caption>, <tr>, <th>, <td>, <col />, <colgroup>, <thead>, <tfoot>, and <tbody>, have been bundled together in the XHTML specifications to form the Table module. While not a required module, this module will be a common component in most XML and XHTML applications.

As you can see from this chapter, tables provide a new level of sophistication for our Web page designs. You will find that as your page designs increase in sophistication, so does the need to rough-draft the design before you start coding. It is one thing to throw together a single, independent Web page; it is another thing entirely to start coding an integrated set of pages that will make up a corporate Web site. In the latter case, some preliminary design work is essential before the coding begins—if for no other reason than that the people paying you will want to approve the content and design first.

EXPLORATION **#7**

Create a new HTML document that contains a table with English-to-Spanish word translations for colors (see example on next page). The table should have a horizontal design and meet the following specifications:

- Caption *English to Spanish Color Translations* under table.
- Border of 5 pixels.
- Dark blue (#336699) border color.
- Table covers the full width of the browser pane.
- Dashed border style.
- Light blue (#CCFFFF) background color.
- Cell spacing of 8 pixels.
- Cell padding of 4 pixels.
- First column contains table headers.
- Remaining columns contain table data.

The title should be *your name's English-to-Spanish Color Translation,* and the table information looks like this:

English	Red	Green	Blue	Yellow	Black	White
Spanish	Rojo(a)	Verde	Azul	Amarillo(a)	Negro(a)	Blanco(a)

Save the file as spanish-colors.html and display it using your favorite browser.

▸▸ KEY TERMS

Border

Caption

Cell

Cell padding

Cell spacing

Column spanning

Frame

Row spanning

Rule

Table

Table body

▸▸ NEW TAGS

```
<table></table>              <colgroup></colgroup>
<tr></tr>                    <col />
<td></td>                    <tbody></tbody>
<th></th>                    <thead></thead>
<caption></caption>          <tfoot></tfoot>
```

▸▸ REVIEW QUESTIONS

1. Define each of the key terms.

2. How is each of the tags introduced in this chapter used?

3. How do you build a table?

4. What is the default width of a table border?

5. What are three different HTML attributes that can turn on a table's default border?

6. What is the recommended way to designate a table's width?

7. What can happen to a table if you make the background of the page too light or too dark?

8. How is a table created using the **border** attribute different from one created using the **style** attribute's border property?

9. What are two ways you can align a table within the browser pane?

10. What is the difference between a margin, cell spacing, and cell padding?

11. What is the order of precedence for attributes within a table definition?

12. What are four attributes designed to use with speech synthesizers?

13. How is the **width** attribute's percentage option handled differently when used in a <table> element versus a <td> or <th> element?

14. Which of the <caption>'s caption-side property values (and associated **align** attribute values) are recognized by the popular browsers?

15. What are two different ways the <colgroup> element can be used to format two or more columns?

16. How is the special form of the proportional **width** attribute "0*" interpreted by HTML 4 compliant browsers?

17. How is the <col /> tag used to align numbers around the decimal point? Hint: **char** plays a big part in this answer.

18. What two problems associated with long tables do the <tbody>, <thead>, and <tfoot> elements address?

19. What HTML tags are associated with the XHTML Table module?

▸▸ EXERCISES

7.1 Many of the visitors to Gwen's page are curious about the prices of the gems and minerals at the shop. Ruby has decided that she needs a page that has the following components:

- The type of stone, gem, or mineral.
- The color of the stone.
- A sample image of the stone.
- The description of the stone.
- The cost of the sample.

Please create a page with a table that has the following design features:

a. The background color for the table should be soft gold, #CCCC99.

b. The text should be dark purple, #330033.

c. The title of the page is "Sample Prices."

d. There should be a level-1 heading of "Gwen's Glorious Gemstone Gallery."

e. There should be a level-2 heading that matches the title.

f. After the level-2 heading there should be three horizontal rules, 25 percent, 50 percent, and 90 percent.

g. Level-1 headings should be in deep green, #003300.

h. Level-2 heading should be in medium green, #669966.

i. All headings should be in a sans-serif font.

j. Use a document-level style sheet when possible; use inline styles unless you must use a deprecated form.

k. The following text must precede the table:

The following are some sample prices for a few of our minerals and gems. Please remember that these particular pieces may be sold before you get a chance to bid on them. We do have others in our stock that are similar to these.

l. The table should occupy 99 percent of the page, and have the following characteristics:

1. The text in the table should be dark blue, #00669, and in a sans-serif font.

2. The background of the table should be cream, #FFFFCC.

3. The table border should be 7 pixels wide, double, and purple, #663366.

4. The cells with headings should have a background color of soft yellow, #FFFF99.

5. The cells with images should have a gray background, #666666.

6. There should be 3 pixels of padding around all cell data.

7. The table's caption should read "Sample Prices" and be below the table.

8. The price data should be aligned on the decimal point.

The table should look like the following, with the images added and the formatting as described. (You will need to add the pictures using the URLs listed.)

Minerals				Gems			
	Code	Desc.	Cost		Code	Desc.	Cost
opaltable.jpg	26411	Raw fire opal in a sandstone matrix (shown)	360.00	rubytable.jpg	21045	A deep purplish red ruby .82ct (shown)	645.00
	26522	Raw black opal, very rough	230.00		31034	Bright red ruby .65ct small inclusion	220.00
	20104	Small, rough, jelly opal with pinpoint fire	89.00		30912	Pair of 3mm ruby hearts. .38ct pair	99.00
berltable.jpg	28318	Raw berl crystals low grade (shown)	69.00	emertable.gif	21045	.26ct .5–.3 mm oval cut deep bluegreen (shown)	120.00
	29110	Very pale berl matrix	85.00		27897	pair, .35ct total, square cut dark green	310.00

Sample Prices

7.2. Create a page that has three tables on it, each table measuring 2 by 3 and each having six elements. The page should be filled with "words" demonstrating how a table can be aligned on the left, right, or center of the page. Use a nice border and background color for the table. The title bar should display "Page Alignment," with your name and the assignment due date included within comment lines.

7.3. Modify the "My Favorite Images" Web page you created in Exercise 6.3 to display the five images within a table. The images should all be in the same column, with a description and credit given in a parallel column. Don't forget to include the **alt** descriptions. Add the new due date to the comment line under your name.

7.4. Retrieve the Homework home page you updated in Exercise 6.4. Add a new "Important Addresses" link to the home page. This link should take you to a new HTML document that contains a table of names and addresses (street and/or email). At a minimum there should at least five names and table headers for Name and Address. The headers should have a different background color. Include your name and the assignment due date within comment lines.

7.5. Retrieve your school's home page that you updated in Exercise 6.5. Add a new "Sports Schedule" or "Performances" link to it. This link should take the user to a new HTML document that contains a table listing the sports, theater, or music performance schedule of your choice. At a minimum there should be four events and table headers for Date and Time. The headers should have a different background color from the rest of the table. Include your name and the assignment due date within comment lines.

7.6. Modify the movies Web page you updated in Exercise 6.6 by taking the five items under the Quick Quiz heading (created in Exercise 4.6) and placing these items in a table of six rows by two columns. The first row has the heading "Question" as the label in cell 1 and "Answer" as the label in cell 2. Place each of the Quick Quiz questions in an open cell in column 1 and the answer in the related cell in column 2. Remove the five-item ordered list that contained the original Quick Quiz questions.

7.7. Create a page that contains a table of sports statistics for four of your favorite athletes. It would be particularly cool if you could find royalty-free images of each player to include in the table. Include your name and the assignment due date within comment lines.

7.8. Create a page that has six tables demonstrating the difference between cell spacing and cell padding. The **colspan** or **rowspan** attribute should be used in every table. The title bar should display "Comparison of Cell Spacing vs. Cell Padding," with your name and the assignment due date included within comment lines.

7.9. Create a small page that uses tables, not to display data but rather to format the top 25 percent of the page. Create a five-cell table, with one row containing a small image in the rightmost and leftmost 10-percent sized cells and a different image in the third cell. The text on the page, following three horizontal rules that take up 50, 75, and 50 percent, respectively, of the width of the page should explain the meaning of the two images. The center, third, cell should be 20 percent of the table width, leaving the even cell numbers with 30 percent of the width each (see accompanying figure).

8

Chapter Eight

Styles: Some Have It and Some Don't

The HTML 4 specifications reflect the new respect Web weavers have for the professional development of the Internet, specifically the World Wide Web. The maturation of the Web from infancy to what could be considered adolescence means acquiring more sophistication—maybe polish is a better word! The emphasis on style sheets as part of the new "dynamic" HTML is a prime example of this growing sophistication. We don't think in terms of developing a single page at a time, but rather of collections of interrelated documents that require continuity among the pages.

CHAPTER OBJECTIVES

After reading this chapter you should be able to do the following:

- Create unique CSS-compliant external style sheets.
- Link external style sheets to specific HTML documents.
- Identify the only HTML element associated with the XHTML Link module.
- Apply generic and tag-level classes to specific HTML code.
- Utilize target names for formatting code.

- Understand the applications for relative and absolute measurements.
- Use the <div> and <span> containers for formatting.
- Format Web pages using common style properties.
- Establish style sheets for printed and aural media.

▸▸ WHAT IS A CASCADING STYLE SHEET?

Cascading style sheets (CSS) establish precedence among style sheets and HTML containers that apply formatting changes to a given element within an HTML document. In this chapter we will focus on cascading style sheets that reflect the W³C CSS1 and CSS2 (May 1998) recommendations. Those recommendations specify that when more than one source tries to change an element's format, the cascading order of precedence is as follows:

1. Inline style changes, like bold or style="font-weight: bold;", take first precedence (they are always used).
2. Then document-level changes specified within the <style></style> container (which is coded in the <head> container) are implemented.
3. Next external files using the .css extensions identify changes.
4. Finally, the default values established by the browser are used if no changes are identified in one of the preceding options.

Let's say that a browser's default font size is 12 points and it loads an HTML document that references an external style sheet setting the font size to 14 points. Furthermore, this HTML document contains a <style> element that sets the font size to 16. Finally, an inline **style** attribute sets a specific paragraph's font size to 18 points. When that document is displayed as a Web page, the paragraph in question is displayed using an 18-point font size. The remaining text in the page is displayed using a 16-point font size.

As you can see, cascading style sheets establish a means of determining which style to use when an HTML element is assigned conflicting style specifications. A general rule of thumb is that the style defined closest to the element takes precedence over any others.

▸▸ WHY USE EXTERNAL STYLE SHEETS?

We introduced inline style changes and document-level style sheets in earlier chapters. Both of these techniques are used to custom-design a single document. They take precedence over external rules and the default properties used by the browser. For home-brew Web designers tinkering with their personal home pages, these design tools are sufficient.

The professional Web weaver, on the other hand, working with dozens, if not hundreds, of HTML documents, needs a way to easily maintain consistency among these large collections of pages. This is the main reason for integrating external style sheets with HTML documents. Professional authors need to keep their pages up to date and looking fresh, which means making frequent changes to the format of documents within a site. Changing the font in a single heading is one thing; changing the level-1 heading's font in 28 related documents is something else—namely, a tremendous expenditure of time and effort! In addition, the possibility of mistakes creeping in increases proportionally with the number of pages that need updating. With external style sheets, you change the font once, in one place, and it is reflected in all the documents that use that external style sheet.

For this reason, the XML and XHTML specifications strongly recommend using external style sheets for formatting Web page content. To emphasize this point, the XHTML 1.0 recommendations have deprecated the Style Attribute module, which supported **style** property:value pairs used for inline formatting. In addition, the W³C cautions Web designers in the same XHTML recommendations that "CSS defines different conformance rules for HTML and XML documents; be aware that the HTML rules apply to XHTML documents delivered as HTML, and the XML rules apply to XHTML documents delivered as XML" (Section C.13). XML coding rules are discussed in detail in Chapter Fifteen.

An external style sheet is downloaded separately from the HTML document and can be used by several Web pages. Thus it reduces the size of all the related HTML documents, because they do not have to contain the code for inline and document-level styles. The smaller the document, the faster it is downloaded to the browser.

▸▸ APPLYING EXTERNAL STYLE SHEETS

An external style sheet is a stand-alone ASCII file with a .css filename extension. Figure 8.1 shows the external style sheet we will use with a weekly Internet newsletter on travel tips. One of the newsletters is found in Figure 8.2. A close look at Figure 8.1 reveals familiar-looking HTML code. External style sheets use the same HTML syntax as the <style> element. A left French, or curly, brace, {, follows the tag name. Properties appear after the brace and are separated from the desired values by a colon. Semicolons separate one property:value pair from another. A right French, or curly, brace, }, closes the style changes. The final semicolon after the last property:value pair is not required, but we strongly recommend that you include it. If it is there, it is easy to add another element to the style-sheet entry, and it doesn't cause an error. Comments are added to the file between /* and */ symbols. This is a common convention for comments used in the C computer programming language.

Figure 8.1

HTML code for an external style sheet saved as an ASCII file with a .CSS filename extension

```
/* External Style Sheet */

body
   {
   background-color: #FFFFCC; /* light yellow */
   margin: 10px;
   }

h1, h2, h3, h4, h5, h6
   {
   font-weight: bold;
   font-family: sans-serif;
   color: #996666; /* rust */
   }

h1
   {
   font-size: 30pt;
   }

h2
   {
   color: #999999; /* dark gray */
   font-size: 16pt;
   }

p
   {
   margin: 20px;
   font-family: "Book Antiqua", serif;
   font-size: 12pt;
   }

ul li
   {
   font-family: "Book Antiqua", serif;
   font-size: 12pt;
   list-style-type: square;
   }
```

More than one tag can be assigned new properties at the same time. For example, all of the heading tags are set to a bold, rust-colored, sans-serif font using this code:

```
h1, h2, h3, h4, h5, h6
   {
   font-weight: bold;
   font-family: sans-serif;
   color:#996666; /* rust */
   }
```

Notice how we aligned the open and close French brace. Aligning them this way can help you debug your code. If you align your braces, then you can look down the screen and ensure that you closed each brace.

Tags that can be nested—for example, lists—are formatted by identifying the main and subordinate elements. In the following code the first-level items in an ordered list are set to be sequenced using Roman numerals (I, II, III, etc.):

```
ol li {list-style-type: upper-roman;}.
```

If you want the second-level items of the ordered list to be sequenced using uppercase letters, the code would look like this:

```
ol li li {list-style-type: upper-alpha;}.
```

You may notice that the preceding examples seem to contradict our suggestion of aligning the open and close curly braces. The general rule of thumb is that if you have *only one property,* you can open and close the braces on the same line. However, as soon as you add a second property, you should put each property on a separate line, and align your braces.

Be careful. If you make even a small mistake in coding your external style sheet, the processing of that tag change does not happen. A forgotten hyphen or missing semicolon is all it takes. The latest browsers are good at compartmentalizing an error and not letting it affect other property changes. Older browsers are not as forgiving, and often none of the style changes that follow the line with the mistake are recognized by them, even if the syntax on those following lines is correct. If your browser is having trouble applying the style sheet, check your syntax. Then check it again, and then have somebody else check it. The browser does not give any warning messages; it just ignores the change!

Let's take a look at how you link an HTML document to this external style-sheet file.

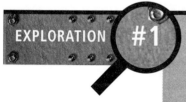

EXPLORATION #1

Using Figure 8.1 as a guide, create an external style sheet with an ASCII editor that does the following:

- Contains a comment line with your name.
- Centers all level-1 headings.
- Displays every paragraph in 14-point Arial font.
- Uses lowercase Roman characters when displaying ordered lists.

Save the file as chapter8.css.

HTML <link>

Description: identifies external files that relate to the document in various ways.
Type: empty.
Attributes: charset, class, dir, **href,** hreflang, id, lang, media, onclick, ondblclick, onkeydown, onkeypress, onkeyup, onmousedown, onmousemove, onmouseout, onmouseover, onmouseup, **rel,** rev, style, target, title, **type.**
Special note: must be coded within the <head> container.
XML: requires ending tag using <link />, for example, <link rel="stylesheet" href="nletter.css" type="text/css" />.

Figure 8.2 HTML code for a document formatted by the external style sheet in Figure 8.1

```
1   <html>
2   <head>
3   <title>External Style Sheets</title>
4   <link rel="stylesheet"
5         href="nletter.css"
6         type="text/css" />
7   </head>
8
9   <body>
10  <h1>Travelers Newsletter</h1>
11  <h2>For People In The Know and On The Go!</h2>
12  <p>In this issue we want to explore Australia. While half-a-world away, you can escape
13  the cold and damp of winter in the North and embrace summer again by traveling there.
14  The people are friendly. The exchange rates are favorable. And there are plenty of places
15  were you can get away from it all!
16  </p>
17
18  <h2>Postcards From Down Under</h2>
19  <p>One of the most pleasant ways to travel in Australia is by train. The rhythmic rumble of
20  the rails provides a soothing backdrop to the beautiful country as it rolls by. Riding the
21  rails gives you time to meet people, appreciate the country side, and to slow down the hectic
22  pace in which travelers may find themselves. AustRail passes are inexpensive and cover 8,
23  15, and 21 days of train travel.
24  </p>
25
26  <h2>Wine, Women and Song</h2>
27  <p>If you like fine, wonderfully priced wines, Australia is the place to visit. Many of the
28  metropolitan areas have wineries a short distance away. Ask your friends in the know about
29  wines if they have tried any of the Aussie wines. We'll bet they have only nice things to
30  says.
31  </p>
32
33  <h3 style="color: #999900">Australian Wine Growing Areas:</h3>
34  <!-- olive font color -->
35  <ul>
36    <li>Barossa Valley Wineries - north of Adelaide </li>
37    <li>Hunter Valley Wineries - north of Sydney </li>
38    <li>Margaret River Wineries - south of Perth </li>
39    <li>Mt. Avoca Wineries - northwest of Melbourne </li>
40  </ul>
```

External Style Sheets

Travelers Newsletter

For People In The Know and On The Go!

In this issue we want to explore Australia. While half-a-world away, you can escape the cold and damp of winter in the North and embrace summer again by traveling there. The people are friendly. The exchange rates are favorable. And there are plenty of places were you can get away from it all!

Postcards From Down Under

One of the most pleasant ways to travel in Australia is by train. The rhythmic rumble of the rails provides a soothing backdrop to the beautiful country as it rolls by. Riding the rails gives you time to meet people, appreciate the country side, and to slow down the hectic pace in which travelers may find themselves. AustRail passes are inexpensive and cover 8, 15, and 21 days of train travel.

Wine, Women and Song

If you like fine, wonderfully priced wines, Australia is the place to visit. Many of the metropolitan areas have wineries a short distance away. Ask your friends in the know about wines if they have tried any of the Aussie wines. We'll bet they have only nice things to says.

Austrialian Wine Growing Areas:

- Barossa Valley Wineries - north of Adelaide
- Hunter Valley Wineries - north of Sydney
- Margaret River Wineries - south of Perth
- Mt. Avoca Wineries - northwest of Melbourne

The <link> tag specifies relationships between the current HTML document and external files—style sheets, scripts, and so on. The <link> tag is the only HTML element included in the XHTML Link module, and like all XML/XHTML-compliant code, it requires an ending tag. We will explore several variations of the <link /> element in subsequent chapters. In this instance, we want to link the external style sheet nletter.css to our newsletter. To do so, we code the following in the document's <head> element:

```
<link rel="stylesheet" href="nletter.css" type="text/css" />
```

rel, href, and type

The **rel** attribute of "stylesheet" establishes that the external file is related to the current document as a style sheet. The hyperlink reference **(href)** identifies the path to the style-sheet file and the file's name. If the file is found at another Web site, then the complete URL needs to be included here. As with images, we urge you not to link across machines and especially not to link across sites for style sheets. That will only cause undue Net traffic, and may well result in your document not displaying as you intended if the remote machine is unavailable. The **type** attribute specifies that the external file is text that follows the CSS specifications.

More than one <link /> container can appear in a document's <head> element. These options are discussed in more detail in later chapters. For now, link your HTML document to a single external style sheet.

The external style sheet in Figure 8.1 was used to create the newsletter shown in Figure 8.2. The HTML code shown in Figure 8.2 is void of any attributes except for a color change to the <h3></h3> heading. This inline style change was included to reinforce the main point of this chapter: inline and document-level style changes are to be used only for custom, one-of-a-kind changes. Professional Web weavers use external style sheets to design their pages and make them easy to maintain.

EXPLORATION #2

Copy the file funfacts.html from the student CD to your personal computer. Open funfacts.html using an ASCII editor, and change the <title> container to *your name's Fun Facts*. Add a link to the chapter8.css external style sheet created in Exploration 1. Save the HTML code as chapter8.html, and display it using your favorite browser.

▸▸ CLASSES OF STYLES

As your page designs become more sophisticated, you may need to apply a set of style changes across multiple elements. For example, the masthead of the newsletter appears at the top of each newsletter document. It contains the name of the newsletter *(Travelers Newsletter)* and the newsletter's logo (For People In The Know and On The Go). Other mastheads might contain the publisher's and editor's names, year of publication, issue number, and so on. Our masthead incorporates centered level-1 and level-2 headings using a green italic Times New Roman font if possible. Otherwise, any serif font will do.

Instead of using inline styles to format each line, we can associate these style changes with the class name, masthead. A *class* is a name given to a set of properties assigned to different HTML elements. The class name always begins with a period. We recommend limiting class names to alphabetic glyphs. At this time Navigator and Opera do not recognize classes that use a number or special character as the first character after the period. The leading period is required syntax—don't forget it. The HTML code to create a class looks like this:

```
.masthead
   {
   color: #009900; /* green */
   font-style: italic;
   font-family: "Times New Roman", serif;
   text-align: center;
   }
```

class

Once a class name has been assigned to a specific set of style changes, either in an external style sheet or by the <style></style> container, it can be applied to elements within the associated HTML document. The code to assign the masthead to the first two headings in the newsletters follows:

```
<h1 class="masthead">Travelers newsletter</h1>
<h2 class="masthead">For People In The Know and On The Go!</h2>
```

The relationship between the external style sheet, the document's HTML code, and the browser's handling of the page display is illustrated in Figure 8.3.

Figure 8.3   HTML code formatted by an external style sheet

External style sheet (nletter.css)

```
.masthead
   {
   color: #009900; /* green */
   font-style: italic;
   font-family: "Times New Roman", serif;
   text-align: center;
   }
```

HTML code using class attribute

```
1   <html>
2   <head>
3   <title>External Style Sheets</title>
4   <link rel="stylesheet"
5         href="nletter.css"
6         type="text/css" />
7   </head>
8
9   <body>
10  <h1 class="masthead">Travelers Newsletter</h1>
11  <h2 class="masthead">For People In The Know and On The Go!</h2>
```

Browser's rendering of code above

> **External Style Sheets**
>
> ## *Travelers Newsletter*
>
> ### *For People In The Know and On The Go!*
>
> In this issue we want to explore Australia. While half-a-world away, you can escape the cold and damp of winter in the North and embrace summer again by traveling there. The people are friendly. The exchange rates are favorable. And there are plenty of places were you can get away from it all!

INHERITANCE

Notice that the masthead class says nothing about the font size, so the headings are displayed in the font sizes assigned to the h1 and h2 headings by the external style sheet. This is an example of *inheritance,* which means that an element maintains (inherits) styles previously defined and will continue to have these styles unless overridden by an acceptable design element closer to the data.

Every style property recognizes the inherit value. Web weavers use this value when they want the browser to pass on properties assigned to the element. But only computed values get inherited. Specified percentage values are not inherited.

GENERIC AND TAG-LEVEL CLASSES

The masthead example presented here is considered a *generic class* because it can be applied to a variety of tags. A *tag-level class* is assigned to a specific tag. In the following examples, three special classes for the <p>paragraph</p> container are established:

```
p.left
    {
    font-family: "Times New Roman", serif;
    left-margin: 3em;
    right-margin: 3em;
    }
```

Table 8.1 Common measurement values

Relative Value	Description
em	Width of M in font-size of active font
ex	Height of x in active font
px	Pixel size relative to viewing device
Absolute Value	**Description**
in	Inch—1 inch equals 2.54 centimeters
cm	Centimeter—1 centimeter equals .3937 inch
mm	Millimeter
pt	Points—1/72th of an inch
pc	Picas—1 pica equals 12 points
Angles	**Description**
deg	Degrees—360 to a circle
grad	Grads
rad	Radians
Time	**Description**
ms	Milliseconds
s	Seconds
Frequencies	**Description**
Hz	Hertz
kHz	Kilohertz

What, you might ask, is an **em**? When we are using *proportional spacing,* an em is the measurement of the horizontal line space taken up by the uppercase letter *M. En* is the measurement of the space taken up by the letter *N.* As a result, a 3-em right indent would indent the paragraph the length of three *Ms.* In this typeface, 3 ems would be MMM long. Since screen sizes vary so much, we would recommend you set margins using relative sizes like ems or percentages (see Table 8.1).

```
p. right
    {
    font-style: italic;
    text-align: right;
    left-margin: 3em;
    right-margin: 3em;
    }
p. centered
    {
    font-weight: bold;
    text-align: center;
    }
```

These tag-level classes can be applied only to the <p> container. However, the HTML syntax is the same as that used with generic classes. The following code would right-align the text and display it in an italic font style by using the right class just defined:

```
<p class="right">Publisher: McGraw-Hill</p>
```

▸ STYLE-SHEET ELEMENTS TO DIVIDE AND SPAN

Once you understand how **class** attributes are used in page design and maintenance, then you will see uses for the <div> element and its smaller cousin, <span>. Consider the newsletter example we have been developing. Special travel advisories, or warnings, need special handling in our document. As a result, a new class, called advisories (Figure 8.4), is created to place a dashed line (border) under any advisories and print the text using a red italic font.

The <div></div> container works with several elements at a time, while the <span> container is limited to inline changes. Let's look at the <div> element first.

HTML `<div>Divide Document</div>`

Description: identifies one or more blocks of text for the purpose of special formatting or identification.
Type: container.
Attributes: *align,* **class,** dir, **id,** lang, onclick, ondblclick, onkeydown, onkeypress, onkeyup, onmousedown, onmousemove, onmouseout, onmouseover, onmouseup, **style,** title.

In Figure 8.4, several elements, including a heading and an ordered list, are enclosed within a <div></div> container set to use the advisories class for formatting. Graphical browsers will use these formatting specifications (dashed border and red italic text) on any objects contained within the <div></div> container as long as no object contains a **style** property that overrides a tag-level format previously set in the style sheet. It is difficult to tell from the figure, but the font color in the level-2 heading "Travel Advisories" remained in gray because this color was specified elsewhere in the style sheet as part of the h2 format (see Figure 8.1). However, the text is displayed in an italic font as specified by the advisories class because text style had not been changed.

Figure 8.4 HTML code using <div> container with **class** and **id** attributes for special formatting

External style sheet
(nletter.css)

```
.advisories
  {
  border-bottom-style: dashed;
  border-color: #FF0000; /* red */
  border-width: 2px;
  color: #FF0000; /* red */
  font-style: italic;
  }

#special
  {
  font-weight: bold;
  margin-left: 1in;
  }
```

HTML code
using class and
id attributes

```
43  <div class="advisories">
44  <h2>Travel Advisories</h2>
45  <p>The U.S. State Department has posted travel advisories for the following countries
46  until further notice:
47  </p>
48  <ol>
49    <li>Afghanistan</li>
50    <li>Bosnia</li>
51    <li>Congo</li>
52    <li>Indonesia</li>
53    <li>Sri Lanka</li>
54  </ol>
55  </div>
56
57  <div id="special">
58  <h2>Editor's Corner</h2>
59  <p>For some of us the grass is always greener after a 4-hour flight to someplace else.
60  However, your own backyard, the one you take for granted, may be someone else's exotic
61  getaway. Over your next three-day weekend, focus your travel expertise at home.
62  Research local food/entertainment, recreational areas, and lodging and take a trip
63  closer to home. If nothing else, you will have ideas for friends who come to visit.
64  </p>
65  </div>
```

Browser's rendering
of code above

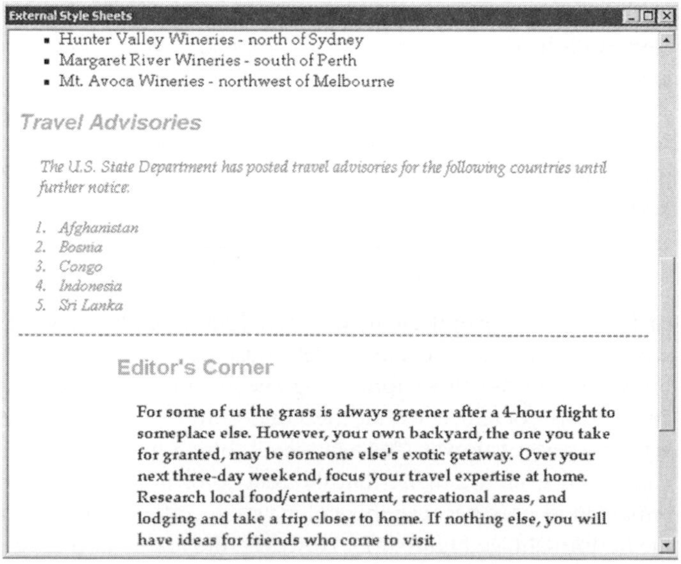

The <div> element can be confusing to some people, because it does not produce any visible change in the browser window when used without attributes. Enclosing several paragraphs of text within a <div> element wouldn't usually have any visual impact on the page. The <div></div> container is also useful for marking off large sections of a page for purposes of identification using the **id** attribute. In other words, it can divide a large document into identifiable sections. If one of those large sections needs special formatting, the Web weaver can also use <div> to selectively apply element-level formatting changes.

This container works best with the **class, id,** and **style** attributes. As shown earlier, the **class** attribute allows the Web weaver to selectively change the format of any HTML elements that fall within the <div></div> container.

The **class** attribute is not the only way to make format changes using a <div> element. The **id** attribute demonstrated in Chapter Three assigned a target name to an HTML element that was used with intrapage links within a document and interpage links from outside the document. This **id** target can also appear in a style sheet (document-level or external) and have unique formats associated with it. For example, the portion of the nletter.css style sheet shown in Figure 8.4 identifies the target #special and sets the font-weight and left margin using this code:

```
#special
    {
    font-weight: bold;
    margin-left: 1in;
    }
```

These formatting codes can then be assigned to any objects within a <div></div> container associated with the #special **id.** The results are shown in Figure 8.4. This application of the **id** attribute is limited to one per Web page because the identifier, like special, cannot be used twice. So, remember, if you choose to use this method to apply formatting to an element, you can do it only once. By the way, in this example, **id** special also serves as the target for an intrapage link.

Furthermore, a <div></div> container can format blocks of HTML code without having a class or target name or even a **style** attribute associated with it. For example, the following code would right-align the elements within the <div></div> container:

```
<div align="right">
<h2>Editor's Corner</h2>
<p>For some of us the grass is always greener after a 4-hour flight to
someplace else. However, your own backyard, the one you take for granted,
may be someone else's exotic getaway.
</p>
</div>
```

In addition, the **style** attribute can be applied to the <div></div> container. In the following code, all the enclosed elements have a 1-inch left margin and are set to bold (see bottom of Figure 8.4):

```
<div style="font-weight: bold;
    margin-left: 1in;">
<h2>Editor's Corner</h2>
<p>For some of us the grass is always greener after a 4-hour flight to
someplace else. However, your own backyard, the one you take for granted,
may be someone else's exotic getaway.
</p>
</div>
```

Yet, the real power of the <div></div> container resides in the ability of the Web weaver to use it for assigning class-level formatting changes to groups of HTML elements.

HTML   <span>Span Area</span>

Description: identifies an arbitrary section of text for the purpose of special formatting.
Type: container.
Attributes: *align,* class, dir, id, lang, onclick, ondblclick, onkeydown, onkeypress, onkeyup, onmousedown, onmousemove, onmouseout, onmouseover, onmouseup, style, title.

The <span></span> container works something like the <div></div> container but is usually used for inline text that needs to be handled in a special way. Use <div></div> for formatting across several elements and <span></span> for inline formatting changes. In the newsletter, a reader's comment is meant to be a travel advisory to others. Since the comment is within an ordered list, the <span></span> container is coded to use the advisories class for formatting—see the highlighted section of Figure 8.5.

Figure 8.5 HTML code with <span> </span> container using advisories class to format text

External style sheet (nletter.css)

```
.advisories
  {
  border-bottom-style: dashed;
  border-color: #FF0000; /* red */
  border-width: 2px;
  color: #FF0000; /* red */
  font-style: italic;
  }
```

HTML code using class attribute

```
63  <h2>Reader's Comments</h2>
64  <ul>
65    <li>AJ from Hackley, Michigan liked our coverage of skiing in the French Alps, but
66      thought we "shortchanged the cross-country skiing in Chamonix."
67    </li>
68    <li>PT from Boulder, Colorado thought we should have been stronger on
69      <span class="advisories"> "the warning to travelers in Thailand about people who
70      try to befriend you in the marketplace. These people have ulterior motives that
71      rarely dovetails with those of the traveler."
72      </span>
73    </li>
74    <li>SY from Tacoma, Washington had several flashbacks when reading our piece on
75      Guadeloupe. "Tell your readers to take a dip in the Cascade Aux Ecrevisses (Crayfish
76      Falls). They will never forget the experience."
77    </li>
78  </ul>
```

Browser's rendering of code above

External Style Sheets

Reader's Comments

- AJ from Hackley, Michigan liked our coverage of skiing in the French Alps, but thought we "shortchanged the cross-country skiing in Chamonix."
- PT from Boulder, Colorado thought we should have been stronger on *"the warning to travelers in Thailand about people who try to befriend you in the marketplace. These people have ulterior motives that rarely dovetails with those of the traveler."*
- SY from Tacoma, Washington had several flashbacks when reading our piece on Guadeloupe. "Tell your readers to take a dip in the Cascade Aux Ecrevisses (Crayfish Falls). They will never forget the experience."

Please contact us at travelnews@newisp.net

As we saw with the <div></div> container, the <span></span> container makes no style changes by itself. It is only by means of the **class, style,** or **id** attributes that elements within the container take on new formats. The <span></span> container can also work with the **id** attribute to identify areas within the document that can be used as a target for intrapage links.

We use these parallel applications of the advisories class (see Figures 8.4 and 8.5) to illustrate how well-designed class designations can be used over and over. One factor that separates the professional Web weaver from the wannabe is the ability to create and use external style sheets with functional design elements and flexible classes.

EXPLORATION #3

Add two new classes to chapter8.css:

1. .computer: sets font to Comic Sans MS and color to #FF0000 (red).

2. .note: sets font to bold and italic with color set to #660099 (purple).

Two level-2 headings (A Computer a Day . . . and They Don't Build Them Like They Used To) use the .computer class. The .note class is used across the heading, paragraph, and order list associated with "The Choice Is Yours" fun fact. Save the external style sheet, and refresh/reload the browser display.

▸▸ COMMON STYLE PROPERTIES

In Chapter Four we covered list item (<li>) values associated with the list-style-type property. In Chapter Five we covered font properties. In Chapters Six and Seven the **style** attribute set various border, margin, and padding properties. What follows is an overview of other properties and associated values we feel are useful when designing Web pages. These properties are often coded in external style sheets and may be used within <style></style> containers or even used inline with tags that recognize the **style** attribute. All of these properties are part of the W^3C's current specifications for HTML, and, as you have heard many times by now, they may not be recognized by older browsers. Common measurements for property values are shown in Table 8.1.

TEXT MANIPULATION AND ALIGNMENT

The **style** attribute's properties shown in Table 8.2 include some of our old favorites. The color property allows you to change the typeface color using the hexadecimal RGB color codes we discussed earlier (see the color insert in the Reference Guide).

The other properties manipulate the look or placement of text on the screen. For example, the text-decoration property runs a horizontal line over, under, or through the text as shown in Figure 8.6—please note that some HTML code has been removed from this code for clarity. When text-align is set equal to justify, the browser should align the words in a line with both the left and right sides of the screen.

Indenting the first line of every paragraph is common to many document designs. The following style code would indent the first line of the paragraph 3 ems to the right:

```
P {text-indent: 3em;}
```

The line-height and vertical-align properties play off each other. Adjustments to the vertical alignment move the text up and down within the vertical line space set aside to display a line of text, that is, the line height. You manipulate the vertical alignment when setting the text to subscript or superscript. The *baseline* is the horizontal plane on which text is normally displayed. You can see where that is by drawing a line connecting the bottoms of all the letters in the line of text. Note that some of the letters have descenders, portions (like the tails on the lowercase g or y) that hang below the baseline. Subscripted text appears below the baseline.

Table 8.2 Text properties and values

Property	Description	Values	Special Notes
color	Changes typeface's color.	Hexadecimal number or color keyword	See color insert for browser-safe color options.
letter-spacing	Increases (+) or decreases (–) spacing between letters.	normal | [length] | inherit |	[length] is measured in ems or cm. Decimals are acceptable.
line-height	Determines vertical space set aside for a line of text.	normal | [number] | [length] | [percentage] | inherit	[number] is the value to be multiplied by the text height.
text-align	Orients text left and/or right or in the middle of a screen.	left | right | center | justify | [string] | inherit	[string] applies to cell alignment in a table based on a string value.
text-decoration	Draws horizontal line through text area or turns area on and off.	none | underline | overline | line-through | blink | inherit	Applies only to text and has no impact on images.
text-indent	Moves start of first line to left or right of text area's default edge.	[length] | [percentage] | inherit	[length] is given in ems. Negative numbers move text left.
text-shadow	Overlays another character image left or right (x), up or down (y).	none | color | x y blur | inherit	Coordinates and blur given in pixels (px): – x goes left, and –y goes up.
text-transform	Standardizes case of text.	none | capitalize | uppercase | lowercase | inherit	Capitalize converts first character of each word to uppercase.
vertical-align	Orients text up and down within vertical line space assigned to each line of text in the text area.	baseline | sub | super | top | text-top | middle | bottom | text-bottom | [percentage] | [length] | inherit	Baseline = '0%' or '0cm'. Positive values raise text above baseline, and negative values lower text.
word-spacing	Increases (+) or decreases (–) spacing between words.	normal | [length] | inherit	[length] is measured in ems or cm.

The line-height property is also used in conjunction with the font-size property. The standard way of figuring the line-height is to take the font-size (in ems) and multiply it by 1.2. This difference between the font size and the computed value of the line height is called the **leading** (pronounced "ledding"). When the line height is smaller than the font size, the tops of the letters on one line touch the bottom of the characters in the line above (called *bleeding*). The following code computes the line height by multiplying the ems of the current 12-point font by 1.2:

```
p {line-height: 1.2; font-size: 12 pt;}
```

A Web author can also set the line height to a specific height. For example, this code sets the line height to a height of 1.1 em:

```
p {line-height: 1.1em; font-size: 12 pt;}
```

In addition, the line height can be set as a percentage of the font size. This HTML code sets the line height at 120 percent of the em in the 12-point font size:

```
p {line-height: 120%; font-size: 12 pt;}
```

Figure 8.6

HTML code for text manipulations

```
4   <style type="text/css">
5   h3 {font-family: sans-serif;}
6   p.em-letterspacing {letter-spacing: 1em;}
7   p.em-wordspacing {word-spacing: 1em;}
8   p.underline {text-decoration: underline;}
9   p.overline {text-decoration: overline;}
10  p.line-through {text-decoration: line-through;}
11  p.gray {color: #999999;}
12  p.caps {text-transform: capitalize;}
13  p.upper {text-transform: uppercase;}
14  p.lower {text-transform: lowercase;}
15  </style>
```

```
19  <h3>Manipulations</h3>
20  <p>normal black text</p>
21  <p class="em-letterspacing">letter spacing @ 1em</p>
22  <p class="em-wordspacing">word spacing for this and that @ 1em</p>
23  <p class="underline">underline</p>
24  <p class="overline">overline</p>
25  <p class="line-through">line-through</p>
26  <p class="caps">capitalize TEXT</p>
27  <p class="upper">uppercase TEXT</p>
28  <p class="lower">lowercase TEXT</p>
29  <p class="gray">gray text</p>
30  <p>normal black text</p>
```

Manipulations

normal black text

l e t t e r   s p a c i n g   @   1 e m

word   spacing   for   this   and   that   @   1em

<u>underline</u>

‾‾‾‾‾‾
overline

~~line through~~

Capitalize TEXT

UPPERCASE TEXT

lowercase text

gray text

normal black text

EXPLORATION #4

Make the following changes to chapter8.css:

1. Add body element, and set color to #000099.
2. Level-1 headings should include letter spacing at 2 mm.

Save the external style sheet again, and refresh/reload the browser display.

background: color | image | repeat | attachment | position

The background property replaces the **backround** and **bgcolor** attributes used within the <body></body> container. In Figure 8.1, we used the background-color property to

Table 8.3 Background properties and values

Property	Description	Values	Special Notes
background-attachment	Determines whether background moves when window scrolls.	scroll | fixed | inherit	
background-color	Sets background color.	[color] | transparent | inherit	[color] is a six digit hexadecimal code or transparent color keyword found inside the book's cover.
background-image	Loads background graphic from designated URL.	[url] (path/filename) | none | inherit	A background image takes precedence over the color.
background-position	Provides xy coordinates for positioning image within page.	% | [length] | top' center or bottom | left, center or right | inherit	[length] measurement can be in either inches (in) or centimeters (cm).
background-repeat	Determines if small background images repeat horizontally (x) or vertically (y).	repeat | repeat-x | repeat-y | no-repeat | inherit	Using repeat makes image repeat vertically and horizontally.
background	Shortcut that combines other background properties.	background-color | background-image | background-repeat | background-attachment | background-position | inherit	Leaves a space (not a comma) between property values.

set the body of the newsletter to light yellow. Background images are set using the background-image property as documented in Table 8.3.

The properties described in Table 8.3 provide the Web weaver with a greater level of control because they are used with a wide variety of elements. For example, the following HTML code would assign the image canvas.png as the background for a level-1 heading (see Figure 8.7):

```
h1 {background-image: url (canvas.png) ;}
```

Figure 8.7

HTML code for setting background images for a specific element

External style sheet
(nletter.css)

```
h1
  {
  background-image: url(canvas.png);
  font-size: 30pt;
  }
```

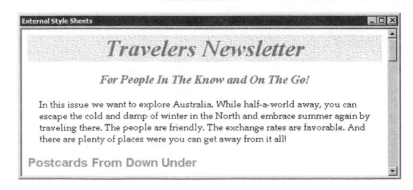

Notice the different syntax of this assignment: rather than setting the URL equal to an address, we used the form url (path/imagename). Background colors are assigned to specific elements in the same way. For example, if you wanted to set a level-2 heading to appear as if it were highlighted (black text on a yellow background), you would code the following:

```
h2 {background-color: #FFFF00;} /* yellow */
```

The background-position property is used when the Web author wants to control the horizontal and vertical location of an image within the Web page. The horizontal coordinates are presented using the following percentages or words:

- 0% (left)
- 50% (center)
- 100% (right)

The vertical coordinates are presented using these percentages or words:

- 0% (top)
- 50% (center)
- 100% (bottom)

Therefore, the horizontal (x) and vertical (y) coordinates together should be interpreted like this (also see Figure 8.8):

- Top left or left top: same as "0% 0%"
- Top, top center, or center top: same as "50% 0%"
- Top right or right top: same as "100% 0%"
- Left, center left, or left center: same as "0% 50%"
- Center or center center: same as "50% 50%"
- Right, center right, or right center: same as "100% 50%"
- Bottom left or left bottom: same as "0% 100%"
- Bottom, bottom center or center bottom: same as "50% 100%"
- Bottom right or right bottom: same as "100% 100%"

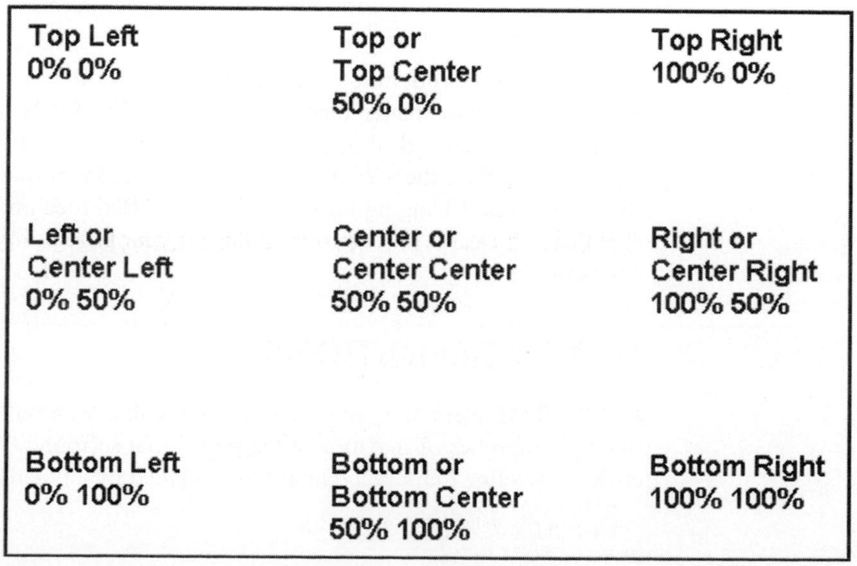

Figure 8.8

Examples of how horizontal and vertical positioning would be used by the background-position property

Top Left 0% 0%	Top or Top Center 50% 0%	Top Right 100% 0%
Left or Center Left 0% 50%	Center or Center Center 50% 50%	Right or Center Right 100% 50%
Bottom Left 0% 100%	Bottom or Bottom Center 50% 100%	Bottom Right 100% 100%

The following HTML code would center the image horizontally and vertically within the page:

```
body
   {
   background-image: url (map.png);
   background-position: center; /* 50% 50% */
   }
```

You can also use inches (in) or centimeters (cm) to identify the xy positioning. However, as with all the other opportunities for coding either an absolute number or percentage, we strongly recommend you use percentages (shown in Figure 8.8).

The CSS2 recommendations also allow for the keyword background to be used as a shortcut when assigning two or more background properties to a document. The acceptable syntax is to include the color, image, repeat, attachment, and position values within the curly braces and separated by spaces. We discourage you from using most shortcuts, since they can confuse both you and your reader. The following code would (1) set the background color to light yellow (#FFFFCC) if the image is not present, (2) use the image paper.png if the image is present, and (3) freeze the image when the screen is scrolled:

```
body {background: #FFFFCC url (paper.png) fixed;}
```

Fixing or *freezing,* the background image is a technique that allows the Web weaver to make sure that the background image does not scroll off the first page.

EXPLORATION **#5**

Use chapter8.css to change the body's background color to #99FFFF. Save the external style sheet, and refresh/reload the browser display.

▶▶ CHANGING LINK COLORS

The colors used to identify links can be changed when the background color or image conflicts. The following code is used in place of the **link, vlink,** and **alink** attributes associated with the <body> element:

```
body {background: #FFFFCC; color: #0000FF;}
   a:link {color: #FF0000;}
   a:visited {color: #00FFFF;}
   a:active {color: #000000;}
```

Although it is possible to change the colors of the link, visited link, and active link, we urge you not to change them unless you are absolutely forced to. Changing these values can cause a great deal of confusion for your users. Users expect the unvisited links on a page to be blue, the visited links to be that funky purple color, and the active link to show up as red. Changing the colors is a Very Bad Idea unless your background requires it. If that is the case, first consider changing your page design to accommodate the default colors instead.

▶▶ BOX DEFINITIONS

Each HTML element is actually enclosed within a virtual "box" that can be used to define the properties of that area of the screen that surrounds the element. That is, the properties that define the screen real estate occupied by an element apply to an area of a page generally referred to as a *box.* The related terminology is similar to the terms used with tables. The white space set aside for margins, together with any borders and padding that surround the HTML element, is known as the ***CSS box model*** (Figure 8.9). This model provides the framework for placing white space around the element, called *padding,* just as similar white space is placed within a table. The CSS model allows for an optional border around the padding as well. Furthermore, it gives the HTML author control of the box's margins, always set to transparent, which define the outside edge of the box. A Web weaver uses the margin properties to specify where the border, if there is one, and the HTML elements are positioned within the box. The box could contain a heading, text, image, or list. When this book was written, the major browsers were just beginning to support these properties. It may take some time before they are fully supported.

Figure 8.9

CSS box model

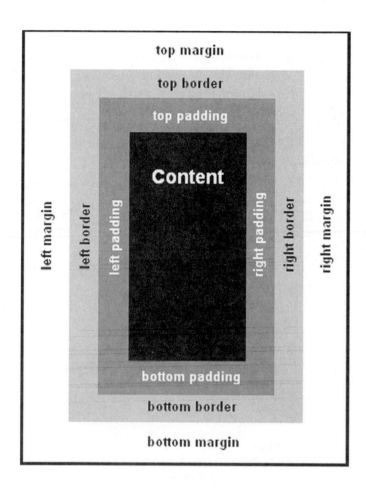

width: [absolute] | [percentage] | auto | inherit

You can establish the horizontal space taken up by a CSS box using the width property. The width is given in a fixed length using ems, pixels (px), English measurements in inches (in), or metric measurements in millimeters (mm) or centimeters (cm). When a percentage is used, the width of the box is computed using the width of the element contained inside the box. When the auto value is used, the width of the box is determined by the values of other properties such as margins, padding, and borders. The following code sets the width of the CSS box that contains the paragraph to 80 percent of the browser's display width:

```
p {width: 80%;}
```

height: [absolute] | [percentage] | auto | inherit

You set how tall a CSS box is by using the height property. Like the width property, the height property is given in a fixed size, a percentage, or is set to auto. The following code establishes a paragraph height of 3 centimeters:

```
p {height: 3cm}
```

visibility: visible | hidden | collapse | inherit

It is even possible to make an object disappear from a Web page without deleting it. When visibility is set to hidden the object still takes up room on the screen but is not displayed. The code to establish #hide as a target that uses the visibility property looks like this:

```
#hide {visibility: hidden;}
```

Any margins, borders, or padding set for the object are not shown but still takes up space on the screen. Knowledgeable Web weavers could write scripts to change this value from hidden to visible that would result in visually turning the object off and on. The collapse value is used only with tables to visually remove specific rows or columns from the table display. If it is used outside a table, the object is hidden.

margin: top | right | bottom | left

Table 8.4 identifies all four margin properties. The only reason to individually identify each property would be if the width of each margin is different.

The following code would set the top margin to 0.5 ems, the right margin to 2 ems, the bottom margin to 5 ems, and the left margin to 10 ems:

```
body
  {
  margin-top: 0.5em;
  margin-right: 2em;
  margin-bottom: 5em;
  margin-left: 10em;
  }
```

The shortcut to this code is to use the margin property is

```
/* top right bottom left */
body {margin: 0.5 em 2 em 5 em 10 em}
```

Table 8.4 Properties and values that affect CSS boxes

Property	Description	Values	Special Notes
margin-bottom	Defines transparent area at the bottom of the CSS box.	[length] | [percentage] | auto | inherit	[length] is measured in ems, cm, or in.
margin-left	Defines transparent area at the left side of the CSS box.	[length] | [percentage] | auto | inherit	[length] is measured in ems, cm, or in.
margin-top	Defines transparent area at the top of the CSS box.	[length] | [percentage] | auto | inherit	[length] is measured in ems, cm, or in.
margin-right	Defines transparent area at the right side of the CSS box.	[length] | [percentage] | auto | inherit	[length] is measured in ems, cm, or in.
white-space	Determines how tabs and repeated spaces are handled.	normal | pre | nowrap | inherit	Both pre and nowrap recognize "\A" as a line-break symbol.

The assumed order when four values are used is top, right, bottom, and left. The newsletter would look like Figure 8.10 if these margins were used.

Figure 8.10

Display of margins as follows: 10 ems for left, 2 ems for right, 0.5 ems for top, and 5 ems for bottom (not shown)

External style sheet (nletter.css)

```
body
  {
  background-color: #FFFFCC; /* light yellow */
  margin-top: 0.5em;
  margin-right: 2em;
  margin-bottom: 5em;
  margin-left: 10em;
  }
```

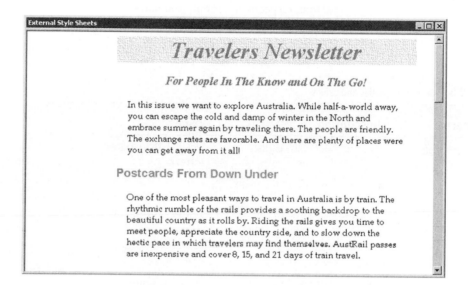

When fewer than four values are used with the margin property, the following rules apply:

- One value: all margins are the same.
- Two values: top and bottom margins are the same, and left and right margins are the same.
- Three values: the first value is for the top, the second value is for the right and left, and the third value is for the bottom margin.

Here is the example from the CSS2 specifications:

```
body {margin: 2em;} /* all margins are set to 2em */
body {margin: 1em 2em;} /* top & bottom=1em, right & left=2em */
body {margin: 1em 2em 3em;} /* top=1em, right=2em, bottom=3em,
left=2em */
```

Using the margin property is one situation where it is appropriate to use a shortcut property. *If* you want all four margins to be the same, it is acceptable to use the margin shortcut as long as you document it in your code.

white-space: normal | pre | nowrap | inherit

The white-space property determines just how the browser handles extra spaces and tabs. Normally additional spaces and tabs are ignored, or, in other words, compressed into a single space. When the white-space property is set to **nowrap** the browser also ignores all line breaks. On the other hand, when the white-space property is set to pre the browser displays every space and tab in the associated container. With nowrap and pre text, line breaks occur only when the <br /> tag is encountered.

border: width | style | color

The border of the CSS box surrounds an element or elements with a line of various styles, colors, and thickness. The distance between the element and the border is determined by the padding, as illustrated in Figure 8.9. You can change the color, line style, and thickness (see Table 8.5) on one, two, three, or all of the sides of a CSS box.

The border-style, border-color, and border-width properties set values for all four borders. When a single value is given, every side is displayed the same way. For example, in the following code, the border's color, style, and thickness are set to blue, solid, and thin, respectively, for all four sides:

Table 8.5   Border properties and values

Property	Description	Values	Special Notes
border-color	Changes color of the border.	[color] | transparent] | inherit	Alternatives: border-top-color, border-right-color, border-bottom-color, or border-left-color
border-style	Changes look of border line.	none | hidden | dotted | dashed | solid | double | groove | ridge | inset | outset	Alternatives: border-top-style, border-right-style, border-bottom-style or border-left style
border-width	Changes thickness, style, and color of border line.	thin | medium | thick | absolute value	Alternatives: border-top-width, border-right-width, border-bottom-width or border-left-width
border-bottom	Changes thickness, style, and color of bottom border.	thin | medium | thick | [length] | hidden | dotted | dashed | solid | double | groove | ridge | inset | outset | [color] | transparent	
border-left	Changes thickness, style, and color of left border.	thin | medium | thick | [length] | hidden | dotted | dashed | solid | double | groove | ridge | inset | outset | [color] | transparent	
border-top	Changes thickness, style, and color of top border.	thin | medium | thick | [length] | hidden | dotted | dashed | solid | double | groove | ridge | inset | outset | [color] | transparent	
border-right	Changes thickness, style, and color of right border.	hidden | dotted | dashed | solid | double | groove | ridge | inset | outset | [length] | transparent	

```
h3
    {
    border-color: #0000FF; /* blue */
    border-style: solid;
    border-width: thin;
    }
```

The following code using the border property provides a convenient shortcut to produce the same border property changes as the preceding code.

```
h3 {border: thin solid #0000FF } /* blue */
```

All of the CSS box properties have this type of shortcut.

The border width can be described in pixels (px), millimeters (mm), inches (in), or with the keywords thin, medium, and thick. Figure 8.11 illustrates the different border

Figure 8.11   HTML code for different border styles and execution with popular browsers

```
4   <style type="text/css">
5   body {background-color: #CCCCCC;} /* light gray */
6   h3 {font-family: sans-serif;}
7   p.dotted {border: dotted;}
8   p.dashed {border: dashed;}
9   p.solid {border: solid;}
10  p.double {border: double;}
11  p.groove {border: groove;}
12  p.ridge {border: ridge;}
13  p.inset {border: inset;}
14  p.outset {border: outset;}
15  </style>
```

```
20  <h3>Border Styles</h3>
21  <p class="dotted">dotted border</p>
22  <p class="dashed">dashed border</p>
23  <p class="solid">solid border</p>
24  <p class="double">double border</p>
25  <p class="groove">groove border</p>
26  <p class="ridge">ridge border</p>
27  <p class="inset">inset border</p>
28  <p class="outset">outset border</p>
```

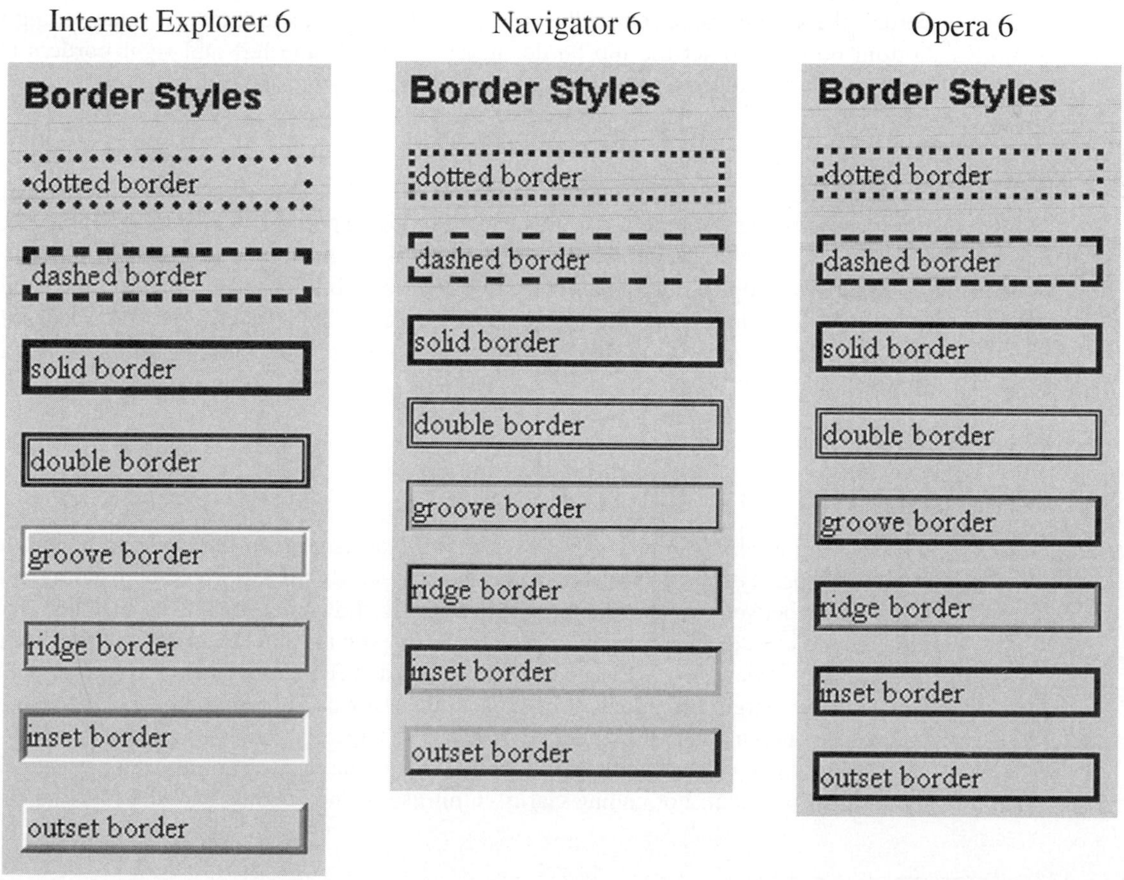

styles—please note that some HTML code has been removed from this code for clarity. You can also designate none or hidden as border styles; in both cases the border width is set equal to zero, with the hidden property taking precedence when table borders conflict. The color property value is best set using hexadecimal RGB color codes, but you can use the color keywords (see Reference Guide).

The ability to independently alter any side of the border creates a wide variety of coding alternatives. Shortcuts like border-style, border-color, and border-width allow the Web weaver to change any of the sides, the top and bottom, left and right, and each side independent of the other. When all four sides are changed, the presentation order of the values is as follows:

1. Top
2. Right
3. Bottom
4. Left

A sample of code that would make each border side a different color is

```
h1 {border-color: red yellow blue green}
```

In this case the top border is red, the right border is yellow, the bottom border is blue, and the left border is green.

When two values are given, the top and bottom borders are the same, and this value is listed first. Then the value for the left and right borders is given. In the following code, the top and bottom borders are dashed, and the left and right borders are dotted:

```
h4 {border-style: dashed dotted}
```

Three values after the property name would result in the first value setting the top border, the second value setting the right and left borders, and the third value setting the bottom border. To set the top border to a thin width, the left and right borders to a medium width, and the bottom border to a thick width, you could use this code:

```
h5 {border-width: thin medium thick}
```

Each of the borders can have the color, width, and style independently changed using the specific border property keywords shown in the "Special Notes" area of Table 8.5 as alternatives. Another way to approach changing the properties of a specific border is to use the border-top, border-right, border-bottom, and border-left properties. Acceptable values would include thin, medium, thick, [absolute value], hidden, dotted, dashed, solid, double, groove, ridge, inset, outset, [color] or transparent as outlined in Table 8.5 and shown in Figure 8.11.

padding: top | right | bottom | left

You can adjust the padding within a CSS box just as you can in a table. Padding and other table properties are discussed in Chapter Seven. In the CSS box the padding is the white space between the content and the border. As shown in Figure 8.12, padding values are given in ems, inches (in), centimeters (cm), or even millimeters (mm), but they cannot be negative—please note that some HTML code has been removed from this example for clarity. Like margin properties, percentage values for padding properties are acceptable, and we encourage you to use either percentages or ems.

The padding values can be individually set, as documented in Table 8.6, or set using the padding shortcut. For coding clarity, limit use of the padding shortcut to those cases

Figure 8.12 HTML code for padding values to centimeters, millimeters, inches, and ems

```
4   <style type="text/css">
5   h3 {font-family: sans-serif;}
6   p.top {border: solid; padding-top: 0.5cm;}
7   p.right {border: solid; padding-right: 5mm;}
8   p.bottom {border: solid; padding-bottom: 0.5in;}
9   p.left {border: solid; padding-left: 5em;}
10  </style>
```

```
14  <h3>Border Padding</h3>
15  <p class="top">top padding</p>
16  <p class="right">right padding</p>
17  <p class="bottom">bottom padding</p>
18  <p class="left">left padding</p>
```

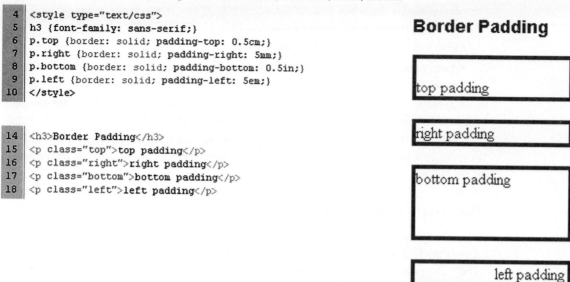

where you are setting all the padding values to the same size. This shortcut, like the margin-property shortcut, is useful when all the values are identical. Otherwise, use the individual properties. When independently changing all four sides to different values, you could use this code:

```
blockquote
  {
  padding-top: 1em;
  padding-right: 3em;
  padding-bottom: 4em;
  padding-left: 5em;
  }
```

The shortcut for the same code would look like this:

```
blockquote {padding: 1em 3em 4em 5em}
```

Table 8.6 Padding properties and values

Property	Description	Values	Special Notes
padding-top	Changes thickness of white space between top of contents and border line.	[padding-width] | inherit	[padding-width] is measured in %, ems, cm, mm, or in.
padding-right	Changes thickness of white space between right of contents and border line.	[padding-width] | inherit	[padding-width] is measured in %, ems, cm, mm, or in.
padding-bottom	Changes thickness of white space between bottom of contents and border line.	[padding-width] | inherit	[padding-width] is measured in %, ems, cm, mm, or in.
padding-left	Changes thickness of white space between left of contents and border line.	[padding-width] | inherit	[padding-width] is measured in %, ems, cm, mm, or in.

As you can see, the same precedence rules apply, with top, right, bottom, and left being the designated order when four values are given. When fewer than four values are used with the padding property, the standard precedence rules also apply:

- One value: all padding is the same.
- Two values: top and bottom padding is the same, and left and right padding is the same.
- Three values: the first value is for the top padding, the second value is for the right and left padding, and the third value is for the bottom padding.

You can avoid all this potential confusion by coding the individual values. Then everybody who looks at your code understands your intent. The color of the padding area is set by the background property.

float: left | right | none | inherit

The float property allows you to align elements side by side. For instance, notice how the text at the bottom of Figure 8.13 starts even with the top of the image, not inline with it. The float property works this way with text, images, and tables. Content flows down the right side of a left-floated box and down the left side of a right-floated box. Currently there is no value that will allow text to flow on *both* sides of the element.

Figure 8.13 Image set for no float (default) and for left float

no float Birds of a feather flock together and in some cases just buddy around.

img {float: left;} Birds of a feather flock together and in some cases just buddy around.

The following code was used to display the image and line of text shown at the top example in Figure 8.13.

```
<img src = "flamingo.gif" >
Birds of a feather flock together and in some cases just buddy around.
```

To float the text as shown at the bottom of Figure 8.13, you would need to add this code to the <style> container or the active external style sheets:

```
img {float: left;}
```

clear: none | left | right | both | inherit

Sometimes you want a paragraph of text to flow to the left or right of an image or table, but you want headings or some other element to start underneath. The **clear** attribute ends the float property's control of the text flow. If you float text next to images as part of a page's design, then the following code will ensure that the headings do not accidentally flow to the right or left of an image:

```
h1, h2, h3, h4, h5, h6 {clear: both;}.
```

The values left and right would work just like <br clear ="left"> or <br clear = "right">, discussed in Chapter Six, in that the respective float properties would be turned off at the time the clear property value was encountered.

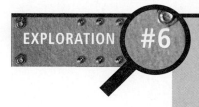

EXPLORATION   #6

Make the following changes to chapter8.css:

1. The body needs

- A double border that is 6 pixels wide and black in color.
- Top and bottom margins at 1 em.
- Left and right margins at 0.5 em.
- Padding on all four sides at 1 em.

2. Paragraphs with a left margin at 2 ems.

3. List items with a left margin at 3 ems.

Save the external style sheet, and refresh/reload the browser display.

▸▸ MEDIA TYPES

Currently, most Web pages are designed for screen displays, but the W³C recognizes that other media will be used to display HTML documents. Therefore, when pages are designed to be printed or used on handheld PDAs or other devices, the Web weaver can identify the intended media type. The default value is *screen,* and other acceptable media values include *braille, embossed, handheld, print, projection, tty, tv,* and *all.* The following code identifies an external style sheet designed for use on a handheld device:

```
<link rel="stylesheet" media="handheld" href="pda.css" type="text/css">
```

▸▸ PAGED MEDIA

Web pages displayed on a screen are continuous. Users scroll through long documents using the browser's scroll bar, and there are no real physical limitations to the length of the document. But HTML documents that need to be printed are not continuous. Every time the content reaches the end of a page, it must be continued onto another page, and the change of page breaks the continuity of the information being presented. HTML documents that are designed for printing need to set the **media** attribute in the <link></link> container to *print.* This paged media uses a new set of **style** properties to establish logical page breaks and other properties based on the printed page (see Table 8.7).

page-break-before: auto | always | avoid | left | right | inherit

When a Web page is designed for printing, the Web weaver must take into account page breaks. One of the most logical places to incorporate page breaks is right before a heading. Page breaks do not affect how the Web pages are displayed on the screen, only when they are printed. The property value **always** is used to set the page break on. The following code forces a page break before every level-1 heading:

```
h1 {page-break-before: always;}
```

The opposite happens when the property value **avoid** is used in setting a page break. In this case, no break occurs before the element is printed. For example, you would probably want to avoid page breaks between a level-1 headings and the paragraphs that immediately follow them. To make sure that no such breaks occur, you could assign every paragraph that falls immediately after a level-1 heading to this class:

```
.first-paragraph {page-break-before: avoid;}
```

Table 8.7 Printed page properties and values

Property	Description	Values	Special Notes
page-break-after	New page started after element is displayed or printed.	auto | always | avoid | left | right | inherit	
page-break-before	New page started before element is displayed or printed.	auto | always | avoid | left | right | inherit	
page-break-inside	Establishes whether a page break can occur within element.	avoid | auto | inherit	Typically used when designer does not want a table or list broken between pages.
page	Designed to be used with **id** attribute and target name.	[target] | auto	Assigns property values associated with target.
size	Specifies size and orientation of page.	[length] | auto | portrait | landscape | inherit	Length sets width and height. One number sets both values. When two values are used, the first sets width.
orphans	Minimum number of lines of a paragraph that must be left at bottom of page.	[number] | inherit	Default is 2. Used with visual and paged media types.
widows	Minimum number of lines of a paragraph that must be left at top of page.	[number] | inherit	Default is 2. Used with visual and paged media types.
marks	Crop marks indicate where page should be cut. Cross marks are used to align sheets.	[crop] | [cross] | none | inherit	Cross marks are also known as register or registration marks.
mark-offset	Positions crop and cross marks.	[length] | [auto] | inherit	

The **left** and **right** values create one and possibly two page breaks, so the content starts on a left page (usually an even-numbered page) or right page (usually an odd-numbered page). Currently the popular graphical browsers do not recognize either the **left** or **right** values.

page-break-after: auto \| always \| avoid \| left \| right \| inherit

Web weavers may also start new printed pages after a specific element is printed using the page-break-after property. This property uses the same values as page-break-before, with the same results. The W[3]C (CSS2 recommendations, section 13.3.6) says the following about page breaks:

- Break as few times as possible.
- Make all pages that don't end with a forced break appear to have about the same height.
- Avoid breaking inside a block that has a border.
- Avoid breaking inside a table.
- Avoid breaking inside a floated element

Some browsers also recognize \A as a page-break-after symbol.

page-break-inside: auto \| avoid \| inherit

To some people it is very annoying to have a table or list break across two pages. It is inconvenient because it requires the reader to flip back and forth when comparing values that fall on different pages. As long as the content of the table or list can reside on a single page, you can eliminate page breaks from occurring by using the following code:

```
table {page-break-inside: avoid;}
```

However, this situation becomes problematic if the table's (or list's) content fills more than one page.

size: [length-width] | [length-height] | auto | portrait | landscape | inherit

The size property is used to change the page dimensions when nonstandard paper is used for printing and to change the orientation of the page. The page orientation defaults to portrait which is taller than it is wide. A landscape page orientation, when recognized by a browser, displays the page's content with the page being wider than it is tall. Portrait and landscape page orientations are common word-processing options, so people are usually comfortable with these terms. This code changes the page orientation to landscape:

```
body {size: landscape;}
```

Most computer systems and printers default to a paper size of 8.5 inches wide and 11 inches tall, which is a portrait-page orientation. When other paper sizes are used to print a Web page, the size property resets the printing dimensions. If a single dimension is given, it is used for both the width and height. For example, this HTML code sets the page size to a five-inch square:

```
body {size: 5in;}
```

In some situations, you could be using one of the following paper sizes:

- U.S. legal-size paper: 8.5×14 in.
- European A4 paper: 210×297 mm
- European A4 paper: 148×210 mm
- European B5 paper: 182×257 mm
- Small index cards: 3×5 in.
- Medium index cards: 4×6 in.
- Large index cards: 5×8 in.

To set the page size for printing on small index cards, you can use the following code:

```
body {size: 3in 5in;}
```

ORPHANS AND WIDOWS

Besides controlling the basic dimensions and orientation of a page, the W[3]C would like browsers to control page orphans and widows. An *orphan* occurs when only the first line of a paragraph fits at the bottom of the page, and the rest of the paragraph must be printed on the next page. When all but the last line of a paragraph fits on a page, the last line of the paragraph on the next page is called a *widow*. Eliminating widows and orphans is both a matter of aesthetics and a practical consideration to help your user see all the text. The Web weaver can choose the minimum number of lines that will be separated by pagination. The default in both cases is two lines. If you want a minimum of three lines in an orphan paragraph (three lines at the bottom of the page before a page break), use the following code:

```
p {orphans: 3;}
```

If less than three lines are available, the whole paragraph will be moved to the next page.

Widows come into play in situations where that last line of a paragraph does not fit on the page. If a single line on the next page is acceptable, you can use this code to override the two-line default:

```
p {widows: 1;}
```

Web weavers concerned about orphans and widows would usually combine these properties within a style sheet. The code to set both to three lines follows:

`p {orphans: 3; widows: 3;}`

Remember, orphans and widows affect only printed Web pages.

CROP AND CROSS MARKS

Also shown in Table 8.7 are properties to turn on and position crop and cross marks. *Crop marks* are short vertical and horizontal lines that indicate the border where an image or page can be trimmed. *Cross marks* are crossed horizontal and vertical lines that are used to precisely align the current page with other pages. Both of these marks are widely used in the printing industry but are not currently recognized by the popular browsers.

▸▸ PRINTER-FRIENDLY WEB PAGES

Web designers have to realize that the content of their Web pages can serve several very different purposes. In most cases this information is needed only temporarily, and a quick look at a screen display is all that is necessary. For example, a weather forecast, sports score, or stock quotation often fall into this quick-look category. Other times users might want to take the information with them, so it needs to be rendered in a form that is useful when printed. Maps, recipes, manual pages, directions, or class assignments sometimes fall into this category. Therefore, some Web pages and their associated style sheets are designed to provide a printer-friendly version.

The properties associated with paged media give designers all the tools they need to create printer-friendly pages. In some cases these Web pages are linked to their screen-oriented counterparts and used only when hard copy of the information is needed. These printer-friendly pages are particularly important when the screen-oriented Web pages use lots of tables or images or when printer-unfriendly designs, like light text on a dark background, are used. In particular, printer-friendly style sheets should incorporate the following design considerations:

- Black text on white backgrounds.
- Font types and sizes that are easy to read.
- Standard margins, usually one inch all around.
- Page breaks to keep important information on the same page. For example, an image and its caption or all the rows in a table on the same printed page.
- Page breaks in logical locations to minimize confusion. Long tables should have page breaks set to occur between rows. These tables should also have the heading data repeated at the beginning of each page.
- Widow and orphan controls.
- A balanced design in which each page contains approximately the same number of lines.
- Page size and orientation that best handles the content. For instance, a table with lots of columns might be better printed in a landscape-page orientation.

Printer-friendly style sheets must be tested before they are implemented on a Web site. This is especially true for the near future because many of the browsers are just starting to recognize these paged-media attributes. However, given that a majority of printers use 8.5 by 11 inch paper, there is no reason why well-designed style sheets cannot be created to print Web pages perfectly on most printers.

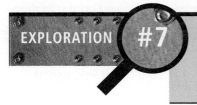

EXPLORATION #7   Add the class .page-break to chapter8.css, and use it to set the page-break before property to **always**. Set the **class** attribute equal to page-break for the "One Big Fish" level-2 heading. Save the external style sheet, and print the Web page using your favorite browser.

▸▸ CONCLUSIONS

Constructing external style sheets is a really good labor-saving and time-saving technique. However, you must be careful when creating any type of style sheet. If a single property is coded incorrectly or if one of the property names is misspelled, that property and all the following style changes might not work. If one or more of your styles do not seem to work, first examine the way you coded each part of the style sheet and make sure the path and filename are correct. In addition to trying your styles with your favorite browser, remember that you need to check how they work with the other browsers as well. Style sheets are great tools, but you need to take the time to make sure they are working properly.

▸▸ KEY TERMS

Baseline
Cascading style sheets (CSS)
Class
CSS box model
Em
Genetic class

Inheritance
Leading
Orphan
Tag-level class
Widow

NEW TAGS

\<div>\</div>
\<link />
\<span>\</span>

▸▸ REVIEW QUESTIONS

1. Define each of the key terms.
2. How is each of the tags introduced in this chapter used? (Provide examples.)
3. What is the order of precedence used by cascading style sheets?
4. Give the main reason for integrating documents with cascading style sheets.
5. What is the basic style-change syntax for an external style sheet?
6. How are comments added to the contents of an external style sheet?
7. How is a link established between an HTML document and an external style sheet?
8. What type of value is inherited?
9. How is the \<div> container used differently than the \<span> container?

10. What is the HTML code that would indent a paragraph 2 ems and print it in the color gray?
11. How would you set the background image to waterfal.png or the color to pink when the image is not available?
12. What are the **style** attributes associated with changing the active link, visited link, and unvisited link using an external style sheet?
13. Identify the four parts of the CSS box model.
14. What order is assumed when four values follow the margin property?
15. What are three border properties?
16. What order is assumed when three values follow the padding property?
17. How does the float property work?
18. Name the nine media types recognized by the HTML 4.0 specifications.
19. Name 10 properties associated with the printed page.
20. List eight printer-friendly page design features.

▶▶ EXERCISES

8.1 Gwen's Glorious Gemstone Web site needs fine-tuning with the design of an external style sheet. Here is what needs to be done:

a. Copy the three boring Web pages (supplied on your student CD) called ch08-styles.html, ch08gems-probs.html, and ch08gems-stones.html to your working directory.

b. You will need to build an external style sheet called ch08-styles.css that has these properties:
   1. The background color should be light tan, #FFCC99.
   2. The standard text color should be deep green, #336600.
   3. Paragraphs should have one of three different margins set:
      i. *narrow*—both right and left margins should be set to 5 ems.
      ii. *medium*—right and left margins should be set to 3 ems.
      iii. *wide*—right and left margins should be set to 3 px.
      These styles should apply only to paragraphs.
   4. There should be three different horizontal rules, with the following widths and names, respectively.
      i. *narrow*—25%.
      ii. *medium*—50%.
      iii. *wide*—99%.
   5. Any element should be able to be set to dark green text, #006600, with a light green background, #CCFFCC, by applying a particular style called *emerald*.
   6. Any element should be able to have a green text, #990033, and a pink background, #FF99CC. The left and right margins should be 3 ems, the top margin should be 2 ems, and the bottom margin 1 em. The font size should be 14 points, and the font weight should be 700. All of these changes should be available by applying the style called *warning*.

c. Now modify each page individually with these specific small changes.
   1. For ch08-styles.html:
      i. Activate the style sheet you created in "b".
      ii. There should be narrow, medium, narrow horizontal rules between the image and the first level heading.
      iii. The first paragraph should have margins of 5 ems.
      iv. The second paragraph should have green text and a green background.
      v. The third and fourth paragraphs should have margins of 3 ems.
   2. For ch08gems-probs.html:
      i. There should be narrow, medium, narrow horizontal rules between the image and the first-level heading.
      ii. The level-1 heading should be color #0066CC.

      iii. Level-3 headings should have a green background and green text. You have a style to do this.

      iv. The <dl> that contains the fakes should have a pink background and dark green text.

      v. The first paragraph of the page should have 3-em margins left and right.

3. For ch08gems-stones.html:

      i. There should be narrow, medium, narrow horizontal rules between the image and the first-level heading.

      ii. The level-1 heading should be color #0066CC.

      iii. In the third row of the table, the word "sold" should have a pink background, green bold text. Use a style.

      iv. Level-3 headings should have a green background and green text. You have a style to do this.

      v. All the item numbers in the table should have green backgrounds and green text . . . think style!

      vi. The word *"Emeralds"* in the line of text above the table should be green on a green background, to match the level-3 headings colorwise.

      vii. The paragraph that starts "We have a series . . ." should have right and left margins of 5 ems.

8.2. Create an external sheet that would describe the page properties for the following writing guide.

- One-inch margins.

- Orphans have at least three lines.

- Widows have at least three lines.

- Portrait-page orientation.

- No page breaks inside a table.

- Level-1 headings are as follows:

  - Page break comes before.

  - Centered.

  - Arial 18-point bold font.

- Paragraph displayed in 12-point Times New Roman regular font.

- Unordered lists use square bullets.

- Ordered lists are as follows:

  - First level uses uppercase roman numerals.

  - Second level uses uppercase alpha characters.

  - Third level uses decimal numbers.

The ASCII file should include comments that document the assignment due date and your name.

8.3. Create an external style sheet that outlines the formatting rules demonstrated in the accompanying box and establishes unique properties for all six heading levels. Provide copies of the CSS file, the HTML document that links to it, and a sample screen display using data of your own choosing. The title bar should display "External Style Sheet Demonstration," with your name and the assignment due date included within comment lines.

8.4. Create an external style sheet for the Homework home page used in earlier exercises, including Exercise 7.4. Establish unique properties for all heading levels, paragraphs, and list items used within the document. Provide copies of the CSS file and the Homework home page that links to it.

8.5. Create an external style sheet for your school's home page or the one you created for the school in earlier exercises, including Exercise 7.5. Establish unique properties for all heading levels, paragraphs, and list items used within the document. Provide copies of the CSS file and the school's home page that links to it.

8.6. Create an external style sheet for your Movies home page or the one you created in earlier exercises, including Exercise 7.6. Establish unique properties for all heading levels, paragraphs, and list items used within the document. Provide copies of the CSS file and the Movies home page that links to it.

8.7. You will need a digital image of yourself or a friend, or a downloaded image of your favorite TV, sports, music, or other personality to complete this exercise. Create an external style sheet that establishes a class called caption. This class should float text to the right of an image. The text should be right-aligned, 12 points in size, and within the sans-serif font family. *A border must appear around the image and the caption.* Provide copies of the HTML document that uses the caption class to display biographical information about your image, the linked CSS file, and a sample screen display. The title bar should display "Float Demonstration," with your name and the assignment due date included within comment lines.

8.8. Create an external style sheet that establishes a class called highlight. This class should display green text with a yellow background. Provide copies of the HTML document that contains a <div> tag, assigning the highlight class to more than two elements of your own choosing. Also provide a copy of the linked CSS file and a sample screen display. The title bar should display "Class Demonstration," with your name and the assignment due date included within comment lines.

Chapter Nine

Multimedia: Watch Your Inclusions

Multimedia, according to the 1990 edition of *The New Lexicon Webster's Dictionary of the English Language,* refers to "a means of communication involving several media, e.g., film and sculpture, print matter, and voices." That's not quite the definition we use when talking about multimedia on the Net. Rather, we take the spirit of the *Webster's* definition and add what could be called a multisensory aspect. When Web weavers speak of **multimedia,** they are referring to sounds, video, animation, and other elements of a page that are not static images and text. We will examine each of these different features in this chapter, concentrating on sounds and video.

CHAPTER OBJECTIVES

After reading this chapter you should be able to do the following:

- Insert a sound or video into a Web page.
- Incorporate Java applets as part of an HTML document.
- Use the <object> element to add multimedia objects to a Web page.
- Preload large multimedia objects to minimize download delays.
- Pass parameters to program applications.
- Identify the HTML elements found in the XHTML Object module.
- Create an aural style sheet.
- Recognize common sound and audio file formats.
- Consider the ethical issues related to intellectual property rights associated with sound and video files.

▸▸ USING MULTIMEDIA

Multimedia is currently the rage on the Web. That has an unfortunate effect on the load on the Net. Multimedia files are HUGE! They download slowly because of the great amount of information that must be transferred. To give you some idea, consider the sound files that are a part of multimedia. One of the most common are the WAV files, discussed under "RIFF WAVE Files" in this chapter. These files require about 10 megabytes of storage for each minute of sound. That's 10 million bytes of storage per minute! Considering the expense of multimedia files in terms of download time and Net traffic, they have to be of great significance before you can justify using them.

Like images, multimedia objects are not available to all the users of a site. Unlike images, most multimedia objects require the user to have additional hardware, some sort of sound card, and speakers. Besides the audio-related hardware, the user must have loaded and configured any additional plug-ins specifically needed by the multimedia object. If the user hasn't installed the plug-in, or if the browser doesn't support such a plug-in, the information available in the multimedia object is lost. If the multimedia object contains essential information, or information that is available only in that format, then those data on the page are not available to the widest audience.

INSERTING OBJECT WITH HREF

Currently multimedia objects are inserted into HTML documents using an <a>anchor</a> container with an **href** attribute identifying the object. When the object is an image we call it an *external image,* because a graphical browser displays it on a new page (Figure 9.1). A sound file is accessible to the user with similar HTML code. For example, a browser plays taps when the user activates the Goodnight! hyperlink generated by the following code:

```
<a href="taps.wav">Goodnight! (WAV file @ 890K)</a>
```

Figure 9.1 HTML code for three different ways to insert an image

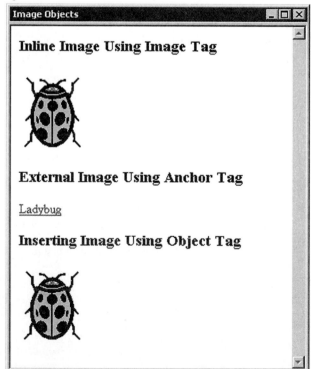

```
<html>
<head>
<title>Image Objects</title>
</head>

<body>
<h3>Inline Image Using Image Tag</h3>
<img src="bug.png" alt="Ladybug" />

<h3>External Image Using Anchor Tag</h3>
<a href="bug.png">Ladybug</a>

<h3>Inserting Image Using Object Tag</h3>
<object data="bug.png" type="image/png">
Ladybug
</object>

</body>
</html>
```

 **<applet>Java Applet</applet>**

Description: initiates the execution of a Java applet.
Type: container.
Attributes: align, alt, archive, class, **code,** codebase, **height,** hspace, id, name, object, style, title, vspace, **width.**
Special Note: deprecated in the HTML 4 recommendations in favor of <object> element.

In the past the only way to handle animated objects was as an image, or *applet*—a small program that runs within a window inside the browser. The <applet></applet> container was designed specifically to handle applets written using the Java programming language and requires the use of the **height, width,** and **code** attributes. The **code** attribute identifies the path and name of the applet file to be inserted (**height** and **width** are self-explanatory). These Java applets provide users with audio, video, and animation as well as allowing them to interact with the Web page. For example, an applet can let you play a video game as part of a Web page (see Figure 9.2). The HTML to insert the ufo_attack applet looks like this:

```
<applet code="UFO_Attack.class"
   width="200"
   height="400">
</applet>
```

The class that you see in this example is a term for a compiled Java applet and should not be confused with the HTML code of class. The <applet> element was deprecated in the HTML 4 specifications because W^{3}C decided that it was too limiting. The reasoning was that Web-based multimedia needed not only to support Java applets but also have the flexibility to incorporate a variety of other multimedia objects and their related plug-ins. The recommendations say this:

> To address these issues, HTML 4.0 introduces the object element, which offers an all-purpose solution to generic object inclusion. The object element allows HTML authors to specify everything required by an object for its presentation by a user agent [browser]: source code, initial values, and run-time data. In this specification, the term "object" is used to describe the things that people want to place in HTML documents; other commonly used terms for these things are: applets, plug-ins, media handlers, etc. (HTML 4 Specifications, Section 13.1)

EXPLORATION #1

To complete the Exploration features in this chapter you will need a blank floppy disk or at least 700 kilobytes of disk space on your personal computer. Copy all the files from the chap09 exploration folder on the Student CD to a blank floppy disk or a disk drive on your personal computer. Open media.html using an ASCII editor, and change the <title> container to *your name's Multimedia Presentations*. Use the <applet></applet> container to insert the UFO_Attack.class applet under the level-3 heading with "*Exploration #1 UFO Attack.*" The applet needs to be 200 pixels wide and 400 pixels high. Save the file as chapter9.html, and display it using your favorite browser. Click on the applet and play the game. Record your scores. When you can stop over 100 UFOs, you will be in league with your humble authors. Note: This applet may not work with some versions of Navigator.

Figure 9.2 HTML code to execute Java video-game applet

```
<html>
<head>
<title>UFO Attack</title>
</head>

<body>
<h1>UFO Attack</h1>
<p>They are invading...</p>
<p> They are jamming the missiles auto-guidance system...</p>
<p> You have to target manually...</p>
<p> <i>And if they land you lose!</i></p>

<applet code="UFO_Attack.class"
        width=200
        height=400>
</applet>

<p> <a href="http://www.rur.com/javacode/UFO_Attack/UFO_Attack.zip">Download</a>
a copy of this page if you like it.
(it may be a bit out of date with the current source!)
This small game is still in development. But you can have the current
<a href="http://www.rur.com/javacode/UFO_Attack/UFO_Attack.java">source code</a>.
</p>
<p>
Please send me your
<a href="http://www.rur.com/feedback.cgi?/javacode/UFO_Attack/">comments + suggestions</a>!
<strong>...Sergio</strong>
</p>

</body>
</html>
```

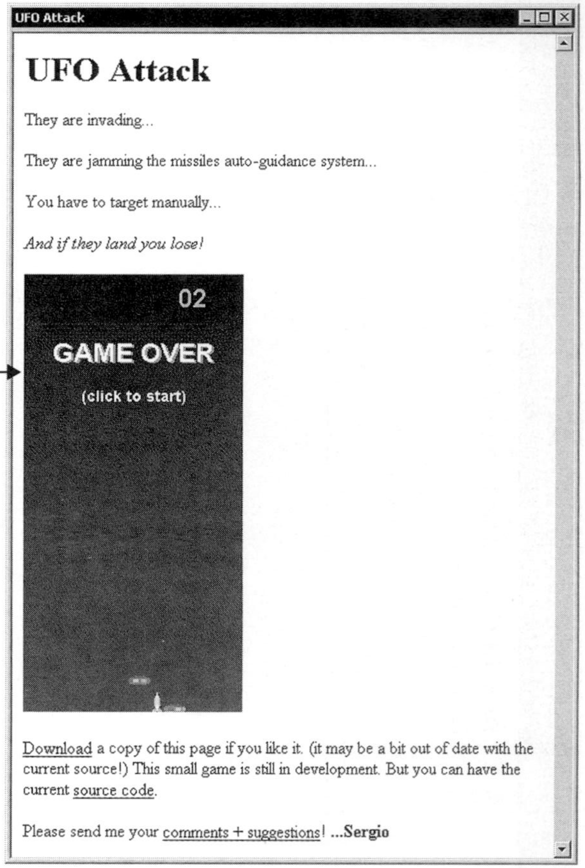

<object>Insert Object</object>

Description: identifies image, html text, sound, video, or other external element for inclusion within the page.
Type: container.
Attributes: align, archive, border, class, **classid, codebase, codetype, data, declare,** dir, **height,** hspace, id, name, onclick, ondblclick, onkeydown, onkeypress, onkeyup, onmousedown, onmousemove, onmouseout, onmouseover, onmouseup, **standby,** style, tabindex, title, **type,** usemap, vspace, **width.**
Special Note: new with HTML 4 recommendations.

Web designers face a dilemma when it comes to using <object> elements to replace <img> and <applet></applet> elements. The former works only on the latest graphical browsers. The latter are tried and true methods for inserting multimedia objects into a Web page. But <applet> has been deprecated and appears to be on its way to obsolescence. Time is on the side of the new <object> element. The farther you are into the new millennium when you read this, the more we would recommend using the <object></object> container to insert multimedia objects into your Web pages. At the time we are writing this, only Opera recognizes the <object> element.

The <object> element can insert images, run Java applets, and play sounds. The HTML code to run the ufo_attack Java applet using <object> is written as follows:

```
<object classid="UFO_Attack.class"
    codetype="application/java"
    width="200"
    height="400">
The UFO Attack game could not be found. You lose.
</object>
```

The contents of the <object></object> container are displayed only when the browser cannot render the object. In the preceding code the alternative message The UFO Attack game could not be found is displayed only when the browser cannot execute the applet. The **alt** attribute serves the same purpose with the <img> tags. Figure 9.1 illustrates how an image is inserted using the <object> tag. We have used several new attributes in these examples that need further explanation.

classid and data

The **classid** and **data** attributes identify the object. It is our understanding that **classid** is used to identify executable objects like applets and scripts. The **data** attribute identifies data—images, sounds, or HTML text (see Figure 9.3). The value of these attributes tells the browser the name of the object and where to find it (URL, path, etc.). For example, the **data** attribute in Figure 9.1 identifies the image bug.png.

codetype and type

The object identified by the **classid** attribute dictates the value of the **codetype** attribute. Likewise, the object assigned to the **data** attribute is reinforced by the **type** attribute. If the **classid** is assigned to a Java applet, then the **codetype** is set equal to application/java. In Figure 9.1, when bug.png is inserted, **type** is set equal to image/png. Although the **codetype** and **type** attributes are optional, their use helps the browser to identify the object it is being asked to insert into the Web page. This information can only help make your HTML documents more robust when working with a variety of browsers.

EMBEDDING OTHER HTML DOCUMENTS

The <object></object> container allows the Web designer to embed other HTML documents within a Web page. For example, a business might want to establish its store hours as an independent HTML document because these hours fluctuate seasonally. Since the hours are posted on several Web pages, embedding the hours.htm code using the <object> element (see Figure 9.3) allows the Web designer to update a single file when the hours change. The following code identifies the HTML document to be embedded:

```
<object data="hours.htm" type="text/html" height="60">
```

In this case the **type** attribute identifies the text as HTML code.

Using the <object> element's **height** and **width** attributes also allows the designer to size the embedded object. Although the example in Figure 9.3 would make more sense if it were sized to show all the hours, we have limited the height to 60 pixels to demonstrate the control you have over an object's size. Notice that scroll bars appear next to the embedded object when it does not completely fit on to the page. The text Business hours not available inside the <object></object> container is displayed only when the object cannot be found. Currently, using the <object> element to embed HTML code into another Web page works only with the Opera browser.

Figure 9.3

HTML code for embedding an HTML document into another Web page

```
<html>
<head>
<title>Our Store</title>
</head>

<body>
<h2>Our Store</h2>
<p>The store is open at convenient hours to better serve you.</p>
<object data="hours.htm" type="text/html" height="60">
Business hours not available.
</object>
</body>
</html>
```

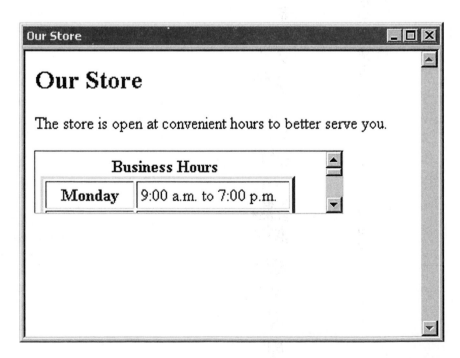

standby and declare

Loading large objects and/or related data takes time and should be avoided whenever possible. Nevertheless, consider a business with an Internet outlet that wants to make a short, but 3 megabytes in size, video of their president talking about the company and his commitment to customer service available on their Web page. When circumstances like this require using large files, the **standby** attribute identifies a message the browser displays during the pause while the file is downloading. This is one of several attributes that provide the skilled Web weaver with a means of creating user-friendly Web pages. The following code displays *Loading welcome message from President* as it downloads a video file:

```
<object data="welcome.mpeg"
   type="application/mpeg"
   standby="Loading welcome message from President. (3 MB)">
Welcome message not found.
</object>
```

Including the **standby** attribute when loading sounds, videos, and large images is one of the things that separate code written by professional Web designers from the Wanna-bes.

The **declare** attribute associates an external object with an HTML document without rendering it in the Web page. In some situations this may mean the browser is able to retrieve large objects before they are needed. The **declare** attribute is Boolean, which means that its appearance within the beginning <object> tag turns on the feature. It is not set to a specific value using an equal sign like most other attributes (see next display of code). When **declare** is present, an **id** attribute must also assign the object a unique name to reference the object.

Declaring the president's welcome video before using it could minimize the wait for loading the large video file. Doing so would allow the browser to start downloading the MPEG file before it is needed. The following code declares the video file and references it as welcome:

```
<object declare
   id="welcome"
   data="welcome.mpeg"
   type="application/mpeg">
Welcome message not found.
</object>
```

The video would not actually appear in the Web page until it is referenced at a later time. For example, this code would run the video:

```
<a href="#welcome">Message for the President (3 MB)</a>
```

Currently none of the popular browsers recognize this attribute; they just render the object at the point the <object></object> container appears within the HTML document.

NESTING OBJECTS

When the popular browsers do embrace all the attributes and alternatives built into the <object></object> container, Web weavers will have a fantastic set of tools to utilize in their Web pages. One of the most important will be the ability to nest <object></object> containers inside one another. This will help designers address one of the most troubling aspects of using multimedia objects: the great variation in browsers and plug-ins available on different user computers.

Back to that business with the video message from the president: nice if it works, but what about potential customers who have computers without the plug-in for the video format to be used? By nesting <object></object> containers, the Web weaver can put in place code that will run the video when possible but if not, will display a picture of the

Figure 9.4   Display the nested image object when the video plug-in of the first choice is unavailable

```html
<html>
<head>
<title>Message From The President</title>
</head>
<body>
<h1 align="center" style="font-family: forte; font-size: 50pt;">Just Perfect</h1>
<h1 align="center">Our President</h1>
<table width="400" align="center">
<tr>
  <td align="center">
  <object data="welcome.mpeg"            ← Not available
    type="application/mpeg"
    standby="Loading welcome message from President. (3MB)">
    <object data="president.jpg"
       type="application/jpeg">
       Every employee of our store is committed to customer service.
       If you are ever displeased with our service please email me
       at president@ourstore.com.
     </object>
  </object>
  </td>
</tr>
<tr style="font-family: Comic Sans MS">
  <td align="center">
  <br />
  "Our customers can always expect the very best customer service
  from myself and every Just Perfect employee."
  </td>
</tr>
<tr style="font-family: Comic Sans MS">
  <td align="center">
    <br />
    <a href="index.html">Home Page</a> --
    <a href="orders.html">Placing Orders</a>
  </td>
</tr>
</table>
</body>
</html>
```

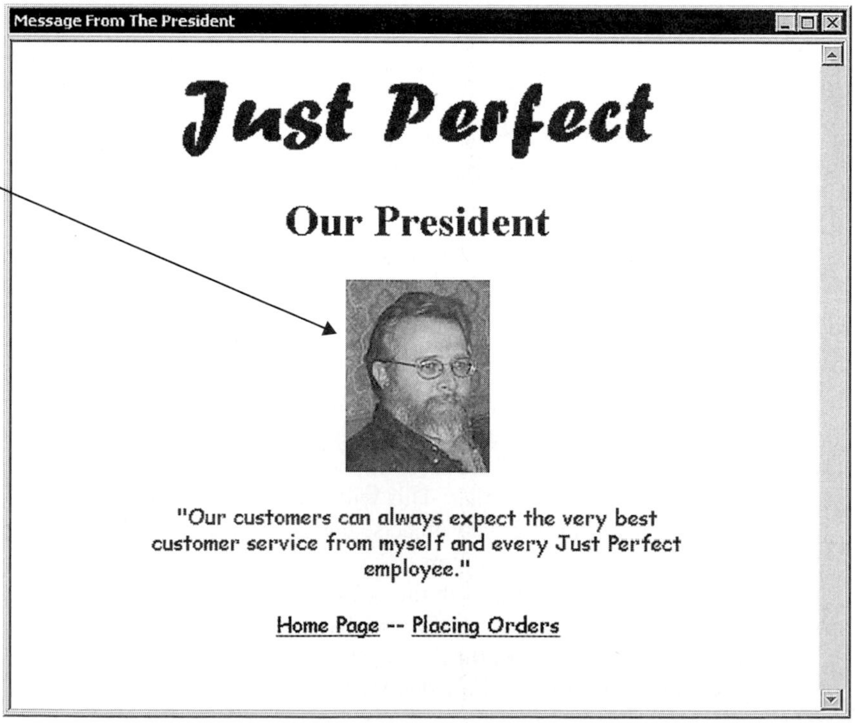

president as shown in Figure 9.4. If nothing else works, a brief statement about customer service will be displayed. All this can be accomplished by nesting each object in the following way:

```
<object data="welcome.mpeg"
   type="application/mpeg"
   standby="Loading welcome message from President. (3MB)">
    <object data="president.jpg"
        type="application/jpeg">
        Every employee of our store is committed to customer service. If you
        are ever displeased with our service please email me at
        president@ourgreatstore.com.
    </object>
</object>
```

EXPLORATION #2 Modify chapter9.html by using the <object></object> container to insert the JPEG file beach.jpg. Place the image under the level-3 heading "*Exploration #2 Image Object.*" Have the browser display the words "*Beach image missing*" as the alternative message. Save the file and refresh/reload the browser display. Note: The <object></object> container currently works only with Opera.

HTML <param>

Description: identifies values needed by object at run time.
Type: empty.
Attributes: id, **name**, type, **value**, valuetype.
XML: requires closing tag using <param /> or <param></param>, for example, <param name="zone" value="EST" valuetype="data" />.

The <param> element is placed inside the <object></object> container before the contents. Originally designed to be an empty tag, it must have an ending tag when used as part of XML/XHTML-compliant code. This tag identifies run-time parameters needed by an object when it is initiated. This is often the case with custom programs. Take, for instance, a Java script that displays a clock. The display is designed to show the current time (see Figure 9.5). The following code includes <param> tags that specify the colors used in the clock face, the clock image, and the time zone parameter.

```
<object classid="billsClock.class"
    type="application/java"
    width="100"
    height="100">
    <param name="BGCOLOR" value="000000" />
    <param name="FACECOLOR" value="FFFFFF" />
    <param name="SWEEPCOLOR" value="FF0000" />
    <param name="MINUTECOLOR" value="008080" />
    <param name="HOURCOLOR" value="000080" />
    <param name="TEXTCOLOR" value="000000" />
    <param name="CASECOLOR" value="000080" />
    <param name="TRIMCOLOR" value="C0C0C0" />
    <param name="LOGOIMAGEURL" value="java.gif" />
    <param name="TIMEZONE" value="5" />
    Unable to run clock.
</object>
```

As you can see, the <object> and <param> elements facilitate the ability of HTML (and XHTML) code to integrate with a variety of plug-ins, like media players, as well as customized program code. In some cases the attributes associated with the <object> </object> container identify program code that animates a Web page, for example, running a Java script that displays Bill's clock. In other cases attributes identify data or parameters that are used by the independent program to determine what is displayed. You will find that the attributes used by the <object> and <param> elements identify three types of information:

1. The URL of the desired object (which could be a file with custom program code) or the actual code itself, such as a script to display a clock.

2. The URL of the data or the actual data to be used when displaying the object, such as the image to use for displaying the clock.

3. Parameters required by the object at run time, such as the colors to use when displaying the clock.

Let's take a closer look at some of the attributes associated with the <param> element.

name and value

When writing a computer program, the programmer uses unique names, called *variable names,* to identify data used by the program. In our clock example, the program code that displays the clock uses the name TIMEZONE to identify the time zone used by the clock. This name identifies an area of the computer's memory where the actual value is stored. The area of memory called TIMEZONE was assigned the value 5 (for Eastern Time Zone) in the previous code and the code shown in Figure 9.5. It could just as easily be assigned the value 6 for Central Standard Time.

Figure 9.5 Clock object displaying current time for Eastern Time Zone

```
<html>
<head>
<title>Java Clock</title>
</head>

<body>
<h1>Bill's Clock</h1>
<object classid="billsClock.class"
  type="application/java"
  width="100"
  height="100">
    <param name=BGCOLOR value="000000" />
    <param name=FACECOLOR value="FFFFFF" />
    <param name=SWEEPCOLOR value="FF0000" />
    <param name=MINUTECOLOR value="008080" />
    <param name=HOURCOLOR value="000080" />
    <param name=TEXTCOLOR value="000000" />
    <param name=CASECOLOR value="000080" />
    <param name=TRIMCOLOR value="COCOCO" />
    <param name=LOGOIMAGEURL value="java.gif" />
    <param name=TIMEZONE value="5" />
  Unable to run clock.
</object>
</body>
</html>
```

Since the names used by the computer program are set when the program is written, the <param> tag's **name** and **value** attributes identify the value to be assigned to a specific name used by the program at the time it is run by the browser. Each <param> tag identifies a single name-and-value-pair. Several <param> tags can be used within a single <object></object> container, as you saw in the clock example. Remember that some computer systems are case-sensitive, so a variable name of TIMEZONE would not match a variable named timezone. Always use the exact name and case of the variables as specified by the programmer. These names are usually found in the documentation that accompanies the program.

valuetype

A <param> tag's **valuetype** attribute identifies three possible values: data (the default), ref, and object. The previous TIMEZONE example could have been written like this:

```
<param name="TIMEZONE" value="5" valuetype="data" />
```

Using this code, the browser assigns the value 5 (Eastern Standard Time) to the variable named TIMEZONE as the clock applet starts. Using a value of 5 is an example of a *data* **valuetype.** In this situation the **value** attribute identifies specific information to be directly used by the object.

When the <param> tag provides a URL to the necessary data (not the data itself), then the *ref* **valuetype** is used. In the following code, the data to be assigned to TIMEZONE is found in a text file in the java directory:

```
<param name="TIMEZONE"
   value="../code/java/zone.txt"
   valuetype="ref">
```

The *object* **valuetype** is used when several objects are active within a Web page, especially when the objects are nested. Setting **valuetype** to object assures that the correct data is passed to the object. There must be agreement between the value assigned to the object's **id** and the value used with the <param> tag's **value** attribute, as follows:

```
<object id="clock"
   classid="http://www.ourstore.com/code/java/billsClock.class"
   codetype="application/java"
   width="100"
   height="100">
     <param name="clock" valuetype="object" />
     <param name="TIMEZONE"
        value="http://www.ourstore.com/code/java/zone.txt"
        valuetype="ref" />
   Unable to run clock.
</object>
```

codebase

The <object></object> container's **codebase** attribute works with the <param> tag to provide a coding shortcut when objects and related parameters require long path and domain names. The **codebase** attribute establishes a path the browser uses with all relative references. For discussion's sake, let's say the object billsClock.class used in the preceding example (and any related files) are found at http://www.ourstore.com/code/java. This address can be set as the base path by using the **codebase** attribute this way:

```
<object id="clock"
   classid="billsClock.class"
   codetype="application/java"
   codebase="http://www.ourstore.com/code/java/"
   width="100"
```

```
height="100">
    <param value="clock" valuetype="object" />
    <param name="TIMEZONE" value="zone.txt" valuetype="ref" />
    Unable to run clock.
</object>
```

Notice that the Web weaver didn't need to code the full path to the zone.txt file; the browser filled it in from the **codebase** value. When there are many different elements that need to be retrieved, **codebase** can save the wise Web weaver a lot of keystrokes. It also makes it easier to move an object from one server to the next. Using **codebase** means changing the path in just one place.

The <object> and <param> elements work together to provide all the information an object needs to execute properly. Since the popular browsers are just beginning to recognize these elements, it is critical that you test your code with a variety of browsers to ensure your Web pages are rendered properly. It would be a mistake to assume the code is working correctly in all the browsers just because it worked in one.

▸▸ XHTML OBJECT MODULE

The <object> and <param> elements form the XHTML Object module. Their inclusion in the XML and XHTML recommendations, along with the <applet> element being declared obsolete (in XML), clearly indicates that these are the tools that will be used to integrate multimedia objects into the next generation of Web pages.

▸▸ WHEN TO USE CODE AUGMENTATION

Using the <object> element to augment HTML code is at the center of what can be good and bad about the evolution of the Internet. The judicious use of images, sounds, animation, videos, and custom programs in Web page design is good. These objects provide the Web weaver with powerful tools for advertising, educating, entertaining, and informing interested users. Misused or overdone, though, these same objects can bore, distract, bother, and confuse these same users. In addition, these objects increase the bandwidth necessary to download your page and so can severely degrade performance.

Furthermore, there are many software tools (we call them *Web utilities*) available to Web designers that will create custom programs that augment HTML code. Unfortunately, they often run only on proprietary plug-ins that need to be installed into the browser before the user can see them. The related software houses like Adobe and Macromedia will usually supply a basic version of their plug-ins for free. We have all visited Web pages created with these products. They can be very sophisticated and have intricate designs that unfold in front of us as we move the screen pointer over the page. Sometimes it even takes a few seconds to figure it out!

This is not written to downplay the importance of these Web utilities. Such software packages can help the serious Web weaver create professional-looking Web pages that integrate lots of information in limited screen space. To do it right takes a lot of work and a good eye for page design. However, Web weavers should ask themselves two basic questions before spending an excessive amount of time and money using these utilities to create complex rollovers, graphics that bounce around the page, or fancy tails that follow the screen pointer:

1. Why is this important?

2. Which group of people do I want to use it?

Not every page in a Web site has the same objectives. It depends on your audience and what you are trying to accomplish.

Consider the Internet-based business mentioned earlier. Besides its home page, its Web site contains information about the company, the youth-oriented products it sells, and a shopping-cart feature that assists the user in purchasing its products. One of the company's objectives for its home page is for it to generate enough interest about its products that users will want to explore the site. Since its target market is young users who can be expected to be Internet savvy, a flashy home page with interesting rollovers and eye-catching animations might be appropriate. However, this design would not appeal to parents or grandparents of those targeted young people. Home pages designed for that older target audience would be wise to forgo the flash and use larger, more readable fonts and images.

In addition, while the home page is designed to capture the users' interest and invite them into the site, once they are past the home page other site objectives come into play. These pages need to clearly identify the company's products and provide ways for users to purchase them. Here flashy pages with animation can distract the user. For these Web pages the Web weaver needs to create logical links between pages with related products and a shopping-cart interface used to purchase items. They must also establish links to the database management program that tracks purchases and maintains the company's product inventory. This is the domain of XML, although some Web utilities, like Macromedia's Cold Fusion, can be effectively used as part of the Web design. Clearly, augmenting HTML code can have a place in good Web design. The trick is to know when and where to employ it and when and where it is a waste of time and bandwidth.

▸▸ ADDING SOUND

Next to images, many people would say that sound is the most common type of multimedia data added to Web pages. The sound you normally hear is a continuous series of different tones and noises. These types of data are called ***analog data*** because the values flow from one to another continuously. Computers don't handle analog data well; they want their input as digital data. ***Digital data*** are discrete, meaning the values are represented by numbers, not by a continuous energy fluctuation. For analog data to be converted to digital data, the data must be captured and encoded as numbers, usually represented as binary 1s (ones) and 0s (zeros). In the case of sound, the more samples taken, the better the sound reproduction is. As you might expect, the files containing sound are much bigger than those without. By the same token, the larger the space used to encode the sound value, the better the sound representation is. In other words, bigger sound files produce more lifelike sounds.

Usually sound files are recorded at sampling rates of 11, 22, or 44 kilohertz. A kilohertz (kHz) is 1,000 cycles per second, or roughly 1,000 samples per second. As mentioned earlier, the more samplings per second, the better the sound quality is. Sound can also be stored as either an 8-bit or 16-bit number. A 16-bit sound file will be much more accurate than an 8-bit sound file.

Thus, the price we pay for quality sound is measured in an audio file's size. An 8-bit, 8-kHz sample is about the quality of a standard telephone call—not very good for audio on a Web page. A 16-bit, 44-kHz sample is nearly the audio quality of a compact disc (CD) player. A minute of 8-bit, 8-kHz sound takes about 1.5 megabytes of file space. A minute of 16-bit, 44-kHz sound takes 10 megabytes. If you want to add stereo, you have to double these numbers! Let's take a look at the different types of sound files.

▸▸ TYPES OF SOUND FILES

Audio files can be found in several different formats. Each format may require a different plug-in (see Figure 9.6), so it is a good idea to limit the format of the sound files on your page to one of the common types. That way the user needs only one plug-in to play all of the sounds you present.

Figure 9.6   Commonly used plug-ins for sounds

Internet Explorer plug-in

Navigator plug-in

Winamp plug-in

Musicmatch plug-in

RealPlayer plug-in

Software packages exist that can convert one type or format of sound file to another. For example, a program called SOX, for PC-compatible machines and Unix boxes (written by Lance Norskog), can convert between most of the common formats and do some simple processing like filtering as well. WAVany, also a PC package (written by Bill Neisius) can also convert most formats to the WAV format. SoundApp (written by Norman Franke) is a similar program for the Macintosh. These products or others like them are often available for downloading from the Internet.

μ-LAW (MU-LAW) FILES

Once widely popular, μ-law (or mu-law) sound files have fallen out of favor except on some Unix sites that hang onto the old formats. Originally developed for the Unix operating system, these sound files use a 2:1 compression ratio and serve as an international standard for compressing voice-quality audio. They are supported by only a few operating systems. A μ-law file usually ends with the extension .au. This type of file supports only *monaural* (single-channel) sound, not stereo (multiple-channel) sound. There is a library of sounds in .au format located at

http://sunsite.unc.edu/pub/multimedia/sun-sounds/

RIFF WAVE FILES

Resource Interchange File Format Waveform (RIFF WAVE) audio format, or WAVE, is a proprietary format that was sponsored jointly by Microsoft and IBM. It is the audio file format most commonly used on Microsoft Windows products. This audio format is also supported by most operating systems. The RIFF WAVE file usually has a file extension of **.wav** (see the HTML code in Figure 9.7).

Figure 9.7

HTML code that uses a sound file

```
<html>
<head>
<title>Sound Objects</title>
</head>

<body>
<h3>Directions to Our Store</h3>
<p>We are easy to find.</p>

<img src="storemap.jpg" alt="Map to Store" height="200" width="300" />
<br>
<a href="directions.wav">Audio directions to our store (WAV file @ 492K)</a>

</body>
</html>
```

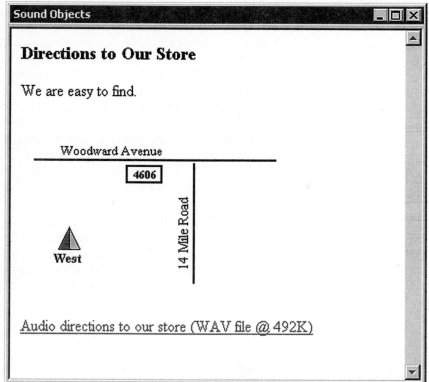

Normally this sound format takes about 10 megabytes of file data to produce a single minute of audio. It is an uncompressed format, so a given WAVE sound file is roughly twice the size of the same sound encoded in μ-law format. There are other encoding techniques—for example, using 8 bits rather than 16 bits to store the sounds—that can be employed in WAVE files to reduce the amount of storage required. The downside of these methods is that they degrade the quality of the sound. The RIFF WAVE format can support both monaural and stereo audio. There is a large collection of sounds in this format at

http://sunsite.unc.edu/pub/multimedia/pc-sounds/

AIFF AND AIFC FILES

Audio Interchange File Format (AIFF) is used to store high-end, complex audio data. It is uncompressed and takes about the same amount of space as WAVE files, 10 megabytes per minute of audio. This recording format can support both monaural and stereo recordings and uses the .aiff filename extension. It was developed by Apple and is most often used by Macintosh and Silicon Graphics software. Because it takes so much space to store audio data in AIFF, Apple developed AIFF-C, better known as AIFC for AIFF Compressed Format. This compression algorithm can compress sounds up to 6:1, but it is a lossy form of compression. As with the lossy JPEG image compression, some of the data bits are removed from the sound file as it is compressed in the AIFC format. The result is a deterioration of the sound. Nevertheless, usually the reduction in quality is not sufficient to outweigh the benefit of the saving of space.

MPEG AUDIO

From the International Standard Organization (ISO) comes the Moving Picture Experts Group (MPEG), which has defined a standard for audio that has the best compression algorithms. These algorithms can compress to a ratio of 4:1 with almost no loss of signal quality. MPEG-compressed audio is the best format for distributing high-quality sound files online. Older MPEG files are usually designated with an extension of .mp2. Since MPEG is also used to store, transmit, and display video, make sure the files you collect for audio are just audio files, not small videos with audio.

MPEG3 audio compression is even more popular and has a lot of people excited about the ability to deliver CD-quality sound files at much smaller file sizes. It takes less than 1 megabyte of storage space to store one minute of music when using MPEG3. It uses a 12:1 compression ratio with very little degradation of sound quality to achieve this storage capacity. Compare these numbers to those of a WAVE file, where one minute of music requires 10 megabytes of storage space. Computers using MPEG3 need a 16-bit sound card. These files have a .mp3 filename extension. This is the file format that is at the heart of all of the controversy about intellectual property and music.

MIDI FILES

The music industry has developed a standard for connecting electric instruments to each other and to computers. The standard is called MIDI, which stands for Musical Instrument Digital Interface. A MIDI recording is not a digital representation of an analog sound, but a description of how to create the sound. The 8-bit code identifies events like note on, note off, pitch-blend changes, control changes, and so on, along with identifying in which of the 16 channels to apply the event. Therefore, the actual sound or music is not stored in a MIDI file. Instead, the 8-bit codes indicate which sound (voice) to play, when a sound is to be switched on or off, the code for the sound (such as 3C for middle C), and a velocity code for volume control. A 10KB MIDI file could easily hold more than a minute of music.

To play a MIDI file, the computer must have access to a WAVE table, synthesizer, or some means of generating the sounds the MIDI data turns on, adjusts the volume of, and turns off. In most cases a sound card contains at least a WAVE table. Selected MIDI codes identify key pressure and after-touch that allow the composer to bend sounds and warble a note. These files have a .mid or .midi filename extension.

OTHER FORMATS

Many other formats can be used to move sound files across the Internet but the ones just discussed are by far the most common. One of the other formats is Creative Voice (.voc) files, used by Creative Lab's Sound Blaster audio cards. Another format, used by

Sun/NeXT computers, usually with an extension of **.snd,** is far less common, but it does show up occasionally.

EXPLORATION #3

Update chapter9.html to include a link to the MIDI file elevator.mid. Use the words <u>elevator music</u> in the paragraph under the level-3 heading of Exploration #3 Sounds as the hyperlink that opens the MIDI plug-in. Add (*midi @ 21KB*) after the hot words. Save the file, refresh/reload the browser display, and play the MIDI file.

▶▶ CHOOSING FORMATS

With all these choices, how does the wise Web weaver decide on the right format? Sometimes the choice is easy. If you find a sound you like, and it is in one of the common formats, or if it is in a format that has an available plug-in for your browser, you will probably decide to use that format. Problems result only if your users don't have the same software you choose to use.

Most Web weavers will agree that .mp3 and .wav are the most useful types of sound files. If you keep all your sounds in one of these formats, you can be assured that the majority of the graphical browsers will have plug-ins able to use them. Remember to do your best to limit all the sounds to a single format on a Web site. That reduces the work the browser has to do, and it could speed up your users' work as well.

Regardless of the format, you should describe the sounds you have included so your user will know what he is downloading. It would be a shame to have a user spend several minutes downloading a sound file in a format he cannot listen to. As with large images, you should give your user an idea about the size of an audio file. That way he can decide if he wants to spend the time necessary to download it.

If you have audio processing and editing software available, you might consider creating a very short sound file that can serve as a lead-in to the larger sound file you have available for download. Then the user can download the smaller sound file first and, based on that, decide if she wants to spend the time necessary to download the actual, large file. It is also common courtesy to use a special, easily recognizable icon to indicate sound files. Politeness is always in fashion, and describing the file a user can download in terms of content, format, and size is indeed polite.

▶▶ AURAL STYLE SHEETS

The HTML 4 and CSS2 recommendations opened a new *design* dimension for our Web pages—sound. Although using music, voices, and other sounds was not new to Web weavers, these recommendations outlined a level of control that made it possible to design how the content is rendered when spoken.

An **aural style sheet** combines auditory icons and speech synthesis. **Auditory icons** are distinctive semantic elements that "bing" and "ping" before or after specific words are spoken. Applications for aural style sheets go beyond the needs of visually impaired users. In Chapter Sixteen we will explore some of these applications, but first you need to know how the different aural properties work.

An aural style sheet is intended for computers with speakers, sound card, and a speech synthesizer. You designate style sheets as aural by setting the **media** attribute. Both the <style> and <link> tags recognize aural as a value for this attribute. When you designate a document-level style sheet as aural, the following code works:

```
<style type="text/css" media="aural">.
```

When you use external style sheets, your code looks like this:

```
<link rel="stylesheet"
    media="aural"
    href="nletter-aural.css"
    type="text/css" />
```

AURAL PROPERTIES

Aural properties present a new way of thinking about the content of a Web page. Instead of font families, aural style sheets use voice families. Do you want the text on the page spoken in a smooth female voice that spells out each word? Or would a rich male voice that pronounces each word work better? Would you like a bell to sound before a level-1 heading is read? Would you like the browser to say good-bye when closing a document?

The following code could be used to present a screenplay in which all level-1 headings are spoken in a male voice, preferably one designated as the "announcer." Walter Cronkite's voice would be good here. The voices of Norton and Trixie have several properties set.

```
h1 {voice-family: announcer, male;}
p.part.norton
    {
    voice-family: norton, male;
    richness: 70; /* max 100 */
    pitch: low;
    pitch-rate: 80; /* max 100 */
    speech-rate: fast;
    stress: 90; /* max 100 */
    volume: loud;
    }
p.part.trixie
    {
    voice-family: trixie, female;
    richness: 40; /* max 100 */
    pitch: x-high;
    pitch-rate: 90; /* max 100 */
    speech-rate: x-fast;
    stress: 90; /* max 100 */
    volume: medium;
    }
```

A complete list of aural properties is found in Table 9.1.

speak: normal | none | spell-out | inherit

One of the most fundamental aural design issues is whether text is spoken or spelled out. When the speak property is set to **normal**, the speech synthesizer uses language-dependent pronunciation rules as the text is reproduced as spoken words. Setting the speak property to **spell-out** means each letter is spoken. This is a good choice for specialized situations, like spelling out medical or technical terminology, but usually not for rendering the full text of a Web page.

volume: [number] | [percentage] | silent | x-soft through x-loud | inherit

The volume property is representative of many of the aural properties in that you can set it with either a keyword like **soft** or a relative value from 0 through 100. A volume value

Table 9.1   Aural properties and values

Property	Description	Values	Special Notes
azimuth	Changes left/right orientation of sound within 360-degree surround-sound environment.	[angle] | left-side | far-left | left | center-left | center | center-right | right | far-right | right-side | behind | leftwards | rightwards | inherit	[angle] is set from −360 to 360 degrees (deg) with center=0deg, right=90deg, behind=180deg, and left=270deg or −90deg. Rightwards=+20deg and leftwards=−20deg.
cue-after	Provides sound after event as auditory icon.	[url] | none | inherit	
cue-before	Provides sound before event as auditory icon.	[url] | none | inherit	
elevation	Changes up/down orientation of sound.	[angle] | below | level | above | higher | lower | inherit	[angle] is set from −90 to 90 degrees (deg) with level=0deg, above=90deg, and below=−90deg. Higher=+10deg and lower=−10deg.
pause-after	Sets time after speaking element's content and before starting next text.	[time] | [percentage] | inherit	Time is measured in milliseconds (ms) and seconds (s).
pause-before	Sets time before speaking element's content.	[time] | [percentage] | inherit	Time is measured in milliseconds (ms) and seconds (s).
pitch	Sets frequency (pitch) of speaking voice.	[frequency] | x-low | low | medium | high | x-high | Inherit	[frequency] is given in hertz (Hz) with low being a lower frequency than medium.
pitch-range	Specifies variation in average pitch.	[number] | inherit	[number] ranges from 0 to 100 with 0 being flat and 100 being animated.
play-during	Specifies sound played as background while element's content is spoken.	[url] mix | repeat | auto | none | inherit	When mix is used, the URL sound is played along with background sound.
richness	Identifies how voice will carry in large room. Rich carries well while smooth does not.	[number] | inherit	[number] ranges from 0 to 100, with 0 being smooth and 100 being rich.
speak	Determines how text is rendered aurally.	normal | none | spell-out | inherit	Normal means language-dependent pronunciation rules are used. Spell-out means each letter is spoken.
speak-header	Works with table headers to determine if header is spoken for each cell or just first one.	once | always | inherit	This property could work with some browsers' handling of the **headers, scope,** or **axis** attributes.
speak-numeral	Controls how numerals are spoken. Pronunciation is language dependent.	digits | continuous | inherit	Digits: "1,2,3" spoken as "one, two, three." Continuous: "123" spoken as "one-hundred twenty-three."
speak-punctuation	Determines if punctuation is spoken.	code | none | inherit	Code means punctuation is spoken.

(continued)

Table 9.1 Continued

Property	Description	Values	Special Notes
speech-rate	Sets speed at which words are read.	[number] | x-slow | slow | medium | fast | x-fast | faster | slower | inherit	[number] given in words per minute with x-slow=80, medium=180, and x-fast=300. Faster=+40 and slower=–40.
stress	Specifies intonation peaks within voice inflection.	[number] | inherit	[number] ranges from 0 to 100, with numbers' meaning depending on language.
voice-family	Sets tenor of speaking voice. *You could even use your own voice.*	[specific-voice] | [generic-voice] | inherit	Generic voices include male, female, and child.
volume	Sets sound's dynamic range.	[number] | [percentage] | silent | x-soft | soft | medium | loud | x-loud | inherit	[number] ranges from 0 to 100, with x-soft=0, medium=50, and x-loud=100.

of zero does not mean the same as silent. No sound is created with **silent** whereas a value of zero means something can be heard, you just have to have really good ears.

Furthermore, there is a difference between the volume property being set to **silent** and the speak property being set to **none**. The former takes up as much time as if the actual text had been spoken, yet no sound is generated. The latter takes no time, and nothing is done. The values for volume are designed to allow the specific browser to accommodate differences in the environment as well. For example, a volume of 50 would produce a very different sound level in a browser used in a library than it would in a browser used in an automobile.

cue: cue-before | cue-after | inherit

Two of the aural properties include shorthand properties. The cue property is used to create auditory icons. Remember that an auditory icon is a special sound played before or after a particular event, like the speaking of a heading. It can set both the **cue-before** and **cue-after** values. If two values are given, the first value is **cue-before** and the second is **cue-after**. If only one value is given, it applies to both properties. For example, the following code initiates the playing of zing.wav before and after a level-1 heading is read:

```
h1 {cue-before: url(zing.wav); cue-after: url(zing.wav);}
```

This code does the same thing:

```
h1 {cue: url(zing.wav);}
```

pause: [time] | [percentage] | inherit

Just as white space is a valuable design tool for visual designs, the use of pauses is important to aural designs. A pause is inserted between the element's content and any **cue-before** or **cue-after** content using the pause property. If two values are given, the first value is pause-before and the second is pause-after. If only one value is given, it applies to both cue-before and cue-after. The following code pauses the speaking for 20 milliseconds after the cue has sounded and waits 30 milliseconds after the words are spoken before sounding the next cue:

```
h1 {pause: 20ms 30ms;} /* pause: before 20ms & after 30ms */
```

This code sets both pauses to 10 milliseconds:

```
h1 {pause: 10ms;} /* pause: before 10ms & after 10ms */
```

SOUND ORIENTATION

The aural properties even let you control which speakers will broadcast different voice families. You actually have control of sound reproduction all around the listener, using the azimuth property if a surround-sound audio system is available. Speaker locations above or below the listener can be manipulated using the elevation property.

All of the properties listed in Table 9.1 are new in the HTML 4 specifications, and we will have to wait for a new generation of browsers before we can use many of them.

▶▶ ETHICAL QUESTIONS

It is very easy to collect sound files from sites all across the Net. All you need to do is look at the URL of the sound site and ftp the sound to your own computer. In addition, many people have built pages that contain a large number of links to sound files that enable you to quickly download the sounds. You can also use tools like Gnutella or WinMX to join a temporary community of users sharing sound, video, and image files. But sounds and music are often copyrighted, just like images, so before you download sounds to use on your page, make sure they are free or get permission from the owner of the sound you wish to use.

Be careful, because the fact that a sound appears on XYZ page does not necessarily mean that the owner of XYZ page has the authority to give you permission to use it. For example, if you were to go to the Oldies Web page, and download a three-minute cut of a Beatles song with the permission of the Web weaver of that page, you could well be in violation of the copyright on the song. You probably need to obtain permission from Michael Jackson, who owns the rights to many of the Beatles' songs!

Show tunes, theme songs, and popular music are all available on the Web, but most of them are copyrighted works. You can get into trouble for using them without permission. Another common mistake Web weavers make is downloading and using short audio snippets from television-program dialog. These, too, are usually copyrighted works.

If you are going to use sound that you have not created yourself, make sure that the sounds you use are in the *public domain,* meaning you can use them without permission. If they are not in the public domain, you will need to obtain permission for their use from the copyright holder, who, as was pointed out earlier, may or may not be the Web weaver of the site where you find the sounds.

You also need to be careful about posting music that you have the right to play. For example, using one of many popular music tools it is easy to take songs from a CD in your collection and "burn" it into MP3 format. You can then use that music on your Web site. However, in all but a very few cases, broadcasting that music violates the copyright of the recording company that created the CD in the first place. You need to be very careful when using any music that you did not personally create.

▶▶ ADDING VIDEO

Video playback is another multimedia design element that is being incorporated into some Web sites to add interest and provide an additional medium for transferring information. As we saw in the previous section, adding audio to a Web page increases the download time because audio objects are large compared with text or even pictures. Video files are a collection of images, usually with a related sound file, so they are larger than either pictures or audio! The following code would make a short video available to the Web user:

```
<a href="bldgdemo.avi">Building Demolition (AVI file @ 3MB) </a>.
```

Figure 9.8 Popular video playback plug-ins

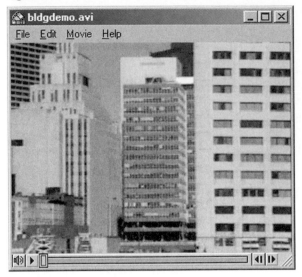

QuickTime plug-in

Windows Media Player plug-in

Capturing analog video at regular intervals and saving each capture as a distinct image, called a *frame,* creates digital video clips. Frames are played back at a particular *frame rate,* which is the number of frames displayed per second. As the frame rate approaches 30 frames per second, the video becomes smooth and looks like a videotape playback or television broadcast. A digital video file may also have an audio track associated with the frames. One job of the video plug-in software (see Figure 9.8) is to synchronize displaying the images with playing the related sounds.

MPEG VIDEO

The MPEG format, devised by the Motion Picture Experts Group, is the most common format for digital video files, or movies, because all the graphical browsers support it, and viewers exist for all the platforms. Unlike the case with AVI, which we will discuss later, anyone with a graphical browser can either download a plug-in or use a browser to play MPEG movies. Although this is the most common type of movie on the Net, it has the disadvantage of being very expensive to create. High-quality MPEG encoders are expensive, requiring equipment costing several thousand dollars. That price is beyond the range of most users. MPEG files usually have file extensions of .mpg on Intel platforms and .mpeg on other systems.

The latest MPEG version, MPEG4, has been released. It is designed to support high-quality video formats, streaming video (see next section) and the next generation of handheld wireless devices. Incompatibilities with the popular MPEG3 audio format and related plug-ins need to be worked out before it can take its place as an industrial standard.

QUICKTIME

QuickTime was developed for the Apple Macintosh. It is nearly as common as MPEG (some of the Macintosh folks say it is more common) and is another Net standard. QuickTime movies can be played on PCs using the QuickTime for Windows (QTfW) software. They can be played using the Xanim program on Unix machines. Usually QuickTime movies have an extension of .qt or .mov on all platforms.

➤ AVI

Microsoft developed Video for Windows (VfW) for the PC. It is the nominal standard for PC video, and a large number of files exist on related platforms. Video for Windows files usually have a file extension of .avi, which stands for Audio/Video Interleave. Internet Explorer allows the Web weaver to incorporate AVI video files as an inline movie without adding a new plug-in. Those of you using older versions of Navigator will need to install an AVI plug-in.

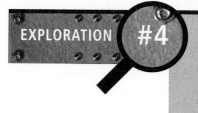

EXPLORATION #4

Insert a short video clip, football.avi, into chapter9.html under the level-3 heading of *Exploration #4 Video*. Use the word <u>football</u> in the paragraph below the headings as the hyperlink that activates the video player plug-in. Add *(avi @ 440KB)* after the hot word. Save the file, refresh/reload the browser display, and play the video.

➤ STREAMING AUDIO/VIDEO

Web-oriented companies like Macromedia and RealAudio are marketing new multimedia formats. As mentioned earlier, they usually make a very basic version of the software's browser plug-in available for free downloading from their corporate Web site. If the user likes the product, she can purchase editing software, more sophisticated plug-ins, and related Web utilities. Movies created with Macromedia's Director program and the company's Flash 3 animation use what they call the Shockwave multimedia format. These multimedia presentations feature *streaming* audio and video, which means that the movie or audio clip starts as soon as the browser plug-in receives a minimal buffering of the file. As the frames are downloaded from the Net, they are loaded into a buffer and then displayed. Ideally, the frames are downloading more quickly than they are being displayed, so the download buffer stays ahead of the presentation. Consequently, the multimedia event begins more quickly because the user doesn't have to wait for the whole file to download.

The drawback to streaming presentations is that a slow Net connection can produce a choppy presentation in which the audio seems to fade in and out. Some streaming audio presentations, like RealAudio, provide a live Net radio broadcast site. On slower computers or modems these broadcasts have the characteristics of old AM radio transmission. The signals sometimes wax and wane, with interference and garbled sound occurring. On faster computers these Net radio broadcasts provide good-quality production of live music and up-to-the-minute news.

However, these Net broadcasts also create an interesting ethical issue. Radio stations pay the huge recording companies a small fee each time they play a song owned by that company. Some of these companies are trying to enforce an extra charge if the radio station is also broadcasting over the Net. This has caused many wonderful radio stations to go "off the Net" until this issue can be resolved. As we mentioned earlier, be very careful when you are providing information on the Net that could be owned by someone else.

Although streaming audio and video is exciting, it places a huge demand on the Net. Other forms of multimedia that require the user to download and store the presentation before it is played affect the Net only while the file is being downloaded. In contrast, streaming technology places a high demand on the Net all through the presentation. As modems become faster and compression becomes better, more and more streaming audio and video will probably appear on the Net. Its presence may have a serious impact on Internet traffic.

‣‣ TO LINK OR TO COPY?

When using multimedia, it is tempting to simply link to a large file on another server rather than store that file on your own server. Indeed, some authors of multimedia ask that you link to their site rather than copying the files to your own server. The advantages of saving space as well as having a current copy of an event make the idea of linking to another server appealing. Yet, this practice increases congestion on the Net. When users make a connection to your Web page, they are putting a certain load on the Net. If you require another connection, to another machine, that increases the load. In addition, making your users wait to retrieve data from another machine adds to the delay. So the idea of linking to resources on another machine is not as good as it first appears. It is best to copy a resource from a remote site and store it on the same server that hosts your page, unless, of course, the resource is copyrighted and you cannot obtain permission to use it. In any case, it is considered proper to put a small credit line on your page indicating where the resource came from, even if it is in the public domain.

‣‣ KEY TERMS

Analog data   Frame
Applet   Frame rate
Auditory icon   Multimedia
Aural style sheet   Streaming
Digital data   Web Utility

‣‣ NEW TAGS

<object></object>
<param />

‣‣ REVIEW QUESTIONS

1. Define each of the key terms.
2. How are each of the tags introduced in this chapter used?
3. What is the major consideration when using multimedia?
4. What <object> attribute identifies multimedia objects that can be downloaded before they are used?
5. How do browsers handle nested <object> elements?
6. Identify three types of information that are provided by the <object> and <param> attributes?
7. What HTML elements are associated with the XHTML Object module?
8. What questions should a Web designer ask before augmenting HTML code with custom programs?
9. Identify six aural properties that change the sound of the spoken word. (This does not mean the orientation or how the sounds are presented, but rather how you would hear it.)
10. What is the filename extension and media type (sound or video) associated with each of the following?
    a. Audio Interchange File Format
    b. Creative Voice Format

c.   Moving Picture Experts Group Audio Format

d.   Moving Picture Experts Group Video Format

e.   Musical Instrument Digital Interface Format

f.   QuickTime Format

g.   Resource Interchange File Format Waveform

h.   μ-law File Format

i.   Video for Windows

11. What should a Web weaver do when using other people's work within a Web page?

12. What is considered a broadcast-quality frame rate for a video?

▸▸ EXERCISES

9.1. Ruby has heard all about the fancy things you have been learning about, and she wants to upgrade her Web page with some of these fancy new inclusions. What she wants you to do is enhance the Web page eme09-raw.htm (on your CD), creating the page eme09-incl.htm with the following features:

     a.   The page should have a title of Pearls, ancient beauty. It should have the standard heading for Gwen's shop followed by a centered, level-2 heading that matches the title.

     b.   The background color should be white, #FFFFFF, and the text should be dark gray, #333333.

     c.   Level-1 headings should be 24 points and light gray, #999999.

     d.   Level-2 and level-3 headings should be 18 points and medium gray, #666666.

     e.   Level-3 headings should be sans serif.

     f.   Since Ruby has really gotten into pearls, she might change her stock on a daily basis. For that reason she would like to have separate pages (freshw.htm, cultured.htm, and natural.htm) show up on her pearls page that list the prices for the three kinds of pearls she sells. At the places indicated in the existing page, insert each of the three pages that contain tables of prices for pearls.

     g.   The tables should be set 5 ems from the left margin of the page.

     h.   At the location indicated in comments in the page, please add a link to the pearl sound file **pearls.wav** right after the initial heading. The text for that line should read Hear <u>Ruby</u> tell you about our newest additions. <u>Ruby</u> is the link that activates the sound file.

     i.   Oh yes, you should use a document-level style sheet for the style information, and make sure that the users of the page know when the particular price lists are unavailable. For example, if the cultured pearl price list is not available, the user should see a message that says Cultured pearl prices are not currently available.

     j.   The screen real estate reserved for each price list should be large enough to see the whole list without taking up excessive space.

9.2. Create a new HTML document with a sound object (which can be a music file) you have found on the Net. Give credit where credit is due, and explain where you found the object. The title bar should display Sounds Incorporated Your Name, with the assignment due date included within comment lines. Create a link to the sites where the objects were found so that your user can go harvest other objects from these sites.

9.3. Place a video object you have found on the Net in a new HTML document. Give the creator credit, and put text on the page explaining where you found the object. The title bar should display Video Incorporated Your Name, with the assignment due date included within comment lines. Create a link to the sites where the objects were found so that your user can download other objects from these sites.

9.4. Retrieve the Homework home page you updated in Exercise 8.4. Use a sound recorder to create a brief aural introduction, and create a link to it on the page. Note: People using Windows have access to a program accessory called the Sound Recorder. Make sure you use language that your mother would approve.

9.5. Retrieve your school's home page that you updated in Exercise 8.5. Incorporate a multimedia object that relates to the school you think reflects positively on you and your fellow classmates. Make sure you include a description that does the object justice. If you cannot find a relevant multimedia object, create a sound file using a sound recorder and use it to complete this exercise. Note: People using Windows have access to a program accessory called the Sound Recorder.

9.6. Retrieve the Web page about your favorite movie you updated in Exercise 8.6. Surf the Internet to find and download an image, video clip, or sound file that relates to the movie or one of the actors. Insert the object into the page. Include descriptions for each object you insert.

9.7. Surf the Net to find an applet, and place it on a new Web page. (May we suggest http://www.jars.com/ as a starting point.) Provide a brief explanation as to where you found it, and include a credit line. The title bar should display *Applet Incorporated your Name,* with the assignment due date included within comment lines. Create a link to the sites where you found the applet so that others can find it.

## Chapter Ten

Frames: Divide and Conquer

Using frames to divide the Web page into smaller "pagelets" used to be a popular way to control the layout of the screen while giving the user a familiar navigation tool and common "look and feel." Each frame is, in essence, a separate HTML document, and you can change the content of each frame individually. However, the use of frames can easily be overdone, creating an unstructured mess that renders the information on your pages difficult, if not impossible, for the user to find and use. In addition, frames make a hash of the careful navigation concepts we have been so carefully building. If you absolutely must use frames you should use them judiciously.

CHAPTER OBJECTIVES

After reading this chapter you should be able to do the following:

- Create an integrated set of Web pages using frames.
- Update target frames using hyperlinks.
- Know how to handle non-frame-compliant browsers when using frames.
- Set the default target frame.

- Use reserve names as special targets.
- Integrate inline frames into Web page designs.
- Identify the advantages and disadvantages of using frames in Web site designs.

▸▸ CONSIDERATIONS WHEN USING FRAMES

Frames were officially anointed in the HTML 4.0 specifications. Popular browsers began to recognize frames before these specifications were released, but older browsers (before Netscape 2.0 and Internet Explorer 3.0) will not support them. For that reason, you should use the <noframes> container to accommodate browsers that don't support frames.

To make matters more "interesting," you can build a framed document that appears within the frame of another framed document! Although frames within frames—and, by extension, frames within frames contained in frames—can show the logical prowess of the Web weaver, they are of little use in most circumstances and may leave the user totally confused.

By the same token, the proper application of frames can create a moderately user-friendly interface that integrates a set of Web pages. When using frames, special consideration should be given to the users' navigation needs. For example, you can build a narrow frame along one of the margins, top, bottom, right, or left (Figure 10.1), that contains a table of contents to your site. The user selects different choices from the table of contents, and the text and graphics for the chosen pages appear in the main (content) frame. That way the user always has her navigation tools available, and she doesn't have to link forward and backward to peruse your site. At the end of this chapter we will demonstrate how similar Web page designs can be executed using tables.

Figure 10.1

HTML code for horizontal frame rows in which the top frame acts as the table of contents

```
<!DOCTYPE HTML PUBLIC "-//W3C//DTD HTML 4.01 Frameset//EN"
"http://www.w3.org/TR/html4/frameset.dtd">
<html>
<head>
<title>Music Hall of Frames</title>
</head>

<frameset rows="15%,*">
    <frame src="toc.htm" />
    <frame src="opener.htm" name="content" />
</frameset>
</html>
```

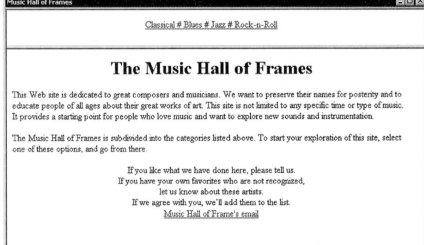

Another factor you need to consider is the way the Back and Forward buttons on some browsers work, or, rather, in the case of frames, don't work. Instead of moving the user from page to page as usual, Back and Forward have a different effect in a framed

document. Most often they will change the contents of the most recent active frame. However, using these buttons may cause results that are very upsetting to your users, like jumping back to the last Web site, not the last Web page.

Another major difference for Web weavers is the way View Source works in a framed document. If you ask to View Source, you will see the source of the main frame document, with the <frameset> tag, and so on. This is usually a tiny page of just a few lines. To view the source of the actual document displayed within the frame, you must right-click on the frame and choose from the shortcut menu either View Frame Source when using Navigator or View Source when using Internet Explorer. Opera uses cascading menus that go from Frame to the View Source option. This, too, can be confusing.

To add even more interest to the life of your users, the URL of the framed document doesn't change, regardless of how many pages you load. That defeats the bookmarking or Favorites tools most users have come to depend upon. Consequently, they may have difficulty finding their way back to a specific part of your site. To help them, you could put the URL of each page that is displayed in a frame somewhere on that page. Then they could at least copy and paste the URL into another document.

In addition, you need to ensure that each page presented in a frame has a way to link to the main page. That way your user always has a reasonable navigation tool available. Let's look at a simple framed document to see exactly what we are talking about.

▸▸ FRAME NAVIGATION

The print medium forces us to show you a series of still frames instead of the dynamic document. Figure 10.1 shows the first screen, called opener.htm. Notice the two frames, one with four navigation links (Classical, Blues, etc.) and the second, larger frame taking up the lower 85 percent of the screen.

Figure 10.2 shows what happens when the user activates the first link, "Classical." The larger content window now displays a second document, called classical.htm. Even though the larger window changed, the smaller navigation window did not. That is one feature of frames that makes them useful. The user can change the text in one frame without losing the control given by the navigation frame.

Figure 10.2   HTML code for the "Classical" link

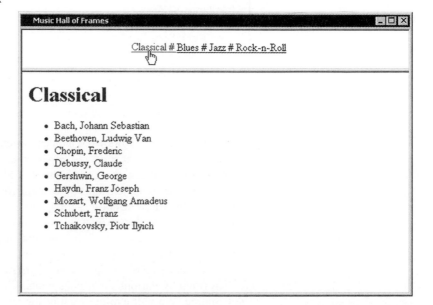

```html
<html>
<head>
<title>Classical</title>
</head>

<body>
<h1>Classical</h1>
<ul>
  <li>Bach, Johann Sebastian</li>
  <li>Beethoven, Ludwig Van</li>
  <li>Chopin, Frederic</li>
  <li>Debussy, Claude</li>
  <li>Gershwin, George</li>
  <li>Haydn, Franz Joseph</li>
  <li>Mozart, Wolfgang Amadeus</li>
  <li>Schubert, Franz</li>
  <li>Tchaikovsky, Piotr Ilyich</li>
</ul>
</body>
</html>
```

Now let's see what happens when the user activates the "Blues" link. As Figure 10.3 shows, the contents of the content window changed again. It now displays the contents of the document blues.htm. The HTML documents displayed in the frame can be any HTML document or any graphic that the browser can display. Using this type of table of contents (the code is shown in Figure 10.3) and a large display window can be very effective for a series of pictures. Use the small frame to allow the user to choose among the images and the larger window to display them.

Figure 10.3

HTML code for the table of contents

```
<html>
<head>
<title>Table of Contents</title>
</head>

<body>
<div align="center">
  <a href="classical.htm" target="content">Classical # </a>
  <a href="blues.htm" target="content">Blues # </a>
  <a href="jazz.htm" target="content">Jazz # </a>
  <a href="rock.htm" target="content">Rock-n-Roll</a>
</div>
</body>
</html>
```

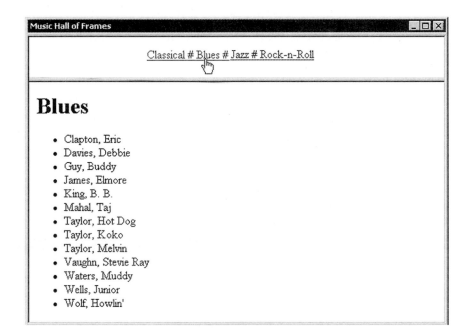

Figure 10.4 also shows what happens when the user activates the "Rock-n-Roll" link. Notice the scroll bar that suddenly appeared on the right side of the content frame. That is another feature you can choose to control or allow the browser to control for you. In this case, the browser detected that the contents of the document were larger than could be displayed in the frame window, so it added the scroll bar to allow the user to see the complete contents of the document.

Figure 10.1 presents the code that generates the frames that display these four documents. Notice that there is no </body> container. The <frameset> container replaces the </body> container. This is the driver, or master document, that builds the frames, which are then filled by various other documents. This is also what the user sees if he activates View Source. We will explore each of the tags and attributes in detail, but for now, just look at the overall structure of the frame document.

Figure 10.4

Browser display of scroll bar that appears when HTML document does not fit in frame

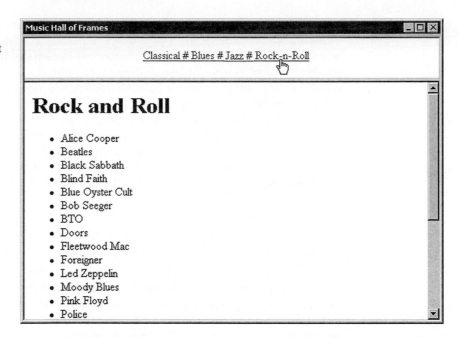

Figure 10.3 presents the code for the menu in our frames example. Figure 10.2 presents the code for the Classical screen. The other HTML documents are basically the same design as the classical screen but with different data. One of the important things to note is that the pages that are placed into the frames look like the documents we have seen all through our experience with HTML. It is an important concept that the documents that fill frames are simply HTML documents placed within frames. They need no special formatting to appear in a frame.

▶▶ FORMATTING FRAMES

Although the documents that fill frames are just like any other HTML document, the document that has frames must be constructed differently from any HTML document we have seen so far. In a framed document, there is no <body></body> container. As you may have noticed in our example in Figure 10.1, the <frameset></frameset> container replaces the <body></body> container for a framed document. This distinction is important, because if a browser encounters a <body> tag before the <frameset> tag, it will ignore the <frameset> altogether. Thus, you can have a traditional HTML document with a <body>, or you can have a framed document with a <frameset>, but not both.

FRAMESET DOCUMENT TYPE DEFINITION

The third HTML document type definition (*DTD*) recognized by the World Wide Web consortium is frameset (the others are Strict and Transitional). The frameset DTD was especially designed for framed documents, as shown in Figure 10.1. Therefore, you must use the following <!DOCTYPE> tag when building one:

```
<!DOCTYPE HTML PUBLIC "-//W3C//DTD HTML 4.01 Frameset//EN"
                        "http://www.w3.org/TR/html4/frameset.dtd">
```

HTML   <frameset>Frame Setting</frameset>

Description: describes how browser window is subdivided into frames.
Type: container.
Attributes: id, class, **cols**, title, style, **onload, onunload, rows.**
Special Note: cannot appear within an HTML document's <body> element.

The <frameset></frameset> container defines a page that contains one or more frames. Although it is possible to have a page with a single frame, most of the time a Web weaver will have at least two different frames within the same page. It is also possible to have a nearly unlimited number of frames defined, but with more than three or four, the user could get lost, and the contents would be difficult to find. The <frameset></frameset> container defines the physical layout of the page, determining how much of the real estate of the screen is given to each of the different frames.

The </frameset> ending tag must never be omitted. Some browsers will not even build the page if this closing tag is left out. All you will see is an empty screen. There are four new attributes used within the <frameset></frameset> container, **rows, cols, onload,** and **onunload.**

rows and cols

Together **rows** and/or **cols** define how many frames are on the screen and how they are oriented. You can use either attribute alone, or you can use both attributes together to define a more complex layout. At least one of these attributes must be coded in the <frameset> open tag. Both have values expressed either in absolute pixels or as a percentage of the screen. As you might expect, it is significantly better coding practice to define sections of the screen as percentage values than to use absolute pixel sizes, because all screens are not of the same resolution as the one you use to build the document.

To make it easier for you to figure out the relative percentages, you can use the asterisk (*) for one of the values, as shown in Figure 10.1. The browser will fill in the asterisk with whatever is left over when your exact percentages are subtracted from 100. For this figure, given the code rows="15%,*", the browser will replace the * with 85%. This feature is also available if you choose to code your rows and cols in pixels.

The browser can help you further with your math: If you were to code cols="25%, 60%, 25%", the browser would actually build three columns that added up to 100 percent, with roughly the proportions you asked for.

Bear in mind that the browsers will also allow the user to resize the frames by dragging the frame dividers unless you specifically prevent it. That means that a savvy user can undo all your careful frame-size calculations.

onload and onunload

Usually the intrinsic events we see as attributes deal with mouse events like clicking on or moving over a place on the screen. The **onload** and **onunload** attributes are a variation of these events, which are discussed in detail in Chapter Twelve. In either case the attribute is used to activate a script or applet. For example, the **onload** attribute is activated when an HTML document finishes loading into a frame. The following code could be used to run the add-one( ) function:

```
<frameset rows="15%,*" onload="add-one ( )">
  <frame src="toc.htm" />
  <frame src="opener.htm" frame="body" />
</frameset>
```

This script uses the add-one ( ) function to count the number of visits to a site. The **onunload** attribute works in similar fashion. It is activated just before the document is removed from the frame. These attributes are also recognized by the <body> element. They activate scripts or applets when the contents of a page are loaded into or unloaded from the browser's window. You will see another example of this when we look at JavaScripts in Chapter Thirteen.

NESTED <frameset> CONTAINERS

"Like a circle in a spiral, like a wheel within a wheel," you can include one or more <frameset></frameset> containers within an outer <frameset></frameset> container. This allows the creation of some fancy (read that as "very complex") formatting, with different numbers of rows or columns across the page.

For an example, examine the code and resulting screen in Figure 10.5. The left column (of size 40 percent), contains only one frame. It displays the document called frame1.htm. The second column contains the nested <frameset> with three rows, occupying 40 percent, 33 percent, and 27 percent, respectively. The three documents—frame2.htm, frame3.htm, and frame4.htm—are displayed from the top to the bottom of that column. You need to be very careful as you construct your nested <frameset>s, because skipping something as simple as a closing angle bracket may produce some strange results.

Figure 10.5

HTML code for nested <frameset> containers that create complex screen layouts

```
<html>
<head>
<title>Nested Framesets</title>
</head>

<frameset cols="40%,*">
  <!--This is the first (leftmost) column -->
  <frame src="frame1.htm" name="area-1" />
  <frameset rows="40%,33%,*">
    <!-- All this is in the second (rightmost) column -->
    <frame src="frame2.htm" name="area-2" />
    <frame src="frame3.htm" name="area-3" />
    <frame src="frame4.htm" name="area-4" />
  </frameset>
</frameset>
</html>
```

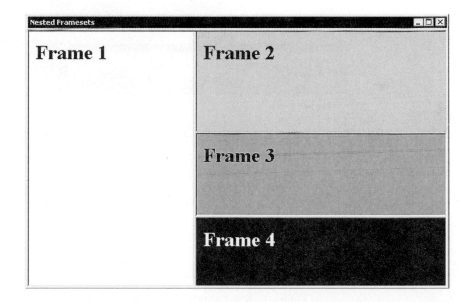

Now let's consider a slightly more complex nesting situation. Figure 10.6 presents the code for two nested <frameset>s, the left one with two rows, and the right one with three. The placement of the </frameset> tag in this example is critical. Although one frameset can be enclosed within another, the end of one frameset cannot occur after the beginning of another. In other words, you cannot overlap framesets as shown in Figure 10.6.

Note that the third frameset is started before the second is closed, causing an overlapping of framesets. The frameset that has two rows, each 50 percent, is still open when the frameset that has three rows, 20 percent, 40 percent, and 40 percent, is opened. The very next line of code closes the second frameset.

Figure 10.6

HTML code in which nested
<frameset> containers
incorrectly overlap

```html
<html>
<head>
<title>Incorrect Nesting of Framesets</title>
</head>

<frameset cols="40%,*">
  <!-- This is the first (leftmost) column -->
  <frameset rows="50%,*">
    <frame src="frame1.htm" name="area-1" />
    <frame src="frame2.htm" name="area-2" />
    <frameset rows="20%,40%,*">
    <!-- This is the second (rightmost) column -->
  </frameset>
      <frame src="frame3.htm" name="area-3" />
      <frame src="frame4.htm" name="area-4" />
      <frame src="frame5.htm" name="area-5" />
    </frameset>
</frameset>
</html>
```

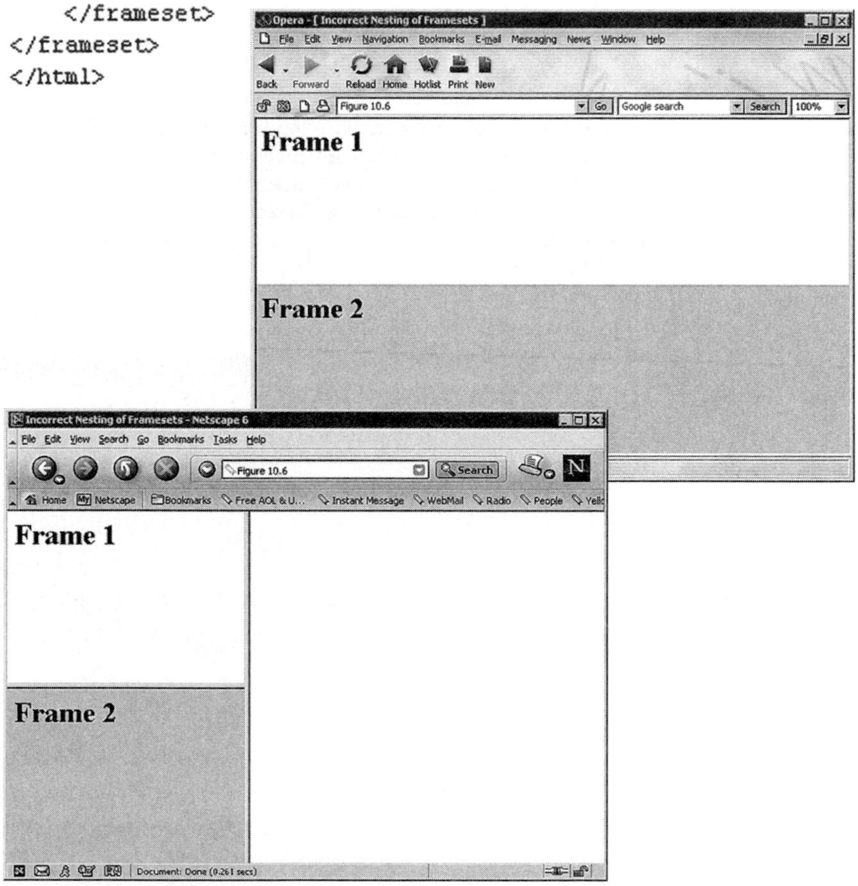

In Figure 10.6, all of the popular browsers become confused, with the Navigator and Internet Explorer browsers taking one course of action and the Opera browser taking another. The Opera browser knows the first column is split into two rows but gets confused after that. Navigator and Internet Explorer start off the first column correctly but cannot infer a close to the frameset, so they ignore the new open <frameset> tag. When they find the closing tag, since they don't understand how <frame> tags can exist within a <frameset> tag, they ignore the closing tag as well. The result is the large empty column on the right. Earlier versions of Navigator do something different yet!

Figure 10.7 presents the corrected code and the proper screen display. The frames now appear as intended. Be aware that this example may have too many frames to be functional. It was designed only to illustrate nested framesets, not to show proper coding or good page layout.

Figure 10.7 HTML code showing correction to nested <frameset> container in Figure 10.6

```html
<html>
<head>
<title>Correct Nested Framesets</title>
</head>

<frameset cols="40%,*">
  <!-- This is the first (leftmost) column -->
  <frameset rows="50%,*">
    <frame src="frame1.htm" name="area-1" />
    <frame src="frame2.htm" name="area-2" />
  </frameset>

  <!-- This is the second (rightmost) column -->
  <frameset rows="20%,40%,*">
    <frame src="frame3.htm" name="area-3" />
    <frame src="frame4.htm" name="area-4" />
    <frame src="frame5.htm" name="area-5" />
  </frameset>
</frameset>
</html>
```

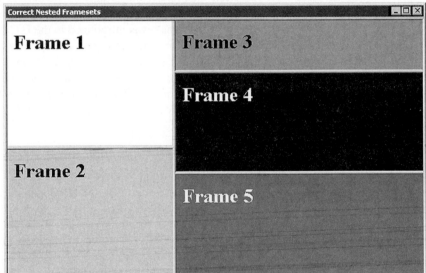

EXPLORATION **#1**

Copy the file recipes.html and the following five files from the student CD to a disk drive on your personal computer.

1. *Appetizer* links to appetizer.html.

2. *Snack* links to snack.html.

3. *Spread* links to spread.html.

4. *Sweet* links to sweet.html

5. *Home Page* links to recipes-homepage.html.

Open recipes.html using an ASCII editor and change the <title> container to *your name's Famous Recipes*. Add hyperlinks to these files using the related word currently in recipes.html as the link.

Save the file as chapter10.html, and display it using your favorite browser, testing each link.

<frame />

Description: identifies the contents of a frame.
Type: empty.
Attributes: class, **frameborder, id, longdesc, marginheight, marginwidth, name,**
noresize, scrolling, src, style, **target, title.**
XML: requires closing pseudo tag syntax using <frame />, for example, <frame
src="opener.htm" name="content" />.

The <frameset></frameset> container is not designed to display any information but just to format, or structure, a page that contains one or more frames. Only elements coded within the <frameset> can present data. There are two types of elements in this class, <frame /> and <noframes></noframes>. The latter will be discussed later in this chapter.

The <frame /> element presents an HTML document within a specific frame on the page. Each <frame /> tag is controlled by a series of attributes defining the properties of the frame as well as specifying its initial content. The various HTML and XHTML specifications have gone full circle on whether the <frame /> element is a container or empty tag. You will find that early implementation of the <frame> element includes the </frame> closing tag. However, <frame> was introduced in the HTML 4 specifications as an empty tag. This was logical because the <frame> container can exist only within the confines of a <frameset>. Since any other tag within the <frameset> would cause the browser to infer a close to the <frame>, the <frame> can be safely treated as an empty tag—at least it could be, until XML and XHTML came along with the requirement that every element have a closing tag. Now proper syntax looks like this:

<frame src="filename.ext" name="frame-name" />

src

The value coded for the **src** attribute is the URL of the document, image, multimedia presentation, or any other displayable object that initially appears in the frame. If you want to create a very complex page, you can even use the URL of another framed document in one of the frames. This **src** attribute may well be the most important attribute for the <frame> tag, because with some early browsers, if there is no **src** and associated value coded in any particular <frame />, that frame can never have any content.

name

The **name** attribute allows the named frame to be the target of other links, so other frames and scripts can change the content of a specific frame. You saw this in Figure 10.1 when we used a framed document to create a table of contents and a text page. In Figure 10.3, the horizontal links (Classical, Blues, etc.) in the table of contents page identify (target) the text page by the name *content*. When the user selects one of the links, the related HTML document is opened in the content frame.

Figure 10.8 provides an example of how the **name** attribute works. Notice that the <frame> descriptor for the second frame has no **src** attribute, but it does have a **name** attribute. In the top screen display Frame 2 seems to be missing its content because no source (HTML document, image, etc.) was specified when the frame was initiated. Activating the link in Frame III (bottom screen display) would supply content to the area where Frame 2 is missing because it has a name—in this case, area-2. This is the HTML code that created the link in Frame III:

<a href="frame2.htm" target="area-2"><b>Link to Frame 2</b></a>

Figure 10.8

HTML code without a source **(src)** for area-2

```
<html>
<head>
<title>Area-2 Missing src</title>
</head>

<frameset cols="40%,*">
  <!-- This is the first (leftmost) column -->
  <frameset rows="50%,*">
  <frame src="frame1.htm" name="area-1" />
  <frame name="area-2">                        ———— Missing src attribute
  </frameset>

  <!-- This is the second (rightmost) column -->
  <frameset rows="40%,30%,*">
    <frame src="frameIII.htm" name="area-3" />
    <frame src="frame4.htm" name="area-4" />
    <frame src="frame5.htm" name="area-5" />
  </frameset>
</frameset>
</html>
```

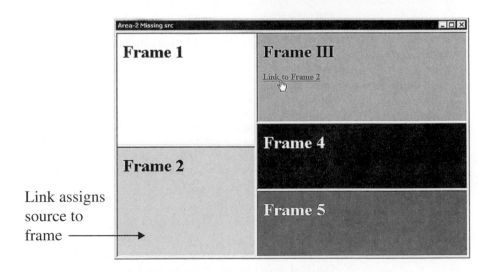

No source
assigned to
frame ———→

Link assigns
source to
frame ———→

Figure 10.9 shows a simple modification of the HTML code in Figure 10.1, where **rows** is replaced by **cols.** The narrow column on the left is now the vertical table of contents (the related HTML code is also shown in Figure 10.9), and the larger frame on the right is the content area of the selected HTML document. As the user activates the various options from the menu on the left, the text that corresponds to that option appears in the frame on the right. If the user activates the Classical choice, the screen looks like the display in Figure 10.9. As with the earlier example, the navigation links do not change when new contents appear in the content area. This is an example of the navigational power of frames and one of the few acceptable uses for frames.

Figure 10.9

HTML code for vertical frame layout, with the table of contents in the left frame

```
<html>
<head>
<title>Music Hall of Frames</title>                    Frameset
</head>

<frameset cols="15%,*">
  <frame src="vtoc.htm" />
  <frame src="opener.htm" name="content" />
</frameset>
</html>
```

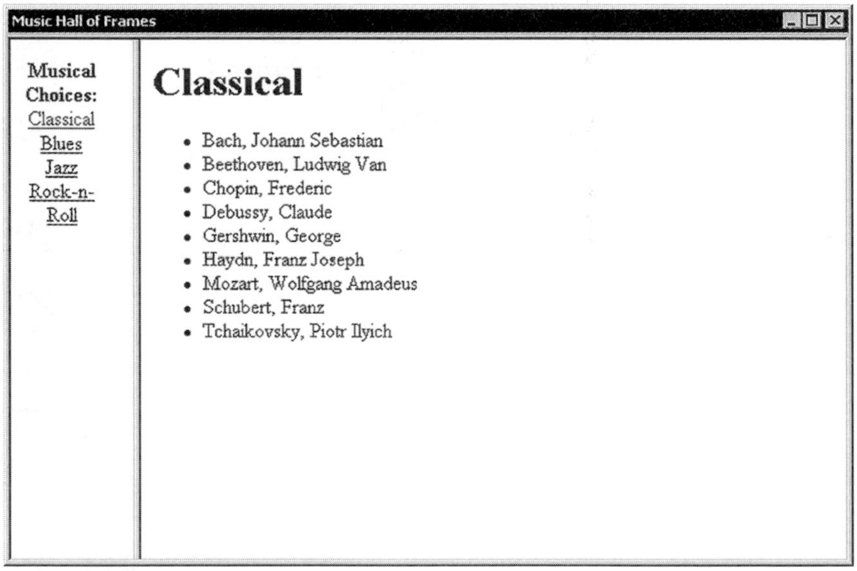

```
<html>
<head>
<title>Vertical Table of Contents</title>
</head>

<body>
<div align="center">
  <b>Musical Choices:</b><br />
  <a href="classical.htm" target="content">Classical</a><br />        vtoc.htm
  <a href="blues.htm" target="content">Blues</a><br />
  <a href="jazz.htm" target="content">Jazz</a><br />
  <a href="rock.htm" target="content">Rock-n-Roll</a><br />
</div>
</body>
</html>
```

Now that you see what the browser can provide, let's take a closer look at the code. The first page, coded in the top of Figure 10.9, is the actual frameset document. It has only two frames defined. The first is for the table of contents, since the frames are built left to right, top to bottom. This frame takes up 15 percent of the whole area of the frames. The second frame gets what is left (roughly 85 percent) and has the name "content" associated with it. It is initially assigned the document opener.htm. The contents are shown in the screen display in Figure 10.1.

Figure 10.9 also shows the code for the table-of-contents document. This menu is simply a list containing the links to the different HTML files that present the data. Each anchor tag has a **target** attribute that directs the browser to place the contents of the HTML file listed in the anchor—for example, jazz.htm—into the frame or window with the name of *content*. This is how one frame, in this case the table of contents, can affect another frame, the content frame. We will examine the **target** attribute in detail later in the chapter.

The code for an actual content page is shown in Figure 10.2. As we said before, an HTML document that appears as the content of a frame requires no special formatting or special attributes. It is simply a regular HTML document placed within a subdivision (frame) of the screen.

id

All throughout this book we have been saying that the **name** and **id** attributes work in the same way. This is not the case with frames. Suppose you replaced the **name** attribute with the **id** attribute so the <frame> code from Figure 10.9 looked like this:

```
<frame src="opener.htm" id="content">
```

The results are dramatically different. Currently both Internet Explorer and Navigator open a new browser window and display the linked files in this new window. Opera replaces the frameset page with the linked file. Since the HTML 4 specifications do not address the issue of targeting frames using the **id** attribute, we do not expect this difference to be resolved in the near future.

scrolling

If the user selects the "Rock-n-Roll" option, the screen will look similar to Figure 10.4, with the appearance of a scroll bar. Unless you force a scroll bar on every frame or prevent scroll bars from being created, the browser will create a scroll bar only when the contents of the document to be displayed extend beyond the boundaries of the browser pane. You can prevent the generation of scroll bars by using the scrolling="no" option with the <frame> tag. Figure 10.10 shows how the "Rock and Roll" page looks with the scrolling="no" option set.

Figure 10.10 HTML code showing **scrolling** attribute set to "no" to prevent browser from displaying scroll bar

```
<html>
<head>
<title>Music Hall of Frames</title>
</head>

<frameset cols="15%,*">
  <frame src="vtoc.htm" />
  <frame src="opener.htm"
    name="content"
    scrolling="no" />
</frameset>
</html>
```

As shown in the "Rock and Roll" example, you can control whether the browser puts scroll bars on the frames you build. If you don't code this **scrolling** attribute, the browser defaults to scrolling="auto", which allows the browser to add scroll bars if the document's content is larger than the frame space allowed to display it. If the entire content of the document can be displayed, then no scroll bar is created. If scrolling="yes" is coded, however, the browser will always create a scroll bar on the frame whether or not the contents extend beyond the boundaries of the frame.

In the previous example, the frame was created with a scrolling="no" option. That prevented the browser from adding scroll bars, even though the content of the document was larger than the frame space. As you can see in the example, some of that content was unavailable. Text outside the frame will always be unavailable if there is no scroll bar to bring it into the visible part of the frame.

Usually it is best to allow the browser to use the default mode of "auto" and place scroll bars on the frame only when necessary. There appears to be no good reason to turn off scrolling.

noresize

In most cases, the user can control the size of the windows on his screen simply by dragging the frame dividers. Thus, he can compensate for any errors in your "guess" as to the best fit. Allowing the user to adjust a frame is usually the browser's default option. But if you have an image that must fit exactly in a space of specific size, and you have placed it in a frame of that exact size, you may wish to restrict the user from playing with the size of that frame. You can do so by coding the **noresize** attribute to the <frame> tag. For instance, we could lock in the size of the left frame with this code:

```
<frameset cols="15%,*">
  <frame src="vtoc.htm" noresize="yes">
  <frame src="opener.htm" names="body">
</frameset>
```

Bear in mind that the **noresize** attribute is set for the whole frame, and for the life of the frame. Like the scrolling option, this attribute sets the characteristics of the frame, not of a specific document shown in the frame. If you code the **noresize** attribute, the frame will never be resizable.

If you have only a few frames on your document, let's say three columns, and you code **noresize** on the center frame, you have effectively locked in the horizontal size of all three frames. The two center dividers cannot be moved, so the size of all three frames is fixed. Use this attribute very judiciously. It is occasionally necessary, but most of the time the user can benefit from being able to resize the frame.

marginheight and marginwidth

The browsers usually place a minimum amount of space between the frame edges and the text within the frame. In some cases this space is so small that parts of the letters may be lost along the margins. To create a better visual effect, especially in a tight frame, use the **marginheight** and **marginwidth** attributes to add spacing along the edges of the frame.

Figure 10.11 presents the code for setting margins in our frame document. The margins are excessively large, chosen to illustrate how the presentation of the document can differ based on these attributes. Normally a margin of 5 to 10 pixels is sufficient to visually separate the contents from the frame. Here the margin height is coded for 25 pixels and the margin width for 50 pixels. To see the difference, compare the screen display in Figure 10.11 with that in Figure 10.1. The default margins are used in Figure 10.1.

title and longdesc

Both the **title** and **longdesc** attributes are used to describe the related object. The **title** attribute provides a short two- or three-word description. The description provided by the

Figure 10.11   HTML code for a content frame with a margin height of 25 pixels and a margin width of 50 pixels

```
<html>
<head>
<title>Music Hall of Frames</title>
</head>

<frameset cols="15%,*" title="Music Hall of Frames">
  <frame src="vtoc.htm" />
  <frame src="opener.htm"
    name="content"
    frameborder="0"
    marginheight="25"
    marginwidth="50" />
</frameset>
</html>
```

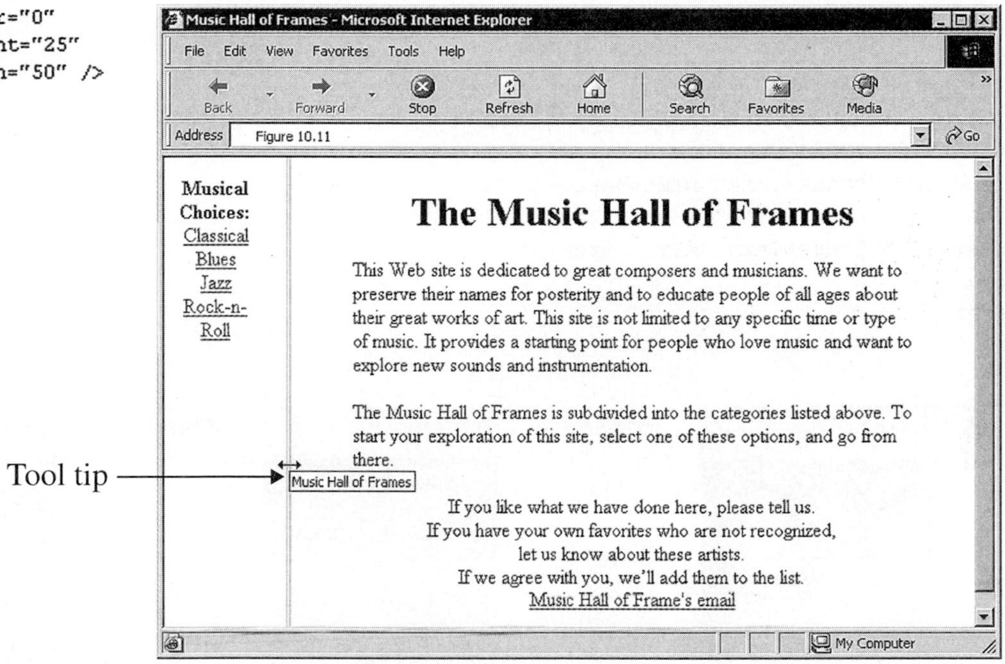

Tool tip

title attribute can be used as the text for a ***tool tip message,*** the popup text box that appears when the screen pointer moves over an object on the screen. Internet Explorer displays the "Music Hall of Frames" tool tip shown in Figure 10.11 using the title attribute found in the <frameset> element. The code looks like this:

```
<frameset cols="15%, *" title="Music Hall of Frames">
```

The **longdesc** attribute specifies a longer description of the contents, one that goes beyond the title attribute's description. The text that makes up the long description is stored as an independent file. You set the **longdesc** attribute equal to the text file's URL, path, and filename. With respect to frames, both of these attributes could be useful for nonvisual users cruising the Web.

frameborder

The **frameborder** attribute is used to turn the frame border on (1) or off (0). The browser recognizes only the value 1 or 0. A frame's border is turned off with the following code:

```
<frame src="vtoc.htm" frameborder="0">
```

Similar code is used in Figure 10.11. Notice in this figure that Internet Explorer still displays part of the border (as oppose to the complete border shown in Figure 10.10) when it is set to "0" using the frame element.

The popular browsers also recognize **frameborder** as part of the <frameset> element. All of the borders are turned off in different ways (see Figure 10.12) with this code:

```
<frameset cols="40%, *" frameborder="0">
```

Figure 10.12 HTML code for turning off frame borders

```
<html>
<head>
<title>No Frame Borders</title>
</head>
<frameset cols="40%,*" frameborder="0">
  <!-- This is the first (leftmost) column -->
  <frameset rows="50%,*">
    <frame src="frame1.htm" name="area-1" />
    <frame src="frame2.htm" name="area-2" />
  </frameset>

  <!-- This is the second (rightmost) column -->
  <frameset rows="20%,40%,*">
    <frame src="frame3.htm" name="area-3" />
    <frame src="frame4.htm" name="area-4" />
    <frame src="frame5.htm" name="area-5" />
  </frameset>
</frameset>
</html>
```

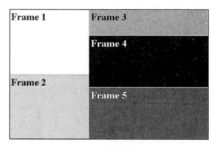

<table>
<tr><td>Internet Explorer</td><td>Navigator</td><td>Opera</td></tr>
</table>

EXPLORATION **#2** Create a Web page that uses the <frameset> element to set up a two-column vertical frame design like that in Figure 10.9. The title bar should display *your name's Famous Recipes*. The left column takes up 20 percent of the browser pane, and the right column takes up the remaining space. Name the left column *links* and display in it chapter10-recipes.html. You will create this HTML document later in this Exploration. The right-column frame should be named *information* and initially open with recipes-homepage.html. Save the file using chapter10-frames.html as the filename.

Open chapter10.html using an ASCII editor. Add a **target** attribute to each source anchor to identify the information frame as the place to open the related file. Save the file using chapter10-recipes.html as the filename. Display chapter10-frames.html using your favorite browser, and test it to make sure each file opens in the information frame.

HTML <noframes>No Frames</noframe>

Description: provides content for browsers that do not recognize the <frameset> element.
Type: container.
Attributes: none.

Not all browsers support frames. Mosaic and early versions of Netscape and Internet Explorer do not support this extension to the HTML language. Browsers that do not recognize HTML codes recommended by the W³C specifications are referred to as **noncompliant browsers.** For users with noncompliant frame browsers, HTML has the <noframes>. . .</noframes> container. Although the use of this tag is not required by the syntax of HTML, you should always code it within your framed document. Otherwise your page will be worthless for users with browsers that don't support frames. Whenever you design a set of documents, always make the contents available to the widest audience.

You can code any HTML tag set within the <noframes> container, even a </body> tag. A frame-compliant browser will ignore the contents of the <noframes></noframes> container, while a browser that doesn't support frames will usually display them.

The way <noframes> works takes advantage of the flexibility of the browsers. When a browser encounters a tag it doesn't know, it ignores that tag. Because a noncompliant browser ignores all the frame tags, including the <noframes> tag, all it finds to display are the contents of the <noframes></noframes> container. There are a few very strict browsers that will not even display the contents of a <noframes></noframes> container and will generate an error message instead, but they are in the distinct minority.

Figure 10.13 shows how a <noframes></noframes> container would be coded and displayed in a noncompliant browser. In this case the browser is Mosaic 3.0. The message within the <noframes> element explains to users with noncompliant browsers that they need to either upgrade their browser or link to an index page. The link will take them to a table of contents document called nftoc.htm that is specifically written for noncompliant browsers. When invoked this way, the table-of-contents page takes up the whole browser window, as shown in the figure. Note that the background color behind the noframe text is light gray in Figure 10.13. This was the default color with older browsers. All the popular browsers now use white as the default background color.

When the user activates one of the links with a noncompliant browser, the browser ignores the **target** attribute. Why? Because there is no frame with that name; therefore, the target doesn't exist for the noncompliant browser. Consequently, the browser loads the image onto the current screen, replacing the table of contents. To get back to the table of contents, the user merely activates the Back button. However, there should also be a link back to the opening page from each of the informational documents. A strategy for handling this situation is discussed in the next section in regard to the special "_parent" target. This is one of several special applications of the **target** attribute you need to know about.

target

As we saw throughout the examples of framed windows, you can specify a label, or **target** attribute, in an anchor (<a>) tag and thus direct the browser to load the document referenced in the **href** into the window or frame specified. For example,

```
<a href="blues.htm" target="content">Blues</a>
```

loads the HTML document blues.htm into the window or frame labeled *content* when the user activates the Blues link. If there is no frame with the **name** attribute of content, the browser will create a new window and call it *content.*

Let's suppose the Web weaver makes a mistake coding the anchor and calls the target text. When the Blues link is selected, the browser cannot put the document into the frame specified in the anchor, because the name text doesn't match the known target name of *content.* Therefore, the browser opens a new window and places the document there. In many cases a mistake like this may even cause the operating system to create a second browser session. It is very important that you code accurate tags when you choose to use targets from a link.

Another common mistake is to forget to include the target with the link. If the user chooses the Blues link from this menu, the framed document will be overlaid by a standard window containing only the data found in the blues.htm document. As just mentioned, when the browser encounters a document that has no target, it will create a

Figure 10.13 Adding the <noframes> element for non-frame-compliant browsers

```
<html>
<head>
<title>Music Hall of Frames</title>
</head>

<frameset cols="15%,*">
  <frame src="vtoc.htm" />
  <frame src="opener.htm" name="content" />
  <noframes>
  <h2>Non-Frame-Compliant Browser</h2>
  <p>I am sorry, but this document is designed to be read by a frame compliant browser. If
     you see this message, your browser doesn't support frames.
  </p>

  <p>You can either update your current browser to one that supports framing, or you can see
     the same content, page by page, using the <a href="nftoc.htm">index</a> and the "BACK"
     button. Sorry for the inconvenience.
  </p>
  The Management
  </noframes>
</frameset>
</html>
```

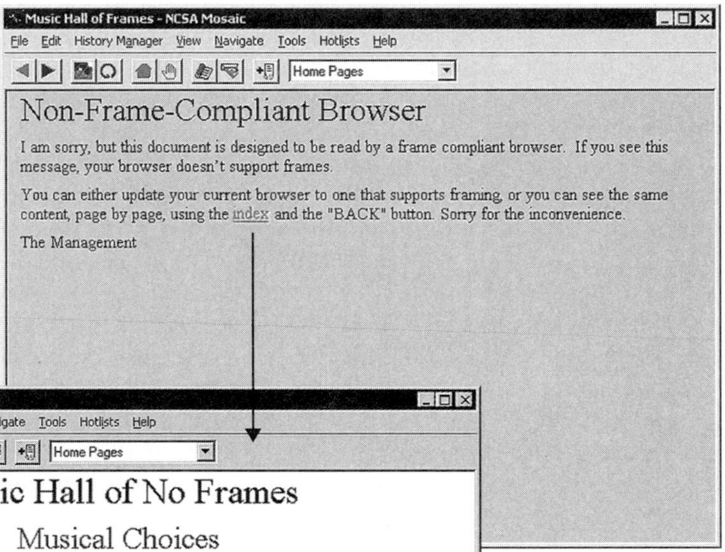

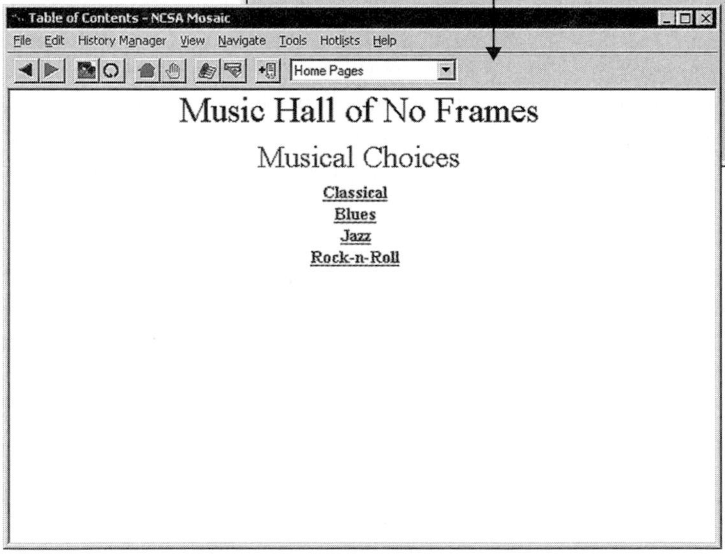

new window for that new document. That sounds almost like a rule, so there must be an exception to it. Our next subject, the <base> tag, provides that exception.

EXPLORATION #3 Add to chapter10-frames.html the ability to handle non-frame-compliant browsers. As part of the message to users, provide a link to chapter10.html.

HTML **<base />**

Description: specifies a document's base URL explicitly. Relative path references then use the base URL as a reference point.
Type: empty.
Attributes: href, **target.**
XML: requires closing tag using <base/>, for example, <base target="content" />.
Special note: must be placed within the <head></head> container.

You can set a default target for each link that uses a specified target by coding the <base /> tag. Thus, we could change the code in the table of contents page as shown in Figure 10.14. This HTML code would produce exactly the same results as the code in Figure 10.9. Notice that the individual links no longer specify a target, yet the page behaves exactly the same as when they did. The <base /> tag with the **target** attribute sets the target for any link that is not explicitly specified. This default target works only on the page that has the <base /> tag, but it will save us some keyboard time and ensure that we have a consistent presentation. The code looks like this:

```
<base target="default-frame" />
```

Figure 10.14

HTML code using <base /> tag to identify *content* as default target

```
<html>
<head>
<title>Vertical Table of Contents</title>
<base target="content" /> ◂
</head>

<body>
<div align="center">
  <b>Musical Choices:</b><br
  <a href="classical.htm">Classical</a><br />
  <a href="blues.htm">Blues</a><br />
  <a href="jazz.htm">Jazz</a><br />
  <a href="rock.htm">Rock-n-Roll</a><br />
</div>
</body>
</html>
```

SPECIAL TARGETS

The browsers support four special targets that serve particular needs. These special target names are called *reserve names* because their spellings have been set aside by the W[3]C to have a specific meaning that cannot be changed. All of these reserve names start with an underscore. The browser will ignore any other target coded with an underscore.

_blank To initiate a newly opened window, the browser uses the _blank target. It is usually used for unnamed windows. This reserve name is often used with an intersystem link to a remote Web page outside the domain of the frameset. For example, if the developers of the Music Hall of Frames want to provide a link to a Web page maintained by an artist's recording company, they could use the following HTML code:

```
<a href="http://recordingcompany.com/~jimbo" target="_blank">
Jim's Home Page
</a>
```

This code opens a new browser window and displays the new home page in it. The browser session with the framed pages is still open. When users have read the new information, they can close the related browser window and continue using the Music Hall of Frames pages.

_self The _self target points to the current frame or window—that is, the one containing the document that is the source for the anchor, <a>. This tag is useful when the Web weaver wants to place a particular document into the frame or window that called it but has a <base> target defined. Otherwise this tag is redundant and unnecessary.

_parent The _parent target causes the document to be loaded into the parent window, which is the window containing the frameset that has the actual hypertext reference. If there is only one level of frame structure, then this is the same as the target of _top.

In our discussion of the <noframes> element, we mentioned that a good Web weaver provides links back to the opening page. Doing so becomes a little tricky when writing HTML code that supports both frame-compliant and noncompliant browsers. One workable solution is to include the following code at the bottom of all the information windows:

```
<a href="mhf.htm" target="_parent">Back to Opening Page</a>
```

Non-frame-compliant browsers ignore the target attribute and return to the opening page (mhf.htm) shown in Figure 10.13. Frame-compliant browsers also return to the opening page and maintain the original frame layout of the parent page. As shown in Figure 10.11, the original layout contained two vertical frames: the left 15 percent of the screen area and the right 85 percent of the screen area.

Interesting results occur in frame-compliant browsers when you do not set target="_parent". Suppose the following code is used as a backward link to the opening page:

```
<a href="mhf.htm">Home Page</a>
```

A frame-compliant browser would place the opening page inside the right frame as shown in Figure 10.15. The correct code would look like this:

```
<a href="mhf.htm" target="_parent">Home Page</a>
```

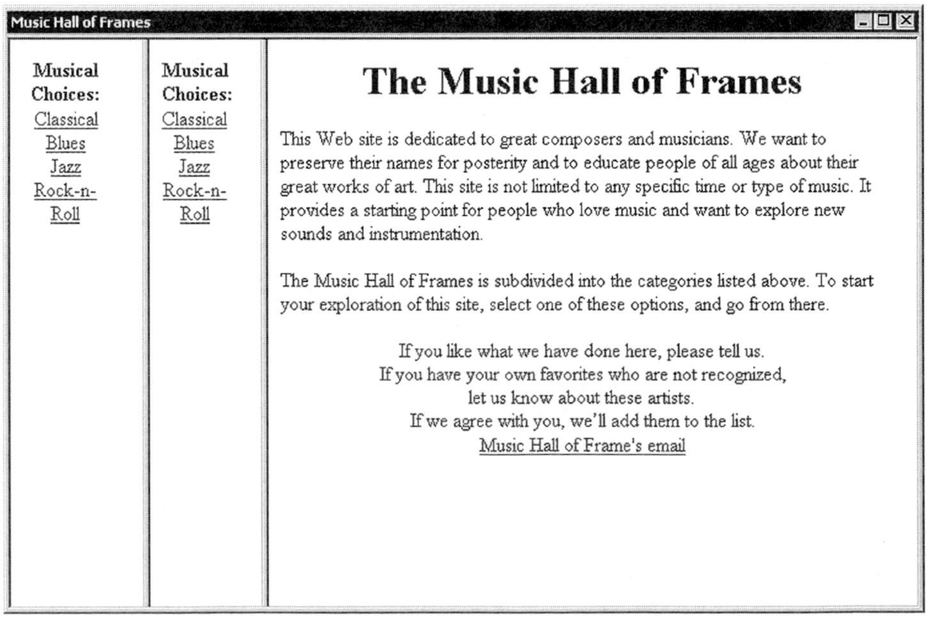

Figure 10.15

Error that resulted when frame-compliant browser reopened the <frameset> page without returning to parent window

_top The most important special target is _top. It causes the browser to load the document into a window without any frames—that is, the top, or initial, window. If you are going to send your user away from your Web site to a remote page (one that is not part of your Web site), you probably won't want to keep your menu on the screen. It would make little sense to your user. As a general rule, when using frames or special formatting, you should always code a target of _top for a link to a remote document. That way, the new document will be loaded into the entire contents of the browser window, not just the portion allocated by your formatting. The code would look like this:

```
<a href="http://www.masters.org/masters.htm "target="_top">
Masters of Music
</a>
```

These results are different than those from using the _blank reserve name, because the same browser window is used for the new Web page. When _blank is used as the target, a new browser window is opened for the designated Web page. You will occasionally see a page where the Web weaver takes pity on users stuck in frames and has a link that says Break free of your frames, which uses this special target to load the user's page into a full-sized window.

EXPLORATION #4

Modify chapter10-recipes.html to add the word *Search* under the Home Page link, and use it as a hyperlink to your favorite search engine. Use the reserve word _blank to open the search engine in a new browser window. Save the file, and display chapter10-frames.html using your favorite browser. Check to see if the search engine opens in its own window.

HTML <iframe>Inline Frame</iframe>

Description: inserts a frame inline with text and other objects.
Type: container.
Attributes: **align,** class, frameborder, **height,** id, longdesc, marginheight, marginwidth, name, scrolling, **src,** style, target, title, **width.**

Inline frames are a new wrinkle the W³C inserted into the world of frames with the HTML 4 specifications. The <iframe> element allows a Web weaver to insert a frame within a line of text. It is no different than inserting any inline element within a section of text. The **align, height,** and **width** attributes allow the author some control over the size and placement of the frame. The information to be inserted inline is identified by the **src** attribute. The HTML code to create a 200-pixel by 500-pixel inline frame looks like this:

```
<iframe src="document.htm"
  height="200"
  width="500">
Text displayed by non-compliant browsers.
</iframe>
```

Only noncompliant browsers display text included within the <iframe></iframe> container. As you can see in Figure 10.16, compliant browsers ignore this text.

Figure 10.16

HMTL code showing application
for inline frames

```
<p>
The Music Hall of Frames is subdivided into the categories listed above. To start
your exploration of this site, select one of these options, and go from there.
</p>
<div align="center">
  <a href="#classical">Classical # </a>
  <a href="#blues">Blues # </a>
  <a href="#jazz">Jazz # </a>
  <a href="#rock">Rock-n-Roll</a>
</div>
<br />
<iframe
  src="classical.htm"
  id="classical"
  height="100"
  width="400">
Text in classical frame can be viewed at
<a href="classical.htm">http://www.mhhe.com/it/eme/classical.htm</a>
</iframe>
<br /><br />
<iframe
  src="blues.htm"
  id="blues"
  height="100"
  width="400">
Text in blues frame can be viewed at
<a href="blues.htm">http://www.mhhe.com/it/eme/blues.htm</a>
</iframe>
<br /><br />
<iframe
  src="jazz.htm"
  id="jazz"
  height="100"
  width="400">
Text in jazz frame can be viewed at
<a href="jazz.htm">http://www.mhhe.com/it/eme/jazz.htm</a>
</iframe>
<br /><br />
<iframe
  src="rock.htm"
  id="rock"
  height="100"
  width="400">
Text in rock-n-roll frame can be viewed at
<a href="rock.htm">http://www.mhhe.com/it/eme/rock.htm</a>
</iframe>
```

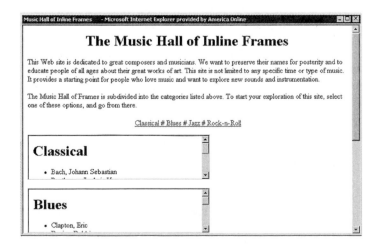

The final variation of the Music Hall of Frames, now called the Music Hall of Inline Frames, is shown in Figure 10.16. As you can see, we have employed an indexed-sequential design with intrapage links to each of the inline frames. The frames are all 100 pixels tall and 400 pixels wide. The **name** attribute assigns each frame a unique target name that is used as the hypertext reference **(href)** in the anchors at the top of the page.

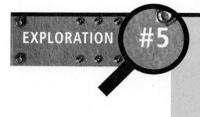

EXPLORATION #5

Make a copy of recipes-homepage.html and call it chapter10-inframe.html. Convert this new file to an intrapage design with internal links to four <iframe> containers within the document. Each <iframe> container displays one of the recipe Web pages: appetizer.html, snack.html, spread.html, and sweet.html in scrolling text areas 400 pixels wide by 300 pixels high. Don't forget to provide links to these files for noncompliant browsers. Save chapter10-inframe.html, and display it using your favorite browser. Test all the links.

▸▸ ALTERNATIVES TO FRAMES

The appeal of using frames in a Web site design is that they lend themselves to a certain amount of consistency in page layout and provides the means to set up and maintain a navigation frame of site links. Although frames provide nice navigation features, a knowledgeable Web weaver can use page designs that incorporate tables to accomplish the goal. To make this point, we have redesigned the Music Hall of Frames example to use a two-row table format to present the data. Row 1 contains the navigation links to other pages. The second row contains the content.

Figure 10.17

Template used to create Web pages for the Music Hall of Frames Web site

```
<html>
<head>
<title>Music Hall Template</title>
</head>

<body>
<table width="100%" border="3" frame="void" cellpadding="20">
<!-- Table Row of Contents -->
  <tr>
    <td align="center">
    <a href="classical-table.htm">Classical # </a>
    <a href="blues-table.htm">Blues # </a>
    <a href="jazz-table.htm">Jazz # </a>
    <a href="rock-table.htm">Rock-n-Roll # </a>
    <a href="opener-table.htm">Home Page</a>
    </td>
  </tr>

  <tr>
    <td>
    <!-- Content goes here -->
    </td>
  </tr>
</table>
</body>
</html>
```

Figure 10.18

Web page using table designed to look like framed page shown in Figure 10.2

```html
<html>
<head>
<title>Music Hall Classical Musician List</title>
</head>

<body>
<table width="100%" border="3" frame="void" cellpadding="20">
<!-- Table Row of Contents -->
  <tr>
    <td align="center">
    <a href="classical-table.htm">Classical # </a>
    <a href="blues-table.htm">Blues # </a>
    <a href="jazz-table.htm">Jazz # </a>
    <a href="rock-table.htm">Rock-n-Roll # </a>
    <a href="opener-table.htm">Home Page</a>
    </td>
  </tr>

  <tr>
    <td>
    <h1>Classical</h1>
    <ul>
      <li>Bach, Johann Sebastian</li>
      <li>Beethoven, Ludwig Van</li>
      <li>Chopin, Frederic</li>
      <li>Debussy, Claude</li>
      <li>Gershwin, George</li>
      <li>Haydn, Franz Joseph</li>
      <li>Mozart, Wolfgang Amadeus</li>
      <li>Schubert, Franz</li>
      <li>Tchaikovsky, Piotr Ilyich</li>
    </ul>
    </td>
  </tr>
</table>
</body>
</html>
```

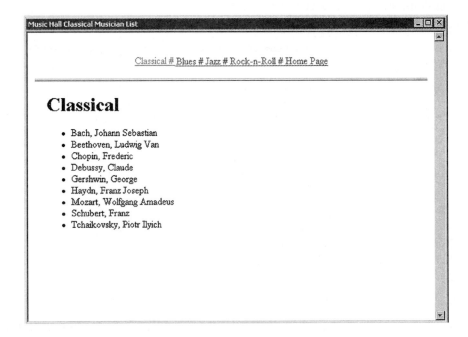

To maintain consistency in the page layout, a template Web page (see Figure 10.17) is developed, tested, and saved without any content. It can then be used over and over again as each page is created and saved with a new filename. One of the resulting pages is shown in Figure 10.18. If you compare it with the framed page shown in Figure 10.2, you will find little difference in the look or how the links work as the user navigates from page to page.

The point of this exercise is to show you that easy-to-navigate Web sites can be designed without using frames. The best approach is to create a site plan in advance. This plan allows the Web designer to conceptualize the overall relationships the Web pages have with each other and decide how users might want to access the related information. Good integration between pages and easy-to-use links don't happen by accident. Once a design is in hand, a navigation bar with appropriate links can be executed without using frames.

▸▸ FINAL COMMENTS

Now that the W[3]C has endorsed frames as an HTML element, it is marginally easier for us to incorporate coverage in this book. Nevertheless, please remember that frames cause navigation problems, especially when users employ Bookmarks or Favorites. As we noted earlier in this chapter, professional Web weavers should always consider other, better ways of designing a Web site. If frames must be used, then the designer needs to minimize the number of frames employed and accommodate non-frame-compliant browsers.

EXPLORATION **#6**

In this Exploration you are going to use tables to create a series of Web pages that look and act like the framed pages from earlier Explorations. Make a copy of recipes-homepage.html and call it chapter10-homepage-table.html. Convert this new file to a design that uses a table to duplicate the vertical-frames layout of chapter 10-frames.html. After you have finalized the layout in chapter10-homepage-table.html, use this same table layout to make the following conversions:

1. Change appetizer.html into chapter10-appetizer-table.html.

2. Change snack.html into chapter10-snack-table.html.

3. Change spread.html into chapter10-spread-table.html.

4. Change sweet.html into chapter10-sweet-table.html.

Each of these new Web pages has the same set of links in the left cell and displays the recipe or home-page opener in the right cell. Test all the links.

▸▸ KEY TERMS

Noncompliant browser
Reserve name
Tool tip message

▸▸ NEW TAGS

<base />
<frame />
<frameset></frameset>

<iframe></iframe>
<noframes></noframes>

▸▸ REVIEW QUESTIONS

1. Define each of the key terms.
2. How is each of the tags introduced in this chapter used? (Provide examples.)
3. What are three disadvantages and one advantage to using frames in designing a Web page?
4. What special formatting is needed for a document to appear within a frame?
5. What attributes must be coded with the <frameset> tag?
6. How is an asterisk (*) used within the <frameset> beginning tag?
7. What is one important rule for nesting one <frameset> element within another <frameset> element?
8. What are the only containers that can present data within a <frameset> element?
9. What happens when a <frame> element does not contain an **src** attribute?
10. Describe how the **name** attribute works with the **target** attribute to allow a specific document to appear in a specific frame.
11. What type of user is most likely to need a descriptive **title** or **longdesc** attribute?
12. What do **frameborder** attribute values of 1 and 0 indicate?
13. When should you use the <noframes> container?
14. What happens when you accidentally use a target name that does not exist?
15. How would you set a frame named text-area as the default target value?
16. Identify and describe four special target names.
17. When do users see the text contained within an <iframe> container?

▸▸ EXERCISES

10.1. Ruby has seen pages that have frames and likes the look for the testimonial pages called "Stories from our Customers" she wants to add to her site. However, after talking to good old Claude down at Computers Etc. she has decided against it. She needs you to build a set of pages that look like a framed document, without actually using frames. Create a four-frame page that looks like the one shown in Figure 10.19. The actual text for each of the "stories" is in the collection of text files named after the writer (ahmed.txt, emmanuelle.txt.gwen.txt., sally.txt, and tom.txt) found on the student data disk. Build the pages with the following characteristics utilizing a document-level style sheet:
   a. The level-1 heading should be medium purple, #660099, centered, and 24 points.

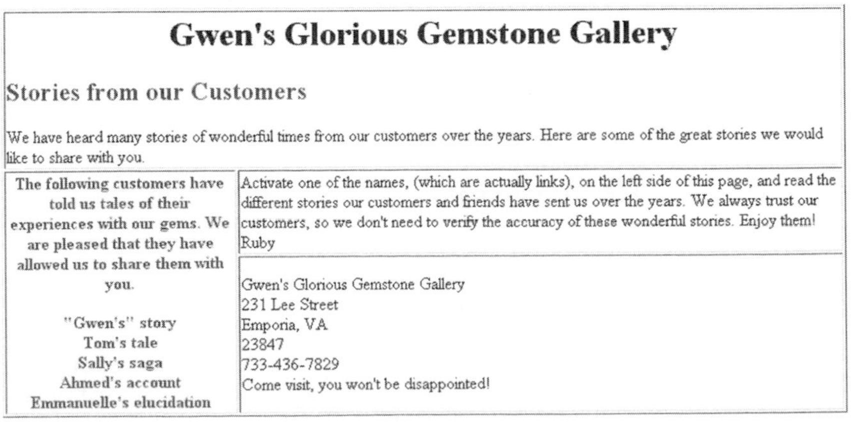

Figure 10.19

Exercise 10.1

Gwen's Glorious Gemstone Gallery

Stories from our Customers

We have heard many stories of wonderful times from our customers over the years. Here are some of the great stories we would like to share with you.

The following customers have told us tales of their experiences with our gems. We are pleased that they have allowed us to share them with you. "Gwen's" story Tom's tale Sally's saga Ahmed's account Emmanuelle's elucidation	Activate one of the names, (which are actually links), on the left side of this page, and read the different stories our customers and friends have sent us over the years. We always trust our customers, so we don't need to verify the accuracy of these wonderful stories. Enjoy them! Ruby
	Gwen's Glorious Gemstone Gallery 231 Lee Street Emporia, VA 23847 733-436-7829 Come visit, you won't be disappointed!

    b. The level-2 headings should be a lighter purple, #9933CC, left-justified, and 18 points.

    c. The data should be enclosed in a table, the left column being the index and the right column the story.

    d. The story side should take up about 85 percent of the table width.

    e. The table should have a pale blue background, #99FFFF, and take up the whole page.

    f. Make sure that there is a dividing line between the index and the story.

    g. The table story text should be dark blue, #336699, and bold.

    h. The table menu text should be deep blue, #0000CC.

    i. There should be the standard footer data on the page.

    j. On each of the customer pages, the particular link to that page should be disabled, of course, and the name should have a light yellow background, #FFFFCC, to highlight that choice.

    k. Each of the customer stories should have a link back to the initial page, as shown in Figure 10.20.

Figure 10.20

Exercise 10.1, part k.

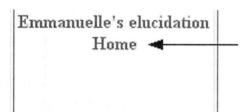

    l. The customer's stories are found on the CD and Web page under their names. These text files need to be incorporated into the various pseudo-framed pages. (Note: the HTML is all done for you in those files.)

    m. Save the main document as `eme10-frm.html`.

10.2. Build a framed document that looks like Figure 10.21. It should have four frames: two vertical frames that are each divided into two horizontal frames. Frame 1 should display text that tells about an image in frame 2. The text in frame 3 should describe the image in frame 4. The title bar should display *Interesting Images,* and your name and the assignment due date should be included within comment lines.

Figure 10.21

Exercise 10.2

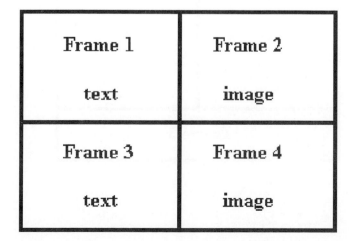

10.3. Build a framed document that looks like Figure 10.22. The top frame should be a table of contents for four of your favorite sports teams or musical groups. The bottom frame should open with a page that identifies the document as a quick reference to when and where you can next see these teams/musicians. The remaining four HTML documents should correspond to options from the table of contents. Each page should identify the group's name, Web site if there is one, and the locations and days for where and when you can see them. If the group is a sports team, provide its schedule. If it is a musical group, provide the next tour dates and locations. The title bar in the <frameset> document should display *your name's Guide To_____* All the HTML documents you create should have your name and the assignment due date included within comment lines.

Figure 10.22

Exercise 10.3

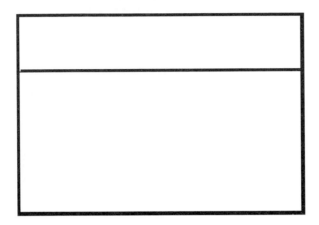

10.4. Redesign the Homework home page used in earlier exercises, including Exercise 9.4, utilizing Figure 10.23 as a model. In frame 1 place your name, an image of yourself if you have one, and links to Web sites you commonly use, like your favorite search engine, your instructor's site, and McGraw-Hill's site for this book. Place links to your homework assignments in frame 2. Frame 3 should contain a personalized footer that includes your email address and your favorite animated GIF file.

Figure 10.23

Exercise 10.4

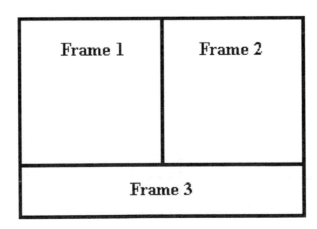

10.5. Redesign your school's home page or the one you created for the school in an earlier exercise, including Exercise 9.5, utilizing Figure 10.24 as a model. In frame 1, center the school's name in large letters, and place the school's address and telephone number in smaller letters under its name. Place a calendar of current school events, like sporting events or concerts, in frame 2. Frame 3 should contain a map to the school or a photograph of the school or of some school event.

Figure 10.24

Exercise 10.5

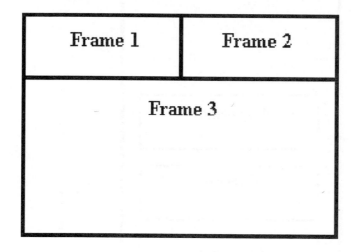

10.6. Create a new movie Web page that uses frames. In frame 1, place links to five images from the movie. Clicking on the link should display the related image in frame 2. Frame 3 should contain a personalized footer that includes your name and email address.

Figure 10.25

Exercise 10.6

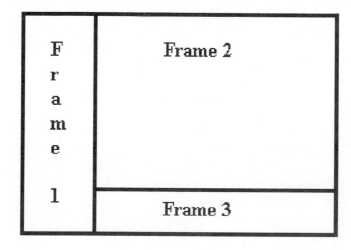

10.7. Create an HTML document that can serve as a takeout menu for a local restaurant. This document must use inline frames for each of the major areas of the menu as shown in the Figure 10.26. At least six options should be available for each area of the menu. The inline frames should be 200 pixels high and 400 pixels wide. The name of the restaurant should appear at the top of the page and in the title bar. All the HTML documents you create should have your name and the assignment due date included within comment lines.

Figure 10.26

Exercise 10.7

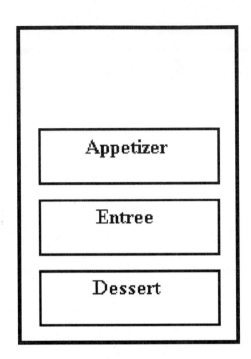

Eleven

Forms and Forms Processing

In this chapter

we will explore ways the Web weaver can design interactive pages that allow the user to input information, and in some cases get a tailored response. Giving the user the ability to enter complex data requires creating a form and processing the data entered. To submit data collected in a form, the user either touches the *Enter* key or activates some sort of Submit button. The browser then sends the data the user has entered to either the server that hosts the page or to an email server. If the data are sent to a Web server, it will process the information using a ***script.*** A script is a program, sometimes written by the Web weaver, that not only processes the data from the form but also creates a response that is sent back to the user via the browser. The alternative of using email is fine for small amounts of data that are infrequently sent, but some problems can result from using email this way when there is a large volume of data or a high message count. We will look at both methods.

CHAPTER OBJECTIVES

After reading this chapter you should be able to do the following:

- Create forms to collect data and send it in an email.
- Control appearance/function of a form.
- Describe uses for intrinsic events.
- Build <input></input> containers to accept various types of data including text, checkboxes, radio buttons, and protected-input areas.
- Correctly use local action controls.

- Create areas on a form for both short and extended text input.
- Use the <select></select> container.
- Identify the HTML elements that make up the XHTML Form module.
- Describe the interrelationship whereby data are sent from a form to the server for processing by a CGI script.
- Code a simple form that sends data to a CGI script for processing.

▸▸ FORM AND FUNCTION

Before we get into the nitty-gritty details of building forms, you need to have an idea of how forms and their data are actually processed. The form shown in Figure 11.1 is an independent HTML document, but it could also be part of an existing document that allows users to input data by performing any of several actions:

- Selecting one of a set of *radio buttons* (shown in Figure 11.1 and discussed in detail later on), sometimes called *option buttons*.
- Choosing one or more checkboxes.
- Using a list box to select an element from a predefined list.
- Entering free-flowing text into a text box as shown in the figure.

After entering all their data, users activate a submission button (such as Submit Query or, as shown in Figure 11.1, Request Catalog) to send the data to the server hosting the Web

Figure 11.1 Code for simple form and sample of completed form

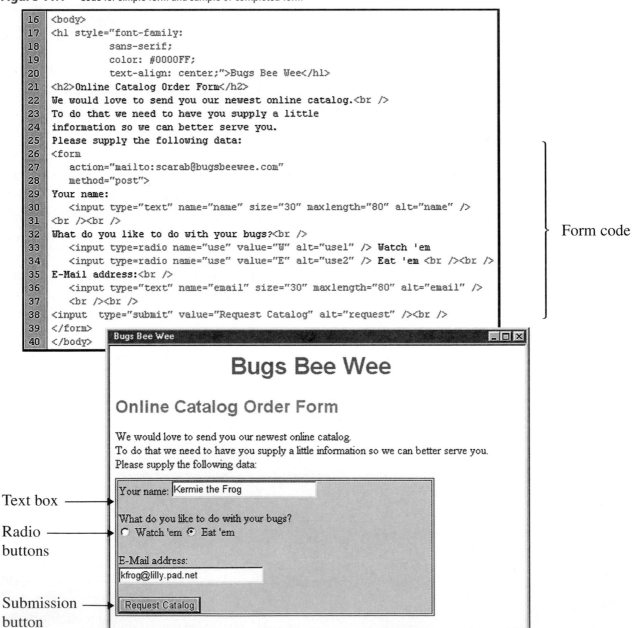

page or to the specified email address. We will use the email approach in the beginning of this chapter and investigate server-based scripts later.

The simple form in Figure 11.1 is designed to allow users to input three fields: their name, their favorite buggy pastime, and an email address for the electronic catalog. After typing in their name, users select one of the two *radio buttons* to indicate what they like to do with bugs and then enter their email address. Finally, they activate the Request Catalog button to send the data to the server for processing. Obviously, this is a simple form, but it will serve as an example to start our exploration of forms. The screen capture in Figure 11.1 shows an example of this form filled out by a user.

When the user activates the Request Catalog control, the Web weaver receives the following email, sent to the email address specified:

name=Kermie+the+Frog&use=E&email=kfrogt%40lilly.pad.net

Let's consider what the Web weaver will need to do with data submitted by email.

▸▸ HANDLING ELECTRONIC MAIL

If you expect to collect a small amount of data from a few users, you may not need to go through the exercise of building a program to handle those data. In our "Bugs" example in Figure 11.1, the form sends an email containing the data that were collected. The <form> beginning tag looks like this (notice the **action** attribute):

<form action="mail to:scarab@bugsbeewee.com" method="post">

In this example, the data will be sent to scarab (actually, Jon Scarab) at the email address of bugsbeewee.com rather than being sent to a program running on the server. Note: You must always use the *post* method instead of the *get* method (both discussed later in this chapter) to send data using email.

The first thing Jon will need to do is to **parse** the data—that is, divide the data into fields. Since he expects only a few catalog requests, this email method is probably a good choice. However, if the Bugs Bee Wee page becomes popular, and many users are sending information, the email method could pose some problems:

- It takes a significant amount of time to process the data, as each form requires several processing steps. Consequently, if there are a lot of responses, the mail server could get bogged down or overloaded. As a result, the user may not get a timely acknowledgement. Jon would have to write back to the user, and that could take a couple of days.

- In order to submit a response, the user must have an email account and must have that portion of his browser correctly configured. Some users, especially those who are using public machines or text-based browser access, might be excluded from responding to the form.

- The user must be willing to send data that are not *encrypted*. Many people prefer to keep their personal information private. So, again, some users might be excluded from responding to the form.

The following data string would show up as part of an email message in Jon's email-box shortly after the user touches the Request Catalog button:

name=Kermie+the+Frog&use=E&email=kfrog%40lilly.pad.net

Notice that there are no spaces in the data string. The spaces between Kermie, the, and Frog are replaced by plus signs (+). The form establishes values for three *variable names* (name, use, and email) chosen by the Web weaver when the form was built. A variable name is a generic way of referring to a location in the computer's memory. The computer stores data at specific addresses in memory, like F7DA42. It is much easier to remember a variable name like email or name than one like F7DA42 or DD8F31. Thus, variable names makes the program more usable and readable by people. The computer always translates the variable name back into an actual memory address before it is used.

These form data were processed by sending them to the browser's mail utility, which then passed them on to the address specified in the action, in this case scarab@bugsbee-wee.com. Jon Scarab will need to decide what to do with these data now, since there will be no automatic processing. Probably he will do the following:

1. Parse the message, changing the plus signs to spaces, removing the leading ampersands (&), and converting the special characters from their encoded values to the normal ASCII characters. If the user uses a special character, like the exclamation point (!), the browsers will usually code it as its hexadecimal value. For example, the string `Froggie the Third!` would look like this: `Froggie+the+Third%21`. The spaces between the three words are replaced by the plus sign, and the exclamation point is coded as hexadecimal 21 (`%21`). In the previous example, @ shows up as `%40`.

2. Store the name, the use, and the email address in a database for later use.

3. Send a copy of the requested online catalog to the user.

Remember that users must have a working mail program available on their computer system to send and receive email. Since the `mailto:` action generates one or more additional screens for users, you should warn them about what will happen before they submit their data. Figure 11.2 shows the warning screen generated by the three major browsers.

Figure 11.2 Warning screens from the "Big Three" browsers when users send unencrypted form data by email

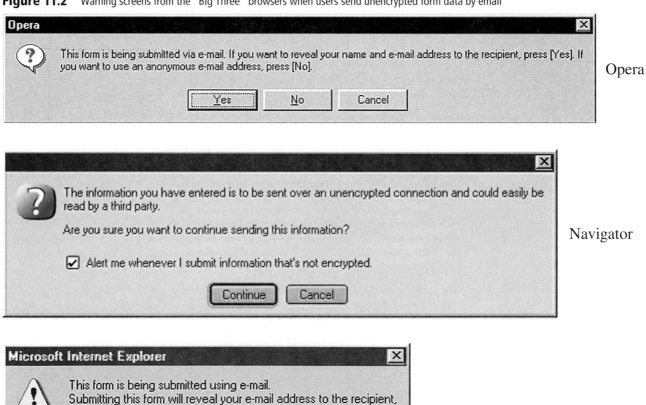

Opera

Navigator

Internet Explorer

▸▸ DESIGNING FORMS

There are no special layout rules for forms other than that they be easy to read and use. You can use the standard HTML elements within a form, so you can control the placement of the fields and text within the body of the form as you would in the rest of the document. The only restriction on forms is that you cannot embed one form within another. While it is indeed possible to code more than one form on a page, this is not considered good practice. Now let's look at the containers used for forms and their attributes.

HTML   `<form>Contents of the Form</form>`

Description: indicates that the contained data define a form.
Type: container.
Attributes: accept-charset, **action,** class, dir, **encytpe,** id, lang, **method, name,** onclick, ondblclick, onkeydown, onkeypress, onkeyup, onmousedown, onmousemove, onmouseout, onmouseover, onmouseup, onreset, **onsubmit, style, target,** and **title.**

The `<form></form>` container holds the contents of the form. The ending tag of `</form>` is never omitted. Although this container currently has 24 attributes, only the **action** and **method** attributes are required. Browsers treat the `<form>` as if it were an image embedded in the text, flowing the rest of the text around it.

Don't code more than one `<form></form>` container on a page unless you create a situation where the user will fill out only one of them.

action

The **action** attribute points to the application that will process the data captured by the form. You can have the data sent to the server and processed by a CGI script, or you can have the data emailed directly to your mailbox.

Common Gateway Interface (CGI) Action If you choose to use the *CGI script* method, described later in this chapter, the URL of the CGI script should specify not only the path but also the filename of the receiving program. Usually the program is in a directory called cgi-bin because that is the place most Web site administrators would put a CGI script. An example of an **action** attribute specifying a CGI script follows:

`<form action="http://www.bugsbeewee.com/cgi-bin/bugorder.cgi">`

In this example, the data entered by the user would be sent to the server at www.bugsbeewee.com. The server would then run the script called bugorder.cgi, located in the cgi-bin directory, and pass the data to it. Most Web site administrators keep all the CGI programs and scripts in a common directory called something like cgi-bin or cgibin. That way, the Web server software, and all the Web weavers, will know where the scripts reside.

Electronic Mail Action As you have seen from the Bugs Bee Wee examples earlier in the chapter (see Figure 11.1), a form can be used to send data via electronic mail by using the mailto: protocol this way:

`<form action="mailto:scarab@bugsbeewee.com" method="POST">`.

When the user activates the submit button, the data from the form are formatted and sent to the email address listed. In this case scarab@bugsbeewee.com will receive an email containing the data.

method

The **method** attribute tells the browser how to send the data to the server. There are two ways to do this: (**get**) or (**post**) named after the http commands that the browser uses to communicate with the server. These two methods place very different demands on both the server and the Net. The mailto: action always requires the *post* method (see Figure 11.1). Let's look a little more closely at these two methods.

When a server gets a request for a CGI script, it handles the request differently than one for just another Web page. Rather than immediately posting the requested document back to the browser, the server looks for the script, or program, specified in the request, or *call,* and tries to run that CGI script. For example, the following line

http://www.bugsbeewee.com/cgi-bin/vote.cgi?goodbug=lb

asks the server, www.bugsbeewee.com, to invoke the script called vote.cgi that resides in the /cgi-bin directory and pass it the variable/value pair goodbug=lb.

Part of preparing the CGI script to run is passing the data from the client to the script on the server. In our present example, the data are a single variable/value pair (goodbug=lb). This format for sending data illustrates the method="get" process. If the method were *post,* the data would not be sent as part of the URL but rather would be included in the body of the message. Different platforms and different operating systems dictate different ways that the CGI scripts get their data.

On Unix systems, a CGI script will get data from one of two sources. If the data are sent via the *post* method, it will appear as standard input, the input file given to all processes created on a Unix system. If the data are sent via the *get* method, they will be placed in a special environmental variable, $QUERY_STRING. Because this is a Unix example, and Unix is case-sensitive, the fact that the variable name is uppercase is critical.

Figure 11.3

Sample CGI script written in Perl language

```
either.pl                                                    _ □ ✕

#!/usr/bin/perl
#               This perl script will take a single variable, in either
#               GET or POST mode, and report back to the user a small
#               HTML page showing the data they sent.  To actually process
#               the data would require further processing at the end of
#               this script.
#
$how = $ENV{'REQUEST_METHOD'};
if ($how eq "GET") {
        $form_data = $ENV{'QUERY_STRING'}
#               with a GET, all data are in QUERY_STRING
                        }
else            {
        $form_size = $ENV{'CONTENT_LENGTH'};
        read (STDIN,$form_data,$form_size);
#               with POST I need to read from standard input
                        }
#               the data are now collected into the variable $form_data
#               let's parse it apart into name and value.
#
($nameis,$valueis)=split (/=/, $form_data);
#
#               the data are now stored in the variables $nameis and $valueis
#
#               Let's create the HTML code
print "Content-type: text/html\n\n";
#
#       Now set up different background colors depending on method:
#
if ($how eq "GET") {print "<body style=\"background-color: #FFFFCC\">\n";}
else {print "<body style=\"background-color: #FFCC99\">\n";}
print "<h1>Your data </h1>\n";
print "<h2>Submitted via the <span style=\"color: #009900\">$how</span>
        method</h2>\n\n";
print "<h2>Variable name          $nameis </h2>\n\n";
print "<h2>Variable value         $valueis </h2>\n\n";
print "Isn\'t that nifty";
exit (0);
```

Figure 11.3 is an example of a simple Perl script, either.pl, that will process a single data element sent with either method *(get)* or *(post)* and create a small HTML page to be sent back to the user. The page that is returned from this script will list the single data element sent from the form (see bottom of Figure 11.4 and Figure 11.5). This script has little value for users except as a testing and *debugging* tool. It illustrates the necessary input and output processing for either the get or post input method. We have included this script on the CD and stored it at the Web site so you can use it as a testing tool. It is rather handy to have this sort of tool available when developing forms.

Figures 11.4 and 11.5 show two different versions of the same page, one sending data using the post method and the other sending data using the get method (look at the submit button). The code is identical for the two pages except for the submission method.

Figure 11.4   HTML code, form, and page returned using the post method

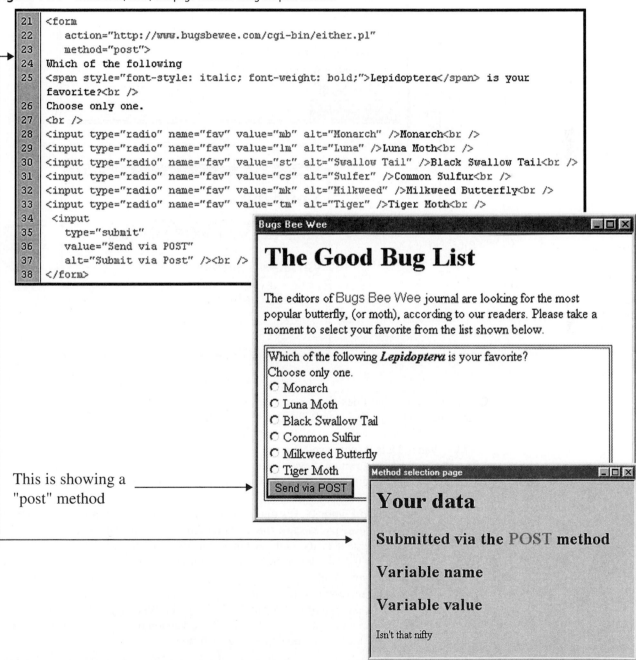

This is showing a "post" method

Figure 11.5

Form and page returned using get method

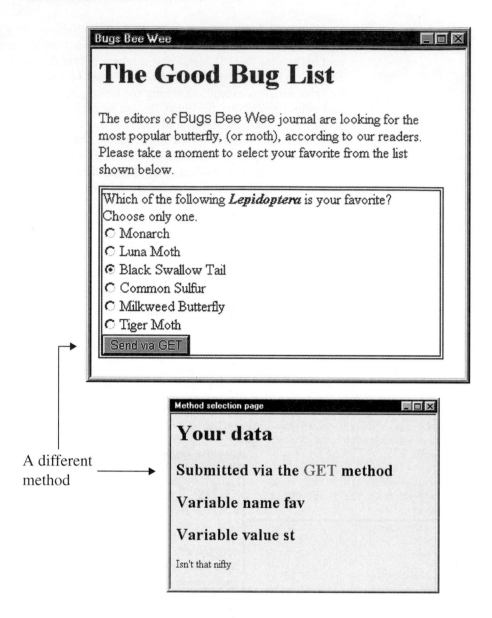

A different method

The script that does the processing, shown in Figure 11.3, is written in the **Perl** scripting language. Perl stands for Practical Extraction and Reporting Language. It has grown and been ported to all of the various Windows platforms, Macintosh, MS-DOS, VMS, Plan 9, Unix, Linux, and even OS/2. It is a very powerful language that is an excellent choice for CGI scripting. Several good books are available to help you learn Perl, the most important being the *Llama* books written by Randal L. Schwartz and published by O'Reilly & Associates.

When the code in Figure 11.3 is run, it creates one of two Web pages, shown in Figures 11.4 and 11.5. These pages show the method used to send the data, and the name and value of the variable sent to it—nothing fancy, but they do illustrate the concept. The script is available on the CD that accompanies this textbook. It is ready to run, and you might want to have your Web administrator install it so you can play with it. Since this isn't a book on Perl, we will not discuss the script in Figure 11.3 in any detail. However, there is a detailed breakdown of that script available on the Web page for the text, as well as on the CD. The name of that file is eitherl.pl. It is a version of the same Perl script, and it contains extensive documentation explaining each step.

enctype

The **enctype** attribute allows you to specify a different encoding format for the data sent from the form to the CGI script. You are unlikely to need this attribute as it is of value only when you are sending binary data or non-ASCII data, usually as part of a file. You would specify an encoding format in this manner:

```
<form enctype="text/plain"
        action="mailto:scarab@bugsbeewee.com"
        method="post">
```

The standard encoding type, specified by the `"text/plain"` value for the **enctype** attribute, is called *application/x-www-form-urlencoded*. This coding is necessary to prevent the data from becoming corrupted during transmission from the browser to the server. We saw an example of this standard encoding when we looked at the data Jon received via email from the browser. Although it is called an "encoding" method, application/x-www-form-urlencoding does *not* protect the user data; the data are quite readable. Application/x-www-form-urlencoded data use the following conventions:

1. All spaces are converted to plus signs (+).

2. Nonalphanumeric characters are represented by their ASCII code, that is, as a two-digit hexadecimal number preceded by a percent sign (%).

3. Each field name except the first is preceded by an ampersand (&).

These conventions are important to remember if you choose to use the `mailto:` action rather than the CGI script action. They are also important to remember when *debugging* scripts.

A second type of encoding, called *multipart/form-data encoding,* encloses the data in a form as several parts of a single document. Each field's data are preceded by a line of 30 hyphens (-) followed by a large random number. The hyphens and the random number serve as dividers between the different data fields. Each field is represented by at least one line of header information, then the actual data. The actual data are not encoded, so there is less possibility of corrupting binary data when transmitted.

Multipart/form-data encoding is normally used to send binary data files, or files that contain non-ASCII characters, so your forms processing will most likely not need to handle them. If you choose to specify multipart/form-data encoding, you must use the *post* method. With this encoding method, each variable ends up as a separate file in the mail message. Each variable is sent as its own plain-text file. If the responses are long, this method might be useful, but in our present example, it makes Jon's job more difficult because he has to open multiple files to collect the data rather than one.

target

The **target** attribute allows the Web weaver to direct the return data from a script to a different window or frame than the one that originally contained the form. This attribute serves the same purpose here as it did for frames, which you saw in Chapter Ten. That is, that **target** can specify a different frame or page than the one containing the form. In addition, a new window can be specified. This attribute is important if your CGI script is used to fill in one frame while the form is in another frame. This attribute wouldn't be used with `mailto:`, but you could create code like this when using a CGI script that returned a page:

```
<form target="buggyframe"
        action="http://www.bugsbeewee.com/cgi-bin/catalog.cgi"
        method="post">
```

The results would be sent to the frame named, or with the **id** attribute set to `buggyframe` in the current document.

style

As you know by now, the **style** attribute was added in the HTML 4 specifications. It is used to create an inline style for the form, overriding any previous style rules. There is a caveat to using **style** within a form. If you code a background color and a special font in

Figure 11.6 HTML code defining inline style and pages as displayed by major two browsers

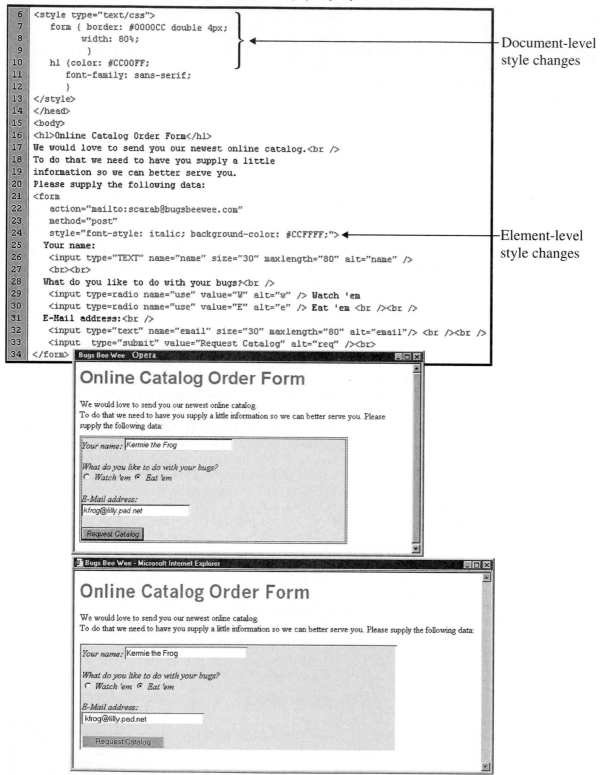

the **style** attribute of the form, those values will apply to the form itself but not necessarily to the contents of button labels, nor to the text areas in which the user will type. Figure 11.6 shows the same form as represented by the two popular graphical browsers. As you can see, the browsers handle the form style somewhat differently. Be aware of this if you choose to employ inline style elements.

name (for <form>)

The **name** attribute is used to identity the form. This name can be used by hyperlinks, JavaScript, and applets to identify the form and to establish an order of hierarchy for specific fields within the form. We will make extensive use of this attribute in later chapters when we build JavaScript scripts to accept data from, or place data into, specific fields within a specific form.

title

The **title** attribute is another way to identify the form. The **name** attribute identifies the form for hyperlinks, applets, JavaScripts and the like. The **title** is most often used to identify the form when the page is presented in nongraphical tools like aural browsers. In the graphical browsers, it functions as a Tool Tip when the mouse pointer hovers over the input area.

INTRINSIC EVENTS

The standard intrinsic events—**onclick, ondblclick, onkeydown, onkeypress, onkeyup, onmousedown, onmousemove, onmouseout, onmouseover, onmouseup**—also apply to the <form> tag. Two new intrinsic events are **onsubmit** and **onreset.** All 12 of these intrinsic events can trigger JavaScript methods, expressions, or functions. We will explore how this is accomplished in the JavaScript chapter. Notice that although you may see these events described elsewhere using a mix of upper and lowercase letters, we are honoring the XHTML precept of coding all attributes in lowercase only.

There are two important reasons to use the **onsubmit** event. The first is to trigger a JavaScript to perform value checking and input validation on the various data fields that the user submitted. That way the server script doesn't have to check each value and send back error screens if the data are incorrect. The second use is to verify for the user that the form has actually been sent. Some authors also blank the fields in the form to further reassure the user that the data have been processed. This is especially important when using the mailto: action.

HTML <input />

Description: creates an input element (control) within a form.
Type: empty tag.
Attributes: accept, accesskey, align, alt, border, **checked,** class, dir, disabled, id, lang, *maxlength,* **name,** onblur, onchange, onclick, ondblclick, onfocus, onkeydown, onkeypress, onkeyup, onmousedown, onmousemove, onmouseout, onmouseover, onmouseup, onSelect, readonly, **size,** src, style, tabindex, **title, type,** usemap, **value.**
Special note: the 4.01 specifications forbid closing tags; however, the form <input attributes /> should be used to be compliant with XML.

The <input /> tag is the tool used to create the actual, user-manipulated areas of a form. Each type of object that collects data or initiates an action within a form is called an *input control* in the HTML specifications. Actually, the specifications speak of two different types of input controls: *successful controls,* which must be coded within the body of a <form></form> container, and *unsuccessful controls,* which are <input> elements coded

Table 11.1 Form input controls and their required attributes.

Control	Required Attribute(s)
Button	**name, value**
Checkbox	**name, value**
File	**name**
Hidden	**name, value**
Image	**src**
Password	**name, value**
Radio	**name, value**
Reset	*none*
Submit	*none*
Text	**name**

within the body of an improperly coded <form></form> container. Remember that a <form></form> container must have an associated action. If you fail to code an action or method for your <form></form>, any input control within that form will be unsuccessful. Unsuccessful controls are often deliberately created as triggers for JavaScript events, as we will see in a later chapter.

Using <input /> controls allows the Web weaver to create text-input fields, selectable images, submission and reset controls, and radio buttons among others. In addition, the HTML 4.01 specifications created a new control called simply a *button,* which we will describe later in this chapter.

With the exception of submission, reset, and button controls, all the different forms of input require the use of the **name** attribute, and every <input /> control requires the **type** attribute. Each input control requires a particular collection of attributes. Table 11.1 shows all of the controls with their required attributes. After presenting some guidelines for forming names, we will explore all these different types of input control along with the applicable attributes for each.

name (for <input />)

The **name** attribute is required by nearly every input control. It specifies the *label,* or variable name, that makes up the left half of the **name=value** pair. The **name,** then, is the identifier, variable name, or label with which the data will be associated when passed back to the server. The other half of the pair is the **value** of the variable, the actual data stored at the memory location specified by the name.

Selecting a good, useful name is important. The rules for names are very flexible, but common practice in programming has provided a few guidelines that will make your work with **name=value** pairs less confusing.

1. Make the name meaningful. While it is acceptable to the browser and script to use names like a, n, and e, they usually make little sense to anyone but the author. Names like age, name, and email tell you and anyone else who is reading your form or script what data you are processing. The few extra keystrokes are more than justified by the ease of understanding that meaningful names provide. Remember that someone else may have to change your code later.

2. Use lowercase letters for the name. Some operating systems, like DOS, don't recognize uppercase and lowercase letters as being different, but other operating systems,

like Unix and Windows XP, do. That means that the variable name Email is different from the variable name email. Always use lowercase variable names. Wise programmers use lowercase for their variable names because

- Lowercase text is slightly easier to read (it has more cues, like descenders).
- Lowercase text usually won't conflict with system variables, which are usually all uppercase.
- It is easier to type all-lowercase text, since there is no need to use the Shift key.

3. Start the name with an alphabetic character. Although you can start the name with nearly any character, if you limit your names to alphabetic characters, there is less chance of either browser or CGI script problems. Avoid special characters like the ampersand (&) and asterisk (*), since they can cause problems by confusing the system.

4. Make the name continuous (no intervening spa ces). With some systems, it is possible to embed blanks in variable names. This may work on your computer, but it is generally considered exceptionally poor programming practice and may well cause problems if you need to move your pages to another computer. To create multiword names, use an underscore rather than an embedded blank. For example, the variable name of "first name" describes the content, starts with an alphabetic character, and is lowercase. It is a good variable name except that it contains a space between first and name. Some operating systems may try to make it into two different variable names, "first" and "name". It would be better to use "first_name", in which the underscore holds the place between the two words.

A properly formed name will make life easier for you and anyone else who chooses to use your form or your script. Take a few minutes to select variable names that make sense and are well formed.

type

The **type** attribute defines which type of input control the form will provide for the user. Each control has a collection of one or more required attributes associated with it. Let's examine each of the values for the **type** attribute—first the "text" value, and later, after discussing some applicable attributes, we'll look at the other **type** values.

type="text"

Text-entry fields, type="text", are probably the most common type of <input /> field. They require little from the Web weaver other than assigning a **name.** However, some of the other attributes can provide additional features. Figure 11.7 presents a very simple form with a text-entry control that uses only default values. This control takes in any number of text characters the user wants to enter, scrolling the window to the left as the user keeps typing. The figure shows that the default text window is 20 characters wide, but as the maximum possible size of the field was not specified, the user can just keep typing, and the most recent 20 characters will show.

Figure 11.7 also shows the code for this simple form. Note that the only attributes for the <input /> tag in this code are **type, name, alt,** and **title.** The **style** information is coded in the header. The 4.01 specifications strongly recommend the inclusion of an **alt** attribute that describes the input element. For that reason, we have included that attribute in many of the examples. Another interesting thing to notice is the Tool Tip that appears when the cursor is moved over the input field. That Tool Tip contains the text associated with the **title** attribute. All the rest of the layout of the control is the default set by the browser.

Careful examination of the code in Figure 11.7 shows that there is no control for submission of the form data. This page represents a special case in forms processing. If the form has only one field, and it is a text-entry field, then the browser will submit the data when the user touches the Enter key. Even though this is a special case, it is well worth

Figure 11.7   HTML code and form showing text-entry control

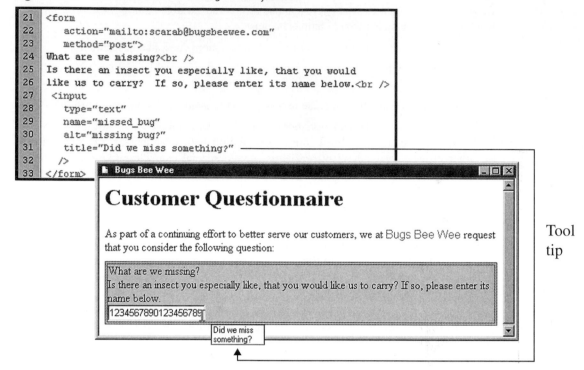

Tool
tip

noting, as there are many forms with only one text-input field, and in those cases users will expect to be able to press the Enter key to submit their forms.

Using all default values is often not a good idea, because the layout will vary among the various browsers. Let's look at some other attributes that should be specified.

size

The **size** attribute specifies the length of the text-entry field. Figure 11.8 shows the same form shown in Figure 11.7 but with a `size="10"` attribute added. As you can see, the

Figure 11.8

Setting size of text-entry field

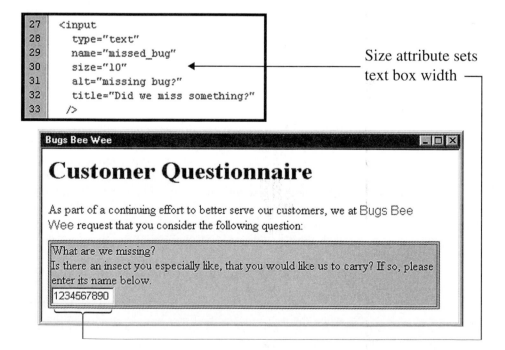

Size attribute sets
text box width

text-entry area is only 10 characters wide. The user can enter as many characters as the browser will allow (normally a very large number), but only the rightmost 10 will show in the window. Note: In this and subsequent screen captures, we will show only the code segment that has changed; the rest of the page is identical to that shown in Figure 11.7.

maxlength

The **maxlength** attribute limits the number of characters the user can enter. Figure 11.9 shows how the form looks with a `maxlength="5"` coded for the text-input control. Only five characters can be typed in the space even though it has a size of 10. This is because the **maxlength** value was set to 5. Setting a **maxlength** that is smaller than the length coded in the **size** attribute can be confusing and frustrating for the user. The browser will sometimes issue a warning sound each time the user tries to type beyond the **maxlength,** so it can be distracting as well. It is best to have the **size** of the text-input field smaller or, ideally, equal to the **maxlength** of that field.

Figure 11.9

Setting maximum length for input field

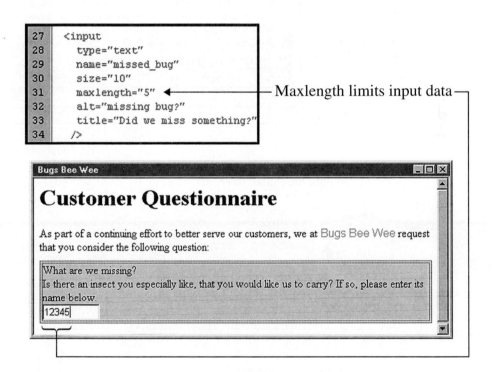

```
27   <input
28     type="text"
29     name="missed_bug"
30     size="10"
31     maxlength="5"          ◄─── Maxlength limits input data
32     alt="missing bug?"
33     title="Did we miss something?"
34   />
```

value

The Web weaver can assign a default **value** to the field so that if users wish to use the default value they need only submit the form as is. Figure 11.10 shows the simple form we have been building with a `value="Default"` coded. (Note: The **maxlength** attribute has been removed.)

   If the user types anything in the field, it is *appended* (added) to whatever was specified as the default by the **value** attribute. Users must delete the data placed in the field before they can enter their own. Use the **value** attribute sparingly—only when you feel quite sure that the user will want to accept it. It takes significantly more work for the users to replace your **value** than to simply type in their own data.

   Regardless of what type of prompt you use, the user can type anything that fits into a text line. If, for example, you want to have the user type a number, she could as well type any combination of letters or characters. There is no way to *validate* her input in the <form></form> container. Your CGI script or a JavaScript must do the validation. Validation can be a long, complex process, so the best bet is to give your user specific instructions as to your expectations. When possible, the wise Web weaver will use other,

Figure 11.10

Using **value** attribute

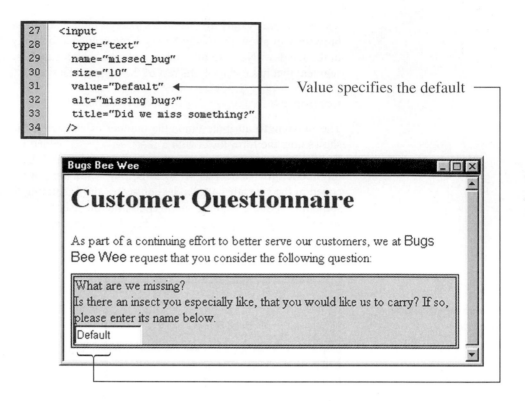

Value specifies the default

```
27    <input
28      type="text"
29      name="missed_bug"
30      size="10"
31      value="Default"
32      alt="missing bug?"
33      title="Did we miss something?"
34    />
```

more precise input controls like checkboxes or radio buttons to focus the user's input and reduce the chance of errors.

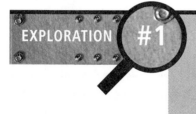

EXPLORATION #1

Create a small form using your email address as the mailto: action. Have the form request that the user enter their first name, middle initial, and last name in a text field that is 26 characters wide. Test your form and notice how the data are formatted. Remember that you don't need to have a submit control if the form contains only one text-entry input control.

type="password"

At times you will want to help users protect the data they are typing from prying eyes at their site. If you set **type** to "password", anything they type will appear as special characters, usually asterisks. Obviously, this is most often used to hide passwords, hence the name, but it can also be used to hide other selection data. Figure 11.11 shows our simple input form with the **type** attribute changed to "password". If you set the control specifier to "password", any default value will also be displayed as asterisks. Generally that is very distracting for the users. Don't code a default value if you use a **type** of password.

Although the data in a field of type="password" are protected from people looking over the user's shoulder at the browser screen, the data are *not* protected when sent to the server. When the data are sent across the Net to the server, they can be intercepted and read.

type="file"

Sometimes the user needs to send a file back along with the form data. For example, if you had a site that would store pages for the users, they could submit some form data and

Figure 11.11

How `type="password"` data are displayed. In this case the text says So Secret

A type value of "password" changes the display

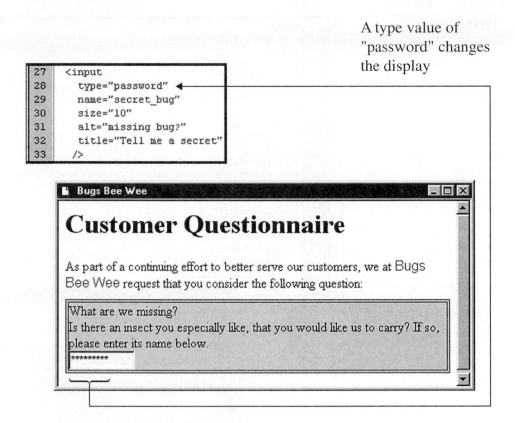

a page for the CGI script to post to the server. It would be possible for them to enter the file's URL in a text field and have the CGI script find and retrieve the file, but that would be cumbersome. Fortunately, the developers of HTML have taken that need into account, and the `type="file"` control has a special feature to help users find the name of the file they want to send.

Figure 11.12 shows a simple form that takes a file as one of the input controls. Look carefully at the screen generated in this figure and compare it to the code. One feature should become obvious quite quickly: there is *no code* that generates the Choose control! That's right: when the browser sees a `type="file"`, it automatically generates a working Choose or Browse button. If the user activates the Choose control, he sees a pop-up window generated with the name of the input control at the top.

Figure 11.13 shows this feature using a bug cuisine data directory on Tim G's machine. As you can see, the user merely activates the button, makes a selection, then activates the Open button (or double-clicks on the filename), and the File Upload screen puts the selected name into the control area. Of course, the user could always simply type in the file path and name just as if it were a text-input control.

One caveat for using this method: the **enctype** attribute of the <form> container must be set to "multipart/form-data" rather than the default, "text/plain." Should the Web weaver forget this step, the browser will send back the *name* of the file rather than its *contents*.

type="checkbox"

Using a set of checkboxes is an easy, fast way for your user to enter data. Checkboxes also minimize data-entry errors! All the user needs to do is select or deselect different items from the control to indicate his preferences. If you design your form efficiently, setting **type** to "checkbox" will allow your users to quickly enter the data you are requesting. Furthermore, you will be able to accurately retrieve those data with less need for data validation, because the possible input data are known and limited. Unlike the case with *radio buttons,* several checkboxes from a series can be selected.

Figure 11.12

HTML code and example of
`type="file"` control

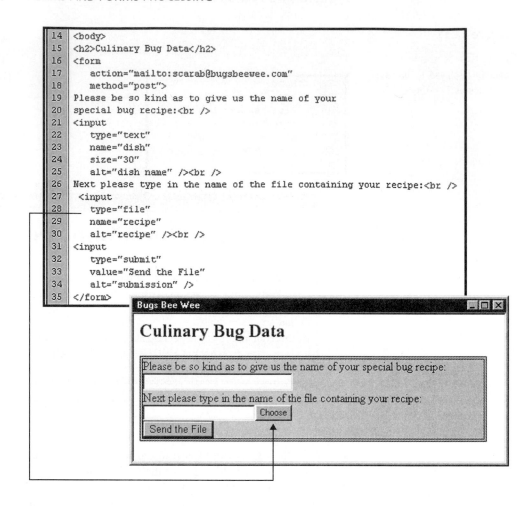

```
14  <body>
15  <h2>Culinary Bug Data</h2>
16  <form
17      action="mailto:scarab@bugsbeewee.com"
18      method="post">
19  Please be so kind as to give us the name of your
20  special bug recipe:<br />
21  <input
22      type="text"
23      name="dish"
24      size="30"
25      alt="dish name" /><br />
26  Next please type in the name of the file containing your recipe:<br />
27   <input
28      type="file"
29      name="recipe"
30      alt="recipe" /><br />
31  <input
32      type="submit"
33      value="Send the File"
34      alt="submission" />
35  </form>
```

Figure 11.14 shows a form with a set of checkboxes allowing users to select the bugs they want more information about. The code shown in this figure is only the snippet that contains the <form></form> container, as the rest of the page is not essential to your understanding of the form. the code for the entire page is available on the CD that accompanies this text, as well as on the Web page.

Notice that each line of code ends in a break (<br />) to force the different selections to appear on individual lines. Leaving out the breaks would cause the checkboxes to appear in a line across the browser window. Careful layout of the form is the job of the Web weaver. The idea is to make the form as easy to understand as possible.

Each instance of the checkbox input control must have a value associated with it. That value will either be sent back to the CGI script or sent as part of the email message. Creating useful, short **value**s is very important. In this example the **value**s for the different checkboxes are short, and all are coded in lowercase letters. These features make the data easier to process on the server and result in shorter email messages as well.

In the example code in Figure 11.14, the Web weaver has given each input control the same name. Assigning the same name option with checkboxes that allows the processing script to more easily handle the data. Using the same name is even more important for radio buttons, as we shall see later in this chapter. When a form contains both checkboxes and radio buttons, using the same names, respectively, provides an easy way to differentiate among the different series of input controls.

The form in Figure 11.14 has been filled out by a user. When the user clicked on a box (checkbox) in front of an insect, the browser marked the selected box with a checkmark (✓). Some older browsers may use an X rather than a checkmark, but all mark the

Figure 11.13

Demonstration of File
Upload window

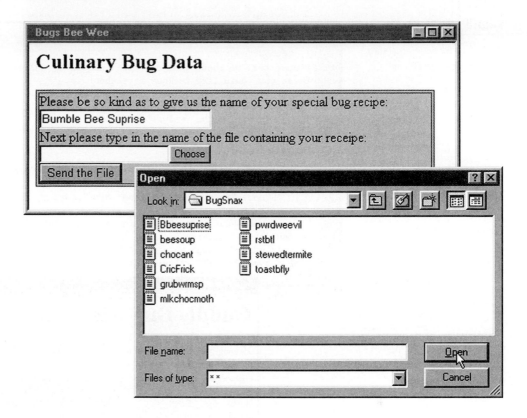

box. Here the user selected three different insects. When he activates the Tell Us control, the browser will send the following data stream back to the server:

favbug=jbug&favbug=hbee&favbug=ewig

Checkboxes are an efficient way to transmit data, both for the Web weaver and the user. On the other hand, using this example, if the user really likes an insect that is not listed, like the dung beetle, the form will not represent his choice. You run the risk of alienating your users if you don't give them enough choices. Probably a text field called "Other" should be added, perhaps with a text box to allow the user to specify his favorite. Be careful, too, to provide some order to your choices when possible, and lay out the form in a way that makes it easy for your user to use.

checked (for checkbox)

As with the text field, you can set a default value or values for a checkbox form. When the user opens the page, one or more of the checkboxes can be shown as already chosen, or checked by adding the **checked** attribute. Figure 11.15 shows how this works. (It can be done for radio buttons, too, as we'll soon see.) When the **checked** attribute is added to the <input /> tag, the form opens with the checkbox already preselected. In this situation, the user must select the checkbox that is marked in order to turn the marking off. This type of form may cause the user extra work, and it may give you invalid data if the user doesn't bother to turn off your preselected choice(s). Figure 11.15 shows XHTML-compliant coding, in which there can be no attribute value names without an assigned value. In this case, it is preferred to code a value of "checked" for the attribute.

type="radio"

As we just explained, checkboxes are most useful when you want the user to be able to select more than one option from the form. But *radio buttons* are best when you want to ensure that the user selects only one option from a list.

Figure 11.14

HTML code for type="checkbox" and completed version of the form

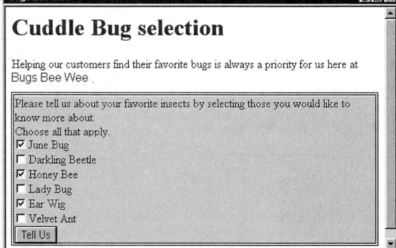

```
18  <form
19      action="mailto:scarab@bugsbeewee.com"
20      method="post">
21  Please tell us about your favorite insects by selecting
22  those you would like to know more about.<br />
23  Choose all that apply.<br />
24  <input type="checkbox"
25         name="favbug" value="jbug" alt="junebug" />June Bug<br />
26  <input type="checkbox"
27         name="favbug" value="dbtl" alt="darkling" />Darkling Beetle<br />
28  <input type="checkbox"
29         name="favbug" value="hbee" alt="honeybee" />Honey Bee<br />
30  <input type="checkbox"
31         name="favbug" value="lbug" alt="ladybug" />Lady Bug<br />
32  <input type="checkbox"
33         name="favbug" value="ewig" alt="earwig" />Ear Wig<br />
34  <input type="checkbox"
35         name="favbug" value="vant" alt="velvetant" />Velvet Ant<br />
36  <input type="SUBMIT" value="Tell Us" alt="Submit" />
37  </form>
```

The term *radio button* needs a little explanation. Not all *that* long ago, car and console radios had a series of mechanical buttons for selecting the radio station. Pushing one button would physically change the position of the tuner and cause the previously pressed button to pop out. As a result, only one selection could be made at a time. It was a somewhat complex, mechanical way of allowing the user to select one—and only one—of a series of preset radio stations. Likewise, the radio-button type of input control in HTML code ensures that only one of a series of choices can be selected.

There are many uses for the radio-button type of input form: salary ranges, age, connection speed, and gender, to name a few. As with checkboxes, you can group a set of radio buttons by giving all of them the same **name** attribute. Unlike the case with checkboxes, assigning the same name is not just an option but a requirement if you want them to perform like true radio buttons. Also like checkboxes, each radio button must have a **value** attribute assigned. The **value** should be different for each button so that the recipient of the email, or the CGI script, can figure out which one the user selected.

Figure 11.16 shows a set of radio buttons that allow the user to select an entomological snack. Unlike the checkboxes in the previous examples, the user can select only one from this series. When she clicks on one of the selections, the "button" changes from a plain circle to one with a dot inside it. If she selects another button, the browser deselects the first choice. That button goes back to the simple circle, and the button for the new selection is changed. In the example in Figure 11.16, the user has selected

Figure 11.15 Demonstration of **checked** attribute.

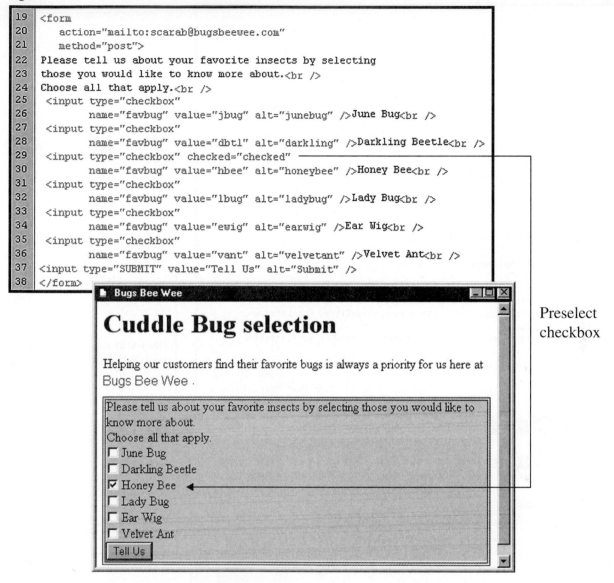

Preselect checkbox

Roast Grub Worm Surprise as her favorite snack. Notice the format of the button in front of that choice.

checked (for radio button)

As with checkboxes, you can preselect one of the radio buttons for your user with the **checked** attribute. Indeed, some browsers will preselect one of the buttons for you, usually the first button in the series. Others don't preselect. It is always a good idea to preselect one of the radio buttons so that you are assured of having a value sent to the server. Unlike the case with preset values in checkboxes, the user can deselect your choice in radio buttons simply by selecting another button. As a result, preselection creates no more work for the user. Remember that if you are trying to code XHTML-compliant code, you should assign a value of "checked" to the **checked** attribute.

Since one of the radio-button controls should be preselected, you should always have more than one radio button on a form. But, remember, radio buttons are for situations when you want your user to make a selection that is exclusive of the others in the list.

Figure 11.16 HTML code and sample use of radio-button input control

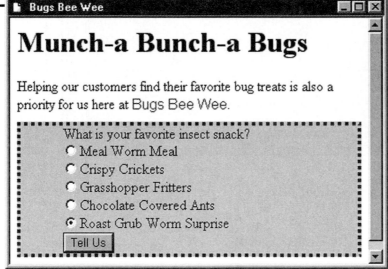

```
 6  <style type="text/css">
 7      form { background:#CCCCCC;
 8            border-color: #0000CC;
 9            border-style:dotted;
10            border-width:4px;
11            padding-left:3em;
12            padding-right:2em;
13            text-align: left;
14            }
15  </style>
16  </head>
17  <body>
18  <h1>Munch-a Bunch-a Bugs</h1>
19  Helping our customers find their favorite bug treats is also a
20  priority for us here at
21  <span style="font-family: sans-serif; color: #0000FF;">
22  Bugs Bee Wee</span>.
23  <form
24      action="mailto:scarab@bugsbeewee.com"
25      method="post">
26  What is your favorite insect snack?<br />
27   <input type="radio"
28         name="snack" value="mwm" alt="meal" />Meal Worm Meal<br />
29   <input type="radio"
30         name="snack" value="cc"  alt="cricket" />Crispy Crickets<br />
31   <input type="radio"
32         name="snack" value="gf" alt="hopper" />Grasshopper Fritters<br />
33   <input type="radio"
34         name="snack" value="cca" alt="ant" />Chocolate Covered Ants<br />
35   <input type="radio"
36         name="snack" value="rgs" alt="grub" />Roast Grub Worm Surprise<br />
37  <input type="submit" value="Tell Us" alt="submit" />
38  </form>
```

Code for the radio buttons

One easy way to cause problems for the script parsing the form data—and to confuse your user as well—is to misspell one of the values used for the **name** attribute. For example, in the code in Figure 11.17, the value for the name ("snak") in the grasshopper line is misspelled. First the user selected Grasshopper Fritters as his favorite, then changed his mind and selected Chocolate Covered Ants. However, since the name was misspelled in the Grasshopper Fritters control, when the user activated the Chocolate Covered Ants control, the Grasshopper Fritters button remained selected. Unfortunately, none of the current validation tools can read your mind and know that you didn't mean to have two

Figure 11.17　Example of what happens when radio button **name** attribute is misspelled

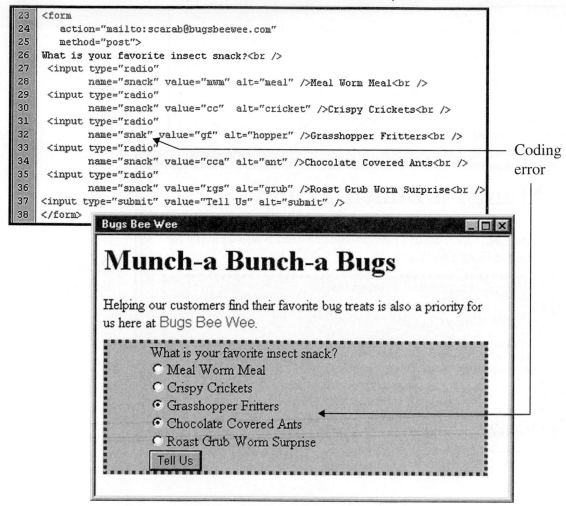

```
23  <form
24      action="mailto:scarab@bugsbeewee.com"
25      method="post">
26  What is your favorite insect snack?<br />
27   <input type="radio"
28        name="snack" value="mwm" alt="meal" />Meal Worm Meal<br />
29   <input type="radio"
30        name="snack" value="cc"  alt="cricket" />Crispy Crickets<br />
31   <input type="radio"
32        name="snak" value="gf" alt="hopper" />Grasshopper Fritters<br />
33   <input type="radio"
34        name="snack" value="cca" alt="ant" />Chocolate Covered Ants<br />
35   <input type="radio"
36        name="snack" value="rgs" alt="grub" />Roast Grub Worm Surprise<br />
37  <input type="submit" value="Tell Us" alt="submit" />
38  </form>
```

Coding
error

Munch-a Bunch-a Bugs

Helping our customers find their favorite bug treats is also a priority for us here at Bugs Bee Wee.

What is your favorite insect snack?
- ○ Meal Worm Meal
- ○ Crispy Crickets
- ◉ Grasshopper Fritters
- ◉ Chocolate Covered Ants
- ○ Roast Grub Worm Surprise
- [Tell Us]

different sets of radio buttons. Therefore, it is critical that you check your code for this kind of sneaky error.

All of the input fields we have examined so far set up data to be sent to Jon Scarab via email. The next three controls cause the *browser* to perform specific actions and are called *local action controls*. You are already familiar with the "submit" control, used to send data to the server or to initiate an email. Now let's look at another type of local action control.

type ="reset"

The **type** attribute set equal to "reset" provides a control that causes the browser to reset, or change, all the input areas back to the way they were when the user entered the page. The **checked** controls will again be set, and anything that the user had entered or selected will be removed, or deselected. Always include a reset button on any form you create. It will enable a user to quickly undo errors or to easily make changes.

Figure 11.18 shows the code for our simple form, now including a reset button labeled Clear Selections to give the user an idea of its function. If you assign a **value** to the <input /> field of a Reset button, as we did here, that **value** will replace the default name of Reset. Sophisticated users will understand the function of a button labeled Reset, but

Figure 11.18 Setting up a "reset" control

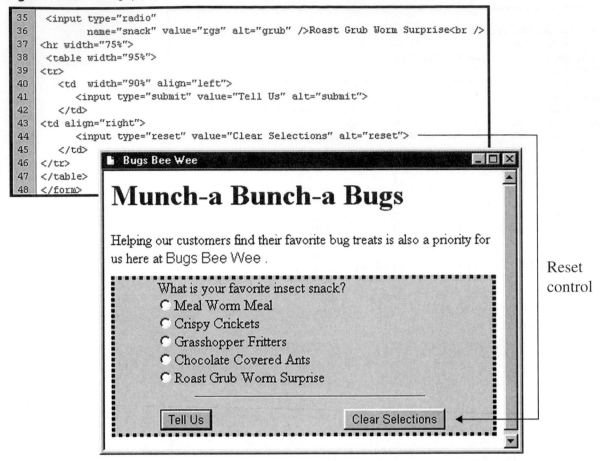

```
35    <input type="radio"
36          name="snack" value="rgs" alt="grub" />Roast Grub Worm Surprise<br />
37    <hr width="75%">
38    <table width="95%">
39    <tr>
40      <td  width="90%" align="left">
41         <input type="submit" value="Tell Us" alt="submit">
42      </td>
43    <td align="right">
44         <input type="reset" value="Clear Selections" alt="reset">
45      </td>
46    </tr>
47    </table>
48    </form>
```

Reset
control

for less Web-wise users, a more explicit label, such as Clear Selections, may help the user understand that he can put the screen back to the way it was before any selections were made. In other words, by activating just one button, the user can undo everything selected. The Web weaver has no control over what is reset when this button is clicked. It is not currently possible to undo only part of a form. A "reset" control resets all the fields on the form.

type="submit"

The type="submit" control does just what it implies—it starts the process by which the browser encodes and sends the information to the server or invokes the browser's associated email program. Like the "reset" control, if you just use a type="submit", the browser creates a small button for the user, in this case labeled Submit Query. As you have seen in the previous examples, if you want to change the label on this submission control, you need to supply a **value** attribute to the input element.

Figure 11.18 shows our simple form but with both the submit (Tell Us) and reset (Clear Selections) controls on the bottom of the form. Notice how one is on the left and the other on the right to help the user avoid activating the wrong one by mistake. One clever way to handle layout of the submit and reset controls is to use a table. The two <input /> fields are put into a table to control their placement on the form. The **width** attributes are used to force the size of the table elements. The **align** attributes are set to "right" and "left" to justify the input fields.

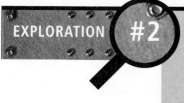

Modify the form you created in Exploration #1 to include the following features:
- Change the single text field for **name** into three fields, First, Middle, and Last names.
- There should be an input field that asks for a secret word. That field should be protected against casual reading.
- Code a single line of five radio buttons that ask users to select their preferred title: Miss, Mr., Mrs., Ms., Dr.
- Code a column of five checkboxes that allows users to select their favorite pet: cat, dog, ferret, goldfish, or turtle. Make dog the default favorite.
- Give users both a submit and a reset control, nicely spaced apart on the bottom of the form.
- As in Exploration #1, have the form send you an email message.

MULTIPLE SUBMIT CONTROLS

You can also supply a **name** attribute to the submit control, and the browser will add the name=value pair to the information sent to the server. This allows you to set up multiple submit buttons, each with a different **name** and **value.** The browser will add the value from the activated control to the input stream. Each submit element can, in this way, signal a different processing step within the CGI script or a different response through email.

For example, you could create a form that allows the user to learn about your product line by requesting information about any of several different catalogs. Alternatively, you could create a form that allows the user to order one of several different products by choosing different submit controls. Figure 11.19 shows a form that lets users choose which of the four different catalogs they want by using different submit controls. When they click on any one of these selections, the data are sent to Jon. These are all submit controls.

Figure 11.19 provides a simple example of using a submit button to send additional information. Notice that all four controls have a **type** value of "submit", all have the same **name,** and each has a different **value,** reflected in its name on the form, signifying its relative contents (its value). Using multiple submit controls can simplify processing for your user. In addition, multiple submit buttons provide an easy way to create an additional variable that can give direction to your CGI scripting or, if you are using email, provide more data in the mail sent to you. In this example, simply by activating one submit control, the user sends information to Jon Scarab, telling him which type of catalog to send. Jon would have to use the "from" field of the user's request to send back the catalog, since the page doesn't have any text area for the user to enter her preferred email address.

type="button"

The HTML 4 specifications gave Web weavers a new control feature called the **button.** With type="button", an author can create a control that has no predefined function. Currently the only use for this control is to initiate a JavaScript event. In all three of the current browsers, they look just like the type="submit" controls but don't submit the form.

Figure 11.19   Form with multiple submit controls

```
6   <style type="text/css">
7      form { background:#CCCCCC;
8            border-color: #0000CC;
9            border-style:dashed;
10           border-width:4px;
11           padding-left:3em;
12           padding-right:2em;
13           padding-bottom:1em;
14           text-align: left;
15              }
16  </style>
17  </head>
18  <body>
19  <h1>Get our Catalog</h1>
20  We have four different catalogs here at
21  <span style="font-family: sans-serif; color: #0000FF;">
22  Bugs Bee Wee</span>.   Please select which of them you
23  would like to receive:<br />
24  <form
25     action="mailto:scarab@bugsbeewee.com"
26     method="post">
27  Which catalog would you like to have us send you?<br />
28   <input
29     type="submit" name="cat" value="Bugs for Eat'en" alt="snack" /><br />
30   <input
31     type="submit" name="cat" value="Cuddle Bugs" alt="cuddle" /><br />
32   <input
33     type="submit" name="cat" value="Pretty Bugs" alt="look" /><br />
34   <input
35     type="submit" name="cat" value="Working Bugs" alt="work" /><br />
36
37  </form>
```

Multiple Submit Controls

Bugs Bee Wee

Get our Catalog

We have four different catalogs here at Bugs Bee Wee. Please select which of them you would like to receive:

Which catalog would you like to have us send you?

- Bugs for Eat'en
- Cuddle Bugs
- Pretty Bugs
- Working Bugs

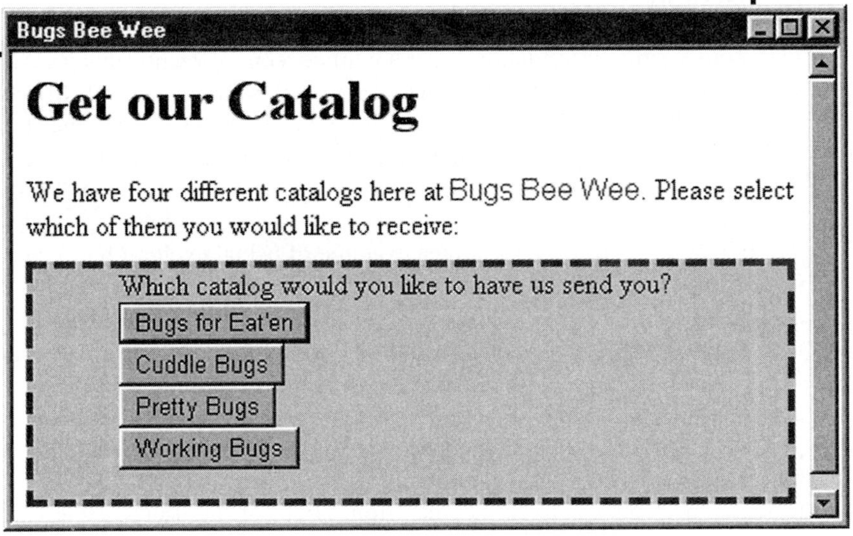

▸▸ GRAPHICAL BUTTONS

You will recall from Chapter Six that when you built anchors that were links, it was possible to include a graphic or image that served as part of the link. It is also possible to do that with the <input /> tag. However, the processing done by the browser is very different in these two cases. In the case of the anchor link, when the user activates the image, the browser loads the file pointed to by the associated address. If the Web weaver adds an image to an <input /> tag, a graphical browser treats it like a mouse-sensitive image map rather than a simple glyph.

type="image"

When the Web weaver has coded an <input> tag with type="image", users see a picture that they can click on. But rather than simply sending the preset value for the name of the input field, the browser sends an X,Y coordinate pair representing the location of the mouse pointer, associated with the **name** attribute. The *script,* or recipient of the email, may process the X,Y pair to determine just where in the image the user clicked. Figure 11.20 shows a simple example of an image used as a button to send in an order.

Figure 11.20   Using image as submit control

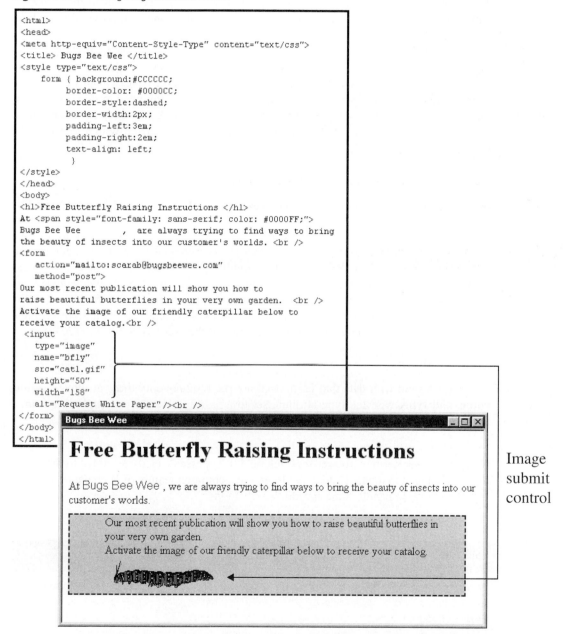

```
<html>
<head>
<meta http-equiv="Content-Style-Type" content="text/css">
<title> Bugs Bee Wee </title>
<style type="text/css">
    form { background:#CCCCCC;
        border-color: #0000CC;
        border-style:dashed;
        border-width:2px;
        padding-left:3em;
        padding-right:2em;
        text-align: left;
        }
</style>
</head>
<body>
<h1>Free Butterfly Raising Instructions </h1>
At <span style="font-family: sans-serif; color: #0000FF;">
Bugs Bee Wee          ,  are always trying to find ways to bring
the beauty of insects into our customer's worlds. <br />
<form
    action="mailto:scarab@bugsbeewee.com"
    method="post">
Our most recent publication will show you how to
raise beautiful butterflies in your very own garden.  <br />
Activate the image of our friendly caterpillar below to
receive your catalog.<br />
 <input
    type="image"
    name="bfly"
    src="catl.gif"
    height="50"
    width="158"
    alt="Request White Paper" /><br />
</form>
</body>
</html>
```

Free Butterfly Raising Instructions

At Bugs Bee Wee , we are always trying to find ways to bring the beauty of insects into our customer's worlds.

Our most recent publication will show you how to raise beautiful butterflies in your very own garden.
Activate the image of our friendly caterpillar below to receive your catalog.

Image submit control

A naive Web weaver might think that the browser will simply submit the order when the user activates the button showing the caterpillar image, but that is not so. The browser will submit the form, but it will also send the X,Y coordinates of the actual mouse position within the graphic in the following form:

bfly.x=84&bfly.y=27.

Here 84 represents the number of pixels in from the *left* edge of the image, and 27 represents the number of pixels down from the *top* edge of the image. The coordinates bfly.x=0 and bfly.y=0 would be the upper left corner of the image.

Notice that the image "catl.gif", is in the same directory as the page, so it is not necessary to code the path to that image. Since the graphic functions as a link, most of the browsers will put a frame around the image, as we saw earlier with images used as links. There may be some specialized need to create a graphical button, but in most cases it simply increases the load time of the page and the load on the Net, so we don't advise using them.

In Chapter Fourteen we will look at the way image maps are used, and how the actual X and Y position of the pointer can contain important data. It is generally not a good idea to use an image as a submit button unless the design of the page demands it.

An important principle is to use only the HTML tools you need to do a job, avoiding the trap of creating fancy code just because you can. A text-only browser can do no more than submit the form, as there is no mouse pointer from which to return the coordinates.

HIDDEN DATA FIELDS

Sometimes you will want to send a CGI script data that you don't want the user to be able to manipulate or even see. For example, if part of the processing involves sending you an email message about some of the contents of the data stream, you would want to send the script to your email address in such a way that the user could not modify the address. Another example of using hidden data fields would be special coding that tells the server exactly which form was used to send the information. Those data, too, should be coded in a hidden field and sent to the server so as to prevent any interference by the user. Finally, one of the more common uses of hidden data fields is to send data that were captured with a previous form. Those data need to be sent, but the user has no need to see them.

type="hidden"

An <input> field with data that users need not see requires only three attributes: **name, value,** and **type,** with the type attribute set to "hidden". Here is a sample line from a form that sends some hidden data to the server:

<input type="hidden" name="mailto" Adephaga@bugsbeewee.com" />

Neither the user nor the browser sees this field. It is passed exactly as coded to the server for processing at that end. Hidden fields are not a common feature of Web pages, but they are a good way to handle some specialized situations.

HTML <button>Button Text and/or Images</button>

Description: indicates that the contained data should be formatted and should function as a button control.
Type: container.
Attributes: class, dir, **disabled,** id, lang, name, onblur, onclick, ondblclick, onfocus, onkeydown, onkeypress, onkeyup, onmousedown, onmousemove, onmouseout, onmouseover, onmouseup, onreset, onsubmit, style, **tabindex,** title, type, value.

The <button> element creates a graphical button icon within a form. All three of the major browsers support this element, which lets the Web weaver imbed both text and an image within the button itself. The difference between the <button> element and the <input type="button" /> control is that the former provides for a more sophisticated set of contents. Images and text can both appear within the container, allowing the Web weaver to create a very attractive button.

There are a couple of attributes we have not yet addressed that are sometimes used with forms. Let's look at them now.

disabled

Controls like <button> can be set as inactive by including the **disabled** attribute inside the <button> tag. Disabled elements will not be sent to the server, nor will they perform their designated actions if the user attempts to activate them. Generally the **disabled** attribute is used only for testing purposes; users should never see disabled buttons.

tabindex

Each element within a form can be selected by using the Tab key. As the user tabs through the form, each different control is successively given *focus*, which in the world of HTML, means that it is made the currently active control and is able to receive input. When an element is given focus, it changes in some fashion, and with input elements, the cursor appears in the input area as well. Normally the order in which the controls will be accessed matches the order they physically appear in the <form> container. The Web weaver can alter this order with the **tabindex** attribute. Thus, setting the value of the **tabindex** attribute determines the order of access of the elements. If you want a particular element to be skipped when the user is tabbing around the form, you can set the **tabindex** to zero. There might be reasons for doing this, in particular if the list is alphabetically ordered, but you would rather have the most popular choices at the beginning. However, it has been our experience that reordering the list is usually more effective than using tabindex to change the order.

INTRINSIC EVENTS

The standard intrinsic events discussed in Chapter Two also apply to the <button> element. Each of these can be used to trigger JavaScript methods, expressions, or functions. We will explore how this is accomplished in Chapter Thirteen.

**<textarea>Optional Text String</textarea>**

Description: creates an area for multiline text-input box.
Type: container.
Attributes: class, **cols,** dir, disabled, id, lang, name, onblur, onchange, onclick, ondblclick, onfocus, onkeydown, onkeypress, onkeyup, onmousedown, onmousemove, onmouseout, onmouseover, onmouseup, onselect, readonly, **rows,** style, tabIndex, title, **wrap.**

All of the input tools discussed thus far limit the user to a single line of input. Even the type="text" input control shows the user only a single line of input. Users can type in an unlimited number of characters if the Web weaver has not set a **maxlength** attribute, but the input appears on only one line, with only part of a large input string visible at a time. The <textarea> container sets the user free from the single-line restriction by creating an area in the browser pane for textual input; </textarea> is never omitted.

It is possible, and even advisable, to include default text in a <textarea> field to give the user instructions. When the form is submitted to the server, the browser takes all the lines of text that have been entered. Each line may or may not be separated by a *carriage-return line feed (CrLf),* called a *newline* in Unix. That long text stream is sent to the CGI script or email address as the value associated with the variable specified by the **name** attribute.

rows and columns

Because the <textarea> container is supposed to describe an area for the user to enter text, the **rows** and **columns** attributes are required. These two attributes define the screen real estate covered by the input area. Not surprisingly, **rows** specifies the number of lines (rows) in the input block, and **cols** is a count of the number of characters (columns) across each line. Together they define a rectangular region on the screen that is set aside for user input.

Figure 11.21 shows a sample form, with rows="7" and cols="60". Be careful using these two attributes, as you can build an area that extends beyond the browser plane if you code large values for these fields. Notice that the text-input area in the figure is

Figure 11.21   Form showing <textarea> for text entry

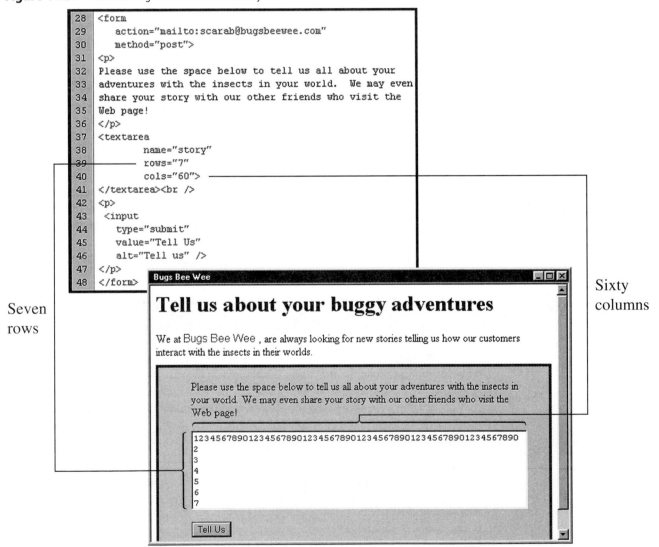

Seven rows

Sixty columns

60 characters. We entered the numbers on the form so you could see the columns and rows. They are not a standard part of the display. There are scroll bars, because the user can enter more than seven lines, and each line can be as long as the user wants. Remember that the browser and the form merely supply a place for the user to enter text. At this point they do not restrict or control how the text looks. Users who type long lines can still lose sight of part of what they have typed.

Because users have become used to the wordwrap feature of most word-processing packages, they may find it annoying to have to keep touching the Return or Enter key to move down to the next line. Again, the designers of HTML have taken that into account by providing the **wrap** attribute.

wrap

The **wrap** attribute causes the browser to break lines on word boundaries as close to the right margin as possible and continue the text on the following line. This is like the word-wrap feature of most word processors. Coding **wrap** will make your <textarea> a friend-lier place for your users. And, indeed, they will expect this feature from a sophisticated Web page. We recommend that you always code the **wrap** attribute. It has three different values: virtual, physical, and off.

wrap="virtual"

When the **wrap** attribute is set to "virtual", it causes the browser to break the input lines at word boundaries in the browser pane. When the text is transmitted to the server, only those *carriage-return line feeds (CrLfs)* that the user actually entered will be in the text stream. Most of the time the text will be passed as a continuous stream with no CrLfs. This is not the ideal choice for most applications.

wrap="physical"

With the **wrap** option set to "physical", the line breaks happen at the browser just as they do with a "virtual" wrap, but the actual CrLfs are *added* to the text the user enters as if the user had actually coded them. This is the preferred option on the **wrap** attribute, because it creates a more readable copy. However, it must be noted that using this attrib-ute option will cause the browser to add data, albeit just CrLfs, to the data the user enters. In addition, the added new line characters need to be handled when processing the data. This could be a consideration if the form is passing data to a CGI script.

wrap="off"

The **wrap**="off" option sets the browser to the standard default processing, where the only CrLfs either shown or sent are those actually entered by the user, and the text can scroll to the right indefinitely. For almost all applications, **wrap**="physical" is a better option than **wrap**="off".

EXPLORATION #3

Modify the form you created in Exploration #2 to include the following additional features:

- Have the form include a text area 8 lines long by 45 characters wide that asks users to de-scribe their favorite pet from childhood. Ask for the animal's name too.
- Change the submit button to an image, preferably a cute image. (We have included **puppy.bmp** and **kitten.bmp** on the CD and the Web site in case you wish to use them.)
- Add a hidden field that contains the words "I am hidden." and has a name of "hidden."

⏩ DROP-DOWN LIST BOXES

All of the controls covered so far in this chapter have occupied consistent screen real estate. They have allowed the user to select from a list that was always completely shown in the browser window (radio buttons or checkboxes) or to enter data into either a text line or text area. The only exception was the file input control, which automatically provided the user with a browse capability. Now we will learn how to use the <select> element to create a drop-down list box with choices for the user.

HTML <select> Set of <option>Elements</option></select>

Description: creates a list box made up of the enclosed <option> elements.
Type: container.
Attributes: class, cols, dir, **disabled,** id, lang, **multiple,** name, onblur, onchange, onclick, ondblclick, onfocus, onkeydown, onkeypress, onkeyup, onmousedown, onmousemove, onmouseout, onmouseover, onmouseup, onSelect, **selected, size,** style, tabindex, title.
Special note: must contain at least one <option> element.

Figure 11.22

HTML code and browser showing <select></select> container

```
23  <form
24      action="http://www.bugsbeewee.com/cgi-bin/vote.cgi"
25      method="post">
26  Which of these insects do you feel is most beneficial
27  in YOUR garden?
28  <br />
29  <select
30      name="goodbug">
31  <option selected>Vote early and often</option>
32  <option>Lady Bug</option>
33  <option>Assassin Bug</option>
34  <option>Lace Wing</option>
35  <option>Praying Mantis</option>
36  <option>Orchard Bee</option>
37  <option>Dung Beetle</option>
38  </select>
39    <input
40      type="submit"
41      value="Send"
42      alt="Select-a-bug" /><br />
43  </form>
```

Bugs Bee Wee Journal

The Good Bug List

The editors of Bugs Bee Wee journal are looking for those insects our readers feel are most helpful in their gardens. Please cast your vote for the insect you feel is your very best helper.

Which of these insects do you feel is most beneficial in YOUR garden?
Vote early and often ▾ Send

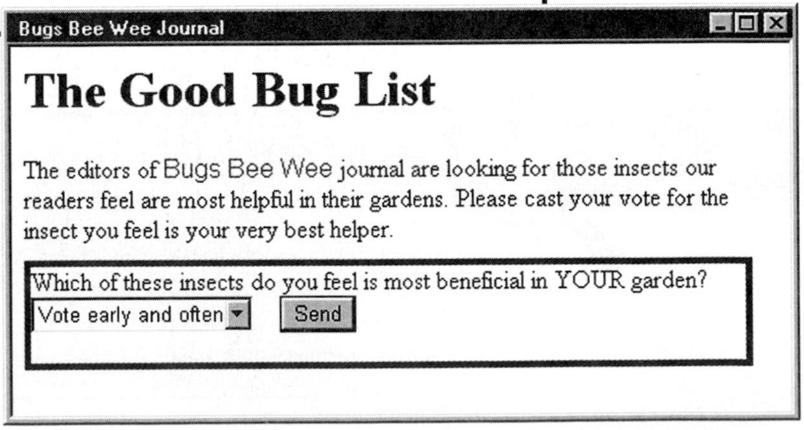

With the <select></select> container you can easily create a drop-down list box of selections. The list will function like a series of radio buttons in that only one of the options in the list can be selected, unless you use the **multiple** attribute, which allows <select> to highlight multiple data elements. (This attribute is discussed in greater detail later in this chapter.) Thus, you have a choice of arranging your drop-down box to allow users only one or more than one selection.

Figure 11.22 shows a screen created with code that includes a <select></select> container. When users look at this screen, the arrow to the right of the selection window tells them that there are more options available. If they activate the down arrow, or any part of the selection box, the list expands as shown in Figure 11.23.

Figure 11.23

Expansion of <select></select> container

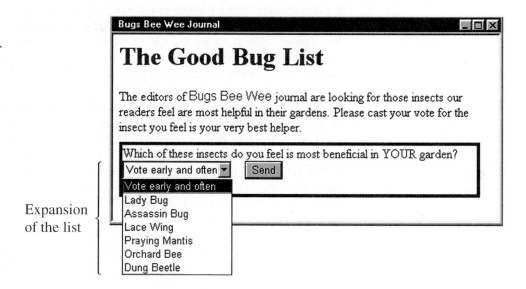

Expansion of the list

When the user activates one of the selections, that option is highlighted and that value is sent back to the CGI script when the Send button is activated. The code in Figure 11.22 shows a nearly generic <select> list box. When the user selects one of the options, the form sends the actual option as the value in the goodbug=value string. For example, if the user selects Lace Wing, then the form sends goodbug=Lace+Wing back to the CGI script. (Remember that spaces are changed to plus signs before data are sent to the server.)

Unlike the case with the other elements we have discussed, if the user does not select an option, and there is no "selected" default option, the value associated with the name attribute is *null*. A null value is a variable that has no value—it is not a value of blank, or zero, but has absolutely no value. Usually null is represented by binary zeros. Because of the null-value problem, and because browsers aren't always consistent about which values to display in the select box, the W[3]C mandates that "authors should insure that each menu includes a default preselected **option**." In the example shown in Figure 11.22 the Web weaver has preselected the "Vote early and often" value. That ensures two things: first that the instruction will always be the value displayed; and second that by default the form will never stuff the ballot box. As we discussed earlier, when you design forms to tally data, you need to be careful not to prejudice the results.

As we have mentioned in earlier examples, XML requires that each attribute have a value associated with it. If you use the selected option, you will need to code

```
selected="selected"
```

rather than just the selected attributes as shown in the example.

Look back at our previous examples of selection sets, checkboxes, and radio buttons. The value returned by those elements could be different from the value in the prompt.

Like the other controls, if Web weavers do not want to use the whole prompt—for example, "Praying Mantis"—they can code a **value** attribute to specify a string other than the prompt. This attribute is discussed later. There are two unique attributes for the <select> container: **size** and **multiple.**

size

The **size** attribute, which should be a positive integer, determines how many of the choices are shown when the list box is first displayed by the browser. The default is a single entry, specified by the **selected** option, with a downward scroll arrow next to it. Figure 11.22 shows how this looks on the screen. By default, only one element, the first in the list, appears. Exactly which one is not specified by the W3C, so it may vary among the browsers. However, when the user activates the down arrow next to the selection (or clicks on any part of the selection box), the whole list of options appears as a drop-down list, shown in Figure 11.23. This is a very handy option. When the user activates her choice, the list contracts back to a single entry, with the choice highlighted and shown in the window. If you want your user to see a fixed number of options and be able to scroll among them, set the **size** to that number. Yet, the default for the **size** attribute, displaying the whole list, is often the most effective choice.

Figure 11.24 shows the same <select></select> container with a **size** attribute of 4. The only difference between the code in Figure 11.24 and the code in Figure 11.22 is this **size** attribute on the <select></select> container. Now the user must scroll down the list, only seeing four choices at a time. This result is less desirable than the default value in most cases, because it takes up more screen area without providing all the list options. The user still must scroll to see all the options. In addition, the default value for "Vote early and often" doesn't work the same way it did when a single choice was displayed. Use the **size** attribute if you must, but in most cases the default is the best choice.

multiple

The **multiple** option allows the <select> element to accept multiple choices. This is the "choose all that apply" rather than "choose only one" option. Used this way, the <select></select> container works like checkboxes rather than like radio buttons. The **multiple** attribute is a *toggle* in the HTML specifications, and is assigned no value; it is just coded as an attribute, as follows:

```
<select multiple name="goodbugs">
 <option>Lady Bug</option>
 <option>Assassin Bug</option>
 <option>Lace Wing</option>
</select>
```

Since the XHTML specifications dislike attributes without assigned values, you should code the open select container like this to be compliant:

```
<select multiple="multiple" name="goodbug">
```

There are three ways for the user to select multiple entries:

1. She can hold down the Shift key and activate different values, in which case *all the values* between the first and second are highlighted and chosen.

2. She can hold down the right mouse button and move the pointer, covering several different contiguous values, *all of which* are chosen when she lifts the mouse button.

3. She can hold down the Control key and then activate any of the selections, highlighting each one that has been activated.

Figure 11.24 HTML code and screen capture demonstrating **size** attribute

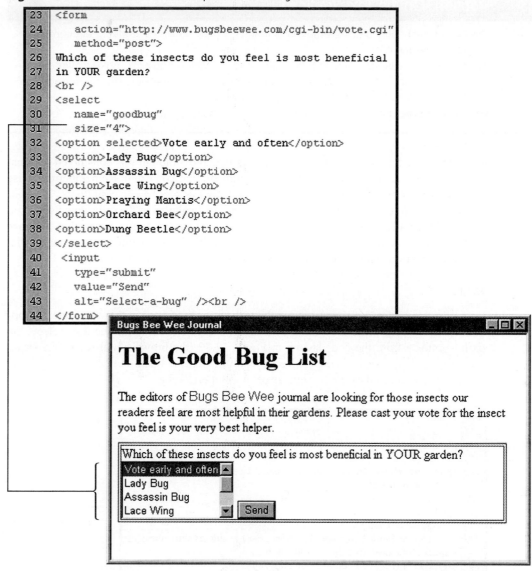

```
23  <form
24      action="http://www.bugsbeewee.com/cgi-bin/vote.cgi"
25      method="post">
26  Which of these insects do you feel is most beneficial
27  in YOUR garden?
28  <br />
29  <select
30      name="goodbug"
31      size="4">
32  <option selected>Vote early and often</option>
33  <option>Lady Bug</option>
34  <option>Assassin Bug</option>
35  <option>Lace Wing</option>
36  <option>Praying Mantis</option>
37  <option>Orchard Bee</option>
38  <option>Dung Beetle</option>
39  </select>
40   <input
41      type="submit"
42      value="Send"
43      alt="Select-a-bug" /><br />
44  </form>
```

If the user simply activates one selection, then another, only the most recent selection is chosen.

disabled

The **disabled** attribute causes a particular element to do nothing. In some browsers, it may even cause that element to be "grayed out." Although **disabled** selections may be good for initial setup and testing, it is *never* a good idea to have them within your final form—unless you want to confuse and frustrate your users. The W³C included the **disabled** option to allow a Web weaver to prevent the execution of an element until a particular condition exists. For example, if you have created a form that requires users to enter a state code before they can select a country code, you could set the initial value of the country <select> element to **disabled.** Then, through the use of a script, the page could change the status of the element by removing the disabled option once the user enters a valid country code. Generally speaking, though, it is a Bad Thing to set elements to **disabled** in any Web page posted for public consumption.

HTML <option>Option Text</option>

Description: defines one element of a menu list created with a <select> element.
Type: container.
Attributes: class, dir, disabled, id, label, lang, onclick, ondblclick, onkeydown, onkeypress, onkeyup, onmousedown, onmousemove, onmouseout, onmouseover, onmouseup, onSelect, **selected,** style, title, **value.**
Special note: should be coded only within a <select> element.

The <option></option> container has a closing tag, and although it is considered optional in the 4.0 specifications, we nevertheless recommend that you use it. Remember that wise Web weavers who want to be XML-compliant always close their containers. The text contained within the <option></option> container is displayed in the drop-down selection box. In almost all cases, the text should be short, only a word or two, rather than a phrase or the Great American Novel. The choices should be distinct from one another so that users clearly know what they are choosing.

value

Normally the <select> element returns the text string contained within the selected <option> element as a value associated with the **name.** For example, if the user selects the sixth <option> from the code shown in Figure 11.22, the browser will return the string bestbug=Orchard+Bee to the CGI script. Notice that the blank between Orchard and Bee has been replaced by a plus sign, as per normal encoding.

Figure 11.25

Adding values to selection to make processing easier

```
23  <form
24      action="http://www.bugsbeewee.com/cgi-bin/vote.cgi"
25      method="POST"
26  >
27  Which of these insects do you feel is most beneficial
28  in YOUR garden?
29  <br>
30  <select
31      name="goodbug">
32  <option selected value="no">Vote early and often</option>
33  <option value="lb">Lady Bug</option>
34  <option value="ab">Assassin Bug</option>
35  <option value="lw">Lace Wing</option>
36  <option value="pm">Praying Mantis</option>
37  <option value="ob">Orchard Bee</option>
38  <option value="db">Dung Beetle</option>
39  </select>
40   <input
41      type="submit"
42      value="Send"
43      alt="Select-a-bug"><br />
44  </form>
```

Notice the values

From Figure 11.22 ⟶

```
29  <select
30      name="goodbug">
31  <option selected>Vote early and often</option>
32  <option>Lady Bug</option>
33  <option>Assassin Bug</option>
34  <option>Lace Wing</option>
35  <option>Praying Mantis</option>
36  <option>Orchard Bee</option>
37  <option>Dung Beetle</option>
38  </select>
```

Look at Figure 11.25, where we have added values to make the CGI script that processes the data a little easier to code. The figure contains both the code from the original list (Figure 11.22), in the box on the bottom of the figure, and the new code. The generated HTML page is identical to the one shown in Figure 11.22.

If the CGI script is to understand the input data from the form, it must be programmed to match the input data string with an expected value. Generally speaking, it takes more work to check for long strings made up of multiple words. When there are spaces in the input string (converted to plus signs), they must either be removed or matched. Establishing a value that is a short string of letters makes it easier to check for expected values. Should the user choose the Orchard Bee from the version of the form in Figure 11.25, the browser will return the string goodbug=ob to the selected script. In the case where the user fails to choose a favorite, the script only has to look for the little string no, rather than Vote early and often. As you can see, it is worth the small effort required to set the **value** attributes, because they make the CGI or JavaScript script much easier to code.

selected

Just like the **checked** attribute for radio buttons and checkboxes, the **selected** attribute preselects the <option> in which it is coded. The **selected** attribute has no value associated with it in the HTML specifications, but it should be assigned the value "selected" if you are coding in XHTML. You can preselect only one option with **selected,** unless the **multiple** attribute is coded within the <select> element. If you try to preselect more than one option without the **multiple** attribute specified, none of them will be preselected.

If you don't specify a **size** attribute, and do preselect one of the options, then that option will appear in the selection box regardless of its position in the list. When the user opens the list, that selection will be highlighted. If the **multiple** attribute has been coded, you can use **selected** to preselect several of the options and each will appear highlighted. Generally, it is considered a good idea to preselect at least one <option>, because if the user doesn't select one, the browser will return a null value for that control. In addition, as mentioned earlier, the W[3]C very strongly recommends selecting one of the <option>s to ensure that all browsers will present the initial expression of the list the same way.

HTML **<optgroup>Collection of <option></option>s</optgroup>**

Description: allows multiple <option>s in a select element to be grouped logically and identified.
Type: container.
Attributes: class, dir, id, **label,** lang, onclick, ondblclick, onkeydown, onkeypress, onkeyup, onmousedown, onmousemove, onmouseout, onmouseover, onmouseup, style, title.
Special note: used only within a <select></select> container.

If you have a long series of <option>s coded within one <select></select> container, you can group them using the <optgroup></optgroup> container. You can specify a label for the collection of <option>s, and some of the browsers will show that label and indicate the subordination by indenting the grouped <option>s under the text specified in each label.

Figure 11.26

Example of <optgroup> and <label> elements

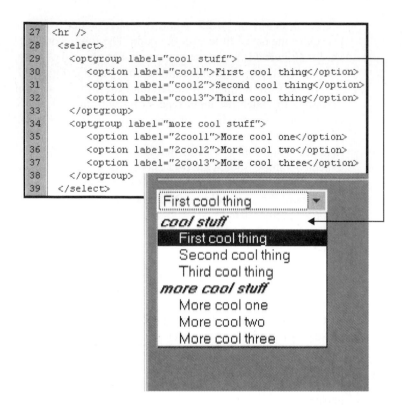

```
27  <hr />
28  <select>
29    <optgroup label="cool stuff">
30      <option label="cool1">First cool thing</option>
31      <option label="cool2">Second cool thing</option>
32      <option label="cool3">Third cool thing</option>
33    </optgroup>
34    <optgroup label="more cool stuff">
35      <option label="2cool1">More cool one</option>
36      <option label="2cool2">More cool two</option>
37      <option label="2cool3">More cool three</option>
38    </optgroup>
39  </select>
```

label

The **label** attribute is a required one. It provides a text label for the group of <option>s contained within the <optgroup></optgroup> container. You should specify a short, precise label for each set of <option>s so that the user can understand your logical groupings. The code portion of Figure 11.26 shows an example of this container:

HTML <fieldset> [<legend>] <input>[s]</fieldset>

Description: defines a grouping of related form controls.
Type: container.
Attributes: class, dir, id, lang, onclick, ondblclick, onkeydown, onkeypress, onkeyup, onmousedown, onmousemove, onmouseout, onmouseover, onmouseup, style, title.
Special note: supported to various degrees by the different browsers but not those at or before the 4.0 level.

In some browsers, the <fieldset> element builds a graphical element around the enclosed controls and <legend> element. This container is designed to help organize a form by grouping like input controls together in one element. It can also be used to better render forms in aural browsers. It was newly added in the HTML 4 specifications. If you choose to use one or more <fieldset>s, we urge you to use the <legend> element as well.

HTML <legend>Text</legend>

Description: provides a caption for the <fieldset></fieldset> container.
Type: container.
Attributes: **accesskey,** align, class, dir, id, lang, onclick, ondblclick, onkeydown, onkeypress, onkeyup, onmousedown, onmousemove, onmouseout, onmouseover, onmouseup, style, title.
Special note: has been deprecated in favor of style sheets.

If you use a <fieldset> element to group your form controls, we urge you to use a <legend></legend> container to provide a caption for the grouping. This element is especially important when you are creating aural or nongraphical pages. Figure 11.27 shows how these two elements, <fieldset> and <legend>, work to define and enclose controls on a form. As you can see, each fieldset physically encloses that part of the form within it, as well as providing a legend or text description of that subset of the form. These two new tools are quite handy.

Figure 11.27   Example of <fieldset> and <legend>

Notice how each fieldset encloses the controls.

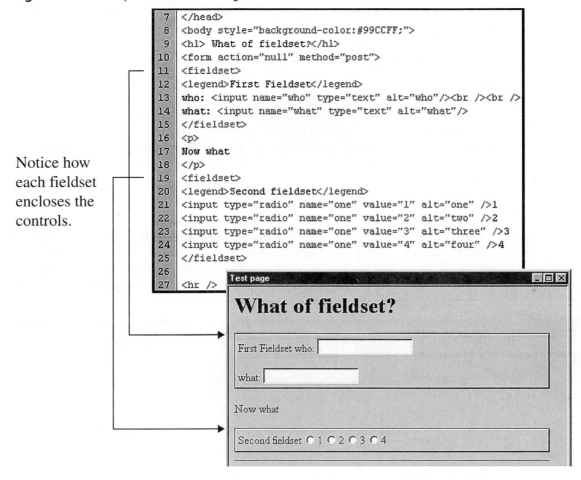

accesskey

The **accesskey** attribute provides a single text key that will bring the associated element into focus. This tool is designed primarily for users with limited mobility. How the browsers support an access key is widely varied. Most of the time an access key is utilized with another special key. For example, in the Windows system the access key is coupled with the Alt key and on Mac systems with the Cmd key.

<label>Text</label>

Description: provides a text label for the associated input control in a form.
Type: container.
Attributes: accesskey, class, dir, **for,** id, lang, onclick, ondblclick, onkeydown, onkey-press, onkeyup, onmousedown, onmousemove, onmouseout, onmouseover, onmouseup, style, title.
Special note: implementation varies widely across the browsers.

The <label> element is another new element that allows the Web weaver to assign text, contained within a container, to a particular input control. It is designed to be used with XHTML pages to have all text enclosed within a container. You can also use it to provide formatting for these text elements through the **style** and **class** attributes. This element is similar to the <legend> element in that it provides a text description for an input control element in a form. You can see how it is used if you look back at Figure 11.26.

for

The **for** attribute allows the <label> element to be associated with a particular input control. The value for this attribute must match one of the values for an **id** attribute of one of the input controls in the form. In our experimentation, this association did not change the physical placement of the contents of the <label> element on the form.

▸▸ XHTML FORM MODULE

The form elements introduced in this chapter—<button>, <fieldset>, <form>, <input />, <label>, <legend>, <optgroup>, <option>, <select>, and <textarea>—have been bundled together in the XHTML specifications to form the Form module. While not a required module, it will be a common component in many XML and XHTML applications.

EXPLORATION #4   Modify the form you created in Exploration #3 to include the following additional features:

- Change the radio buttons to a select menu.
- Add a drop-down menu of important features for a pet. Include as a minimum the following: cuddly, protective, nonshedding, warm-blooded, quiet, and intelligent.
- Remember to save the original version of your page each time you make a change.

▸▸ PROCESSING DATA AUTOMAGICALLY (CGI)

Using the techniques you have learned so far, you can create forms that will enable your users to send you all sorts of interesting and useful data. However, as we mentioned earlier, when your site becomes more popular, or the volume of your data increases, using email becomes cumbersome. So let's look at ways to automatically process data sent by a form.

Up until now, we have looked at forms only from the perspective of the browser and passing data back to the Web weaver via email, but the real work with forms occurs at the server. Remember that the form is a tool for collecting and delivering data from the user. In most cases, after the data are collected, the browser packages them up and ships them to the server for processing. The server runs a set of programs that takes these data from the browser, processes them, and passes them to a script that does *something* with the data. This process can be confusing, so let's look at the terms for a minute.

The set of programs that handles the data formatting and passing is called the ***Common Gateway Interface (CGI).*** The user-written program that processes the user data and sends the results back to the user is usually called a ***script.*** A script is the name we give to programs, usually written by the Web weaver, that perform the actual data processing. Figure 11.28 shows how we directed the browser to send the data to a script for processing. Look at the action line in the script. You will notice that it specifies that the form data should be sent to a script rather than to an email address.

Figure 11.28

Invoking script with form instead of using email

Code to invoke
the vote.cgi script

```
23  <form
24      action="http://www.bugsbeewee.com/cgi-bin/vote.cgi"
25      method="post">
26  Which of these insects do you feel is most beneficial
27  in YOUR garden?
28  <br />
29  <select
30      name="goodbug">
31  <option selected value="no">Vote early and often</option>
32  <option value="lb">Lady Bug</option>
33  <option value="ab">Assassin Bug</option>
34  <option value="lw">Lace Wing</option>
35  <option value="pm">Praying Mantis</option>
36  <option value="ob">Orchard Bee</option>
37  <option value="db">Dung Beetle</option>
38  </select>
39    <input
40      type="submit"
41      value="Send"
42      alt="Select-a-bug"><br />
43  </form>
```

Exactly what the *something* is that a script does with the data can vary greatly. If the script is poorly constructed, it may appear as a black hole to the user—the data go in but nothing comes out. A simple script may thank users for their input and tuck that input away in a file. On the other hand, a finely crafted script may run a sophisticated search program, retrieve some collection of data from a database, and create an HTML document to present those data back to the users, as shown in Figure 11.29. Actually, the only limitations on what a script can do are those imposed by the imagination of the scriptors.

CGI provides the standards and format that browsers use to send data to the server, as well as the format the server uses to hand off the data to a script. That program, usually called the *CGI script,* does whatever is necessary to process the data and, it is hoped, send something back to the user.

Three ways to obtain a CGI script are as follows:

1. You can write your own, usually in either the Perl or C programming languages or as a *shell script* on your Unix machine. Although Perl and C are the most common high-level languages used for CGI scripting, theoretically any high-level language can be used for this purpose.

2. If you are not a programmer, you can hire a programmer to write the script for you.

3. You can search across the Net, find a script that will work for you, download it to your server, and use it.

If you choose this last course, respect the *intellectual property* of others. Copy only *public domain* software, or *freeware.* The problem with this third method of obtaining a

Figure 11.29

Results of CGI script that presents data back to users

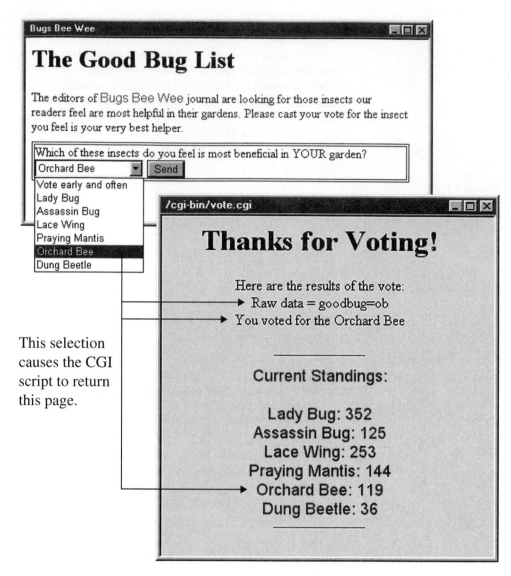

This selection causes the CGI script to return this page.

CGI script is that you must adapt your form to use the tools available from some source on the Net rather than having a tool crafted to your exact needs. Using "off the Net" scripts is fine for simple applications and for testing, but if you are contemplating a complex response to the user, you will usually need to find a way to create, or have someone else create, your own specialized CGI script.

Teaching programming is beyond the scope of this text. Instead, we will present some simple scripts to show you how the process works. If you already know how to program in a high-level language, you can use the introduction to CGI in this chapter and the additional exploration in the next chapter to help you create your own CGI scripts on your server. Even if you are not a programmer, you can use the simple script presented in this chapter and those in the next chapter to get started, then have a programmer build specialized scripts for you. CGI is becoming an essential forms-processing tool.

▸▸ HOW CGI WORKS

CGI is a collection of programs the Web server uses to communicate with scripts that are kept on the server. The most common use for CGI is processing forms, but there are other, more sophisticated ways to use CGI to pass data. We will look at using CGI to process data from forms, since that is the most common usage. Following are the steps for using a CGI script on a server to process a form:

1. The browser requests a form from the server.

2. The user fills out the form and activates the submit control.

3. The browser sends the form data to the server.

4. The server recognizes the CGI *call* and passes the script name and the associated data to the set of programs called CGI.

5. The CGI application massages the data and creates a set of environmental variables, then starts the requested script.

6. The CGI script runs, generating a response to the user along with the other processing.

7. The CGI software passes the response created by the script back to the server.

8. The server passes the processed data and response back to the browser.

9. The browser displays the processed data and response to the user.

The only parts of this process that concern the Web weaver are creating and presenting the form the user fills out and crafting the CGI script that processes the data and sends them back, along with a proper response, to the user. The rest can be considered part of the "magic of http."

When a server gets a request for a CGI script, the server handles it differently than the request for just another Web page. Rather than immediately posting the requested document back to the browser, the server looks for the script, or program, specified in the request, or *call,* and tries to run that CGI script. For example, the following line

http://www.bugsbeewee.com/cgi-bin/vote.cgi?goodbug=lb

asks the server, www.bugsbeewee.com, to invoke the script called vote.cgi that resides in the /cgi-bin directory.

Part of preparing the CGI script to run is passing the data from the client to the script on the server. In our present example, the data are a single variable (goodbug=lb). This format for sending data illustrates the method="get" process. If the method were post, the data would not be sent as part of the URL. Different platforms and different operating systems dictate different ways that the CG scripts get their data.

EXPLORATION #5 Create a new form that sends the data to either.pl on your own machine or on your school's server. Send the script a value selected from a drop-down menu. First send the data via the post method. Then send it again, in a different iteration of the form, via the get method. Confirm that both methods work. Print the page that was returned to you from each method. (You will need access to a machine running Perl for this exercise. If you don't have access to Perl on your server, you should talk to your instructor about this exploration.)

▸▸ KEY TERMS

Button	Perl
CGI	Radio button
Focus	Script
Input controls	Variable name
Parse	

▸▸ NEW TAGS

<button></button>
<fieldset></fieldset>
<form></form>
<input />
<label></label>

<legend></legend>
<optgroup></optgroup>
<option></option>
<select></select>
<textarea></textarea>

▸▸ REVIEW QUESTIONS

1. Define each of the key terms.
2. How is each of the tags introduced in this chapter used? (Provide examples.)
3. What is the easiest way to distribute data collected with a form?
4. Name three disadvantages to using the distribution method identified in Question 3.
5. What attributes are required with every <form> element?
6. What are the two methods used to send data from a form to a CGI script on the server? Which is preferred?
7. How are data that were encoded using the application/x-www-form-urlencoded encryption altered?
8. Name the two intrinsic events that are unique to forms.
9. List ten types of input controls.
10. What information does a **name-value** pair provide to the CGI script?
11. Summarize the authors' guidelines for creating variable names.
12. How is a checkbox control different from a radio-button control?
13. What is the easiest way to clear a user's form entries?
14. Which control starts the process of the browser encoding and sending information to the server?
15. How is a text box different from a text area?
16. How is a list box different from other input controls?
17. Give the rationale for using short strings of letters for option values.
18. Which HTML tags are associated with the XHTML Form module?
19. How can you obtain a CGI script?

▸▸ EXERCISES

11.1. Ruby wants to collect some data from her customers. She needs you to build a page that includes a form that asks for the following information:
   a. The customer's favorite gemstone, (use a set of radio buttons, one per line, with a name of "fav", and a value set to the lowercase of the first letter of the gemstone. The gemstones are: Ruby, Sapphire, Pearl, Emerald, and a final choice of "I love them all" which should have a value of "a".
   b. A set of checkboxes, one per line, that allow the customer to select other gems they might be interested in. The values should be: Amber, Carnelian, Hyacinth, Jet, and Turquoise. The value for each should be the lowercase first initial of the gem. The name should be "new."
   c. A text box name "email" that is 24 characters long used to collect the user's email address.
   d. A set of options which describe the user's knowledge of gemstones. The name should be "know", and the choices should be: Expert, Knowledgeable, Literate, Novice, and Newbie.
   e. A 60 column by 6 row text area named "suggest" with physical wrap where the users can enter their suggestions.

    f. A table on the bottom of the page that contains both submit and reset buttons. The buttons should be labeled "Tell Us" and "Reset Form" respectively. The table should be 99% of the form, with the center column taking up 50% of the table.

    g. Have the form send you an email with the data so you can see how the data look to a script. Make sure you use the "post" method.

    h. The page should have the following styles set in an on page style sheet:

        1. The body should have a light green background, #CCFFCC, the text should be darker green, #336633, the font weight should be 500.

        2. Level 1 headings should be dark green, #006600, centered, and 24 point.

        3. Level two headings should be bright green, #339933, centered, and 18 pt.

        4. The form should have a bright green background, #99FF99, with deep green text, #006633, a double, medium, bright green, #993333, border, with a sans-serif font of size 14 and weight of 600, and 1 em of padding all around.

    i. Use the page eme11-raw.htm from the Web site or your student disk as the beginning text, and save your final page as eme11-data.htm.

11.2. Create a new HTML document containing a form. The title bar should display Operating System Survey by *your name,* with your name and the assignment due date included within comment lines. Form results should be sent to your email account or an email account given to you by the instructor. At a minimum the form should contain the following:

    a. Text boxes to accept the person's name and email address.

    b. Checkboxes with **name** and **value** attributes for these operating systems:

        (1) CP/M

        (2) Macintosh OS

        (3) Windows 2000

        (4) Unix

        (5) Windows XP

    c. Radio buttons with **name** and **value** attributes that correspond to the operating systems listed in Exercise 10.1. These buttons need to allow the user to rate the systems as follows:

        (1) Good

        (2) Bad

        (3) Never used it

    d. Submit control

    e. Reset control

11.3. Create a new HTML document containing a form. The title bar should be Bugs Bee Wee Order Form, with your name and the assignment due date included within comment lines. Form results should be sent to your email account or an email account given to you by the instructor. At a minimum the form should contain the following:

    a. Text boxes to accept the person's name and email address.

    b. Checkboxes with **name** and **value** attributes for these bugs:

        (1) Ladybug

        (2) Praying mantis

        (3) Cricket

        (4) Honey bee

    c. Text box for the credit card number.

    d. Radio buttons for these credit card companies:

        (1) American Express

        (2) Discover

        (3) Master Card

        (4) Visa

    e. Submit control

    f. Reset control

11.4. Retrieve the Homework home page you updated in previous exercises. Create a new HTML document containing a form and a link to this page on your home page. The title bar on the page with the form should display Personal Survey by *your name*. Include your name and the assignment due date within comment lines on the form page. The form should collect information from the user that is sent to your email account or an email account given to you by the instructor. It needs to contain submit and reset controls. The information collected must include the user's name and email address, along with any or all of the following:

    a. Favorite musicians and related songs.
    b. Favorite athletes and related teams.
    c. Favorite actors and actresses.
    d. Favorite television shows.
    e. Favorite movies.

11.5. Retrieve your school's home page updated in previous exercises. Create a new HTML document containing a form and a link to this page on the home page. The title bar on the page with the form should display Course Request Form. Include your name and the assignment due data within comment lines on the form page. The form should collect information from the user that is sent to your email account or an email account given to you by the instructor. It needs to contain submit and reset controls. The information collected must include the user's name and email address, along with all of the following:

    a. Course prefix and number.
    b. Course name.
    c. Radio buttons identifying the semester/term and the year the user wants to take the class.
    d. Reason the user needs that class.

11.6. Retrieve the movies home page updated in previous exercises. Create a new HTML document containing a form and a link to this page on the home page. The title bar on the page with the form should display All Time Favorite Movies Survey. Also include your name and the assignment due date within comment lines on the form page. The form should collect information from the user that is sent to your email account or an email account given to you by the instructor. It needs to contain submit and reset controls. The information collected must include the following:

    a. Movie's name.
    b. Radio buttons identifying one of the following movie categories in which the user would place the film:
        1. Comedy
        2. Horror
        3. Science fiction
        4. Love story
        5. Action/adventure
    c. Text area for brief description of the user's favorite scene.

11.7. Create a new HTML document containing a form. The title bar should display Complaint Form, with your name and the assignment due date included within comment lines. Form results should be sent to your email account or an email account given to you by the instructor. At a minimum the form should contain the following:

    a. Text boxes to accept the person's name and email address.
    b. Text area for complaint.
    c. Radio buttons with **name** and **value** attributes for these options:
        (1) I just wanted you to know.
        (2) Please respond to the email address given.
        (3) Contact my lawyer.
        (4) Go to #!$#*.
    d. Text boxes to accept the lawyer's name and address.
    e. Submit control.
    f. &Reset control.

11.8. Create a new HTML document containing a form. The title bar should display Voting Form, with your name and the assignment due date included within comment lines. Form results should be sent to your email account or an email account given to you by the instructor. At a minimum the form should contain the following:

   a. Text boxes to accept the person's name and email address.

   b. At least five radio buttons the user can use to vote for a candidate for some office.

   c. Text box for write-in alternative.

   d. Checkboxes with name and value attributes for these options:

   (1) This is the first time I have voted online.

   (2) I have periodically voted online.

   (3) I always vote online.

   (4) Online voting is not patriotic.

   e. Submit control.

   f. Reset control.

11.9. Craft a form that allows the user to select one entry from a drop-down menu of six different milk shake flavors. Send the output to the either pl script and have it return both the method used to send the data (get or put), and the **name-value** pair from the script. Verify that your script is correctly pointing at the CGI script by displaying your form and then seeing the returned page. After you have the form working correctly (this may entail having your instructor or system administrator help you determine the correct path to the CGI directory on your computer, as it varies from machine to machine), modify the form to use the other submission method. Verify that the script correctly identifies the method.

Twelve

CGI, Metatags, and Other Tricks of the Trade

As mentioned in the last chapter, data collected in a form are often sent to a Web server for processing by a script as an alternative of using email when there is a large volume of data or a high message count. In this chapter we want to take a closer look at these server-side scripts, in particular, the popular *Common Gateway Interface (CGI)* scripts. Although the focus of this book is HTML, not CGI scripting, discussing CGI scripts allows us to introduce several HTML techniques that can bring added life to your pages. Some, like *searchable documents* or *server-based dynamic documents,* may require close work with your Web administrator. In addition, you need to know about HTML *metatags,* which assist search engines in properly categorizing your Web pages and help validators find syntax errors.

CHAPTER OBJECTIVES

After reading this chapter you should be able to do the following:

- Describe the interrelationship whereby data are sent from a form to a server for processing by a CGI script.
- Code a simple form that sends data to a CGI script for processing.
- Describe the functioning of the <isindex> tag, and code the recommended replacement.
- Use <meta /> tags to supply additional information on Web pages.
- Use <meta /> tags to create a series of auto-loading pages.
- Create multicolumn pages using tables.
- Build pages with headlines and sidebars using table tags.
- Use pseudo-elements and pseudo-classes to alter the look of pages.

⏵⏵ PROCESSING DATA AUTOMAGICALLY (CGI)

Using the techniques you have learned so far, you can create forms that will enable your users to send you all sorts of interesting and useful data. Up until now we have looked at forms only from the perspective of the browser and in terms of passing data back to the Web weaver via email, but the real work with forms occurs at the server. Remember that the *form* is a tool for collecting and delivering data from the user. In most cases, after the data are collected, the browser packages them up and ships them to the server for processing. The server runs a set of programs that take these data from the browser, process them, and pass them to a script that does *something* with the data. This procedure can be confusing, so let's look at the terms for a minute.

The set of programs that handle the data formatting and passing is called the *Common Gateway Interface (CGI)*. The user-written program that processes the form data and sends the results back to the user is usually called a *script*. Scripts are programs, usually written by the Web weaver, that perform the actual data processing.

Exactly what that *something* is that a script does with the data can vary greatly. If the script is poorly constructed, it may appear as a black hole to the user: the data go in, but nothing comes out. A simple script may thank the users for their input and tuck it away in a file. On the other hand, a finely crafted script may run a sophisticated search program, retrieve some collection of data from a database, and create an HTML document to present those data back to the users. Actually, the only limitations on what a script can do are those imposed by the limitations of the imagination of the scriptors!

CGI provides the standards and format that browsers use to send data to the server, as well as the format the server uses to hand off the data to a script. That program, usually called the *CGI script,* does whatever is necessary to process the data and, in the case of the best scripts, sends something back to the user. There are three ways to obtain a CGI script:

1. You can write your own, usually in either the Perl or C programming languages or as a *shell script* on your Unix machine. Although Perl and C are the most common high-level languages used for CGI scripting, theoretically any high-level language can be used for this purpose.

2. If you are not a programmer, you can hire a programmer to write the script for you.

3. You can search across the Net to find a script that will work for you and download it to your server.

If you choose this last course, respect the *intellectual property* of others. Copy only *public domain* software, or *freeware.* The problem with this third method of obtaining a CGI script is that you must adapt your form to use the tools available from some source on the Net rather than having a tool crafted to your exact needs. Using off-the-Net scripts is fine for simple applications and for testing, but if you are contemplating a complex response to the user, you will usually need to find a way to create, or have created, your own specialized CGI script.

Teaching programming is beyond the scope of this text. Instead, we will present two simple scripts to show you how the process works. If you already know how to program in a high-level language, you can use the introduction to CGI in this chapter and the additional exploration in the next chapter to help you create your own CGI scripts on your server. Even if you are not a programmer, you can use the simple scripts presented in this chapter and those in the next chapter to get started, then have a programmer build specialized scripts for you. CGI is becoming an essential forms-processing tool.

⏵⏵ HOW CGI WORKS

CGI is a collection of programs the Web server uses to communicate with scripts that are kept on the server. The most common use for CGI is processing forms, but there are other, more sophisticated ways to use CGI to pass data. We will look at using CGI to process data from forms, since that is the most common usage. Following are the steps involved in that process:

1. The browser requests a form from the server.
2. The user fills out the form and activates the submit control.
3. The browser sends the form data to the server.
4. The server recognizes the CGI *call* and passes the script name and the associated data to the set of programs called CGI.
5. The CGI application massages the data and creates a set of environmental variables, then starts the requested script.
6. The CGI script runs, generating a response to the user along with the other processing.
7. The CGI software passes the response created by the script back to the server.
8. The server passes the processed data and response back to the browser.
9. The browser displays the processed data and response to the user.

The only parts of this process that concern the Web weaver are creating and presenting the form the user fills out and crafting the CGI script that processes the data and sends them back, along with a proper response, to the user. The rest can be considered part of the "magic of http."

When a server gets a request for a CGI script, the server handles it differently than the request for just another Web page. Rather than immediately posting the requested document back to the browser, the server looks for the script, or program, specified in the request, or *call,* and tries to run that CGI script. For example, the following line

http://www.bugsbeewee.com/cgi.bin/vote.cgi?goodbug=lb

asks the server www.bugsbeewee.com, to invoke the script called vote.cgi that resides in the cgi-bin directory.

Part of preparing the CGI script to run is passing the data from the client to the script on the server. In our present example the data are a single variable (goodbug=lb). This format for sending data illustrates the method="get" process. If the method were set equal to "post", the data would not be sent as part of the URL. Different platforms and different operating systems dictate different ways that the CGI scripts get their data.

UPDATING DATABASE WITH CGI

One of the other common uses for a form is updating a database. In Chapter Eleven the either.pl script was the first CGI script used to process the "favorite bug" vote. Figure 12.1 shows the form you saw in Figure 11.24 modified simply by changing the CGI script so that it could be used to update a database on the bugsbeewee server. As you can see, the page now invokes the script vote.cgi. This script is just a little more complex than the one we saw in Chapter Eleven. It is on the CD and on the Web site. If you wish to run it on your server you, too, could create a wonderfully informative database of insect preferences.

Figure 12.2 shows the user sending in her vote, and the response from the server. Each time a user votes, the database is updated to reflect her choice. This type of online voting is very popular across the Net. You will find polls about all sorts of interesting information—none as interesting as our favorite insect report, but worth checking out anyway.

EXPLORATION **#1**

Create a Web page with a form that has a list box showing five of your favorite television shows, and send the user's selection to **either.pl** on your own machine, or on your school's server (**either.pl** is found on the CD that comes with this book). Include your name in the Web page's title. First send the data via the POST method. Then send it again, in a different iteration of the form, via the GET method. Confirm that both methods work, and print both confirmation Web pages.

Figure 12.1 The "favorite bug page" as modified to update database on server

```
23  <form
24      action="http://www.bugsbeewee.com/cgi-bin/vote.cgi"      ← Code to invoke
25      method="POST"                                                the vote.cgi script
26  >
27  Which of these insects do you feel is most beneficial
28  in YOUR garden?
29  <br />
30  <select
31      name="goodbug">
32  <option selected value="no">Vote early and often</option>
33  <option value="lb">Lady Bug</option>
34  <option value="ab">Assassin Bug</option>
35  <option value="lw">Lace Wing</option>
36  <option value="pm">Praying Mantis</option>
37  <option value="ob">Orchard Bee</option>
38  <option value="db">Dung Beetle</option>
39  </select>
40    <input
41      type="submit"
42      value="Send"
43      alt="Select-a-bug" /><br />
44  </form>
```

Figure 12.2 Voting for a favorite bug and getting results back from server

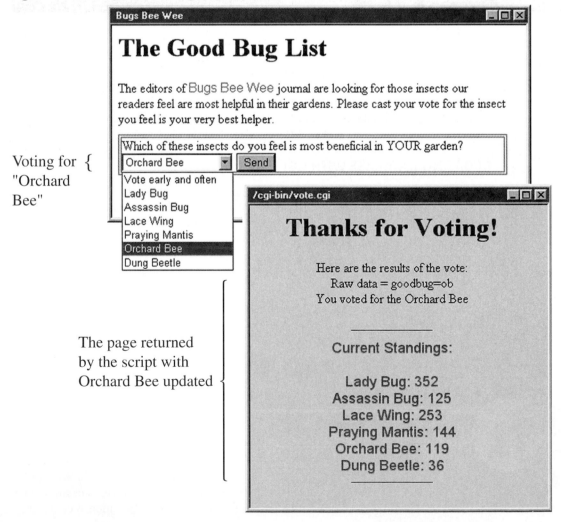

Voting for { "Orchard Bee"

The page returned by the script with Orchard Bee updated

SEARCHABLE DOCUMENTS

Another excellent application for CGI scripting is to support an HTML document that runs a search on a Web site, called a *searchable document.* This document enables users to run a keyword search on a site, or on a subset of the files on a site, to find specific information. Searchable documents can present a security concern for your Web server administrator, though. As mentioned earlier, you need to be aware of the presence of unethical users on the Net. Just as you should carefully review your CGI scripts with your Web server administrator, so should you review any searchable documents.

Here's the reason for the security concerns. The server normally expects to return an HTML document to the browser and then go on to something else. When a search is involved, the server has to run a search program and send the results back to the browser. As with a document that executes a CGI script, a searchable document invokes a user-written search script that could access any file on the Web server. This is dangerous, because sensitive files could be accidentally exposed within the search domain. Careful and conscientious consultation with your system administrator can ensure that the code you build will not compromise your server. It is very important that you consider security concerns any time you build scripts to run on a machine that is exposed to the Internet. Please take this easy step before exposing your server to potential attack.

HTML **<isindex/>**

Description: indicates that the document contains a tool to perform searches.
Type: empty tag.
Attributes: action, class, dir, id, lang, prompt, style, title.
XML: this tag is not an XML recognized element.
Special notes: deprecated in the HTML 4.0 specifications in favor of the <input> element. The specifications require that the tag be coded in the <head> container, but most browsers support its inclusion in the <body> element as well. In the latter case, the browser will place the search field where the <isindex> element is positioned.

The <isindex> element was another way to link to the server. This tag is much like the <a>anchor</a> and <submit> tags. The difference is that <isindex> passes only one or more keywords to the server as a string to be matched by the search script. The HTML 4 specifications have deprecated the <isindex> element in favor of the <input> element discussed in Chapter Eleven, so we will use the recommended method in our examples, but be aware that older pages may use the <isindex> element.

▸▸ DATA ENTRY USING <INPUT> ELEMENT

Using the <input> element (see Figure 12.4, which occurs a little later in this chapter) instead of <isindex> requires additional code, and a little more work to create the CGI script that does the work; but, hey, we want to be HTML 4-compliant, right? A sample script (`search1.cgi`) is included on the CD and is available on the Web site. The *search script* may look at the contents of a single file or database, or it may search across one or more directories. It may even search every file on the server to locate specific data requested by the user. If you are designing the script to search more than a single file, *be sure* to check with your Web site administrator to ensure that any sensitive files are protected from the script.

CALLING DOCUMENT

You can include a search element on one of your Web pages, but it is often more useful for your users, and easier to code, if you create a separate page to serve as the search-form page. A *calling document* is then needed to bring the search page up. Figure 12.3 shows an example of a calling document.

Figure 12.3 Initial calling page with code

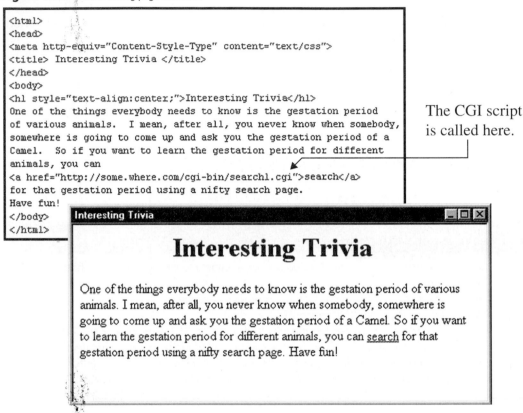

```
<html>
<head>
<meta http-equiv="Content-Style-Type" content="text/css">
<title> Interesting Trivia </title>
</head>
<body>
<h1 style="text-align:center;">Interesting Trivia</h1>
One of the things everybody needs to know is the gestation period
of various animals.  I mean, after all, you never know when somebody,
somewhere is going to come up and ask you the gestation period of a
Camel.  So if you want to learn the gestation period for different
animals, you can
<a href="http://some.where.com/cgi-bin/search1.cgi">search</a>
for that gestation period using a nifty search page.
Have fun!
</body>
</html>
```

The CGI script is called here.

Interesting Trivia

Interesting Trivia

One of the things everybody needs to know is the gestation period of various animals. I mean, after all, you never know when somebody, somewhere is going to come up and ask you the gestation period of a Camel. So if you want to learn the gestation period for different animals, you can <u>search</u> for that gestation period using a nifty search page. Have fun!

Notice that the link invokes a CGI script on the server. The user can activate the link that acts as a request for information, and a new screen will pop up to allow him to perform the search. When the user activates <u>search</u>, the link invokes a CGI script on the server called `search1.cgi`. He can enter the data he wants on the search page, touch the Enter key, and see another screen that gives the results of his search. There is a single CGI script that either sends the user the search form or sends back the results of the search. This is a more sophisticated script than those we have seen so far, but it is not beyond understanding with a little careful study.

SEARCH REQUEST PAGE

In Figure 12.3, no data were passed to the script from the calling document. Therefore, the script assumed the user wanted to see the Search Request page, that is, the form for entering data, as shown in Figure 12.4. Here the browser displays the Web page that was generated by the search script and waits for the user to type in an animal name and touch the Enter key. This entire page was created by the script! It is not a pre-built page. The user has asked for the gestation period of a camel. Smart user! He will be ready with the answer when asked! The browser sends the requested word, Camel, back to the address specified in the **action** attribute of the form that contains the <input> element. (This is the same URL that was requested with the link to the search itself.) This step works like the CGI examples you saw earlier. The difference is that there is no <submit> control.

Figure 12.4   Search Request page as generated by script

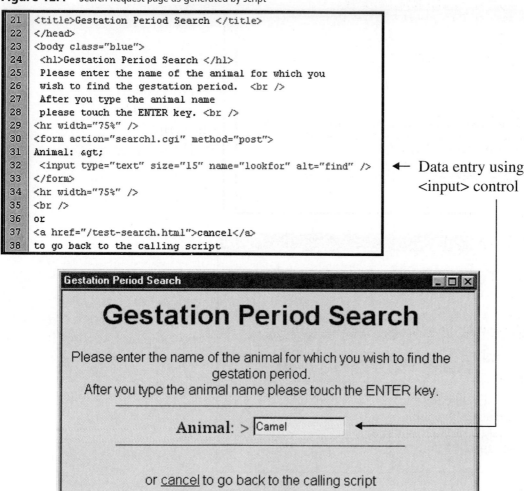

```
21  <title>Gestation Period Search </title>
22  </head>
23  <body class="blue">
24   <h1>Gestation Period Search </h1>
25   Please enter the name of the animal for which you
26   wish to find the gestation period.  <br />
27   After you type the animal name
28   please touch the ENTER key. <br />
29  <hr width="75%" />
30  <form action="search1.cgi" method="post">
31  Animal: &gt;
32   <input type="text" size="15" name="lookfor" alt="find" />
33  </form>
34  <hr width="75%" />
35  <br />
36  or
37  <a href="/test-search.html">cancel</a>
38  to go back to the calling script
```

← Data entry using
   <input> control

Gestation Period Search

Gestation Period Search

Please enter the name of the animal for which you wish to find the
gestation period.
After you type the animal name please touch the ENTER key.

Animal: > | Camel | ◄

or cancel to go back to the calling script

One of the less than obvious features of a form with a single text <input> control is that the user can submit the form simply by touching the Enter key. This is a handy bit of knowledge to tuck away, and we will employ it now. The address to which the browser sends the data is the address of the search script, so this works just fine.

Beware, however, if you choose to use the <input> tag from within a regular HTML document rather than using the technique presented here. There could be a problem with your document handling the return data. The <input> tag will send the data *back to the URL of the page that contains it.* That means that the URL of the page that contains the <input> must be able to process the data returned to it. The <base> tag, discussed later in this chapter, is very useful, as it modifies the URL of the document to the one specified in the tag.

SUCCESS PAGE

After the user sends a request to the server for an animal that is in the database, the same script that created the Search Request page builds another, different HTML page—the Success page. This page contains the requested data, which the server sends back to the user. Notice that the user has the option of canceling the search by activating cancel on the search page (Figure 12.4). Figure 12.5 shows the Success page generated by the search1.cgi script that is returned when the browser finds one or more matches in the database.

Figure 12.5 Success page generated by CGI script

```
21   <title> Search results for:  camel </title>
22   </head>
23   <body class="green">
24   <h1>Search results for: camel </h1>
25   Here are the results of your search: <br />
26   <hr width="75%">
27 <h3>  Camel - 13 Months</h3>
28   <hr width="75%">
29   Do another <a href="/cgi-bin/search1.cgi">search</a><br />
30   Back to the <a href="/test-search.html">calling page</a><br />
31   Add an animal to the list? <br />
32   If so, send
33   <a href="mailto:html_doc@hotmail.com">the authors</a>
34 an email.
35   </body>
```

All this code is generated by the script

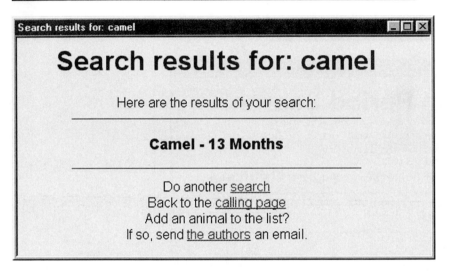

Besides presenting the user with the results of the search, this document also provides some additional navigation tools. As shown in Figure 12.5, if the user wants to search for a different animal, she can activate the search link and go back to the search page. If the user is finished searching, she can activate the calling page link and go back to the document that originally offered the search link. If the user wants to request an additional animal be added to the database, she can also send an email to the authors doing so.

If the user chooses the Back button on the browser, it will display the search page as well. Additional navigation tools are essential, because the page may have been bookmarked, and the user might want to return to it. In that case, the browser would be sent to the search engine with the word requested, and the search script would return the same results page. The URL stored in the bookmark file would be http://some.where.com/cgi-bin/search1.cgi. Notice that this looks suspiciously like the CGI calls we saw before. Why? Because the <input> element is part of the CGI we have already studied!

If the user had only bookmarked this screen, and if there were no navigation links on the screen, the browser would be able to return to the search itself but not to the page that called the search. The URL of the calling page would not be available in the computer's *cache,* that is, in the memory accessible to the browser. Navigation links are essential on *all* the pages you create!

MISS PAGE

Now let's look at the case when the search script doesn't find a match—that is, when the search was unsuccessful and generated a "miss." If the user requests data about an animal that is not in the database (see Figure 12.6), he is politely told that there is no entry for that animal. The user is then allowed to either start a new search, go back to the page that sent the browser to the search in the first place, or send the authors an email requesting that they add his animal to the database. As we saw with the Success page, this kind of navigation tool is also critical.

Figure 12.6 shows the screen the user sees (the Miss page) when requesting the gestation period of a toad. Remember, the same script, search1.cgi, generates all three of these pages, the Search Request page, the Hit page (Success page) and the Miss page. The user is given the same navigation tools here as those presented in the case of a match. The screen looks similar to the screen that gives the results if the search is successful. It is important to keep some consistency of style, or similarity of layout, across related screens in a series. (Note: Toads are amphibians, so they lay eggs. The time it takes an egg to hatch is usually called the *incubation* period not the *gestation* period.)

Figure 12.6 Miss page, seen when search fails

The same script, search1.cgi, also generated this code.

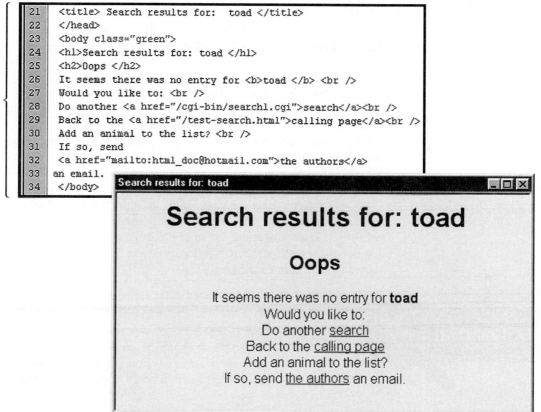

Remember that one CGI script on the server generated all the code you have seen with the Search Request page, the Success page, and the Miss page. Your authors built the script, but the script creates a unique page each time a user requests a particular gestation period. This kind of extremely responsive coding is a perfect example of DHTML, the D standing for Dynamic. If you wish to study the script, it is included on the CD and at the Web site for the text. If you have access to a Unix server, you can install the script and run it as well. Since this isn't a text on CGI, we won't examine the script in detail.

THE DATA FILE

Even though we are not going to examine the code for the CGI script, it is worth a moment to discuss the way the data file was built. Well-designed data files make the job of scripting much easier. Take a look at Figure 12.7. It is a partial listing of the data file for

Figure 12.7

Part of data file for gestation search

```
<h3>  Anteater - 6 months</h3>
<h3>  Ardwolf - 3 months</h3>
<h3>  Aardvark - 7 months</h3>
<h3>  Bear - 7-9 months</h3>
<h3>  Beaver - 4 months</h3>
<h3>  Bison - 9 months</h3>
<h3>  Bobcat - 2 months</h3>
<h3>  Bow Head Whale - 12 months</h3>
<h3>  Bush Baby - 4 months</h3>
<h3>  California Sea Lion - 12 months</h3>
<h3>  Camel - 13 Months</h3>
<h3>  Caribou - 8 months</h3>
<h3>  Cat - 2 months</h3>
<h3>  Cow - 9 months</h3>
<h3>  Cheetah - 3 months</h3>
<h3>  Deer - 5 months</h3>
<h3>  Elephant - 18 - 22 months</h3>
<h3>  Fox - 2 months</h3>
<h3>  Gazelle - 5 months</h3>
<h3>  Giraffe - 15 months</h3>
<h3>  Goat - 5 months</h3>
<h3>  Gorilla - 8.5 months</h3>
<h3>  Gray Squirrel - 44 days</h3>
```

This is a sample of the data file for the search.
Notice how each entry is coded as a level 3 heading.

the gestation period search. Each entry in the file was created as an HTML heading (<h3>) element, so when the script retrieved the line or lines from the file, they were already formatted for use in the document.

In an alternate form of this code, the data file could be composed of list <li> entries, and the list structure could be generated to surround the elements and make them into a list. Each line in Figure 12.7 is an <h3> level heading, so no matter how many are retrieved, they stand out one from another and produce an attractive screen.

Correctly designing the data file is an important part of setting up for almost any searchable structure or set of files. If your user is going to select data from several different files, it may be necessary to add code to your script to format the data. That kind of additional formatting was not necessary in our example, because the data file was designed to work with the script.

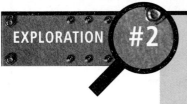

EXPLORATION #2　Assuming you have available to you a Unix machine, or that you can get to the script on the McGraw-Hill Web site, create an HTML document that uses a form to initiate a search for an animal with gestation periods ranging from 2 to 18 months. The content of the form needs to describe the importance of knowing gestation periods, then ask the user to submit a number representing the gestation period in months. Include your name in the title, and print the results of a gestation search using 5 months as input.

▸▸ <base />

At times you might be referencing a series of objects that are not on the same server as your page. For example, you might be using a set of images from the company's image server, which is a different machine than the one you are using for your page. This is when the <base> is necessary.

In Chapter Three we discussed two ways to refer to an address (URL) within a page. An absolute path has all the parts of the address coded, as follows:

http://www.myserver.edu/mydir/neatpage.html

Alternatively, a relative path is not a complete URL and might look like this:

`href="pagetwo.html"`

With the relative URL, the browser supplies all of the related path information. In this example, the browser would fill in the address of the server hosting the current document. Suppose `neatpage.html` is the current page, and we are using a relative link to `pagetwo.html`. The browser would complete the address for the link as follows:

`http://www.myserver.edu/mydir/pagetwo.html`.

We are able to use relative—that is, partial—addresses because the browser fills in the missing pieces. Normally, the browser simply uses the URL of the current page as the basis for this completion. Sometimes, however, it would be handy to be able to tell the browser to use a path other than the one for the current page when it completes relative paths. For example, suppose we wanted to access a series of 19 images on the company image server, a different server from the one housing the current page. We would have to code the absolute address for each of the 19 images—what a pain!

Fortunately, the authors of HTML have anticipated this need. The <base /> tag allows the Web weaver to specify a different base address for the browser to use when completing relative addresses. The browser uses the address specified in the <base /> tag when completing all relative URLs instead of using the address of the current page.

The <base /> element must be coded inside the <head></head> container. It changes the way relative addresses are specified for all the <a>, <img>, <link>, <frame>, and <form> elements in the whole document. The <base /> tag is the only element in the XHTML Base module.

Although <base /> is a very powerful and useful tag, you must be careful with it. If you insert it into an existing document that is already using relative addressing, the additional data necessary to complete the relative URLs will be taken from the tag instead of from the actual URL of the page. Therefore, you need to either (1) change all relative addresses to absolute URLs or (2) move the items being relatively addressed.

href

The **href** attribute is the only required attribute for the <base /> tag. It is used to specify the address of the URL that is to become the new base for relative addressing. The specified URL can be an absolute address or a relative address. For example, we can code

`<base href="/docs/" />`

for the previous example, and the browser will then complete the relative URL, making it the completed URL where the documents would be stored:

`http://www.myserver.edu/docs/`

target

The popular browsers also support **target** as a second attribute to the <base /> tag. As we saw in Chapter Ten the **target** attribute can specify a particular named frame as the default frame where the browser will display redirected documents. In addition, if the Web weaver sets a `target="_top"` in the <base /> tag, any framed document will be forced out of frames and displayed in a full browser window. You will not need to code <base/> in most of the documents you build, but when you need it, it is extremely useful.

▸▸ CREATING NEW TAGS

As if there weren't enough HTML tags to learn about already, we will now look at one that allows the Web weaver to create new tags, the <meta /> tag. In everyday parlance, the term *meta* means "about," or "information about some topic." *Metalanguage* is information about language, and so forth. The choice of the word *meta* in this instance allows the user to add information about the HTML page.

HTML | **<meta />**

Description: supplies additional information about the document.
Type: empty tag.
Attributes: content, dir, **http-equiv**, lang, **name**, scheme.
XML: requires closing tag using <meta />, for example, <meta name="keywords" content="black hole, event horizon" />.
Special note: can appear only within <head> container. Several can occur within the same <head> container and each <meta /> element must specify a property/value or name/value pair.

The use and importance of the <meta /> header element is growing, and it will become more important in the future. If you have been following the development of HTML from 1.0 through 4.1 and on to XHTML, you have seen the <meta /> element take on more and more significance and usefulness. The <meta /> tag is the only element in the XHTML Metainformation module.

This tag can be placed only in the <head>. . .</head> container. It provides some interesting options to Web weavers. Many of the <meta /> attribute values are still under discussion, and not all browsers and search or indexing engines use the same ones, nor do they all use them the same way. While debate still rages about some of the <meta /> tags, they have become more important and valuable in each successive release of the specifications.

Some of the <meta /> attribute values are already useful. One of the emerging standards is the *Dublin Metadata Core Element Set* (or *Dublin Core*), proposed by the March 1995 Meta Data Workshop in Dublin, Ohio, and updated for the HTML 4.0 specifications. It specifically addresses information stored in documents as opposed to other forms of data, like image or sound files. You can find a great deal of information on these values by searching the Web for "Dublin Core" or "OCLC/NCSA Meta Data Workshop Report."

The <meta /> tag can have six different attributes: **http-equiv, content, name, lang, dir,** and **scheme.** The two language attributes, **lang** and **dir,** have been discussed elsewhere. Two of these attributes, **http-equiv** and **name,** are mutually exclusive; you can use one or the other, but not both. Each <meta /> tag must be coded in one of these two forms:

<meta http_equiv="name" content="value" />

or

<meta name="name" content="value" />

The "name" in this code is the name of one of the special attributes, and the "value" is the content, or value, assigned to that name. For example:

<meta name="keywords" content="Argentina, Patagonia" />

Following is a discussion of the attributes for the <meta /> tag.

http-equiv

Coding an http-equiv="name" is the same as including that "name" in the http header. These values are often used by browsers, search engines, and *spiders* (automated search programs that traverse the Web and build indicies for search engines) to perform specialized actions. Let's look at the more commonly used **http-equiv** names. This list is not exhaustive, and it will change and grow over time.

expires The expires value for the **http-equiv** attribute sets a date and time after which the page should be considered outdated and so must be reloaded from the server. When some of the browsers pull a document from cache rather than requesting the document from the Net, they will check to see if there is an expires value. If the document has "expired," then the browser will generate a Net request and download a new copy of the document. This is something like the "sell by" date on dairy products. For example, if a Web page were to post a daily weather forecast for a resort, the Web weaver should set the page to expire each day to force the browser to reload the page from the server the next day. That way the user would never run the risk of getting out of date weather reports.

An example of this <meta /> attribute follows:

```
<meta http-equiv="expires" content="Wed, 29 Mar 2004 00:00:00 GMT" />
```

This code will mark the page that contains it to expire at midnight March 29, 2004. The format of the date field must be coded exactly correctly, or the browser will consider it an invalid date. When the browser encounters an invalid expiration date, it considers the date to be *now* and reloads the page. If the expires value is zero, the browser will never use the page in cache and will always consider the page expired and reload it from the source.

content-type A value of content-type can be used to direct the browser to load a specific character set before it displays the page. This value is used by validators and it can be important if the page contains special text characters or is designed to be displayed in a nonstandard character set. Sample HTML code looks like this:

```
<meta http-equiv="content-type" content="text/html; charset="ISO-8859-1" />
```

This value is taking on greater significance as the browsers and validators begin to better support the HTML 4 standard, using scripting language and the style-sheet language for the document.

content-language If you are designing a page to be read in a specific language, like British English rather than whatever the browser defaults to, you can use the content-language value. The language must be specified as a "language-dialect" paired value, for example content="en-GB", which signifies that the language to be used is en (English) with the GB (Great Britain) dialect. The complete tag looks like this:

```
<meta http-equiv="content-language" content="en-GB" />
```

window-target The most common use for the window-target value is to stop a document from appearing in a frame. Specifying the following <meta /> tag attribute and value will normally cause the document to appear in a full window rather than being displayed inside a frame:

```
<meta http-equiv="window-target" content="_top" />
```

This value works much like the **name** attribute we have already discussed in relationship to the <form> and <frame> tags. The window-target value works with some browsers but not all of them, and it is not always reliable, so don't depend upon it.

pics-label The **http-equiv** attribute's value of pics-label stands for Platform for Internet Content Selection. This value is a way to specify the type of content for the document or page. Some legislators want to require ratings on all Web pages as a way to get around the Supreme Court's rejection of the Exon amendment, the Digital Decency Act, and other such attempts to censor the Internet as unconstitutional. The initial scheme of pics-label use is flexible and intended for other purposes as well as censorship, but some are concerned that this rating scale might eventually be imposed on Web weavers by an outside agency. As a Web professional, you need to become aware of the ways pics-label values can be used or abused. Then you should educate others about your findings.

More useful and ethical uses for the pics-label values are to manage privacy, intellectual property, and code management. For these uses, pics-label is a useful and functional tool.

refresh The refresh value is one of the most dynamic and exciting tools currently available for the <meta /> tag. It allows the Web weaver to specify when a page should be reloaded from the server ("refreshed"). This is very handy when the contents of a page change at regular intervals. For example, if you have the ultimate "watch me work in my cube" or the greatest "fish tank" page, and the digital camera puts out a new picture every 30 seconds, you can have your Web page refresh each 30 seconds as well. If you code an expires value and a refresh, the user will always get the newest picture.

The refresh value enables Web-potatoes to watch the scene on the screen change without even having to expend the energy to click their mouse to update the page: the ultimate in convenience. It is also helpful if your page is driven from a CGI script that updates data on a regular basis. You can force your page to reload at regular intervals to capture the new, updated information.

Furthermore, refresh allows the skillful Web weaver to mimic *push technologies.* To the users, this reload attribute is invisible. All the users know is that at specific intervals the page refreshes itself with new data. It is really a *pull technology,* since the client is asking the server to refresh the page, but it looks like push. Browsers use pull technology where the browser requests data from the server, "pulling" the data from the source. A push technology is one where the server sends data to the browser, "pushing" it, without the browser requesting it.

Another exciting way this attribute can be used is to display a series of pages without the user having to do anything. This is very handy if you are creating a kiosk or other Web-driven attention-getting display, but it can easily be abused, as we will discuss later.

Figure 12.8 HTML code for first two of four refreshing pages

refrsh1.htm

```
4   <head>
5   <title> A refresh series page 1 </title>
6   <meta http-equiv="refresh"
7   content="3; url=FILE:///C|/evenmoreex/emel2/refrsh2.htm" />
8   <!--This screen will wait for 3 seconds, then refresh with
9    the second screen in the set...-->
10  <meta http-equiv="Content-Style-Type" content="text/css" />
11  </head>
12  <body style="background-color: #FFFFCC;">
13  <h1>First screen in a refresh series</h1>
14  This screen will display for 3 seconds,<br />
15  then it will be replaced by the second screen in the series.<br />
16  The background color will change too, to make it obvious <br />
17  that the screens are changing.
```

After 3 seconds

refrsh2.htm

```
4   <head>
5   <title> A refresh series page 2 </title>
6   <meta http-equiv="refresh"
7   content="5; url=FILE:///C|/evenmoreex/emel2/refrsh3.htm" />
8   <!--This screen will wait for 5 seconds, then refresh with the
9    third screen in the set...-->
10  <meta http-equiv="Content-Style-Type" content="text/css" />
11  </head>
12  <body style="background-color: #CCFF99;">
13  <h1>Second screen in a refresh series</h1>
14  This screen will display for 5 seconds,<br />
15  then it will be replaced by the third screen in the series.<br />
16  The background color will change too, to make it obvious that the<br />
17  screens are changing.
```

You can also use refresh to cycle among a set of pages in one small frame on a page or to reload a table page in which an image changes.

For example, if you have a business selling fruit, you can create a framed Web page with one of the frames or cells containing a set of "refreshing" documents, each of which presents a picture of your orchards at different seasons. Thus, one corner of your Web page will have a pretty, attractive frame of small pictures to attract your customers. Subsequent pages will produce a loop of pages, each pointing to the next in the series. Figure 12.8 shows the code for the first two pages in a series of four integrated pages. The resulting Web pages are found in Figure 12.9. Each page in the series uses the refresh value to prompt the browser to request the next Web page after a preset number of seconds. The fourth page points back to the first page to start the cycle over again.

These pages have a very short refresh, so it is easy to see them work. They are available on the CD that comes with this book and on the Web site for this book. Notice the <meta /> line shown in Figure 12.8. It is the only new code in this page; you have seen the rest many times before. The **http-equiv** is assigned the value of refresh, and the related content value is set equal to

1. The time to wait before the screen is refreshed (3 seconds).

2. The address of the new file to refresh from after that time interval.

Take a closer look at the syntax for the **content** attribute:

content="3; url = http://www.mgh.com/eme/refrsh2.htm"

The time and the URL are both contained within the same set of quotation marks, and the URL is separated from the time by a semicolon. In addition, the URL must always be specified as an absolute path; this element *cannot* use relative path names. Because we can't know where you are putting the files, you will most likely need to modify the path names to make this set of pages work on your machine.

Some search engines will not load pages with a refresh set in this way because this technique can be used to create *spam*. This is especially true for pages with very short refresh rates like these samples. It is good practice to warn your users if you are creating a page that will auto-refresh, as it will put an additional burden on the client machine, and on the Net.

Figure 12.9 How the first two refreshing screens look in the browser

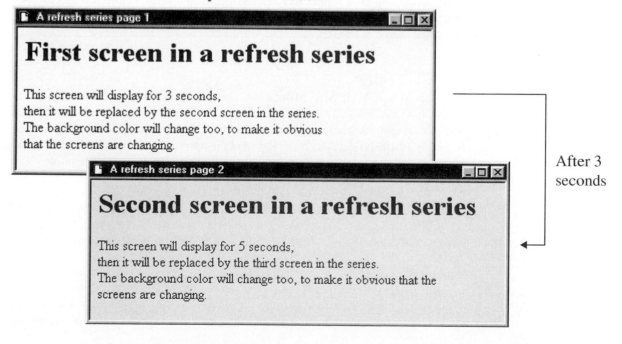

If you make a mistake in coding **refresh**, the results can be very interesting. For example, if you use two sets of quotation marks at the beginning of the **content** attribute's value, the screen will begin to refresh at once, reloading the same page that contains the <meta /> tag with an interval of close to zero. If there are any mistakes in coding the URL, such as using a relative path, some browsers will simply ignore the URL and refresh the *current page* at the interval specified. Other browsers will report that they can't find the page. Correctly coding the value for the **content** is critical, but refresh is well worth the effort, for when it works, it is really a neat effect.

If you use a stopwatch to time the screens, you will see that the refresh values are not exact measures of time. Rather, the intervals specified are guidelines, or "relative" time intervals. A window that refreshes after 10 seconds will change more slowly than one that refreshes after 8 seconds. This is especially true the first time you run the series, if you have to download the pages across the Net. Don't try to create a time-sensitive series with this sort of **refresh**. With timing, as with formatting, you are a bit at the mercy of the browser.

The third screen in the series changes only the URL, the delay time, and the background color. If you go to the Web site for the book and look at this series, or if you code them yourself, you will notice that the delay is getting progressively longer on each screen—3, 5, and then 7 seconds. Like the other screens of the series, the fourth screen in the series has a different duration, color, and URL. This page sends the user back to the first screen to start the whole process over again. It has a short duration of only 3 seconds. This set of four screens is designed to illustrate how pseudo–push technology can be accomplished with the **refresh** value.

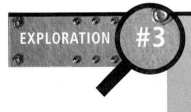

EXPLORATION #3

Copy refrsh1.html, refrsh2.html, refrsh3.html, and refrsh4.html from the CD or the Web site, and place them in your working HTML directory. Then hack the code so that the paths in the four <meta /> tags point to the files on your system. (Hint: One way to get the correct path is to use the browser's File menu Open option to display the Web page. The correct path is played in the Navigation/Address box.) Once you have the four pages working as built, change the refresh rate so that all of them refresh on 10-second intervals. Warning: Have the pages cycle through three complete cycles, then try to stop them. If you are successful, use the Back button, and notice what has happened to your history!

Notification When Web Site Moves Another interesting and user-friendly way to use refresh is to automatically redirect the user to a new URL when a page or Web site moves. For example, the home page at the old URL might say something like the message in Figure 12.10 and then automatically send the user to the new page. Notice that the screen allows the user to go to the new site manually as well. This is a nice, polite, "I'm sorry to inconvenience you" way of telling the users that you have moved your site. The new address is shown so that they can write it down, cut and paste it, or activate it and then bookmark the site. After about 20 seconds, the browser will refresh the screen with the data from the new URL. The first screen the users see at the new location should remind them to bookmark the new site and edit their list of bookmarks to remove the old URL.

You should always give users the option of activating the new URL rather than waiting for your code, and give them enough time to read the screen before you send them off. If the user activates a link within the page, the browser will interrupt the **refresh** timer and load the page from the link the user selected. User input always has precedence

Figure 12.10

Using refresh to redirect users to new site

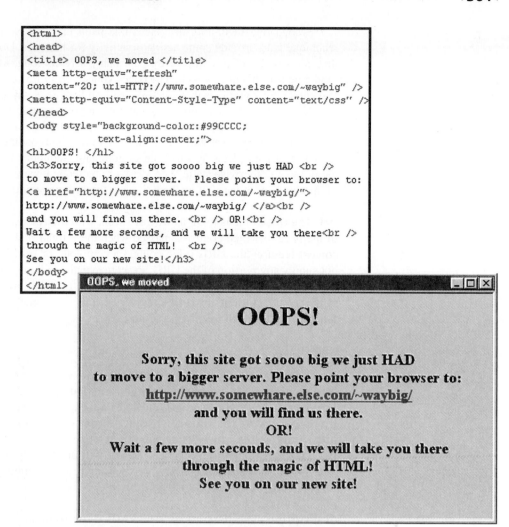

```
<html>
<head>
<title> OOPS, we moved </title>
<meta http-equiv="refresh"
content="20; url=HTTP://www.somewhare.else.com/~waybig" />
<meta http-equiv="Content-Style-Type" content="text/css" />
</head>
<body style="background-color:#99CCCC;
             text-align:center;">
<h1>OOPS! </h1>
<h3>Sorry, this site got soooo big we just HAD <br />
to move to a bigger server.  Please point your browser to:
<a href="http://www.somewhare.else.com/~waybig/">
http://www.somewhare.else.com/~waybig/ </a><br />
and you will find us there. <br /> OR!<br />
Wait a few more seconds, and we will take you there<br />
through the magic of HTML!  <br />
See you on our new site!</h3>
</body>
</html>
```

over automatic refresh. For that reason, you should give your users a link to activate, rather than forcing them to endure the series you have created. The code in the four-screen refreshing loop in our previous example has no such links, so it locks the user into the series. This is an error of design.

Look at the code in Figure 12.10, and notice that in the <meta /> tag, the absolute URL is typed out, and the refresh time is a reasonable one for allowing the user to read the screen. Remember, however, that the older browsers don't recognize this <meta /> tag. Therefore, you should always give your users the option of activating a link to go to the address that refresh will send them to. This is true even if you are simply refreshing the current screen to update the information.

GUIDELINES FOR USING REFRESH

Like all the other neat tools we have discovered, refresh can be abused. That is why some search engines will not collect sites using it. There are a few rules of thumb that should be followed so as not to abuse refresh and thus abuse your user.

First, give the user enough time to read the contents of the screen before you refresh it. As the Web weaver, you probably wrote the page you are refreshing, so you know the content. When you read the page, you are really just skimming it because you already know what it says. You are reading it *much* faster than the average reader will. Give your readers ample time to read the wonderful content you have provided before you send them to a new page.

Second rule of thumb: use pages that paint up quickly. The whole purpose of this technique is to provide some action or activity for the user. Don't have pages in your set that contain lots of graphics or that are many screens long, as that will violate the first guideline and this one as well. The pages you set up in this sort of series should be small and contain few graphics that are also small, so the pages will paint up quickly.

Third rule of thumb: provide a way for your user to stop the series. As was noted earlier, the browser will always take user input over a refresh. If the user activates any link in the page, the browser will follow the link rather than loading the new page or reloading the existing page. Usually this type of automatic sequence is used to provide some dynamics to an otherwise static Web kiosk or unattended browser. Give the users a way out of the series, or at least allow them to go to the new page without waiting.

url The URL value is used, as we have seen, with the **refresh** value. It specifies the URL of the page to which control is passed when the refresh time expires. The syntax for this context requires the URL value contain a complete, or *absolute,* path. The browser will not supply any portion of the URL, so *relative* paths will not work. The URL itself should be enclosed in quotation marks and be separated from the time value by a semicolon. The syntax of the **content** for **refresh** is very critical; any mistake may cause the refresh to fail, possibly refreshing only the current screen.

name

The **name** attribute is used for data that do not correspond to the standard http header tags. In other words, you will use **name** when you specify data that are not recognized by **http-equiv.** You can declare additional data for use by your own software using the different values of the **name** attribute. Some of the **name** values will move into **http-equiv** as the browsers become more sophisticated. For example, the **keywords** value is almost universally recognized and will most likely move into **http-equiv** in the near future. We will look at **keywords** in more detail shortly. Here is a partial list of <meta /> tags you can code using the "name=" format.

description The **description** value will allow some search engines to capture a description of your page. Normally the search engine takes the first few lines from the page content as the description, but if you have a framed document, or one with extensive formatting, those lines may not tell what your page is about. You can code the following to give the search engines a better idea of the content of your site:

```
<meta name="description" content="A collection of great . . . " />
```

Always make sure that your description is accurate and brief.

keywords Just as the **description** content value helps the search engines display the true content of your site, so the **keywords** value allows the index-based search engines to have a better idea of the topics available on your site. Usually the index-based search engines take the keywords from the title of the document. Using this <meta /> tag attribute value of **name="keywords"** will give those search engines a better set of words for referencing the content of your site. Code the tag like this:

```
<meta name="keywords" content="Unix, Ferengi, HTML" />
```

Notice that the **content** is a list of keywords separated by commas and enclosed in quotation marks. The **keywords** value is important if you want the index-based search engines to accurately represent the content of your site. Some of the validators even recommend including it. As the number of pages on the Net increases, it becomes more and more important to the wise Web weaver to help search engines find their pages.

author The **content** of the **author** value should be self-explanatory, but just in case it is not, here's the definition: **author** is the name of that wonderful individual who wove the

Table 12.1 Elements in Dublin Core set

Title	Resource Type	Author
Format	Keywords	Resource identifier
Description	Source	Publisher
Language	Other contributor	Relation
Coverage	Date	Rights management

page. This is a nice feature to include, as long as you are proud of the work you have done. One of Tim T's Web pages could contain the following <meta /> tag:

```
<meta name="author" content="Timothy N. Trainor" />
```

OTHER COMMON NAME VALUES

Many other values exist for the **name** attribute, most of them specific to a particular application or browser. New values will be incorporated into the standard, and the <meta /> tag will take on additional importance in future versions of the HTML standard. Table 12.1 lists the current 15 elements in the Dublin Core set. The contents associated with most of these are pretty self-evident. They are used to provide additional information to the browser or other user-agent that reads the page.

scheme

The **scheme** attribute allows the Web weaver to provide browsers with additional information about the context of the data. The following two examples are discussed in the HTML 4 specifications:

```
<meta name="date" scheme="Mo-Day-Year" content="06/05/05" />
```

and

```
<meta name="identifier" scheme="ISBN" content="024772-2" />
```

In the first case, the **scheme** explains that the date is June 5th, not May 6th, as some Europeans may interpret the date, because they traditionally use a day-month-year format. In the second example, the **scheme** indicates that the identifier is actually the ISBN number. The **scheme** attribute is a valuable addition to the HTML 4 specifications.

▶▶ MULTICOLUMN PAGES

If you want your page to look like a magazine or newspaper, you will need to construct multicolumn pages. Currently there is no HTML code designed specifically to create the multicolumn layout, but as we have seen over and over, a creative Web weaver can use an existing container to perform tasks other than that for which it was specifically designed.

We will use a table to create our multicolumn page. Figure 12.11 shows the code, and how it looks in the browser. Although the figure looks like a simple columnar text, the source code shows what was done to force the text into this format. HTML code works differently than a word processor, which simply creates columns and then flows the text into them. In HTML code, the text needs to be manually placed into the columns. If one of the columns contains more text than the other, the results look most strange, as we can see in Figure 12.12.

The text in the left column in Figure 12.12 seems to float, somewhat suspended, whereas text fills the right column. If you are going to present text using this technique, it

Figure 12.11 Creating multicolumn page using tables

```
<html>
<head>
<title> Showing off a three column page </title>
</head>
<body>
<table border="0" cellspacing="10" width="99%">
<tr>
<td width="48%"> This is the text that will appear
in the first column of the table.  You could use this
format to display text that looks like a newspaper or
magazine layout.  It is interesting to note that the
data in this column appears without borders, as it
should, because the Web weaver set the <b>border</b>
attribute to zero which did away with the borders.
</td>
<td> <br /><br /></td> <!-- This gives a blank column -->
<td width="48%">This is the second column.  You could
control the width of the different columns by setting
the <b>width</b> attribute. In this instance, the width of
the two columns is set to 48%, that means that
the middle column has all of 4% left.  The middle column
contains a pair of line breaks, &lt;br&gt; and that is all.
The line breaks are necessary to hold space.
</td>
</tr>
</table>
</body>
</html>
```

Left column

Center (blank) column

Right column

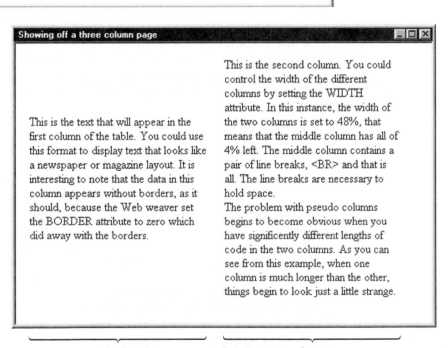

Showing off a three column page

This is the text that will appear in the first column of the table. You could use this format to display text that looks like a newspaper or magazine layout. It is interesting to note that the data in this column appears without borders, as it should, because the Web weaver set the **border** attribute to zero which did away with the borders.

This is the second column. You could control the width of the different columns by setting the **width** attribute. In this instance, the width of the two columns is set to 48%, that means that the middle column has all of 4% left. The middle column contains a pair of line breaks, <br> and that is all. The line breaks are necessary to hold space.

Figure 12.12

Multicolumn pages with unequal amounts of text

Showing off a three column page

This is the text that will appear in the first column of the table. You could use this format to display text that looks like a newspaper or magazine layout. It is interesting to note that the data in this column appears without borders, as it should, because the Web weaver set the BORDER attribute to zero which did away with the borders.

This is the second column. You could control the width of the different columns by setting the WIDTH attribute. In this instance, the width of the two columns is set to 48%, that means that the middle column has all of 4% left. The middle column contains a pair of line breaks, <BR> and that is all. The line breaks are necessary to hold space.

The problem with pseudo columns begins to become obvious when you have significantly different lengths of code in the two columns. As you can see from this example, when one column is much longer than the other, things begin to look just a little strange.

Notice how unequal amounts of text
result in unbalanced column length

is best done after all the text has been written, so you can balance the two columns, keeping approximately the same number of lines in each. Obviously, the task becomes more difficult as the number of columns grows. This technique is valuable, but it is somewhat more difficult to apply than other text presentations.

▸▸ HEADLINES

By using the **colspan** attribute and changing the font, you can create headline-like text. Figure 12.13 provides an example. Several tags were used here. Notice that we added a new row of code to handle the headline, and we forced alignment, increased the font size, and bolded the text. The result looks like a headline, and that is what we were shooting for.

Figure 12.13   Using <table> element and **colspan** attribute to create a headline look

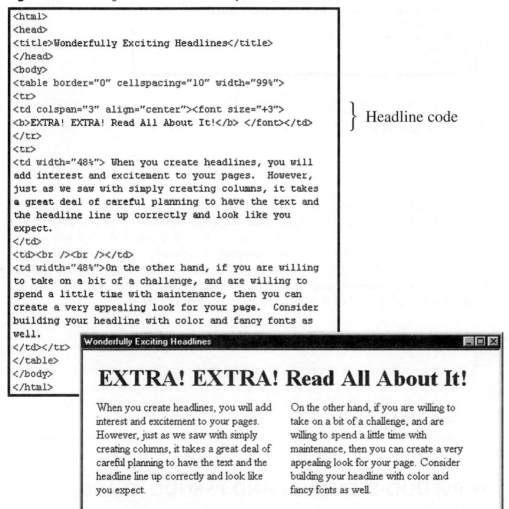

```
<html>
<head>
<title>Wonderfully Exciting Headlines</title>
</head>
<body>
<table border="0" cellspacing="10" width="99%">
<tr>
<td colspan="3" align="center"><font size="+3">
<b>EXTRA! EXTRA! Read All About It!</b> </font></td>
</tr>
<tr>
<td width="48%"> When you create headlines, you will
add interest and excitement to your pages.  However,
just as we saw with simply creating columns, it takes
a great deal of careful planning to have the text and
the headline line up correctly and look like you
expect.
</td>
<td><br /><br /></td>
<td width="48%">On the other hand, if you are willing
to take on a bit of a challenge, and are willing to
spend a little time with maintenance, then you can
create a very appealing look for your page.  Consider
building your headline with color and fancy fonts as
well.
</td></tr>
</table>
</body>
</html>
```

} Headline code

Wonderfully Exciting Headlines

EXTRA! EXTRA! Read All About It!

When you create headlines, you will add interest and excitement to your pages. However, just as we saw with simply creating columns, it takes a great deal of careful planning to have the text and the headline line up correctly and look like you expect.

On the other hand, if you are willing to take on a bit of a challenge, and are willing to spend a little time with maintenance, then you can create a very appealing look for your page. Consider building your headline with color and fancy fonts as well.

If you find your code causes you to use a lot of tags, like the code in Figure 12.13, you might consider better utilizing the HTML you know, especially style sheets. The code shown in Figure 12.14 will produce the same output as the code for the headline in Figure 12.13, but with fewer tags and better compliance with the new specifications.

Figure 12.14

More "state of the art" code for headlines

```
 5  <title>Wonderfully Exciting Headlines</title>
 6  <style type="text/css">
 7  .headline {
 8          text-align:center;
 9          font-size:24pt;
10          font-weight:700;
11          }
12  </style>
13  </head>
14  <body>
15  <table border="0" cellspacing="10" width="99%">
16  <tr>
17  <td colspan="3" class="headline">
18  EXTRA! EXTRA! Read All About It!</td>
19  </tr>
20  <tr>
21  <td width="48%"> When you create headlines, you will
22  add interest and excitement to your pages.  However,
23  just as we saw with simply creating columns, it takes
24  a great deal of careful planning to have the text and
25  the headline line up correctly and look like you
26  expect.
27  </td>
```

Using styles rather than inline code for headlines

▸▸ SIDEBARS

Sometimes it is handy to have a *sidebar,* or side head, to set the heading off from the rest of the text of the document. Figure 12.15 shows what sidebars look like and how to code them.

Sidebars take up a lot of screen real estate, but they make a nice visual division of the page. In addition, they can help your user find things more easily on your page. While they are not a good idea for long pages, because you need to put all the text into a table, they are excellent for smaller pages where the content is divided into specific thoughts.

As you can see, the sidebar here takes up 10 percent of the width of the screen. That is a significant amount of space in a long document. This technique is best used for shorter pages, and only when it is needed to draw the reader's attention.

EXPLORATION #4

Code a sample page called cars.html that demonstrates how sidebars, columns, and a headline can add excitement to a page. Use the data on the carfacts.txt page on the CD or the Web page. Be sure to use color, and use only styles to control the formatting.

▸▸ PSEUDO-ELEMENTS AND PSEUDO-CLASS

In the original specifications, the experts at the W^{3}C tied all of the tools for style sheets to specific structures of a document. Thus, certain styles could be associated with headings, even different styles for different headings. That was a wonderful invention as far as it went. However, in practice the designers found that there were elements of a document that were not addressed by the existing structural design elements. For example, there was no element that referred to the first line of a paragraph or the first letter of a word. In the second set of style-sheet specifications, CSS2, the Web designers of the W^{3}C addressed these needs by creating pseudo-elements and pseudo-classes.

Figure 12.15 Creating and using sidebars

First sidebar ⟶

Second
sidebar ⟶

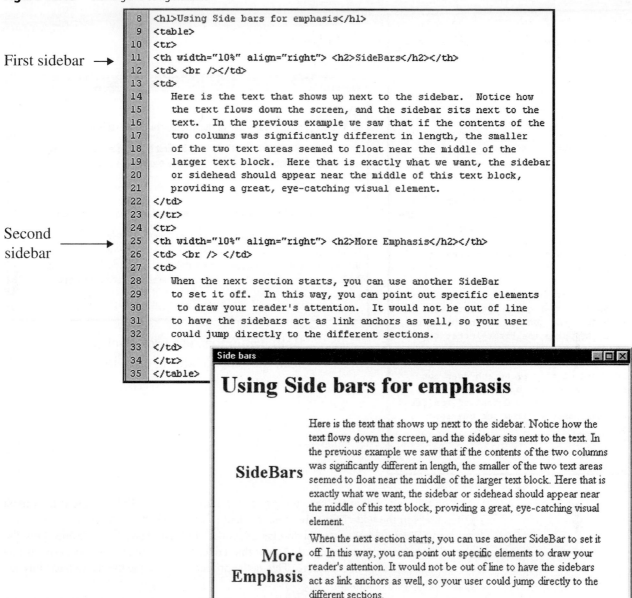

```
 8  <h1>Using Side bars for emphasis</h1>
 9  <table>
10  <tr>
11  <th width="10%" align="right"> <h2>SideBars</h2></th>
12  <td> <br /></td>
13  <td>
14    Here is the text that shows up next to the sidebar.  Notice how
15    the text flows down the screen, and the sidebar sits next to the
16    text.  In the previous example we saw that if the contents of the
17    two columns was significantly different in length, the smaller
18    of the two text areas seemed to float near the middle of the
19    larger text block.  Here that is exactly what we want, the sidebar
20    or sidehead should appear near the middle of this text block,
21    providing a great, eye-catching visual element.
22  </td>
23  </tr>
24  <tr>
25  <th width="10%" align="right"> <h2>More Emphasis</h2></th>
26  <td> <br /> </td>
27  <td>
28    When the next section starts, you can use another SideBar
29    to set it off.  In this way, you can point out specific elements
30     to draw your reader's attention.  It would not be out of line
31    to have the sidebars act as link anchors as well, so your user
32    could jump directly to the different sections.
33  </td>
34  </tr>
35  </table>
```

Using Side bars for emphasis

SideBars Here is the text that shows up next to the sidebar. Notice how the text flows down the screen, and the sidebar sits next to the text. In the previous example we saw that if the contents of the two columns was significantly different in length, the smaller of the two text areas seemed to float near the middle of the larger text block. Here that is exactly what we want, the sidebar or sidehead should appear near the middle of this text block, providing a great, eye-catching visual element.

More Emphasis When the next section starts, you can use another SideBar to set it off. In this way, you can point out specific elements to draw your reader's attention. It would not be out of line to have the sidebars act as link anchors as well, so your user could jump directly to the different sections.

A *pseudo-element* allows style sheets, both document-level and external, to address aspects beyond those specified by the document's basic design. Some of the currently defined pseudo-elements include :first-line, :first-letter, :before, and :after. Pseudo-elements must be associated with a subject tag. Figure 12.16 shows how they can be used. As I am sure you have come to expect, all the browsers don't support these pseudo-elements the same way, and at the time of this writing, Internet Explorer doesn't recognize the :before pseudo-element at all.

A *pseudo-class* is similar to a pseudo-element in that it allows designers to address Web page characteristics other than their name, attributes, or content. Pseudo-classes may be static, like :first-child, or they may be dynamic like :hover, :active, and :focus. Pseudo-classes can be used anywhere and need not be associated with a particular element. Some pseudo-classes are quite complex. We will stick to some of the more straightforward and generally well-supported pseudo-classes.

Figure 12.16 Examples of pseudo-elements

```
<html>
<head>
<title>Playing with pseudo-classes</title>
<style type="text/css">
p {font-size: 12pt;
    }
p:first-letter {font-size: 36pt;
                font-style: italic;
                }
p.special:before {content: "Wowsers!;"}
p.special:first-letter {color: #33CCFF;}
</style>
</head>
<body>
<p>Notice how the first letter of
this paragraph has a different appearance
than the rest of the text.  The first
letter of a paragraph was not uniquely
identifiable before the existence of
this pseudo-element.
</p>
<p class="special"> This paragraph uses
the &quot;special&quot; class to add
text before the content of the paragraph,
as well as using the first-letter to add
color to the first letter of the addition.
Please look at the browser rendering, the
first word of this paragraph does not
appear here in this paragraph.
Notice how the size and font of the first
character cascades from the previous
style.
</p>
</body>
</html>
```

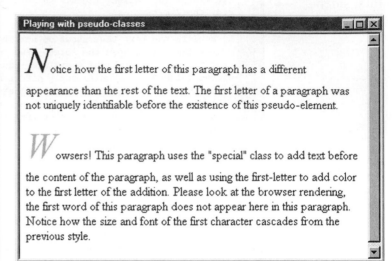

Both paragraphs use pseudo-classes, with the second adding style info to the first

You will notice that the screen capture in Figure 12.17 is a little different than most of the others in the text. That is because we had to show you three different states of the browser to illustrate how the pseudo-classes work. The first class, :link, defines how the links in the page will be formatted. As per that code, links are blue and sans serif, just as you see in the first browser capture. This is the proper way to code the deprecated **link** attribute on the body element.

The second browser capture shows what happens when the user puts her mouse over the link but hasn't yet activated it. This is the :hover pseudo-class. In truth, this feature is the one that caused us to explore pseudo-classes in the first place. It is quite elegant and powerful, and one we encourage you to use. It allows you to control how the text is formatted when users let their screen pointer linger over it—for example, the background color, font weight, color, and so forth. All of the current popular browsers support both :link and :hover.

It is interesting that the spelling of one of the hot words used for the link changes when it is in :hover mode. Can you figure out why? Right—because the browser has assigned the space needed for Look Closely, and when the :hover pseudo-class changes the size and weight of the font, there is insufficient space to display all of the larger characters. Therefore, the browser chooses to preserve the rest of the surrounding text and cuts off the ly in Closely.

The third screen capture works only in the Opera browser at this time. Navigator seems to ignore it, and Explorer applies the pseudo-class after the user has clicked on the link. The color and font of the link text change when the user activates the link. This is

Figure 12.17 Examples of pseudo-classes

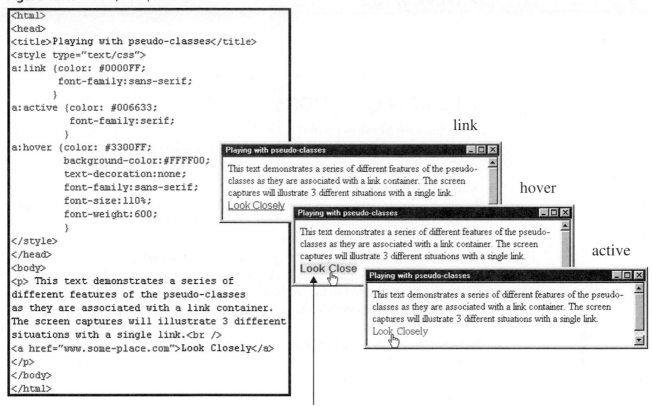

Spelling appears
to have changed

the stylish way to set the **alink** attribute. We used :link and :active as examples, but we don't encourage you to alter the default colors of a link. But we do encourage you to use the extremely useful :hover pseudo-class.

Please load the figure into your browser and experiment with it. These pseudo-classes are so helpful, and the two-color format of this text does not do the page justice. The potential for other pseudo-elements and pseudo-classes is staggering. Now that you have all of these great techniques in your repertoire, it is time to put them to use.

EXPLORATION #5 Modify the **cars.html** file you created in Exploration 4 to use the hover pseudo-class with each of the car names used as the sidebar. Change the background color to black and the text color to white when the screen pointer hovers over the car name.

►► KEY TERMS

Calling document   Push technology
Pseudo-class   Search script
Pseudo-element   Searchable document
Pull technology

▸▸ NEW TAGS

<base />
<meta />

▸▸ REVIEW QUESTIONS

1. Define each of the key terms.
2. How is each of the tags discussed in this chapter used? (Provide examples.)
3. List the three ways you can obtain a CGI script.
4. What is the security concern associated with searchable documents?
5. When using searchable documents, why should the page showing the results also contain navigation buttons back to the calling document?
6. When would you use the <base /> tag?
7. What type of information is identified by a <meta /> tag?
8. How could you use the <meta /> element's **http-equiv** attribute to redirect users when your Web site has moved to a new URL?
9. What are the authors' guidelines for using <meta /> elements to refresh a screen?
10. How can <meta /> tags be used to help register your Web page with a search site?
11. How can you create a multicolumn page layout?
12. How do pseudo-elements differ from standard elements?
13. What does the pseudo-class :hover control?

▸▸ EXERCISES

12.1. Ruby would like to see a different "look and feel" for a new page describing the adventures of her sister. Please take the text in **eme12-raw.htm** and format it according to the following instructions, saving the page as **eme12-adv.htm**. Each paragraph should be one column of a three-column page. Ruby would like the page to have a headline of "The Adventures of Emmy" and a sidebar of "All New." She would like you to use an external style sheet to format the page. Call the external sheet **eme12.css.** Please build the page with the following characteristics:

1. Level-1 headings should be sans serif, centered, and hot pink, #CC0066.
2. The background color should be light gray, #CCCCCC.
3. The text should be cherry red, #990033.
4. Headlines and sidebars should be brick red, #993300, sans serif, and in a font weight of 800. Headlines should be centered and 22 points. Sidebars should be 16 points. These values should be set using classes "headline" and "sidebar" from the external style sheet.
5. Each column should start with a single letter that is deep red, #660000, sans serif, and 16 points. You should use a pseudo-element—in the style sheet, of course—to achieve this effect.
6. At the bottom of the page, you should have a link back to your home page. The link should change to have a background color of light cream, #FFFFCC, and a text color of deep purple, #9900CC, when the user moves his mouse over it. Use a pseudo-class for this effect.

12.2. Build a framed document with three sections as shown in Figure 12.18. In the top left frame (Frame 1), use a set of three HTML documents that each display one image or graphic from a series of three. Your name and the assignment due date must be included as comment lines within each document. The document that appears in Frame 1 should contain a <meta /> tag with a **refresh** attribute that waits 5 seconds and then has the browser display the next page in the sequence. The last page should reference the first page.

Figure 12.18

Used for Exercise 12.2

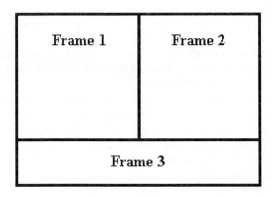

Frame 2 contains text that describes the images or graphics in Frame 1. Frame 3 should contain your name, email address, the page's creation date, and any other information you would like to include in a page footer.

12.3. Build the same integrated Web pages as you did in Exercise 12.2, but use tables instead of frames as shown in Figure 12.19.

Figure 12.19

Used for Exercise 12.3

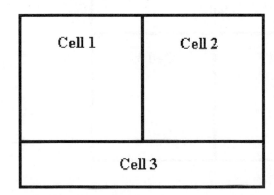

12.4. Your Homework home page is going to move to a different Web site. In preparation for this move, create a new HTML document that supersedes the home page. Change the filename for the current home page to **index2.htm** or **index2.html**. Create a new HTML document, and save it using the old home-page filename, most likely **index.htm** or **index.html**. The title bar should say *your name's* Personal Homepage is Moving. Add your name and the assignment due date to comment lines within the HTML document. The page should contain the following:

a. Your name.

b. Date the move will take place.

c. Link to **index2.htm** or **index2.html**.

d. Footer with date the page was created.

12.5. Modify the school home page you have been working on as a part of these end-of-chapter exercises to incorporate the :hover pseudo-class for all occurrences of the school's name. When the screen pointer hovers over the school name, the background color should change to one of the school's colors.

For example, if your school's colors are blue and gold, have the background color change to gold. Also, use the pseudo-elements to create an initial-cap format for all paragraphs on the home page. Your initial cap should be italic and at least twice as large as the normal text. Make sure your name and the assignment due date are included in comment lines within the HTML document.

12.6. Modify your movies home page to include a form with a list box of six of your favorite movies, and send the user's selection to **either.pl** on your own machine, or on your school's server (**either.pl** is found on the CD that comes with this book). Include Adventures of *your name* as one of the movie titles. Select the option with your name, and send the data via the post method. Print the confirmation Web page.

12.7. Create three HTML documents, each containing a table of the same size. The tables should have two columns in one row and another row that spans the two columns as shown in Figure 12.20. The bottom right cell (cell 3) of each page should display a different image or graphic from a series of three. All the title bars should display Another Application for the META Tag. Your name and the assignment due date must be included as comment lines within each document. Each document should contain a <meta /> tag with a refresh value that waits 2 seconds and then has the browser display the next page in the sequence. The last page should reference the first page. Cells 1 and 2 are the same in all three documents. Cell 2 contains text that describes the images or graphics in cell 3. Cell 1 contains a brief title that corresponds with the table's contents.

Figure 12.20

Used for Exercise 12.7

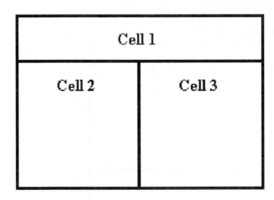

12.8. Create a Web page to present a two-column online newsletter. The HTML document should include comments containing your name and the assignment due date. Use a table that contains no borders and 10-pixel cell spacing. If you are not feeling creative, you can use the *Traveler's Newsletter* we developed in Chapter Eight.

13

Chapter Thirteen

JavaScript Programs for Your Pages

In this chapter, we overview the JavaScript language and related syntax; but it would take another book like this to explain everything you need to know to become a JavaScript programmer. Be aware that although this chapter focuses on the scripting language of JavaScript, you can substitute any other scripting language, like Tcl, Visual Basic, or the like, in using the principles explained here.

CHAPTER OBJECTIVES

After reading and studying this chapter you should be able to do the following:

- Explain the difference between Java and JavaScript.
- Use the <script></script> container to identify a simple JavaScript.
- Program and execute a simple JavaScript.
- Create examples of the three basic programming structures.
- Explain why JavaScript is considered an object-oriented language.
- Use the Document, Window, and Navigator JavaScript objects in program code.
- Determine how different browsers handle JavaScript.
- Explain why eye candy isn't a good tool for Web weavers.

►► WHAT IS JAVASCRIPT?

JavaScript was added to Netscape way back in 1995. It is an example of ancient technology that is still useful today. Actually, JavaScript started life as an addition to Navigator 2.0. Back in those days, it was called LiveScript, as it was part of the Netscape LiveWire server product. It was initially designed as a scripting language used to write queries to the server and handle the daily administration tasks of server management. When the folks at Netscape Communications Corporation, now part of America Online/Time Warner (AOL), started a collaboration with the developers of the computer programming language Java at Sun Microsystems, they renamed the product JavaScript. Browsers starting with Navigator 2.0 and Internet Explorer 3.0 support it. Today JavaScript is recognized as a powerful programming tool that can enhance your Web pages in wonderful ways.

►► MISCONCEPTIONS ABOUT JAVASCRIPT

Before we look at JavaScript and how it is used in your pages, there are a couple of serious misunderstandings that we need to dispel. So let's do that right off the bat.

JAVASCRIPT IS NOT JAVA "LITE"

JavaScript is *not* Java, and it is not related to Java. It did not evolve from Java or into Java. It is a *scripting language,* which is a somewhat simplified programming language that provides only some of the features of a full-blown programming language like COBOL (or Java!). For example, JavaScript cannot read from files on the hard drive, write files to the hard drive, create temporary files, or perform other file-related activities.

JavaScript has no stand-alone output functions; it uses only the output features of the browser. Short, single-purpose programs, especially those written in the Unix environment, are often called *scripts.* JavaScripts, in keeping with the "script" portion of the name, are usually short and are designed to perform a specific task.

Java had already made an impact on the Net when JavaScript was developed. Some say it is unfortunate that the Netscape folks decided to use the Java moniker. JavaScript does look something like Java . . . if you don't look too closely, that is.

JAVASCRIPT IS NOT A WIMPY LITTLE PSEUDO-LANGUAGE

While JavaScript may not have the incredible programming power of Java, it is not a "wimpy li'l thang" (in Texas parlance), either. It is a very useful language that will enable you to build and maintain sophisticated code that adds functionality and *verve* to your pages. Some of the applications of JavaScript are quite powerful; and, as is true with most programming languages, the limitations of what you can create are mostly the limitations of your own imagination, not of the language.

There are many sophisticated applications for JavaScript already in use across the Net, and many more are being developed. JavaScript will enable you to create Web applications that are dynamic. Actually, the term *DHTML,* or *Dynamic HTML,* is mostly a reference to JavaScript-enhanced HTML pages. It will enable you to build powerful, client-based applications. However, there are a few things that JavaScript can't do for you. Let's look at them next.

WHAT JAVASCRIPT CAN'T DO

There are four major areas where JavaScript lacks ability; all are related to either personal computer security concerns or the browser environment. First, JavaScript doesn't have any graphical abilities. Second, it can't read or write files on the client machine—the computer running the JavaScript. This is a very serious security matter. To maintain personal computer security, you wouldn't want a strange piece of software to be able to read from or write to your hard disk. There is a small exception here, in the area of *cookies.*

Although JavaScript itself cannot read to or write from any drive on your computer, it may request that the browser write a small file, called a *cookie,* into permanent storage. We will learn about cookies in Chapter Fourteen. Those data are written by your browser at the bequest of the JavaScript, not actually by the JavaScript code, so you can choose *not* to allow the cookie to be created.

The third area in which JavaScript lacks power is networking. JavaScript supports networking only as it is involved in downloading the contents of specified HTML pages from URLs. The fourth area of lack is that no ***multithreading*** capabilities are built into JavaScript, meaning the CPU cannot be shared among multiple JavaScript tasks, or threads.

While we are talking about things that JavaScript cannot do, we need to address the subject of *JScript,* Microsoft's version of JavaScript. It seems that JScript is Microsoft's attempted implementation of a JavaScript-like scripting language. It supports most of the major features of JavaScript, plus some enhancements that can be used only by the Microsoft Internet Explorer. What that means to us is that whereas JavaScript is understood by all the major browsers, JScript is understood, in it entirety, only by Internet Explorer. Therefore, as we want to be as browser-neutral as possible, we will not explore the special features of JScript in this text.

WHAT JAVASCRIPT CAN DO

JavaScript is an object-oriented language designed to interface with HTML. It recognizes objects like document, browser, and date that make our job of page design easier and a lot more fun! Here are some of the more common things you can find JavaScripts doing on progressive Web pages:·

- **Control browser features**—Using JavaScript the author can control various features and elements of the browser. Some of the more common controls are to display simple messages, open new windows, and even generate HTML code on the fly.

- **Modify document appearance**—JavaScript allows the author to set up controls on the page that enable the user to change the appearance of the page. For example, the background color and text color can be altered.

- **Modify document content**—JavaScript allows the author to create code that runs only on the client, changing the page content on the fly. Before JavaScript came along, using CGI scripts on the server was your only way to generate dynamic content.

- **Store and use information about user**—One of the more controversial uses for JavaScript is the creation and use of *cookies.* These small data elements are actually stored by the browser and then read by JavaScript. They allow the author to keep track of information about users.

- **Interact with applets**—Java applets can extend the functions of your pages. JavaScript can control aspects of a Java applet, even deciding whether to run it or not. As you learned in Chapter Nine, an *applet* is a small Java program, whereas a *script* is a program written in a scripting language like JavaScript.

- **Manipulate images**—JavaScript can allow the user to select one from a set of images on the page. In addition, using the concept of *rollover,* a JavaScript can change images on the page, using intrinsic events like **onmouseover** or **onmouseout** as the user moves his screen pointer around.

- **React to state of browser and client system**—JavaScript enables the author to create pages specifically tailored to the browser and user accessing that page. It can pick up local information and respond to those data by creating additional content or modifying the content of the page.

As you can see, JavaScript provides the Web weaver with a wide assortment of tools to help present information to users. However, this isn't a book about writing JavaScript, only one chapter. Thus, we will present a couple of JavaScript examples to examine and write only one simple JavaScript program from scratch. Our focus is not on teaching you JavaScript, but rather on showing you how to incorporate it into your HTML pages.

Figure 13.1 The "Hello World" function, both code and execution

```
<html>
<head>
<meta http-equiv="Content-Style-Type" content="text/css" />
<style type="text/css">
.wow { font-size:24pt;
       font-style:italic;
       text-align:center;
     }
</style>
<script type="text/javascript">
// <!-- Protection from older browsers it's not really necessary
// This function will display the famous phrase "Hello World"
//
function Hello() {
var OutputString = "<p class='wow'>Hello World </p>"
document.writeln(OutputString)
              }
// -->
</script>
<title>My First Function</title>
</head>
<body style="background-color: #FFFFCC">
<h1>The Output from the Hello() function</h1>
<script type="text/javascript">
Hello()                                          ———— This is the function call
</script>
<p>That&#039;s all she wrote, folks<br />
Wowsers, wasn't that exciting!
</p>
</body>
</html>
```

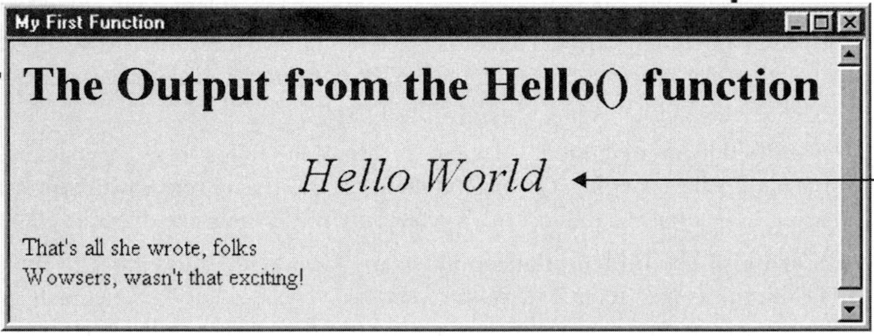

My First Function

The Output from the Hello() function

Hello World ←———— This is the output

That's all she wrote, folks
Wowsers, wasn't that exciting!

▸▸ INTRODUCING JAVASCRIPT

Before we get into actually writing JavaScript, we need to look at a few programming concepts. Figure 13.1 shows a simple JavaScript function that puts the phrase "Hello World" on the screen. A *function* is small piece of code that performs a single well-defined task that can accept a value to be processed. While this isn't exactly computing the trajectory to the moon, the "Hello World" function will serve as a good introduction to JavaScript.

Compare the screen capture with the code in Figure 13.1. Notice that the function itself is coded within a <script></script> container placed inside the <head></head> container. The function shown in this example writes the infamous words "Hello World" on the screen.

We write functions for two reasons:

1. They allow us to reuse the same code more than once in the same page.

2. They allow us to move the code from page to page easily.

Let's look at how we built the script. The first new feature is the <script> container.

 **<script>Script(s)</script>**

Description: encloses the actual elements of the scripting language—JavaScript, Vbscript, etc.
Type: container.
Attributes: charset, **defer, language, src, type**.
Special note: often includes commands that generate HTML code as well as JavaScript.

The <script></script> container encloses all the JavaScript (or other scripting language) code within an HTML page. Any scripting code must be enclosed within this container, or the browser won't be able to recognize it as a script and will most often simply display it as text.

src

The **src** attribute can be used to specify the URL of an external script in the same way you insert images into your document. If you want to use a function or script from an external file, you need to specify the URL of the JavaScript file as the argument to the **src.** The external Javascript file must use a .js filename extension, as shown in the following code:

```
<script src="neatscript.js" >
```

This source file should contain only JavaScript, no native HTML code.

Using **src** is a nice way to standardize a set of functions across several pages and keep the updating maintenance task to a minimum. For example, if all the pages in a site need to use the same function, linking each page to the function with the **src** attribute will allow all of them to use the same code. Moreover, the Web administrator can make a change in one place (the script file), and that change will be reflected across all the pages at once.

If you don't use an external function, each page will have to have a copy of the function, and the Web administrator will need to change the code in each HTML document. Having to maintain the same code on many pages is a cumbersome and error-prone task.

type

Unless coded in a <meta> tag, the **type** attribute should always be used with <script></script> container. It specifies the scripting language used for the particular script. Some of the possible values are "text/javascript", "text/tcl", and "text/vbscript". The HTML code would look like this:

```
<script type="text/javascript">
      some great JavaScript commands
</script>
```

If you don't code a **type** attribute value, the browser may pick a default value for your scripts. Currently JavaScript is the default used by the popular browsers, but it is much better to explicitly code the value so there will be no mistake. The W³C is very clear on this point. It explains that this attribute must be coded, and that you should not expect a default value for it. Even if a browser currently defaults to a specific language, there is no guarantee that it will continue to do so in the future. By coding a **type** attribute for each <script> element, your code will work even if the browser creators decide to use a different default.

<meta />

You can also use a <meta /> tag to set the default for the whole page. Two examples of the format are as follows:

```
<meta http-equiv="Content-Script-Type" content="text/javascript" />
<meta http-equiv="Content-Script-Type" content="text/tcl" />
```

Using one of these <meta /> tags in the <head></head> container will set the default scripting language for the whole page. If you code the **type** attribute in a <script> element, it will override the value set in the <meta> tag.

defer

The **defer** attribute tells the browser whether the code in the script is necessary to build the page. The value set for defer is a toggle. If defer="true", then the browser doesn't have to wait for the execution of the script as it builds the page.

language

In previous versions of HTML, the **language** attribute was used to identify the script's language to the browser—for example, "vbscript" or "JavaScript". In the HTML 4 specifications, the W^{3}C has deprecated this attribute in favor of the **type** attribute. However, wise Web weavers will code both.

Now that we know about the <script> element, let's take a closer look at the script coded in Figure 13.1. The first collection of three lines constitutes the *comments*. Comments start with a double right slash (//). Here are the first three comment lines:

```
// <!- - Protection from older browsers
// This function will display the famous phrase "Hello World"
//
```

The first line of the comments also shows a second type of comment code with which you are already very familiar. It is the HTML comment you have come to know, love, and use(!). Some programmers think there is a need to hide scripts from older browsers that don't understand JavaScript, just as you hid the document-level style sheets. Other programmers don't think there will be that many folks running version 3 and earlier of the browsers. We will protect some scripts and not others so you can see that both ways work. The second comment line explains what the function does.

▶▶ THE HELLO() FUNCTION

The next section of the code is the actual "Hello World" function taken from Figure 13.1. It displays the famous phrase "Hello World." The reason "Hello World" is famous is that many wise programming instructors require their noble students to build their first program to display those words. This tradition has a long and honorable history. It started with a paper called "The Programming Language B," written in 1973 by Johnson and Kernighan. (The B language was the precursor to the C programming language, still in use today.) In this paper, which was formatted partly as a technical report by Johnson and partly as a tutorial by Kernighan, the first instance of a "Hello World" program was presented. And you thought history was boring!

```
function Hello() {
var OutputString = "<p class='wow'>Hello World </p>"
document.writeln(OutputString)
            }
```

Note that the first line tells the browser that what follows is a function. It also gives the function a name and tells the browser that there are no *parameters* for the function. A parameter is a value passed to the function. The function then uses the parameters to perform some action. For example, if we built a function that adds two numbers and outputs the total, we could pass two numbers as parameters. The code would look like this: function sum(num1, num2), in which num1 and num2 are the parameters to the function sum.

In the "Hello World" function shown in Figure 13.1, the open curly brace following the parentheses marks the actual beginning of the function code. This looks a lot like setting up a document-wide style sheet.

The next line creates the variable name OutputString and stores the text string with the HTML code to display "Hello World" at the memory location assigned to Output-String. In the world of programming, a *variable name* is a handy way to reference a place in the computer's memory. It is a name we give to a location in the memory of the computer. It is much easier to ask the computer to store a value at a place called OutputString than to use the actual memory address of F9DB742A.

Once we have defined a variable name, we can assign a value to that location. Since this value can change, we call it a *variable*. The value (variable) assigned to a variable name is the information that appears on the right side of the equal sign (=) in an assignment statement. For example, in

```
var OutputString = "<p class='wow'>Hello World </p>"
```

the value is the following **string:**

```
"<p class='wow'>Hello World </p>"
```

A string is a series of characters enclosed in either single or double quotation marks that are displayed as ASCII text.

The third line of the function actually displays the string in the browser. For this simple function, we didn't need to create the variable OutputString to display "Hello World." We could have simply coded

```
<script type="text/javascript">
document.writeln("<p class='wow'>Hello World </p>")
</script>
```

which would have produced the same results as those shown in Figure 13.1. However, this style of coding is considered poor practice, because it is often more difficult to modify. Therefore, it is preferable to use the variable OutputString as presented earlier. That is the professional way to craft maintainable code.

Just as a left curly brace opened the function, a right curly brace is required to mark the end of the function code. It is possible to code several functions within the <script></script> container. You will see an example of that later on in Figure 13.8. But since there is only one function in this page, we can close the <script></script> container after we close the function.

Notice that just before we close the </script>, we close the HTML comment block. Using comments to protect the script used to be important because browsers before the 4th generation didn't support scripting, so some of the code showed up. Since very few folks use those older browsers, protecting the script with comments is no longer essential. We will protect some scripts and not others throughout the chapter.

One rule of defensive coding that we try to promote is to always put the open and close curly braces on a line by themselves. That way they are easy to find. It also helps if you align them vertically so that they are visually in the same column.

▸▸ INVOKING FUNCTIONS

This is the actual code to invoke the hello( ) function:

```
<script type="text/javascript" >
//<!- - Protection starts
Hello()
//- ->
</script>
```

The first thing we notice here is a return of the <script></script> container. Each time we declare *or use* a script, we need to use the <script></script> container. That way the browser knows that the element(s) enclosed within the container are to be executed as scripts rather than simply output to the screen as text. Figure 13.2 shows what would happen if we forgot to enclose the **function call** in a <script></script> container. The

Figure 13.2 Failing to enclose JavaScript function call within <script></script> container

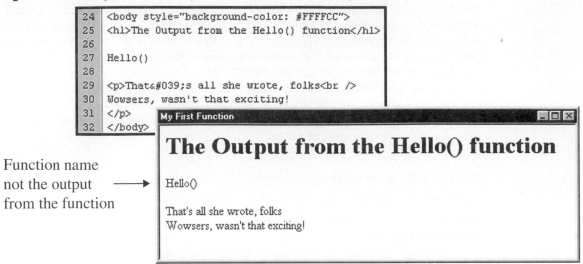

Function name not the output from the function

function call is the place in the code where we request the results returned from the function. In this case, the function call shows where we want the string "Hello World" to appear.

Obviously, the browser doesn't have any way of knowing that the string "Hello()" is supposed to call a function rather than be output as text. The actual invocation (*call*) of the function, "Hello( )", tells the browser to find a function called Hello and pass no parameters to the function. Here is where some function magic happens!

One rule of functions says that when the function is executed, the function call is replaced by the results of that call—the output from the function. In the page the browser sees this:

Hello( )

The browser replaces the function call line with the large, centered, italic words: *Hello World.*

Now that we know what a function looks like and a little about how to use one, we need to examine some programming concepts that will help us better understand how to use, modify, and finally write JavaScript.

EXPLORATION **#1**   Create, run, and debug a small Web page that demonstrates the hello( ) function. Change it so that it displays the line Hello *your name* to personalize your page.

▸▸ BASIC PROGRAMMING STRUCTURES

Every program or script is composed of statements that are rendered in the language of that particular programming language. Each language has a syntax that dictates how any specific action verb is used within the language. You are already used to dealing with the syntax of HTML, where attributes must be coded within the angle brackets of the beginning tag and the like. Now we need to learn something about JavaScript syntax.

All programs in any language are composed of the three standard building blocks of (1) sequences of statements, (2) selection of one set of statements over another, and (3) groups of statements that are iterated. Let's take a look at these basic programming structures using JavaScript syntax.

SEQUENCE OF STATEMENTS

A *sequence* is simply a set of statements that are executed one after the other, in the order they appear in the program. Figure 13.3 shows a snippet of JavaScript that demonstrates a set of instructions that form a sequence. This sequence of code writes out a descending set of numbers starting with 10 and ending with 1. You will see this code again in a couple of figures; it is an excellent example of a sequence. As you can see, each of the lines of code is executed one after the other, resulting in a descending series of numbers. Between each output statement, the script subtracts one from the counter.

Figure 13.3

Sequence of code

```
16  document.writeln("<div style='color: #336600;'>");
17  document.writeln("<img src='rocket.gif' alt='rocket' align='right' />");
18      count=10;
19      document.writeln("T minus = "+count+"<br />");
20      count--;
21      document.writeln("T minus = "+count+"<br />");
22      count--;
23      document.writeln("T minus = "+count+"<br />");
24      count--;
25      document.writeln("T minus = "+count+"<br />");
26      count--;
27      document.writeln("T minus = "+count+"<br />");
28      count--;
29      document.writeln("T minus = "+count+"<br />");
30      count--;
31      document.writeln("T minus = "+count+"<br />");
32      count--;
33      document.writeln("T minus = "+count+"<br />");
34      count--;
35      document.writeln("T minus = "+count+"<br />");
36      count--;
37      document.writeln("T minus = "+count+"<br />");
38  document.writeln("</div>");
39  document.writeln("We have ignition...we have liftoff!");
```

SELECTION OF CODE

The *selection* of one sequence of code over another is the heart of most programs. This structure allows us to create code that can respond to a variety of conditions. Figure 13.4 shows a script that checks to see if the browser is actually Java-enabled. The script uses an IF/ELSE statement to display one of two messages. Notice that first the code opens a division and sets the color for the text within it. Then it builds the beginnings of a level-2 heading. Next the IF statement tests to see whether or not the browser supports Java. Based on that result, the code outputs the correct message as the rest of the heading.

Let's take a closer look at this IF/ELSE statement. The way to read this code is as follows:

- if: If the navigator.javaEnabled( ) function resolves to a value of *true,* write the lines that indicate that the browser is Java-enabled.

- else: Since the navigator.JavaEnabled( ) function *does not resolve to a value of true,* write the lines that indicate that the browser is not Java-enabled.

In some books on programming, this is called an IF/THEN/ELSE statement. Since JavaScript doesn't use the THEN command, it is just an IF/ELSE statement for us.

TESTING FOR JAVASCRIPT

By the way, some students have asked how to use JavaScript to determine if the browser supports JavaScript, just as we tested for Java-enabled browsers. If you think about it,

Figure 13.4   An example of selection and its results in JavaScript

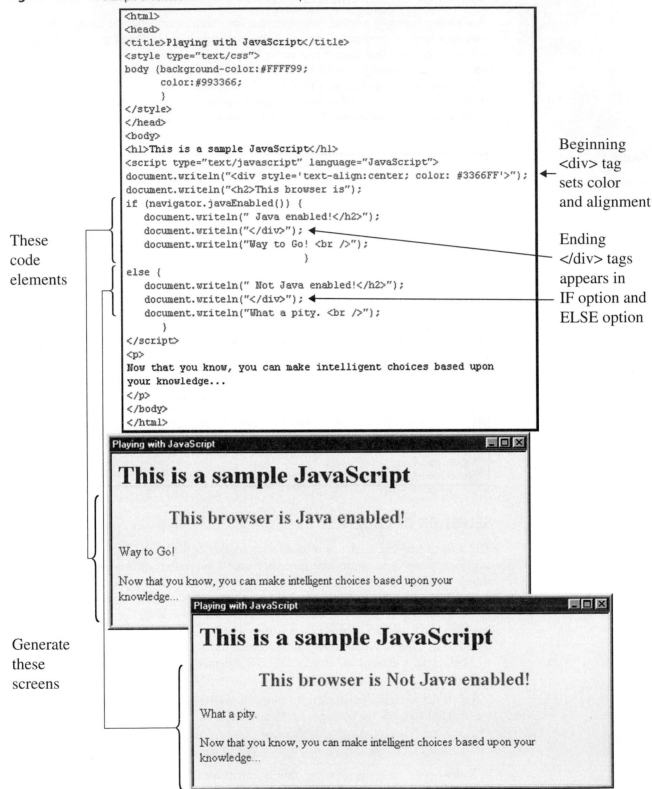

These code elements

Beginning <div> tag sets color and alignment

Ending </div> tags appears in IF option and ELSE option

Generate these screens

there is actually only one sure way of determining whether your browser supports JavaScript or not. Simply use JavaScript to write a line or two to your screen. If you see the text, then your browser supports JavaScript. If it doesn't write the text, then you can assume that your browser does not support JavaScript. You can code a little script that says, "If you can see this, then your browser supports JavaScript."

ITERATION OF STATEMENTS

To *iterate* is to repeat a sequence of instructions. (To irritate, on the other hand, is to annoy!) In programming parlance, an iteration construct is characterized as an initial condition, an iterative step value, and a termination condition. Another name for iteration is **loop.** Here is an example of a very simple loop. The code counts down from 10 to 1, by 1s.

```
for (var count=10; count >=1; count--)
    {
    document.writeln( "T minus = "+count +" <br />" )
    }
document.writeln( "We have ignition . . . We have lift off!" )
```

The initial condition has the value of the variable count equal to 10. The iterative step decrements (subtracts) 1 from the value of count each time the loop is executed. That is the count-- part, which says "decrement count by 1 after you use it." The ending condition is the second part of the for statement, and it says, "keep doing this while the value of count is greater than or equal to (>=) 1."

Now consider this statement:

```
"T minus = "+ count +" <br/>"
```

It tells writeln that it should output the string "T minus =", then concatenate, or add, the value stored at the variable name of count, and then concatenate the string "<br/>" on to the end of that line. Those plus signs (+) indicate concatenation, or combination, rather than addition.

An example of how this code works is shown in Figure 13.5. This figure also shows the output of the loop. Notice that using an iteration construct, a programmer can get 10 lines of output with just four lines of code (two of them being curly braces!).

Usually iterative code replaces a fairly large block of sequential code. For example, the code in Figure 13.6 will accomplish the same result as the loop in Figure 13.5, but it is much longer. It becomes fairly obvious that it is much simpler and more efficient to code the little loop of four lines than to code 22 lines to achieve the same result. In this way, loops allow us to reuse instructions, making our programs far more efficient.

You know how three building blocks look using JavaScript. Every script you build will be composed of some or all of these three building blocks. Let's take a closer look at this language.

EXPLORATION #2 Copy the code from Figure 13.5 from the student CD and modify it so the code displays the text "Almost There!" when the count equals 5.

▸▸ OBJECT-ORIENTED CONCEPTS IN JAVASCRIPT

Object-oriented programmers use the term **object** to mean an entity like a document, a button, or a form. JavaScript is an *object-oriented language,* meaning that it is based on a set of specialized entities called objects. Although the whole of the JavaScript

Figure 13.5   Iteration code and resulting page

```
<html>
<head>
<title>Up, up, and away with JavaScript</title>
<style type="text/css">
body {background-color:#FFFFFF;
      color:#993366;
      }
</style>
</head>
<body>
<h1>Another sample JavaScript</h1>

<script type="text/javascript" language="JavaScript">
document.writeln("<div style='color: #336600;'>");
document.writeln("<img src='rocket.gif' alt='rocket' align='right' />");
for (var count=10; count >=1; count--)
   {
      document.writeln("T minus = "+count+"<br />");
   }
document.writeln("</div>")
document.writeln("We have ignition...we have liftoff!")
</script>
<p>

Wowsers,<br /> such excitement!
</p>
</body>
</html>
```

Iteration using
For statement

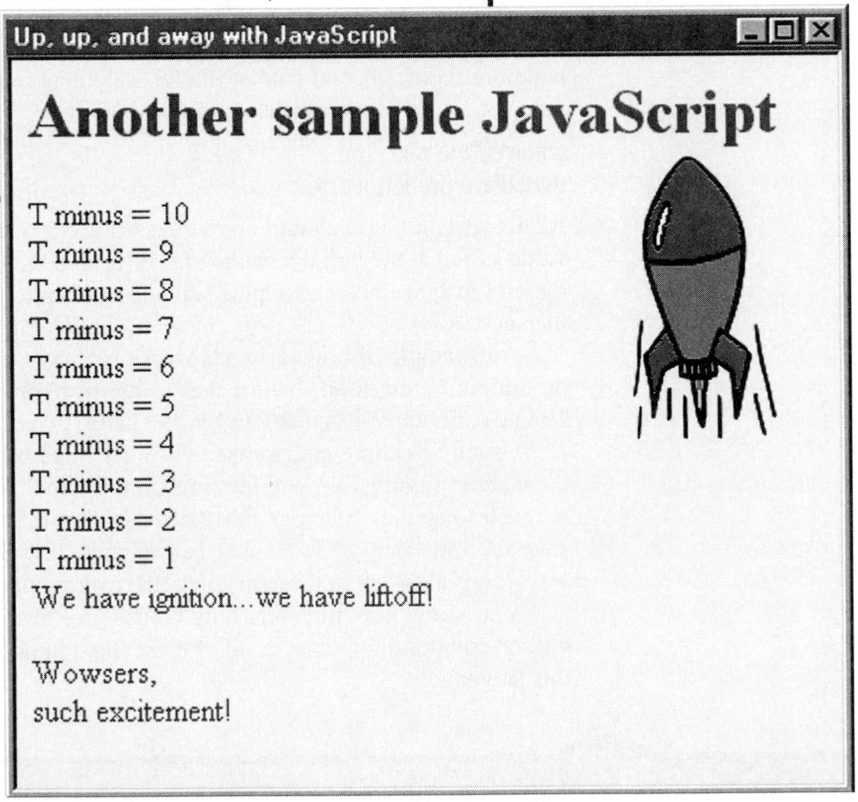

Up, up, and away with JavaScript

Another sample JavaScript

T minus = 10
T minus = 9
T minus = 8
T minus = 7
T minus = 6
T minus = 5
T minus = 4
T minus = 3
T minus = 2
T minus = 1
We have ignition...we have liftoff!

Wowsers,
such excitement!

language is far beyond the scope of this text, we will examine four different objects that are very handy for Web weavers: date, document, window, and navigator. Although many other objects are available in JavaScript, these four are particularly useful. If you want to learn more, you will need to consult one of the many books devoted solely to JavaScript or visit one of the many Web-based tutorials on the subject.

More than one example of each object is possible. Each example is called an *instance* of the object. Some JavaScriptors call objects by their numbers, like form [1] or button [0]. This practice is rather like calling two students Student0 and Student1. We would prefer to see you use the **name** attribute to label each object something that reflects its use of function.

Figure 13.6 Sequential code that duplicates looping code in Figure 13.5

This code outputs 10 countdown lines and then the ignition line... it is a little longer than the loop!

```
18      count=10;
19      document.writeln("T minus = "+count+"<br />");
20      count--;
21      document.writeln("T minus = "+count+"<br />");
22      count--;
23      document.writeln("T minus = "+count+"<br />");
24      count--;
25      document.writeln("T minus = "+count+"<br />");
26      count--;
27      document.writeln("T minus = "+count+"<br />");
28      count--;
29      document.writeln("T minus = "+count+"<br />");
30      count--;
31      document.writeln("T minus = "+count+"<br />");
32      count--;
33      document.writeln("T minus = "+count+"<br />");
34      count--;
35      document.writeln("T minus = "+count+"<br />");
36      count--;
37      document.writeln("T minus = "+count+"<br />");
38 document.writeln("</div>");
39 document.writeln("We have ignition...we have liftoff!");
```

Every object has **properties,** which are attributes, or features, of the object, like the color of the text, links, and background of a document. Every object also has **methods,** which are predefined functions that manipulate data, like the navigator.javaEnabled() method we saw in Figure 13.5, and the writeln() method for the document object we used to display variables. Table 13.1 shows the four objects that will be discussed here

Table 13.1 Some properties and methods for four common HTML objects

Object	Properties	Methods
Date	Prototype	(getDate), (getDay), (getHours), (getMinutes), (getMonth), (getSeconds), (getTime), (getYear), (getMilliseconds) JavaScript 1.3
Document	alinkColor, anchors, applets, bgColor, cookie, fgColor, images, lastModified, linkColor, links, referrer, title, URL, vlinkColor	(close), (open), (write), (writeln)
Window	closed, defaultStatus, document, frames, history, location, locationbar, menubar, name, opener, parent, self, status, statusbar, toolbar, top, window	(alert), (back), (close), (confirm), (find), (forward), (home), (open), (print), (prompt), (scroll), (stop)
Navigator	appCodeName, appName, appVersion, language, mimeTypes, platform, plugins, userAgent	(javaEnabled), (plugins.refresh), (preference)

with their associated properties and methods. This table does not list all of the properties and methods for each of the objects, only some of the more common ones. These are the ones we will discuss in this text.

Remember, the concept here is that a Web page has properties—physical things that are parts of it. Using a puppy as an analogy, it has the properties of big brown eyes, soft fur, and wet nose. It also has methods: chase the laser, tug the pants leg, and sleep. Let's explore the four commonly used objects shown in Table 13.1 and see how to use their methods and manipulate their properties.

▶▶ DATE OBJECT

The date object returns the current time and date. If you have spent any time browsing the Net, you have seen many pages that show you the time. Most of those pages use a CGI script to display the time and date. Remember, using a CGI script means at least one call to the server and one return from the server. If the clock updates each second, there is a call to the server at least 60 times every minute! This is not a good way to reduce Internet traffic. In addition, unless you compensate for the difference in time zones, the time you display will be server time, not client time.

To make our point, we are going to introduce you to Valerie, owner of Valerie's Venerable Volume Vault, a used-book store in Little Horse, Texas. Valerie wants to incorporate a clock in one of her Web pages. The page shown in Figure 13.7 demonstrates a JavaScript that does its magic at the client side, so requires no extra data to be passed across the Net. That means two transmissions are saved each second, and the clock will be accurate even if the Internet connection is lost!

Figure 13.7

Using date () object in JavaScript to create clock

The screen in Figure 13.7 gives the day of the week and the time to the nearest second. Figure 13.8 presents the code for that screen. Don't let all that code bother you; we will look at it in detail later, but for now we are interested in the part of the code that uses the date object. Two user-created functions, whatTime() and whatDay(), create a new object that contains the current date. The line now = new Date() ; creates a new object, another instance of the date object called now in the whatTime() function. That object inherits its properties from the Date object, and we use it to collect all of the date information we need in order to determine the time. We will reuse this function about once a second to keep the display current. The whatDay() function in Figure 13.8 creates the new object when which is also an instance of the Date object we use to determine the day of the week.

Figure 13.8   HTML code for the Exceptional clock

```
<html>
<head>
<meta http-equiv="Content-Style-Type" content="text/css" />
<title>An Exceptional little clock example</title>
<script type="text/Javascript" language="JavaScript">
<!-- No protection for these scripts...by design -->
function driver() {
//       This function will call the two day and time functions.  This just
//       makes it easier to run them both "on page load".
   whatTime();
   whatDay();
          }
function whatTime() {
//       Create an instance of the date called "now"
   now = new Date();
//       Using the "now" instance parse out the hours data
   hours = now.getHours();
//       Parse out the minutes
   minutes = now.getMinutes();
//       Parse the seconds
   seconds = now.getSeconds();
//       Add the hours to a string called timeVal
   timeVal = " " + ((hours > 12) ? hours - 12 : hours);
//       What this does:  If the hours are greater than 12 (it is afternoon),
//       subtract 12 from the hours number we will put on an AM/PM indicator.
   timeVal  += ((minutes < 10) ? ":0" : ":") + minutes;
//       if the minutes are less than ten, put in the leading zero.
        timeVal  += ((seconds < 10) ? ":0" : ":") + seconds;
        timeVal  += (hours >= 12) ? " PM" : " AM";
      document.time.timer.value=timeVal;
        setTimeout("whatTime()",1000);
                      }
function whatDay() {
        when= new Date();
   day = when.getDay();
   if (day == 0) day=" Sunday";
   if (day == 1) day=" Monday";
   if (day == 2) day=" Tuesday"
   if (day == 3) day="Wednesday";
   if (day == 4) day="Thursday";
   if (day == 5) day=" Friday";
   if (day == 6) day="Saturday";
        document.time.day.value=day;
                     }
</script>
</head>
<body style="background-color: #CCCCFF" onload="driver();">
<h1 style="text-align: center">Valerie's Venerable Volume Vault</h1>
<div style="text-align: center">
<form name="time" action="noop">
<table width="99%" summary="formatting">
<tr>
<td align="left"><img src="flylf.gif" height="127" width="162" alt="books"></td>
<td align="center"><h3>Don't let your reading time fly away!</h3></td>
<td align="right"><img src="flyrt.gif" height="127" width="162" alt="books"></td>
</tr>
</table>
Today is:<br />
   <input type="text" name="day" size="9" alt="dayofweek"><br />
And it is already: <br />
   <input type="text" name="timer" size="13" alt="hour:minute:second"><br />
Make sure you get your reading done today!
</form>
</div>
<hr />
</body>
</html>
```

driver() function

whatTime() function

whatDay() function

Load driver() function when Web page opens

The first function listed in Figure 13.8 is a small function called driver(), whose only purpose is to invoke the two date functions. Using this driver function makes it easier to start the programs running when the page loads. Look at the first line of the code including this function:

```
<body style= "background-color: #FFFFCC" onload= "driver();" >
```

▸▸ INTRINSIC EVENTS

We have a new attribute coded here, the **onload** attribute. This is an example of an intrinsic event. These events can be used to trigger JavaScript code. In this case, when the **onload** event happens, the function driver() is executed to call the time and day functions.

Table 13.2 shows some of the intrinsic event names and what they mean.

Although you can't see it in the book, when you execute the page shown you will see that the time value in Figure 13.8 updates roughly each second. (JavaScript counts time in thousandths of a second, that is, in milliseconds.) This time value is a handy and very workable dynamic addition to a Web page. Although Valerie's "Reading Time" page isn't all full of bells and whistles, it was designed to show you how the date object

Table 13.2 Intrinsic events

Intrinsic Event	What Triggers This Event	Associated Tags
onblur	The user moves off the object by moving the mouse pointer or tabbing.	\<button>, \<input>, \<label>, \<select>, \<textarea>
onchange	The user alters the contents of the object.	\<input>, \<select>, \<textarea>
onclick	The user clicks the mouse button on the object.	*Most tags.*
ondblclick	The user double-clicks the mouse on the object.	*Most tags.*
onfocus	The user moves to the object either by mouse movement or tabbing.	\<button>, \<input>, \<label>, \<select>, \<textarea>
onkeydown	The user presses a key over the object.	*Most tags.*
onkeypress	The user presses and releases a key over the object.	*Most tags.*
onkeyup	The user releases a key over the object.	*Most tags.*
onload	The browser finishes loading a window or all the frames within a \<frameset>.	\<body>, \<frameset>
onmousedown	The user presses the button on the mouse while the pointer is over the object.	*Most tags.*
onmousemove	The user moves the pointer while it is positioned over the object (different from **onmouseover**).	*Most tags.*
onmouseout	The user moves the pointer off, or away from the object.	*Most tags.*
onmouseover	The user moves the pointer onto the object.	*Most tags.*
onmouseup	The user releases the mouse button over the object.	*Most tags.*
onreset	The user activates the reset control.	\<form>
onselect	The user selects some text in a text field.	\<input>, \<textarea>
onsubmit	The user activates the submit control.	\<form>
onunload	The browser removes the element from the window or frame.	\<body>\<frameset>

works. To learn JavaScript, you should build small pages like this that allow you to experiment this way with a single concept or a set of related tools. There are more uses for the date object; we will examine one of them in Chapter Fourteen on Dynamic HTML.

EXPLORATION #3

Modify the page you created in Exploration #1. Change it so that it displays the current date in a small form field. Do not use the same names (time, day, and timer) that we did. When you make it work using different names, you will better understand how naming happens in Web pages.

▸▸ DOCUMENT OBJECT

The document object is one of the most common objects JavaScript programmers use. Some of the methods, like document.write() or document.writeln(), are used to display lines on the page. The example in Figure 13.9 uses document.writeln to output the data. This object helps you change the colors of some of the features of the page. Values like bgColor, fgColor, linkColor, alinkColor, and vlinkColor are grouped under the title Display Properties. Here are some additional properties of the document object:

- The document.cookie property allows a browser to store data that the script can access to keep information about users, like their preferences. You have probably opened some pages on the Web that set *cookies* for you. We will explore cookies in more depth in Chapter Fourteen.

- The document.referrer property allows JavaScript to access the URL of the document that contains the link that sent the browser to your document.

- JavaScript maintains list of the anchors (document.anchors), the links (document.links), the images on the page (document.images), and the applets used with a page (document.applets). It even keeps track of the different forms on your page in the document.forms property.

- There are also some interesting methods associated with the document object. For example, document.open() and document.close() control moving data into an existing window. In addition, the document.clear() method is supposed to clear the contents of the browser window. In practice, document.clear() doesn't usually work. A *workaround* is used instead as a way to achieve the results of a command that doesn't work by using other commands that were not designed for that effect but can nevertheless produce the desired result. In this case, the workaround is to either issue a document.open() or just do a document.write() with no contents in the document.write().

- The document.lastModified property takes the last changed data from the file information stored on disk, so the browser always displays the correct, last updated, date.

Figure 13.9 provides an example of the use of the document.lastModified property. As you can see, the date the document was last modified appears at the bottom of the screen. The format of the date has changed since the previous edition of the text. This shows the evolution of the browsers. In previous versions of the browsers, the document.modified() function data were displayed like this:

02/10/05 22:27:40

That date would not be considered internationally correct, since it could be either the 2nd of October, or the 10th of February. An internationally correct format would be

10/Feb/2005

which leaves no room for doubt.

Figure 13.9 Using document.lastModified property to date a page

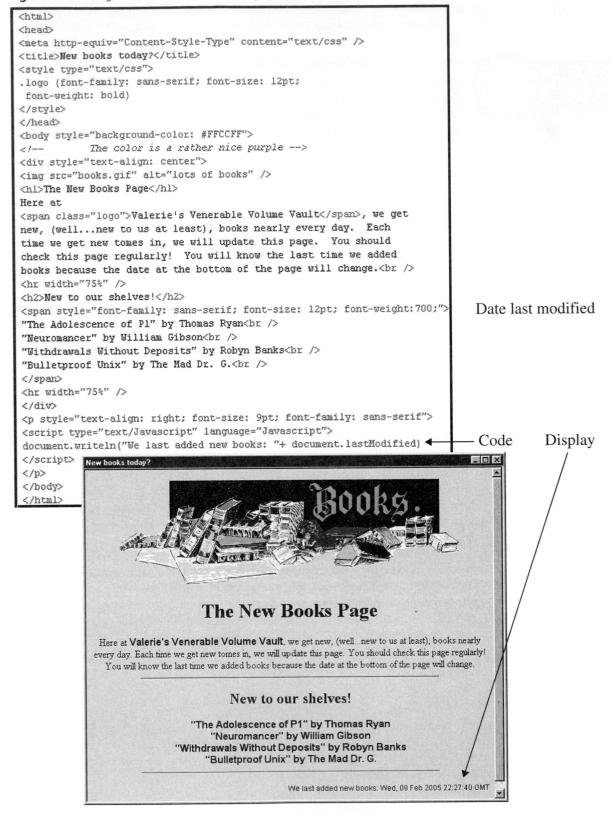

```
<html>
<head>
<meta http-equiv="Content-Style-Type" content="text/css" />
<title>New books today?</title>
<style type="text/css">
.logo {font-family: sans-serif; font-size: 12pt;
 font-weight: bold}
</style>
</head>
<body style="background-color: #FFCCFF">
<!--       The color is a rather nice purple -->
<div style="text-align: center">
<img src="books.gif" alt="lots of books" />
<h1>The New Books Page</h1>
Here at
<span class="logo">Valerie's Venerable Volume Vault</span>, we get
new, (well...new to us at least), books nearly every day.  Each
time we get new tomes in, we will update this page.  You should
check this page regularly!  You will know the last time we added
books because the date at the bottom of the page will change.<br />
<hr width="75%" />
<h2>New to our shelves!</h2>
<span style="font-family: sans-serif; font-size: 12pt; font-weight:700;">
"The Adolescence of P1" by Thomas Ryan<br />
"Neuromancer" by William Gibson<br />
"Withdrawals Without Deposits" by Robyn Banks<br />
"Bulletproof Unix" by The Mad Dr. G.<br />
</span>
<hr width="75%" />
</div>
<p style="text-align: right; font-size: 9pt; font-family: sans-serif">
<script type="text/Javascript" language="Javascript">
document.writeln("We last added new books: "+ document.lastModified)
</script>
</p>
</body>
</html>
```

Date last modified

Code   Display

Using two of the big-three browsers, we see the date correctly displayed in an internationally correct fashion. The only browser that holds to the US-oriented format is Explorer.

Notice, too, that the <script> in Figure 13.9 uses the document.writeln() method to output the document.lastModified property. This means that each time Valerie adds a book to her New Books Page or makes any other changes to the page, the browser will automatically update the date last modified. This great little JavaScript property keeps Valerie from having to hand-code the date each time she changes the page (leaving her more time for reading).

▸▸ WINDOW OBJECT

The window object sits at the top of or at the beginning of the hierarchy of JavaScript objects. Because of that, it has some unique and useful properties. The control of an *existing* window is very limited, but if you generate a new window, your script can control many of its properties.

One of the most unusual attributes of the window object is that you don't need to reference it directly or by name; it is assumed. Earlier we used the document.writeln() method. Actually, the correct reference to that method is window.document.writeln(), but because everything takes place in a window, the window part is assumed. That in and of itself is a very special feature to have in an object-oriented programming language.

STATUS BAR

Among the things you can control in an existing window is the status bar. Now, whether or not you *should* change or control the status bar is another question. Some Web weavers think the status bar should never be altered, as your users have come to expect certain predictable things there. Other Web weavers believe that their users never even think to look at the status bar, so putting information there is a waste of time. Nevertheless, there is a cadre of Web weavers who believe that if the status bar is there, they should put content in it. Figure 13.10 shows an example where the status bar changes to an author-supplied message when the user moves the screen pointer over a link.

Notice how in using the intrinsic event **onmouseover,** we reset the status-bar message by giving the property window.status a new value generated by the code on the page. This tool is a simple way to alter the status bar. The code following the semicolon return(true), is required to tell the browser to perform the update of the status bar. As we saw with the display of the date, the different browsers handle some events differently. At the time of this writing, Internet Explorer handles **onmouseover** as expected. Opera requires the user to click and hold on the link to see the status bar change. The old Netscape Navigator 4.6 handles the change perfectly, but Netscape 6.0 seems to ignore it altogether. Please test the page with your browser to see what happens. This is yet another example of why you need to test your pages with several browsers.

One difference we have noticed is that with the default status message, the message changes when the pointer is moved off the link. The updated version uses the **onmouseout** event to blank out the status line when the mouse pointer moves off the image.

The default message placed in the status bar tells the user the target (URL) of the link. That is not as informative a message as the ones coded in Figure 13.10. Sometimes it is useful to tell users where they are going rather than what they are going to see. This field can, in some cases, be of help to your users. However, as with all the other neat features we have learned, resist the temptation to overuse it.

It is also possible to set up a scrolling status-bar message. There is but one word of discussion necessary about creating a scrolling status-bar message: *Don't!* Such messages are annoying and distracting, so don't build them. Actually, it is possible to create other scrolling features, too. A good rule of thumb is that if you are considering creating a

Figure 13.10 Changing data in status bar **onmouseover**

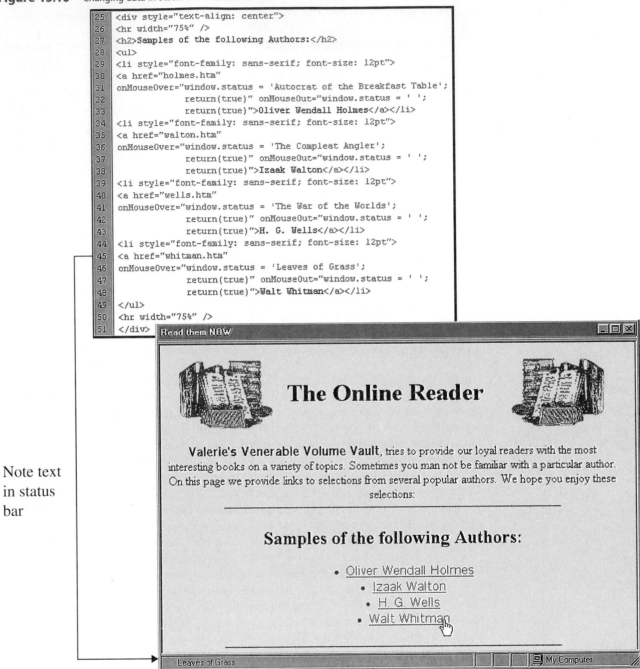

Note text in status bar

scrolling "anything," take a deep breath, walk calmly away from the computer, and wait until the urge passes. It will be better for all parties concerned.

DIALOG BOXES

Three methods associated with the window object produce a dialog box that requires the user's input: `window.alert()`, `window.confirm()`, and `window.prompt()`. Figure 13.11 shows the code and samples of each of the different dialog boxes. Please note that the screen here is a composite screen; in real life each of the dialog boxes would appear on its own screen and have to be closed before the next would appear. These dialog boxes are said to be **modal,** which means they will stay on the screen and prevent the user from doing *anything else* until she responds to them. Alert boxes, in particular, are very useful when you debug your JavaScript scripts. However, in day-to-day use, having to constantly respond to a modal dialog box is very annoying.

Figure 13.11   Composite showing three types of dialog boxes

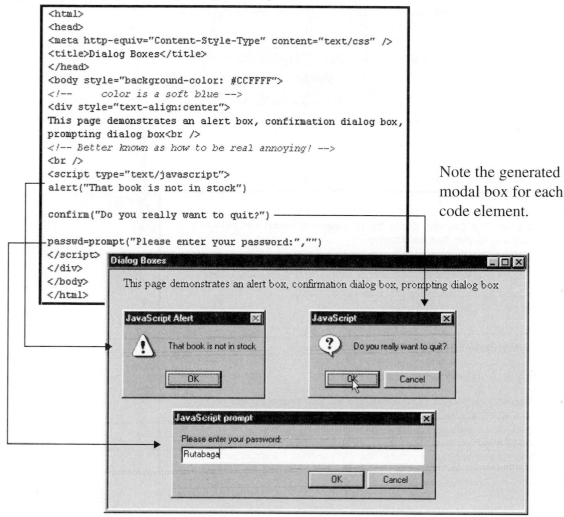

```
<html>
<head>
<meta http-equiv="Content-Style-Type" content="text/css" />
<title>Dialog Boxes</title>
</head>
<body style="background-color: #CCFFFF">
<!--     color is a soft blue -->
<div style="text-align:center">
This page demonstrates an alert box, confirmation dialog box,
prompting dialog box<br />
<!-- Better known as how to be real annoying! -->
<br />
<script type="text/javascript">
alert("That book is not in stock")

confirm("Do you really want to quit?")

passwd=prompt("Please enter your password:","")
</script>
</div>
</body>
</html>
```

Note the generated modal box for each code element.

Each of the dialog boxes has different requirements. The *alert dialog box* simply requires the user to activate the OK button. The *confirm dialog box* asks the user to activate either OK or Cancel. Usually the confirm box is used with an IF/ELSE statement, because it returns a value of "true" or "false." The *prompt dialog box* asks the user for input. In this case, it asks for a password. Notice how the password is *not* protected from casual view.

The Web weaver can set a default value for the input string, and the user can simply activate the OK button to accept it. If there is a default value, it shows up as a highlighted string so the user doesn't have to delete it before entering his own value. All he needs to do is start typing. To send his response to the prompt, the user needs to activate the OK button. To abandon the response, he can activate the Cancel button.

Dialog boxes can be functional tools if they are not overused. One of the worst offenders in overuse is the alert box. Some unwise Web weavers use them far too often. Use them only when absolutely necessary.

EXPLORATION #4

Create a small Web page that demonstrates each of the dialog boxes as follows:

1. Alert the user to the fact that the page just opened.

2. Ask the user to confirm that he wants to continue displaying the page.

3. Prompt the user to input her name.

4. Prompt the user to input his school's name.

5. Ask the user to input her instructor's name

6. Ask the user to confirm that he is done.

7. Alert the user to the fact that data entry is complete.

Open the document and test it to make sure all of the boxes open correctly.

Figure 13.12 Page set up to create new window

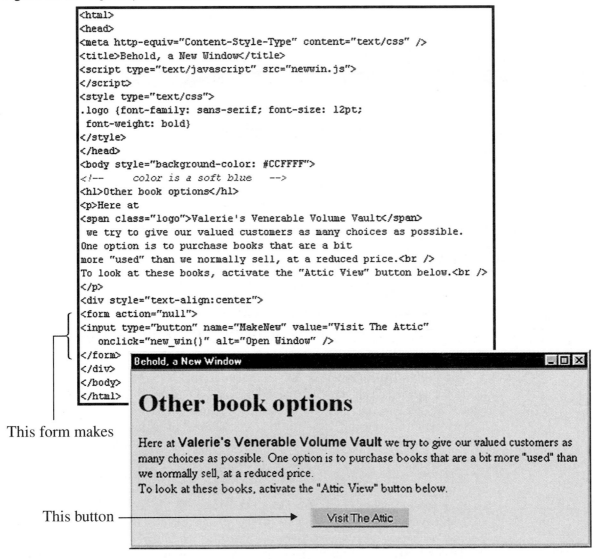

```
<html>
<head>
<meta http-equiv="Content-Style-Type" content="text/css" />
<title>Behold, a New Window</title>
<script type="text/javascript" src="newwin.js">
</script>
<style type="text/css">
.logo {font-family: sans-serif; font-size: 12pt;
 font-weight: bold}
</style>
</head>
<body style="background-color: #CCFFFF">
<!--    color is a soft blue   -->
<h1>Other book options</h1>
<p>Here at
<span class="logo">Valerie's Venerable Volume Vault</span>
 we try to give our valued customers as many choices as possible.
One option is to purchase books that are a bit
more "used" than we normally sell, at a reduced price.<br />
To look at these books, activate the "Attic View" button below.<br />
</p>
<div style="text-align:center">
<form action="null">
<input type="button" name="MakeNew" value="Visit The Attic"
   onclick="new_win()" alt="Open Window" />
</form>
</div>
</body>
</html>
```

This form makes

This button ⟶

Behold, a New Window

Other book options

Here at **Valerie's Venerable Volume Vault** we try to give our valued customers as many choices as possible. One option is to purchase books that are a bit more "used" than we normally sell, at a reduced price.
To look at these books, activate the "Attic View" button below.

Visit The Attic

NEW WINDOWS

Another useful tool is the ability to open a completely new window. Unlike frames, new windows give the user a separate entity with which to interact. The new window is under the Web weaver's control as far as size and features go.

Writing the content to the new window is a little more complex than building the HTML code in an editor, because it all needs to be packaged in one large *character-string variable* that is written with one document.write() call. In Chapter Fourteen we will examine more of the options, but for now, let's look at a sample page in Figure 13.12 that creates a new, small window. The code for the **calling page** here doesn't contain many new features except the external call to the JavaScript in the <head> and the <form></form> container that houses the button that invokes the script. A calling page is simply the page that calls, or invokes, the function in question. The <form> contains the "Visit The Attic" button that, when activated, invokes the JavaScript that creates the new window. Figure 13.13 illustrates what happens when this button is activated.

The Web weaver can control the following window features:

- Size

- Appearance of a toolbar, status bar, or scrolling bars

Figure 13.13 What happens when the "Attic" button is activated

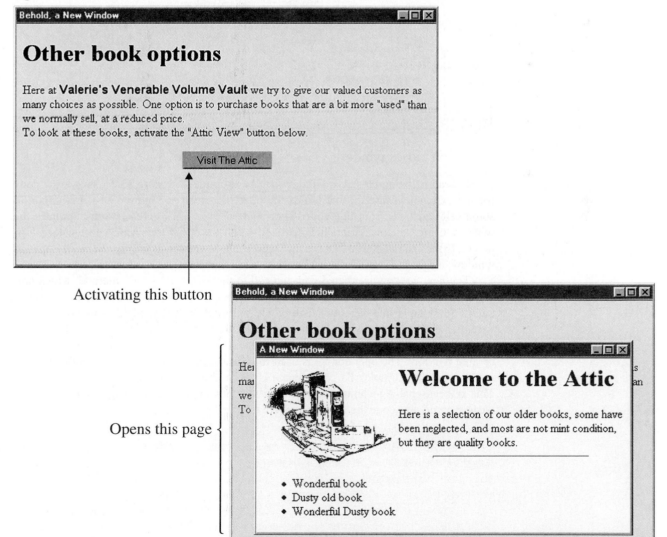

- Whether or not the window is resizable

- Contents

One thing that is outside the author's control is where the window appears. It will always be placed wherever the browser wants it—either inside or overlapping the existing browser window. For now at least, where the window is generated is not an option.

A new window can open another HTML document, which is very handy for applications in which the primary use of a window is to view documents. Each newly created window can contain a different document.

In addition to creating new windows, you can allow the user to close them. Figure 13.14 shows our new window with a button added to close the window. This way the user won't have to activate the close X button in the top right corner of the window.

Figure 13.14

Self-closing window

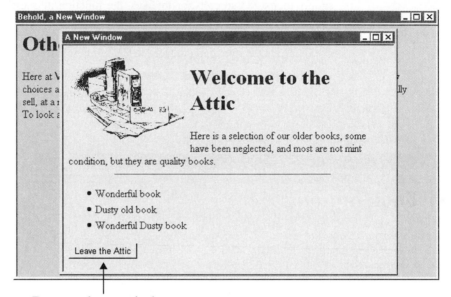

Button closes window

Instead of being closed, a window can be minimized. Figure 13.15 shows the code for the external JavaScript that builds the page presented in Figure 13.14. Let's look at some selected lines from this code. The function new_win() creates and populates the window using the JavaScript. It is invoked when the "Visit the Attic" button (see Figure 13.13) is activated. The "Leave the Attic" button, created as part of the newly opened window, closes the new window when the user activates it.

The new window is created with the call to the window.open() method, which creates a new window of a size specified by the Web weaver that also has a menu bar, scroll bars, and a status line. This instance of the window.open() method is assigned to the variable NewWindow, which is the very creative name of the newly created window. The variable Content stores one very large text string that is the content of the newly created window. The operator += is used to *concatenate* additional pieces to the original contents of the variable. To concatenate is to combine two (or more) strings into one. This is a reasonable technique for creating the contents of the new page. A foolish Web weaver could also code the whole page like this:

```
var Content="<html><head><title>A New Window</title></head><body style=
'background-color: #FFFFCC'><img src='atticbk.gif' align='left' alt='books'
height='140' width='180'><h1>Welcome to the Attic</h1>Here is a selection of
our older books, some have been neglected, and most are not mint condition,
but they are quality books. <hr width='70%'><ul><li>Wonderful book</li>
<li>Dusty old book</li><li>Wonderful Dusty book</li></ul><form action='null'>
<input type='button' name='Clunk' value='Leave the Attic' onclick='close()'>
</form></body></html>"
```

Figure 13.15   HTML code that creates new window in Figure 13.14

This is the external JavaScript file that creates the window

Code to create button that closes window

```
1   /*==================================================================
2       new_win()
3
4       Description:
5           This function creates a new window, and writes
6           a single line to it.   The file name is newwin.js
7
8   ================================================================== */
9   function new_win() {
10  var NewWindow = window.open("","Newbie","height=340,width=500,status,menubar,scrollbars, resizable")
11  if (NewWindow != null) {
12  //            Test to make sure the window actually opened.
13  //            If it did, build the content for it.
14      var Content="<html><head><title>A New Window</title></head>"
15      Content += "<body style='background-color: #FFFFCC'>"
16      Content += "<img src='atticbk.gif' align='left' alt='books'"
17      Content += "height='140' width='180' />"
18      Content += "<h1> Welcome to the Attic </h1>"
19      Content += "Here is a selection of our older books, "
20      Content += "some have been neglected, and most are not "
21      Content += "mint condition, but they are quality books."
22      Content += "<hr width='70%'><ul> <li>Wonderful book</li>"
23      Content += "<li>Dusty old book</li>"
24      Content += "<li>Wonderful Dusty book</li></ul>"
25      Content += "<form action='null'>"
26      Content += "<input type='button' name='Clunk' value='Leave the Attic'"
27      Content += "onclick='close()' />"
28      Content += "</form>"
29      Content += "</body></html>"
30  //    Notice that the whole content for the page is put
31  //    in one long string.  However, if you build a complex
32  //    page, you can use the technique shown above to keep
33  //    the individual parts of the page separated just a
34  //    bit for readability
35  //
36  //    Now we build the new page
37      NewWindow.document.write(Content);
38      NewWindow.document.close()    // close the input stream for the
39  //                                   new window.
40                          } // End of if block
41                      }       // End of function
```

We think that is a bit harder to understand. Spacing it out makes the page easier to code, and easier to understand if we need to fix it later.

The next two lines with the NewWindow object output the value associated with Content into the window, then close the data stream for the new window. This last step is important, because if the input stream is not closed, the browser doesn't know that the document is complete and may wait for it to be completed. The delay can cause some browsers to hang up. Also, results can be unpredictable. Always close the input stream with this code.

NewWindow.document.close()

Opening windows is a very handy way to add functionality to your pages. Rather than writing all of the code for the page, as in our example, you can also specify the URL of a different page to be opened in the new window. Your user can see a new page, and you can control many of the features of the window. If you want to open an existing document in a new window, simply code the URL as the first argument. If the first argument is null, the browser won't load any document into the new window, and you must supply the content. For example,

```
window.open("newt.htm", "newt", "height=100, width=200, scrollbars")
```

would open a new window named "newt", 100 by 200 pixels, with scroll bars, containing the content of the HTML document "newt.htm". This is a very useful technique; it differs from the <object></object> method in that it creates a whole new window rather than opening a page in the existing page.

onload and onunload

In addition to the methods and properties we have already discussed, two event handlers can be very important when designing pages. The **onload** and **onunload** attributes (event handlers) can be used to trigger JavaScript functions. The **onload** event occurs when the page has completed the loading process. The loading process includes moving images from the server, loading and starting Java applets, and loading and starting all of the plug-ins. The following line, found in Figure 13.8, invokes the script function called driver() when the page finishes loading.

```
<body style="background-color: #CCCCFF" onload="driver();">
```

The **onunload** event or events occur just before the document is cleared from the browser window. Obviously, you wouldn't want to run user-interactive scripts just as the window closed. Usually **onunload** events are used for housekeeping or statistical purposes.

The window object has many other features beyond those discussed here. As you begin to use the window object, you will discover the features most important to you.

▸▸ NAVIGATOR OBJECT

One point that could be confusing about the navigator object is its name. Navigator is, of course, the name of a popular browser, yet the navigator *object* speaks to any browser and to the platform upon which the browser is running. The major browser manufacturers all recognize and support the navigator object.

This object is often called an "advanced object" because it doesn't really fall within the normal JavaScript hierarchy. It isn't a large object, having only two methods and 11 properties, as shown in Table 13.3 (p. 402).

It is most often used to gather information about the client platform—for example, to see if the platform running the browser supports the Java language. You may wish to check whether a user has the latest and greatest browser, one capable of utilizing your fancy page. If you wish to use browser-dependent features, you may create different versions of your pages, specifically tailored to each version of each of the browsers. Most Web weavers are too busy to build that many versions of the same page, but it can be done.

An amusing use for the navigator object is to tell your user about the computer system she is using, as shown in Figure 13.16. Figure 13.17 illustrates how the JavaScript works after the user activates the "Tell Me!" control.

Figure 13.16 Initial page to invoke script displaying Navigator object data

```html
<html>
<head>
<meta http-equiv="Content-Style-Type" content="text/css" />
<title>New Window Creation</title>

<script type="text/javascript" src="research.js">
<!--
Using an external script keeps the page size down and
allows us to easily use the same tool in several pages.
-->
</script>
<style type="text/css">
.logo {font-family: sans-serif; font-size: 12pt;
 font-weight: bold}
</style>
</head>
<body style="background-color: #FFCCFF;">
<div style="text-align: center">
<img src="smiley.gif"  alt="A woodcut of a smiley fellow" />
<h1>And just what have I learned about you?</h1>
</div>
Here at
<span class="logo">Valerie's Venerable Volume Vault</span>
we too, do our research.  Our chief researcher, Dusty Tomes
keeps track of our users.  Activate the button below, and
let's see what he has discovered about you!
<form action="noop">
<input type="button" name="TellAll" value="Tell Me!"
   onclick="NavData()" alt="open function" /><br /><br />
</form>
</body>
</html>
```

This small form

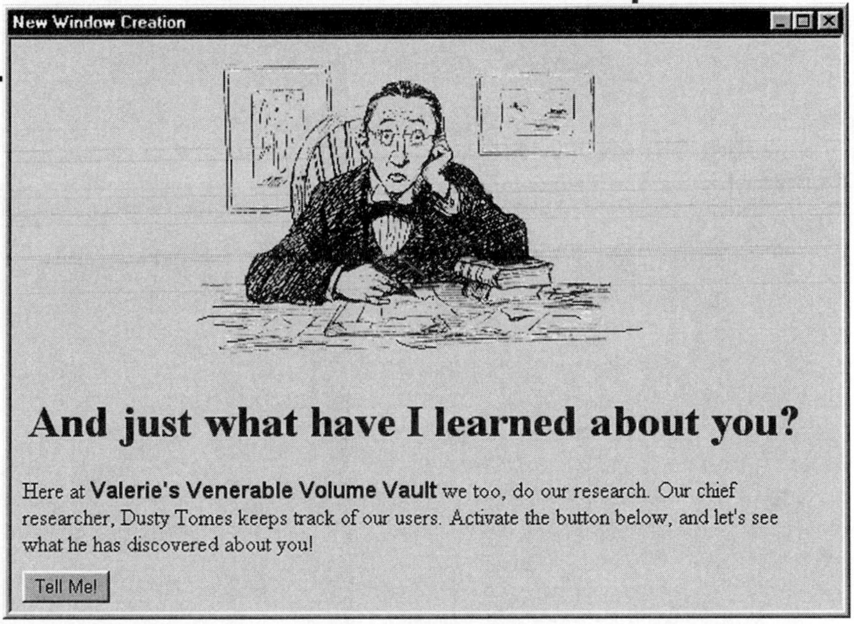

Generates this button

New Window Creation

And just what have I learned about you?

Here at **Valerie's Venerable Volume Vault** we too, do our research. Our chief researcher, Dusty Tomes keeps track of our users. Activate the button below, and let's see what he has discovered about you!

Tell Me!

The navigator object will most likely take on more features as the browsers continue to evolve and JavaScript matures. For now it is useful if you want to capture information about the browser your user is employing. With those data, you could build different versions of the page based on the browser in use. Figure 13.18 shows the code for the pages in Figure 13.17.

You should notice that much of the code looks a lot like that in Figure 13.15. Reusing code that works is called *code leveraging.* Why invent a new way to do the same thing every time you need to redo it? Code leveraging has three advantages:

1. Coding is faster, because you don't need to "reinvent the wheel" each time.

2. Debugging is minimized, because presumably the existing code works, so you won't need to debug it.

Figure 13.17 What happens when user invokes script

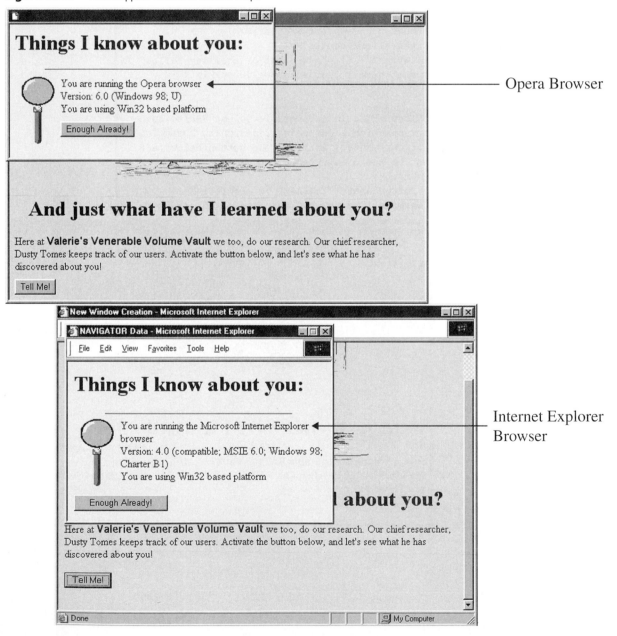

Figure 13.18 This is file research.js, an external JavaScript function

```
1   var NewWindow = null;
2   //          This variable, NewWindow, must be global so both the
3   //          function and the onClick can reference it.
4   //
5   /*===================================================================
6     NavData()
7
8     Description:
9           This function creates a new window, and loads in the
10          NAVIGATOR data.  It includes a close button too.
11
12  =================================================================== */
13  function NavData() {
14  NewWindow = window.open("","Smilie","height=200,width=400,status, menubar")
15  if (NewWindow != null) {
16  //          Test to make sure the window actually opened.
17  //          If it did, build the content for it.
18      var Data="<html><head><title>NAVIGATOR Data</title></head>"
19      Data +="<body bgcolor='#CCFFCC'>"
20      Data += "<h1>Things I know about you:</h1>"
21      Data += "<hr width='75%' />"
22      Data += "<img src='magglas1.gif' height='100' width='50' align='left'"
23      Data += " alt='Magnifying Glass' hspace='10' />"
24      Data += "You are running the "+ navigator.appName+" browser<br />"
25      Data += "Version: "+ navigator.appVersion + "<br />"
26      Data += "You are using " + navigator.platform + " based platform<br />"
27      Data += "<form> <input type='button' name='s' value='Enough Already!'"
28      Data += " onclick='window.close()' />"
29      Data += "</form>"
30      Data +="</body></html>"
31  //
32  //          Now we build the new page
33      NewWindow.document.write(Data);
34      NewWindow.document.close()     // close the input stream for the
35  //                                    new window.
36              } // End of if block
37          }      // End of function
```

This is file research.js, an external JavaScript function

3. The code is faster to maintain. Once you learn how one JavaScript works, you also know about any others that employ the same code.

All in all, code leveraging makes good sense, provided that the first time you write the code, you make it good, maintainable, readable code.

The new navigator properties are shown in the code in Figure 13.19. These three navigator properties capture the *application name* and *version* and the *platform* that is running the browser. Notice that the window.close() method is coded *inside* the new window. Look back at Figure 13.17. The button marked "Enough Already!" activates this method and closes the window from inside the page. With this technique the window is actually closed, not just minimized. Play with these screens either on the Web site for the book or copy them from the CD. You really need to see them in action.

EXPLORATION #5 — Create a new Web page that displays to the user today's date, the Web browser he is using, and the version of that browser, as well as the operating system currently running his computer. Test this page on two of the popular browsers.

Figure 13.19 JavaScript-generated HTML code using Navigator object

Note the three navigator properties selected by this code

```
18    var Data="<html><head><title>NAVIGATOR Data</title></head>"
19    Data +="<body bgcolor='#CCFFCC'>"
20    Data += "<h1>Things I know about you:</h1>"
21    Data += "<hr width='75%' />"
22    Data += "<img src='magglas1.gif' height='100' width='50' align='left'"
23    Data += " alt='Magnifying Glass' hspace='10' />"
24    Data += "You are running the "+ navigator.appName+" browser<br />"
25    Data += "Version: "+ navigator.appVersion + "<br />"
26    Data += "You are using " + navigator.platform + " based platform<br />"
27    Data += "<form> <input type='button' name='s' value='Enough Already!'"
28    Data += " onclick='window.close()' />"
29    Data += "</form>"
30    Data +="</body></html>"
```

Table 13.3 Methods and properties of navigator object

Method	Explanation
navigator.javaEnabled()	Returns "true" if the browser supports Java applets; otherwise returns "false."
navigator.plugins.refresh()	Checks to see if there are newly installed plug-ins; if so, enters them into the plugins [] array and may reload pages using them.
Property	**Explanation**
navigator.appCodeName	The coded name of the browser (usually Mozilla in both Netscape and Microsoft browsers).
navigator.appName	The name of the browser.
navigator.appVersion	The version of the browser.
navigator.cookieEnabled	Boolean that returns "true" if cookies are allowed and "false" if they are not (IE4+, Netscape 6+).
navigator.language	The language supported by the browser (Netscape 4+).
navigator.mimeTypes[]	An array of all the MIME types recognized by the browser (Netscape 3+.)
navigator.platform	The platform on which the browser is running, such as Linuxi586 or Win32.
navigator.plugins[]	An array of all the plug-ins that are installed in the browser (Netscape 3+.)
navigator.systemLanguage	The system-level language code (IE 4+).
navigator.userAgent	The string passed to the browser as the http user agent in the request.
navigator.userLanguage	Like navigator.language.

Figure 13.20   Example of a more interesting rollover

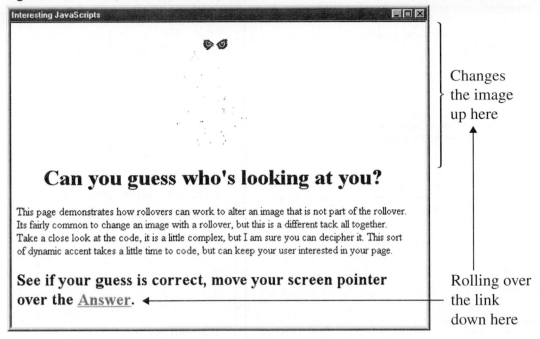

Changes the image up here

Rolling over the link down here

►► ANOTHER INTERESTING BIT

The first script in this section is very interesting in that it uses a *rollover* to change an image away from the screen pointer. It is fairly common to see pages with images that change when you move the screen pointer over them. This example shows how you can use some fairly intricate JavaScript to change an image somewhere else on the page. Take a look at the screen capture in Figure 13.20; it is the opening screen of the series. When the user moves her screen pointer over the Answer link, the figure changes to reveal who is looking at her.

No, we won't show you the answer—you will have to experiment yourself. Figure 13.21 shows the code for the page in Figure 13.20. Notice we have built the functions in the <head> and then called them from the body. Notice, too, that we preload the images. You will see this technique again. It saves time for your users, as they won't have to wait for images to load from across the Net.

Let's take a closer look at the code in Figure 13.21. First we create and initialize some variables. In lines 13 through 21 we set the variables we will be using to control the appearance and disappearance of the images. Then, in lines 25 through 32, we build the *array* holding the eight images we are going to use in the animation. An *array,* also called a *subscripted variable,* is an area of memory reserved for a series of data elements. With all the data set up, we preload the images into the array in lines 34 through 37.

Each element takes up one array numeric designation or subscript. Usually each array element is the same size and type. In this case the eight array elements are named `imagearray[0]` through `imagearray[7]` since JavaScript starts counting with zero. With an array the programmer can easily load and access a series of variables employing the iteration programming structure, as we did in lines 34 through 37.

There is a very interesting method called `eval()` that executes the enclosed code. Using it twice, we first declare a new instance of the `Image()` object and then assign that new instance to the `imagearray` matrix. This is a very subtle use of a powerful method.

Notice that all of the lines of the script, except the functions, are executed as the page initially loads. That way the images are ready and waiting for our user when she makes her guess.

Figure 13.21 Coding remote rollover

```
3   <html>
4   <head>
5   <meta http-equiv="Content-Style-Type" content="text/css" />
6   <title>Interesting JavaScripts</title>
7   <script language="JavaScript" type="text/javascript">
8
9   <!-- The initial idea for this script and many more are  -->
10  <!-- available free online at The JavaScript Source!! -->
11  <!-- http://javascript.internet.com -->
12
13  var maximages = 8; //  count of images or steps in the fade sequence.
14  var appearspeed = 100; // appearance time in milliseconds;  100 = 100 ms
15  var disappearspeed = 250; // it disappears more slowly.
16
17  var appeartimer;
18  var disappeartimer;
19  var appearcount = 0;
20  var disappearcount = maximages-1;
21  var imagearray = new Array(maximages);  // space for the fade images
22  // the first item should be 0, then numbered
23  // through 1 less than your maximages
24
25  imagearray[0] = "owl0.gif";
26  imagearray[1] = "owl1.gif";
27  imagearray[2] = "owl2.gif";
28  imagearray[3] = "owl3.gif";
29  imagearray[4] = "owl4.gif";
30  imagearray[5] = "owl5.gif";
31  imagearray[6] = "owl6.gif";
32  imagearray[7] = "owl7.gif";
33  // preloads fade images
34  for (var i = 0; i < maximages; i++) {
35  eval('pic' + i + ' = new Image();');
36  eval('pic' + i + '.src = imagearray[i];');
37                              } // end  preload loop
38  function appear() {
39  clearTimeout(disappeartimer);
40  document.images['roll-pic'].src = imagearray[appearcount];
41  if (appearcount != maximages-1) {
42  appearcount++;
43  appeartimer = setTimeout('appear()', appearspeed);
44                              }
45  else {
46  clearTimeout(appeartimer);
47  appearcount = 0;
48      }
49                  } // end of appear function
50  function disappear()  {
51  clearTimeout(appeartimer);
52  document.images['roll-pic'].src = imagearray[disappearcount];
53  if (disappearcount != 0) {
54  disappearcount--;
55  disappeartimer = setTimeout('disappear()', disappearspeed);
56                      }
57  else {
58  clearTimeout(disappeartimer);
59  disappearcount = maximages-1;
60      }
61                      }  // end of disappear function
62  </script>
63  </head>
64  <body>
65  <div style="text-align:center;">
66  <p>
67  <a name="roll-pic"></a> <!-- here to serve as a target -->
68  <img src="owl0.gif" name="roll-pic" alt="mystery pic" /><br />
69  </p>
70  <h1>Can you guess who's looking at you?</h1>
71  </div>
72  <p>
73  This page demonstrates how rollovers can work to alter
74  an image that is not part of the rollover.  Its fairly
75  common to change an image with a rollover, but this is
76  a different tack all together.  Take a close look
77  at the code, it is a little complex, but I am sure
78  you can decipher it.  This sort of dynamic accent
79  takes a little time to code, but can keep your user
80  interested in your page.
81  </p>
82  <h2>See if your guess is correct, move your screen pointer over the
83  <a name="solution" href="#roll-pic"onmouseover="appear()" onmouseout="disappear()">
84  Answer</a>.</h2>
85  </body>
86  </html>
```

Create variables and assign values to them.

Preload images

Appear() function

Disappear() function

Using intrinsic attributes to call the functions

Lines 38 through 61 define the two functions appear() and disapper(). They should look very much the same, the difference being that disappear() loads the images from image7 to image0, and appear() loads the images from image0 to image7. Another difference is the time increment before the image changes. In appear() the time interval is shorter, so the images appear more quickly than in disappear(). Other than that, the two functions work just exactly in reverse order. If you think about it, that is pretty much the way you would expect them to work.

With the two functions defined, and the data preloaded into an array, it's time to hand control over to the actual page code. There should be little that is new to you in the <body> of the page. Let's look at the rollover. Line 68 in Figure 13.21 identifies, by name, a target for a later anchor to link to. That way the anchor container won't generate an error if the user tries to activate the link. Since **onmouseover** and **onmouseout** work most reliably with links across different browsers right now, we use that format. The functions point to the actual image name, for example:

document.images ['roll-pic']. src= imagearray[appearcount];

Therefore, when we invoke the function, it already knows which image to alter. We would have to code another function to alter a different image. When the user rolls, slides, moves, tabs, or spins his screen pointer over the word Answer in the level-2 heading (line 84 in Figure 13.21), the function appear() begins executing. As it does, the image at the top of the page resolves through eight steps, becoming more and more defined. When users move their screen pointer off from the word Answer, the disappear() function reverses the steps and makes the image diminish until it appears again like it was in the beginning.

This is an excellent example of *eye candy,* a feature that exists simply to be cute or to demonstrate the prowess of the Web weaver. Using this sort of code judiciously is one of the greatest challenges for Web weavers. In this case, we spent almost eight hours creating our eye-candy code, which actually serves no real purpose other than to be cute. Sometimes being cute is reason enough to expend this time and effort if it amuses or brings your user back, but you need to be ever so careful not to load your pages or your site with too much of this sort of empty feature.

▸▸ THINGS JAVASCRIPT SHOULD NOT BE FORCED TO DO

Sometimes a language makes it easy to become really obnoxious with your Web pages. For example, the Navigator browser has the *nefarious* <blink> tag that can be used to create visually distracting pages. JavaScript has some of these unrecommended uses, too. In fact, coding JavaScript can enable you to build some terribly ugly pages. Not only can you make text blink, but you can make it blink in a series of colors! Here are some general guidelines for avoiding the misuse of JavaScript:

- Don't use the alert, confirm, and prompt dialog windows just to display text. These functions should be reserved for their intended purposes, not used just because they are available. In your experience with JavaScript, you will probably see more of these boxes than you would like to see. Don't be among those who overuse them!

- Don't scroll messages on the status bar. The status bar can be an important tool. When you really need to put information there, do so, but don't scroll it. A scrolling status bar is distracting; it pulls your user's eyes away from the content of the page, and it also becomes annoying in very short order.

- Actually, it is best not to scroll anything. Some Java applications use scrolling to good effect if it scrolls from more than one direction. However, with most JavaScript scripts the scrolling will move in only one direction. That is boring, distracting, and should be considered passé.

Chapter Fourteen will address some exciting uses for JavaScript creating truly dynamic HTML pages using and expanding upon the techniques you have learned here.

▸▸ KEY TERMS

Array	Modal
Calling page	Multithreading
Code leveraging	Object
Concatenate	Parameter
Function	Properties
Function call	Scripting language
Instance	String
Loop	Workaround
Methods	

▸▸ NEW TAG

<script></script>

▸▸ REVIEW QUESTIONS

1. Define each of the key terms.
2. How is the <script> tag used? (Provide an example.)
3. What was JavaScript, a.k.a. LiveScript, originally designed to do?
4. Name four things JavaScript does not do.
5. Identify and give an example of two different ways to specify which scripting language is used by a script.
6. In what two places can you find JavaScript code?
7. Why are two different types of comment lines used within JavaScript?
8. What special characters are used to identify the beginning and ending of the function code?
9. What happens to a function call when the function is executed?
10. List four JavaScript objects that are useful to Web authors.
11. How is running JavaScript different from running a CGI script in regard to Net traffic?
12. How does JavaScript count time?
13. What is a unique feature of the Window object?
14. Identify three different kinds of modal dialog boxes and describe the differences between them.
15. When opening a new window, what are four things the author can control through JavaScript and one thing the author cannot control?
16. Why should you always close the input stream with JavaScript code?
17. How is the navigator object most often used?
18. What are three advantages to code leveraging?
19. What are three things JavaScript should not do?

▸▸ EXERCISES

13.1. Now that you can build JavaScripts, Ruby wants you to modify her existing raw page (**eme13-raw.html** on the CD or Web site) so she can add it as a new page on her site. She wants it modified as follows:

a. Have the page look like the "standard page with the following particulars" (set, of course, in a document-level style sheet):

 1. The page should have a title of "Colors, A Rainbow of Beauty." It should have the standard heading for Gwen's shop followed by a centered level-2 heading that matches the title.

 2. The background color should be soft gray, #CCCCCC, and the text should be a mellow brown, #996600.

 3. Level-1 headings should be 24 points, light blue-green, #336633, and centered.

 4. Level-2 and level-3 headings should be 18 points and medium green, #339933.

 5. Level-2 and level-3 headings should be sans serif.

b. Ruby would like to have the text on the page change color when the user selects a particular "favorite gem." Use the following color chart to set the gems and colors to build the "Rainbow":

 1. Ruby, #CC0000

 2. Citrine, #FF9966

 3. Topaz, #FFFF00

 4. Emerald, #006600

 5. Sapphire, #6699CC

 6. Tanzanite, #003399

 7. Amethyst, #660099

c. You can find a JavaScript function that changes the color of the text on the page in another page called **colors.htm,** located on the CD and the Web site. Explore that page, and adapt the colors you find there for the page for Ruby. You will need to be careful to set up the page exactly as you see it on the "colors" page. We have set the **id** of the page for you; you will need to change the colors to match.

d. The form should list each color on its own line. The form elements should be two inches from the right margin, in a column.

e. Save the page as **eme13-js.htm.**

f. If you code the page correctly, the colors of the body of the text will change, but the level-1 and level-2 headings, as well as the contact information at the bottom of the page, will not. Research this and decide whether or not style data takes precedence over styles set with scripts.

13.2. Create a new HTML document that includes JavaScript code displaying the following:

a. Your name.

b. The course prefix, number, and name of your HTML class.

c. The instructor's name for this class.

The document's title bar should display "Sample JavaScript Code" with your name and the assignment due date included within comment lines.

13.3. Create a new HTML document that includes JavaScript code displaying a modal dialog box prompting the user to enter his mother's maiden name. The document's title bar should display "Internet Privacy Concerns," with your name and the assignment due date included within comment lines. The content of this new page should discuss privacy concerns as they relate to Internet applications. In addition, somewhere within the page, display a button that calls the JavaScript shown in Figure 13.19. This code opens a new window that displays information about the user's computer platform.

13.4. Retrieve the Homework home page you updated in previous exercises. Add to the page footer the call to a JavaScript that displays the last date the page was modified.

13.5. Retrieve your school's home page that you updated in previous exercises. When the user moves the screen pointer over the school's name, a JavaScript should be called that displays a team cheer in the status bar. For example, if your school colors are black and blue, and the team name is the "Banana Slugs," you could display "Go Black and Blue!" or "Slime-em Slugs!"

13.6. Retrieve the movies home page you updated in previous exercises. Add the HTML code to create a button labeled "Rent this Video" someplace on the page. When the user activates the button, a JavaScript should be invoked that opens a new window displaying the name of a movie you would recommend for everyone to watch. This JavaScript code should include a button that closes the window when activated. Test the code on two popular browsers.

13.7. Create a new HTML document that includes a button that calls a JavaScript to open a new window. The new document's title bar should display "Used Computer Equipment," with your name and the assignment due date included within comment lines. The page content should look like a want ad, advertising at least one used computer for sale. Under the description of the sale item(s), place a button labeled "Warranty." When this button is activated, it should open a new window that displays the company name, address, telephone number, email address, and cost for a one-year warranty.

13.8. Create a new HTML document that includes JavaScript code modifying the count-down loop shown in Figure 13.5. The modification should count *up* from 1 to 15. The document's title bar should display "Count Up From 1 to 15," with your name and the assignment due date included within comment lines.

14

Chapter Fourteen

Dynamic HTML: Charismatic Pages

In this chapter we will explore a set of dynamic ways to present information. Chapter Thirteen set the stage by introducing the fundamentals of JavaScript. We can now expand on these skills and put JavaScript to work enhancing our page designs. *Dynamic* means having action, motion, or responding to the user. Most of the dynamic features that we will explore in this chapter are centered in JavaScript, but some, like *image maps,* are enhancements to good old HTML, and others, like CGI scripts, visit that idea. We have included these particular examples because we think they represent a good cross section of what is available to the wise Web weaver. Feel free to copy these examples, modify them to meet your needs, and incorporate them in your own documents.

CHAPTER OBJECTIVES

After reading this chapter you should be able to do the following:

- Explain to others the differences between server-side and client-side processing.
- Use image maps to create a set of related links.
- Create pop-up windows to present data.
- Code image rollovers to add dynamic events to a page.
- Build JavaScript events to alter the color on the page.
- Create cookies to store data about the user.
- Employ JavaScript code to validate user input.
- Use a CGI script to update a data file reporting results back to the user.

▸▸ IMAGE MAPS

Image maps allow the user to select different parts of an image to cause an event to happen. These areas, called **hot spots,** can act as links to other pages or can invoke JavaScript programs. Each hot spot is associated with some event, usually a link to a new page or to a target within the current page. There are two ways to implement image maps in HTML: on the client side or on the server side.

SERVER-SIDE IMAGE MAPS

In *server-side mapping* the work is done on the server side of the exchange. Data are sent by the browser to the server to be processed by a CGI script, which returns the results to the browser for the user to see. We mentioned this method, and discouraged its use, when we looked at using images as submit buttons in Chapter Eleven. Server-side image mapping has fallen from favor in the Net community because it has the following disadvantages:

- **Increased Net traffic.** Each time the user activates any part of a server-side image map, the browser must send the coordinates of the screen pointer to the server. This process increases the traffic on the Net, because the browser doesn't know if the coordinates selected will map to an actual URL or not, and each activation causes another transaction over the Net.

- **Confusion for the user.** Normally, when the user moves the mouse pointer over a link, the URL is displayed on the screen. In a server-side model, the browser has no idea what URL, if any, is associated with any part of the image. Therefore, the browser displays either the URL of the image-map program or the X and Y coordinates of the screen pointer location. Neither is very helpful for the user.

- **Much slower response for the user.** In a server-side model each response back to the user must be generated by the server. That means that the browser has to send a signal to the server requesting that the server process the information about a mouse click. Then the client has to wait until the server receives, processes, and returns the information before it can continue processing. If there is much congestion on the Net, that response can take a long time to reach the client. The user has to wait for the request from the client to reach the server, then for the server to process the request and reply to the client. As you well know, since you are one, users don't like to wait!

- **Local testing is impossible.** To test a server-side image map, the Web server must run a special image-mapping program and process the X and Y coordinates sent from the client. Thus, it is impossible to test the functionality of a server-side image map without being connected to a Web server. This is a big hindrance for many Web weavers who work "off-line" at home or in the office.

- **There are several different server-side mapping packages.** If the Web weaver chooses to use server-side image mapping, he must decide which type of image mapping software is run on the Web server. Two of the most common are the W^3C (CERN) httpd server and the NCSA (National Center for Supercomputing Applications) httpd server. Each requires different, incompatible coding from the browser. Therefore, if the Web weaver tries to move her code to a server that uses an incompatible encoding method, she will need to recode her pages.

- **Often a system administrator must set up the server code.** Although it is possible in some circumstances for the Web weaver to also maintain the Web server, in most cases the Web weaver doesn't control the server. Consequently, the Web administrator must load the software necessary to receive, process, and reply to the image. Loading the software adds another step in implementing new Web pages.

For all these reasons, server-side image mapping is not used as much as it once was. Client-side image mapping (discussed next) poses none of the problems of server-side mapping. If you are forced to use server-side mapping, you will need to do some research into the **ismap** attribute for the <img /> container. The <img> element's **ismap** attribute is the only HTML code option found in the XHTML Server-side Image Map module.

CLIENT-SIDE IMAGE MAPS

Client-side mapping, where the work is done on the client side of the exchange, means that the client (user's computer) does all the work and no data need be transmitted across the Net. The browser processes any reaction to the image activation locally. This is a newer methodology, and most Web weavers prefer it to server-side mapping because it has the following advantages:

- It is usable by people browsing with nongraphical browsers.
- It provides immediate feedback as to whether the pointer is over an active region (hot spot) of the image.
- It decreases loading on the Net, allowing faster response to the user.
- It can be tested and modified without having a connection to the server already up and running.
- It can be accomplished by the Web weaver with no outside help from the Web administrator.
- It is endorsed by Forces for Good within the community.

A minor drawback to client-side mapping is that it is supported only by relatively newer browsers, like Netscape 2.0+ and Internet Explorer 3.0+. Nevertheless, with most of the industry moving to new browsers as soon as they are released, this is a small price to pay for all the benefits that client-side mapping provides.

IMAGE COORDINATES FOR HOT SPOTS

Before coding an image map a Web weaver must identify the coordinates to all the hot spots to be used as image links. Image editors and drawing packages (Photoshop, Paint Shop Pro, and even Paint) display the XY coordinates of the screen pointer as it moves over an image. However, identifying the coordinates of all the map's hot spots (all those pairs of numbers that follow the **coords** attribute in Figure 14.1), can be a time-consuming task. Software like Mapedit, CuteMap, or Mapthis makes the creation of client-side maps very simple by allowing the Web weaver to outline the proposed hot spot on the map using the screen pointer. The mapping software then converts the outline into the proper XY coordinates

Figure 14.1 shows a simple page containing an image that is set up as a client-side image map. There are just a few differences between the page shown in Figure 14.1 and the HTML code you have been building thus far. What follows is a discussion of these differences, including the additions to the HTML code necessary to create an image map using the <img>, <map>, and <area> elements. The <map> and <area> elements combine together to form the XHTML Client-side Image Map module.

usemap

The first attribute we need to discuss in regard to image maps comes in the <img> container:

```
<img src="newbooks.gif" usemap="#newbooks" border="0" />
```

The **usemap** attribute specifies a target name for the client-side image map as opposed to the **ismap** attribute, which is used with server-side mapping. This attribute assigns the

Figure 14.1 Image map and related code

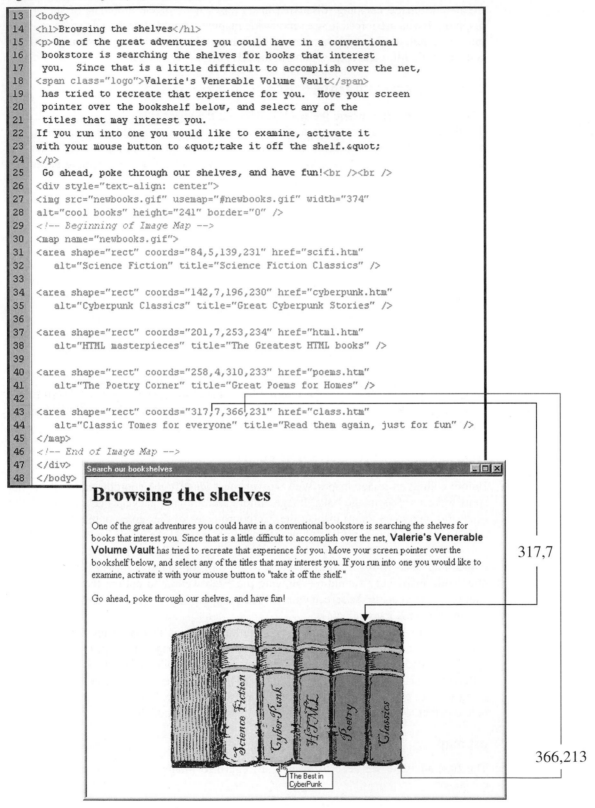

target name of #newbooks.gif in Figure 14.1, which identifies the actual mapping information found in the <map></map> container and the related <area /> tags (both will be discussed in turn). In some cases the **usemap** attribute identifies the URL of map information that is an independent file. Usually, though, the URL is simply the internal target name preceded by an octothorp: #newbooks.

In Figure 14.1, our <map> tag is assigned the target name of newbooks.gif in the body of the HTML document. It is best to use the same name for the map information and the image it maps. That way, especially if you have several image maps, you can easily know which map is associated with which image. However, we could have named the map "phred" and the code would have worked equally well. Notice that all the code necessary to process the image map is contained within the HTML document.

Here is the way the image map works: When the user activates any part of the image, the X and Y coordinates of the position of the screen pointer are captured. Then the browser on the client computer processes them using the coordinates provided by the <map> container. When the browser receives the coordinates, it compares them with each of the different sets of <area /> coordinates.

For example, suppose the screen pointer appears within a rectangle that has a top left corner of 317,7 and a bottom right corner of 366,231, the <area /> associated with classic works. When the user activates his mouse anywhere within the boundaries of that part of the image, the browser transfers control to the hypertext reference **(href)** associated with that area of the image map. You can overlap the <area /> definitions, but the first one the browser encounters, working from top to bottom, will take precedence. As a result, you need to arrange your <area />s from most precise to most general, or from smallest to largest.

HTML   **<map>Contents of Image Map</map>**

Description: encloses client-side image map data specified by the **usemap** attribute.
Type: container.
Attribute: class, del, dir, id, **name,** onblur, onclick, ondblclick, onfocus, onkeydown, onkeypress, onkeyup, onmousedown, onmousemove, onmouseout, onmouseover, onmouseup, rev, style, tabindex, target, **title,** type.
Special note: requires **name** attribute.

The <map></map> container encloses all the HTML code that defines a client-side image map. The **name** attribute is required to identify the container as a target for the <img /> element's **usemap** attribute, just as anchor (<a>) elements use an anchor name as a target. The browser associates the value assigned to the **name** attribute with a particular set of mapping instructions. The following HTML code is used in Figure 14.1 to identify the coordinates of the image map named newbooks.gif.

```
<map name="newbooks.gif">
```

This **name** attribute value is then assigned to the **usemap** attribute in the <img /> tag to identify the image map. Therefore, the name must be unique from any other map name on that page. Like anchor elements, the leading octothorp (#) in the **usemap** attribute value signifies that the source URL (name) is local to the document. This code identifies newbooks.gif as the image and #newbooks.gif as the local source for the image coordinates:

```
<img src="newbooks.gif" usemap="#newbooks.gif" />
```

The octothorp is omitted from the **name** attribute of the <map></map> container because it identifies where the image map coordinates are located—that is, the target.

In addition to the **name** attribute, the <map></map> container holds a set of <area> tags, one for each hot spot in the image.

title

The **title** attribute, introduced in the HTML 4 specifications, has taken on new significance with the current crop of browsers, starting with Navigator 6 and Opera 6. The text associated with the **title** attribute is displayed when the user holds his mouse pointer over the image, or in this case over the hot spot defined by the <map></map> container. Older browsers used to display the text associated with the **alt** attribute. Today's popular browsers do not display the **alt** text; they use the text assigned by the **title** attribute instead. We have found you can add a **title** to all sorts of interesting elements, like headings, tables, links, etc., with results in a similar effect.

alt VERSUS title

One small but annoying concern with image maps is that since our Web pages are client-side, they are dependent upon the good graces of the browser builders. You need to be very careful about testing your code with the current browsers. As just mentioned, past releases of the browsers showed the data assigned to the **alt** attribute as a tool tip when the mouse pointer hovered over the corresponding hot spot. That made building useful image maps very straightforward. However, the text associated with the **alt** attribute is designed to be displayed only when the image is broken or not available. Therefore, the current versions of both Navigator and Opera no longer display those data when the pointer merely hovers over an image or image hot spot. With the new versions of these browsers, the text associated with the **title** attribute is displayed when the pointer is held over an image or hot spot.

To summarize, the older versions of the browsers don't support the **title** attribute; they show the **alt** content. Newer versions don't support **alt** on mouse-over; they use **title** content. You must never assume that just because version 6.8 of any given browser supports a particular feature that version 6.9 will still support it. Constant testing to ensure that your pages still work should be an ongoing task.

HTML **<area />**

Description: defines the coordinates and link for one region of a client-side image map.
Type: empty tag.
Attributes: accesskey, **alt,** class, **coords, href,** id, lang, **nohref,** onblur, onclick, ondblclick, onfocus, onkeydown, onkeypress, onkeyup, onmousedown, onmousemove, onmouseout, onmouseover, onmouseup, **shape,** style, tabindex, target, **title.**
XML: requires closing tag using <area />.
Special note: requires the **coords** and either the **href** or **nohref** attributes.

The real work of a client-side image is described by the <area /> tag. This empty tag defines each hot spot in the image map and tells the browser what to do if the user activates it. XML specifications require the closing tag format <area />. When the user moves the screen pointer over any area that has been defined by an <area /> tag, the pointer changes to a pointing finger, and the browser displays the URL of the related link in the status bar. Six commonly used attributes for this tag are **alt, title, shape, coords, href,** and **nohref.** We discussed **title** earlier. Let's consider each of the others now in turn.

alt

In older browsers, and some of the current browsers, the value for the **alt** attribute is displayed when the user "hovers" over the area. You should always use the **alt** attribute with each <area /> element to help your users understand where they are going. In view of the current state of affairs with older and newer browsers, you should code both an **alt** and a **title** for your hot spots.

shape

The **shape** attribute works with the **coords** attribute (discussed next) to define the hot spots on the page. This attribute tells the browser how to process the coordinates. It also, as its name implies, describes the general shape of the hot spot. There are four valid shapes:

1. Circle
2. Rectangle (or rect)
3. Polygon (or poly)
4. Default

Browsers are not consistent in their treatment of these values. Navigator doesn't recognize the value rectangle but all the popular browsers recognize rect, so the abbreviated name is the preferred usage. On the other hand, Internet Explorer doesn't understand the "default" shape (fourth in the preceding list), so defining a polygon shape="poly" for the whole image is better than coding shape = "default". How you define the shape of the hot spot is important. There are two schools of thought about this issue. The first is that either circle or rect should be used whenever possible because a simpler shape makes setting up the **coords** simpler. The other school of thought is that the hot spot should be as exact as reasonable, following the actual outlines of the objects in the image. There is strong support for both schools of thought. We advise you to pick one and stick to it.

coords

The **coords** attribute is required. It describes the boundaries of a hot spot. Each entry in the **coords** list is an XY coordinate pair. All coordinates are measured in *pixels* on the original image. The **coords** attribute can be the vertices of polygons or the XY coordinates of the center of a circle and the radius of the circle. Following are the three types of shapes with the required **coords** values for each:

- circle="x,y,r" requires the XY coordinates of the center of the circle and the length of the radius (r).
- poly="x1,y1,x2,y2,x3,y3 . . ." requires the XY coordinates for each vertex, or corner, of the shape. Usually poly is used to describe odd-shaped areas, like the shape of a country when a map of the world is used as an image map.
- rect="x1,y1,x2,y2" requires two sets of coordinates (see Figure 14.1). The first is the XY coordinates for the *top left corner,* and the second is the XY coordinates for the *lower right corner* of the rectangle. The rectangle is a specialized form of polygon—you need specify only two points to define it.

href

Each <area /> must have an associated **href** or have the **nohref** attribute coded. Usually the **href** attribute describes the URL of the HTML document to be displayed when the user clicks the mouse button with the screen pointer within the defined area of that <area />. If you are using the identified area to link to a local HTML document, or to a target within the existing document, simply code the URL of the document or the target name as the value for this attribute. The following code establishes thailand.htm as the Web page to open when the user activates the Thailand area of the "world" image map:

```
<area
    shape="poly"
    coords="372,131, 376,154, 380,153, 380,153, 380,139, 378,134"
    alt="Thailand"
    title="Thailand"
    href="thailand.htm" />
```

nohref

The **nohref** attribute defines an area that the user can activate but that contains no link. Thus, the user can activate the hot spot described by the <area />, but *nothing will happen.* There are only two reasons for using this attribute. If you are building a large image map and want to define all the areas in the beginning but don't have URLs created for some of the hot spots, you could bring up the page and fill in the **href**s later. The other reason for using this attribute would be if you want to annoy your users. This attribute creates hot spots that the user can activate with no response. That could be very frustrating.

HTML 4 CONSIDERATIONS

In the HTML 4 specifications, the W^{3}C introduces the technique of using an <object> container rather than the <img /> tag to identify a client-side image map. It also discusses using <a> tags within the <map> element rather than <area /> tags to identify the actual mapped areas within the image. At the time of this writing, the popular browsers vary widely in their support of these techniques, so we will show no example. Opera brought up the image just fine, but didn't consider it an image map and so it had no hot spots. Internet Explorer didn't even open the image when it was contained within the <object> element. Netscape correctly used the <object> element when the map used <area />s, but refused to acknowledge a <map> built of <a> tags. *Caveat emptor* (buyer beware) is especially appropriate when talking about how browsers will handle an image map.

MAKING IT EASY

It is fairly simple to use an image-mapping software package (like Mapedit by Boutell.Com, Inc) to create the <map> container for you. Software packages like this are usually WYSIWYG tools that take as input an HTML file with the image(s) to be mapped already coded in one or more <img> tags. The software asks which image you wish to map. It then displays that image. You simply outline each region you want to be a hot spot. The software prompts you for the URL and other data to be associated with that hot spot, and it creates the <map> container for you, right in the HTML document specified.

If you don't have access to an image-mapping program, you can use an image editor or any drawing package—like Paint, shown in Figure 14.2—to determine the required points of reference on any figure.

Most drawing packages allow the user to find the XY coordinates of points within the image. In that case, you will need to record those coordinates and create your own <map> container. For example, Figure 14.2 shows one of the boundary points in the cyberpunk area of the image. The point identified—138,10—is the first point in the set of coordinate pairs in the <area /> data as well. Manually recording and entering the top left and bottom right corners would give us the coordinates necessary to specify that rectangle in the <area> element.

OTHER CONSIDERATIONS

Not all browsers support client-side images. In fact, not all browsers support image mapping. To make your pages as friendly as possible for the whole range of potential users, you could include your image map within an anchor tag. That way if the user cannot use image maps, she at least has the option of linking to a page that provides her with more useful options. If she doesn't have a browser that supports client-side image mapping, she can click anywhere on the image and see the document you defined, which should contain a set of links to all of the documents available from the image map. Hence, a majority of users will be able to access your information.

If you choose to build a graphics-dependent page using image maps, you should also build a parallel page designed for the text-only browser. Many professionally designed sites allow the user the choice of seeing a graphical rendering or a text-only page right from the home page. This technique will win you the gratitude of the text-only users on the Net.

Figure 14.2

Using drawing tool to identify coordinates of points in image

Drawing tool

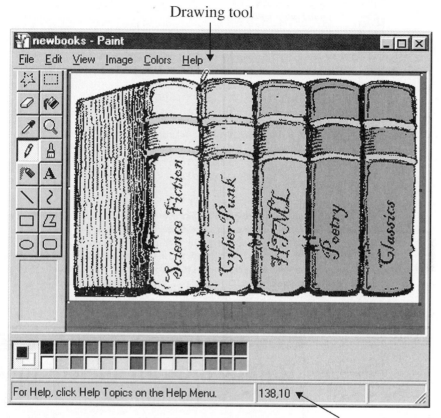

The X,Y address of the drawing tool

EXPLORATION #1

Create a small page that uses the image palette.gif on the student CD and the Web site for the book. Have your page use the image as an image map, asking the user to select his favorite color from the seven on the palette. Be sure to create a large area to cover the areas outside the colors, so you can warn users if they choose an area outside one of the colors. When the user clicks on the color, open one of the seven pages, red.html, orange.html, yellow.html, green.html, blue.html, indigo.html, or violet.html, which are also on the student CD.

▸▸ SIMPLE ROLLOVERS

We introduced you to rollovers in Chapter Thirteen. There you saw an interesting example. Now let's look more closely at a simple rollover that shows the minimal way to use this tool.

Figure 14.3 A rollover page, before the rollover

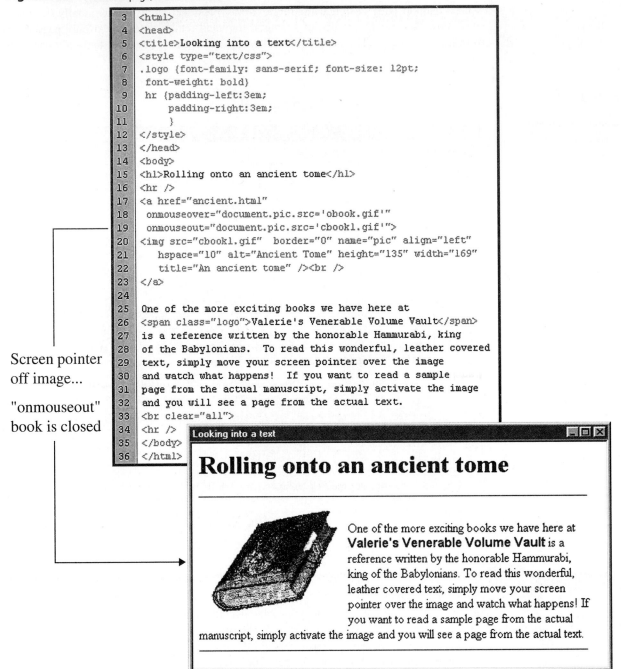

```
3   <html>
4   <head>
5   <title>Looking into a text</title>
6   <style type="text/css">
7   .logo {font-family: sans-serif; font-size: 12pt;
8    font-weight: bold}
9    hr {padding-left:3em;
10       padding-right:3em;
11       }
12  </style>
13  </head>
14  <body>
15  <h1>Rolling onto an ancient tome</h1>
16  <hr />
17  <a href="ancient.html"
18   onmouseover="document.pic.src='obook.gif'"
19   onmouseout="document.pic.src='cbookl.gif'">
20  <img src="cbookl.gif" border="0" name="pic" align="left"
21     hspace="10" alt="Ancient Tome" height="135" width="169"
22     title="An ancient tome" /><br />
23  </a>
24
25  One of the more exciting books we have here at
26  <span class="logo">Valerie's Venerable Volume Vault</span>
27  is a reference written by the honorable Hammurabi, king
28  of the Babylonians.  To read this wonderful, leather covered
29  text, simply move your screen pointer over the image
30  and watch what happens!  If you want to read a sample
31  page from the actual manuscript, simply activate the image
32  and you will see a page from the actual text.
33  <br clear="all">
34  <hr />
35  </body>
36  </html>
```

Screen pointer off image...

"onmouseout" book is closed

Rolling onto an ancient tome

One of the more exciting books we have here at **Valerie's Venerable Volume Vault** is a reference written by the honorable Hammurabi, king of the Babylonians. To read this wonderful, leather covered text, simply move your screen pointer over the image and watch what happens! If you want to read a sample page from the actual manuscript, simply activate the image and you will see a page from the actual text.

Usually rollover applications involve images and even image maps. The screen capture in Figure 14.3 shows a very simple image rollover before the screen pointer "rolls over" the image. You know how to make a page look like this by simply inserting an image and setting the **align** attribute or the **style** attribute's float property to left. However, look at Figure 14.4, and see what happens when the user puts the screen pointer on the book image. Notice that the image of the closed book is replaced by one of an open book. By simply moving the screen pointer, the user causes the page to, dare we say, dynamically change the image on the screen. Figure 14.3 also shows the code for the page. Pay particular attention to the <a></a> container; this is where the enhancement happens.

Look at the code for the anchor tag duplicated in Figure 14.5. Here we are using the **onmouseover** and **onmouseout** events to trigger changes in the **src** for the object named

Figure 14.4   A simple rollover, rolling over

onmouseover
book is open

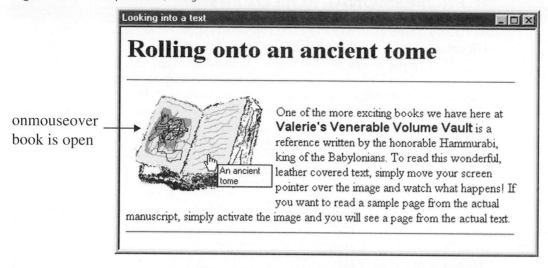

Figure 14.5

The code for the rollover

```
17  <a href="ancient.html"
18    onmouseover="document.pic.src='obook.gif'"
19    onmouseout="document.pic.src='cbookl.gif'">
20  <img src="cbookl.gif"  border="0" name="pic" align="left"
21     hspace="10" alt="Ancient Tome" height="135" width="169"
22     title="An ancient tome" /><br />
23  </a>
```

pic in the current document. Back in Chapter Thirteen we talked about how naming objects was the preferred way to address them. When the user moves the screen pointer over the image, the **onmouseover** event is triggered, and the source for the image named "pic" is changed from cbookl.gif to obook.gif. In other words, using the concepts of JavaScript and object-oriented programming, we can cause the value of the **src** attribute for the named object "pic" to change when the user moves his screen pointer over the image. When the user moves his screen pointer off the image, the **onmouseout** event is invoked, and the cbookl.gif image is put back as the image in the space named "pic". This is a very nice way to add a dynamic element to your pages.

The only attribute necessary to address the space on the page by name is name="pic", which gives the image object a name we can reference as we change the content. Of course, the image can change in a variety of ways. It could be a button that goes from dark to light, or a word that becomes outlined in color when the screen pointer moves over it. One of the more sophisticated uses for rollover images is loading an image map as the second image. That presents more of a coding and design challenge, but it can be very effective.

Remember, in all of our discussions of images, that they are available only to users with graphical browsers, so it isn't wise to become too dependent on them. One of the problems with images in general, and specifically with rollovers, is that a second image can increase the download time for the user. We will address this problem in the next section.

EXPLORATION   #2   Create a page that demonstrates an image rollover using the two images frown.gif and smile.gif on the student CD and the Web site. The image should be centered on the screen. Use an image 251 pixels wide and 251 pixels high. When the user moves her screen pointer over the frown image, it should change to the smile image. Have the image change back to the frown when the user moves her screen pointer off the image.

▸▸ PROFESSIONAL ROLLOVERS

Actually, this section could be called "no-wait rollovers" because the technique we will demonstrate reduces the "wait time" (which is the download time) for the user by preloading the images while the page is building. This code also takes into account the problems of older browsers and browsers that cannot handle JavaScript. With this code, the page will look and work the same as it does in Figures 14.3 and 14.4. The difference is that the images will already be in cache when the intrinsic event calls for them, so they will load very quickly. Figure 14.6 shows a code snippet for this new version.

Figure 14.6

HTML code that preloads images

Here we pre-load the images as the page builds.

When we need the images they are already in cache.

```
13  <script type="text/javascript">
14  <!-- Image caching at its finest -->
15  if (document.images){
16      openbook = new image();
17      closebook = new image();
18      openbook.src = "obook.gif";
19      closebook.src = "cbook1.gif";
20                      }
21  else {
22      document.pic=" ";
23      closebook=" ";
24      openbook=" ";
25          }
26  // <!-- end of fine caching code -->
27  </script>
28  </head>
29  <body>
30  <h1>Rolling onto an ancient tome</h1>
31  <hr />
32  <a href="ancient.html"
33   onmouseover="document.pic.src='openbook.src'"
34   onmouseout="document.pic.src='closebook.src'">
35  <img src="cbook1.gif"  border="0"  name="pic" align="left"
36      hspace="10" alt="Ancient Tome" height="135" width="169"
37      title="An ancient tome" />
38  </a>
```

The only difference between the code in Figure 14.3 and Figure 14.6 is the JavaScript in the <script> element in the <head></head> container. The script at the beginning of the page does two things. First, it checks to see if the browser can identify images. If it can't, then it simply sets the images to blanks. Only browsers that support JavaScript 1.1, like Navigator 3.0+ and Internet Explorer 4+, have the document. images object. If the browser can support images, then the script creates two new image objects, openbook and closebook. Once these objects are created, the browser uses the **.src** property to begin loading the images into the objects. This image-loading takes place while the rest of the screen is building and while the user is reading the screen. When the user moves the mouse over the image, the image has already been loaded into cache and so is available to quickly load into the page. This technique makes the image rollover much smoother; it looks more professional.

You would not notice a change if you took the images from the CD that comes with this book, but you should see a difference if you load the pages from the Web site for this book. If you are using the Web site, be sure to flush your cache before you download the page, because it uses the same images as those in Figures 14.3 and 14.4.

▸▸ COLOR-CHANGING ON THE FLY

One of the least complex changes you can make is to allow users to alter the background color of the page while they are looking at it. Although we are always at the mercy of the browser when it comes to the final appearance of our documents, JavaScript allows us to make some changes on the fly. One common change is to allow the user the choice of background colors. It is fairly easy to give users a set of radio buttons, or even a simple text field, and allow them to alter the color of the background.

Altering the color of the foreground is a tad more complex; we will see a JavaScript that allows the user to play with both foreground and background colors in a bit. It is also possible to change the colors of the links—like the **alink, vlink,** and **link** options on the <body> tag. All in all, JavaScript allows you to build an environment that gives the user some control over the way the page looks. This can be a nice touch.

Figures 14.7 and 14.8 show a Web page created just to demonstrate the user's ability to change the background color. Figure 14.7 shows the default version of the screen just as the user encounters it. Notice that in Figure 14.7 we have shown you only the code related to the color changing. We have snipped out the plain text to make the figure shorter. However, the whole script is on the companion CD and the Web site for the book.

Figure 14.8 shows the screen after the user chose the Blue background. This screen is not particularly dynamic, but it gives the users some control over their screen displays, which many users appreciate.

COLOR PREFERENCES

Research into color preferences among users has revealed that a large majority of them prefer to read dark text on a light background—a combination that has been around for thousands of years and is generally your best bet. Unfortunately, some novice Web weavers seem to delight in creating pages with dark backgrounds and light text. As we have mentioned before, this is not a good idea. One option is to let your users decide what type of background color they prefer. If you wanted to expand on this, you could have the form send you an email each time your users change the background color. Then you could tally up the counts of the colors they preferred, doing your own empirical research on user color preferences.

One of the important things to notice about Figure 14.8 is that the blue color does not fill the entire browser pane. The way the code is designed, color changes are applied to the entire body of the document, but since the document does not occupy all of the real estate within the browser pane, only those portions that are part of the <body> element change background color.

We have mentioned before that different versions of the browsers support different features. The HTML document for this figure is an example. In previous editions of this page, the authors used the document.bgColor property to change the color of the entire background. With newer versions of the browsers, this code stopped working. It seems the newer browsers want to have the background color set using a **style** attribute instead of the document property. Your humble authors have made the decision to present code that works with the newer browsers, with the caution that if you're using an older version of the browsers, you should be prepared for the possibility that this code will not work. We have included versions of these pages that work with older browsers but not the newer browsers on the CD (see the old-code directory).

KEEPING FORMS HTML-COMPLIANT

In Figure 14.7 the <form></form> container is used only to contain the elements used to activate the JavaScript. While the validators require every form to have an associated action, we have not coded a submit button, so the "null" action would never be taken. It is

Figure 14.7 Initial color-changing page

```
12  <script type="text/javascript">
13  var color; // Global variable
14  function switchbg(color){
15  wholedoc.style.backgroundColor=color;
16  }
17  </script>
18  </head>
19  <body id="main">
20
21  <!-- use id not name to identify -->
22  <script type="text/javascript">
23  var wholedoc=document.getElementById("main"); //get div identity
24  </script>
```

Plain, old, boring code removed

```
36  <form action="null"> <!-- no real action, just holds buttons -->
37  <!-- Must pass color as a string ' ' -->
38  <script type="text/javascript">
39  var wholedoc=document.getElementById("main"); //get identity
40  </script>
41  <p>
42  I would like the background color to be:
43  </p>
44  <input type="button" name="bgcol" alt="white" value="white"
45     onclick="switchbg('#FFFFFF');" />
46  <input type="button" name="bgcol" alt="cream" value="cream"
47     onclick="switchbg('#FFFFCC');" />
48  <input type="button" name="bgcol" alt="lilac" value="lilac"
49     onclick="switchbg('#FFCCFF');" />
50  <input type="button" name="bgcol" alt="yellow" value="yellow"
51     onclick="switchbg('#FFFF33');" />
52  <input type="button" name="bgcol" alt="green" value="green"
53     onclick="switchbg('#CCFFCC');" />
54  <input type="button" name="bgcol" alt="blue" value="blue"
55     onclick="switchbg('#66CCFF');" />
56  <input type="button" name="bgcol" alt="indigo" value="indigo"
57     onclick="switchbg('#6600FF');" />
58  <input type="button" name="bgcol" alt="violet" value="violet"
59     onclick="switchbg('#9900F9');" />
60  <input type="button" name="bgcol" alt="black" value="black"
61     onclick="switchbg('#000000');" />
62  </form>
```

First color changer page ▫◻✕

Colors to read by

In our continuing effort to provide our users with the most pleasant viewing experience we at **Valerie's Venerable Volume Vault** are always trying to make our site as friendly as possible. To help you enjoy our page more, please use the buttons below to set the background of the page to a color with which you are comfortable.

I would like the background color to be:

| white | cream | lilac | yellow | green | blue | indigo | violet | black |

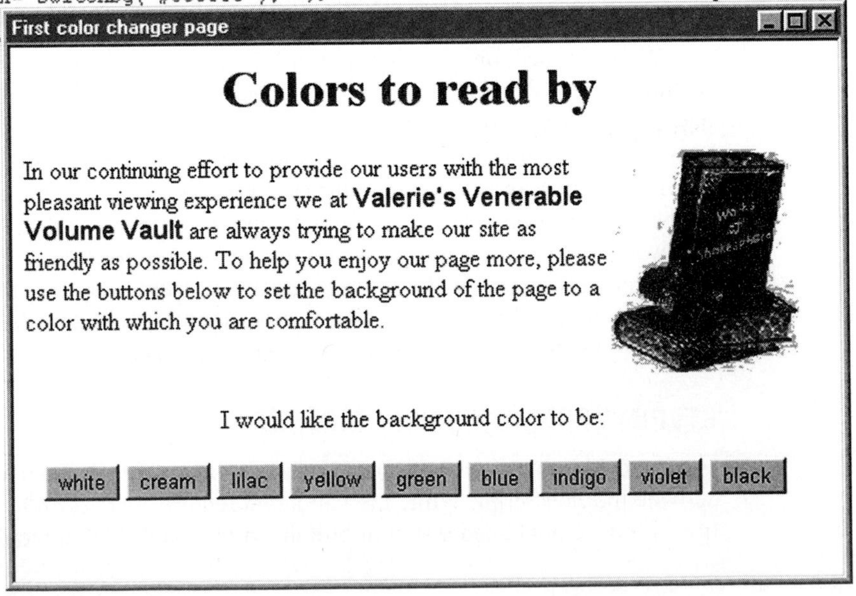

Figure 14.8

How screen looks when changed to blue

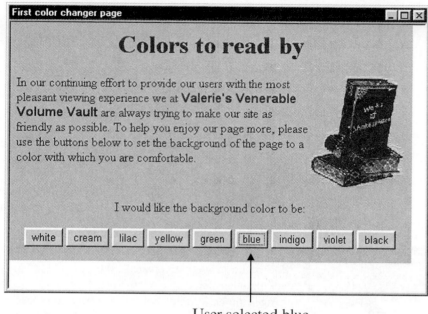

User selected blue

there only to satisfy the requirement of the validators. Let's take a detailed look at the interesting bits of code from Figure 14.7.

The first interesting part of the page is the JavaScript, a variable declaration and a little function, located in the <head></head> container:

```
<script type="text/javascript">
      var color; // Global variable
      function switchbg(color) {
      wholedoc.style.backgroundColor=color;
                                    }
</script>
```

The global variable color holds the hexadecimal code passed by the <button> element down in the form. The function itself is all of one line and simply sets the background-color property of the style of the object called wholedoc to the color passed by the function. This is another example of the object-oriented nature of JavaScript. In this case, the entire document (an object) is given an identity of wholedoc. Then the background color for the style for that object is set to the color specified by the user. Notice that when used in this context, background color is not a hyphenated variable name.

INVOKING THE SCRIPT

The next collection of code that enables this function to work occurs early in the <body></body> container:

```
<body id="main">
   <!--use id not name to identify -->
   <script type="text / javascript">
   var wholedoc=document.getElementById("main"); //get div identity
   </script>
```

This code illustrates one of the uses for the **id** attribute. As the comment describes, you must use the **id** attribute, not the **name** attribute, to identify a section of the page if you're going to use this type of JavaScript to identify a portion of the page. The next three lines are a JavaScript that establishes an identification for the whole body of the page using the getElementById method of the document object. We mentioned that in the last section, and now you know how it is accomplished. This is necessary so that we can apply the style property to that entity.

Now let's consider the code that evokes the function to change the background color:

```
<input type="button" name="bgcol" alt="blue" value="blue"
    onclick="switchbg('#66CCFF');" />
```

We could have used radio buttons instead of the generic button input control. However, using the button element reduces the amount of screen real estate necessary, and gives a pleasant appearance. When the user activates this particular button, the onclick intrinsic event runs the switchbg( ) function, passing the color value of #66CCFF to the function. The function then modifies the value of the style property backgroundColor, and the browser reflects the change.

This is a simple yet elegant way to give users some control over the browsing environment. Now let's look at a way to give them even more control.

EXPLORATION #3 Modify the image map created using palette.gif in Exploration #1 to change the background color of the Web page. Create a page that has a set of buttons that changes the background color of the page to colors corresponding to the colors in the palette when the user activates the selected button.

▸▸ A LITTLE FANCIER COLOR-CHANGING

Changing the foreground color is no more complex than changing the color of the background if you use style properties. Figure 14.9 shows the new page, with the modifications we made to the previous color changer to allow the user control over the foreground color as well as the background color.

The obvious difference between Figure 14.7 and Figure 14.9 is the second set of buttons that asks users for their choice of text color (foreground). You could create a page like this to test various background/foreground color combinations. This page gets very interesting for users if they select something like black text and a black background. Makes reading the text a bit challenging!

The new code shown in Figure 14.9 is simply a tiny modification of the JavaScript function we already built to change background color. This is another example of *code leveraging* to generate new code. Wise programmers always try to leverage their code; it cuts down on development time and debugging time. The only difference we need to point out between the code in Figure 14.7 and Figure 14.9 is changing the function name from switchbg( ) to switchfg( ), and the change in the style property, which is modified from style.backgroundColor to style.color.

While the change in the way the browsers handled JavaScript made the coding of the background color more difficult, it actually made coding the foreground color change easier. It should be no surprise to you that this method of changing the foreground, or text, color won't work with older browsers. As we did for the page that changed background color, we have included the older style example in the old_code directory on the CD. In the past generations of browsers, the only way you could change the text color was to run a JavaScript that called a modal prompt box to ask users their color preference before the page was built. That meant users had one chance to set their text color. With the advent of the modern browsers, at least this generation of browsers, users can change their text color and their background color as often as they like.

Figure 14.9   Changing both background and foreground colors

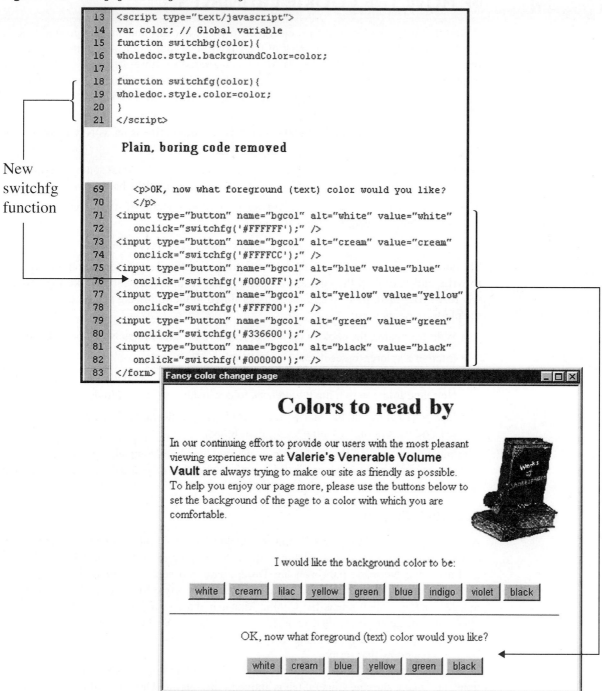

```
13   <script type="text/javascript">
14   var color; // Global variable
15   function switchbg(color){
16   wholedoc.style.backgroundColor=color;
17   }
18   function switchfg(color){
19   wholedoc.style.color=color;
20   }
21   </script>
```

Plain, boring code removed

```
69      <p>OK, now what foreground (text) color would you like?
70      </p>
71   <input type="button" name="bgcol" alt="white" value="white"
72      onclick="switchfg('#FFFFFF');" />
73   <input type="button" name="bgcol" alt="cream" value="cream"
74      onclick="switchfg('#FFFFCC');" />
75   <input type="button" name="bgcol" alt="blue" value="blue"
76      onclick="switchfg('#0000FF');" />
77   <input type="button" name="bgcol" alt="yellow" value="yellow"
78      onclick="switchfg('#FFFF00');" />
79   <input type="button" name="bgcol" alt="green" value="green"
80      onclick="switchfg('#336600');" />
81   <input type="button" name="bgcol" alt="black" value="black"
82      onclick="switchfg('#000000');" />
83   </form>
```

New switchfg function

Colors to read by

In our continuing effort to provide our users with the most pleasant viewing experience we at **Valerie's Venerable Volume Vault** are always trying to make our site as friendly as possible. To help you enjoy our page more, please use the buttons below to set the background of the page to a color with which you are comfortable.

I would like the background color to be:

| white | cream | lilac | yellow | green | blue | indigo | violet | black |

OK, now what foreground (text) color would you like?

| white | cream | blue | yellow | green | black |

EXPLORATION #4   Modify the page you created in Exploration #3 by adding a second set of buttons that allows the user to change the foreground color to any of the colors in the palette when they activate one of them.

▸▸ HOW THE COOKIE CRUMBLES

Now that we can allow users to select their favorite background and foreground colors, maybe it would be nice to keep track of their favorite combination so that they can see it the next time they visit the site. To do that we need to store a **cookie** on the user's browser. A cookie, or more precisely, a *persistent cookie,* is a small data file stored by the user's browser on the user's computer. If you are using cookies, you need to be aware of some limitations of this methodology:

- There can be a maximum of 300 cookies in the cookie file as far as Navigator is concerned.

- Internet Explorer doesn't limit the number of cookies, other than setting the limit on the size of the folder that holds the cookies to 2 percent of the hard-drive space.

- A cookie can contain only 4 kilobytes (4,000 characters) of data. That total is the sum of both the cookie's name and value.

- The browser will store a maximum of 20 cookies per server or domain.

Since JavaScript cannot access the hard drive directly, it must depend on the browser to write and later read the cookie. A cookie is stored in a file called **cookies.txt** somewhere on your hard drive. We found cookies stored in the following places, depending on the platform being used:

- With Navigator, the cookies.txt file is located in Program Files\Netscape\Users\ttg.

- Internet Explorer tosses its cookies in Windows\Profiles\ttg\cookies.

- On Macintosh computers, Navigator has a file called MagicCookie stored in the Netscape folder within the Preferences folder inside the System folder.

- Internet Explorer on the Mac stores its cookies in a file called Internet Preferences in the Preferences folder within the System folder.

You must *not* hand-edit the cookie file using an editor like Notepad. Cookies are created by the browsers and must be preserved *exactly* as they are or you risk breaking a link and inhibiting the browser's ability to process them.

DELETING COOKIES

Although you should not directly edit the cookie file using an editor like Notepad, you can use tools built into or available with each browser to edit cookie files. To delete cookies using Netscape 6.0, open the Tasks menu and select the Privacy and Security submenu. From the next cascading menu choose the Cookie Manager and activate View Stored Cookies which opens the Cookie Manager dialog box. Within the Cookie Manager you can delete individual cookies or all of them. An example of that manager is shown in Figure 14.12 (later in this chapter), where we display the contents of one of the cookies created by that script.

To delete cookies built by Internet Explorer 6, select the Tools menu's Internet Options, and make sure the General tab is active in the Internet Options dialog box. You can choose to delete all of the cookies by pressing the Delete Cookies button. Unfortunately, there's no tool to delete individual cookies.

Opera 6 does not provide cookie management within the browser itself. However, you can download the freeware program O4FE. The Opera 4 File Explorer allows you to manipulate the cookie file, cache, global-history file, and even the visited-links list. This toolkit gives you incredible control over the data that the Opera browser stores. It is by far the best tool of the three.

In day-to-day use you probably won't need to modify the cookies file—or any other files your browser gives you access to. However, when you are testing a script that creates cookies, it's often very valuable to be able to manipulate the cookies file to remove the unwanted cookies stored there during testing and development.

A NOTE ON TESTING

While we were building and testing the code for this chapter we encountered a strange happenstance. It seemed that the Opera browser is designed so that it won't build cookies at all if the page that contains the JavaScript is local. That means that if you test your cookie-baking scripts in Opera, you will need to have them on a server, not just local to your machine. This points out the importance of first of all having access to good technical support for your tools, and also of doing all you can to learn the particular habits of your tools.

CHECKING FOR COOKIES

As you know, JavaScripts cannot actually modify the contents of the hard drive of the client machine, nor can they read from the hard drive of the client machine. However, they can *ask the browser* to store and retrieve small amounts of data (cookies) for them. In the "old days" these data were shipped across the Net to a CGI script, which then processed them. Now JavaScript can use the data locally as well, often eliminating the need for the slower CGI scripts.

Cookies allow the Web page to act as if it has a little bit of memory. For example, the page in Figure 14.10 is designed to ask users for their name the first time they come to the page. By storing the data in a cookie the HTML document can "remember" and display their name each time they revisit the page, as shown in Figure 14.11. This would be impossible without the use of cookies. The first time the user comes to the page a prompt box asks for her name. When she leaves the page, a JavaScript asks the browser to create a small cookie on her hard drive that contains her name and the number of times she has come to the page.

Figure 14.10 Page shown to user on first visit

This prompt box and HTML code was generated by the first script in Figure 14.13

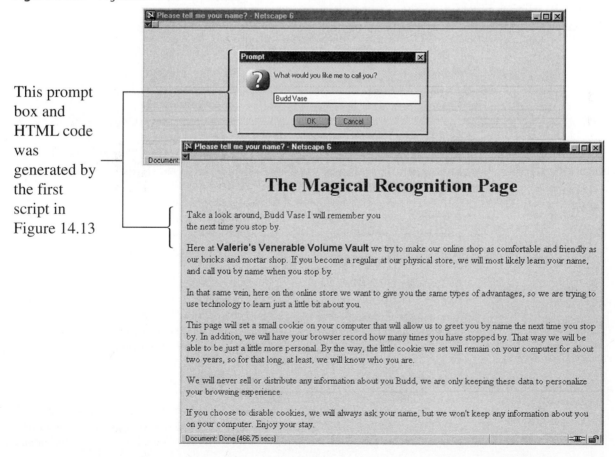

Upon subsequent visits, or if the user reloads the page; the JavaScript checks to see if a cookie already exists. If it does, the script takes the name stored in the cookie and builds a slightly different page, and of course does not prompt the user for her name.

Saving information like this is also called *maintaining state.* In some circumstances it is useful to allow the browser to save information about the state of a particular page. Users may appreciate feeling that they are important enough for you to ask for and remember their names or preferences.

One of the most significant advantages of cookies is their persistence. Once set, they can remain on the client machine for days or months or even years. The cookie in our example in Figure 14.12 will remain, or persist, for two years from the date it was created. If the user comes back to the site any time in the next two years, the page will remember, and call her by name.

PROMPT BOX TO INPUT NAME

On a user's first visit, a prompt box like the one shown in Figure 14.10 should ask for his name. The bottom of the figure shows the screen capture of the user's initial page. He'll never see this page again if his computer accepts cookies. We could use the same technique to remember other information about the user, such as color preferences, clothing sizes, hobbies, and so forth.

Figure 14.11   How page looks on second visit

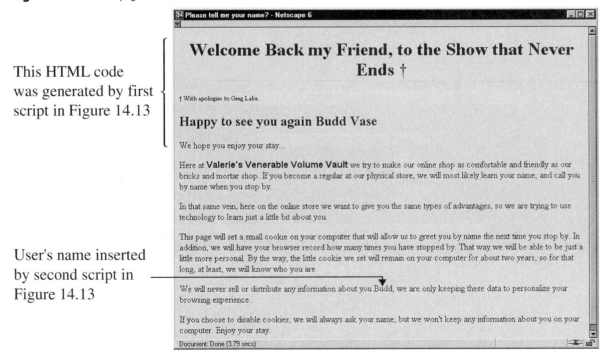

This HTML code was generated by first script in Figure 14.13

User's name inserted by second script in Figure 14.13

Figure 14.11 shows the page the user will see on subsequent visits. Notice that he is not prompted for his name, and that the page displays different first-level and second-level headings than before (compare with Figure 14.10). This is the page the user will see from now on. If you're going to use cookies to keep track of customer information, you should tell your customers how you're going to use those data, and explain to them that by turning off cookies they can prevent the page from keeping any data. Now let's peek behind the curtain and see how all the magic happens.

Figure 14.12 shows the code that allows the page to "remember" the user's name. It also shows this cookie as it is displayed by the Netscape cookie manager. Taken as a whole, the code looks somewhat complex, so let's break it down into manageable hunks.

We will dissect it one function at a time. In an effort to save trees, and reduce the size of the screen capture, we've removed all the comments—small white lines between some of the numbers indicate where they were excised. The entire page, with all of its comments, is available on the CD and the Web site if you wish to peruse it.

There are three functions in the large script contained at the beginning of the document. We will examine them one by one and then look at a couple of small scripts embedded in the body of the page that make the changes to the code for the page.

Figure 14.12 Baking cookies with JavaScript

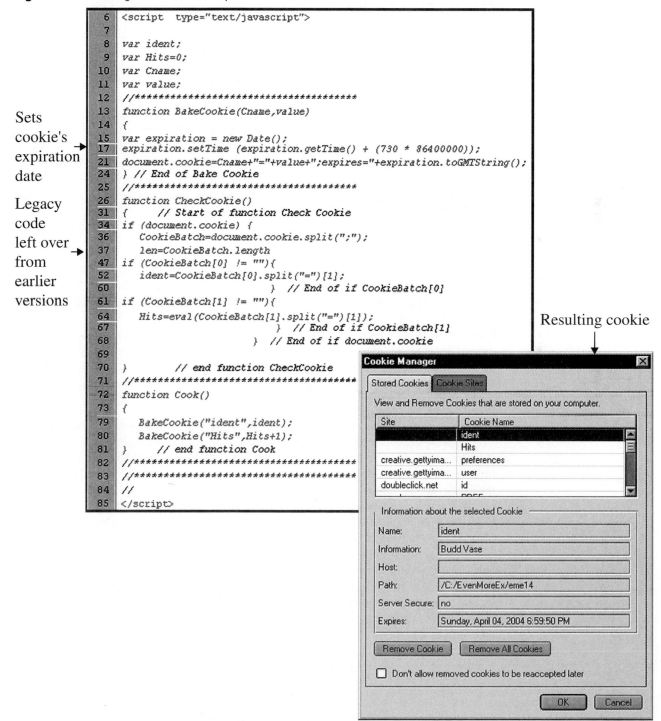

Sets cookie's expiration date

Legacy code left over from earlier versions

Resulting cookie

```
 6  <script   type="text/javascript">
 7
 8  var ident;
 9  var Hits=0;
10  var Cname;
11  var value;
12  //**********************************
13  function BakeCookie(Cname,value)
14  {
15  var expiration = new Date();
17  expiration.setTime (expiration.getTime() + (730 * 86400000));
21  document.cookie=Cname+"="+value+";expires="+expiration.toGMTString();
24  } // End of Bake Cookie
25  //**********************************
26  function CheckCookie()
31  {        // Start of function Check Cookie
34  if (document.cookie) {
36     CookieBatch=document.cookie.split(";");
37     len=CookieBatch.length
47  if (CookieBatch[0] != ""){
52     ident=CookieBatch[0].split("=")[1];
60                    }  // End of if CookieBatch[0]
61  if (CookieBatch[1] != ""){
64     Hits=eval(CookieBatch[1].split("=")[1]);
67                    }  // End of if CookieBatch[1]
68                  }  // End of if document.cookie
69
70  }        // end function CheckCookie
71  //***********************************
72  function Cook()
73  {
79     BakeCookie("ident",ident);
80     BakeCookie("Hits",Hits+1);
81  }      // end function Cook
82  //***********************************
83  //***********************************
84  //
85  </script>
```

Cookie Manager

Stored Cookies | Cookie Sites

View and Remove Cookies that are stored on your computer.

Site	Cookie Name
	ident
	Hits
creative.gettyima...	preferences
creative.gettyima...	user
doubleclick.net	id
	PREF

Information about the selected Cookie

Name: ident
Information: Budd Vase
Host:
Path: /C:/EvenMoreEx/eme14
Server Secure: no
Expires: Sunday, April 04, 2004 6:59:50 PM

Remove Cookie   Remove All Cookies

☐ Don't allow removed cookies to be reaccepted later

OK   Cancel

GLOBAL VARIABLES

The first four lines of the script identified four variables that are used throughout the page. These *variable names* are declared here so they can be used as ***global variables,*** which are values stored at a location that is known to all of the functions in this page. A ***local variable,*** in contrast, is known only to the function in which it is created. Had we declared the variables inside one of the functions, only that function would know about these local variable names and the values (variables) stored there. But instead, as global variables, all of the functions can read and modify the same variables.

SETTING COOKIE'S VALUE

The first function, BakeCookie(Cname,value), actually sets the cookie value. The term *cookie* leads to all kinds of wonderful word plays, and someone must have had that in mind when the feature was named. This function takes two parameters: the name of the cookie and the value to be assigned to that name. In addition to the variable name and value, which looks a lot like the name-value pairs we saw in the chapter on CGI, a cookie must have an expiration date. This expiration date determines how long the cookie will remain, or persist, on the user's machine before it becomes inactive. The default expiration date is the current date, so that the cookie will disappear when the browser closes. The expiration date is calculated in milliseconds. In our example, the cookie is supposed to stay active on the user's machine for two years from the time it was set. Looking at the code, we see the expiration time is calculated as follows:

```
var expiration = new Date();
expiration.setTime (expiration.getTime() + (730 * 86400000));
```

First a local variable name of expiration is created as an instance of the Date() object. Next the getTime() method is used to find the current time. Finally, 730, the number of days in two years, is multiplied by 86,400,000, the number of milliseconds in a day. (The number of milliseconds in a day is obtained as follows: 24 hours * 60 minutes/hour * 60 seconds/minute * 1,000 milliseconds/second.) The result is added to the current time to get the date that we store as the variable expires. Whew! Now we use the cookie property of the document object to ask the browser to store the name=value pair with the expiration date in the cookie file:

```
document.cookie=Cname+"="+value+";expires="+expiration.toGMTString();
```

This line of code concatenates a series of values—either values stored in variables like Cname and value, or values explicitly coded as strings like "; expires=". The entire concatenated series makes up a cookie as shown at the bottom of Figure 14.12. That last little bit of code tells the browser to convert the time to Greenwich Mean Time format, the format that the browser expects.

If we make even a little mistake in coding the expiration date, the browser will replace our time with the current time, and the cookie won't be stored. This seems a lot of work just to store some data, but the effect is certainly worthwhile.

The BakeCookie() function is called twice, once to store the user's name, and once to increment the number of times the user has been to this page. It is called by the function Cook(), which happens to be the third of the three functions we will look at. The Cook() function is very simple. *It is invoked* when the browser *exits* this page, and it represents the technique of building a simple function to invoke other functions.

CHECKING TO SEE IF COOKIE EXISTS

The second function, CheckCookie(), asks the browser to see if a cookie has been stored on the user's hard drive for this particular page. If a cookie exists, we assume it's a cookie we built. This may be an invalid assumption if the page creates other cookies. However, for the sake of this discussion, we will accept that if a cookie is stored, then we were the ones who stored it. Should the first statement resolve to false, meaning that no cookie has been stored, the function simply terminates and the variables Hits and ident have no value. Note: One of the features of cookies is that only the server that created the cookie may read that cookie. Therefore, we don't have to worry about naming our cookies a unique name, since our version of Hits and ident are associated with our server.

On the other hand, if a cookie has been stored, then the function divides that cookie string into its individual elements. All of the cookies for a particular server are stored as a semicolon (;) delimited series. So the cookie that was stored when Budd left the page the first time looks like this:

```
ident=Budd Vase;Hits=1;
```

As you can see, the different cookies (name-value pairs) are separated by semicolons. By using the the split() method on the document.cookie object, we create an array of individual cookies we call a CookieBatch.

LEFTOVER LEGACY CODE

The next line of code is an example of an artifact sometimes referred to as *legacy code.* What that means, in this case, is that it's a line of code that is no longer used; it was left behind when the page was updated. We left it here to show you that when you dissect a page, you might well discover bits of code left over from previous incarnations of a function. What could tip you off in this case is that the variable len is referenced nowhere else in the code.

CHECKING COOKIE'S IDENTITY

The next line, an IF statement, checks to make sure that the first element of the CookieBatch has something in it. The first element of the array must not be null or empty. Notice that the first element of the array is numbered 0, not 1. JavaScript begins counting with 0 rather than 1.

If the first element is not empty, the script executes a very complex line:

```
ident=CookieBatch[0].split("=")[1];
```

This line defines the value of the ident variable by splitting the first element of the CookieBatch array on the equals sign and then taking the second part of that newly created array. In other words, since there's something in the first element of the CookieBatch array, we know that its form is going to be name=value. We also know that **name** is going to be ident, so all we care about is what appears on the right side of the equal sign. In our example, when the user came to the page the second time, the value of ident was "Budd Vase".

After collecting the user's identity, the script needs to determine whether the user has been there before. I suppose you could say this is redundant, because if there's a cookie with that user's name, he must have been there before, but knowing how many times he has shown up might be useful. So the script duplicates the logic it used to discern the user's identity using the second element of the CookieBatch array and stores the value into the Hits variable.

Figure 14.13   JavaScripts from body of document

Visited before

First time visitor

```
95   <body onunload='Cook()' id="main">
96   <script type="text/javascript">
97
98   CheckCookie()        // Call the function to get the values
99   if (Hits > 0 ) {  // They have been here before
100      document.write('<h1>Welcome Back my Friend, to the Show that Never Ends &#134;</h1>');
101      document.write('<span style="font-size:8pt;">&#134; With apologies to Greg Lake.</span>');
102      document.write('<h2>Happy to see you again ' + ident + '</h2>');
103      document.write('We hope you enjoy your stay...');
104                    } //End of if part
105  else {            //  First time user
106      document.write('<h1>The Magical Recognition Page</h1>');
107      ident=prompt("What would you like me to call you?");
108      document.write('Take a look around, ' + ident +' I will remember you');
109      document.write('<br /> the next time you stop by.');
110      }        // end of else part
111  //
112  </script>
135   We will never sell or distribute any information about you
136   <script type="text/javascript">
137   //
138   // Here foist is the first part of their
139   // name.  If they use just a first name,
140   // like wilbur, then the
141   // first (zeroth) element of the array is
142   // the whole name.  If they use john smith
143   // then the first element is john.
144   // It personalizes it a bit more.
145   foist=ident.split(" ")[0];
146   document.write(foist + ",");
147   //
148   </script>
149  we are only keeping these data to personalize your
150   browsing experience.
157  </body>
```

USING COOKIE DATA

Now that you're familiar with the functions that the page uses, let's take a look at the little JavaScripts embedded in the body of the page. Figure 14.13 shows an abbreviated version of the body of the document. The first script begins execution right after the browser builds the body element, as shown in Figure 14.11. The first thing the script does is run the CheckCookie() function. This script then checks to see whether or not the Hits variable contains a value greater than zero. If the user has been to the page before, it generates the "welcome" HTML code that results in Figure 14.11. Otherwise, it's the user's first visit to the page, so the JavaScript generates the magical header, and opens the prompt dialog box that captures the user's name in the variable ident, as illustrated in Figure 14.10. Since the prompt dialog box is one of the modal boxes, if you run this script locally you may not see anything except the background color before being prompted for your name. That's what happened in the first screen capture in Figure 14.10.

The second script in Figure 14.13 is only two lines long, not counting the excessive documentation, and generates only the user's first name followed by a comma. Since we wanted to personalize this line, we used the split method to pick off just the first name. It's that kind of nice little touch that JavaScript can perform so elegantly in a dynamic HTML page.

We made an interesting discovery when we were working with this code. It seemed natural to use the **onLoad** event to trigger the CheckCookie function. However, when we did that, the only content for the page was either a blank screen the first time the page was invoked or the welcome message on subsequent loads. Apparently, the browser considers the code generated by the function as the *only* content for the page if it encounters it before the rest of the content starts to build—a surprising "feature" of the browser.

USING COOKIES APPROPRIATELY

Cookies can be misused to track users' habits. The 2000s seem to be the decade of privacy. Users are concerned about what data are kept about them, for them, or against them. Many users automatically disable storing cookies, because some nefarious Web weavers have misused this technology. If you're going to use persistent cookies in an attempt to make your users' browsing experience more personal, be sure to tell them exactly what data are being kept and how long those data will be kept. If you're conscientious about keeping the user informed, and store only those data that you tell the user you're storing, you can avoid violating your user's trust.

EXPLORATION #5   Modify Exploration #4 to use a cookie to keep track of the background and foreground colors the user chose when she left the page. Then, on any subsequent visit, tell her what these colors were.

▸▸ KEY TERMS

Client-side mapping
Cookie
Dynamic
Global variable
Hot spot

Image map
Local variable
Maintaining state
Server-side mapping

▸▸ NEW TAGS

<area />
<map></map>

▸▸ REVIEW QUESTIONS

1. Define each of the key terms.
2. How is each of the tags introduced in this chapter used? (Provide examples.)
3. What are the advantages to using client-side mapping?
4. Identify two different ways the coordinates for image-map hot spots are found.
5. What <img> attributes are used to create server-side and client-side image maps?
6. List the HTML elements found in the XHTML Server-side Image Map and Client-side Image Map modules.
7. What is the order of precedence when <area /> definitions overlap hot spots within an image map?
8. How is the **name** attribute used to identify the source image for the image map?
9. Why are both the **alt** and **title** attribute values needed when coding image maps?
10. Name three valid shapes that can define an image map hot spot, and give the format of the associated coordinates for each.
11. What is the secret to "no wait" rollovers?
12. What is the conclusion of research into users' screen-color preferences?
13. How do you keep a form HTML-complaint when it calls a JavaScript?
14. What are the limits to the size and number of cookies the browser can maintain?
15. How do you delete cookies maintained by your favorite browser?

16. What is the default cookie expiration date?

17. What guidelines do the authors give conscientious Web weavers about the use of cookies?

▸▸ EXERCISES

14.1 Ruby wants to incorporate an image map onto her site. She wants to have a page that allows customers to "browse" a collection of jewelry, and if they activate one of the gems, transfers them to a page that shows other gems of the same type. Use the image gems.gif on the first page, and have that image open the pages rubies.htm, sapphires.htm, emeralds.htm, and amethysts.htm. Make the page eme14-dyn.raw your starting point. The main page should have the following characteristics:

a. Background should be color #CCFFFF.

b. Text should be color #003366.

c. Headings 1 and 2 should both be centered and in sans serif type. Level-1 headings should be color #660099, and level-2 should be color #0099CC.

d. Image map should be called gems.gif.

e. The Red gemstone should link to rubies.htm, show the words "Wonderful rubies await you!" when the user hovers over it, have an **alt** value of Rubies, and display the image rub1.gif in place of the display case when the user moves his mouse over that image. When the user moves his mouse off that gem and back to the background of the page, the image of the display case should reappear.

f. The Blue gemstone should link to sapphires.htm, show the words "Here are beautiful sapphires!" when the user hovers over it, have an **alt** value of Sapphires, and display the image sap1.gif in place of the display case when the user moves her mouse over that image. When the user moves her mouse off that gem and back to the background of the page, the image of the display case should reappear.

g. The Green gemstone should link to emeralds.htm show the words "Nothing compares with the beauty of emeralds!" when the user hovers over it, have an **alt** value of Emeralds, and display the image eme1.gif in place of the display case when the user moves their mouse over that image. When the user moves his mouse off that gem and back to the background of the page, the image of the display case should reappear.

h. The Purple gemstone should link to amethysts.htm, show the words "Breath-taking amethysts are but a click away!" when the user hovers over it, have an **alt** value of Amethysts, and display the image ama.gif in place of the display case when the user moves her mouse over that image. When the user moves her mouse off that gem and back to the background of the page, the image of the display case should reappear.

i. Use the page ch14-raw.htm on your CD or on the Web site as a beginning to create your image map to map the image gems.gif.

j. Save your completed page as ch14-dyn.htm.

Recommendation: Get each feature to work at a time. Don't try to make them all work at once—that way lies madness . . . even for your humble authors. We built this page one design element at a time. First get the image map to link to the pages. (They are also on the CD and on the Web site.) Then get the rollover to work. Then get the display case to come back.

14.2. Create a new HTML document with text that uses at least three different examples of jargon or slang with which you are familiar. The title bar should display "Jargon Revealed" with your name and the assignment due date included within comment lines. Create a rollover that displays the jargon's definition for each jargon example.

14.3. Retrieve the "Internet Privacy Concerns" page you created in Exercise 13.3. Add the code to create a cookie that stores the browser name and computer platform used by the person reading the Web page.

14.4. In Exercise 6.4 you added an image of yourself to the Homework home page. Use a digital camera, scanner, or free-drawing software to create another image of yourself. Modify the Homework home page so that the second image is displayed over the first when the screen pointer is held over the first image.

14.5. Update the school's home page to include a rollover with an image or graphic already used on one of the related pages. The choice is up to you. Here are some ideas for the image:
  • Your school in summer with rollover of same view in winter.
  • Basketball player dribbling with rollover of same player shooting.
  • Drummer hitting drum with rollover of drummer with sticks in the air.
  • Student in library reading with rollover of same student sleeping on book.

14.6. Modify the movies home page by adding a prompt box to ask users to enter the name of their favorite movie when the page is opened the first time. Save the name of the movie in a cookie that expires in two days. The next time the Web page is opened within two days, it should automatically display the name of the movie stored in the cookie and the words "Good Movies" about it.

14.7. Create a new HTML document that is designed to display a single work of visual art. The title bar should display the artwork's title and the artist's name. Your name and the assignment due date must be included within the document as comment lines. The page should include the image, the artist's name, and creation date if it is known. The document should also incorporate the code introduced in this chapter that lets the user select radio buttons to change the screen's background color.

14.8. Create four new HTML documents. One document should contain a client-side image map. The map needs at least three hot spots. Activating a hot spot should open one of the three HTML documents. Each hot spot should open a different document. Your name and the assignment due date must be included within each document as comment lines.

Chapter Fifteen

XML: The Next Best Thing

XML is everywhere. You read about it in magazines, see it referred to on the Net, hear people talking about in restaurants, and now you can even read about it in this book! It seems that anyone who is anyone is doing something with XML. This chapter will give you an overview of XML, how it works, the types of tools you need to develop XML applications, and why XML is important to you. Although XML is still in its infancy and yet unproven, it is a tool that you as a wise Web weaver need to understand, because we can promise you that XML, in some form or other, is in your future. No need to fear, though—as we have shown you throughout this book, you can easily write XML-compliant HTML code. And now it's time to take a closer look at this fairly new arrival on the Web scene.

CHAPTER OBJECTIVES

After reading this chapter you should be able to do the following:

- Explain the general purpose for XML.
- Describe how XML data are displayed on multiple platforms.
- Recognize well-formed XML code.
- Understand the role document type definitions (DTDs) play in validating documents.
- Explain how XHTML relates to XML and HTML.

- Identify the steps in the tool chain that handles XML code.
- Recognize software tools used to build XML applications.
- Identify applications for XML and XHTML.
- Understand the relationship between style sheets and XML.

▸▸ WHAT IS XML, ANYWAY?

XML stands for "eXtensible Markup Language." It is the latest and greatest coding scheme for *describing data* across numerous applications, only one of which is displaying those data in a traditional browser. XML was developed by the W³C and is described by them in their press release dated February 10, 1998, as "a system for defining, validating, and sharing document formats on the Web."

What that means to you is that XML provides a mechanism to create new definitions for your data, describe how the various data elements are related, and—if you want to go the full course—define what the data look like when displayed on various platforms. Since XML is still in its infancy, using this new technology may push you to the "bleeding edge" of the development process (more about that later). But soon, possibly within a couple of years, many of the tools you need will be readily available.

In this chapter we will explore one of the more commonly used applications of XML to give you just a taste of what's involved in the process. Lest you think you have to cover wholly new ground here, relax. You already know many of the techniques required by XML, because we have carefully guided you so that you have been building proper—or, in XML parlance, "well-formed"—HTML pages. Well-formed HTML pages are procedurally just one small step away from well-formed XML pages.

One way to look at XML is simply as a large collection of logical style containers. As we're sure you remember, we spoke of logical style containers as describing *how the data were used,* or what the container contained, rather than *what the data should look like* when displayed. This is, by formal definition, the absolutely correct use for markup language. From the coding point of view, all XML does is give you a series of containers to describe exactly the types of data you are presenting. It's up to other tools, like cascading style sheets (CSS) or extensible-style language (XSL) to determine what the data actually *look like* when displayed on the page.

Imagine for a moment that the <cite></cite> container didn't change the way the data on the page were presented by putting it in italics, but only identified those data as a citation. You could, by creating either external or document-level style sheets, describe exactly the way you want your citation presented in the browser. That's the way XML was designed to work. You can describe the content of your data in one document and how it should be presented in another. You already know how that process works, because you have built cascading style sheets that define the way data are presented on your pages. The authors of XML simply preserve and enforce the distinction between describing *what the data are* and *how the data are presented.* This becomes especially important when you look at presenting the same information across several platforms—for example PCs, personal digital assistants (PDAs), and cell phones. We will look at this type of presentation in the next chapter.

▸▸ THE LANGUAGE OF XML

Like any other technology, XML uses a series of terms you need to understand in order to discuss it fluently. The first term, which we have already alluded to, is *well-formed.* A well-formed document has the following characteristics:

1. All container tags have distinct start and end components. For example, the first element in the following list would be well-formed, as the element is closed. But the second element would not, because, the Web weaver has forgotten the closing tag on the <li>.

```
<ul>
    <li>I am correctly formed</li>
    <li>Ooops, I am mal-formed
</ul>
```

That omission would cause that element, and hence that list, and in fact that entire page to be malformed instead of well-formed.

2. All tags are correctly nested. (No crossed containers.)

3. The values for all attributes are enclosed in quotation marks.

4. All empty tags are correctly terminated. (Empty tags are terminated by a /> string.) For example, <hr> is an incorrectly terminated empty tag. Coded as <hr />, it is correctly terminated.

5. Since XML is supposed to be case-sensitive, all elements are coded in lowercase. (Actually, this isn't really a hard rule yet, but it is expected to be required shortly.)

Since you have been following our guidelines, you have been building well-formed HTML documents right along. Those documents, because they are well-formed, are valid XHMTL documents. Aren't you impressed? You have been writing XHTML all along and didn't even realize it! If you follow the logic of the XML developers, there is no such thing as a "malformed" XML document, for if it isn't well-formed, it isn't XML!

Another XML term is **valid,** meaning all the elements follow the rules as set out by the document type definition (DTD). For example, you would not code the src attribute in a <br /> tag, because there is no valid use for src within <br />. Since, we believe, you have been validating all your HTML code, you are already producing valid HTML and, therefore, valid XHTML.

Note: a document can be well-formed without being valid, and it can be valid without being well-formed. And for the real language buffs among you, the XML developers have coined two very specific terms to define the states of validity. A document may be valid under one DTD but not under another. So instead of *valid* and *invalid,* they prefer the terms *type-valid* and *non-type-valid.*

An **element** is the basic unit of XML—by formal definition, a container and its contents, bounded by <container> </container> tags, or a well-formed empty tag. The DTD defines the rules for elements.

An **entity** is any chunk of data that needs some sort of special handling. You have been using *character entities* like < and &, to add special characters to your document. With XML you can create your own *special characters* that can be glyphs, strings, or even blocks of text.

A construct you will use in XML is **XSL,** Extensible Style Language. Along with cascading style sheets, XSL is used to define the way data appear when enclosed within a particular container.

The "parent" language for the XSL is **DSSSL,** Document Style Semantics and Specification Language, just as SGML was the parent language for XML. In proper W[3]C parlance, we would say that DSSSL is a *superset* of XSL, just as SGML is a superset of XML. Or, to really muddy the waters, we can say XSL is a subset of DSSSL, and XML is a subset of SGML. There, we think we've covered the bases well.

↠ DTD UP CLOSE AND PERSONAL

Figure 15.1 shows an example of a small part of the HTML 4.01 DTD. Isn't it amazing that you have been using—actually, requesting that the browser use—these rules to describe your page, and you never even realized it. Yes, you have! Where, you ask, did you specify the DTD for your document? Take a close look at the very first line of each of your pages. If you followed our recommendation (and built pages that validated correctly), you coded the following line as the very first line of each of your files:

```
<!DOCTYPE HTML PUBLIC "-//W3C//DTD HTML 4.01//EN"
   "http://www.w3.org/TR/html4/strict.dtd">
```

Remember that? Now look at exactly what it is asking for. See that bit in there that says DTD HTML 4.01? Yup, that is where you told the browser what rules to follow. And even better than that, see the bit that says http://www.w3.org./TR/html4/strict.dtd? That is the location the browser will go to download the DTD that will parse your page. Let's look at a little part of the DTD and dissect it.

Figure 15.1

A tiny part of the HTML DTD

```
<!ENTITY % StyleSheet "CDATA">
    <!-- style sheet data -->

<!ENTITY % Text "CDATA">
    <!-- used for titles etc. -->
```
These attributes define what kind of data are allowed within these entities.

```
<!ENTITY % coreattrs
 "id          ID          #IMPLIED
  class       CDATA       #IMPLIED
  style       %StyleSheet; #IMPLIED
  title       %Text;       #IMPLIED"
  >
```
These attributes are defined as the "core" attributes.

```
<!ELEMENT br EMPTY>   <!-- forced line break -->
<!ATTLIST br
  %coreattrs;
  >
```
This is our old friend <br>, notice the attributes allowed for this tag.

Figure 15.1 shows just a small portion of the DTD for HTML. Small as it is, it shows how a DTD is organized and laid out. So that you wouldn't have to read pages and pages of DTD data, we cut and pasted the relevant parts into the figure. The first two small sections define two individual entities called "StyleSheet" and "Text" that can contain character data (CDATA). Then there is another entity, coreattrs, that contains four different individual data items. Two of them are new, **id** and **class,** and they can contain data of types ID and CDATA, respectively. The second pair of data items, **style** and **title** can contain data of the types %StyleSheet and %Text. Notice how part of the DTD is reused to define other parts. This is a principle the W^3C tries to reinforce: reuse things that work; don't reinvent the wheel.

Finally, with all the entities defined, we are ready to define an element. The last part of the image shows how our old friend the <br> element is defined in the HTML DTD. Notice that it allows the core attributes in the <!ATTLIST/ container. All of those attributes are allowed, and none are required. If a <br> element is coded with any other attribute, it will be an invalid element.

So that is a DTD—or, rather, a part of a DTD. We think from that portion you can see how the W^3C can define exactly how a DTD can describe particular tags. Now let's look at the bigger picture.

▸▸ THE REASON FOR XML

The developers at the W^3C realized that HTML was being pushed far beyond its initial usefulness. They were especially concerned because people were trying to use HTML to define *how* data should appear in the browser and on other platforms, and that isn't the purpose of a markup language. Rather, a markup language should simply define *what the data are,* and allow some other entity, in this case style sheets, to define how those data should look when displayed on various devices.

This attempt to use HTML beyond its limits was one motivation for developing XML. The other motivation was the fact that many folks were developing content for devices other than the standard browsers. For example, there is a big push to display content on cell phones and PDAs. The developers decided that if they created a markup language that was used only to describe the data, other folks could build tools to display those data in different formats on different devices. The extensible (X) part of this new markup language allows users to build unique descriptions of their data in ways that are meaningful to them. If several different but related businesses want to share a set of definitions, then with XML they have the flexibility to do so.

➤➤ DTD MODELS

Through the constructs of XML, one set of definitions can be used by different individuals and groups. This sharing has caused the development of a multitude of different DTDs. Five of the more common right now are the XML/EDI, OFX, GedML, dbXML, and DocBook models.

XML/EDI MODEL

The XML version of the electronic exchange for business data is the XML/EDI model. Businesses sharing data with the XML/EDI model are using the same descriptors for data like invoices and project data. One of the goals of the XML/EDI project is to build a tool for business data transfer that will make it easier and faster to set up electronic commerce sites. If you wish to research this model further, please check out http://www.xmledi-group.org/xmledigroup/start.htm.

OFX MODEL

Microsoft and Intuit are building a financial data model based on Microsoft Money and Quicken called the OFX model. The goal of the OFX model is to standardize the way financial packages and institutions label and format their data so that they can transfer information more easily. This model will also make it easier to do online banking. You can further research it at http://www.ofx.net.

GEDML MODEL

The Church of Jesus Christ of Latter Day Saints (Mormons) keeps the largest genealogy database in the world. The Mormons decided that XML was the ideal tool to use to describe genealogy data so they devised GedML, a new markup language written in XML and derived from their existing GEDCOM format. You can see the fruits of this effort at http://users.iclway.co.uk/mhkay/gedml/index.html. Do check it out; the DTD is very nicely crafted.

DATABASE MODELS

Any one of a number of industries have seen XML, specifically dbXML, as a way to bring all of their diverse databases into alignment. Most of the major database companies have embraced XML as a data description standard. For example, Oracle supports an extensive range of database tools for customers building database applications because they believe that XML, now described as "the Internet standard for information exchange," is such an appropriate and necessary language to use in database applications. The traditional database companies are moving to XML as the latest and greatest way to represent data.

DOCBOOK MODEL

The DocBook model is an example of an SGML/XML vocabulary designed to standardize the production of online and printed documentation. It is maintained by OASIS, the Organization for the Advancement of Structured Information Standards, which defines itself on its Web page as "a nonprofit, international consortium that creates interoperable industry specifications based on public standards such as XML and SGML, as well as others that are related to structured information processing." You can visit OASIS at http://www.oasis-open.org.

DocBook was originally created by the Davenport Group to address the needs of software vendors attempting to produce a common set of Unix documentation. The first widely used open-source publishing system for DocBook was based on the ISO/ITC international standard, DSSSL. DSSSL formatting allowed DocBook documents to be published in a variety of forms, including but not limited to PostScript, PDF, RTF, HTML, and HTML help.

More recently, development has accelerated on the expansion of publishing tools based on the W^{3}C XSL Recommendations. At the time of this writing the XSL style sheets can produce HTML, HTML help and PDF documentation. Norman Walsh is currently maintaining the DocBook mailing list and DTD. Later in this chapter we will explore DocBook in greater detail. You can read more about DocBook at the OASIS site, or you can read Mr. Walsh's book describing DocBook at http://www.docbook.org/tdg. However, if you are going to be working with DocBook, you really should buy the hard copy of the text. Then you can annotate it and make it an even more valuable resource.

Each of these DTD models has a core of loyal supporters as well as a large following, and in the first two examples, those loyal supporters are historical competitors like Microsoft and Intuit. Everyone will benefit if we use a common model for the data in an industry that allows sharing of data across corporations and applications. XML will facilitate that.

EXPLORATION #1

Visit one of the four sites listed in the preceding section, and look at the DTD shown. See how the different elements are built from entities and how the various entities in elements are defined. We recommend the GedML, site since the DTD is so easily found, or the DocBook page because we'll be discussing it later, but you can take your pick of at least one of the four:

- http://users.iclway.co.uk/mhkay/gedml/index.html
- http://www.ofx.net
- http://www.xmledi-group.org/xmledigroup/start.htm
- http://www.docbook.org/tdg

▸▸ RELATIONSHIP BETWEEN XML AND XHTML

One question you might be pondering is, "Just how does this XML stuff relate to all the wonderful HTML I've been learning?" That is a really great question. We are so glad you asked it. Take a look at Figure 15.2. As the figure demonstrates, SGML is the parent of both HTML and XML. A number of markup languages have been spawned from Standard Generalized Markup Language, but we are interested in just these two. The developers at the W^{3}C attempted to address two different but related issues: first, HTML was being pushed beyond its limits, because the data being represented were more complex than the W^{3}C had initially anticipated. Second, although SGML allowed developers to design their own languages, it was an extremely complex process for doing so. XML was created by crafting a subset of SGML to augment HTML and thus supply developers with a simpler tool for describing data. Then XML was added to the latest HTML specifications. The result was ***XHTML.*** The latest recommendation, XHTML 1.0, says in part:

> XHTML 1.0 is the first major change to HTML since HTML 4.0 was released in 1997. It brings the rigor of XML to Web pages and is the keystone in W^{3}C's work to create standards that provide richer Web pages on an ever increasing range of browser platforms, including cell phones, televisions, cars, wallet-sized wireless communicators, kiosks, and desktops.
>
> XHTML 1.0 is the first step and the HTML Working Group is busy on the next. XHTML 1.0 reformulates HTML as an XML application. This makes it easier to process and

Figure 15.2

The relationship between HTML and XML

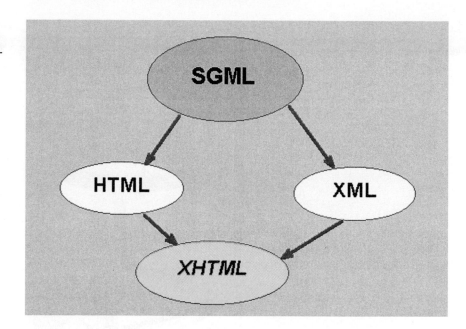

easier to maintain. XHTML 1.0 borrows the tags from W³C's earlier work on HTML 4 and can be interpreted by existing browsers, by following a few simple guidelines.

http://www.w3.org/MarkUp/#recommendations

As you can see, the W³C envisions XHTML as the next iteration of the HTML Web markup language.

▸▸ XML IS MORE THAN A MARKUP LANGUAGE

Many of the tools you use in HTML have been developed and packaged in ways that make their use very simple. XML is more complex.

Figure 15.3 shows all the processes that must be accomplished to render an XML document on the screen. First, the XML document is passed to a parser application, which uses the DTD associated with the document to create an intermediate file. You can run a validator before the parsing step, or you use a parser that is also a validation engine. However, many parsers are nonvalidating so don't count on your parser alerting you to problems, other than by breaking. This step determines if your document is valid *(type-valid)* or invalid *(non-type-valid)*. If you don't specify a DTD, then your document is valid by default, since there is no standard against which to check it.

After passing the parsing step, the XML code is passed to a processing application. Here the code is formatted for a particular display based on the style sheet associated with the file. One of the strengths of XML is that you can use the same data and simply process it differently for different displays: typical monitor, cell phone, PDA, aural output device, printed document, and so on. It is this flexibility that was one of the major driving forces behind the development of XML. Notice that nothing in the parsing step has anything to do with the format of the display. Nor does anything in the DTD. All of the formatting is done with style sheets.

Finally, after being parsed, processed, bent, folded, spindled, and mutilated, the code is presented in the device of choice—in this case on a monitor.

To be absolutely honest, the procedure in Figure 15.3 is an oversimplification. The actual process of creating a display from an XML source document is a bit more complex, and the complexity is growing all the time. For example, a whole set of tools, called XLink, is involved in creating links, and two other sets of tools, XPath and XPointer, are necessary to add search capabilities to your pages. On top of that, other tools are needed

Figure 15.3

Processes involved in rendering
XML document to HTML

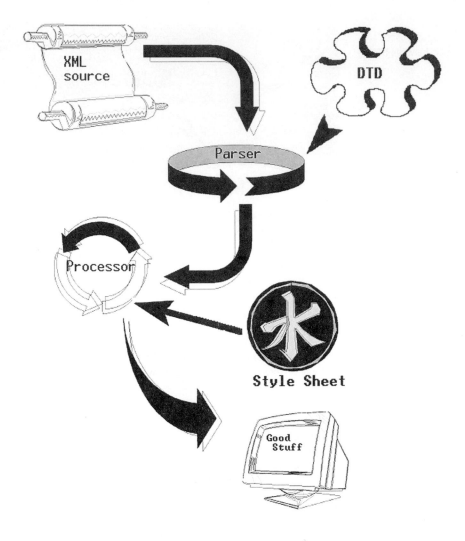

to convert one form of DTD data into another, to create programming to drive XML, and
so forth. XML developers have coined the term ***tool chain*** to describe a particular collection of tools necessary to render XML into a displayable format. Following is a list of
some of the tools you would need to study if you wanted to perform particular tasks as far
as massaging/presenting/archiving/basing your data:

- XML, SGML—for designing a DTD to describe your documents.

- DTD—for authoring DTDs, structuring new data, or simply validating particular
  data files. Note: A DTD can be XML-compliant or SGML-compliant but not both.

- CSS, DSSSL, XSL-FO, XHTML—for formatting, presenting, and publishing data in
  pages on devices.

- XSLT—for transforming one DTD into another.

- RDF, XTM—for associating different file types with an existing application.

- Xlink, Xbase, Xinclude—for linking documents together, or linking data into existing documents.

- Xpath, Xpointer, Xquery—for creating searchable pages, or searching documents or
  query databases described with XML.

- DOM—for representing XML data in a tree format.

- SAXON, XLAN XT—for programming directly in XML. These tools can also be
  embedded into other Java applications. Excellent tools, but complex to learn.

• LibXML, LibXSLT/XSLTproc—for creating XML/XSLT-aware C applications. This is a very exciting direction as it allows programs to generate and use XML data directly.

If it seems that there's a great deal to learn and many significant choices to make, you're right. To give you some idea of the complexity of trying to use XML correctly, your humble authors spent five full days just trying to install and use the tools necessary to take a very simple XML page, using the DocBook DTD, and render that page into HTML. With the help of several great folks on the DocBook mailing list, we managed to have a very simple XML page appear as HTML on our very own computers.

▸▸ BUILDING HTML FROM XML

The simple page shown in Figure 15.4 was created using xsltproc, which runs in the Windows environment and combines the parsing and processing steps using an *XSLT* (e*X*tensible *S*tylesheet *L*anguage *T*ransformer) procedure to perform the actual transformation into a predefined display format like HTML.

Figure 15.4

Simple DocBook, (XML) document

```
<?xml version="1.0"?>
<!DOCTYPE article  SYSTEM "./docbookx.dtd">
<article>
<title>There and Back Again</title>
<artheader>
  <author>
  <firstname>Bilbo</firstname>
  <surname>Baggins</surname>
</author>
<pubdate>Long Ago</pubdate>
</artheader>
<para>
<abbrev>LOTR</abbrev> stands for Lord of the Rings.
In this paragraph we could discuss
the intricate details of the construction
of a most proper hole in the ground.
</para>
<bridgehead>Now, a wonderful quote!</bridgehead>
<blockquote>
  <para>
  There were many paths that lead up into those
  mountains, and many passes over them.  But most
  of the paths were cheats and deceptions and
  lead nowhere or to bad ends; and most of the
  passes were infested by evil things and
  dreadful dangers.
  </para>
  <citation>Page 64 of
      <citetitle>The Hobbit</citetitle>
    by J. R. R. Tolkin
  </citation>
</blockquote>
</article>
```

Let's look at some of the highlights of this simple little DocBook (XML) document. The first line of the figure shows the required XML-version specification line. We used version 1.0 because it is the only version available at this time. The second line should look somewhat familiar to you. The differences in this instance are the Doctype of article and the DTD of docbookx.dtd. The third line begins an actual document container, in this case the <article></article> container. This <article> element takes the place of the <html></html> container you're used to using. The fourth line defines the title for the article. That container should look very familiar to you, although, as you'll see in a moment, it has greater usage in DocBook.

Line 5 begins the article header, which contains the author and publication date containers. Following the article header container is the body of the article. Notice that there is no special container that describes the body—rather, paragraphs enclose the body data. After the first paragraph is another container we're sure you are familiar with: <blockquote></blockquote>. Not surprisingly, blockquote functions very much the same way in DocBook as it does in HTML.

The container at the end of the blockquote is very interesting. It is a complex container called <citation></citation>, which holds the bibliographic information, in this case about the quotation. Notice that it also contains another container, <citetitle></citetitle>, which holds the title of the cited work. Finally, the last line of the file shows the closing article tag.

Since you're familiar with building HTML files, take a look at Figure 15.5 to see what this XML file generates when we run it through xsltproc and ask for HTML as out-

Figure 15.5   HTML code generated from XML code in Figure 15.4

```
<html>
<head>
<meta content="text/html; charset=ISO-8859-1"
    http-equiv="Content-Type">
<title>There and Back Again</title>
<meta name="generator" content="DocBook XSL Stylesheets V1.45">
</head>
<body bgcolor="white" text="black" link="#0000FF"
    vlink="#840084" alink="#0000FF"><div class="article">
<div class="titlepage">
<div><h2 class="title">There and Back Again</h2></div>
<div><h3 class="author">Bilbo Baggins</h3></div>
<div><p class="pubdate">Long Ago</p></div>
<hr>
</div>
<div class="toc">
<p><b>Table of Contents</b></p>
<dl></dl>
</div>
<p>
LOTR stands for Lord of the Rings.
In this paragraph we could discuss
the intricate details of the construction
of a most proper hole in the ground.
</p>
<h2>
<a name="id5298179"></a>Now, a wonderful quote!</h2>
<blockquote class="blockquote">
<p>
    There were many paths that lead up into those
    mountains, and many passes over them.  But most
    of the paths were cheats and deceptions and
    lead nowhere or to bad ends; and most of the
    passes were infested by evil things and
    dreadful dangers.
    </p>[Page 64 of
        <i>The Hobbit</i>
     by J. R. R. Tolkin
]</blockquote>
</div></body>
</html>
```

Generated HTML

```
<?xml version="1.0"?>
<!DOCTYPE article SYSTEM "./docbookx.dtd">
<article>
<title>There and Back Again</title>
<artheader>
  <author>
  <firstname>Bilbo</firstname>
  <surname>Baggins</surname>
</author>
<pubdate>Long Ago</pubdate>
</artheader>
<para>
<abbrev>LOTR</abbrev> stands for Lord of the Rings.
In this paragraph we could discuss
the intricate details of the construction
of a most proper hole in the ground.
</para>
<bridgehead>Now, a wonderful quote!</bridgehead>
<blockquote>
  <para>
  There were many paths that lead up into those
  mountains, and many passes over them.  But most
  of the paths were cheats and deceptions and
  lead nowhere or to bad ends; and most of the
  passes were infested by evil things and
  dreadful dangers.
  </para>
  <citation>Page 64 of
      <citetitle>The Hobbit</citetitle>
   by J. R. R. Tolkin
  </citation>
</blockquote>
</article>
```

DocBook code

put. Wow, that tool sure did a lot for us. Notice that it generates pretty good-looking HTML, with a couple of little departures from the norm. The box on the right shows the original XML code that was processed, along with the generated HTML, so you can see where particular bits of HTML code came from.

There are several features of generated code you need to pay close attention to:

1. Notice the <meta> tags in the head container. The second one tells us that this page was generated by DocBook XSL stylesheets.

2. It's interesting that the xsltproc combines both the use of color words (only those that are appropriate), and the more proper hexadecimal codes in the <body> tag.

3. Moving down the code, we see that the first and last names of the author are combined in a level-3 heading.

4. Although XML requires each container to be closed, xsltproc and the DocBook DTD generate unclosed horizontal rule elements because they are building to the HTML 4 specifications.

5. The next division of the generated code is very interesting—the XML parser generates a table of contents for us without any direct request. It assumes that any article has a table of contents, so that division with its associated directory list is (automagically) created for us whether we need it or not.

6. In this instance of the generation of HTML code, the <abbrev></abbrev> container generates no special coding in HTML.

7. The <blockquote></blockquote> container functions just as we expect.

8. But look at what this citation does for us! The procedure xsltproc does some special processing of citations: it creates an open square-bracket pair around the whole of the citation and places the title of the work, enclosed in the <citetitle></citetitle> container, in italics.

Figure 15.6

How the generated DocBook code looks in a browser

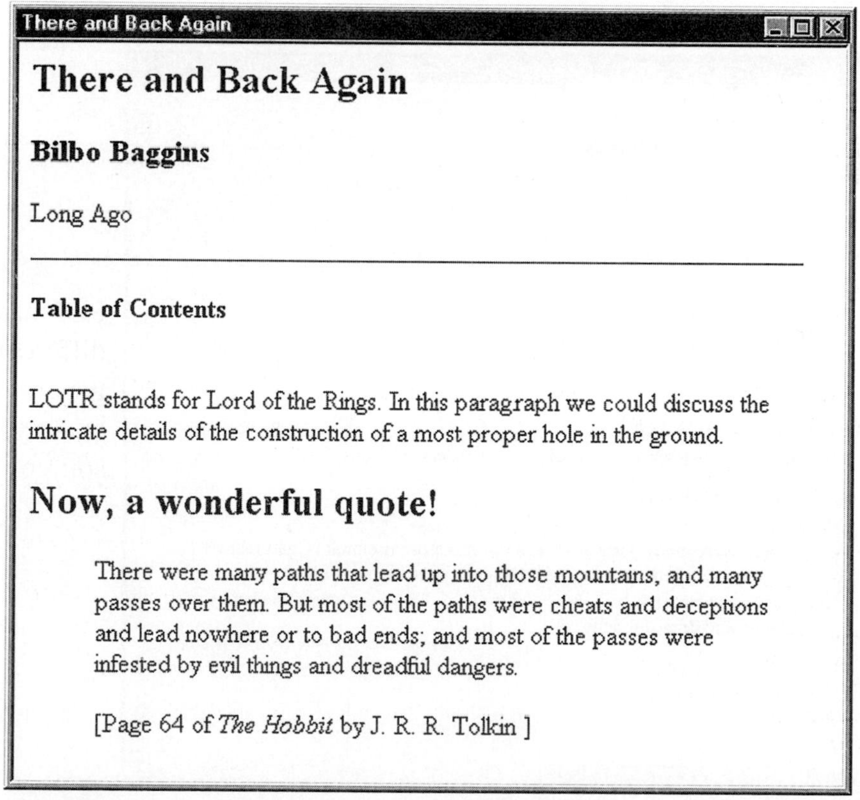

> **There and Back Again**
>
> **There and Back Again**
>
> **Bilbo Baggins**
>
> Long Ago
>
> _____
>
> **Table of Contents**
>
> LOTR stands for Lord of the Rings. In this paragraph we could discuss the intricate details of the construction of a most proper hole in the ground.
>
> **Now, a wonderful quote!**
>
>> There were many paths that lead up into those mountains, and many passes over them. But most of the paths were cheats and deceptions and lead nowhere or to bad ends; and most of the passes were infested by evil things and dreadful dangers.
>>
>> [Page 64 of *The Hobbit* by J. R. R. Tolkin]

The output of the HTML code generated from Doc Book

We think you can see from this example how data encoded in DocBook format can be converted to very useful HTML code. In addition, please remember that we did nothing special other than using a processor to convert the data, marked up in XML, to HTML. Figure 15.6 shows how the browser displays those data.

We'll admit that on initial inspection, Figure 15.6 probably isn't the most exciting Web page you have ever seen but, just remember that we *wrote no HTML* to generate this page! Instead we had xsltproc take our lovely XML code and generate HTML from it. To say that again, in XML parlance, what we did was use a processor to take our code, represented in XML format, and transform it to HTML for presentation in a browser. We could have just as well used a different option on the same processor to transform the same important data into another format, for example, Adobe's portable document format (PDF).

▸▸ CREATING PDF OUTPUT FROM XML

Simply by changing the DTD we could have xsltproc build output designed to go into a different type of processor to create printed text. In this case xsltproc using the FO DTD allows us to generate a "Format Output" file. Then we can run xsltproc again, using a different DTD, and create an FOP-formatted version of the file. FOP, which stands for *Formatting Objects Processor,* is the type of the file used as input to the text-processing tools like Apache's FOP processor.

In all honesty, the method of getting the FOP processor to work eluded us for several days. Part of the reason is that the XML we initially wrote had a small error. It seems that the <blockquote></blockquote> container cannot contain plain text. All the text must be enclosed within another container. We were trying to generate the page shown in Figure 15.7 with the text of the blockquote by itself inside the container. With some guidance from the great folks on the DocBook list, we discovered our error and corrected it by putting a paragraph container around the text.

Figure 15.7   Printed (PDF) version of same XML code shown in HTML in Figure 15.6

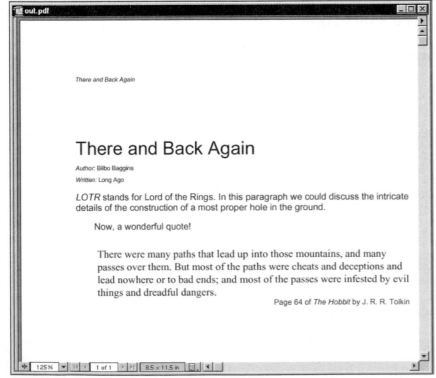

PDF has a totally different "look" generated from exactly the same source.

The displayed version of the PDF code generated from Doc Book.

The FOP processor is more demanding than the XSLT processor. Figure 15.7 shows how the XML file we've been using looks when rendered through the FOP Processor and displayed in Adobe Acrobat.

Remember, this is exactly the same XML file that generated the HTML page shown in Figure 15.6. That is the beauty of XML: the same input file can be processed using different DTDs, style sheets, and tools to render output suitable for display or presentation by a variety of devices. For example, we could use a tool like FOP to create PDF output, or we could use different tools to create output for a PDA, a cell phone, a PowerPoint display, Microsoft Word, or even some sort of audio browser. The whole idea behind the development of XML is that you have one file to describe the data, totally independent of the way that data are to be presented to the world. Then by applying DTDs and style sheets, you modify or tailor the output to show those data in a myriad of devices.

This cross-platform applicability is reminiscent of the initial concept behind the Java programming language: write once, run anywhere. Unfortunately, the proprietary interests of some of the initial supporters of the Java language were more important to them than true interoperability. Since the XML standards are supported by the W³C and not by commercial interests, we can hope that it will not suffer the same fate. Obviously, HTML is still supported across the browsers of multiple companies, and XML, at least so far, has also been untainted by proprietary interests.

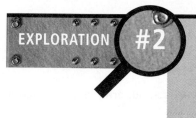

EXPLORATION #2

To give you a better idea of how the W³C views the importance of cross-platform compatibility using XSLT tools, take a look at how it expects XSLT to be used. Use your favorite browser to display the following URL: http://www.w3.org/TR/xslt#data-example Check out what the W³C is saying. It's slightly more complex than the example we've been studying this chapter.

▸▸ WHAT NEXT?

A logical question is, "So what's next with XML?" The answer depends upon whom you talk to. For example, according to the OASIS "about" page, it serves as a repository for a wide range of different XML- and SGML-based projects. XML is starting to define a number of different human relationships outside cyberspace as well as addressing a plethora of different hardware/software platforms. For example, the HumanMarkup technical committee (TC) has defined its goals this way: "The HumanMarkup TC is set forth to develop the HumanML and associated specifications. HumanML is designed to represent human characteristics through XML. The aim is to enhance the fidelity of human communication."

HumanML is set forth to be an XML Schema and RDF Schema specification, containing sets of modules that frame and embed contextual human characteristics, including physical, cultural, social, kinesic, psychological, and intentional features within conveyed information. Other efforts within the scope of the HumanMarkup TC include messaging, style, alternate schemas, constraint mechanisms, object models, and repository systems, which will address the overall concerns of both representing and amalgamating human information within data.

Examples of human characteristics include emotions, physical descriptors, proxemics, kinesics, haptics, intentions, and attitude. Applications of HumanML include agents of various types, AI systems, virtual reality, psychotherapy, online negotiations, facilitations, dialogue, and conflict resolution systems. That's pretty amazing—developing the markup language to describe people! And you thought XML was a dry topic.

In other words, the future of XML extends far beyond the World Wide Web. The idea of building tools to describe data and relationships among particular elements of data has caught on and is growing. Currently this whole endeavor is limited only by the fact that it's very new. In the next few years XML applications and XML tools will proliferate, and XML will become part of most data-description scenarios. Understanding how XML works, and the role it will play in data communications as well as in human communications, will be an essential part of your education in just a few years.

EXPLORATION **#3** Check out the OASIS site at http://www.oasis-open.org/ Investigate two or three of the wide range of different XML applications supported by OASIS.

▸▸ XML AND DATABASES

As we mentioned earlier, Oracle and the other major players in the database community have embraced XML as an ideal tool for encoding data. The XML concept fits into the existing database model because it describes the contents of various bits of data, rather than simply describing how they will be displayed. Take, for example, a simple database for a college class. We will first look at the class data as described by HTML, then as it could be described by XML.

The data about your class probably contains the following elements:

- Room number
- Department code and course number
- Course name
- Instructor
- List of students

These data could be presented in HTML as shown in Figure 15.8. As you can see from the figure, all of the data are presented in a tabular format. Each element of the data is there, and all you need to know is the layout of the page. However, it wouldn't be that easy to code a program to go into this page and extract particular elements of the data, such as the instructor's name. Your program would have to know exactly where to look in the data to find the required information. Another challenge would be to write a program to count the students in the class. What this shows us is that HTML is excellent for *presenting* and *formatting* data, but it isn't so good at helping us analyze those data.

Figure 15.8

Representing classroom data in HTML

```
 9  <table>
10  <tr>
11     <th>2431 Jones Hall</th>
12     <th>COMP 2981 Web Weaving</th>
13     <th>Ben Thare</th>
14  </tr>
15  <tr>
16     <td>Sally Smart</td>
17     <td>William Wise</td>
18     <td>Bonnie Bright</td>
19  </tr>
20  <tr>
21     <td>Sam Sharp</td>
22     <td>Anna Able</td>
23     <td>Quinn Quick</td>
24  </tr>
25  </table>
```

Figure 15.9 shows us a sample of a hypothetical XML page that presents the same data, but in XML format. The first thing that catches our eye is that the page is longer! The expanded data give us a great deal more control over both how the data are represented and how they are processed. Look back at Figure 15.8 for a moment. With your knowledge of HTML, you can probably look at that page and pretty much know how the data will look. Now do the same with Figure 15.9. Any idea how the data will look on the page? Nope. That is because XML is a proper markup language, and merely describes the data rather than trying to both describe the data and dictate its placement and appearance. All that said, we are sure that you could, with your knowledge of CSS, create a style sheet that would describe exactly how those data would appear on the page using the tags in Figure 15.9.

Figure 15.9

Representing classroom data in XML

```
<?xml version="1.0"?>
<Classroom>
    <Course>
        <Name>Web Weaving</Name>
    <Department>COMP</Department>
    <CNumber>2981</CNumber>
    <Instructor>
        <Name>
            <Last>Thare</Last>
            <First>Ben</First>
        </Name>
    </Instructor>
    <Room>
        <Building>Jones Hall</Building>
        <Number>2431</Number>
    </Room>
    <Student>
        <Name>Sally Smart</Name>
    </Student>
    <Student>
        <Name>William Wise</Name>
    </Student>
    <Student>
        <Name>Bonnie Bright</Name>
    </Student>
    <Student>
        <Name>Sam Sharp</Name>
    </Student>
    <Student>
        <Name>Anna Able</Name>
    </Student>
    <Student>
        <Name>Quinn Quick</Name>
    </Student>
    </Course>
</Classroom>
```

But what of the other questions we ask of the data? Would it be possible to extract the instructor's name from the data in Figure 15.9? Sure, that would be easy—just search for the container <Instructor></Instructor> and extract the contents. What about counting students? That would be easy, too. All your program would need to do is count the number of <Student></Student> containers. All in all, XML would enable you to create any display you wanted with style sheets and a DTD, and it would give you relatively easy access to the actual data.

The other advantage of XML, one that is becoming more and more important in our wired world, is that XML data can be displayed on different devices, in different formats, without recoding. For example, Ben (the instructor) could display the class in a seating chart on hard copy, have the student names on a Web page in the classroom, and use those same data to enter grades on his wireless PDA as he rode the subway home from school each evening. Each device would have its own tool chain to present the data for that particular platform. We will examine this procedure more closely in the next chapter.

The bottom line is that storing data in an XML format gives anyone who must deal with those data more access and more flexibility. As Web weavers, we will be interfacing with XML data as we build our pages. You already have a solid grounding in XHTML, and we know you are ready to move into this exciting and powerful new paradigm as XML becomes more prevalent in our sphere of influence.

EXPLORATION #4 Go to the Oracle site at http://www.oracle.com and look at "Oracle9i Case Studies—XML Applications." Read what Oracle has to say in this outstanding discussion of XML and how it applies to Web weavers.

▸▸ KEY TERMS

DSSSL	Well-formed
Element	XHTML
Entity	XML
Tool chain	XSL
Valid	XSLT

▸▸ REVIEW QUESTIONS

1. Define each of the key terms.
2. How are XML containers like logical HTML style containers?
3. What determines how XML data are displayed or printed?
4. What is the difference between "well formed" and "valid" XML code?
5. How are data descriptions, entities, and elements combined together into DTDs?
6. List three current examples of large-scale data integration using XML.
7. Which W³C recommendation updates the HTML 4.01 specifications?
8. Explain why XML folks say, "Write once, display anywhere."

▸▸ EXERCISES

15.1. Use the following imaginary markup language to answer the questions at the end.

```
<paper>
<heading>
        <title>How I spent my Summer Vacation</title>
        <author>Robyn Banks</author>
        <datewritten>November 11, 2004</datewritten>
        <instructor>Dusty Tomes</instructor>
</heading>
<para>
This summer I found a new career option. I became an author. The book
I am writing is called "Withdrawals Without Deposits." I must admit that
```

doing the research for this book is a little daunting. I really don't like having to watch out for police officers all the time. However, I hope the book, and the research, provide me a good retirement income.
</para>
</paper>

    a. Describe all of the physical characteristics of the paragraph text.

    b. Describe all the physical characteristics of the date in the heading.

    c. Describe all the physical characteristics of the author's name.

```
para {
      left-margin:3em;
      right-margin:2em;
      font-size: 12pt;
      font-style:"Times New Roman";
      }
heading {
      text-weight:900;
      text-align:center;
      text-family:sans-serif;
      }
author {
       font-style:italic;
       }
```

15.2. Using the data in Figure 15.9, construct a style sheet that would produce the following output:

    a. Instructor's name, centered, bold, sans serif, 14 points, blue (#0033CC).

    b. Student names, left-justified, bold, serif, 12 points, green (#006633).

    c. Building name, right-justified, italic, 16 points, blue (#0033CC).

    d. Course name and number, italic, 14 points, serif, black (#000000).

Chapter Sixteen

Pragmatic Hypertext: It Ain't All Pictures!

To the novice HTML author, Web weaving means building home pages, or maybe creating an e-commerce site replete with graphics, dynamic content, and lots of artistic effort. We have been helping you hone those skills in the preceding fifteen chapters. There is another side to delivery of content on the Web, and it doesn't have all that much to do with pictures. Rather, it has to do with delivering content to different classes of devices besides the traditional monitor/keyboard combination. You might build a Web page that interacts with a user's cell phone, or even design content that is geared toward a spoken delivery, presenting your company's information over the phone in an aural fashion.

CHAPTER OBJECTIVES

After reading this chapter you should be able to do the following:

- Explain the importance of nongraphical Web sites.
- Describe different formats used to deliver data to a client.
- Use a browser to read an online text.

- Describe the role of XML in a multiplatform environment.
- Explain the use of WAP technology to build Web pages.
- Describe uses for aural Web pages.

▸▸ COMMON MISCONCEPTIONS

A common misconception that neophyte Web weavers have is that building Web pages means building pages only for public consumption on the World Wide Web. In today's world of private intranets, there is growing corporate and private use of the browser interface to provide access to information. In this environment, many professional Web weavers find themselves creating extremely large documents that will never be viewed by the public, using only the linking and display features of the browser.

▸▸ TEXT

Text-only documents don't use graphics, sound, or dynamic features; they simply supply massive amounts of text, often with hyperlinks to other documents. Many of these documents are sent to the browser as plain text, which means that they won't even be recognized as HTML files. They are usually displayed in a monospaced font like Courier. Figure 16.1 shows an example of this type of file, and, as you can see, plain text is really plain. It is just text, without bold, italics, or second-color enhancements. The text-only format is useful for moving lots of text data—not as pretty to read as a proportional font, but very functional and extremely quick to code. Another significant advantage of plain text is that it can be presented on nearly any device, even aural ones.

Figure 16.1

Plain-text page

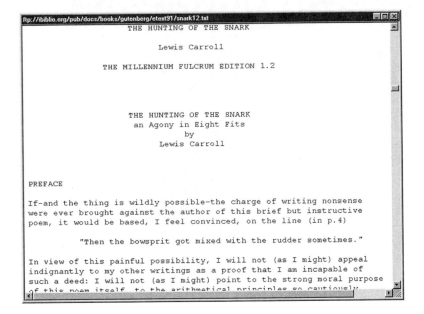

Several classes of documentation are beginning to appear on the Web. Among these are literature, corporate/government documentation, electronic books, Web-based instruction manuals, online help, and online education. In addition, the advent of mobile devices like cellular phones and handheld *PDAs* tied into wireless networks means that more and more classes of devices are trying to access Web content. Most of these devices have the following characteristics in common:

- They have small screens. For example, a typical cell phone has only four lines for text, one for a heading, and one for *softkey* definitions. A softkey is a user- or application-defined key on the existing keyboard, or in this case keypad. These softkeys allow easy entry of special application-specific data like a request for pricing or such.

- They have a *very* limited color palette, usually only a few shades of gray.

- The input device is extremely limited in many cases. For example, a cell phone has a small number of keys, a PDA may allow only stylus input, and none of the handheld devices we have seen have large keyboards.

• The content should be deliverable in a short time frame; users don't want to wait five minutes for a large page to download.

Now let's look at the different types of pages that are delivered across this wide range of devices.

▸▸ LITERATURE

Selfless groups have hosted some interesting examples of great works of literature on the Net. In Chapter One you saw some of the offerings from the University of Virginia's online library. A list of several collections of this type is included at the end of this chapter. Check them out and enjoy some classic reading. The usual caveat applies, however, that the addresses of some of these sites may have changed between our reading of them and your reading of this text. Figure 16.2 shows a partial list of the works available from Bartleby.com. Many other collections of literature are out there for your online reading enjoyment. A TEOMA search for online literature showed 10,500 matches. We are sure that there will be more tomorrow. Building libraries of electronically available books is currently in fashion.

Figure 16.2

Screen capture from Bartleby.com site

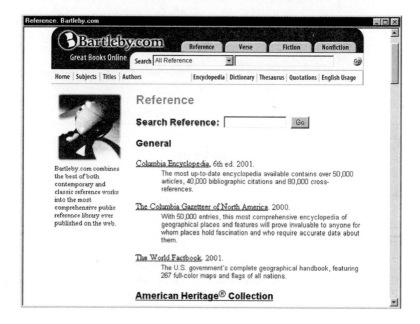

BASIC TEXT

Many text-only documents are simply online versions of the paper originals. In some cases, they include translator's notes, but most are simply long, text-only documents. They don't involve many of the features of the browser and have no links to word definitions. All they do is present the text, either in the plain version we saw in Figure 16.1 or in proportional fonts like the one used in this book. Such projects are a wonderful use for the Web. They give anyone with even the most basic Web access the opportunity to read a great variety of literature, often in the original language.

Figure 16.3 shows a pair of screen captures from different sites. The upper of the two is a screen capture from Sir Arthur Conan Doyle's *A Scandal in Bohemia* as presented in plain ASCII text (monospaced font) at Project Gutenberg. The lower is another mystery, this time *The Murders in the Rue Morgue* by Edgar Allen Poe, presented as an HTML page in proportional font from the Electronic Text Center of the University of Virginia Library. Both qualify as text-only because there are no illustrations along with the text.

Figure 16.3

Two examples of text only documents

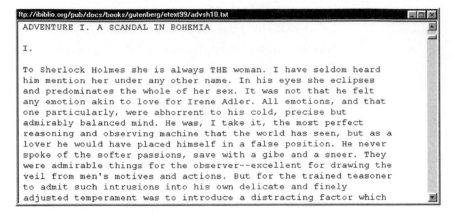

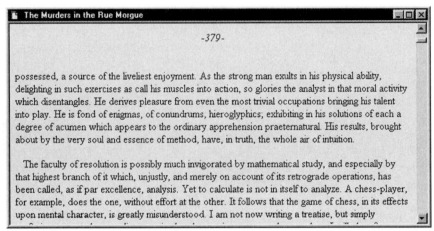

TEXT AND ILLUSTRATIONS

Other literature collections provide their readers with some illustrations to accompany the text. As Alice wondered, "[A]nd what's the use of a book . . . without pictures or conversations?" on the first page of *Alice's Adventures in Wonderland.* Many other developers of online material feel the same way. For example, one of the versions of Alice's adventures has scans of some of the accompanying illustrations. Figure 16.4 shows a screen capture of one of the pages. Notice that the illustration has a nicely textured background that makes it look even more like a paper text. Actually, it is in color and quite nice to see if you visit. The address is in the list at the end of this chapter.

Figure 16.4

Example of a document built with both text and illustrations

HYPERLINKED TEXT

The most powerful use of HTML in presenting text occurs when the Web weaver uses links to tie several documents together. In some cases these documents give the reader actual links to documents that are referenced, or they may provide an online glossary or dictionary that supplies the definitions of certain **hot words**, which are text (usually underlined) that the user activates to open another Web page. Figure 16.5 shows a screen capture from the online version of *The New Hacker's Dictionary,* also known as *The Jargon File* (in its paper version). The words that look like links are actually links to other words in the dictionary. (By the way, this is a great place to learn new jargon! Fair warning, however: you can lose hours exploring this wonderful document.)

Figure 16.5   Screen capture of part of a page showing hyperlinks within the document

Notice the links to other parts of the document.

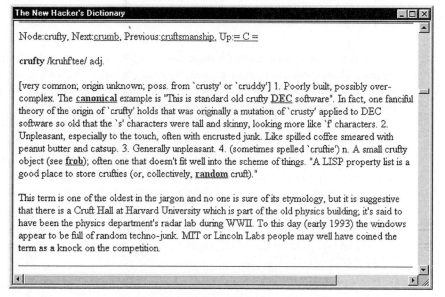

The New Hacker's Dictionary

Node:crufty, Next:crumb, Previous:cruftsmanship, Up:= C =

crufty /kruhf'tee/ adj.

[very common; origin unknown; poss. from 'crusty' or 'cruddy'] 1. Poorly built, possibly over-complex. The canonical example is "This is standard old crufty DEC software". In fact, one fanciful theory of the origin of 'crufty' holds that was originally a mutation of 'crusty' applied to DEC software so old that the 's' characters were tall and skinny, looking more like 'f' characters. 2. Unpleasant, especially to the touch, often with encrusted junk. Like spilled coffee smeared with peanut butter and catsup. 3. Generally unpleasant. 4. (sometimes spelled 'cruftie') n. A small crufty object (see frob); often one that doesn't fit well into the scheme of things. "A LISP property list is a good place to store crufties (or, collectively, random cruft)."

This term is one of the oldest in the jargon and no one is sure of its etymology, but it is suggestive that there is a Cruft Hall at Harvard University which is part of the old physics building; it's said to have been the physics department's radar lab during WWII. To this day (early 1993) the windows appear to be full of random techno-junk. MIT or Lincoln Labs people may well have coined the term as a knock on the competition.

Using hyperlinks to retrieve definitions or to branch the user to supplementary documents brings to bear the power of the Net. The previous examples in this chapter show how the Web can be used to emulate a paper-and-print text. The fourth example, from *The Jargon File,* shows how a wise Web weaver can utilize the hyper part of Hyper Text Markup Language to create a document with features that were previously unheard of.

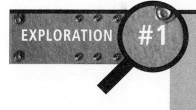

EXPLORATION #1

Log into one of the sites mentioned, such as the Jargon file at http://www.tuxedo.org/~esr/jargon/ or the University of Michigan at http://hti.umich.edu/. Now read a bit of one of the texts. We recommend *Alice's Adventures in Wonderland* at the U of M, or anything in *The Jargon File.* Print one of the pages.

▶▶ CORPORATE/GOVERNMENT DOCUMENTATION

Many applications in government and the corporate world require building large collections of HTML pages to replace hard-copy documentation. Some of these uses are policy and procedure manuals, employee manuals, current legislation, government reports, budgets, and the like.

Figure 16.6

A sample of a government use

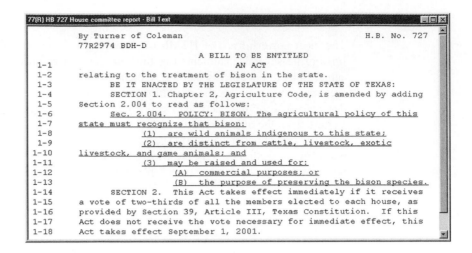

Figure 16.6 shows part of a page from the Texas Legislature Online pages. It is a simple, unadorned text document, easy to read and well indexed. If anyone in the state, such as a prospective rancher, wants to read recent laws that apply to his situation, he can do so any time of the day or night, provided the server is up.

There are several good reasons to produce manuals and other documents online rather than in a paper version:

- Probably the most important benefit is that each user will always have access to the most recent data. Doctors, for instance, can have access to the latest government research without having to wait for it to be published in a medical journal.

- The expense of publishing online is usually much less than printing many paper copies. In addition, it is supposed to save trees, although in practice most people go ahead and print copies of the pages.

- Updates to existing online documents are available across the whole user community as soon as they are entered. This reduces the chances that some subset of an organization will not be informed of a change in policy.

- Online documents are available anywhere there is an Internet connection. A user at a remote location can have immediate access to the whole set of corporate documentation in the field.

- In addition, other companies or government agencies can look at an organization's methods to help formulate their own.

Creating and maintaining a set of online corporate/government documents is a monumental task, because accuracy and availability are always essential issues. However, in our rapidly changing world, people need access to the most recent updates in policy, procedures, or even laws. Online publishing of these kinds of data meets those users' needs very well. With the addition of wireless access, it is becoming possible for users to be in constant touch with the Net wherever they roam. We will discuss the wireless phenomenon later in this chapter.

►► ELECTRONIC BOOKS (EBOOKS)

With the right hardware and software, you can use an electronic book, or *ebook,* nearly anywhere, and on a wide range of devices. When we wrote the last edition of this book, ebooks were a new development, and pretty much restricted to a couple of hardware vendors' specialized devices. Now, ebooks are available for many handheld and PDA platforms, as well as for use with laptop and desktop computers. It won't be long before it will be common practice to have ebooks supplement, or even replace, books like the one you are holding. A number of companies are building software and ebooks. If you search the Net, you will find hundreds of sites that deal with ebooks, ebook readers, and ebook emulators.

Figure 16.7

Ebook reader, emulated on PC

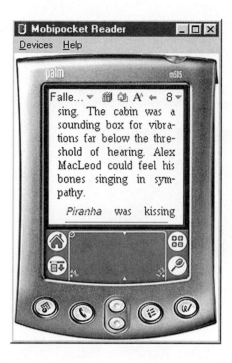

Figure 16.7 shows one of the ebook emulators in use. In this instance the software is emulating a Palm device, displaying the text from a free ebook, *Fallen Angels,* by Larry Niven, Jerry Pournelle, and Michael Flynn, from the Baen Library. We anticipate that there will be more and more movement to publish in this medium as people become more comfortable with and dependent upon their PDAs.

Some advantages of ebooks are that they may have an internal dictionary so you could find the meanings of words you didn't know. In addition, depending upon the device, you could have available thousands of pages of text and graphics, so you could have several texts in the book at the same time. Features would include adjustable fonts, multiple bookmarks, limited note taking, and even highlighting. Readers would buy the text online, download it to their PC, and then transfer the data to their electronic book or PDA.

In most of the implementations we have seen, once the book is on your system, you can pretty much treat it as it if were a paper-and-ink text. If you wanted to lend the text to a friend, you could loan her the whole electronic book or just copy the file for her to read. Please note that while many ebooks are free to download and distribute, others are not free and should not be copied. It could be a great boon to students, who would only have to carry one, electronic, book with them, having the equivalent of several textbooks in a three-pound package. For some folks, reading an ebook is not nearly as satisfying as having a paper-and-ink tome to cuddle up with. However, it is much more convenient to read a book on your PDA than use a paper text while standing in line, or sitting in a boring lecture. Did we really say that? It is also more discreet. We believe that ebooks will become more popular in the near future, and that many books, reference manuals, and guides will be published in this format.

▸▸ WEB-BASED REFERENCE MANUALS

You can find out how to do almost anything on the Net these days, from tying knots (see top of Figure 16.8), surgical and otherwise, at http://www.ethiconinc.com/

wound_management/procedure/knot/index.htm to building crystal-set radios at http://www.midnightscience.com. The bottom of Figure 16.8 shows a screen capture of part of the plans for building a crystal radio that takes no electric power to run.

Figure 16.8

Example of online instructions

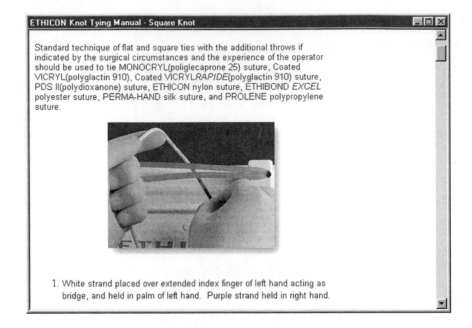

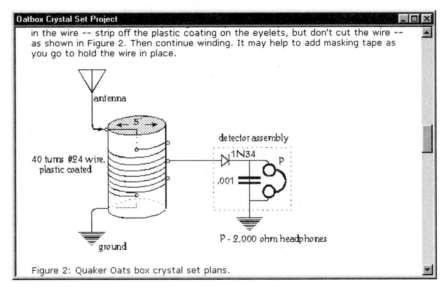

As with online corporate/government documentation, online instruction manuals have several benefits for both the author producing them and the user.

- The online reference can be as current as the author is willing to keep it. The company who owns the product can update the online manual to reflect problems, features, or even misunderstandings conveyed to them by their customers.

- Users can't lose an online reference. Unlike hard-copy manuals, they don't get lost behind the refrigerator, under the couch, or buried in a file drawer.

- If the customer buys a device secondhand, the requisite documentation is still available even if the original owner lost the paper version.

- Should customers want to print the manual, they can do so at their own expense.

- Using the full range of HTML, CSS, JavaScript, and multimedia tools, a careful Web weaver can create a multimedia user's guide that is far more comprehensive than a printed manual could ever be. In addition to written instructions, a Web site can supply actual MPEG video clips showing how the product is to be used, along with narration to help the user through more complex tasks, like software installation.

- With the development of wireless Web browsers, online instruction manuals can be available when and where you need them, simply by linking to the server from a wireless device.

All in all, online manuals provide a superior way to supply many forms of user's guides, manuals, and reference works. If you end up supporting almost any type of device, seriously consider putting your manuals and user's guides online. Your customers and users will thank you for the convenience.

▸▸ ONLINE HELP

Another area where Web weavers are increasingly involved is in the creation of Help files for packages and programs. Microsoft has abandoned its traditional WinHelp format and gone to a new tool called HTML Help. That means that now Microsoft Help files are written using a variant of HTML rather than the previous format. Unfortunately, Microsoft has chosen to use Active-X controls in this package, so it isn't useful across all the browsers. However, when a major player in the computing field begins to use HTML-based help, it won't be long before there are other, more compatible packages available. If you want to explore this tool, download the Microsoft HTML Help creation tool. You can visit the Microsoft site for a description of the product, the process, and the actual software.

Of course, Netscape is not about to be left out in the cold, so it developed NetHelp, another HTML-based Help tool. It uses Communicator, which isn't cross-platform compliant either. You can find out more about NetHelp by visiting

http://home.netscape.com/eng/help/home/home.htm

Figure 16.9

Sample of NetHelp page

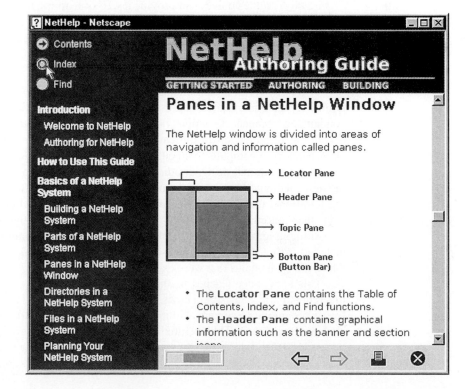

You can download the NetHelp SDK (Software Development Kit) from this site. Figure 16.9 is a screen capture from the Netscape site showing a sample page from the NetHelp 2 page. Notice that the Help screen looks much like a regular Web page—that is the whole idea!

▸▸ ONLINE EDUCATION (DISTANCE LEARNING)

One arena where the Web has had a major impact is in training. Both in-house corporate training and distance learning in schools and colleges have jumped on the HTML bandwagon. While other forms of distance learning have slowed in growth or are even dwindling, Web-based education has become a hot topic. There are several reasons for this:

- Online education is available whenever and wherever the student can find a computer tied into the World Wide Web. Students can learn at their own pace, and on their own schedule. They don't have to wait for a professor, nor are they limited in how quickly they can complete a unit of instruction. By the same token, they don't need to commit to a specified block of time in a classroom at a regularly scheduled interval.

- A college doesn't need the overhead of a physical plant to conduct online classes. All it needs do is supply a host or server computer, the necessary software, and the content. There is no need for classrooms, desks, whiteboards or chalkboards, a cafeteria, or even a parking lot.

- All the students receive the same instruction. This fact can be good or bad. The quality of the experience depends, in part, on the skills of the author building the course.

- Once instruction has been developed, it takes less effort to update and modify it. Of course, this advantage depends on the sponsoring organization recognizing and committing itself to the necessity of regular updates. As neophyte Web weavers, you already know the importance of checking and maintaining your pages on a regular basis. Unfortunately, not all the folks in management do.

- Finally, online courses can provide a web of learning that exceeds the scope of a single professor. A science course could be designed using the expertise of a dozen or more specialists, all writing Web pages about their own areas of study, or it could include the use of original sources available only via the Web. No single professor can duplicate that!

There is a fly in the ointment, however. Each of the points just listed has a counterpoint. George Santayana's famous saying that "those who do not learn from the past are condemned to repeat it" applies here. *Computer-assisted instruction (CAI)* was going to revolutionize education in the early 1980s by replacing professors with terminals and classrooms with computers and cubicles. The revolution didn't happen. The major reason was that educational designers didn't take into account the limitations and strengths of the new medium. Along with the many problems with CAI was the impossibility of forcing traditional teaching methods into the new medium. CAI courses were often nothing more than automated page-turning tools. Students spent hours and hours reading text on eye-straining terminals, all alone. One of the biggest complaints voiced by students subjected to early CAI was that they were lonely. Overall, the CAI effort failed to yield even a fraction of the gains that were expected of it.

This experience teaches us that authors of Web-based education must consider the inherent strengths and weaknesses of the medium. They can't treat it like a traditional delivery system with a screen. Multimedia offers possibilities that are completely new in the history of education. The potential is staggering. But so is the development effort. Building good Web-based distance learning is not a job for a single faculty member any more than filming an epic movie would be for a single film maker. When colleges and universities realize that building good multimedia online courses requires hundreds of hours of development for each hour of delivered material, we will see the beginnings of great distance learning.

Figure 16.10

Online discussion topic for distance-learning course

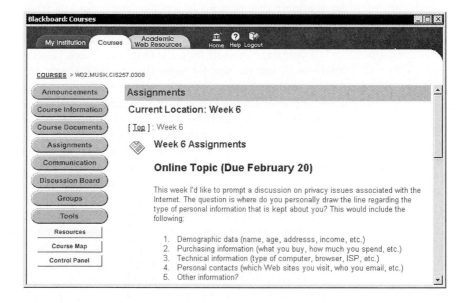

Figure 16.10 shows one screen from an online course. This screen is from a set of pages designed around software that supports online courses. The discussion topic on privacy shown in this figure is meant to focus online students on an issue that would normally be part of a dialog between teacher and students in a traditional on-campus class. Other support services provided the online student are announcements, quizzes, assignments, and the email addresses of fellow students. Coupled with email support, this course can provide instruction to students widely scattered around the country.

Online courses of this nature are not built by a team of specialists, but by individual teachers. It is a very useful course, built around a good textbook, and is intended to replace the teacher's lectures. Successful students must bring to online classes of this nature an ability to read the textbook for content along with the time-management skills to take tests on time, accomplish weekly assignments, and post their thoughts on the discussion topics in a timely manner.

Perhaps the very best instructional delivery system is a professor sitting on one end of a log and the student on the other. That kind of one-on-one teaching/learning is probably the ideal. However, in our widely scattered world, HTML-based teaching seems to be the best method of distance learning we have ever had.

EXPLORATION #2 Online learning and you. Check out one of the free online courses at Barnes and Noble University or Code warrior U. http://www.barnesandnobleuniversity.com or http://codewarrioru.com Sign up for a free course that interests you and experience online learning for yourself.

▸▸ THE WIRELESS WEB

Mobile computing, wireless Web, even deskless workstations—they all describe the same thing—using part of the electromagnetic spectrum to broadcast data without having the client physically attached to the Internet. One of the most daunting tasks for this new medium is the wide variety of physical characteristics in the lineup of devices. A cellular phone has a tiny, usually black and white screen and a limited keyboard, but it can present and receive aural messages. A PDA can manage limited color graphics and may have a more extensive set of input controls, but will most likely not handle aural data. Then there are all the devices in between. This plethora of platforms makes designing Web content challenging indeed for the wireless Web weaver.

If you limit yourself to just HTML—or, much better, XHTML—your problems are fairly small and can usually be handled by style sheets. However, let's look at the problem of presenting streaming video on three different devices: a laptop PC, a PDA, and a cellular phone. On the PC, with its powerful processor, you can just transplant the video and let it play. On the PDA, with limited processor power, you must reduce the video stream to a slide show, probably without sound. When you direct the presentation to a cell phone, you will need to simply display a set of captions to the slides instead of the slides themselves.

As you can see, as you move farther and farther away from the power and resources of the PC, your medium degrades. On the other hand, you gain flexibility and mobility. You can check the performance of your stocks, perform trading transactions, locate the nearest Mongolian restaurant, or even buy a soda with just your cell phone. All of these are possible today in Europe. North America is a bit behind the development and deployment curve in the wireless arena. Try to do all that with your PC while cruising down the street on your ProPed scooter. The point is that the mobile user will be using one of a wide range of devices to access the content you are providing. Now let's talk a bit about how you build those data into usable form.

In Chapter Fifteen we looked at how you can build a document in XML and through the use of conversion tools or style sheets present it in many different formats. In addition to CSS and XSL and the other formats discussed earlier are WML (Wireless Markup Language) and VoiceXML, the voice-driven markup language. There is a strong movement to simply incorporate these alternative browser requirements within the body of XHTML, since modularization has already been built into the language. The W^{3}C has been actively researching compatibility among various devices since 1998. Let's look at a representative sample of these different ways to present Web content.

WAP (WIRELESS APPLICATION PROTOCOL)

WAP (Wireless Application Protocol) is a proposed standard that is quickly gaining favor in the wireless community. It has a strong foothold in Europe. The WAP Forum, http://www.wapforum.com lists many specifications tying XHTML and XML to WML (Wireless Markup Language.) Actually, this whole wireless environment has provided the acronym generators with a field day. So you can read the documentation with minimal distraction, here is a list of acronyms:

CARD—the equivalent of page in HTML (shades of Hypercard!)
WAE—Wireless Application Environment
WML—Wireless Markup Language
WSP—Wireless Session Protocol
XHTMLMP—Extensible Hypertext Markup Language Mobile Profile (the convergence of XHTML and WAP/WML)
XWML—Extended Wireless Markup Language

As you can see, there are a lot of new acronyms. The important thing to realize is that WAP, or WML, is being built as an extension of XHTML. That means that the conversion from/to XHTML should be relatively easy. Another important consideration is that WAP is an open standard, not tied to any industry, so it can grow and develop without worrying about paying allegiance to any particular subset of the business.

WIRELESS INTERNET

Looking at what is happening in Europe and in Japan, where DoCoMo, the mobile communications arm of Nippon Telephone and Telegraph, is serving over 6 million users now. Projections are that by the year 2004 there will be over 1.3 billion folks using wireless Internet. DoCoMo was the first company in the world to offer cellular phone technology to their customers. The stumbling block in the United States is conflicting standards. Currently three competing methods exist for delivering WAP to users. When that issue has been resolved, the industry will be poised to move into the arena in large scale.

▸▸ KNOWLEDGE IS POWER

The only real hindrance to building tools that work on multiple platforms is thinking outside the traditional box. For example, let's say you have a Web-enabled mobile phone. You are standing in your favorite bookstore and find a new text, an Even More Excellent text, you wish to buy. Rather than just walking to the register, you log into bn.com and enter the ISBN number of the book. If the price is lower than the store shows, you have a couple of options:

1. You can simply order the book from Barnes and Noble online.
2. You can take your phone to the cashier and ask if he is willing to match the price.

In either case, you come out the winner. Imagine doing something like that when you purchase cars or anything else. This situation gives you, the consumer, great leverage.

WIRELESS DATA

Sure, but what about the other side? What about you, the Web developer? Are you going to have to build a dozen different pages/cards to handle a dozen different platforms? Do you have to build three different pages to handle three different browser types now? Nope. You just rely on the tools to handle the content. Building pages in XML will enable you to use different *resolvers,* hardware/software combinations that render XML into different formats, to deliver your content across the multitude of platforms. The general idea is shown in Figure 16.11, which details the three layers of this new protocol. (Notice how much it looks like the XML process we examined in the last chapter.)

Figure 16.11

Model for WAP delivery of HTML/WML content

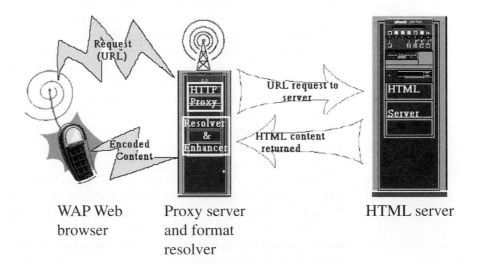

WAP Web browser   Proxy server and format resolver   HTML server

As you can see from Figure 16.11, the WAP browser (in the cell phone) requests data from a proxy server. The proxy server is designed to take data from wireless devices, recognize what type of device is making the request, and decode the URL requested by that client. After decoding the URL, the proxy server sends the request to the HTML/HTTP server. The HTTP server provides the content to the proxy server, which reformulates and styles it to the specifications of the particular client device before sending it to the WAP client. The proxy server handles all of the magical formatting tasks, deciding which of the mobile formats to use, PDA, cell phone, and so on. If you build the code in XML or XHTML rather than in HTML, then the same model will work across a wider range of browsers.

AURAL DATA

The next logical step is to get rid of the text part of the content, since cell phones are designed to handle data in an audio/aural form and many PDAs are coming equipped with aural add-ons. VoiceXML seems to be the logical extension of the HTML to XHTML to WML path. Aural data might include taking voice instruction and providing audio output of the content. This technology is not as advanced as WAP, but we don't think it will be long before an existing Web page can be served up in a variety of sound formats.

It is important to realize that any of these new platforms will want to take advantage of the existing profusion of pages already on the Net. It wouldn't make sense to build a platform that required only a specialized data format like WML without a means to take HTML and present it in that format.

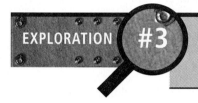

EXPLORATION **#3**   Check out the different standards for phone service in the U.S., Japan, and Europe. Log onto http://www.ou.edu.engineering.ecm/standard.html and read about it.

▸▸ WEB SITE VS. WEB PAGE

In Chapter Three you saw four different organizations of pages: sequential, indexed sequential, hierarchical, and custom. You saw that you could create a single page to serve as a table of contents and linkage point for a series of poems. That was just a tiny example of a Web site. In addition, Chapter Three mentioned the importance of *storyboarding* your site so you could design both the flow of the pages and the way the user would interact with that flow. Now we will build on those ideas.

Consider for a moment what the design of an encyclopedia site would look like. The initial design would probably be sequential, simply flowing from one page to the next, just as users would read a book if they were reading it front to back. But that model doesn't work for an encyclopedia, because it is a reference work, and people don't usually read it from front to back for entertainment. (Mind you, if you haven't tried that, you might enjoy it. It's amazing what you can learn just by picking up a volume of a good encyclopedia and reading for a few dozen pages.) Another problem with using a sequential design here is that a single page containing the whole content of a good encyclopedia would take a *long* time to download.

The model best suited for the online version of a book or class is as follows: The first step is to include a set of *intrapage* links that allow the user to select any of the letter of the alphabet and jump to the first page that has entries starting with the letter. *The Jargon File,* Figure 16.5, is an excellent example of this sort of design. You can download the whole Jargon file as one big page; it has links to each beginning letter and to definitions of words within other definitions.

Back to our online encyclopedia, the next step might be to divide the page into 26 different pages, one for each letter of the alphabet, as shown in Figure 16.12. The master table of contents, or index, should contain links to each chapter. Each of those pages could have its own index to allow selection of entries from that page.

Figure 16.12

Example of single page with links to several different pages

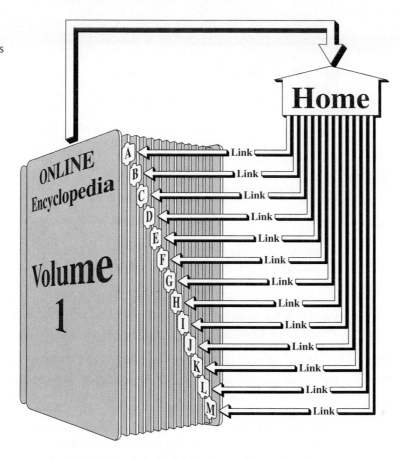

Finally, each letter of the alphabet could have its own page, with a large list of links to various topics, each of which has its own page. This model could easily involve hundreds or even thousands of pages. In such a model, the design would have to be carefully crafted to ensure that the pages are tied correctly forward and backward. Indeed, this type of design creates a set of links so complex it would justify the term Web weaving!

▸▸ MIGRATING FROM TEXT TO HYPERTEXT

When an individual or an organization decides to migrate from a paper-based document system to an online document model, a lot of initial work is involved. The first step is to design, or storyboard, the site, showing the linkages among all of the different documents and pages within those documents. This is a critical step, because navigation is often where online sites fail. Users must be allowed to find and retrieve the information they need with little or no hindrance. The relationships need to be carefully crafted to enable free-flowing movement across the whole of the content.

The second step, designing a page's "look and feel," is almost as critical as the first. This is another area where some companies fail to consider their users. On the one hand, a page layout that is too busy, too loud, or loads too slowly is a disservice to the user. On the other hand, plain vanilla pages using black text on stark white do little to make the user's experience pleasant.

You learned about page footers in Chapter Three. During the page-layout stage, details such as footers will also need to be finalized. A small graphic of the company's logo in a header may help unify and define the documents. However, remember that headers and footers will appear on each page as it is printed. The way the documents will look when printed is an important consideration. In fact, the appearance of the printed page is of such import that many sites offer a version of the page that is "printer friendly." We discussed this in the chapter on styles. You need to consider hard copy as yet another medium into which your page may be rendered.

OPTICAL SCANNING

Finally, the most interesting question: How will the actual content be migrated from paper to Web-based format? We won't attempt to deal with a document that exists only in paper format. The operations of selecting *OCR* (optical character recognition) software, scanning the text, converting it to an electronic format, and proofreading it for correctness and completeness are beyond the scope of this text.

TEXT CONVERTERS

Assume that you are starting with a document that exists in some electronic form—for example, a document in a word-processor format like Word 2000—you can choose from a pantheon of packages that claim to take text in some form like ASCII, RTF (rich text format), MS Word, PostScript, WordPerfect, and so on, and convert that text into HTML. Some of these packages perform better than others. On the W³C's Web site alone, more than 70 different converter packages are listed. Some are freeware, some are shareware, and others are commercial products. All of them claim to create HTML from some other application format. None that we tested did a perfect job. In every case, the output needed some tweaking to make it useful.

We discussed *text-to-HTML converters* in Chapter One, so we have no need to go into detail about them here. Suffice it to say, we did some serious research on such converters using the various tools available and found that all of the conversion packages— using built-in word processor tools, external conversion tools, or importing the text into an HTML editing package—created documents that still needed additional work. For example, almost all of the conversion programs consider each sentence a separate unit and encode all of the formatting tags each time. As of now, none of them generates style sheets.

Nevertheless, the HTML documents produced by such converters most likely require less work than a plain ASCII file would if you had to add all of the HTML features. Moreover, using external style sheets could ease the job of standardization and allow for quicker conversions.

If you are faced with the task of converting a set of text files to HTML, the best bet would be to get samples of several of the conversion programs. Run all of them against one example file that has the features found in the target files, and look at the resulting HTML files. Find the one that is most complete, or that requires the least manipulation, and then acquire that package. Over time, packages like Web Publisher, StarOffice, and Microsoft Word will become increasingly complete, creating HTML documents with a high degree of reliability.

AURAL BROWSING

Not everyone in the Web community uses a visual browser. Some 3 percent of users (as per the W³C) have a visual condition that renders the traditional Web page less than ideal for them. An additional 4–5 percent don't use a graphical browser for reasons of connection speed, hardware limitations, or because they choose not to be bothered by distracting graphics. In addition, the wise Web weaver will take into consideration users who cannot appreciate graphical content because of various other circumstances. Web browsers are now available for your cell phone, your PDA, and even your car. It is great to cruise the Web while cruising down the highway—but not with graphics! You don't want to be looking at pictures instead of the road! In the auto-browser and in many cell phone applications, the user will select an aural, meaning "relating to the ear" or "hearing," presentation and voice input rather than a graphical one.

One of the noteworthy features of the HTML 4 specifications, according to the W^{3}C, is a significant increase in the support for accessibility. Using an aural component on your page allows those Web cruisers who are not using graphical browsers to implement other possibilities.

The following code adds aural presentation to a page:

```
h1 { voice-family: heidi;
       volume: medium;
       richness: 30
     }
```

Please note that aural presentations are a combination of both audio cues, or *audio icons,* and synthesized speech as covered in Chapter Nine. Audio icons are used much like graphical icons to delimit parts of the text, to highlight specific phrases, and to call attention to changes in the content. Unlike the current practice of converting the Web page to plain text and then passing it to a text-to-speech reader that simply reads all of the characters passed to it, the aural styles allow the rich environment of the Web page to be transferred to an aural modality.

The aural rendering of the page can be considered separate from the graphical, as images will be replaced by the values of their **alt** attributes, and the various characteristics of the text, such as headings, will be represented by aural cues. Yet the major content will be the same as before adding aural capabilities. Aural characteristics include properties that control the volume, speech properties, pausing before or after, cue before or after, and playing an aural content during another type of activity. In addition, a rich set of voice properties is available, the most interesting being the voice family designated by names like paul, heidi, peter, and goat!

The aural presentation space is three-dimensional, so with proper audio gear, a Web weaver can design sounds that come from different directions and elevations. Of course, users who have that sort of surround-sound stereo setup correspond to graphical users with 21-inch, 64-million-color monitors. The wise Web weaver won't require that level of hardware commitment.

Let's look at the code again. It will set level-1 headings to be played in the very smooth voice of heidi, at mid-level volume:

```
h1 { voice-family: heidi;
       volume: medium;
       richness: 30;
     }
```

If this were coded as part of a document's style sheet, and if the user had a sound-equipped browser, level-1 headings would be presented in sound, and perhaps in text as well. Currently there is no way to test aural styles in the standard browsers, but new and better browsers are being created all the time. One new thrust is in the realm of telephone-based Web browsing, allowing the user to employ a telephone as her browser of choice, navigating the site with voice input and audio replies.

INTERNATIONAL CONSIDERATIONS

The world seems to grow smaller every day, and the World Wide Web is one of the major forces that seem to be shrinking it. Content on a Web page is available to anyone, worldwide, who has a browser and access to the Net. In light of that fact, the W^{3}C added a significant number of features to the HTML 4 specifications to take into account people who want to host pages in languages other than English.

As you have seen, attributes are available on nearly every tag that allow the Web weaver to specify both the language for that element and the direction that the language is to be read. The direction is important for punctuation marks and the like. As you cruise the Web, you will see more and more sites that provide content in languages other than

English. The internationalization of the HTML specifications is an important step to promote accessibility worldwide. For example, you might see a page with a <meta /> tag that specifies

<meta http-equiv="content-type" content="text/html; charset=iso-8859-5">

which specifies the Cyrillic alphabet, or

<meta http-equiv="content-type" content="text/html; charset=iso-8859-2">

which is used to present Central European languages like Croat, German, Hungarian, Polish, Romanian, Slovak, and Slovenian. Then there is

<meta http-equiv="content-type" content="text/html; charset=iso-2022-jp">

which specifies Japanese.

As Web authors, we should strive to make our content available to as wide an audience as possible, both those folks who have preferences as to their chosen form of input and those who don't speak our langauge. Over time, the browsers will allow more and more people access to our content.

▸▸ ONLINE TEXT SITES

Here are some of the more interesting sites that have text documents available on the Web.

- http://www.hti.umich.edu/all/unrestrict.html This is a list of links to famous and not so famous works. Several religious texts are included. (Notice that the site address looks like a hypertext link. If this were an online document, you could just click on the address and go to that site. Alas, you are reading this on paper and so must go elsewhere to link to the site.)

- http://etext.lib.virginia.edu/ebooks/subjects-illclas.html The University of Virginia is collecting classics in both HTML and ebook format. This is a good resource for free ebooks.

- http://home.earthlink.net/~lfdean/carroll/nursery/chapter01.html The first chapter of *Alice's Adventures in Wonderland*. You can read many of Lewis Carroll's works at this site.

- http://www.tuxedo.org/~esr/jargon Technically this is called *The Jargon File*, and the paper version, published by MIT press, is *The New Hacker's Dictionary*. It is a wonderful site that can consume your time on many a rainy afternoon, providing chuckles, chortles, and even a few guffaws as well as giving you an understanding of the world of the hacker. Check it out!

- http://www.promo.net/pg/ Project Gutenberg is attempting to make 10,000 electronic editions of books available on the Net before the year 2003. This project has the following philosophy:

  The Project Gutenberg Philosophy is to make information, books and other materials available to the general public in forms a vast majority of the computers, programs and people can easily read, use, quote, and search.

- http://www.ipl.org/ The Internet Public Library is just what its name implies—a large collection of electronic documents available for your perusal.

- http://onlinebooks.library.upenn.edu/ This is called the *online books page*. It boasts over 7,000 titles, including a very interesting list of books that have been banned by one group or another.
  Note: Between the first and last versions of this edition of this text, two of the URLs previously listed above either disappeared or moved. Such is life on the Web.

▸▸ KEY TERMS

ebook   resolver
hot word   softkey

▸▸ REVIEW QUESTIONS

1. Define each of the key terms.
2. Identify four characteristics of handheld wireless devices.
3. What is the most powerful use of HTML in presenting text?
4. What are five benefits to maintaining documents online?
5. List five advantages or features that the authors speculate will be available with electronic books.
6. How could you benefit from learning online?
7. What is one of the most daunting tasks in developing wireless applications, and how it is handled by XHTML?
8. Explain how WAP and VoiceXML are different.
9. Why would a sighted person use an aural browser?

▸▸ EXERCISES

16.1. Ruby has heard that you are getting close to the end of the class, and she wants us to give you her best wishes on your final. She also thanks you for all the hard work you have done for her site. She urges you to work hard on your final project.

16.2. Use the online references provided in this chapter to find out how many books are currently available from Project Gutenberg.

16.3. Use the HTML format of *The New Hacker's Dictionary* to find the definition of *hamster.*

16.4. Create a link to *The New Hacker's Dictionary* on your homework home page.

16.5. Create a link to the University of Virginia ebook Web page on the school home page you created in earlier exercises.

16.6. Find an online book (using the recommended links) that was made into a movie. Create a new Web page that provides information about the movie and a link to the related online book. Add a link on this new page to the movies home page you created in earlier exercises.

16.7. Send an email to the software house of the browser you use. Ask it when the next release of its software will be available. Include in the email at least one inquiry about an HTML-recommended feature you would like to see supported—for example, aural style sheets. If you use Internet Explorer, email Microsoft. If you use Navigator, email Netscape or America Online.

16.8. If you have a PDA or Web-enabled phone, download one of the free Web browsers for your device, then go to one of the free ebook sites, get an ebook, and thus experience the cutting edge of technology. However, don't read it while your instructor is lecturing!

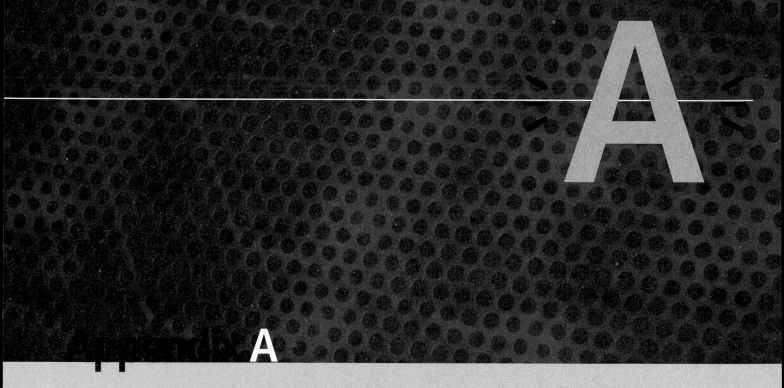

A Style Manual

Style—we all feel we have it when we are building our pages, and our pages always look good to us. But there are some guidelines that will make your Web pages more readable and more usable. Or, as Robert Burton (1576–1640) said, "It is most true [that] 'stylus virum arguit,' our style betrays us."

The following style guidelines—and they are just that, guidelines not rules—come to you from a number of different sources. First, they reflect the page-design experience of the authors of this textbook, plus the experiences of their students. Some of these endeavors worked, and some serve as good examples of what not to do.

Second, these guidelines come from many different style guides found across the Net. They are too numerous to mention, but a collection of some URLs that served as resources appears at the end of this section. Third, these guidelines were derived from the ranting and raving of many users who have written in mail groups, left messages, and generally made their feelings clear about what they like and don't like about different sites.

▸▸ GENERAL GUIDELINES

- **Have a purpose for your page.** Don't create a Web page just because you can. Have a distinctive unique purpose for your pages, and let the reader know, up front, what that purpose is.

- **Be consistent.** Consistency is critical. Decide on things such as how you are going to use headings, what colors will mean, how site navigation will be accomplished, and then stick with that design across all your pages. In addition, use consistent images when you mean the same thing, and use a consistent background image or color (plain color being better than an image because the page loads faster), to tie all your pages together. Using a different but consistent background to identify related collections of pages is also a good strategy. Always use the same navigation controls on all your pages, like Back, Forward, and Home.

• **Design for both graphical and nongraphical browsers.** Not everyone uses a graphical browser, so if you want your information to be accessible to all users, design your pages to be accessible to nongraphical browsers. In fact, in large areas of the world, most folks depend on fast, small, text-only browsers. Advancements in hands-free applications of Web-based information and the needs of the visually impaired add weight to this point. Always look at your page in Lynx, a text-only browser, or turn off Image Loading in your graphical browser to see what your page looks like as plain text. One site recently visited looked like this in Lynx:

[LINK]

[LINK]

[LINK] [LINK] [LINK]

[LINK]

That is not very helpful, now, is it?

• **Don't try to be "slick."** Fancy, powerful animated images and applets are wonderful toys, but most users don't appreciate a page full of distracting elements that get in the way of finding what they need on your page. Pages that use the very latest Web technology will probably be of value only to a small minority of users who play on the cutting edge. For the majority of users, your innovations will either be invisible (at best) or render your page useless (at worst). Don't design pages to simply show off how complex you can make them. Remember our discussion of "eye candy," and don't fill your pages with empty, content-void graphics just because you have the tools to do so. Always remember that your primary goal is to create a page that enables users to efficiently and enjoyably find the information they seek.

• **Use big pages and images only when absolutely necessary.** Size *is* important! Big, slow-to-load pages do not reflect good design. If you need to display a large image, put it on a page by itself and give the user a link to that page. One nice way to do that is to use a *thumbnail image* as the link. When using thumbnails, make sure you tell the user how big the image is or how long it may take to download. Your home page should download very quickly. A good rule of thumb is to keep your home page with all its images smaller than 1 megabyte of disk space. That way it will be relatively quick to download. A good test is to link to your page from a browser connected through a modem and see if you can hold your breath until your page fully loads. If you can't, consider making the page smaller.

• **Maintain your page!** After you have spent the time to create a page, it's worth a little extra time to ensure that all links on that page work and that the other elements of the page are correct. Plan to spend some time each week checking your page. It is always more fun to create new content for your pages, but your users deserve to find a good, useful, accurate page when they make the effort and take the time to come to your site. Make sure your links work and that the information you put on your page is accurate. It is a good idea to incorporate the "date last modified" code we showed you, it may encourage you to update your page frequently, because that shows users the date of the last change.

• **When you update your site, do it all at once.** Don't upgrade a site piecemeal. If you are changing the look of your site, plan the effort so that you bring all the pages with your new look online at the same time. It can be confusing for your users if they move from screen to screen of your site and find significant differences among the pages.

• **Don't change the colors of the linking text unless your design absolutely forces you to.** Should you feel forced by your design to change the colors of the linking text, it might be better to change your design. Coding colors for the **alink, link,** and **vlink** attributes that are different from the defaults can confuse your users. Even though the default colors are not necessarily the very best, and there may be good arguments for changing them, users still expect unvisited links to be blue and visited links to be purple. Stick with that color scheme whenever possible.

- **Use background images with care.** A background image will, *without a doubt,* interfere to some extent with the readability of your page. Use background images when necessary, but know that you will be reducing, albeit slightly in some cases, the readability of the text on your page.

- **Use light backgrounds with dark text when you can.** They are easier to read than dark backgrounds with light text. If you doubt this, ask yourself if it is easier to drive a car during the day or at night. Dark backgrounds make seeing more difficult. In addition, white text on a dark background will not usually print out if the user tries to print your page. And white text doesn't show up well on a white page! We realize that there is some attraction to creating pages with very dark backgrounds. However, as your experience with the Web increases, you will find that style less and less attractive. Generally, those pages with dark backgrounds are built by Web newbies. Experienced Web weavers know that dark text on light background has been with us for a long time. It has been the style of choice for thousands of years—to be exact, 5,000 years—ever since papyrus sheets were used in place of the later invented paper. Unless there is a very compelling reason for the opposite, use light backgrounds with dark text.

- **Use color sparingly.** Color is a powerful tool, but too much color on a page is worse than no color. Color can focus the attention of your user, or it can distract from the content. One of the glaring mistakes that novice Web weavers make is to create pages that are a veritable riot of colors. Bright colors for text and background, color images, initial caps in a contrasting color to the rest of the text—color, color, color everywhere. Those pages are visually brutal to view and downright difficult to read. Subtle use of color is always better than the assault on the senses employed by some Web weavers.

- **Choose browser-safe colors.** Several places throughout the text we have mentioned browser-safe colors. Those 216 colors that are browser-safe should provide as much of a palette as any designer needs. We have included them on the color insert in the *Reference Guide* you purchased with this book to make your job easier. Remember, too, that all platforms will not render even the browser-safe colors *exactly* the same way.

- **Be very careful if you choose to use fancy animation tools.** There are a number of tools on the market now that you can use to create impressive, expansive, beautiful animations and flash images. While they are indeed visually exciting, they have no place in a serious Web site, other than perhaps on an initial or "flash" screen. They are slow to load, and far more often overdone that done right. We strongly urge you to avoid the glitter of these glitzy additions to your page and stay with solid, well-designed, carefully crafted content that provides your users with what they came for, information, not time-wasting flash.

- **Build your pages so any browser can use them.** It doesn't really make much sense to create pages that contain features that are supported by only one of the browsers. We have been careful to show you things that will work in both of the major graphical browsers. Avoid the trap of building a page "best viewed with ExplorerScape." There is a campaign on the Net to encourage Web weavers to create browser-neutral pages. Visit the home page for this movement at

www.anybrowser.org/campaign/

Look for buttons like the one in Figure A.1 as you cruise the Web. The movement is growing!

Figure A.1

Best Viewed in Any Browser!

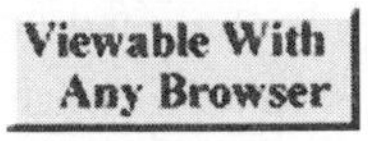

Viewable With Any Browser

- **Always provide a way for the user to get in touch with you.** You will want your users to be able to tell you of problems they found or give you kudos for things they liked. Your email address should be on your home page or on the main page of a collection. This way, since all the other pages will have navigation links back to the home page or to the central link for a series of pages, the user can always get to the page with your address on it by means of the mailto link. Make sure that the mailto link is documented as well. A cute, animated GIF is nice, but it is invisible in a text-only browser.

- **Cross-link all the pages in your site.** Avoid deadend paths that force people to use the Back button on their browser. If you have a worthwhile page, people will bookmark it. When they come back to your page using a bookmark, they will need to be able to move back to the rest of your site. They must have a set of navigation tools to do that. One of the more useful tools is a small one-row table at the bottom (or top) of each page (see Figure A.2) that contains links around your site. See the section on making a table of contents for an example of this structure.

- **Date your pages.** Always include the date on your pages so the user knows when the site was last updated. For example, it does the user no good to have a site that lists all the important astronomical events for 1994. It might be interesting in a historical context, but it's not of much interest to the user who is trying to find out when to look for the next Perseid meteor shower. You owe it to your readers to date your page. Besides, it may encourage you to keep your page up to date if the time of your last update is noted there for everyone to see. Along this same line, when you put the date on your page, use the formal style of "Last updated March 4, 2003" rather than "Last updated 03/04/03." Why? Because in Europe that date means April third, not March fourth. (Europeans place the day number first, then the month number.) Using the "date last modified" JavaScript code Chapter Fourteen is an easy way to accomplish this.

- **Don't have several links to the same content on the same page.** It is horribly confusing for your user to see links to interesting material more material that is interesting, even more interesting material, all of which point to exactly the same page. In fact, you should beware of using too many links as a general principle. A page that is filled with many links of any type can be confusing for the user. Link to important sites, but don't overdo the links—unless you are creating a page of links, that is. A page of links is usually not a good use for a Web page, but in specialized cases it can be useful. If you are going to have a page of links, consider putting them in a table to better arrange them for your user.

- **Make sure your page is unique.** Okay, this sounds like a social issue, not a style issue, but your page should exist only if it supplied some unique content to the Net. It is not sufficient to be a page of links, or a page of quotes from other pages, or a page of images, ahem, "borrowed" from other sites. Your page should provide something unique to the world. If it doesn't, why should it take up space on the Net? Perhaps the only thing unique about your page is your history, your vision, and a collection of your holiday pictures. Well, let's forget that last bit—but the first two items are reason enough to create a Web page. No one else has your exact history and vision. The point is, your page should provide something new to the Web, something that is available only on your pages. Without that, all the rest of these issues become merely smoke.

• **Ensure that your page will degrade in a graceful manner.** When a particular browser doesn't support one of the features on your page, be it a tag, an attribute, or even a JavaScript, your page degrades in that browser. Test your pages to ensure that they degrade gracefully, without losing the essential content. One example is to turn off Image Loading or use a nongraphical browser to see how your page looks, and works. If you have no essential data in images, your page should be fine. On the other hand, if you included critical data in an image, your page would not degrade in a graceful fashion.

▸▸ READABILITY OF YOUR HTML CODE

• Hard-code newlines (carriage return line feeds) after column 50 or so. That way when your users do a View Code they won't have to scroll to the right to read your code.

• Use white space to break up your code. Since the browsers remove excess spaces, it doesn't cost anything to put blank lines between design elements. Remember, easy to read is easy to fix.

• Indent to show subordination. For example, put <li></li> containers two spaces right of the <ol> tag so that the <ol> and the </ol> will line up with the <li>s indented, making it easy to see where the list starts and ends. The same is true for coding tables. Align the <table> with the </table>, indent and align the <tr>s, and indent again and align the <td>s or <th>s. Frames within a frameset and controls within a form should also be indented.

• If a container spans more than one line, try to align the starting and ending tags so the ending tag is easy to find.

• Use comments liberally, explaining <i>why</i> you are doing what you are doing, not just <i>what</i> you are doing.

▸▸ STYLE IN THE <head>

• **Use a title, and make it a meaningful one.** Often the title is all a potential user has to go on to determine if she wants to go to your page. Make your title descriptive and accurate. A good title is usually less than 50 characters long. Remember, if users save your page in a Bookmarks/Favorites file, your title is the description that will be stored to help them find your page again.

• **Include <meta> tags that contain complete and accurate data.** An example of a good <meta> tag follows:

```
<meta http-equiv="Content-Type" content="text/html; charset=ISO-8859-1" />
```

This <meta> tag is used to identify the character set you want to the browser to use with the Web page. It is especially important to employ this type of <meta> tag when you are using special symbols or a foreign language with special characters.

The following <meta> tag documents the content of a Web page:

```
<meta name = "keywords" content = "style guide, excellent" />
```

Both of these tags help search index your page and create accurate links to it. The list of keywords will often be displayed by the search engine as well.

• **Use external resources when possible.** It is usually more maintainable to link to style sheets and JavaScripts than to code them in the <head> container. If you use a style sheet or JavaScript in more than one page, make them external and link to them.

➠ THE <body> OF STYLE

- **Don't use frames unless you must.** While there are some good uses for frames, which we have discussed, as a general rule, you shouldn't use them. They take up screen real estate, they can slow processing, and they functionally disable some useful browser tools like the Back button and bookmarking (saving favorite pages). If you absolutely must use them, be sure to provide your users with a prominently displayed way to exit from the framed document lest they be trapped in your frames.

- **Use headings in level order.** The <h1> headings are for important, main ideas. <h2> should come next, then <h3>, and so on. Always use headings in order. Don't skip a level unless your design forces you to. And if it does, consider changing your design. In addition, don't employ headings just as a formatting tool. If you want text to be in a small bold font, use the **style** attribute's font-size and font-weight properties, not an <h6></h6> container.

- **Use the cascading styles.** The HTML specifications gave us cascading style sheets. You have seen numerous examples of how those are used throughout this text. To summarize our advice:

  1. If you are providing style data for more than one page, use an external style sheet and link to it.

  2. Use document-level style data.

  3. Use inline style for specific, unique style changes that happen only once on a page.

- **Put equal spacing between elements of equal importance.** Add extra spacing between elements that are of distinct categories. For example, if you have two tables on your page, add a blank line or two between them so the reader has a chance to see that the code for one table stopped and then another began. By the same token, a blank line between paragraphs makes the code much more understandable.

- **Use horizontal rules to separate different elements on the page.** Horizontal rules, <hr />, provide a good visual break. But don't code them with too large a **size** attribute. According to some Web weavers, it is considered bad form to code more than one <hr /> in succession. Others use a series of two or three <hr />s of different sizes to create an interesting border or divider. If you code more than one <hr />, don't go overboard like Ruby did on some of her pages in the exercises.

- **Keep your pages to a reasonable length.** There is great debate on what is a "reasonable" length for a page. It is like when Abraham Lincoln was asked how long a man's leg should be, and he gave the famous reply, "Long enough to reach the ground." Your Web page should be long enough to reach the ground, too. Hmmm . . . okay, how long would that be? How about long enough to cover the concept or idea you are presenting? If the page is too short, the user wastes time waiting for it to paint up. (However, sometimes it is an excellent idea to have small pages that serve as footnotes to your larger page.) If the page is too long, users may not want to view all of it. There is some evidence that most users will not scroll down more than one or at the most two screens on a page. That is a good measure for your home page, as well as for index pages or pages at the head of a set. Yet, it makes little sense to break up the posting of a scientific paper that runs to 15 screens just for the sake of brevity. If you are putting a book on the Net, it is usually a good idea to break it down by chapters, or even by large sections. But don't break a book into 20-line chunks and force your reader to flip from page to page to follow your narrative. The proper length, then, depends on the content.

- **Always have a table of contents for your site.** If you have a complex site with several different areas of interest, try to have a main *table of contents* (TOC) that links to the sublevel TOCs. This way your user can navigate about your site more easily.

Each page should have a link back to the sublevel TOC at a minimum. It is good to also have a link to the main TOC. A series of pages should have links from each one to the next. Don't force your user to bounce back to the TOC to see each successive page of a document. The pages should have Next and Back links to help the user navigate.

This is not to say that your TOC must look like a TOC! It is easy to create a little table of links that serves as a TOC or to incorporate an image map as a TOC. This way the user has a navigation tool, but you don't sacrifice the "look and feel" of your page. Figure A.2 provides an example of a table used as a navigation bar.

Figure A.2

Table of links as example of navigation element

- **Test your page with the Lynx browser or by telling your browser not to display images.** Lynx is available for download to your server (check with your systems manager) or for use from several sites. The Web page for this book has a link to Lynx in case you can't find one closer to home.

- **Print your page.** This sounds like a simple test, but it is sometimes amazing how bad a page can look when printed. A good Web weaver will always consider the printed version of their page even though the Web is designed to save trees. You should create printer friendly versions of your pages if you expect them to be printed often.

- **Always indicate the status of your page.** Some pages are created for a specific purpose and require no updating. You should tell your user when the data on your pages are final versions and not subject to revision. On the other hand, most pages are constantly under revision. If that is the case, tell users and give them some idea as to when the next update will happen. However, don't use the cute "under construction" GIFs or, worse, the "under construction" *animated* GIFs. Everybody knows that everyone's pages are almost always "under construction"; you don't need to include those graphics.

- **Always use the shortest URL you can get away with when referencing pages within your site.** Remember that the browser will complete the left portion of the URL if you allow it to. Use relative URLs whenever possible.

- **Don't use <blink>!** There really isn't any compelling reason to, now, is there?

- **Don't change the URL of your page unless you absolutely must.** Cruising the Net, one finds the "page not found" message far too often. It seems that people just move their pages from place to place. Plan where you are parking your page, and keep it there. Moving pages is really a disservice to your users. If you must move your page leave a page to forward to your new page.

- **Make sure the text within an <a></a> container explains the target of the link.** Remember, some text-only browsers display link text just like any other text, so the explanation is critical.

- **Use the height and width attributes on images whenever possible.** Using the **height** and **width** attributes will make the text appear more quickly on your page because the browser doesn't have to download the entire image before determining the image's screen footprint.

- **Ensure that each image element contains a descriptive alt.** Every image must be described by a line of text. This rule allows nongraphical browsers and browsers with the image loading turned off to know the content of the images. Creative use of the **alt** value allows the user with the nongraphical browser to get the general idea in some cases. For example, if you have a graphic for "New," you can code the **alt** attribute like this: alt = ">NEW<". A graphical bullet could be coded this way: alt = " * " or alt = "@".

- **Use the title attribute.** Nearly every element now supports the **title** element. Your users will see that content as a tool tip when they hover their screen pointer over the element with the newer browsers. Use that feature to give your user more direction or information. Be sure to use a **title** attribute with every image.

- **Use the new, nonvisual styles as they are developed.** Creating pages that can be heard, not just read, will bring your content to more users. As the multisensory techniques and tags evolve, make an effort to use them so as to allow the widest audience possible to enjoy your efforts.

- **Use a good HTML validation program to test your page.** Several good HTML validation packages are available that will check the code on your site. The one we recommend is located at http://validator.w3.org. Don't be surprised if this validation package finds many little errors.

▸▸ ETHICAL/MORAL CONSIDERATIONS

- **Leave your eyepatch and Jolly Roger at home when you cruise the Web and when you design and code Web pages.** A plethora of wonderful images and applets and animated GIFs and backgrounds are out there that people have spent a great deal of time and effort to create. Don't pirate them for your site. Take only those that are clearly marked as free, and always give credit to the site where you found them.

- **Don't link to images or multimedia across the Net unless the owner of the site requires it.** Linking will slow the loading of your page and create additional congestion on the Net as well. Always harvest the images or other resources you are going to use and host them locally. Of course, you must have permission from the owner of the resource before you harvest it. Don't make the mistake of thinking that if you find a copyrighted image, you can link to it rather than copy it. The actual display of that image is controlled, and the owner of the copyright won't appreciate your using it without permission.

- **Be careful about the content of your pages.** In the United States we have the Constitution to protect our right to free speech. This is not a universal right. Some countries restrict the content of any material allowed across their borders. In addition, many organizations and parents are beginning to use blocking software to limit access to sites on the Net. If you have valuable content to share—and why else would you have a Web page—you don't want access to your site blocked because you have used offensive language or graphics. If you are compelled to use language or graphics that a significant portion of your audience may find offensive, put them on a page or pages of their own, and tell your users what they are linking to. Remember as well that unless you own your own Internet feed and the computer hosting your page, somebody else may feel responsible for what you post.

- **Pay attention to the people who take the time to comment on your page.** For every one that writes a complaint, there will have been dozens who left your page in frustration and will not return.

▸▸ LANGUAGE AND WRITING

- **Write in gender-neutral language whenever possible.** However, the line, "A wise Web weaver always checks *his/her* links," is gender-neutral but seems clunky, obvious, and interrupts the text flow. A better choice might be, "Wise Web weavers always check *their* links."

- **Spell-check your pages!**

- **Proofread your pages.** A spell checker checks only spelling. As you cruise the Web, you will notice sites where the Web weaver did use a spell checker but probably never reread the page. Eye yam shore ewe no thee kinks of problems eye yam tanking abut! My spell checker had *no* problem with the preceding line.

- **Now proofread it again; then have somebody else proofread it.**

- **Avoid regional slang.** You are writing for an international audience, and slang can cause serious problems for non-native speakers of your language. As regional dialects continue to evolve, non-native speakers may include people from the other half of your country as well as folks from outside your national borders. I am sure y'all know what I mean dude.

- **Don't use the phrase "click here."** Not only is the effect obnoxious, but the phrase assumes the user has a mouse.

- **Try to avoid politically inflammatory, racist, or religiously biased language on your page.** If you feel compelled to use any of this kind of language, put it on pages that your users can choose to link to, and be sure to tell users what they are linking to. For example:

  These are my <u>feelings</u> about the Unix operating system. Note: I'm a Unix aficionado!

  That line tells users that they will be linking to a page that is probably a pro-Unix rant. If they don't want to read it, they don't have to. Don't put rants on your home page, forcing users to see them when first seeing your page.

- **Avoid specifying fonts by name if possible.** With the new font-oriented **style** properties in the HTML 4 specifications, it is very tempting to find some "fun" fonts on your machine and incorporate them into your page. While this can result in a very vibrant page, it can also cause two different problems:

  1. If the user's platform doesn't have the particular font you requested, it will default to another font that may not give the results you desire.

  2. If the user has a font on her system that has the same name but different glyphs than the one you specified, the page may well be unreadable when displayed. For these reasons, we recommend the following restrictions when specifying the font family.

     a. If you must use a named font, like New Century Schoolbook, follow it with a generic style that will also work, like serif, sans-serif, or monospace. (Avoid cursive and fantasy.)

     b. Test your page with the generic font to ensure that it looks correct.

     c. The named fonts of Times New Roman and Courier are probably generally available. Others are subject to the whims of the users and their platform.

- **Create pages you are proud of, and then keep them that way.** Regularly scheduled maintenance will keep your car running longer and your Web pages fresh and exciting. Don't let your content get stale. Stay aware of the changes and improvements in the specifications, and keep your pages up to date with those suggestions. Change your oil every 3,000 miles. And, finally, have fun!

▸▸ STYLE GUIDELINES

The following sites contained style guides at the time this book was written. With the rate of change on the Net, some of these sites will have disappeared by the time you read this. However, other sites will have come online. Searching with a search engine will allow you to find others.

www.useit.com/alertbox/9612.html

www.sun.com/960416/columns/alertbox/index.html

www.tlc-systems.com/webtips.shtm

www.sysmag.com/web/html-style-old.html

www.w3.org/Provider/Style/All.html

www.anybrowser.org/campaign/

www.w3.org/Provider/Style/Overview.html

info.med.yale.edu/caim/manual/contents.html—This is a whole book online.

The most important thing you must do as a Web weaver is be considerate of your users first, last, always, and design your pages for them.

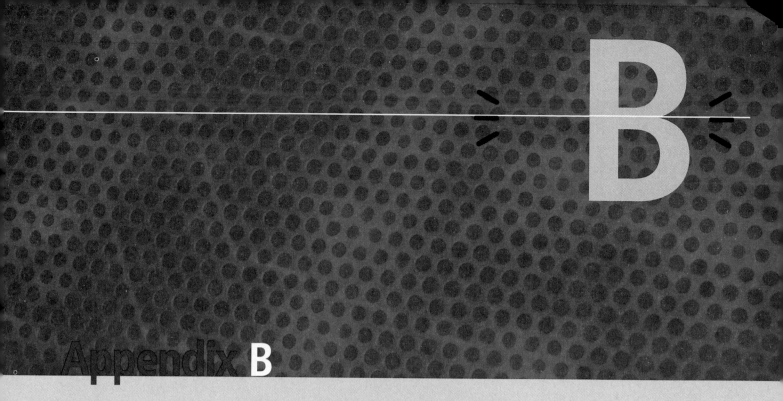

File Transfer Protocol

File transfer protocol (ftp) is an Internet protocol for copying files from one computer to another. It replaced the older UUCP, (Unix to Unix CoPy) command. Software that supports ftp is the tool most often used to *publish* a new Web page—that is, to copy an HTML document onto an active Web server for public access. You can use ftp to copy interesting files from other places on the Net to your computer. That process is called *downloading.* Or you can use ftp to copy files on your local machine to other computers on the Internet. That process is called *uploading.* You can retrieve or send text files, images, icons, or any other type of file using ftp.

Ftp software is available for most operating systems, but it was originally a Unix tool, so the commands for standard ftp look very Unixlike. In the first part of this discussion we will look at the Unix ftp commands used if you are working on a Unix-based computer. Other operating systems also support this command-line version of ftp. In addition, many enhanced ftp software packages are available to make it easy to transfer files. We will take a look at these graphical alternatives after we examine the command-line methodology, and then consider secure ftp at the end of this appendix.

▸▸ COMMAND-LINE FTP

Table B.1 shows some of the common ftp commands. You may choose to use more graphical ftp software, which will do more of the work for you, but even then, the steps described here must be accomplished for ftp to work.

Table B.1   Common ftp commands

Command	Description	Example (note: ftp> is the prompt)
	CONNECTION COMMANDS	
open	Opens a specific connection (a particular user on a particular device).	ftp> open sammy.dcdcd.edu
close	Closes the current connection, but usually ftp continues to run.	ftp> close
bye	Ends the ftp session. If connected it will first close the connection.	ftp> bye
?	Very important command that lists all the ftp commands available.	ftp> ?
help	Gives a one-line explanation of each of the commands.	ftp> help
	SWITCHES/TOGGLES	
prompt	Used when copying multiple files, this switch turns off or on a file by file-confirmation process. It is on by default. Turn it off if you are copying multiple files.	ftp> prompt
verbose	This switch turns on file transfer statistics.	ftp> verbose
hash	Turning on this switch tells ftp to output a hash mark, or octothorp (#) each time it transfers a particular number of bytes. This is very useful if you are copying a large file since it tells you ftp is working. It is also called the ftp user's sanity-saver command.	ftp> hash
	TRANSFER MODES	
ASCII	Used only to copy text files.	ftp> ascii
bin(ary)	Used to copy all but text files. Can be used to copy text files as well, but it is slower with text files than ASCII mode.	ftp> bin
	NAVIGATION COMMANDS	
cd	Changes the directory on the *remote* computer.	ftp> cd new-dir
pwd	Shows the current directory on the *remote* computer.	ftp> pwd
lcd	Shows or changes directory on the *local* computer.	ftp> lcd
ls	Lists the files in the current directory on the remote computer.	ftp> ls
dir	Produces a longer version of ls, showing information about each file.	ftp> dir
	FILE TRANSFER COMMANDS	
put	Copies *a single file* from the local computer to the current directory on the remote computer.	ftp> put coolfile
get	Copies *a single file* from the remote computer into the current directory on the local computer.	ftp> get waycoolfile
mput	The "m" stands for "multiple." This command transfers *multiple files* from the local computer into the current directory of the remote computer. You might want to turn off the prompt feature if you don't want to confirm each transfer.	ftp> mput myfiles*
mget	This command transfers *multiple files* from the remote computer into the current directory of the local computer. You might want to turn off the prompt feature if you don't want to confirm each transfer.	ftp> mget files*
delete	This command will remove one or more files from the remote computer. This is a very dangerous command. It is usually disabled, but you should never experiment with it. The only time you might need to use it is to remove files you have mistakenly uploaded to the remote computer.	ftp> delete badfile

BINARY VERSUS ASCII FILE TRANSFERS

Ftp software can operate in one of two transfer modes, either ASCII or binary. If you are copying images, sounds, or programs, you need to copy them as binary files. Binary transfers take a little longer, but they are usually copied without errors. Use ASCII only for copying text files. If you try to copy a binary file in ASCII mode, ftp will try to convert the binary to an ASCII representation. This often involves padding with extra zero bits, which will corrupt a binary file. If you download a program and it doesn't seem to work, chances are you downloaded it in ASCII rather than binary. Download it again, using binary transfer mode, and it will probably work. Some of the graphical programs also have a transfer method called *automatic,* which tries to look at the data and determine what transfer method to use. We recommend that you always set your method, unless you have time to redo the transfer if the software guesses incorrectly.

Figure B.1   Starting ftp session on command line

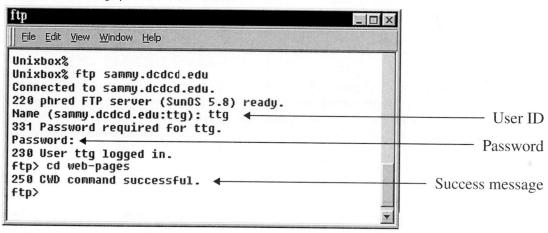

A normal ftp session is shown in Figure B.1. You start a file transfer with the ftp command, which initiates a connection between the local computer (the one you are sitting at) and a remote computer (the one that either has the files you want or is where you want to send files). The remote computer is usually a Web server. In Figure B.1, the user *ttg* has connected to *sammy,* a Unix-based computer that has an ftp server set up for registered users only. Some ftp sites are set up to allow *anonymous ftp* connections in which the user can use the name "anonymous" and thus need no password. In the case of Figure B.1, the user was required to enter his name and then a password. This is the way it will most likely be when you move pages up to your Web server.

In Figure B.1, *ttg* types his user ID, then his password. The ftp server on *sammy* responds with the "logged in" message. Notice that the prompt changes to ftp>, indicating that the ftp program is now active. Next, the user changes directories with the cd web-pages command, making the web-pages directory active. This is where the Web pages for that user are stored. Each time the user enters a command, ftp tells him whether the command worked or not. For example, in Figure B.1, the ftp server told ttg that he had successfully changed directories by issuing the response,

250 CWD command successful

This response tells the user that his CWD (Change Working Directory) command succeeded. It is an important feature of ftp; the user is always provided with immediate feedback.

DOWNLOADING FILES USING COMMANDS

Now that *ttg* is in the correct directory; the real work can begin. Since *ttg* knows that he wants to download a file that starts with an htmll he asks the computer to list the files in the current directory that begin with htmll using the command is htmll, as shown in

Figure B.2

Successful listing of files

```
ftp                                                              _□×
 File  Edit  View  Window  Help
Ftp> ls html1*
200 PORT command successful.
150 ASCII data connection for /bin/ls (309.122.220.221,36428) (0 bytes).
htmllab1.html
htmllab10.html
htmllab2.html
htmllab3.html
htmllab4.030900
htmllab4.html
htmllab5.html
htmllab6.html
htmllab7.html
htmllab8.042500
htmllab8.html
htmllab9.html
htmllabec1.html
htmllabr8.042500
htmllabr8.html
htmllabr9.html
htmllabrfinal.html
htmllabtest.html
226 ASCII Transfer complete.
remote: html1*
290 bytes received in 0.02 seconds (13.89 Kbytes/s)
ftp>
```

List of files

Figure B.2. After looking over the list of files, *ttg* decides that the file he really wants is htmllab4.html, a file containing the exercises for the fourth lab in his HTML class.

Figure B.3 shows the screen capture after *ttg* downloads htmllab4.html to his local Unix computer. First, the he issued a get htmllab4.html command. The ftp program informs him that the file is 4,146 bytes long. Then ftp begins to download the file. As it is a rather small file, there was no need to turn on the **hash** function. Notice that the ftp program tells the ttg the name of the file on both the local and remote computers. Finally, all of 0.012 seconds later, ftp reports that 4,234 bytes have been downloaded. On close examination the file seems to have grown by 88 bytes in the download! Why? Because ttg forgot to set the transfer mode to *binary!* Even though the file is actually an ASCII file, as are all HTML files, the ftp program pads the file with some bytes of binary zeros to round things out. The zeros won't make any difference in this case, as we will see in a moment, since they are discarded after the transfer. However, were the file an image, the results would be horrible.

Figure B.3   Moving files from and to a server

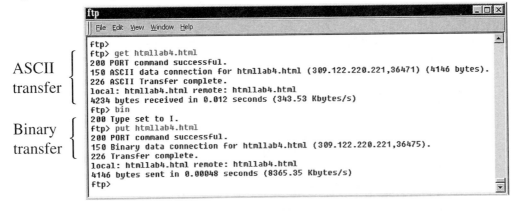

ASCII transfer

Binary transfer

```
ftp                                                              _□×
 File  Edit  View  Window  Help
ftp>
ftp> get htmllab4.html
200 PORT command successful.
150 ASCII data connection for htmllab4.html (309.122.220.221,36471) (4146 bytes).
226 ASCII Transfer complete.
local: htmllab4.html remote: htmllab4.html
4234 bytes received in 0.012 seconds (343.53 Kbytes/s)
ftp> bin
200 Type set to I.
ftp> put htmllab4.html
200 PORT command successful.
150 Binary data connection for htmllab4.html (309.122.220.221,36475).
226 Transfer complete.
local: htmllab4.html remote: htmllab4.html
4146 bytes sent in 0.00048 seconds (8365.35 Kbytes/s)
ftp>
```

This scenario serves only as an example of how to retrieve a file with ftp. Usually the user would modify the file in some way before putting it back. In this case nothing was done to the file, but ttg decides he should set the transfer mode to binary. That is the next line in the code. Then he sends the file back to the server with the put htmllab4.html command. Notice that ftp moves exactly the right number of bytes this time.

This is the normal sequence of events using ftp. It is not a complex tool to use. The biggest problem most students have with ftp is figuring out where the files should come from or where they went after they were uploaded or downloaded, and that problem disappears with a little practice.

▸▸ GUI-BASED FTP

Many software tools are available to make the ftp process more intuitive. The first one we will consider is called CuteFTP. It was designed to run in Microsoft Windows' mouse-oriented "point and click" environment. CuteFTP is a very powerful program with lots of options. At this time, however, we will look at only the bare bones of this tool. It is available for download from www.cuteFTP.com with a 30-day trial. CuteFTP is *shareware*. If you use the product after the 30 days of free trial, you are obligated to pay the author, GlobalSCAPE Inc., an amount under $50.00 for the time and effort necessary to create this product.

SETTING UP CuteFTP

The screen captures in Figures B.4 through B.8 show the steps in setting up and using CuteFTP. The first screen, Figure B.4, shows how to set up CuteFTP to find a particular computer. Here we set up "Way cool site" at IP address 123.123.123.123. This may or may not be a valid IP address; it is for demonstration purposes only. Do not try to use it. Notice that we can set the user ID and the secret password as well, so CuteFTP can go to the site and log in for us. In the box below User Id we can set the radio button to use anonymous ftp if that is the type of site we intend to access.

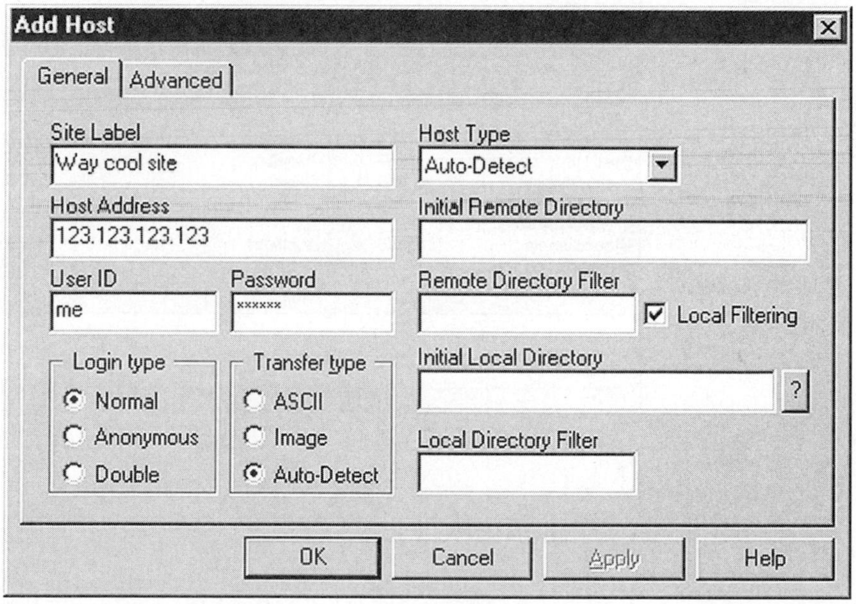

Figure B.4

Setting up account login with CuteFTP

Figure B.5 shows the first screen we normally see when starting CuteFTP. It allows us to select a site from a series of folders. When we click on a site, CuteFTP will connect us to it. In this case the user has selected the server *sammy* from the list of servers on the right.

Figure B.5

Initial CuteFTP screen to select site

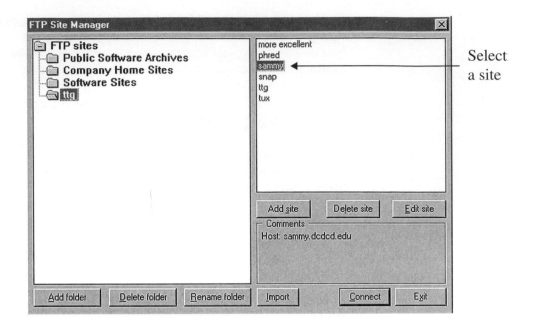

Select a site

In Figure B.6, CuteFTP has connected to *sammy,* and we will select on the web-pages subdirectory to open that set of files. Notice that the interface is a complete mouse-oriented graphical interface. In this example we want to download a file from *sammy* to our local computer.

Figure B.6

After successful login, both computers are represented

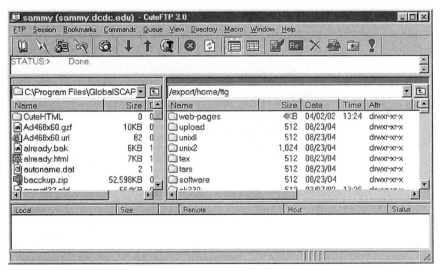

Local computer   Remote computer (sammy)

DOWNLOADING FILES

As Figure B.7 shows, the file we want to download is syl2484.html from *sammy.* To download, we simply double-click on the filename. If we click on the server side, CuteFTP will download the file to our PC. If we click on the local side (left), CuteFTP will upload the file to the server. It really makes the ftp process simple. Another way to select a file and download it is to simply drag the file from the remote computer side of the screen to the local side of the screen. CuteFTP will then download the file.

Figure B.7

Selecting file to download

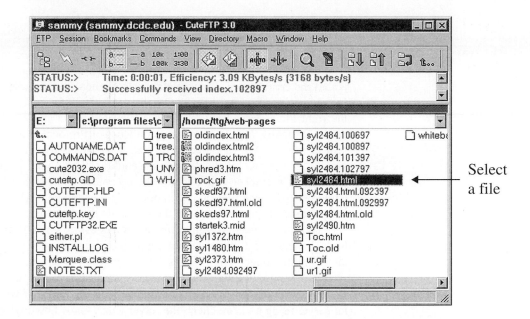

Select a file

In Figure B.8, CuteFTP has successfully downloaded the file from *sammy* to our home PC in .05 seconds. Programs like CuteFTP make it much easier to move files across the Net. Even old command-line pros like your humble authors use graphical ftp software on their home computers. It is a great tool that makes ftping much easier.

Figure B.8   File successfully downloaded

File successfully downloaded →

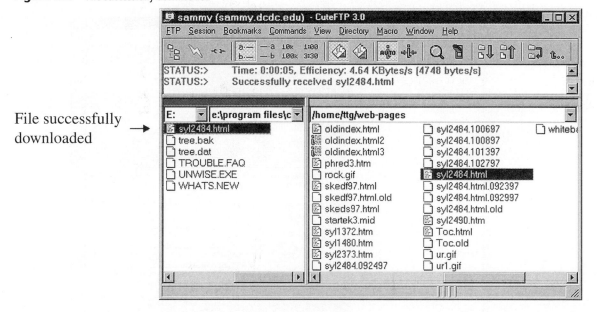

As you can see, it isn't all that difficult to download a file using this type of graphical ftp program. Uploading is exactly the opposite of downloading. You either double-click on a file on the local side of the screen, or drag a file from the local side of the screen to the remote side. CuteFTP then uploads the file or files selected.

▸▸ SECURE FTP

Although plain vanilla ftp may work for most users, some system administrators are beginning to require their users to employ more secure transfer tools. The reason for this is that the crackers are getting better tools. Some of those tools allow the cyber criminals to read each packet that moves over the network. It does take time, but with practice and the right tools, a cracker can watch as your login ID and password move over the network. Normally TCP/IP (Transmission Control Protocol / Internet Protocol) packets are sent as normal ASCII, called *clear text.* That means that if a cracker is watching when you log in using an ftp client, he or she could read both your login ID and password. With those tools a cracker could access the computer and pretend to be you. The next step could be to damage files on the computer, and he or she might use your ID to do it, causing your system administrator to think you did the damage.

To prevent unauthorized criminals from stealing your ID and password, you can use tools that encrypt all the data that are passed across the network. This encryption process takes slightly longer, but it makes the transmission of data more secure.

One important consideration is that you must have a secure ftp server set up on your HTML server before you connect using a secure ftp client. If you try to connect to a regular server using a secure client, the server won't know how to decrypt the data.

Setting up a secure ftp session is a little more complex than just pointing CuteFTP at the regular ftp server. Figure B.9 shows the account setup screen in one of our favorite secure ftp tools. It is called *ssh,* which stands for *secure sh*ell and is available from ssh.com. This particular product provides both a secure ftp client and a secure telnet client. It uses secure shell encryption at the highest level available. There are many different secure shell clients available. You should consult with their system administrators to see which one or ones they recommend. Follow their recommendations, since they know exactly what kind of secure server they are running. Note: you can only use a secure shell if that software is installed on your server.

Figure B.9

Setting up ssh

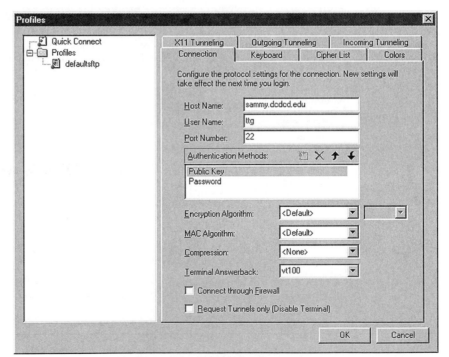

Figure B.10 shows how to use this particular ssh client to connect to a particular server. Notice our friend *sammy* is there in the list. All we would have to do is click on *sammy* and the client would connect us to that server, using the login ID and password we had stored.

Figure B.10

Selecting a particular server
with ssh

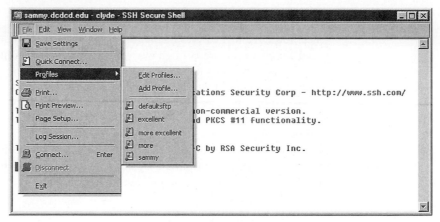

Selecting a server using a profile

SAVING PASSWORDS

Another important security issue involves, of course, your password. Don't let software remember your password. If someone else sits down at your computer, he can log into servers as if he were you, using your login ID. That is not a good idea, ever, and especially if your computer is not in a secure location. For example, there was a problem at a local college where someone was logging into the server and then using their account to download inappropriate files from the Net. It was very easy for the system administrator to determine who was downloading the files, since this person logged into the system using his or her school ID. When the faculty member with that ID was accused of downloading unacceptable files, she pled innocence. After further research, the systems folks discovered that the downloads were all happening between 10 PM and 2 AM. The faculty member was able to document several occasions when she was off campus with witnesses when the downloads happened. Finally, one evening the systems administrator stayed on campus and waited for the downloads to begin. Once the suspect ID logged in, the campus police went to the faculty member's office. There they discovered one of the custodial staff using her computer. The reason that individual could imitate the faculty member was that she had stored both her login ID and password in a program. All the custodian needed to do was run her login program and the system thought he was the faculty member.

Figure B.11

Secure ftp ready to download

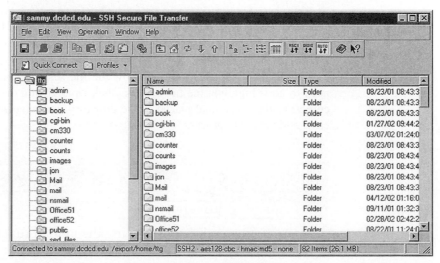

Successful login

DOWNLOADING SECURE FILES

Once you have logged into the target server, ssh looks much like CuteFTP. It is a GUI-based ftp client. Figure B.11 shows what the screen looks like. Although this screen initially looks very much like the CuteFTP screen, if you look closely, you will see the difference: both sides of the screen show the same directory structure, but secure file transfer shows you only the target computer, or server, initially. If you choose to upload a file, the program will open a second window to allow you to find the file or files you want to upload on your hard drive. If you choose to download a file, as the user did in Figure B.12, the software will open another window to allow you to specify where you want the file(s) placed. As you can see from the figure, ssh allows the user to select exactly where to put the file being downloaded. If you have chosen multiple files, ssh will place all of them in the directory specified.

Figure B.12

Download target selection box

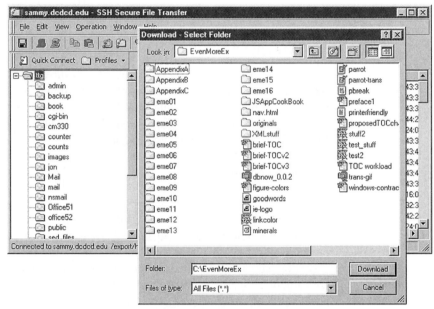

The download file selection screen

UPLOADING SECURE FILES

As with downloading, if you choose to upload one or more files, you can click on the upward pointing arrow in the command bar, shown in Figure B.13, and ssh will produce a file selection box that allows you to select which file or files will be uploaded to the server. You need to select the target directory on the server before you tell ssh you want to upload files. Figure B.14 shows how the file selection box for upload looks. All you need to do is highlight the file or files, click Upload, and the files will be transferred, securely, to the server and placed in the directory you have already specified. It is a very easy, and very safe process.

Figure B.13

Upload selection arrow

Selecting the upload function
from the function bar

Figure B.14

Files selection box for upload

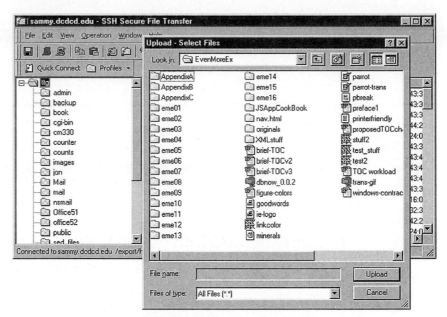

The file upload selection screen

BAD FILE-NAMING PRACTICES

One final note about uploading files to your Web pages directory: You need to be very careful about the tools you use. Some of our students have used tools that assume that the first letter of each filename is uppercase. That works on Windows machines, because they are not case-sensitive, but it causes no end of problems for students using computers running Unix because Unix recognizes the difference between myimage.gif and Myimage.gif. If your page is looking for the former, and your ftp client makes the first character uppercase, like the latter example, the Web server won't see it. Finding and fixing those errors is very difficult.

By the same token, some operating systems allow you to put spaces into your filenames. Adding spaces is an exceptionally bad practice because other operating systems will interpret the space as the end of the first filename. So if you have named a file My image.gif, many operating systems will see that as two distinct files, My and image.gif, neither of which exist. If you use an operating system that allows spaces in filenames, don't fall into that trap! Never put spaces in filenames; it is an evil practice.

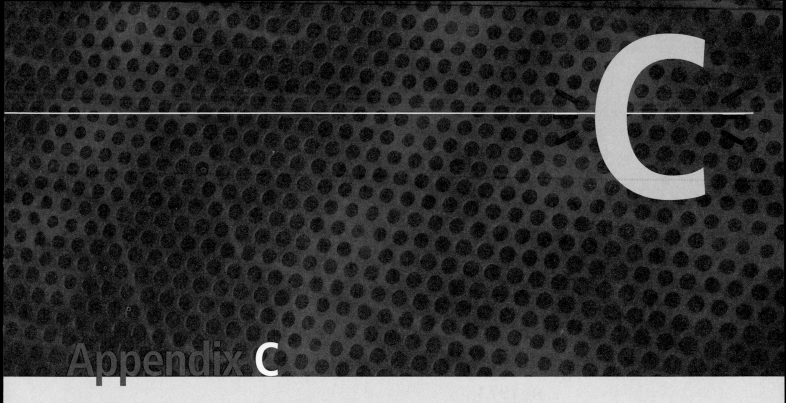

History of the Internet

Since everything we have discussed happens via the Net, we thought it important that you understand where this whole thing started. This appendix provides a condensed history of the Internet, from its simple beginnings, through its growth and development as a tool of the academy, to the globally encompassing World Wide Web we know and love today. Let's go back in time to the world before the Web, or even before the Net!

▸▸ 1957

The USSR (Union of Soviet Socialist Republics) successfully launched *Sputnik,* the first artificial satellite ever sent into orbit in 1957. This accomplishment brought the military in the United States to the realization that if the USSR could launch an object into orbit, it could also send a missile to the United States carrying a nuclear device. If all of the command and control elements of the United States military were congregated around Washington, the whole leadership would be vulnerable to destruction with one weapon. Thus, the United States formed ARPA (Advanced Research Projects Agency) to determine technological and scientific ways to mitigate this threat.

▸▸ 1962

The RAND Corporation (actually a government agency) was commissioned by the U.S. Air Force in 1962 to determine how it could maintain command and control communications in the event of a nuclear event. It devised the concept of *packet switching,* the current model for the Net, to allow for multiple redundancy of messages. The significant concept of this methodology is

1. A message is broken down into fixed-length "packets."

2. Each packet is sent into the network independently and makes its way to the receiver without referencing any other packets.

3. If a packet fails to arrive at the destination, the sender is notified and the packet is resent.

4. Each element or node in the pathway is responsible for forwarding each packet using the best path available. Therefore, each packet takes its own path through the network as it travels to its final location.

Packet switching allowed the proposed network to be "self-healing"—that is, to be able to direct packets around damage. This is why it is nearly impossible to censor the Internet. The Net treats censorship as it would damage and simply routes traffic around it. Research flourished around this new communications model.

When ARPA wanted to build the ARPANET, it awarded the contract to BBN (Bolt, Beranek and Newman, Inc.). BBN selected Honeywell minicomputers for the nodes and established them at the University of Utah, Stanford Research Institute (Stanford), the University of California at Santa Barbara, and the University of California at Los Angeles. In addition to providing command and control for the military, ARPANET served as a test bed for academic work in networking. Graduate students did the majority of the research in this new field, research that was critical to the nation and that led to the development of the Internet.

▸▸ 1971

Gradually new nodes were added to the network. By 1971 there were 19 nodes and a planned capacity of 30. The reason for the slow growth was the complexity of the interface hardware and software and the amazing array of different hardware platforms that were to be part of the network.

▸▸ 1972

In October 1972, at the International Conference on Computer Communications in Washington, researchers who had built the ARPANET demonstrated it to the world. At that conference, the INWG (International Networking Working Group) was formed. Later in 1972 the first email program was built by Ray Tomlinson at the BBN. The year 1972 also saw ARPA renamed DARPA (Defense Advanced Research Projects Agency), acknowledging its military sponsorship. At this time the network was using NCP (network control protocol) to transfer data among like machines. The problem with this protocol was that it depended upon each node having the same interface hardware. That was like requiring everyone on the network to use the same modem. Several different groups were working on more robust protocols that would allow different types of hardware to communicate with each other.

▸▸ 1973

In the fall of 1973 the very first draft of the TCP/IP protocol was released. Initial work on TCP/IP (Transmission Control Protocol/Internet Protocol) was done at Stanford, the University of Sussex, and the University College London. Even in its infancy, the protocol of the Net was an international effort.

▸▸ 1974

The first true TCP/IP specification was released in 1974. It was based primarily on the work of Vinton Cerf and Bob Kahn. The importance of this new protocol was that it was for all intents and purposes hardware-neutral. It allowed anyone to use the network regardless of the hardware used to connect to it. This interoperability was important, because the early Net used not just cable connections, but also satellite communications and packet radio to transmit packets. In an article on the new TCP protocol, Vinton Cerf and Bob Kahn used the term *Internet* for the first time.

▸▸ 1975

The year 1975 was an important one because in July the ARPANET was transferred to DARPA as a working network tool. In essence, the network became a commercial success. It was renamed DARPANET and continued to do double duty, serving as a place for the development and testing of network theory while also serving as the emergency command-and-control communications medium for the military.

▸▸ 1976

Robert Metcalfe developed the Ethernet, a way to move data very quickly using coaxial cables in 1976. This development was crucial to the later implementation of local area networks (LANs). Even this early in the history of the Net, we must mention the Unix operating system. Although Unix was only about seven years into development, in 1976 the UUCP (Unix to Unix CoPy) program was created at AT&T Bell Labs. This program was developed because Unix programmers felt it was terribly inefficient to have to transfer data from one computer to another by physically carrying the magnetic tapes from one computer to the other even when the physical distance was only inches. They asked a simple question: "Why not just hook a wire between the two computers and use it to pass data?" This was the beginnings of rapid data exchange over wire. Although there are other, often faster protocols now, UUCP is still a viable Unix command and is used in many data centers to push data from one Unix box to another. TCP/IP is the protocol of choice on the Internet.

▸▸ 1979

As far as applications are concerned, probably one of the most significant tools ever built for the communication of ideas is Steve Bellovin's USENET, the decentralized news program that was based on UUCP and created in 1979. This collection of thousands of groups of email articles covers nearly any topic you can think of. It is the repository of a gigantic body of knowledge and a mechanism for people to convey information to one another. It was the first truly public use of the Internet that gave a glimmer of its tremendous potential for information sharing.

Remember, at this point data were transferred as text files. Graphics, if they were moved at all, were moved as large encoded strings of ASCII characters that had to be decoded and reassembled by the recipient before they could be viewed. The tools to do this were *uuencode* and *uudecode*. It is easy to see the UUCP heritage in their names.

Unlike other text-based tools, such as Archie and Gopher, Usenet has grown and thrived and remains an outstanding source of information and support. *Archie* is a search tool designed to search an international base of anonymous ftp servers. Usually data archived on Archie is text-only. Although the graphical part of the Net, represented by the World Wide Web, has taken the forefront recently, Archie was and remains an excellent research tool. Another really useful feature of Archie is that you can submit requests and retreive data via email. *Gopher* was developed at the University of Minnesota, home of the Golden Gophers, as a tool to "burrow through the Net and find information." It is another technology that is still active and viable but has been pushed aside because it didn't have a graphical format.

Also in 1979 IBM created BITNET, which stands for "Because It's Time NETwork." This network is important because it is the source of the *store-and-forward* concept whereby a host holds messages until they can be delivered. (This concept is the heart of any email client you currently use.)

▸▸ 1981

In an effort to provide network support for colleges and universities that didn't have access to DARPANET, the National Science Foundation created CSNET in 1981. Very quickly, Vinton Cerf proposed a way to interconnect the two networks. Then 3Com released UNET, a Unix-based TCP/IP product running on Ethernet.

▸▸ 1982

After eight years of testing and research, the U.S. Department of Defense decided in 1982 that all DARPANET traffic would be performed in TCP/IP rather than NCP. In the summer of that year the main network hubs stopped accepting NCP packets for one day. This action caused a tremendous problem for institutions that had not yet converted to TCP/IP. Later, in the early fall, those same hubs rejected all NCP packets for two days.

▸▸ 1983

On January 1, 1983, DARPANET stopped accepting any NCP packets, it became and remains a TCP/IP network. Another very significant step in making the Net easier to use also occurred in 1983. At the University of Wisconsin researchers created the DNS (domain name system), which allowed nodes to have easy-to-remember names rather than just the four-triplet IP address. For the first time a machine could be called my.cool.unix.box and you could connect to it because the domain name server translated that name to the actual IP address 144.163.21.141 for the Internet user.

▸▸ 1984

As the number of hosts on the network continued to grow, the government decided to divide the DARPANET into two segments. In 1984 MILNET was designated for strictly military use and ARPANET to support the research component. MCI was given the contract to upgrade the slow CSNET to high-speed communication (T1) lines. The new network with the new, high-speed backbone would be called the NSFNET.

▸▸ 1985

In 1985 there was an explosion of development in Internet products as vendors realized that there were significant commercial applications for the Internet. The vast majority of these products were Unix-based and the weblike nature of the Internet became apparent as Unix networks and local area networks began to join together, creating wide area networks (WANs) that then linked into the Internet. In 1985 DARPA requested that TCP/IP be built into Berkeley Unix, and since version 4.2 of the Berkeley Standard Distribution (BSD) was issued, TCP/IP has been built into the operating system. This feature allowed companies like Sun Microsystems to begin building hardware designed to run commercial Internet applications using the Unix operating system.

▸▸ 1987

Two of the older networks, BITNET from IBM and CSNET, the older and slower NSF network, combined in 1987 to form the Corporation for Research and Educational Computing (CERN), another part of the National Science Foundation.

▸▸ 1990

Tim Berners-Lee working for CERN (European Organization for Nuclear Research in Geneva, Switzerland) not to be confused with the US CERN, developed a hyperlinked system to allow members of the international community of high-energy particle researchers efficient access to information. This was the beginnings of the technology that fostered the World Wide Web. At this time Tim Berners-Lee also began work on a hypertext editor and browser.

▸▸ 1992

CERN (in Switzerland) released the first command-line browser to the world in 1992. It was made available through ftp (file transfer protocol) sites and given to the community for free. The *World Wide Web,* a phrase coined by Berners-Lee, was officially born.

▸▸ 1993

Marc Andreessen at NCSA (The National Center for Super-Computing Applications) presented the alpha release of the fully graphical Mosaic browser for X-windows (the Unix GUI) systems in 1993. Suddenly the graphical side of the Internet became viable. By September of 1993 World Wide Web traffic made up a whopping 0.1 percent of all the traffic on the NSFNET. In November NSCA released versions of the Mosaic browser for Microsoft's Windows on the PC, Apple's Macintosh operating system, and Unix's X-Windows graphical interface. By the end of the year there were over 200 http (HyperText Transport Protocol) servers on the Web.

▸▸ 1994

By June 1994 there were already over 1,500 registered Web servers, and traffic had increased 1,000 times the level it had been three years earlier. Another landmark date is October 1, 1994, when MIT and CERN founded the W^{3}C. The first W^{3}C meeting was held on December 14 of that year at MIT.

▸▸ 1995

Starting in late 1994, and continuing in 1995 the number of Web servers expanded at an amazing rate. This expansion continues today. From this point onward there are few landmark events. Some, like the malconceived Communications Decency Act of 1995, also known as the Exon amendment, attempted to cripple the Web by grossly limiting the content available to those topics that could not be offensive to anyone under the age of 18. As Web weavers we must maintain constant vigilance to protect the freedom and information on this wonderful medium.

▸▸ 2003

Publication of *Even More Excellent HTML with an Introduction to DHTML, XHTML, XML, and JavaScript,* probably the seminal text on creating Web pages, written by two authors who are clueless to what the future really holds for the Internet but we do know it's going to be one heck of a ride.

Note: This glossary contains words beyond those indicated as key words in the text. It is designed to be a bit more comprehensive than the run-of-the-mill glossary. If you have any words that you think should have been included, please send your suggested additions to (ttg@phred.dcccd.edu). We will consider any additions that will make this glossary more complete, and more fun! We look forward to your suggestions.

Absolute path: The full path from the root directory to a document. Absolute paths always start with a leading slash (/).

Absolute path name: Also called **absolute URL,** the complete description of the path to a resource.

Absolute width: Width measured in pixels. *See also* Relative width.

Abstract Window Toolkit (AWT): Includes user interface features like windows, dialog boxes, buttons, checkboxes, menus, scroll bars, lists, and text fields.

Abstraction: Results from taking the essential characteristics out of an object and creating data to represent those characteristics.

Access: To retrieve data from a storage medium like a tape or disk.

Access time: The time it takes the read/write head to find requested data on a storage medium.

ACM: *See* Association for Computing Machinery (ACM)

Active directory: The directory or subdirectory that the operating system or application program uses as a default when accessing programs or data files from disk.

Address: Unique number assigned to each memory location within a computer's processing hardware.

AI: *See* Artificial Intelligence (AI)

AIFC: *See* AIFF Compressed Format (AIFC)

AIFF: *See* Audio Interchange File Format (AIFF)

AIFF Compressed Format (AIFC): Sound format developed by Apple because AIFF required so much storage space. Compression is lossy.

Algorithm: Statement of the steps to be followed in solving a problem or performing a process.

Alphanumeric data: Another name for textual data.

American National Standards Institute (ANSI): Group that develops programming language standards for use by industry and computer manufacturers.

American Standard Code for Information Interchange (ASCII): Code for storing data that uses 7 bits to a byte and is commonly used in microcomputers; an extended version of ASCII uses 8 bits per byte.

Analog data: Data that consist of continuous series of sounds and tones.

Analog signals: Signals representing data as patterns of frequencies, like sounds.

Analog sound: Sound in which values flow from one to another continuously.

Anchor name: The anchor container with the name attribute, serving as a target anchor.

Animated GIF: A series of GIF images that are quickly changed in order to create simple animation.

Animation: Visual images of motions produced by rapid presentation of drawn or computer-generated graphics.

Anonymous ftp: Allows use of ftp without entering password; users give "anonymous" as name and their e-mail address as a password.

ANSI: *See* American National Standards Institute (ANSI)

Append: To attach additional material to a data stream or file, usually adding data to the end of the file or data stream.

Applet: Small program, usually written in the Java language, that runs within a window inside the browser.

Applet viewer: Allows user to view applets without a browser.

Application software: Class of programs that solve specific user-oriented processing problems like word processors, spreadsheets, or browsers.

Arithmetic operation: Ability of a computer to do mathematical functions like addition and subtraction with numerical data.

Array: Also known as a subscripted variable, a series of identical data elements stored contiguously in memory.

Artificial Intelligence (AI): Software application that stimulates human thought and judgment by the use of heuristic problem-solving techniques.

ASCII editor: Produces an ASCII file; also called a *text editor.*

Attributes: HTML elements that modify tags; they are coded within the open tag of a container.

Audio icons: Used like graphical icons to delimit parts of the text, to highlight specific phrases, and to call attention to changes in content, but they are composed solely of sound.

Audio Interchange File Format (AIFF): Sound format developed by Apple and used most often by Macintosh and Silicon Graphics to store high-end audio data. It has an uncompressed format, and it supports stereo.

Audio Video Interface (AVI): Provided by Internet Explorer for inline movies.

Audiovisual data: Data that people can hear or see, like voice, music, drawings, photographs, and video sequences.

Auditory icon: Distinctive audio cues used to highlight spoken specific phrases, delimit text, and call attention to changes in content.

Aural style sheet: A style sheet that contains auditory icons and speech synthesis for use with Web pages.

AVI: *See* Audio Video Interface (AVI)

AWT: *See* Abstract Window Toolkit (AWT)

Backup: Extra copy of data or programs on a disk or tape that is kept for use in case the original is destroyed or corrupted.

Backup procedures: Making a copy of important files and programs on another tape or disk. This is essential to prevent loss of your work in the event your system or disk is damaged.

Bad thing: Something that has no redeeming social value. Contrast with good thing.

Base URL: The URL of the page that invokes an applet, image, or new page (unless the <BASE> attribute is coded).

Baseline: Imaginary line that runs across the bottom of the text letters, not including descenders.

Benchmark test: Compares software and hardware performance against a minimum standard agreed upon by management and the application development team.

Berners-Lee, Tim: Invented the World Wide Web in late 1990 while working at CERN, the European Particle Physics Laboratory in Geneva, Switzerland. He wrote the first WWW client and the First WWW server, along with most of the communications software, defining URLs, HTTP, and HTML. A graduate of Oxford University, Tim is now the overall director of the W^3C.

Beta releases: Experimental versions of software that test new features before they become part of the current release.

Beta test: Prerelease testing of commercial software by potential outside users.

Binary: Code pattern of on/off bits used to represent data or computer operations.

Binary digit: The on or off state of a single computer circuit, represented as one and zero, respectively; also known as *bit*.

Binary file: File of machine-readable code composed of ones and zeros.

Bit: The on or off state of a single computer circuit, represented as one and zero, respectively; also known as *binary digit*.

Bit mapping: Pattern of pixels making up a graphic image; also known as *pixel graphics*.

Bits per pixel (bpp): Determines the number of colors in an image.

Bits per second (bps): A measurement of data transmission speed.

Bleeding: When color from one pixel affects an adjacent pixel.

Blocked element: Elements that are formatted as separate blocks of text, such as headings, paragraphs, tables, or lists.

Block-level element: An element, like the <hr />, that automatically forces a new line before and after it.

BMP: Standard Microsoft Windows image format, usually created by Paintbrush program and used for the wallpaper in Windows. It supports 1, 4, 8, and 24 bits per pixel. It is usually not compressed.

Bogon: Analogous with proton/electron/neutron and doubtless reinforced after 1980 by the similarity to Douglas Adams's "Vogons"; see the bibliography in Appendix C of the "Hacker's Dictionary," and note that Arthur Dent actually mispronounces "Vogons" as "Bogons" at one point. 1. The elementary particle of bogosity (*see* quantum bogodynamics). For instance, "The Ethernet is emitting bogons again" means that it is broken, or acting in an erratic or bogus fashion. 2. A query packet sent from a TCP/IP domain resolver to a root server, having the reply bit set instead of the query bit. 3. Any bogus or incorrectly formed packet sent on a network. 4. By synecdoche, used to refer to any bogus thing, as in, "I'd like to go to lunch with you but I've got to go to the weekly staff bogon." 5. A person who is bogus or who says bogus things. This was historically the original usage, but it has been overtaken by its derivative senses (1–4). *See also* Bogosity; bogus.

Bogosity: 1. The degree to which something is bogus. At CMU, bogosity is measured with a bogometer; in a seminar, when a speaker says something bogus, a listener might raise his hand and say, "My bogometer just triggered." More extremely, "You just pinned my bogometer" means you just said or did something so outrageously bogus that it is off the scale, pinning the bogometer needle at the highest possible reading (one might also say, "You just redlined my bogometer"). The agreed upon unit of bogosity is the microLenat. 2. The potential field generated by a bogon flux.

Bogotify: To make or become bogus. A program that has been changed so many times as to become completely disorganized has become bogotified. If you tighten a nut too hard and strip the threads on the bolt, the bolt has become bogotified, and you had better not use it any more. This coinage led to the notional *autobogotiphobia,* defined as "the fear of becoming bogotified"; but is not clear that the latter has ever been "live" jargon rather than a self-conscious joke in jargon about jargon. *See also* Bogosity; bogus

Bogue out: To become bogus, suddenly and unexpectedly. "His talk was relatively sane until somebody asked him a trick question; then he bogued out and did nothing but flame afterwards." *See also* Bogosity; bogus.

Bogus: 1. Nonfunctional. "Your patches are bogus." 2. Useless. "OPCON is a bogus program." 3. False. "Your arguments are bogus." 4. Incorrect. "That algorithm is bogus." 5. Unbelievable. "You claim to have solved the halting problem for Turing Machines? That's totally bogus." 6. Silly. "Stop writing those bogus sagas." Astrology is bogus. So is a bolt that is obviously about to break. So is someone who makes blatantly false claims to have solved a scientific problem. (This word seems to have some but not all of the connotations of *random*—mostly the negative ones.) It is claimed that *bogus* was originally used in the hackish sense at Princeton in the late 1960s. It was spread to CMU and Yale by Michael Shamos, a migratory Princeton alumnus. A glossary of bogus words was compiled at Yale when the word was first popularized. The word spread into hackerdom from CMU and MIT. By the early 1980s it was also current in something like the hackish sense in West Coast teen slang, and it had gone mainstream by 1985. A correspondent from Cambridge reports, by contrast, that these uses of *bogus* grate on British nerves; in Britain the word means, rather specifically, "counterfeit," as in "a bogus 10-pound note."

The bogon has become the type case for a whole bestiary of nonce particle names, including the *clutron* or *cluon* (indivisible particle of cluefulness, obviously the antiparticle of the bogon) and the *futon* (elementary particle of randomness, or sometimes of lameness). These are not so much live usages in themselves as examples of a live meta-usage: that is, it has become a standard joke or linguistic maneuver to "explain" otherwise mysterious circumstances by inventing nonce particle names. And these imply nonce particle theories, with all their dignity or lack thereof (we might note parenthetically that this is a generalization from "[bogus particle] theories" to "bogus [particle theories]"!). Perhaps such particles are the modern-day equivalents of trolls and wood-nymphs as standard starting points around which to construct explanatory myths. Of course, playing on an existing word (as with *futon*) yields additional flavor.

Boilerplate: Partially completed document with spaces or codes for specific fields that are added later.

Boole, George: (1815–1864) developed two-state (true or false) logic theory from mathematical expressions during the nineteenth century. His theories later became the basis for binary code.

Border: Margin of an element, such as a cell in a table or the table itself.

Bpp: *See* Bits per pixel (bpp)

Bps: *See* Bits per second (bps)

Browser: Software that translates the HTML codes into a presentation on the screen; used to cruise the World Wide Web.

Browser pane: The part of the screen that is normally visible to the user.

Buffer: Internal memory set aside for temporary data storage.

Bug: An error within a computer program. The first bug was a moth that was trapped in a relay in one of the first computers. Grace Hopper taped the moth in the log book and explained how they had "de-bugged" the computer. Actually the term *bug,* in entomology, refers to the family Hemiptera. Computer bugs fall into two classes, syntax errors and logic errors. A *syntax error* is an actual error in the formation of the computer code. A *logic error* is correct syntactically but produces an incorrect answer. For example, coding <HR width="5%"> when you want a line half the screen width would be a logic error (you should code it "width= "50%".)

Bullet: A graphic, traditionally a dot, that prefaces a list item to highlight or itemize it.

Bulleted list: One type of list in which each list item is preceeded by a bullet. These are also known as unordered lists since there is no hierarchical ordering explicitly defined by numbers or letters preceding each element.

Buttons: Elements that perform some action when clicked with a mouse button or activated with the Enter key.

Byron, Augusta Ada: (Countess of Lovelace, 1815–1852) annotated and published Charles Babbage's work in the 1840s. Her detailed instructions for operation of the Analytical Engine are considered a precursor to modern programming. Actually Ada was really the first programmer. She was also the daughter of Lord Byron, the famous poet.

Byte: A group of bits representing a single character or digit of data, usually 8 bits.

C: High-level programming language used in system programming and graphics. It is portable and easy to structure but is a complex language to learn.

Cache: To store data that may be needed again, either on disk (in the case of caching pages) or in memory.

CAI: *See* Computer-assisted instruction (CAI)

Call: Request for a program.

Calling document: Page that contains the link that brings up a search page.

Calling page: The Web page which calls a function, such as a JavaScript function.

Camera-ready copy: A printed document ready to be photographed for a traditional printing plate. Its current meaning is a document ready to be copied.

Caption: Text that further explains the content of a table.

Cards: HyperCard pages.

Carriage-return line feed (CrLf): New line of text, usually the result of touching the Enter or Return key. Called a *newline* in Unix parlance.

Cascading style sheet (CSS): An established precedence among style sheets and HTML containers that instructs the browser how to display a Web page.

Case-sensitive: An operating system or other software than can recognize the capitalization of characters is used to differentiate letters.

Case sensitivity: Recognizing the difference between uppercase and lowercase letters.

Cathode ray tube (CRT): An output peripheral by which a visual display is shown on a screen; also known as *monitor.*

CD: *See* Compact disc (CD)

CD-ROM *(compact disc read-only memory):* A high-capacity removable optical disk that permanently stores data and cannot be changed; also known as *CD* or *compact disk.*

CD-RW (compact disc read/write): A high-capacity optical disk with a surface that can be written upon, then erased and rewritten upon.

Cell: Intersection of a row and column in a table.

Cell padding: The amount of space between the cell rules and its contents

Cell spacing: Amount of space between adjacent cells, as well as between the outer edges of the cells and the edges of the table.

Central processing unit (CPU): Processing hardware of a computer, containing a processor and memory.

CGA: *See* color graphics adapter (CGA)

CGI script: A program, running on a server, written in any one of several popular languages, most often Perl or a Unix shell language, to process data sent from an HTML form.

Channel: Division of audio data representing a single voice or instrument.

Character: Smallest unit of data, a single digit, letter, or symbol.

Chip: Small silicon wafer on which resides integrated circuits and other processing circuitry.

Checkboxes: Type of input item that allows a user to make more than one selection by activating boxes next to each choice.

Class: A feature of style sheets that define several different styles for a tag.

Click: To press a mouse button once to select a menu option or icon.

"Click here": Sentence to be avoided. Anyone who has read this book will *never* use this outmoded and vulgar phrase.

Client/server: Network design in which the client—that is, any end-user's computer—takes on processing tasks traditionally handled by a network server.

Client software: Program that is resident on your computer but interacts with other programs or data across the Net.

Client-side mapping: Image map controlled by client rather than server. This is the preferred type of mapping because it reduces the load on the Net.

Clip art: Graphics and images on paper or disk that are purchased for use by designers.

Close box: Icon found in the top right corner of a window. Clicking on the close box deactivates that associated window, which usually returns the window back into its original icon.

Code: Written program instruction.

Code leveraging: Reusing existing code by slightly modifying it into new code to perform a different operation.

Coding: Writing a computer program or HTML page.

Color graphics adapter (CGA): Color monitor standard that displays 640 by 200 pixels in 16 colors.

Column spanning: Extending a cell across two or more columns in its row.

Comments: Documentation of choices made while writing a program or HTML page, including explanations of why those choices were made.

Common Gateway Interface (CGI): Program that processes the information sent in on a form.

Compact disc (CD): Removable disk that permanently stores data and cannot be changed; also known as *CD-ROM*.

Compiler: High-level language translator that checks an entire program for errors while it is translating all the code into machine language. If there are syntax errors, a list of errors is output by this program.

Computer architecture: The physical characteristics of the computer, for example, a 40 GHz Pentium processor with a graphics card of 16 billion colors and a quad stereo sound card.

Computer-assisted instruction (CAI): Using the computer to present material to students. A type of self-paced learning popular in the 1980s that is making a resurgence through the use of Web-based training.

Concatenate (concatenation): Sequentially join two or more strings together.

Concatenation: Adding to the end of an element or file.

Container elements: *See* Containers

Containers: Used to modify the contents placed within them. They consist of a beginning and closing tag. Although the closing tag can sometimes be inferred, it should never be eliminated.

Content: What a document says versus how a document looks (layout).

Content-based style: *See* Logical style

Cookie: A small quantum of data, stored by the browser, that is associated with a particular HTML page on the Net. Usually cookies are used to store and retrieve information about the user. In most cases, cookies live only for the life of the browsing session and disappear when the browser is closed. The reason for the term *cookie* is lost in the mists of antiquity, but there are a couple of good possibilities. First, the term *magic cookie* was used to describe a small chunk of data that allowed access to some special functions of a computer program. These small data elements were used in the mainframe days. Another rendition of the cookie was the cookie-monster program. That was arguably one of the first computer virus programs. The user would be working along and all at once the computer would clear the terminal screen and say "Give me a cookie." If the user responded with any input except the word "cookie," the program would continue to demand a cookie. The absolutely proper name for a cookie is a *persistent client state HTTP cookie,* but the term *magic cookie* is much more fun.

Cracker: One who breaks into computers for nefarious reasons. These are the bad guys.

CrLf: *See* Carriage-return line feed (CrLf)

CPU: *See* Central processing unit (CPU)

Crash: Term generically used to describe a computer failure but can also be used to describe the failure of any part of a computer system or a software failure. Always a bad thing.

CRT: *See* Cathode ray tube (CRT)

CSS box model: Style sheet formatting model that assumes that each element results in one or more rectangular boxes. This model provides the framework for placing whitespace around elements of the Web page.

Cursor: Blinking line or box that highlights where the computer is going to display the next keyboard entry.

Cursor control: Use of keys on keyboard to move the cursor up, down, left, or right through a document.

Cut and paste: Process of changing the location of data or formulas within a document or page; also known as *Move.*

Data: Facts, figures, and images, the stuff of data processing. Note: Data is a *plural* word; the singular is datum.

Data compression: To reduce data storage space by replacing data redundancies with special notations that take up less space. Data compression can be lossy, meaning some of the data in the sound or image are lost, or lossless, meaning all the data are preserved in the compression.

Debug: To remove the errors from a program. *See* Bug.

Default value: The choice that the program will make for you if you fail to specify a value.

Definition list: List formatted like a dictionary or glossary.

Deprecated (deprecated element): An element or tag that is deprecated is one that has been outdated either by a new element or tag, or by a change in the specifications. Deprecated elements may become obsolete in future versions of the specifications.

Deprecated tags: Tags that are still supported by software but are targeted for replacement and will become obsolete in the near future.

DHTML: *See* Dynamic HTML (DHTML)

Dialog box: Window that prompts the user to enter text, select options from a list, or click on an icon to initiate or cancel some program option.

Digital data: Data that consist of discrete values, typically binary (1 or 0).

Digital sound: Sound in which values are represented by numbers rather than by a continuous stream.

Digital video: Created by capturing analog video at regular intervals and saving each capture as a distinct image called a *frame*. Frames can then be played back to give the appearance of motion, that is, to create a movie. Digital video files may have audio tracks associated with the frames.

Direct call: Process of retrieving a file by name.

Discrete data: Data represented by numbers (digita data).

Distributed program: Program that runs on computers across the Internet, such as an HTML browser.

Dithering: Replacing one uniform color with repeating patterns of other colors that approximate the initial color, or blending two colors to create a third color. Dithering can reduce compressibility and usability.

DNS: *See* Domain Name Server (DNS)

Document: The HTML code for a page.

Document-level style sheet: Establishes formatting rules that affect all elements in a document's <body> container.

Document type definition (DTD): The specifications that define the structure and syntax standards used to create an HTML document.

Domain: The computer that runs the server software.

Domain name: Substitutes for the numeric IP address; an alphabetic name, such as "www.McGraw-Hill.com."

Domain Name Server (DNS): Program that translates domain names into IP addresses.

Download: Transfer of data or a file from a remote machine to the local machine.

Downloading: Copying a computer-readable file from another computer to your computer.

Drag: To move an object on the screen by pointing at it and holding down a mouse button while you move it to a new screen location.

Driver: Master document that builds the frames of a framed document.

Drop-down menu: Menu options that stay hidden in a menu bar at the top of the screen until the user selects it. When the menu is selected, the menu opens to list program options. Once an option is selected, the menu rolls back up into the menu bar. Also known as *pull-down menu.*

DSSSL: Document Style Semantics and Specifications Language, the parent language for XSL. The language describes how such documents are presented or mapped to other formats.

Dublin Metadata Core Element Set (Dublin Core): Standard for the META tag.

Dynamic content: Refers to the spectrum of active features, including images, sound, animation, and interactivity.

Dynamic document: Document with active features that could include images, sound, animation, and interactivity.

Dynamic HTML: Web page content that changes each time it is viewed through the use of JavaScript as well as new HTML extensions that enable Web page reaction to user input without contacting the server.

Ebook: Electronic books that are published and available for download via the Internet.

Echo: The Unix command that sends a data stream to the output device.

Element: A basic unit in XML that consist of a container and its contents.

Em: The measurement of the horizontal line space taken up by the uppercase letter M when using proportional spacing.

email: The preferred spelling of E-mail.

Empty element: *See* Empty tag

Empty element (empty tag): Used primarily for page formatting, an element with no content or closing tag.

Empty tag: A tag that does not enclose any text, so it has no closing code—for example, <BR>.

Encapsulation: Feature of object-oriented programming in which data and the operations necessary to manipulate those data are collected together into a usable module.

End user: Person who can use computer technology to organize data, stimulate new ideas, solve problems, and communicate the results to others. This individual is also called a *user*. In HTML parlance, the user is that individual for whom we create pages.

Entity: Special symbols in XML that need special handling. Entities are coded with an ampersand (&) at the beginning and end with a semi-colon (;).

Executable file: Binary file.

Extended graphics adapter (EGA): Color monitor standard that displays 720 by 350 pixels in 16 colors.

Extended graphics array (XGA): Color monitor standard that displays 1024 by 768 pixels in 65,536 colors.

External image: An image that is placed on a page by itself, and a link is provided to it.

Field: Related group of letters, numbers, and symbols, as in a name or address.

File Transfer Protocol (ftp): Allows you to move files across the Net.

Filename: Unique set of letters, numbers, and symbols that identifies a data file or program.

Filename extension: A Combination of three or four letters that is added to the end of a filename, preceded by a period, to identify the file format. For example, hypertext markup language files are identified by the filename extensions .htm or .html.

Firewall: Program that protects one or more computers from attack from across the Net.

Flagitious: According to *Webster's Dictionary of the English Language,* flagitious comes from the Latin *flagitiosus* and means grossly wicked. Rhetorically it means guilty of enormous crimes. Perhaps a bit strong to apply to the <blink> tag, but it is a fun word, and after you have looked at as many blinking pages as we have, well, they do seem grossly wicked at that.

Floating image: An image that can be placed by the browser in either margin.

Floating-point number: A number with a decimal point.

Flood filling: Creating a large colored area by using height and width attributes to expand a very small image across the screen.

Focus: Identifies the currently active control that is able to receive input.

Font: The typeface, weight, style, and size of the text.

Form: An HTML document, or part of an HTML document, that allows the user to provide input and then returns an HTML document in response, either giving requested information or simply thanking the user.

Frame: 1. The division of a framed page. Each frame contains a HTML document. 2. Created by capturing analog video at regular intervals and saving each capture as a distinct image. Frames can be played back to create a movie.

Frame rate: The number of displayed frames per second.

Freeware: Software in the public domain.

Ftp: *See* File Transfer Protocol (ftp)

Full justification: Both right and left margins of a document are aligned. Full justification is not often seen in HTML documents.

Function: Predefined formula or code segment that performs common mathematical, financial, or logical operations. We often use JavaScript functions in HTML pages.

Function call: The point from which a function is called and data is returned from the function. It contains any parameters that are passed to the function.

Functions keys: Keyboard keys that activate special software features (the F1–F12 keys on most keyboards.)

Generic class: A style class not associated with a particular tag.

GIF: *See* Graphic Interchange Format (GIF)

Gigabyte: 1 billion bytes of memory.

GIGO: "Garbage in, garbage out," meaning errors in data produce useless information.

Global variable: A value stored at a location known to all the functions on a page.

Glyph: A variety of symbols that provides the appearance of a letter, number or other symbol. Arabic numbers and English letters are examples of common glyphs.

Good thing: Something that is inherently good or results in uniformly positive outcomes. Recoding our pages in compliant XHTML is a good thing.

Graphic Interchange Format (GIF): The most common image format on the Web, supporting 8-bit color and having lossless compression. The three types of GIF are plain, transparent, and animated.

Graphical user interface (GUI): Program that uses images to facilitate users' selections of commands by means of a pointing device like a mouse.

Grep: A Unix tool used to find particular lines in one or more files. Stands for Global Regular Expression Print.

Grunt work: Also called *scut work.* The boring part of any task. In building an HTML document, coding the <html>, <head> . . . skeleton could be considered grunt work.

GUI: *See* Graphical user interface (GUI)

Hacker: Self-taught computer expert who tends to try to find unauthorized ways to access computer systems. These are the good guys. Contrast with cracker.

Hard return: A carriage return entered into the text when the user presses the Return or Enter key.

Hardware: Computer and other associated equipment. Generally, if you were to kick the hardware with your bare foot, it would hurt.

Harvest: To collect resources from the Net, such as images, sounds, and applets.

Hierarchical model: Model in which data items and their references are organized in a top-down fashion; larger parts are composed of smaller parts.

High-level language: Programming language that resembles human language. Programs written in high-level languages, like BASIC and Pascal, must be translated into the computer's machine language before being used.

Highlight: To increase the intensity of certain characters on a screen for emphasis.

Home page: The highest level page on a Web site.

Horizontal rule: Tag that places a horizontal line, or rule, on a page.

Hosting: Making a Web page available on a known domain.

Hot spot: A defined area in an image or section of text that activates a function or link to another Web page when selected.

Hot word: Text that is used as a reference or link to another web page.

Hoze: To completely break or mess up. Often used to describe the results of a logic error. For example one might say, "I forgot to code the closing tag on the italics container and it hozed the rest of the page."

HREF: *See* Hypertext reference (HREF)

HTML: *See* HyperText Markup Language (HTML)

HTML author: The person who creates a Web page.

HTML editor: Software used to produce HTML code.

HTML text-file converter: Converts existing word-processor files to HTML code.

HTML validator (HTML verifier): A Web tool that validates HTML syntax and structure. Validators will also confirm that any hyperlinks contained in the document are valid.

HTML verifier: Makes sure your links are valid and your HTML syntax and grammar are correct.

HTML viewer: Lets you see what your document may look like on a browser.

Http: *See* Hypertext Transport Protocol (http)

HyperCard: Forerunner of HTML; Macintosh feature that allowed users to create buttons that would perform certain actions.

Hyper document: Document that contains links.

Hypertext document: Document that contains links.

HyperText Markup Language (HTML): The tool use to build Web pages; not a true programming language.

Hypertext reference (HREF): A required attribute of the LINK tag; it points to some valid http address.

Hypertext Transport Protocol (http): The protocol used to send HTML documents across the Net.

Icon: Picture of item, action, or computer operation.

IF . . . THEN: Programming statements used to perform actions based on the value of a given condition. IF a particular condition is true, THEN perform the associated action(s).

Import: To add graphics, images, or text created by other software to a document.

Image editor: Allows you to modify images, add special effects, and convert from one file format to another.

Image map: Image that serves as a map in that users can click on various parts (links) of the image to retrieve information. There are two types: server-side maps and client-side maps.

Infinite loop: A series of instructions within a computer program that are repeated continuously without exit.

Information: Knowledge derived by processing data, usually in the form of a printed report or screen display. The only reasons we build Web pages is to provide information.

Inheritance: Feature of object-oriented programming in which one class can receive data structures and methods or procedures from a previous class.

Inline element: Part of an HTML page that is placed within the current line of text.

Inline image: An image that occurs within the line of text. In HTML, images are placed inline unless the author codes one of the **align** attribute values.

Input controls: Multiple number of form data input types, such as buttons, text fields, multiple-choice lists, drop down boxes, etc.

Instance: In object oriented programming, an individual object.

Integer: A whole number, without a decimal point.

Intellectual property: Material resulting from ideas, or mental processes; usually protected by a copyright.

Interactivity: Exists when the user can input information to a page and receive a response. Java provides a degree of interactivity that allows users to play games, live, on the Net.

Internet address: *See* Internet Protocol (IP) address

Internet Protocol (IP) address: Numeric address assigned to each machine on the Internet. Consists of four sets of one, two, or three octal digits separated by periods. *See also* Domain name

Internet Service Provider (ISP): Company that specializes in providing access to the Internet.

Interpreter: Translates source code into binary code, one line at a time.

Intersystem link: Link to an item in a different system.

Intranet: Computer network like the Internet except that it contains only the computers of a specific company.

Intrapage link: Link to an item located within the current document or page.

Intrapage target name: A target within the current document or Web page.

Intrasystem link: Link to an item within the current system.

Intrinsic events: Mouse activities, like clicking, and document changes, like loading.

IP address: *See* Internet Protocol (IP) address

ISP: *See* Internet Service Provider (ISP)

Iteration: *See* Loop

Jacquard, Joseph Marie: (1752–1834) Developer in 1801 of mechanized looms using punched cards for patterns.

Java: High-level programming language that uses object-oriented techniques, works across the Internet, is translated line by line, is safe and hard to crash, runs on many different computer platforms, and does powerful things quickly.

Java applet: A small program written in the Java language that serves as an extension to an HTML document, providing visual and other effects, including animation. Applets are a subset of Java. They are called from an HTML program and run on a browser.

Java compiler: Translates Java source code into bytecode; called Javac.

Java development kit (JDK): Includes a Java compiler (Javac), Java bytecode interpreter to run stand-alone programs, a Java debugging tool, and an applet viewer.

JavaScript: Specialized programming language for building programs that are embedded in an HTML document and perform simple tasks; not related to Java. JavaScript gives the HTML programmer tools such as looping and conditional statements.

JavaScript editor: Software package that helps Web authors create JavaScripts, taking much of the grunt work out of creating JavaScript.

Java Virtual Machine: Java interpreter.

Javac: Java compiler; translates Java source code into bytecode.

JDK: *See* Java development kit (JDK)

Joint Photographic Experts Group (JPEG): Image format on the Web that supports 8-bit and 24-bit color and is available on all browsers. Compression is lossy. *Progressive JPEGs* create an effect similar to an animated GIF.

JPEG: *See* Joint Photographic Experts Group (JPEG)

Just-in-time programming: Involves multithreading, in which a program can start running before all of it is downloaded.

Justification: The alignment of text along the margins (right, left, full).

K: *See* Kilobyte (K)

Kerning: Adjusting the spacing between printed characters according to the shape of the characters.

kHz: *See* Kilohertz (kHz)

Kilobyte (K): Consists of 1024 bytes of memory, or 2^{10} bytes.

Kilohertz (kHz): Roughly a thousand samples per second.

Late binding: Choosing the correct method to handle an object at run time.

Latin-1 character set: List of common letters, numbers, symbols, and punctuation marks used in Western languages, each with a numeric value and some also with names; designed by the International Standards Organization (ISO).

Layout: How a document looks versus what it says (content).

LCD: *See* Liquid crystal display (LCD)

Leading: The difference between the font size and the computed value of the line height.

Left justification: Alignment of text in a document along only the left edge.

Line break: Tag to end a line on a page and start a new one.

Linear programming: Type of programming wherein an optimum solution for a problem is found for a given set of requirements and constraints using a top-down method.

Liquid crystal display (LCD): Monitor in which an electric field causes configurations of molecules to align and light up, producing characters.

Link: Specially marked place on the screen that will cause something to happen when you activate it. Links can open another HTML document, move you to another place in the current document, display a picture, play a sound, or run a video clip.

List box: Displays a list of names or options. When the list is too long to fit in the box, scroll arrows move the list up and down to display different items within the list box.

Local action buttons: Buttons that cause the browser to perform specific actions within the client (browser), instead of involving a CGI script on the server.

Local area network (LAN): Privately owned collection of interconnected computers within a confined service area.

Local variable: A value known only to the function in which it was created.

Logic error: Program error that is translatable but does not produce correct results.

Logical operation: Ability of a computer to compare two values to see which is larger or if they are equal.

Logical operator: Symbol (<, >, =) indicating which logical operation is to be used in an IF . . . THEN statement.

Logical style: Using specific style containers that describe the way the text within a container is used rather than simply how it looks.

Loop: *See* Iteration

Lossless compression: Compression that keeps all the data bits in the image so that image or sound quality does not degrade.

Lossy compression: Compression in which some pixels are discarded, causing image or sound quality to degrade.

Lynx: The most common text only browser.

Machine code: An operating language unique to each computer that is made up of bits (0 or 1) representing electronic switches (off or on); also known as *machine language.*

Mailto: Refers to a directive in a form that causes data to be sent to an electronic mail (e-mail) address rather than being sent to be processed by a CGI script.

Maintaining state: Term used to describe the process of storing some aspect or aspects of user information for later retrieval. Examples include color choices, last time visited, places visited at the site, and other data that may be important to the user. Most often cookies are used to maintain state in a browser.

Maintenance: Keeping one or more of a computer system's components or programs up to date.

Maintenance programmer: A person who modifies programs or Web pages already in use in order to reflect a change in content.

Marker: Bullet used in an unordered list.

Marquee: Display of animated (moving) text that scrolls horizontally or vertically on the page.

Maximize button: Windows icon with two overlapping boxes found in the top right corner of the title bar next to the minimize button. Clicking on the maximize button expands the related window to fill the screen.

McLuhan, Marshall: (1911–1980) Author of books relating technology to society. His ideas have influenced present-day data communications and multimedia.

Megabyte (MB): 1 million bytes of memory.

Megahertz (MHz): 1 million clock cycles per second; a measurement of processing hardware speed.

Memory: Computer circuitry that temporarily stores data and programs. Usually grouped by storage capacity of thousands (K) or millions (M) of characters; for example, a computer with 8M of memory can store up to 8 million letters, numbers, or symbols.

Menu: List of program options that allows a user to activate an option by highlighting it or by entering a single letter or number.

Menu bar: Horizontal area that runs across the top of a window and displays menu titles.

Method: In object-oriented programming, a method is a way of manipulating data. Objects have methods associated with them to process the data, which are called *properties* of the object. Some of the methods are things like getMonth( ) or write (). One way to identify a method is that it will usually return a value or values, and it usually ends with parentheses. Methods can also act on data that are passed to them through parameters contained in the parentheses. For example, document.write("Hello World") will write the phrase "Hello World" to the current document.

Microsecond: One millionth of a second; used to measure the speed of a computer's processing.

Millisecond: One thousandth of a second; used to measure the access time of a computer's disk drive.

Minimize button: Windows icon with an underscore found in the top right corner of the title bar next to the maximize/restore button. Clicking on the minimize button converts the window back into an icon or sends it to the taskbar.

MIPS: 1 million instructions per second; a measurement of a computer's processing speed.

MIME: *See* Multipurpose Internet Mail Extensions (MIME)

Modal: Term usually meaning to have modes or be associated with a particular mode. However, in this instance we will use the Microsoft definition. In MS-speak, a modal window will stay on the screen and claim any input the user enters until it is closed. You can access other windows only after the modal window is closed. Such a window would typically be used to warn the user of an error or problem. The alert( ), confirm( ), and prompt( ) dialog boxes are all examples of modal windows in JavaScript.

Modular: A modular language, like JavaScript, allows the coder to create small sections of code that perform one task.

Monaural sound: Single-channel sound as opposed to multiple-channel (stereo).

Mondlock, Buddy: Famous folk singer, known worldwide . . . or at least he should be.

Monitor: An output peripheral by which a visual display is shown on a screen; also called a *screen* or *CRT*.

Monochrome monitor: Single-color monitor, that is, a monitor that shows one color against a black background.

Monospaced font: Font in which each letter takes up the same amount of space. *See also* Proportionally spaced font

Movie: Digital video file, sometimes accompanied by audio file. *See also* Audio/Video Interleave (AVI)

Moving Picture Experts Group (MPEG): Video or audio format with the best compression algorithms, providing high-quality online files.

MPEG: *See* Moving Picture Experts Group (MPEG)

Mu-law (µ-law): Sound file originally developed for Unix, now an international standard for compression voice-quality audio, supported by almost all operating systems. Does not support stereo. Extension is ".au."

Multimedia: Includes sound, pictures, and animation.

Multiprocessing: Linking several computers together to work on a common problem.

Multipurpose Internet Mail Extensions (MIME): Tells the browser what kind of file data are being sent across the Net.

Multitasking: One computer running two or more independent programs concurrently.

Multithreading: Allows access to different parts of the same program at the same time. This allows a program to begin execution before it has completely downloaded from the Net.

Nanosecond: One billionth of a second; used to measure the speed of a computer's processor.

Nesting lists: Lists within lists; lists with sublists.

Netcology: Conservation of Net resources; coined from the term *ecology.*

Newline: Term used in Unix to describe a carriage-return line feed.

Noncompliant browser: Browsers that do not comply with W³C specifications for HTML codes.

Null: No value. Literally, binary zeros in a field.

Object: Section of program code in object-oriented programming that contains both the processing code and descriptions of related data to perform a single task. Each object is an instance of a class; it has a state and a behavior. It is the term used to describe an element, like a button, form, the actual browser, the document, or even the current date. The data contained within the object are called the *properties,* and the instructions for manipulating the data or causing the object to interact with other objects are called *methods.*

Object instance: A particular occurrence or use of a class (in object-oriented programming).

Object-oriented programming (OOP): Programming methodology whereby a program is organized into objects, each containing both descriptions of the data and processing operations necessary to perform a task.

Obsolete tags: Tags that are no longer supported by updated browsers.

OCR: *See* Optical character recognition (OCR)

Octothorp: #, hashmark, pound sign, number sign, tic-tac-toe board, and even thud.

Offline: State of hardware when it is not communicating with the computer. This is also used to indicate a process that happens when the computer is not connected to the Internet, for example "offline viewing."

Online: Direct input and processing of data by a computer.

OOP: *See* Object-oriented programming (OOP)

Open standard: A standard that is still developing; anyone is free to use it and make suggestions about inclusions.

Operating system: A collection of system programs that oversees the execution of application programs, manages files, and controls the computer system's resources— monitor, keyboard, disk drives, memory, etc.

Optical character recognition (OCR): Process in which a device like a scanner is used along with special software to take a picture of a page of text, analyze the picture, and produce a file of machine-readable data from the analysis. For example, if you were to process this page of the glossary using OCR, you would end up with a file containing all of these words that you could process with a word processor.

Ordered list: List with items numbered or lettered.

Orphan: The first line of a paragraph that appears as the last line on a page.

Package: Set of directory names, starting from the URL, with each element of the package separated from the others by a dot. Or, something you get at Christmas or on your birthday. (I like the second definition better than the first . . . oh, well.)

Padding: White space around elements such as cells, tables, or images.

Page: What you see when a document is displayed on your screen by a browser.

Page footer: Appears at the end of an HTML document and provides basic information about the creator of the page plus a list of the navigation links used. Should contain the date last modified as well.

Palette: Displays the color options available in a graphics package.

Pane: *See* Browser pane

Paragraph: Identifies a continuous string of text within a page; used to break up text into smaller units. In HTML, defined by the <p> . . . </p> container.

Parameters: Attributes that give the Web weaver some control over applets or values passed to a function or routine.

Parent class: A superclass in object-oriented programming; a feature of inheritance.

Parent window: The window containing the hypertext reference to another page.

Parse: To divide into component parts. We parse a sentence into words using white space and punctuation. The browser must parse HTML code into its components so it can interpret it.

Password: Special combination of letters, numbers, or symbols that is theoretically known only to the user, and allows access to protected computer systems and data.

Path: Set of directory names that lead to a specific document.

PCX: Image format on the Web that was developed by Zsoft for the PC Paintbrush program. Supports 1, 4, 8, and 24 bits per pixel but does not seem to support compression.

PDA: *See* Personal digital assistant (PDA)

PDF: Image format on the Web that is created with a special software package called Acrobat from Adobe. PDF documents can look like a magazine page, with multiple columns. PDF documents support "on page" searching.

Perl: An elegant little programming language developed by Larry Wall, often used to write CGI scripts. Perl stands for Practical Extraction and Report Language.

Personal digital assistant (PDA): Class of devices like the PalmPilot VI, the Avigo, or any of a series of small, usually palmtop devices used to manage personal information.

Physical style: Describes the way the text within a container is supposed to look when displayed by a browser. *See also* Logical style

Picosecond: One trillionth of a second; used to measure speed within a computer's processor.

Pitch: The number of characters printed per inch in a document.

Pixel: Stands for "picture element"; one of the many tiny dots that make up the display on your screen. In a color monitor, each pixel is actually three small dots, one each red, blue, and green. (No, we don't know where the "x" came from.)

Platform: Describes the specific type of computer and its operating system, browser, and so forth.

Platform independence: Can be run on a variety of platforms; this is an important goal for HTML code.

Plug-in: Additional software program that works with a browser and is required to display multimedia or other special formats.

PNG: *See* Portable Network Graphics (PNG)

Point: Unit of measure for type size. One point equals 1/72 of an inch.

Pointers: Variables that contain the addresses of other data.

Polymorphism: Having the same name for more than one, usually related, method. The two types of polymorphism are overloading and overriding.

Port number: Must be specified when the server is set up to receive http traffic on a network port other than the default port.

Portability: Characteristic of being viewable by all sorts of computers.

Portable Network Graphics (PNG): Relatively new but important image format on the Web that supports 8-bit and 24-bit color but is an open standard and is not supported by all browsers. Compression is lossless. Compression is excellent, so there are many Web weavers that are trying to help PNG become the standard on the Net.

Pragma: Normally used to indicate information a compiler uses. In this instance it means "extra data the browser uses."

Prepend: To add data to the beginning of a file, variable name, or data stream. For example, accessing the data stored at a memory location in Unix is accomplished by prepending a dollar signs ($) to the variable name.

Preventive maintenance procedures: Running diagnostic checks and cleaning computer hardware to prevent a crash from occurring; running diagnostic checks, link-viability checks, and the like to ensure that a Web page is healthy, wealthy, and wise.

Primary storage: Another name for a computer's internal memory.

Procedural approach: Traditional approach to program design in which data are separate from instructions and the programmer lists the steps needed to solve a problem.

Progressive image: A file saved as layers that display the image data in several passes, each pass making the image better.

Property: Object-oriented term used to describe the data associated with an object. Some examples of properties are the colors of the text, links, and background of a document, or the current date and time. Properties are the data that an object's methods use or modify.

Properties: Attributes or features of a element or object.

Proportional spacing (proportionally spaced font): A font in which different characters have different widths. (*See also* Monospaced font.)

Protocol: Tells the browser what kind of resource it is accessing and allows different machines or programs to communicate. HTTP and plain text are two examples.

Pseudo-class: A style sheet feature that allows designers to address overall Web page characteristics. They are not associated with a particular element.

Pseudocode: A method of representing program logic by using English phrases in an outline form.

Pseudo-element: A style sheet feature that address typographical items rather than structural elements. They must be associated with a subject tag.

Public: Available to other applications, either as a direct call or through the import statement.

Public domain: Not copyrighted; can be used for free, without obtaining permission. It is always a good idea to give credit to the source of public domain material—that is just polite.

Publish: To move a Web page to the server that will host it, making it available to the world.

Pull-down menu: Menu options that stay hidden in a menu bar at the top of the screen until the user selects it. When the menu is selected, the menu opens to list program options. Once an option is selected, the menu rolls back up into the menu bar. Also known as *drop-down menu*.

Pull technology: Starts with the client requesting data from the server. Almost all HTML screens are "pulled." The client is in control.

Push technology: Starts with the server deciding to send data to the client without a request from the client. This is still rare on the Net. Broadcast television is an example of push technology. The client (your TV) doesn't request the data; it is just sent by the server (the TV station), and your client can use it if so desired.

Radio button: Type of input item than ensures that only one of a series of choices can be selected by the user. So called because it resembles an old-fashioned pushbutton radio.

Readability: How easy a page is to read. Two of the factors that determine readability are (1) the proper use of white space to separate design elements and (2) starting new lines of code where appropriate. Not only is the readability of a page important, but so is the readability of the HTML code.

Relative path: The path to a document that starts from the current directory.

Relative path name: As opposed to *absolute path name,* does not start with a right slash, because it starts with the current position in the file structure. The browser fills in all of the missing data to the left of the information provided.

Relative width: Width measured as a percentage of the screen. *See also* Absolute width

Reserve name: Special target names whose spellings have been set aside in W³C specifications. These names all begin with an underscore and their specific meanings cannot be changed. The currently reserved names are **_blank, _self, _parent,** and **_top** and some say phred is also reserved.

Resolution: A measure of graphic image sharpness in bits (pixels) per inch or bits per line. The higher the resolution, the sharper the graphic image is.

Resolver: Hardware and software combinations that render XML into different formats.

RGB number: Number representing a specific mixture of red, green, and blue colors; expressed as a six-digit (hexadecimal) number in HTML. An example is #FFCC99.

Resource Interchange File Format Waveform Audio Format (RIFF Wave): Proprietary sound file format sponsored jointly by Microsoft and IBM and most commonly used on Microsoft Windows products. It is supported by most operating systems, has uncompressed format, and supports stereo. File extension is ".wav."

Reverse video: Putting text into the opposite colors expected on a screen; done for emphasis. For example, white characters on a black background would be reverse video.

RGB monitor: Monitor using red, green, and blue (RGB) pixels in combinations to form a variety of colors.

RIFF WAVE: *See* Resource Interchange File Format Waveform Audio Format (RIFF WAVE)

Right justification: Alignment of text in a document along the right edge.

Rollover: A feature on a page that changes as the mouse pointer moves over it.

Robust: Strongly constructed.

Row spanning: Extending a cell across two or more rows in its column.

Rule (a): The horizontal or vertical line that separates the rows and columns of cells in a table or the horizontal line across the page dividing different content areas.

Rule (b): Part of a style sheet. The rules in a style sheet provide the direction for the browser as it builds specific elements of the page.

Sans-serif type style: A type style in which the printed characters lack tails, resulting in a simple block style of text.

Scalar: One of the two ways information can be accessed in a computer program. With scalar values, the data are present in the command, without ever being stored in a specific location in memory. For example, the following print statement uses a scalar value:

> print "Hello World".
> The character data string "Hello World" is a scalar value.
> The other choice is to use *variables.* A variable is a handy name for a location in memory. In the following example, the data are stored in the variable string:
> string = "Hello World"
> print $string

Then the contents of that variable are printed. (Note: this is a Unix example, so the $ that precedes the variable name is required. What it is saying is, "Print the contents of the variable 'string,' not the word 'string.'")

Scalable Vector Graphics (SVG): A language for describing two-dimensional graphics in XML. A new Web standard format.

Screen pointer: An icon, usually an arrow, on a screen that moves when the mouse or some other pointer device is moved. Program options are activated by using a mouse to move the screen pointer over the desired icon and clicking the mouse button.

Script: A program, usually written in a scripting language like Perl or JavaScript or one of the Unix shells. A script usually has one well-defined function and is relatively small.

Scripting language: A language used to write scripts, for example, JavaScript, Perl, or Unix shell languages.

Scroll: To roll data up, down, and sideways on a screen for viewing long or wide documents.

Scroll arrows: Arrows found at both ends of a scroll bar. Users change the view of a window or list box by clicking on one of the scroll arrows.

Scroll bar: Area that appears on the right or lower edges of a window or list box when only a partial view is available. A scroll bar contains a scroll box and scroll arrows.

Scroll box: Square within a scroll bar that identifies which portion of the window or list box is currently being viewed. Users can change the view by dragging the scroll box within the scroll bar.

Search script: A CGI script that performs a search across the contents of a single file or across one or more directories.

Search site: Specialized Web page designed to help people find data from other pages by means of one or more keywords.

Searchable document: Document containing ISINDEX tag; it allows the user to search one or more files on the server.

Secure environment: Created by a programming language that cannot write to disk drives or cause overflow errors; an environment safe from viruses.

Security manager: Runs at all times in Java to enforce the rules of applet behavior.

Selection: Basic structure in a computer program that allows execution of one of two different sets of code based on some condition; often called an *IF-THEN structure.*

Sequence: Basic structure of a computer program whereby instructions are executed in the order they appear in the program.

Serif type: A type style in which short line segments are added to print characters to help the reader's eye flow across the page.

Server redirection: Technique for returning a CGI script in which a Location: header is coded instead of a Content-type: header.

Server-side include: Directives placed within the HTML document that execute other programs or output data such as environment variables or file statistics. Server side includes are executed on the server and the results are displayed on the Web page sent back to the browser.

Server-side mapping: Image map controlled by server; that is, the server decides what client should do.

SGML: *See* Standard Generalized Markup Language (SGML)

Shareware: Software that you can legally copy and use but for which you should register and pay the registration fee.

Shell script: A program, often a small program, written in one of the Unix shell languages. Most scripts are written to run in the Bourne shell.

Snail mail: Regular postal service.

Softkey: A user or application defined key on a keyboard.

Source: Origin of a link.

Stacks: HyperCard documents.

Stand-alone program: Runs on a single, local machine and is complete on that machine.

Standard Generalized Markup Language (SGML): Language for coding Web pages that can be viewed by all types of computers, all across the world. HTML is a subset of SGML.

Static Web page: A Web page that does not contain any links to other Web pages, and in which information does not change unless the HTML source code is changed.

Status line: Area of a browser pane that displays pertinent information about what is happening within the browser. Often the status line shows the address to which a link points.

Stereo sound: Multiple-channel sound as opposed to single-channel (monaural).

Storyboard: Diagram illustrating how two or more Web pages relate to one another.

Streaming: Method for transferring data in such a manner that it can be processed as a steady and continuous stream, such as with video or audio files. This data is buffered so that playback can start as soon as a minimal amount of data has been downloaded.

String: A series of characters enclosed in either or double quotation marks that are displayed as ASCII text.

Style: Describes a way to set off a group of characters from the surrounding text block.

Style sheets: Added in the new HTML standard to give the Web weaver more control over the placement and appearance of various elements on the page and to allow the creation of aural entries. There are two types of style sheets: *external,* which are files called when the browser opens the page, and *internal,* which usually apply only to the page in which they occur.

Super VGA monitor: Color monitor standard that displays 1024 by 768 pixels in 256 colors.

SVG: *See also* Scalable Vector Graphics.

Syntax: Word order, spacing, abbreviations, and special symbols used by a command-driven interface or programming language.

Syntax error: An error in the formation of the computer code.

Table: Data arranged in rows and columns.

Table body: A group of one or more rows within a table that will scroll between the header and footer when the table is too long to be fully displayed. There can be multiple table bodies defined for a table.

Tagged Image File Format (TIFF): Image format use to exchange documents between different computer platforms. Supports 1, 4, 8, and 24 bits per pixel.

Tag-level class: A style class that is applied to a specific tag.

Tags: HTML codes that are enclosed in angle brackets and are used to format the text. *See also* Containers

Target: When referencing Web pages, it is the end of a link. In <form> elements, an attribute that directs return data to a window or frame different from the current document.

Telnet: Allows you to work remotely on computers across the Net.

Template: An HTML skeleton with labels and scripts, but no test or pictures, that is formatted for a specific application where it is copied and reused. Templates are very useful to increase efficiency and reduce grunt work.

Terabyte: 1 trillion bytes of memory.

Text: Nongraphical data composed of ASCII characters.

Text box: Accepts keyboard entries from user to identify new filenames or disk locations. Text boxes are often used within a dialog box.

Text file: File consisting of just text, with no embedded word-processing codes; consists of only ASCII characters. Also called a *plain ASCII file.*

Thumbnail image: Very small version of the actual image, created using special thumbnailing software.

TIFF: *See* Tagged Image File Format (TIFF)

Tile: To repeat an image; for example, you can use a small image as the background of a Web page by tiling it, or repeating it to fill the screen.

Title bar: Horizontal area across the top of a window that displays the window's title. A window can be moved by clicking on the title bar and dragging it to a new screen location.

Toggle: Switch; turns a preset feature on and off.

Tool chain: A common term that describes a particular collection of tools necessary to render XML into a displayable format.

Tool tip message: A pop-up text box that appears when the screen pointer moves over an object on the screen.

Turing, Alan: (1912–1954) Developed the Turing test for artificial intelligence and provided some basis for computer science theory.

Unicode: Modeled on the ASCII character set, but it uses 16-bit encoding to support full multilingual text. No escape sequence or control code is required to specify any character in any language. According to the Unicode standard, any glyph in any language should be able to be represented.

Uniform Resource Identifier (URI): The most general identifier for Web resources; the URL is a component of the URI.

Uniform Resource Locator (URL): The Internet address, or location, of a resource, whether it is a Web page or a specific part of a Web page.

Universal Resource Name (URN): A more general identifier for Web resources, not yet completely defined.

Unordered list: *See* Bulleted list

Uploading: Sending data or programs directly to another computer.

URI: *See* Uniform Resource Identifier (URI)

URL: *See* Uniform Resource Locator (URL)

URN: *See* Universal Resource Name (URN)

User friendly: Term for an attribute of computers meaning "easy to use" that is horribly overused. It is included here to beg you not to use it when describing your pages!

Utility applets: Useful, practical applets usually designed for commercial sale.

Valid: All elements of a document follow the syntax and structure rules as set out by the DTD.

Vaporware: Computer programs that have been promised but do not exist.

Variable name: A generic way of referring to a location in the computer's memory.

Variable value: The data stored at the location in memory specified by a variable name.

Vector graphic: Graphics that use mathematical geometric formulas to represent images instead of a grid of pixels.

Verification program: *See* HTML verifier

VGA: *See* Video graphics array (VGA)

Video display terminal (VDT): A screen that provides temporary output of information.

Video graphics array (VGA): Color monitor standard that displays 720 by 400 pixels in 256 colors.

Virus: Harmful software that destroys other software on the target machine and can reproduce itself and spread from machine to machine.

Void: Will not return a value.

Web administrator: Person who maintains a Web server.

Web master: Person responsible for a collection of pages on a Web site.

Web server: Computer on the Internet with a recognized domain name or IP address that runs one of the Web server packages like Apache.

Web site: A series of related Web pages.

Web utility: Available software tools for Web designers that create custom programs to augment HTML code. These tools often require special plug-ins to be installed in the browser before they can be used.

Web weaver: Person who creates a Web page.

Well-formed: A complete and correctly formatted document.

What You See Is What You Get (WYSIWYG): Started as a tool for word processing and desktop publishing to show what the end result would look like. Now it has come to refer to any application that shows the user what the output will look like as the code is being generated.

White space: Spaces, tabs, and blank lines; those areas on the screen that are not covered by text or graphics.

Widow: The last line of a paragraph that is carried over as the first line of a page.

Wizard: Program that helps you code and will identify errors in your code.

Word wrap: Feature in which the word processor senses the margins and moves words to the next line as needed without carriage returns being necessary.

World Wide Web Consortium (W³C): International organization that sets standards for HTML protocols and tags (www.w3c.org).

Workaround: Term used to describe an action or set of actions that take the place of some other, often broken, action. Usually a workaround is less than elegant but does provide the user with a way to accomplish the desired task.

W³C: *See* World Wide Web Consortium (W³C)

WYSIWYG: *See* What You See Is What You Get (WYSIWYG)

XHTML: Extensible Hypertext Markup Language, a combination between HTML and XML specifically designed for standardized net device displays. This extensibility ensures that the presentation of the pages is consistent regardless of platform.

XML: Extensible Markup Language, a language used for describing data across numerous applications. It allows designers to create their own customized tags, enabling the definition, transmission, interpretation and validation of data.

XSL: Extensible Style Language, a style sheet specification for separating content when creating HTML or XML web pages. Similar to CSS, but additionally allows developers to dictate how web pages are printed, and contains specifications allowing the transfer of XML documents across different applications.

XSLT: Extensible Style Language Transformation, language in XSL style sheets used to transform XML documents into other XML documents.

Your Mileage May Vary (YMMV): An expression that indicates that there are differences between browsers and platforms. For example, "The page looked good on my machine at home, but YMMV."

Zipped file: Compressed file.

Zorro: Ok, so he has nothing to do with HTML, he was still a neat historical figure.

Index

a

a. *See* Anchor (**a**)
abbr. *See* Abbreviation (**abbr**)
abbrev, 447
Abbreviation (**abbr**), 122,
  124, 128
  in tables, 190
above, 174, 259
Absolute paths, 63–64
  refreshing and, 362
  relative vs., 64, 65–66,
    354–355
Absolute values, 214, 228, 230
accesskey, 59, 335
Acrobat, 140, 449
acronym, 122, 124, 128
action, 299, 301, 350
Active-X, 463
add-one (), 272
address, 122, 123, 128
Addresses. *See also* Internet
  address; Uniform Resource
  Locator (URL)
  variable names for, 299
  in Web documents, 123
Adobe, 140, 448, 449
"Advanced" object, 398
Advanced Research Projects
  Agency (ARPA), 497,
  498, 499
advisories, 215–219
".aero," 11
AI. *See* Artificial intelligence
  (AI) systems
AI Internet Solutions, 21, 24
AIFC. *See* AIFF Compressed
  Format (AIFF-C or AIFC)

".aiff," 256
AIFF. *See* Audio Interchange
  File Format (AIFF)
AIFF Compressed Format
  (AIFF-C or AIFC), 256
Alert dialog box, 393, 405
align, 13, 14, 418. *See also*
  text-align
  caption and, 195
  char and, 185
  float vs., 180–181
  in forms, 321
  in frames, 287–289
  headings and, 40
  horizontal alignment and, 150
  horizontal rule and, 43
  images and, 146
  paragraphs and, 42
  style vs., 150
  for table captions, 171
  for table text, 184, 187–188
  vertical alignment and,
    152–153
Alignment
  horizontal, 146, 150–151
  style and, 219–221
  of table caption, 194, 195
  of table text, 183–186,
    187–188, 199
  vertical, 146, 152–153
alink, 48–49, 224, 369, 476
  JavaScript and, 389, 421
all, 174, 233
alt, 144, 146–147, 148
  area and, 414–415
  aural browsers and, 471
  creative use of, 481–482
  in forms, 309, 310
  title vs., 414

Alta Vista, 24
always, 233, 234, 259
America Online (AOL), 8, 18
America Online/Time
  Warner, 374
American Standard Code for
  Information Interchange
  (ASCII), 16, 470, 487
Ampersand, 128, 129, 130, 131
  with **enctype,** 305
Analog data, 253, 256, 262
Anchor (**a**), 48, 59–63
  area vs., 416
  attributes of, 59
  for external images, 142, 242
  frames and, 283
  image links and, 161–162
  image maps and, 416
  intersystem source, 66–68, 71
  intrapage source, 70–71
  mailto protocol and, 75
  placement of, 71–72
  rollovers and, 418–419
  _self and, 286
  source, 59–62, 66–68, 69,
    70–71
  style guidelines regarding, 481
  target, 59 (*See also* Targets)
  URLs and, 9, 66–67
Anchors, JavaScript and,
  389, 405
Andreessen, Marc, 501
Angle brackets, 4, 28
Angles, 214, 259
Animations, 138, 481. *See also*
  Rollovers
  with applets, 243
  param and, 250
  streaming audio/video for, 263

style guidelines regarding, 476,
477, 478
target audience and, 253
Anonymous ftp, 487, 489, 499
AOL. *See* America Online
(AOL)
appear, 404, 405
Apple Macintosh, 2, 56, 501
applet. *See* Java applets (**applet**)
Application name/version,
JavaScript and, 401, 402
Application/x-www-form-
urlencoded, 305
Archie, 499
area, 414–417
a vs., 416
map and, 413, 414, 416
usemap and, 411–413
ARPA. *See* Advanced Research
Projects Agency (ARPA)
ARPANET, 500
Arrays, 403–405
article, 445, 446
Artificial intelligence (AI)
systems, 449
ASCII. *See* American Standard
Code for Information
Interchange (ASCII)
ASCII character set, 128–129
ASCII editor, 16, 42
Ask Jeeves, 24
Asterisks, 312
AT&T, 499
Attributes, 13–14, 28
common errors involving, 37
deprecated, 87–88
DTDs and, 22
for mouse activities, 35
null, 329
recognized by anchor tag, 59
style sheets and, 34
".au," 254
Audio browsers. *See* Aural/audio
browsers
Audio files, 253–257. *See also*
Sound
AIFC, 256
AIFF, 256
with applets, 243
best-quality, 256
copyrighted, 261
lead-in, 257
MIDI, 256
most useful, 257
MPEG, 256
μ-law (m-law) files, 254
RIFF WAVE, 255
sharing, 261
size of, 253, 257
streaming video and, 262, 263
videos with, 256
voice-quality, 254
Audio Interchange File Format
(AIFF), 256

Audio/Video Interleave (AVI),
262, 263
Auditory/audio icons, 257,
259, 471
Aural/audio browsers, 9, 455,
470–471
abbr for, 190
alt and, 146
forms and, 307, 334, 335
plain text and, 456
stereo for, 471
table summaries for, 178
title and, 307
wireless devices and, 466
XML and, 449, 468
Aural data, 468
Aural properties, 258–261
Aural style sheets, 164, 257–261
author, 362–363
auto, 225, 226, 233, 234, 259
Automatic file transfer, 487
Automatic image loading,
turning off, 144, 146, 147,
148, 164
Automatic refreshing, 359,
361, 362
".avi," 263
AVI. *See* Audio/Video Interleave
(AVI)
avoid, 233, 234
axis, 191
azimuth, 259

b

b. *See* Bold (**b**)
B programming language, 378
Back button, 5, 56, 66
CGI scripts and, 352
frames and, 268–269, 283, 479
intrapage links and, 71
one-way streets and, 73
background, 45–48, 49,
221–224, 232
background-attachment, 222
background-color, 221,
222, 223
Background color (**bgcolor**),
44–45, 221
background image and, 45–47
default, 45, 283
in forms, 306–307
JavaScript and, 389, 421–425
readability and, 46, 47, 49
refreshing and, 360
in tables, 177–178, 181,
188, 195
text color with, 45–48, 49,
177–178, 421, 424, 477
background-image, 222, 224
Background image
(**background**), 45–48, 49,
221–224

saving, 48
URLs and, 45, 47–48
background-position, 222,
223, 224
background-repeat, 222
Backgrounds
images as, 45–48, 222,
224, 477
for printer-friendly pages, 236
readability and, 45–48, 49, 477
sound, 259
style guidelines for, 475, 477
Backup copies, 42
Baen Library, 461
Bandwidth, 252, 253
Bartleby.com, 457
base, 33, 284, 285–287, 354–355
_self and, 286
target and, 355
Base module, 355
basefont, 132
baseline, 184–185, 199, 219
BBN. *See* Bolt, Beranek and
Newman, Inc. (BBN)
behind, 259
Bellovin, Steve, 499
below, 174, 259
Berkeley Standard Distribution
(BSD), 500
Berkeley Unix, 500
Berners-Lee, Tim, 501
Beta releases
of Navigator, 8
W3C and, 15
bgcolor. *See* Background color
(**bgcolor**)
Bibliography, 125, 446. *See also*
citation; Citation (**cite**)
big, 121
Binary code, 253, 305, 487
enctype for, 305
ftp and, 487
Bit-Mapped Picture (BMP), 140
BITNET, 499–500
Bits per pixel (BPP), 141
reducing, 144
".biz," 11
_blank, 285–286, 287
Blank lines, 2, 41, 131
for readability, 100
style guidelines for, 480
Bleeding, 220
Blinking text, 405, 481
Blocked (block-level) elements,
88–90, 126
del and, 127
ins and, 127
Blocking software, 482
blockquote, 125–126, 128
pre and, 131
XML and, 446, 447, 448
".bmp," 140
BMP. *See* Bit-Mapped Picture
(BMP)

body, 34, 221–222
  attributes for, 34–35, 44–49
  head and, 32
  JavaScript and, 405, 421
  noframes and, 283
  onload and **onunload**
    with, 272
  replaced by **frameset,** 270, 271
  style guidelines for, 480–482
  style sheet and, 111
Bold (**b**), 12, 116, 120
  font-weight and, 118–119
  inline elements and, 88,
    120–121
Bolt, Beranek and Newman, Inc.
  (BBN), 498
Bookmarking, 33, 478, 479
  CGI scripts and, 352
  in ebooks, 461
  frames and, 269, 291, 480
  intrasystem targets and, 73
  refreshing and, 360
Books, 2, 4. *See also* Electronic
  books (ebooks); Online
  books
Boolean operations, JavaScript
  and, 402
border, 171, 172–175, 178–181
  background color and, 177
  CSS box and, 228–230
border-bottom, 228–230
border-color, 157, 178–179,
  180, 228–230
border-left, 228–230
border-right, 228–230
border-style, 156, 157, 163,
  178–179, 228–230
border-top, 228–230
border-width, 156, 157,
  178–179, 228–230
Borders, 156–158
  for boxes, 225, 226, 228–230
  browsers and, 229
  for frames, 281–282
  for image links, 162–163
  page breaks and, 234
  for tables, 171, 172–175,
    177–181, 182
  thick or thin, 228, 230
  transparent, 180, 228, 230
  types of, 229
bottom, 153, 195, 226, 230–232
  for table text, 184–185, 199
Boutell.com, Inc., 416
box, 174
Boxes, 224–233. *See also* List
  boxes; Text-entry
  fields/boxes
  borders for, 228–230
  dialog, 392–394
  padding for, 225, 228, 230–232
BPP. *See* Bits per pixel (BPP)
br. *See* Line break (**br**)
Braille browsers, 9, 233

Broadcasts, streaming
  audio/video for, 263
Browser layout, 2, 109
  of borders, 156, 229
  of boxes, 225, 229
  comments and, 115
  fonts in, 110
  of headings, 5, 40
  inline styles and, 120
  of lists, 94, 97
  physical styles and, 120–121
  readability and, 100
  special characters and,
    128–129
  style sheets and, 208
  of tables, 170, 175–180, 186,
    187, 199
  text-only, 9
  titles in, 33
  turning of formatting for, 130
  word processing and, 17
Browser pane, 325–327
  color in, 421
  defined, 131
Browsers, 5–9, 19, 477–478. *See
  also* Internet Explorer;
    Netscape Navigator; Opera
  applets and, 245
  ASCII editor and, 16
  audio (*See* Aural/audio
    browsers)
  audio files and, 257
  background and text color
    in, 48
  background color and, 421
  background images and, 48
  borders and, 156, 229
  Braille, 9
  CGI scripts and, 339
  chain of links formed by, 2
  changing standards and, 178
  and closing containers, 13, 14
  color and, 144, 477
  command-line, 501
  content-type and, 357
  cookies and, 426, 427, 431, 432
  customized, 18
  degrading in, 479
  Dublin Core and, 363
  embedded HTML code
    and, 246
  expires and, 357
  File menu options on, 6
  first ones, 501
  fonts and, 116–117
  forms and, 299, 301, 307,
    319–321, 323–324, 329
  frames and, 174, 178, 268–269,
    274, 283
  function calls and, 380
  graphical (*See* Graphical
    browsers)
  graphical buttons and, 322, 324
  head inferred by, 32

HTML codes displayed by, 5,
    7, 19
  HTML editors and, 19
  HTML supported by, 449
  http-equiv and, 356, 362
  image displays and, 144,
    148, 165
  image formats and, 138–140
  image maps and, 411, 413–414,
    415, 416
  and Internet history, 501
  for intranets, 456
  Java-enabled, 381–383
  JavaScript and, 374, 375, 377,
    381–383
  JavaScript color coding
    and, 424
  JavaScript document object
    and, 389
  JavaScript navigator object
    and, 398–400, 401, 402, 405
  JavaScript window object
    and, 396
  layout controlled by (*See*
    Browser layout)
  metatags and, 356
  Mosaic, 115
  multimedia and variation in,
    247, 252
  navigation buttons on, 5, 6, 56
  newer, 482
  noncompliant, 91–92, 283,
    286, 287
  nongraphical (*See* Text-only/
    nongraphical browsers)
  older (*See* Older browsers)
  path names and, 65
  places to get, 22–23
  previewing document in, 16–17
  pseudo-classes and,
    368–369
  refresh and, 358
  scheme and, 363
  standby and, 247
  status bar and, 391
  style recognized by, 87–88
  tables and, 175, 178, 180
  tags inferred by, 32, 42
  technical support for, 18
  telephones as, 471
  text-only (*See* Text-only/
    nongraphical browsers)
  title and, 414
  unencrypted data and, 300
  URLs and, 9, 355
  videos and, 262, 263
  View menu options on, 6
  W^{3}C and, 15
  wireless devices and, 466
  XML and, 15, 449, 468
BSD. *See* Berkeley Standard
  Distribution (BSD)
Budgets, 459
Buffers, 263

Bullets
in headings, 40
images as, 160–161
in lists, 92–94, 97, 113,
160–161
"Burning," 261
Business data, XML/EDI model
for, 441
button, 324–325, 423, 424
Buttons
browser, 5, 6, 56
in forms, 307, 308, 321–325
radio (*See* Radio buttons)

C

C programming language, 209,
337, 346
B programming language
and, 378
XML and, 445
Cable connections, 499
Cache, 143, 352
expires and, 357
rollovers and, 420
CAI. *See* Computer-assisted
instruction (CAI)
Call, 380. *See also* Function call
Calling document, 350, 352
Calling page, 395–396
caption, 193–195
caption-side, 195
Captions
for images, 236
page breaks and, 236
for tables, **171,** 193–195
CARD, 466
Carriage-return line feed (CrLf),
326, 327, 479
line breaks as, 43
white space and, 2
Cascading style sheet (CSS), 34,
87–88, 438
box model, 225–233
CSS1, 208
CSS2, 118, 208, 234, 366
DTD and, 444
guidelines for using, 480
for manuals, 463
reason for, 208–209
type and, 113
wireless devices and, 466
XML and, 439, 451
Case sensitivity, 61
image files and, 146
intrapage targets and, 71
multimedia and, 251
of Unix, 63, 309
uploading, 495
in well-formed documents, 439
Cataloging program, 33
Catalogs, forms for requesting,
299–300, 322
CDs, 261

cellpadding, 182–183, 192
Cells, 170–171, 172. *See also*
Table data (**td**)
alignment of text in, 184–186
audio and, 259
background color in, 177
borders around, 179
height of, 192–193
padding around, 173, 181, 192
spacing around, 181–183
width of, 191–192
cellspacing, 173, 182–183
Cellular phones, 455, 466, 467
aural data and, 468
streaming video for, 466
text-only documents and, 456
XHTML and, 15
XML and, 438, 440, 449
Censorship, 357, 457, 498
center, 154–156
for audio, 259
for table text, 184–185,
188, 199
Centering
of images, 151, 154–156
of paragraphs, 155–156
Centimeters (cm), 214
Cerf, Vinton, 498, 499, 500
CERN. *See* Corporation for
Research and Educational
Computing (CERN);
European Organization for
Nuclear Research (CERN)
CGI. *See* Common gateway
interface (CGI)
CGI scripts, 312–313, 337–339,
346–353
calling document and, 302,
350, 352
data file for, 353–354
get vs. post and, 302
hidden data on, 324
JavaScript and, 386
miss page, 352–353
obtaining, 337–338
Perl and, 302, 303
refresh and, 358
search, 349, 351, 352–353
search request, 350–351, 353
searchable documents and, 349
select and, 329
server-side image maps
and, 410
Submit button and, 321
success page and, 351–352
target and, 305
for updating databases,
347–348
URL of, 301, 302
validation by, 311
value and, 333
wrap and, 327
char, 184, 185, 188
Character entities, 439
Character sets, nonstandard, 357

Character-string variable,
395–396. *See also* Text
strings
charoff, 186
charset, 59
Charts, 138
Checkboxes, 298, 308, 313–315
vs. radio buttons, 313
with radio buttons, 314
to reduce chance of errors,
312, 313
checked, 315, 317–318, 319
circle, 415
Circles, 415
citation, 446, 447
Citation (**cite**), 122, 125,
126, 438
del or **ins** and, 127
XHTML Edit module
and, 128
cite. *See* Citation (**cite**)
citetitle, 446, 447
class, 213, 216, 219
div and, 217
DTD and, 440
for forms, 336
headings and, 40
for Java applet vs. HTML
code, 243
Classes, 212–215
generic vs. tag-level, 214–215
pseudo-, 366–369
classid, 245
clear, 153–154, 232
Clear text, 492
"Click here," 74
Client-side image maps, 410,
411, 416
Client system
JavaScript and, 375, 398, 399
secure ftp and, 492
Closing/ending tag, 14, 28, 37,
40, 42
common errors involving, 37
empty tags and, 28
"cm." *See* Centimeters (cm)
CNET Shareware, 24
COBOL, 374
code, 121, 128
with applets, 243
for audio, 259
Code leveraging, 400–401, 424
codebase, 251–252
codetype, 245
Coding/code
augmentation of, 252–253
avoiding line breaks in, 164
binary, 253, 305, 487
browser display of, 5, 7, 19
common errors in, 36–37
design before, 115
destructive, 77
"eye candy," 405
HTML-compliant vs.
noncompliant, 91–92

JavaScript, 376 (*See also* JavaScript)
legacy, 431
maintenance of, 401
for margins (white space), 158–159
pics-label and, 358
in pixels (*See* Pixels [px])
readability and, 100, 479 (*See also* Readability)
reuse of, 400–401
shorthand in, 119–120
source, 39
structure of, 31
symbols in, 129
syntax of, 21, 31, 113, 210, 383
of tables, 171, 176, 179, 188
"tricks" for, 163–164
type size used in, 110
col, 191, 197–198
ColdFusion, 23, 253
colgroup. *See* Column group (**colgroup**)
collapse, 226
Colon
in property:value pair, 113
vertical bar vs., 64
Color
background, 44–45 (*See also* Background color [**bgcolor**])
bits per pixel (BPP) and, 141, 144
of borders, 228–230
browsers and, 144, 477
dithering of, 49, 142
in good design, 49–50
hexadecimal codes for, 44–45, 180
JavaScript and, 389, 421–425
of links (*See* Link color)
in literature, 458
for printer-friendly pages, 236
standard names for, 44–45, 180, 447
style guidelines for, 475, 477
in tables, 177–178
of text boxes, 307
text-only documents and, 456
of text with background, 45–48, 49, 177–178
user preferences in, 421, 424
wireless devices and, 466
XML and, 447
color, 132, 219, 220
Color monitor, 7
Color scanners, 140
cols, 174, 272, 326
colspan, 188, 189, 365–366
Column group (**colgroup**), 191, 195–196, 198
Column spanning (**colspan**), 188, 189
Columns
in forms, 326–327
multiple, 363–365

proportional, 198, 199
in tables, 170–171, 174, 188–189, 195–199 (*See also* Cells)
".com," 11
Command-and-control communications, 499
Command-line browser, 501
Command-line ftp, 485–489
Commas, in table text alignment, 185
Comments, 30, 38–39, 115
in external style sheets, 209
JavaScript and, 378, 379
readability and, 479
in server-side includes, 77
user complaints as, 482
Commercial Web sites, images for, 146
Common gateway interface (CGI), 301, 336–339, 346–353. *See also* CGI scripts
Communications Decency Act, 501
Composer (HTML editor), 19
Compression
for audio files, 254, 256
for graphic files, 139
lossless, 139
lossy, 139, 256
for MPEG files, 256
streaming audio/video and, 263
CompuServe, 138
Computer-assisted instruction (CAI), 464
Computer code (**code**), 121, 128. *See also* Coding/code
avoiding line breaks in, 164
samp compared to, 124
var compared to, 124
Concatenation, 383, 396
Confirm dialog box, 393, 405
Conflict resolution systems, 449
Constraint mechanisms, 449
Containers, 12, 28. *See also* Tags
anchors and, 71
closing of, 13, 14
three parts to, 14
in well-formed documents, 438–439
in XML, 439
Content, 470, 475, 478
aural browsers and, 471
ethical/moral considerations concerning, 482
free speech and, 482
vs. information about page, 32
international languages and, 471–472
JavaScript to modify, 375
vs. layout, 2 (*See also* Browser layout)
metatags and, 357–358
offensive, 482, 483, 501
vs. pictures, 455

size in relation to, 480
in tables, 178
content, 356
author and, 362–363
keywords and, 362
refresh and, 359, 360, 362
Content-based styles, 122
content-language, 357
content-type, 357
continuous, 259
Control. *See* Input controls
Converters, 18, 20, 23, 470
Cookies, 375, 389, 426–433
deleting, 426
expiration date for, 430
navigator object and, 402
persistent, 426, 433
setting values for, 430–431
using, 432–433
".coop," 11
Coordinated universal time (UTC), 127
Coordinates. *See* X,Y coordinates
coords, 411, 412, 415
Copying. *See also* Downloading
ftp for, 10, 485 (*See also* File Transfer Protocol [ftp])
linking vs., 264
Copyrights, 261, 264, 482
Corel Corporation, 23, 24
Corporate documentation, 456, 459–461
Corporation for Research and Educational Computing (CERN), 500–501
Country name extensions, 11
Crackers, 492
Creative Voice files, 256
Credit, giving, 39, 264, 482
CrLf. *See* Carriage-return line feed (CrLf)
Crop marks, 234, 236
Cross marks, 234, 236
CRT monitor, 44
CSE validator, 21, 24
CSNET, 500
CSS. *See* Cascading style sheet (CSS)
".css," 208, 209
CSS1, 208
CSS2, 118, 208, 234, 366
CSS box model, 225–233
cue-after, 259, 260
cue-before, 259, 260
Curly braces, 112–113, 378, 379. *See also* French braces
Currency symbols, 128
Cursive typefaces, 111, 116
Cursor, focus and, 325
Custom bullets, 160–161
Custom design, 57
Custom programs
param for, 249–251
Web utilities for, 252

d

CuteFTP, 489–492
CuteMap, 411
Cybercrime, 492

DARPA. *See* Defense Advanced
 Research Projects Agency
 (DARPA)
DARPANET, 499, 500
Dashed borders, 228, 229, 230
Data
 analog, 253, 256, 262
 analyzing, 450
 aural, 468
 describing, 438, 441, 449–451
 digital, 253, 256, 262
 encrypted (*See* Encryption)
 formatting, 450 (*See also*
 Formatting)
 hidden, 177, 324
 human information within,
 449–450
 manipulation of, 385
 parsing, 299, 300, 443,
 444, 447
 presenting, 450, 451
 relationships among elements
 of, 449–450
 rows and columns of, 170–171
 (*See also* Tables)
 wireless, 467–468
data, 245, 251
Data entry, 349–354
 automatic refreshing and,
 360–361
 for search request, 350–351
Data transmission, multimedia
 and, 7
Database companies, 441
Database management program,
 links to, 253
Databases
 CGI for updating, 347–348
 forms and, 300
 genealogy, 441
 XML and, 441, 444, 450–452
Date
 European vs. U.S. format for,
 363, 389, 391
 expires and, 357
 JavaScript and, 386–388,
 389–391
Date last modified, 389–391,
 476, 478
Date object, 384, 385
datetime, 127
Davenport Group, 442
DbXML, 441
dd, 102
Debugging
 alert boxes and, 393
 CGI scripts for, 303

enctype and, 305
 readability and, 100
 reusing code and, 400, 424
Decimal points, in table text
 alignment, 185
declare, 247
Decryption, 492
Default message, 391
Default text, 326
Default value, 13, 14
 changing, 49
 in dialog boxes, 393
 for forms, 310, 312, 329
 JavaScript and, 377, 378
 of link colors, 48–49, 59, 61,
 224, 369, 476–477
 for shape, 415
 style sheets and, 208
Defense Advanced Research
 Projects Agency (DARPA),
 498, 499, 500
defer, 378
Definition (**dfn**), 122, 124, 128
Definition (in list of definitions)
 (**dd**), 102
Definition lists (**dl**), 100–103
 images in, 161
Definition terms (**dt**), 102
"deg," 214
Degrading, 479
Degrees (deg), 214
del, 126–127
Delete (**del**), 126–127
Deprecated attributes, **style** vs.,
 87–88
Deprecated list forms, 103–104
Deprecated tags, 13, 15, 31,
 132–133
 font-handling, 132–133
 strict DTD and, 31
Describing data, 438, 441,
 449–451
Describing images, 481–482
Describing people, 449
description, 362
Design, 35. *See also* Formatting;
 Layout; **style;** Style sheets
 to avoid maze, 56
 code augmentation in, 252
 color and, 49–50
 custom, 57
 document-level style sheets
 and, 115
 external style sheets and, 212
 of forms, 301–307, 310, 314
 hierarchical, 57, 60, 73, 307
 images and, 49–50
 indexed-sequential, 56–57, 58,
 62, 289
 links and, 55
 printer-friendly, 236
 professional, 50, 208
 pseudo-elements/classes and,
 367–369

rough drafts for, 201
 sequential, 56–57, 62, 468
 server-side includes and, 77
 sound and, 257
 storyboards for, 56–58,
 468, 469
 style manual for (*See* Style
 manual)
 of tables, 171, 179, 182
 tables in page, 201
 of Web site, 201
Desktop computers, ebooks
 for, 460
Destination (of link), 59
Development software, 23
dfn, 122, 124, 128
DHTML. *See* Dynamic HTML
 (DHTML)
Dialog boxes, 392–394, 424
 cookies and, 427–428, 432
 overusing, 405
 types of, 393
Dictionary, online, 459, 461
Digital data, 253
 in MIDI files, 256
 videos and, 262
Digital Decency Act, 357
digits, 259
dir. *See* Directory (**dir**)
Director program, 263
Directories
 case sensitivity and, 71
 images and, 145–146
 list items in, 88
 as lists, 103–104
 paths and, 62, 63–66
 sub-, 145
 in URL, 12
Directory (**dir**), 29, 31
 charoff and, 186
 as deprecated list form,
 103–104
 head and, 32
 metatags and, 356
 title and, 32
disabled, 325, 331
disappear, 404, 405
Distance learning, 464–465
Dithering, 49, 142
div. *See* Divide document (**div**)
Divide document (**div**), 128,
 215–218
 centering images with, 154
 id and, 217
 JavaScript and, 382
dl, 100–103
DNS. *See* Domain Name Server
 (DNS)
DocBook model, 441–442,
 445–448
DoCoMo, 467
DOCTYPE, 28, 30, 31–32
 head and, 32
 version vs., 31

Document-level style sheets, 111–120, 133–134
aural, 257–258
vs. external style sheets, 208, 212
guidelines regarding, 480
vs. inline style, 34
list items and, 113
pseudo-elements and, 367
style and, 33
Document object, 384, 385, 389–391, 423
Document Style Semantics and Specification Language (DSSSL), 439, 442, 444
Document type definition (DTD), 22
DOCTYPE and, 30, 31–32
frameset, 271
in well-formed documents, 439
XML and, 439–442, 443, 444, 449, 451
Documentation
in code, 38 (*See also* Comments)
corporate/government, 456, 459–461
Documents
content vs. information about, 32 (*See also* **meta**)
dividing (*See* Divide document [**div**])
editing, 42
elements of, 28–42 (*See also* Elements)
embedded HTML, 246–247
filenames of, 12 (*See also* Filenames)
hyper (*See* Hyper documents)
JavaScript to enhance, 375
large, 68, 72, 217 (*See also* Online books)
large vs. small, 72
metatags in, 356 (*See also* Metatags)
moving around in or among, 56 (*See also* Navigation/moving)
pages vs., 2 (*See also* Pages)
saving, 42
text-only, 456–457
valid, 439, 443
well-formed, 438–439
Dogpile, 24
DOM, 444
Domain, 11–12
Domain name, 11
href and, 66
IP address vs., 66–67
Domain Name Server (DNS), 11, 66, 500
DOS operating system, uppercase vs. lowercase and, 308
DOS text, 16

Dotted borders, 228, 229, 230
Double borders, 228, 229, 230
Downloading, 8. *See also* "Wait time"
of audio plug-ins, 254, 263
defined, 485
ftp for (*See* File Transfer Protocol [ftp])
of images (*See* Image downloading)
of multimedia files, 242
problems in, 487
of sound files, 254, 261
standby while, 247
streaming audio/video and, 263
of video files, 261
of video plug-ins, 263
Drawing packages, 411, 416, 417
Drawings, 138
Dreamweaver HTML editor, 19, 21, 23
Driver function, 388, 398
Drop-down list box, 328–331
DSSSL. *See* Document Style Semantics and Specification Language (DSSSL)
dt, 102
DTD. *See* Document type definition (DTD)
Dublin Core, 356, 363
Dynamic HTML (DHTML), 353, 374, 409–435
cookies and, 426–433 (*See also* Cookies)
date object in, 389
for image maps, 410–417

e

Ebook emulators, 461
Ebook readers, 461
Ebooks. *See* Electronic books (ebooks)
Edit module, 127
Editing, 42
Editors
ASCII, 16, 42
HTML (*See* HTML editors)
image, 140, 411, 416
and Internet history, 501
JavaScript, 18, 21, 22
text, 16, 17, 426
Unix vi, 16
XML, 18, 22, 24
".edu," 11
Education, 456, 464–465
Electronic books (ebooks), 4, 456, 460–461. *See also* Online books
Electronic commerce (e-commerce), 441, 455
Electronic mail. *See* Email

Electronic Text Center. *See* University of Virginia's Electronic Text Center
Elements, 28–42, 128
blocked (block-level), 88–90, 126, 127
body, 34–35
container, 28
defined, 439, 440
Dublin Core, 356
empty, 28
floated, 234
head, 32
html, 29–32
inline, 88–90, 367 (*See also* Inline elements)
input (*See* Input controls)
picture, 43, 138
pseudo-, 366–369
relationships among, 449–450
separating, 43, 480
style guidelines regarding, 480
title, 32–33
in well-formed documents, 438–439
XML and, 438
elevation, 259
Ellipsis, 128
em (emphasized text), 122, 124, 128
"em" (measurement), 182, 214, 215
Email. *See also* mail program; mail utility; **mailto**
BITNET for, 500
for forms, 297, 299–300, 301
links to open, 75, 76
links to your, 478
mailto and, 75, 76
Submit button and, 321
USENET and, 499–500
Embedding
of blanks, 309
of codes (in word processing), 16
in forms, 301, 325
of HTML documents, 246–247, 301
of quotes, 126
of text and images within button, 325
Embossed media, 233
Emphasized text (**em**), 122, 124, 128
Employee manuals, 459
Empty elements, 28
Empty tags, 12, 28
common, 42–44
format of, 14
in HTML vs. XML, 43
in well-formed documents, 439
XML and, 13
en (language code), 29, 30

Encoding. *See also* Coding/code
  application/x-www-form-
    urlencoded, 305
  enctype for, 305
  multipart/form-data, 305
Encryption, 492
  forms and, 299, 300
  secure shell (ssh), 492,493, 494
enctype, 305, 313
Encyclopedia, online, 468–469
English language code, 29, 30
Entities, 129, 439, 440
Ethernet, 499
Ethics, 482
  pics-label and, 357
  for sound files, 261
Europe, 467, 472
European Organization for
  Nuclear Research
  (CERN), 501
"ex" (measurement), 214
Excite, 24
Exon amendment, 357, 501
expires, 357, 358, 362
Extended Wireless Markup
  Language (XWML), 466
Extensible HyperText Markup
  Language Mobile Profile
  (XHTMLMP), 466
Extensible HyperText Markup
  Language (XHTML), 15. *See
  also entries beginning*
  XHTML
  aural data and, 468
  DTD and, 444
  empty tags in, 43
  extension of, 466, 468
  external style sheets and,
    111, 208
  forms and, 336
  modules for (*See* XHTML
    modules)
  well-formed documents in, 439
  wireless devices and, 466
  XML and, 442–443
Extensible Markup Language
  (XML), 4–5, 13, 14, 437–453
  advantages of, 451–452
  aural data and, 468
  conversion of, 466, 467
  databases and, 441, 444,
    450–452 (*See also* DbXML)
  DocBook model of, 441–442,
    445–448
  DTDs and, 439–440, 441–442,
    449, 451
  empty tags in, 43
  external style sheets and,
    111, 208
  flexibility of, 22, 443, 452
  forms and, 307, 315, 317, 329
  future of, 449–450
  horizontal rule in, 43
  HTML compared against,
    450–452

HTML rendered from,
  443–448
human communication and,
  449–450
id vs. **name** in, 70
links and, 253
multimedia and, 252
PDF created from, 448–449
reason for, 440–441
shorthand coding and, 120
SVG images and, 139
symbols (entities) in, 129
tables and, 201
terminology in, 438–439
W³C specifications for, 15–16
well-formed documents in,
  438–439
wireless devices and, 466, 467
XHTML and, 442–443
Extensible-style language (XSL),
  438, 439
  style sheets for, 442
  wireless devices and, 466
  XML and, 447
Extensible Stylesheet Language
  Transformer (XSLT), 445
Extensions, 11
  for audio files, 254–256
  for backup copies, 42
  for HTML documents,
    16, 42, 64
  for images, 138–140
  for JavaScript, 377
  server-side includes and, 77
  for video, 262–263
External images, 142, 242
External style sheets, 111,
  208–215, 216, 237
  applying, 209–210
  aural, 258
  background-image and, 222
  body and, 480
  div and, 216
  head and, 479
  link and, 33
  pseudo-elements and, 367
  reason for, 208–209, 237
  span and, 218
  for text-to-HTML
    converters, 470
"Eye candy," 405

f

face, 132, 133
Facilitations, 449
Fantasy typeface, 111, 114, 116
far-left, 259
far-right, 259
Favorites, 33, 479
  frames and, 269, 291
  intrasystem targets and, 73
Feedback
  in ftp, 487

image maps and, 411
  mailto for, 10
fieldset, 334, 335
File menu options, 6, 42
File protocol, 10
File Transfer Protocol (ftp), 10,
  485–495
  anonymous, 487, 489, 499
  Archie and, 499
  binary vs. ASCII, 487, 488
  command-line, 485–489
  CuteFTP and, 489–492
  downloading with commands,
    487–489
  downloading with GUI,
    490–491
  downloading with secure, 494
  example of, 487
  graphical, 485, 489–491
  GUI-based, 489–492
  images and, 488
  and Internet history, 501
  list of commands for, 486
  secure, 492–495
  uploading with, 485, 491,
    494–495
Filenames, 12. *See also* Names
  case sensitivity and, 71, 495
    (*See also* Case sensitivity)
  extensions to (*See* Extensions)
  for images, 145–146, 161–162
  paths and, 63
  spaces in, 495
  uploading and bad, 495
Files
  copying (*See* Copying;
    Downloading)
  with forms, 312–313
  multimedia, 242, 261 (*See also*
    Multimedia)
  paths to (*See* Paths)
  reading, 10
Financial data, OFX model
  for, 441
Firewall, 66
Flash, 23, 263
float, 146, 150, 180–181, 418
  in boxes, 232
  clear and, 232
Floated elements, page breaks
  and, 234
Flood filling, 148–150
Focus, 325, 335
font, 132–133
font-family, 110, 116–117
font-size, 110, 117–118, 220
font-stretch, 119–120
font-style, 117, 118
font-variant, 119
font-weight, 118–119
Fonts, 110–111, 116–120
  bold (*See* Bold [**b**])
  changing, 116
  deprecated tags and, 132–133
  in ebooks, 461

in forms, 306–307
italic (*See* Italic (**i**))
monospaced, 111, 116, 456
normal, 117, 118
oblique, 117, 118
for printer-friendly pages, 236
for quotations, 125
serif vs. sans serif, 110, 111
size of, 110, 117–118,
   120–121, 132
style guidelines for, 480, 483
wider vs. narrower, 119–120
Footers, 75–76, 469
FOP. *See* Formatting Objects
   Processor (FOP)
for, 336
Foreground color (**fgcolor**), 389,
   421, 424–425
form, 299, 301–307
   input and, 307–308, 311, 325
   JavaScript and, 395, 421–422
Form module, 336
Formatting, 109–136. *See also*
   Design; Layout
   vs. analyzing, 450
   comments and, 115
   content-based styles in, 122
   description and, 362
   of different tags
      simultaneously, 114–115
   fonts and, 110–111, 116–120
   of frames, 271–275
   glyphs and, 110, 128
   guidelines for, 480
   of headings, 40 (*See also* **head**
      [**h1,h2,. . .**])
   inline styles in (*See* Inline
      elements; Inline style)
   of list items, 113
   logical styles in, 122–128
   physical styles in, 120–121, 122
   for readability, 100 (*See also*
      Readability)
   since HTML 4 specifications,
      133–134
   special characters and,
      128–130, 131
   style for, 34–35
   style sheets for, 208 (*See also*
      Style sheets)
   symbols in, 128–130, 131
   turning off, 130–132
Formatting Objects Processor
   (FOP), 448–449
Forms, 298–343
   attributes for, 301–307, 308
   browsers and, 299, 301, 307,
      319–321, 329
   button text/images on,
      324–325
   checkboxes on, 298, 308,
      313–315
   collection of options in,
      333–334
   default text for, 326

default values for, 310, 312, 329
designing/layout of, 301–307,
   310, 314
drop-down lists for, 328–331
email for, 297, 299–300, 301
encryption and, 299, 300
examples of simple, 298, 299,
   310, 314
files submitted with, 312–313
graphical buttons on, 322–325
hidden data on, 324
images as buttons in, 322–325
input (control) elements in
   (*See* Input controls)
input validation in, 307
intrinsic events in, 307, 325
JavaScript and, 389, 421–423
local action controls for,
   319–321
multiple selections on,
   328–334
optional text string in, 325–327
options in, 328–334
passwords for, 312
processing of, 297, 298–299,
   336–339
radio buttons on (*See* Radio
   buttons)
resetting data on, 319–320
scripts for, 301 (*See also* CGI
   scripts)
set of option elements for,
   328–331
submitting data on, 309–310,
   320–321 (*See also* Submit
   buttons)
Tab key and, 325
text-entry fields for, 309–312
text for buttons on, 324–325
validation of input on, 311
value checking in, 307
Forward button, 5, 56, 268–269
Forward slash, 63, 64
frame, 174–175, 178, 276–282
Frame rate, 262
frameborder, 281–282
Frames
   alternatives to, 289–291
   attributes for, 287–289
   base and, 285–287
   browsers and, 268–269,
      274, 283
   formatting of, 271–275
   within frames, 268
   inline, 287–289
   navigation in, 267, 268,
      269–271
   nesting of, 272–275
   noframes and, 268, 282–284
   readability of code for, 479
   refresh and, 359, 362
   resizing of, 280
   style guidelines for, 479, 480
   in tables, 172–173,
      174–175, 199

target and, 279, 283–284, 355
   in videos, 262, 263
   View Source in, 269, 270
   for Web pages, 267–296
   window-target and, 357
frameset, 269, 271–275, 286
   attributes for, 272
   body replaced by, 270, 271
Frameset DTD, 31
Franke, Norman, 254
Free speech, 482
Freeware, 18, 337, 346
French braces, 209, 210. *See also*
   Curly braces
Frequencies, 214, 259
FrontPage, 21, 23
Ftp. *See* File Transfer Protocol
   (ftp)
Function call, 379–380, 395
Functions
   defined, 376
   driver, 388, 398
   invoking, 379–380
   parameters for, 378, 380
   predefined, 385
   rollovers and, 405
   src and, 377
   user-created, 386

g

GEDML model, 441
Genealogy database, GEDML
   model for, 441
Generic class, 214–215
Get method, 299, 302–304, 339
".gif," 138
GIF. *See* Graphics Interchange
   Format (GIF)
GifCruncher, 144
Global variables, 423, 430
GlobalSCAPE Inc, 489
Glossary
   lists for, 100–103
   online, 459
Glyphs, 110, 128, 439
Gnutella, 261
Google, 24
Gopher, 10, 499
".gov," 11
Government documentation, 456,
   459–461
"grad" (measurement), 214
Graphical browsers, 5, 6, 7–8,
   48. *See also* Internet
   Explorer; Netscape
   Navigator; Opera
   background and text color in,
      48, 49
   background images and, 48
   changing standards and, 178
   links in, 59 (*See also* Link
      color)
   text-only mode of, 9

Graphical buttons, 322–325. *See also* Images, for submit buttons
Graphical user interface (GUI)
ftp and, 489–491
of Unix, 501
Graphics, 138. *See also* Charts; Images; Pictures; Tables
in ebooks, 461
tips regarding, 142–144
wireless devices and, 466
Graphics designer, 50
Graphics Interchange Format (GIF), 48, 138–139, 140, 142
animations with, 138, 478, 481
definition lists and, 161
Greater-than symbol, 128, 131
Greenwich Mean Time, 127
Groove borders, 228, 229, 230
groups, 174
GUI. *See* Graphical user interface (GUI)

h

h1, h2. . . *See* **head (h1, h2. . .)**
Handheld devices, 8, 233
ebooks for, 460
MPEG4 for, 262
text-only documents and, 456
videos for, 262
XHTML and, 15
Handicap-sensitive designs, 111
Hard copy. *See also* Paper documents
layout that considers, 470
replacing, 459, 460, 462
Hardware
for aural browsers, 471
elecronic books and, 460–461
and Internet history, 498
for multimedia files, 242
resolvers and, 467
site for obtaining reviews of new, 24
storage, 7, 242
XML and, 449
hash, 488
head (h1, h2. . .), 32, 39–40, 128
base and, 355
JavaScript and, 395, 403, 423
link and, 212
meta and, 356, 378
results of missing ending tag for, 37
rollovers and, 420
script and, 376
style and, 112
style guidelines for, 479
style sheet and, 111
tags used with, 33
title and, 32

with and without inline | styles, 35
XML and, 447
Head (of link), 59
Headers, 469
http, 356
meta and, 356
spanning columns, 188, 189
spanning rows, 188–189, 190
for tables, 186–193, 199
headers, 190, 191
Headings, 30, 32. *See also* **head (h1,h2. . .)**
anchors and, 71–72
CGI scripts and, 354
images in, 40
levels of, 39–40
purpose of, 40
side, 366, 367
style guidelines for, 480
titles vs., 33
XML and, 447
Headlines, 365–366
height, 148–150
with applets, 243
for boxes, 226
with frames, 287–289
with **object,** 246
style guidelines regarding, 481
with tables, 192–193
Help, online, 442, 456, 463–464
Hertz (Hz), 214
Hexadecimals, 44–45, 180
with **enctype,** 305
for special characters, 300
XML and, 447
hidden, 226, 228
Hidden data, 177, 324
Hidden/protected scripts, 378, 479
Hierarchical design, 57, 60
of forms, 307
intrasystem targets and, 73
high, 259
High-resolution screen, 176
higher, 259
Highlighting, in ebooks, 461
Home button, 5, 56
Home page, 12
defined, 8
downloading of, 476
image links to, 161–162, 163
image maps and, 417
links on, 63
links to, 73, 75
multimedia for, 253
paths and, 63
size of, 480
Honeywell, 498
Horizontal alignment, 146, 150–151
Horizontal margins, 158
Horizontal positioning, 223–224
Horizontal rule (**hr**), 43–44, 176
physical tags with, 122
shading of, 44

style guidelines for, 480
XML and, 447
Horizontal table layout, 187, 188, 189
Hosting, 16, 500
Hot List, 33
Hot spots. *See also* Image maps
area and, 413
shape of, 415
that won't activate, 416
Hot words, 59, 459
Hotbot, 25
HotDog, 23
HoTMetaL, 24
Housekeeping, **onunload** for, 398
hover, 368–369
Hovering, 368–369, 414–415
tool tip message and, 482
hr. *See* Horizontal rule (**hr**)
href. *See* Hypertext reference (**href**)
hreflang, 59
hsides, 174
hspace, 158, 159
".htm," 16, 42, 64
".html," 16, 42
HTML. *See* HyperText Markup Language (HTML)
html (or **HTML**) container, 29, 32
HTML editors, 16, 17–20, 42, 501
full-feature, 21
sites for downloading, 23
XML editors and, 22
HTML Help, 442, 463–464
HTML specifications, 14, 15, 34
empty tags in XML vs., 43
formatting since version 4, 133–134
metatags in 1.0 through 4.1, 356
older, 120
regarding frames, 268
regarding Java applets, 243
regarding **name** vs. **id,** 70
HTML validators
description of, 21
DTD and, 31
sites for downloading, 24
Http. *See* Hypertext transfer protocol (http)
http-equiv, 356–363
Human communication, XML and, 449–450
HumanMarkup TC, 449
HumanML, 449
Hyper documents
defined, 2
http and, 10
large vs. small, 72
links in, 2.4, 56 (*See also* Links)
vs. standard text, 4

HyperCard, 2, 56
Hyperlinks
  CERN and, 501
  in forms, 307
  in text-only documents, 456, 459
Hypertalk, 56
HyperText Markup Language (HTML). *See also entries beginning* HTML; Hyper documents
  attributes in, 13–14 (*See also* Attributes)
  audio and, 9 (*See also entries beginning* Audio)
  aural data and, 468 (*See also* Aural/audio browsers)
  browsers and, 5–9, 19 (*See also* Browser layout; Browsers)
  CGI scripts and, 354 (*See also* CGI scripts)
  changing paper-based system to, 469–472
  code augmentation of, 246–247, 252–253
  code format for, 14 (*See also* Coding/code)
  containers in, 12 (*See also* Containers)
  content and, 455 (*See also* Content)
  conversion to, 18, 20, 23, 470
  defined, 1, 2
  DocBook and, 442
  for documents/pages (*See* Documents; Pages)
  for embedding HTML document into another Web page, 246–247
  Extensible (*See* Extensible HyperText Markup Language [XHTML])
  external style sheets and, 208 (*See also* External style sheets)
  in forms, 301, 324 (*See also* Forms)
  in frames, 271 (*See also* Frames)
  JavaScript and, 375 (*See also* JavaScript)
  links and, 55 (*See also* Links)
  for manuals, 463
  meaning of, 2–5
  metatags and, 356 (*See also* Metatags)
  migrating from text to, 469–472
  multicolumn pages and, 363–365
  object to augment, 246–247
  programming languages vs., 56
  SGML and, 4, 31
  standards for, 14–16
  tags in, 12 (*See also* Tags)

  template for, 28–31
  terminology for, 12–14
  tools for, 16–22
  URLs and, 9–12 (*See also* Uniform Resource Locator [URL])
  for various devices, 455
  W³C and, 14–16 (*See also* World Wide Web Consortium [W³C])
  well-formed documents in, 438, 439
  wireless devices and, 466 (*See also* Wireless devices)
  XML and, 5, 13, 442–443
  XML compared against, 450–452
  XML rendered into, 443–448
  XSL and, 442
Hypertext module, 59
Hypertext reference (**href**), 61, 62, 66, 212
  base and, 355
  frames and, 283, 289
  image maps and, 413, 415, 416
  inserting objects with, 242–249
  intrapage source anchors and, 70–71
  mailto and, 75, 76
Hypertext transfer protocol (http), 10, 356–357
  and Internet history, 501
  wireless data and, 468
Hyphens, 177
  with **enctype**, 305
  lang and, 29
Hz. *See* Hertz (Hz)

I

i. *See* Italic (**i**)
IBM, 255, 499
ICANN. *See* Internet Corporation for Assigned Names and Numbers (ICANN)
Icons, 138
  alt as substitute for, 146
  auditory/audio, 257, 259, 471
  graphical button, 325
  in headings, 40
  place-holder, 148
  reusing images for, 143
  that change, 35
id, 74, 216
  div and, 217
  DTD and, 440
  forms and, 305, 336
  frames and, 279
  headers and, 190
  intrapage links and, 68–70
  JavaScript and, 423
  object and, 251
  span and, 219
  target and, 305

IF statement, 431
IF/ELSE statement, 381
IF/THEN/ELSE statement, 381
iframe, 287–289
Illustrations, 138, 458
Image downloading, 138, 140–141, 165
  reducing "wait time" for, 420
  in rollovers, 419
  style guidelines regarding, 476, 481
  thumbnails and, 476
Image editors, 140, 411, 416
Image links, 161–163
Image maps, 410–417
  client-side, 410, 411, 416
  parallel text-only page for, 417
  in rollovers, 418, 419
  server-side, 148, 410–411
  software for, 411, 416
  X,Y coordinates in, 324
Image module, 144
Image-reduction software, 144
Images, 137–167. *See also entries beginning* Graphic; **img;** Pictures
  applets as, 243–244 (*See also* Java applets [**applet**])
  background, 45–48, 477
  base and, 354–355
  BMP, 140
  borders for, 156–158
  browsers and, **5**
  as bullets, 160–161
  captions for, 236
  centering of, 151, 154–156
  colors in, 141, 142–144 (*See also* Color)
  for commercial sites, 146
  common problems with, 146
  deciding to use, 164–165
  in definition lists, 161
  and degrading of page, 479
  directories for, 145–146
  dithering of, 49
  downloading of (*See* Image downloading)
  enlarging small, 148
  expanding of, 148–159
  external, 142, 242
  flood filling of, 148–159
  formats for, 138–141
  GIF (*See* Graphics Interchange Format [GIF])
  in good design, 49–50
  in headings, 40
  on home page, 476
  inline, 146, 147
  input and, 322–324
  inserting, 242
  JavaScript and, 375, 389, 398, 403–405
  JPEG, 48, 139, 140, 142
  large, 142, 143, 247

links to, 142, 143, 144–146
    (*See also* Image links)
in list items, 88
long description of, 147
low-resolution, 163
manipulating, 375
margins of, 158–159
multimedia and, 138
object and, 245–249
PDF, 140
PNG, 48, 139, 140
preloading of, 143, 403,
    404, 420
progressive, 139
reducing size of, 144
reusing, 143
rollover, 143, 418, 420 (*See
    also* Rollovers)
sharing, 261
size of, 137, 140–141, 144
    (*See also* Bits per pixel
    (BPP); **height; width**)
standby and, 247
style guidelines for, 476, 477,
    479, 481
for submit buttons, 410 (*See
    also* Graphical buttons)
SVG, 139
thumbnail, 143, 148, 149, 476
TIFF, 140
tips regarding, 142–144
transparent areas on, 45 (*See
    also* Transparent GIF)
vector graphics for, 139
in video files, 261–263
img, 144–153, 242, 411
"in" (measurement), 214
Inches (in), 214
Indents, 479
Index, 61. *See also* Table of
    contents
    abbreviations and, 124
    acronyms and, 124
    for encyclopedia, 468
    http-equiv and, 356
    keywords and, 362
    metatags and, 356
    path names and, 63
index, 61
Indexed-sequential design,
    56–57, 58, 62
    with inline frames, 289
".info," 1
Information sharing, 499–500
inherit, 225, 226, 227, 228, 232
    for audio, 258, 259
    for paged media, 233, 234
Inheritance, 214
Inline elements, 88–90
    external style sheets
        and, 111
    frames as, 287–289
    styles vs., 366
Inline frames, 287–289
Inline images, 146, 147

Inline style, 34–35, 87–88, 113,
    120–130
    content-based, 122
    vs. external style sheets,
        208, 212
    forms and, 306–307
    guidelines regarding, 480
    logical, 122–128
    nesting, 120–121, 124
    physical, 120–121, 122
    span for, 218
    tables and, 179
input, 307–321
    data entry with, 349–354
    form and, 307–308, 311, 325
    graphical buttons and, 322–324
    images and, 322–324
    name for, 308–309
Input controls, 307–321
    fieldset for, 334
    focus and, 325
    graphical buttons
        and, 322–325
    grouping of, 334, 335
    order of access to, 325
    readability of code for, 479
    successful vs. unsuccessful,
        307–308
    types of, 309–310, 312–321
Input devices, text-only
    documents and, 456
Input validation, 307, 311
ins. *See* Insert (**ins**)
Insert (**ins**), 126–127
Insert object (**object**), 245–249
Inset borders, 228, 229, 230
Instance, 384
Institut National de Recherche en
    Informatique et en
    Automatique in Europe, 14
Instruction manuals, 456,
    462–463
Intel, 262
Intellectual property, 337,
    346, 358
Interactive images
    applets as, 243 (*See also* Java
        applets [**applet**])
    SVG, 139
Interactive pages, 298. *See also*
    Forms
International Conference on
    Computer
    Communications, 498
International considerations,
    471–472
    abbreviations and, 124
    in design, 111
    in Internet history, 500–501
    symbols and, 128–129
International name extensions, 11
International Networking
    Working Group
    (INWG), 498
International search, 499

International standards, 14–16, 29
    for audio, 254
    ISO/ITC, 442
International Standards
    Organization (ISO), 30, 31
    Latin-1 character set of,
        128–129
    MPEG of, 256
    name and, 70
Internet. *See also* World Wide
    Web
    backgrounds from, 48
    browsers to download from,
        22–23
    censorship on, 457, 498
    corporate documentation on,
        456, 459–461
    editors to download from,
        23, 24
    first use of term, 499
    government documentation on,
        456, 459–461
    history of, 497–501
    for information sharing,
        499–500
    instruction manuals on, 456,
        462–463
    literature on, 456, 457–459,
        460–461
    manuals on, 456, 459, 460,
        461–463
    streaming audio/video and, 263
Internet address, 5, 9, 11. *See
    also* Internet Protocol [IP]
    address; Uniform Resource
    Locator (URL)
Internet Corporation for
    Assigned Names and
    Numbers (ICANN), 11, 25
Internet Explorer, 5, 7, 8. *See
    also* Browser layout;
    Browsers
    description of, 8
    JScript and, 375
    plug-in for, 254
    site for downloading, 23
Internet organizations, 25
Internet Protocol (IP) address, 11
    domain name vs., 66–67, 500
    href and, 66
Internet protocols, 10, 498, 499
    http, 10, 356–357, 468, 501
    IP, 11, 66–67, 500
    mailto (*See* Mailto)
    TCP/IP, 492, 498, 499, 500
Internet Public Library, 472
Internet Service Provider (ISP),
    16, 17–18
Internet traffic, 48, 77, 212, 242
    ethics and, 482
    image maps and, 410, 411
    streaming and, 263
    Web percentage of, 501
Intersystem anchors, 66–68, 71
Intersystem links, 71

Intersystem URLs, examples
of, 67
Intonation, 260
Intranet, 110, 456
Intrapage links, 58, 62
case sensitivity and, 71
for encyclopedia, 468, 469
source, 70–71
in table of contents, 68, 478
target, 68–70, 217, 219
Intrapage source anchors, 70–71
Intrapage targets, 68–70
links back using, 73
URLs with, 71
Intrasystem links, 60, 62, 71, 72
links back using, 73
Intrasystem source anchors, 72
Intrasystem targets, 73–74
Intrinsic events, 34, 35
forms and, 307, 325
frames and, 272
JavaScript and, 388–389,
391, 404
rollovers and, 420
Intuit, 442
INWG. *See* International
Networking Working Group
(INWG)
IP. *See* Internet Protocol (IP)
addresses
isindex, 33, 349
ismap, 411
usemap vs., 411
ISO. *See* International Standards
Organization (ISO)
ISO/ITC standard, 442
ISP. *See* Internet Service Provider
(ISP)
Italic (**i**), 116, 117, 118, 120
cite and, 122, 125
dfn and, 124
em and, 124
inline elements and, 88,
120–121
vs. oblique, 117, 118
Iteration of statements, 383,
384, 403

j

Japan, 467, 472
Jargon File, The, 459, 468, 472
Java, 449
JavaScript and, 374, 375
XML and, 444
Java applets (**applet**), 243–244
in forms, 307
frames and, 272
JavaScript and, 375, 389, 398,
402
object and, 245–249
scripts vs., 375
Java-enabled browsers, 381–383

JavaScript, 373–408
basic structures in, 380–383
for blinking text, 405
color and, 389, 421–425
comments and, 115
cookies and (*See* Cookies)
date object in, 384, 385,
386–388
degrading and, 479
dialog boxes and, 392–394
Display Properties in, 389
document object in, 384, 385,
389–391, 423
for dynamic HTML, 405, 409
(*See also* Dynamic HTML
[DHTML])
for forms, 307, 308, 311,
321, 333
head and, 479
"Hello World" example of,
376, 378–379
image height and width
in, 148
intrinsic events and, 35,
388–389, 391, 404
for manuals, 463
misconceptions about,
374–375
navigator object in, 394, 395,
398–403
as object-oriented language,
383, 391, 423
objects in (*See* JavaScript
objects)
onload and **onunload** with, 272
param and, 250
for rollovers, 403–405, 420
(*See also* Rollovers)
script and, 33
scrolling and, 391, 395, 405
selection of code in, 381
sequence of statements in, 381
status bar and, 391–392, 395,
405
testing for, 381–383, 391
triggering functions in, 398
window object in, 384, 385,
391–398
JavaScript editors, 18, 21, 22
JavaScript objects, 383–403
date, 384, 385, 386–388
document, 384, 385,
389–391, 423
navigator, 394, 395, 398–403
window, 384, 385, 391–398
Johnson, S. C., 378
Joint Photographic Experts
Group (JPEG), 48, 139,
140, 142
".jpeg," 139
JPEG. *See* Joint Photographic
Experts Group (JPEG)
".jpg," 139
JScript, 375
Justifying, 115

k

Kahn, Bob, 498, 499
kbd, 121, 128
Keio University, 14
Kernighan, B. W., 378
Keyboard (**kbd**), 121, 128
Keyboards, text-only documents
and, 456
Keypads, 456
Keywords, 5, 7, 479
keywords, 362
"kHz." *See* Kilohertz (kHz)
Kilohertz (kHz), 214, 253
Kiosk, 358, 362

l

label, 334, 336
landscape, 234
lang. *See* Language (**lang**)
language, 378
Language (**lang**), 29–31
char and, 185
head and, 32
metatags and, **356**
for quotations, 126
title and, 32
Languages
audio files and, 259
codes for, 29–31, 357, 402
international, 86, 87, 471–472
JavaScript navigator object
and, 402
metatags and, 356, 357
programming (*See*
Programming languages)
quotes in different, 126
scripting, 33, 357
symbols in different, 129
system-level, 402
wireless devices and
markup, 466
LANs. *See* Local area networks
(LANs)
Laptops, 460, 466
Latin-1 character set, 128–129
Layout. *See also* Design;
Formatting
consistency of, 289, 291
content vs., 2 (*See also*
Browser layout)
importance of, 469
Leading, 220
LED monitor, 44
left, 150, 188, 195, 226, 230–232
for audio, 259
for paged media, 233, 234
left-side, 259
leftwards, 259
Legacy code, 431
legend, 334–335

Legislation, 459, 460
Length
of borders, 228, 230
of paged media, 234
Less-than symbol, 128, 131
letter-spacing, 220
level, 259
lhs, 174
li. *See* List item (**li**)
LibXML, 445
LIbXSLT/XSLTproc, 445
Ligatures, 29
Line art, 139
Line break (**br**), 43, 128
DTD and, 440
img and, 144, 146, 153–154
in plain-text list, 84
Line breaks, preventing, 164
line-height, 219, 220
Lines. *See also* Borders
long, 131
in tables, 173 (*See also* Rows, in tables)
link, 33, 48–49, 210, 212, 224, 476
href and, 61
JavaScript and, 389, 421
media and, 233
pseudo-classes and, 368, 369
Link color, 48–49, 59, 224, 369, 476–477
href and, 61
JavaScript and, 421
Link module, 212
Link rot, 66, 72
Linked style sheets, inline style vs., 34
Links, 55–80. *See also* Hyperlinks
anchors and, 59–63 (*See also* Anchor [**a**])
"broken," 21
"click here," 74
color of (*See* Link color)
copying vs., 264
to database management program, 253
defined, 2
for encyclopedia, 468, 469
ethics and, 482
frames and, 269–271, 283, 285, 286, 289, 291
graphical buttons and, 321–324
on home page, 63
to home page, 73, 75
as hot spots, 410 (*See also* Hot spots; Hot words)
http and, 10
image maps and, 416 (*See also* Image maps)
to images, 142, 143, 144–146 (*See also* Image links)
images as, 322–324
intersystem, 71

intrapage, 58, 62, 68–70, 217, 219
intrasystem, 60, 62, 71
intuitive (logical), 56
multimedia and, 253, 264
navigation, 352 (*See also* Navigation/moving)
one-way streets with, 72–74
to open email, 75, 76
page footers and, 75–76
pseudo-classes and, 368
refreshing and, 360, 361, 362
rollovers and, 403–405
to shopping-cart interface, 253
to sound files, 56, 261
storyboards and, 56–58
style guidelines for, 478, 481
testing, 21, 66, 67, 72, 476
thumbnail images as, 143
URLs and, 9
visited and active, 224
XML and, 253, 443, 444
List boxes, 298, 328–331
List item (**li**), 83–104
described, 88
formatting, 113
in ordered list, 83–88
style sheets and, 113
List module, 103
list-style-image, 161
list-style-type, 86–88, 89, 113, 161, 219
outside vs. inside for, 94–96
Lists, 81–108
blocked elements in, 88–90
bullets in, 92–94, 97, 113, 160–161
of definitions, 100–103
deprecated forms of, 103–104
HTML-compliant code for, 91–92
inline elements in, 88–90
in list items, 88
nesting, 97–99, 210
ordered, 82–88
page breaks and, 234–235
plain-text, 82, 83–84
pre and, 132
readability of, 100, 479
style sheets and, 113
sublists in, 96–99
tables vs., 169
tags for, 82
unordered, 82, 92–96
Literature, 456, 457–459, 460–461
LiveScript, 374
Llama books, 304
Loading, 35, 77
Local action controls, 319–321
Local area networks (LANs), 499, 500
Local variables, 430
Logical styles, 122–128, 438
emphasized text, 122, 123–124
nesting, 124

Login ID, 492, 493. *See also* User ID
Logos
files for, 146
in headings, 40
in page footer, 75
updating of, 146
longdesc, 147–148, 280–281
Loops
JavaScript and, 383, 384
refresh and, 359, 361
sequential code vs., 383, 385
Lossless compression, 139
Lossy compression, 139, 256
loud, 258, 260
low, 259
Low-resolution image (**lowsrc**), 163, 164
Low-resolution screen, 158, 176
lower, 259
lowsrc, 163, 164
LTR, 29
Lynx, 5, 476
description of, 8–9
site for downloading, 23
using, 481

Macintosh, 2, 56, 501
access key on, 335
AIFF files for, 256
path names on, 64
plug-ins for, 254, 262
Simple Text editor of, 16
Macromedia, 21, 23, 253, 263
Mail program, 10
Mail utility, 300
mailto, 10, 75, 76. *See also* Email
forms and, 301, 302, 305, 307
for your email address, 478
Maintaining state, 428
Maintenance
of code, 401
external style sheets for, 212
of pages, 476, 483
of tables, 191
Manuals, 456, 459, 460, 461–463
map, 413–414, 416
title and, 414
usemap and, 411–413
Mapedit, 411, 416
Mapthis, 411
margin, 158–159, 226, 227
margin-bottom, 226
margin-left, 226
margin-right, 226
margin-top, 226
marginheight, 280
Margins
for boxes, 225–227
for images, 158–159
justifying text at, 115

for printer-friendly pages, 236
for tables, 181, 182
marginwidth, 280
Markers (in lists), 92–93, 113
Massachusetts Institute of
    Technology (MIT), 14, 501
maxlength, 311, 325
MCI, 500
Measurement values, 214,
    225–227, 230, 231
Media, 233–236. *See also*
    Multimedia
media, 233, 257–258
Media Player plug-in, 262
Media players, 250, 262
Medical terminology, 258
medium, 259
Medium borders, 228, 230
menu, 103–104
Menus
    intrapage links in, 68
    list items in, 88
    as lists, 103–104
Messaging, 449
meta, 355–363
    profile and, 32
    style guidelines for, 479
    XML and, 447
Meta Data Workshop, 356
Metainformation module, 356
Metatags, 355–363
    Dublin Core and, 356, 363
    frames and, 357
    future of, 363
    http-equiv, 356–363
    importance of, 356
    JavaScript and, 377–378
    refresh, 358–363
Metcalfe, Robert, 499
method, 302–304
Methods
    of document object, 389
    of navigator object, 402
    vs. properties, 385, 386
Microphone, 7
Microsoft, 255, 442, 449. *See
    also* Windows
    FrontPage of, 21
    Help files of, 463
    JScript of, 375
    video by, 263
Microsoft Money, 441
Microsoft Office, 23
Microsoft Paint, 140
Microsoft Quicken, 441
Microsoft Word, 23, 449, 470
".mid," 256
middle, 152
".midi," 256
MIDI. *See* Musical Instrument
    Digital Interface (MIDI)
Millimeters (mm), 214
Milliseconds (ms), 214
MILNET, 500
MIME, 402

Misspelling, 318–319
MIT. *See* Massachusetts Institute
    of Technology (MIT)
mix, 259
"mm." *See* Millimeters (mm)
Mobile computing, 465–467. *See
    also* Wireless devices
Modal dialog box, 393, 424, 432
Modems, 49
    slow, 164
    streaming audio/video and, 263
Modules
    Human ML and, 449
    W³C and, 16
    wireless devices and, 466
    XHTML (*See* XHTML
        modules)
Momma, 25
Monaural sound, 254, 255, 256
Money (Microsoft), 441
Monitors/screens
    color on different, 49
    CRT vs. LED, 44
    devices other than
        traditional, 455
    high-resolution, 176
    low-resolution, 158, 176
    monochrome, 144
    small, 456
Monospaced font, 111, 116, 456
Moral considerations, 482
Mormons' genealogy
    database, 441
Mosaic, 115, 501
Moscow University's Sternberg
    Astronomical Institute, 24
Mouse
    hovering with, 368–369,
        414–415
    intrinsic events and, 35
    JavaScript and, 375 (*See also*
        Rollovers)
    and pseudo-classes of **link** and
        hover, 368–369
    SVG images and, 139
    X,Y coordinates of position of,
        323, 324
".mov," 262
Movies, 263
Moving. *See* Navigation/moving
Moving Picture Experts Group
    (MPEG), 256, 262, 463
Mozilla, 402
".mp2," 256
".mp3," 256, 257, 261
".mpeg," 262
MPEG. *See* Moving Picture
    Experts Group (MPEG)
MPEG3, 256, 261, 262
MPEG4, 262
".mpg," 262
"ms." *See* Milliseconds (ms)
Mu-law (m-law) files, 254, 255
Multicolumn pages, 363–365
Multiline text, 325–327

Multimedia, 7, 241–266
    animations for, 263 (*See also*
        Animations)
    aural style sheets and, 257–261
    for education, 464–465
    images and, 138 (*See also*
        Images)
    inserting objects in, 242–249
    links in, 264
    for manuals, 463
    Shockwave, 263
    sound for, 242, 253–261 (*See
        also* Audio files; Sound)
    streaming audio/video in,
        262, 263
    using, 242–252
    videos for, 261–263 (*See also*
        Video games; Videos)
    XML and XHTML
        recommendations for, 252
Multipart/form-data encoding,
    305, 313
multiple, 329, 330–331, 333
Multisensory tags, 482
Multithreading, 375
Multiword variable names, 309
".museum," 11
Music
    copyrighted, 261
    design and, 257
    MIDI files for, 256
    MPEG files for, 256
    streaming audio/video
        for, 263
Musical Instrument Digital
    Interface (MIDI), 256
Musicmatch plug-in, 254

n

name, 307–310, 326
    for checkboxes, 315
    common values for, 363
    frames and, 279, 289
    graphical buttons and, 323–324
    http-equiv and, 362
    image maps and, 413–414
    intrapage links and, 68–70
    JavaScript and, 384, 423
    metatags and, 356
    misspelling for, 318–319
    option and, 332
    param and, 250–251
    for radio buttons, 316
    rollovers and, 419
    for submit control, 321
".name," 11
Name extensions. *See* Extensions
Name-value pair, 308–309, 321
Names. *See also* Filenames;
    Variable names
    http-equiv, 356–357
    meaningful, 308
    reserve, 285–287

National Center for Super-Computing Applications (NCSA), 501
National Science Foundation, 500
Navigation/moving
  browser buttons for, 5, 6, 56
  CGI scripts and, 352
  frames and, 267, 268, 269–271, 289, 291
  ftp commands for, 486
  importance of, 469
  intrapage targets for, 68–70
  links for, 56, 469
  storyboards and, 56–58
  style guidelines for, 475, 478
  TOC for, 480–481 (*See also* Table of contents [TOC])
Navigator. *See* Netscape Navigator
Navigator object, 384, 385, 398–403
NCP. *See* Network control protocol (NCP)
NCSA. *See* National Center for Super-Computing Applications (NCSA)
Neisius, Bill, 254
Nesting
  of frames, 272–275
  of inline style containers, 120–121, 124
  of lists, 97–99, 210
  of objects, 247–249
  of quotes, 126
  in well-formed documents, 439
".net," 11
NetHelp SDK, 463–464
Netscape Communications Corporation, 8, 374, 463
Netscape Communicator software package, 19, 463
Netscape Navigator, 5, 7. *See also* Browser layout; Browsers
  description of, 8
  JavaScript and, 374
  plug-in for, 254
  site for downloading, 22
Netscape's Composer, 19
Network control protocol (NCP), 498, 500
Networking, 375, 499
New Hacker's Dictionary, The, 459, 472
Newline, 326, 479
News protocol, 10, 499
Newsgroups, 10
next, 61
Nippon Telephone and Telegraph, 467
No line break (**nobr**), 164
nobr, 164
noframes, 268, 282–284, 286
nohref, image maps and, 415, 416
Non-type-valid, 439, 443

Noncompliant browsers, 91–92, 283, 286, 287
none, 174, 228, 232
  for audio, 258, 259
  for paged media, 234
Nongraphical browsers. *See* Text-only/nongraphical browsers
Nonstandard character sets, 357
noresize, 280
normal, for **speak,** 258
Normal font, 117, 118
Norskog, Lance, 254
Northern Light, 25
noshade, 44
Note taking, in ebooks, 461
Notepad editor, 16, 17, 426
NoteTab, 23
nowrap, 193, 227–228
NSFNET, 500, 501
Null argument/action, 398, 421
Null value, 329
Number, 234, 259

O

OASIS. *See* Organization for the Advancement of Structured Information Standards (OASIS)
object, 245–249, 398
  applet vs., 245
  to augment HTML code, 252–253
  for embedding HTML documents, 246–247
  img vs., 245, 416
  param and, 249–252
Object models, 449
Object module, 252
Object-oriented language, 375, 383, 391, 419, 423
Objects
  "advanced," 398
  inserting multimedia, 242–249
  in JavaScript (*See* JavaScript objects)
  nesting of, 247–249
  run-time parameters for, 249–251
  tables as, 180
Oblique font, 117, 118
Obsolete tags, 13, 15
OCLC/NCSA Meta Data Workshop Report, 356
OCR. *See* Optical character recognition (OCR)
Octothorp (**#**), 37, 70, 129
OFX model, 441
ol. *See* Ordered lists (**ol**)
Older browsers, 115, 180, 210, 268
  background color in, 421, 424
  image maps and, 411, 414
  JavaScript and, 379, 380
  rollovers and, 420

onblur, 388
once, 259
onchange, 388
onclick, 35, 307, 388, 424
ondblclick, 307, 388
onfocus, 388
onkeydown, 307, 388
onkeypress, 307, 388
onkeyup, 307, 388
Online banking, OFX model for, 441
Online books, 2, 4, 10, 456, 457. *See also* Electronic books (ebooks)
  design for, 56–57
  Web sites for, 472
Online dictionary, 459, 461
Online education/training, 456, 464–465
Online encyclopedia, 468–469
Online glossary, 459
Online help, 456, 463–464
Online negotiations, 449
onload, 35, 272, 388–389
  cookies and, 432
  purpose of, 398
onmousedown, 307, 388
onmousemove, 307, 388
onmouseout, 307, 375, 388, 418
  reliability of, 405
  status bar and, 391
onmouseover, 35, 307, 375, 388, 418, 419
  reliability of, 405
  status bar and, 391, 392
onmouseup, 307, 388
onreset, 307, 388
onselect, 388
onsubmit, 307, 388
onunload, 272, 388
  purpose of, 398
Open-source publishing system, 442
Open standard, 139, 466
OpenNIC, 11, 25
Opera, 5, 7, 8. *See also* Browser layout; Browsers
  description of, 8
  downloading of images in, 165
  site for downloading, 22–23
Operating systems, 308–309
  CGI scripts and, 302, 339
  ftp and, 485
optgroup, 333–334
Optical character recognition (OCR), 470
Optical scanning, 470
option, 329–331, 332–333
Option buttons, 298
Oracle, 441, 450
Ordered lists (**ol**), 82–88
  nesting, 97–99
  options for, 86–87
  style sheets and, 113
  unordered lists within, 96–99
".org," 11

Organization for the Advancement of Structured Information Standards (OASIS), 441, 442, 449
Orientation, 236, 259, 261
orphan, 234
Orphans, 234, 235–236
Output (**samp**), 122, 124, 128
Outset borders, 228, 229, 230

p

p. *See* Paragraph (**p**)
Packet switching, 497–498
Packets, 499, 500
Padding
  around cells, 173, 181, 192 (*See also* **cellpadding**)
  for boxes, 225, 228, 230–232
padding, 230–232
padding-bottom, 231
padding-left, 231
padding-right, 231
padding-top, 231
page, 234, 235
page-break-after, 234
page-break-before, 233–234
page-break-inside, 234–235
Page breaks, for printer-friendly pages, 236
Page footers, 75–76, 77
Page viewer, 23
Paged media, 233–236
Pages. *See also* Web pages
  browser display of, 5, 7 (*See also* Browser layout)
  collection of, 206, 208 (*See also* Web sites)
  content of (*See* Content)
  degrading of, 479
  description of, 33 (*See also* **title**)
  design of (*See* Design)
  documenting, 38 (*See also* Comments)
  documents vs., 2 (*See also* Documents)
  elements of, 28–42, 128 (*See also* Elements)
  home (*See* Home page)
  interactive, 297 (*See also* Forms)
  layout of (*See* Layout)
  loading and unloading, 35
  "look and feel" of, 469, 481
  maintenance of, 476, 483
  modifying, 39
  moving around in, 56–58 (*See also* Navigation/moving)
  multicolumn, 363–365
  orientation of, 236
  refreshing of, 358–363
  series of, 358–359
  size of, 142, 236, 476, 480

status of, 481
storyboards for, 56–58, 468, 469
style manual for (*See* Style manual)
testing, 161
Paint programs, 140, 411, 416, 417
Paint Shop Pro, 140, 411
Palm device, 461
Paper documents, 469. *See also* Hard copy
Paragraph (**p**), 13, 14, 40–42
  centering of, 155–156
  pre and, 131
  tag-level classes and, 214, 215
  in XHTML Edit module, 128
Paragraphs, in lists, 91–92
param, 249–252
Parameters, 378, 380
  run-time, 249–251
_parent, 283, 286
Parsing, 299, 300, 443, 444, 447
Passwords
  dialog boxes and, 393
  for forms, 312
  ftp and, 487, 489, 492
  saving, 493
  telenet and, 10
Paths, 12, 62, 63–66
  absolute, 63–64, 65–66
  for images, 145–146, 161–162
  relative, 64–66
pause, 260–261
pause-after, 259
pause-before, 259
"pc" (measurement), 214
PCs
  AVI for, 263
  and Internet history, 501
  plug-ins for, 254
  QuickTime for, 262
  streaming video for, 466
PDAs. *See* Personal digital assistants (PDAs)
".pdf," 140
PDF. *See* Portable Data Format (PDF)
Percentage measurements, 225, 226
  asterisk in, 272
  for audio, 259
  with frames, 272
  inheritance and, 214
  vs. pixels, 44, 176, 191, 192, 198, 215, 272
  vs. words, 223
Periods
  for classes, 213
  in table text alignment, 185
Perl, CGI scripts and, 302, 303, 304, 337, 346
Permission, 48, 261, 264
Persistent cookies, 426, 433
Personal digital assistants (PDAs), 438, 440, 466

Photographic images, 138
Photoshop, 140, 411
Physical styles, 120–121, 122
Picas (pc), 214
pics-label, 357
Picture element, 43, 138
Pictures, 137. *See also* Drawings; Graphics; Illustrations; Images
  links and, 56
  two-dimensional, 138
pitch, 259
pitch-range, 259
Pixels (px), 43, 148, 192
  asterisk and, 272
  in borders, 156, 157, 173, 174, 178–179
  with frames, 272
  in lossless vs. lossy compression, 139
  in margins, 158, 159
  vs. percentage measure, 44, 176, 191, 192, 198, 272
  for table margins, 182
  vs. vector graphics, 139
  for width of table, 176, 191–192
  X,Y coordinates and, 324
Plain GIF, 138
Plain text, 130, 456–457
Plain-text lists, 82, 83–84
plaintext, 130
Platform for Internet Content Selection, 357
Platforms
  CGI scripts and, 302, 339
  color and, 477
  and Internet history, 498
  JavaScript navigator object and, 398, 401, 402
  pics-label and, 357
  "portable across," 5
  wireless devices and, 466, 467–468
  XML and, 438, 449, 452, 467
play-during, 259
Plug-ins, 5, 23, 140
  for audio, 253, 254, 257
  code augmentation and, 252
  JavaScript and, 398, 402
  for multimedia, 242, 247, 263
  param and, 250
  for video, 262, 263
Plus sign, 300, 305, 383
".png," 139
PNG. *See* Portable Network Graphics (PNG)
Pointer. *See also* Mouse
  change in, 61 (*See also* Rollovers)
  hovering with, 368–369, 414–415, 482
  image maps and, 411, 413
Points (pt), 110, 117, 118
  values instead of, 132

Policy manuals, 459
poly, 415
Polygons, 415
"Portable across platforms," 5
Portable Data Format (PDF),
    140, 442, 448–449
    aural data and, 468
    ebooks for, 460, 461
    streaming video for, 466
    text-only documents and, 456
Portable Network Graphics
    (PNG), 48, 139, 140
portrait, 234
Post method, 299, 302–303
    CGI scripts and, 339
    for multipart/form-data
        encoding, 305
PostScript, 442, 470
PowerPoint, 449
pre. *See* Preformatted text (**pre**)
Preformatted text (**pre**),
    130–132
    boxes and, 227–228
    plaintext vs., 130
    tables and, 169
    var and, 124
    in XHTML Edit module, **128**
Preloading, 143
Presentation module, 122
previous, 61
Print media, 233
Printer-friendly pages, 236,
    469, 481
Printing, 469. *See also* Paged
    media
    from browser, 5
    paged media for, 233–236
    as test, 481
Privacy, 358. *See also*
    Encryption
".pro," 11
Procedure manuals, 459
Processor
    for converting XML to HTML,
        445–448
    streaming video and, 466
Professional design, 50, 208
profile, 32
Programming languages
    basic structures in, 380
    CGI scripts and, 337–338, 346
    Hypertalk, 56
    JavaScript and, 374, 378
    scripting languages and, 374
    XML (*See* Extensible Markup
        Language [XML])
Progressive image, 139
Project Gutenberg, 472
Projection media, 233
Prompt dialog box, 393, 405,
    427–428
Proofreading, 483
Properties, 385–386, 402
Property-value pairs, 86–87,
    88, 112

for inline formatting, 208
in tables, 177
Proportional spacing,
    110–111, 215
Proportional width, 198, 199
Proposed recommendation (to
    W³C), 14, 15
Protocols. *See* Internet protocols
Proxy servers, 467–468
Pseudo-classes, 366–369
Pseudo-elements, 366–369
Psychotherapy, 449
"pt." *See* Points (pt)
Public domain, 48, 261, 264,
    337, 346
Publishing
    defined, 485
    online vs. paper, 460
    tools for, 442
Pull technology, 358
Punctuation, 259, 471
Push technologies, 358, 360
"px." *See* Pixels (px)

q

q, 125, 126
".qt," 262
QTfW. *See* QuickTime for
    Windows (QTfW)
Query databases, 444
Quicken, 441
QuickTime for Windows
    (QTfW), 262
QuickTime plug-in, 262
Quotation marks
    forgetting, 37
    href and, 61
    for image files, 145–146
    lang and, 29
    for pixels, 148
    refresh and, 359, 360, 362
    single vs. double, 126
    in well-formed documents, 439
Quotations
    inline styles for, 125–126
    short vs. long, 126
Quote (**q**), 125, 126

r

"rad," 214
Radians (rad), 214
Radio broadcasts, 263
Radio buttons, 298–299, 308,
    315–319
    for changing background color,
        421, 424
    vs. checkboxes, 313
    with checkboxes, 314
    preselecting, 317
    to reduce chance of errors, 312

RAND Corporation, 497
Random numbers, 305
Ratings scale, 357
RDF Schema, 449
Readability, 479
    background and, 45–48, 49, 477
    of code, 479
    curly braces and, 112
    of lists, 100, 479
    of tables, 188, 191, 479
RealAudio, 263
RealPlayer plug-in, 254
Recommendations (to W³C),
    14, 15
rect, 415
rectangle, 415
Red, green, and blue
    (RGB) numbers, 44–45, 132
ref, 251
Reference books, 468
Reference manuals, 456, 459,
    460, 461–463
References, 125. *See also*
    Bibliography
refresh, 358–363
Refresh button, 5, 42
rel, 61, 212
Relative paths, 64–66,
    354–355
    refreshing and, 362
    style guidelines regarding, 481
Relative values (measurements),
    214, 215
Reload button, 5, 42
Reloading
    expires and, 357
    refresh and, 358, 359
repeat, 259
Repository systems, 449
Reserve names, 285–287
Reset button, 319–320
Resolution, 158, 163, 176
Resolvers, 467
Resource Interchange File
    Format Waveform (RIFF
    WAVE), 255, 256
Reusing, of images, 143
rev, 61–62
RGB. *See* Red, green, and blue
    (RGB) numbers
RGB numbers, common errors
    involving, 37
rhs, 174
Rich Text Format (RTF),
    442, 470
richness, 259
Ridge borders, 228, 229, 230
RIFF WAVE. *See* Resource
    Interchange File Format
    Waveform (RIFF WAVE)
right, 150–151, 188, 195, 226,
    230–232
    for audio, 259
    for paged media, 233, 234
rightwards, 259

Rollovers, 35, 143, 375
    examples of, 403–405,
        417–419
    professional, 420
    target audience and, 253
row, 191
rowgroup, 191
Rows
    in forms, 326–327
    in tables, 170–171 (*See also*
        Cells; Table row [**tr**])
rows, 174, 272, 326
rowspan, 188–189, 190, 192
RTF. *See* Rich Text Format
    (RTF)
RTL, 29
Rules, 172, 173–175. *See also*
    Horizontal rule (**hr**)
rules, 173–175
Run-time parameters, 249. *See
    also* **param**

S

s. *See* Strikethrough (**s** or **strike**)
"s" (measurement), 214
samp (output), 122, 124, 128
Sans serif typeface, 110, 111, 117
Satellites, 499
Saving, 42, 48
SAXON, 444
Scalar Vector Graphic (SVG), 139
Scanners, 140
Schemas, 449
scheme, 356, 363
Schwartz, Randal L., 304
scope, 191
Screens. *See* Monitors/screens
script, 376, 377–378, 379–380
ScriptBuilder, 21
Scripting languages, 33
    content-type and, 357
    programming languages and, 374
Scripts, 374
    applets vs., 375
    CGI (*See* CGI scripts)
    defined, 337, 346
    for forms, 297, 301 (*See also*
        CGI scripts)
    frames and, 272
    graphical buttons and, 323
    protecting/hiding, 378, 379
Scrolling
    background image and
        slower, 49
    of big tables, 199–201
    of embedded objects, 246
    frames and, 270, 279–280
    JavaScript and, 391, 395, 405
    line breaks and, 164
    links to avoid, 57, 68
    of long lines, 131
    status bar and, 391
    warning about, 391–392

Search engines, 479, 499
    description and, 362
    http-equiv and, 356
    images and, 164
    international, 499
    metatags and, 356
    refreshing and, 359
Search request page, 350–351, 353
Search script, 349, 352
    miss page and, 352–353
    success page and, 351–352
Search sites, 5, 7, 124
    lang and, 29
    list of, 24–25
    profile and, 32
    titles and, 33
Searchable documents, 349,
    354, 444
Searching, **isindex** and, 33
Second cascading style sheet
    (CSS2), 118, 208, 234, 366
Seconds (s), 214
Secure ftp, 492–495
Secure shell (ssh), 492, 493, 494
Secure telenet, 492
Security. *See also* Encryption;
    Passwords
    with ftp, 492–495
    JavaScript and, 374
    searchable documents and, 349
select, 328–334
selected, 330, 333
_self, 286
Semicolon, 129, 130
    with property:value pairs, 113
    refresh and, 359, 362
Separating elements, 43. *See also*
    Headings; Horizontal rule
    (**hr**); Line break (**br**)
Sequence, 381, 383, 385
Sequential design, 56–57, 62, 468
    indexed, 56–57, 58, 62, 289
    one-way streets with, 72–73
Serif typeface, 110, 111, 117
Server-side image maps, 148,
    410–411
Server-side includes, 77
Servers
    CGI scripts and, 302
    forms and, **307,** 324, 336–339
    ftp and, 487, 492
    hidden data and, 324
    JavaScript and, 374
    path names and, 63
    proxy, 467–468
    searchable documents and, 349
    URLs and, 354–355
SGML. *See* Standard
    Generalized Markup
    Language (SGML)
SGML/XML vocabulary, 441
shape, 415
Shareware, 18
    CuteFTP as, 489
    sites for, 24

Shell script, 337
Shockwave, 263
Shortcuts, 158, 179
    for borders, 229, 230
    codebase, 251–252
    for margins, 227
    padding, 230–231
".shtml," 77
Sidebars, 366, 367
silent, 258, 260
Silicon Graphics, 256
Simple Text editor, 16
Site manager, 21
size
    font and, 132–133
    horizontal rule and, 43
    paged media and, 234, 235
    select and, 330
    of text-entry field, 310–311
small, 121
".snd," 257
soft, 258, 260
Softkey, 456
SoftQuad, 24
Software
    audio processing and
        editing, 257
    blocking, 482
    ebooks for, 460
    for ftp, 485 (*See also* File
        Transfer Protocol [ftp])
    Help packages for, 442,
        463–464
    for image maps, 411, 416
    image-reduction, 144
    resolvers and, 467
    for server-side image maps, 410
    site for obtaining reviews of
        new, 24
    sites for downloading, 22–24
    for testing links, 66
    utility, 252, 253, 263
    W3C and, 15
    XML and, 449
Solid borders, 228, 229, 230
Sound, 242, 253–261. *See also*
    Audio files; Aural/audio
    browsers
    choosing format for, 257
    copyrighted, 261
    design and, 257
    ethics involving, 261
    library of, 254
    links and, 56, 261
    monaural, 254, 255, 256
    object and, 245–249
    orientation of, 259, 261
    plug-ins for, 5
    quality of, 253, 255, 256
    single- vs. multiple-channel, 254
    standby and, 247
    stereo, 253, 255, 256
    types of files for, 253–257
    in video files, 256, 261, 262
Sound Blaster audio cards, 256

Sound card, 7, 242
  aural style sheets and, 257
  WAVE table on, 256
SoundApp, 254
Source anchors, 59–62, 69
  intersystem, 66–68
  intrapage, 70–71
  intrasystem, 72
Source code, comments and, 39
Source (**src**), 144–146
  forms and, 308
  frames and, 277
  JavaScript and, 377
  rollovers and, 418–419, 420
SOX, 254
Spaces, 2
  in boxes, 226, 227
  in filenames, 495
  in frames, 280
  lang and, 29
  proportional, 110–111, 215
  for readability, 100
  style guidelines for, 480
  in variable names, 309
Spam, 359
span, 195, 196, 218–219
  col and, 197, 198
  in XHTML Edit module, 128
speak, 258, 259
speak-header, 259
speak-numeral, 259
speak-punctuation, 259
speak-rate, 260
Speakers, 242, 257
Special characters, 128–130, 131,
  300, 309
  content-type and, 357
  meta and, 479
  XML and, 439
Special targets, 285–287
Speech synthesizers, 9,
  123–124, 257
  aural style sheets and, 257, 258
  headers for, 190
  image links and, 161
  lang and, 29
Spell checkers, 124, 483
spell-out, 258, 259
Spiders, 356
src. *See* Source (**src**)
Ssh. *See* Secure shell (ssh)
Stacks, 56
Standard Generalized Markup
  Language (SGML). *See also*
  DOCTYPE
  HTML and, 4, 31, 439, 442, 444
  standards for, 441
  XML and, 439, 442, 444, 449
Standardization, of designs, 111
Standards
  changing, 178–181
  for HTML, 14–16
  ISO/ITC, 442
  open, 139, 466

SGML, 441
  for tables, 178–181
  for wireless devices, 466–467
  for XHTML, 15–16
  XML, 441
standby, 247
Stanford Research Institute, 498
StarOffice, 20, 23, 140, 470
start, 62, 84, 85
Start (of link), 59
Starting/beginning tag, 14, 28
StarWriter, 20
Statements
  iteration of, 383, 384, 403
  sequence of, 381
Static Web page, 55
Statistical operations, **onunload**
  for, 398
Status bar, 391–392, 395, 405
Status of page, 481
Stereo sound, 253, 255, 256
Storage hardware, 7, 242
Store-and-forward concept,
  499–500
Storyboards, 56–58, 468, 469
Streaming audio/video, 262,
  263, 466
stress, 260
Strict DTD, 31
strike, 121
Strikethrough (**s** or **strike**), 121
Striking through, **del** and, 127
Strings. *See* Character-string
  variable; Text strings
strong, 122, 123–124, 128
Strongly emphasized text
  (**strong**), 122, 123–124, 128
Structure module, 36
style, 33, 34–35, 111–113,
  208, 418
  align vs., 150
  background color and, 421
  basefont and, 132
  in boxes, 228–230
  common properties of,
  219–221
  div and, 217
  DTD and, 440
  font and, 132
  for forms, 306–307, 309,
  310, 336
  guidelines for, 480
  headings and, 40
  images and, 156–158
  for list bullets, 93–94
  list items and, 113
  in lists, 84, 85, 86–90, 97–99
  nowrap vs., 193
  paged media and, 233
  style sheet and, 111, 208
  in tables, 177–181, 191–193,
  196
  tag-level classes and, 215
  type and, 113

Style Attribute module, 208
Style manual, 475–484
  regarding animation, 476, 477
  regarding applets, 476
  regarding background, 475
  regarding **body,** 480–482
  regarding browsers, 476,
  477–478, 479
  regarding color, 475, 476–477
  regarding consistency, 475
  regarding content, 475,
  478, 480
  regarding degrading, 479
  regarding "eye candy," 476
  regarding fonts, 483
  regarding **head,** 479
  regarding images, 475, 476,
  477, 479, 481
  regarding language/writing,
  482–483
  regarding links, 478, 481
  regarding maintenance,
  476, 483
  regarding navigation, 475, 478,
  480–481
  regarding readability, 479
  regarding size, 476, 480
  regarding updating, 476,
  478, 481
  regarding URLs, 481
  regarding Web sites for
  guidelines, 484
Style properties, 219–224
Style sheets, 111, 207–240
  aural, 164, 257–261
  cascading (*See* Cascading style
  sheet [CSS])
  checking, 237
  content-type and, 357
  dividing and, 215–219
  document-level (*See*
  Document-level style sheets)
  external (*See* External style
  sheets)
  headers and, 190
  headings and, 40
  headlines and, 365
  inline style and, 34–35, 120,
  208 (*See also* Inline style)
  lacking, for text
  converters, 470
  orphans and, 236
  precedence among, 208 (*See*
  also Cascading style sheet
  [CSS])
  for printer-friendly Web
  pages, 236
  pseudo-elements and, 367
  second set of specifications for,
  366 (*See also* CSS2)
  spanning and, 215–219
  style and, 88, 179
  tables and, 179
  widows and, 236

wireless devices and, 466
XML and, 443, 444, 447, 449
XSL, 442
Styles, 207–240
  of box definitions, 224–233
  classes of, 212–215
  common properties of, 219–221
  conflicting, 208, 230
  headlines and, 366
  human, 449
  inherited, 214
  of link colors, 224
  logical (*See* Logical styles)
  media types and, 233
  precedence for, 208, 230, 232
    (*See also* Cascading style
    sheet [CSS])
  shortcuts for (*See* Shortcuts)
Stylus, 456
Subdirectories, for images, 145
Submit buttons, 298, 301, 320–324
  get vs. post method and, 303–304
  graphical, 322–324
  multiple ones, 321, 322
  server-side image maps
    and, 410
Subscripted variables, 403–405
Subscripts (**sub**), 121, 219
summary, 178
Sun Microsystems, 23, 257, 374, 500
Sun/NeXT, 257
sup, 121
Superscripts (**sup**), 121, 219
SVG. *See* Scalar Vector Graphic
  (SVG)
Switches, 44, 486
Symbols, 128–130, 131, 479
Syntax, 383
  DTD and, 31
  for list items, 113
  style sheets and, 210
  validating, 21
Synthesizer, 256. *See also*
  Speech synthesizers
System-level language code, 402
System/Web administrator, 16
  client-side image maps and, 411
  path names and, 63
  security concerns and, 349, 492
  server-side image maps
    and, 410
  server-side includes and, 77

t

T1 lines, 500
Tab key, 325
tabindex, 59, 325

table, 171–182
  frame and, 174–175, 178
  width and, 176–177
Table body (**tbody**), 199, 200, 201
Table data (**td**), 186–193
  align and, 187–188
  nowrap and, 193
  precedence of attributes
    with, 187
Table footer (**tfoot**), 199, 200–201
Table header (**th**), 186–193
  align and, 187–188
  audio and, 259
  colspan and, 188
  precedence of attributes
    with, 187
  rowspan and, 188–190
Table header (**thead**), 199, 200
table-layout, 177
Table module, 201
Table of contents (TOC), 480–481
  for encyclopedia, 468
  frame as, 268, 279, 283, 285
  index as, 61
  intrapage links in, 68, 478
  XML and, 447
Table row (**tr**), 183, 184–186
Tables, 169–205
  background color of, 177–178
  borders for, 171, 172–175, 177–182
  captions for, 171, 193–195
  cells in, 170–171 (*see also*
    Cells)
  changing standards and, 178–181
  columns in, 170–171, 174, 188–189, 195–199
  for creating multicolumn
    pages, 363–364
  deciding against, 164
  description of, 178
  designing, 171
  dividing, 182–183
  vs. frames, 268, 289
  frames in, 172–173, 174–175
  headers for, 186–193, 199, 200
  long, 199–201, 236
  losing data from, 177
  margins of, 181, 182
  new codes for, 199–201
  as objects, 180
  page breaks and, 234, 235, 236
  readability of, 188, 191, 479
  rows and columns in, 170–171
  rules in, 172, 173–175
  scrolling of long, 199–201
  summaries of, 178
  tags for, 171
  text alignment in, 183–186
  text/data in, 186–193

  text outside, 180–181
  white space in, 179, 181–183, 193 (*See also* Borders, for
    tables)
Tabs
  in boxes, 226, 227
  pre and, 132
  for readability, 100
  white space and, 2
Tag-level class, 214–215
Tagged Image File Format
  (TIFF), 140
Tags, 12. *See also* Containers
  closing/ending, 14, 28, 37, 40, 42
  creating new, 355–363
  deprecated, 13, 15, 31, 132–133
  DTDs and, 22
  editing, 42
  empty (*See* Empty tags)
  meta- (*See* Metatags)
  nested (*See* Nesting)
  obsolete, 13, 15
  older, 15
  starting, 14, 28
  in XHTML Structure module, 36
Tail (of link), 59
target
  base and, 355
  forms and, 305
  frames and, 279, 283–284, 355
Targets, 59, 62–63, 219
  default, 285
  frames and, 283–284, 285
  image maps and, 413
  intrapage, 68–70, 71, 73–74, 217
  intrasystem, 73–74
  IP address vs. domain name
    for, 67
  reserve names for, 285–287
  in rollover, 405
  special, 285–287
  status bar and, 391
  style guidelines regarding, 481
tbody. *See* Table body (**tbody**)
Tcl, 373
TCP/IP. *See* Transmission
  Control Protocol/Internet
  Protocol (TCP/IP)
td. *See* Table data (**td**)
Technical terminology, 258
Telenet, 10, 492
Telenor, 9
Telephone-based Web
  browsing, 471
Teletype machine, 120
teletype (**tt**), 121
Template, 28–31, 289, 291
Tenor, 260
TEOMA, 25, 457
Testing
  of aural styles, 471
  CGI scripts for, 303
  client-side image maps and, 411

of cookies, 427
for degrading, 479
disabled for, 325
JavaScript and, 381–383, 391
of links, 21, 66, 67, 72, 476
by printing, 481
server-side image maps and, 410
Text
clear, 492
color of background with, 45–48, 49, 177–178, 421, 424, 477
default, in forms, 326
default color for, 48
DOS, 16
emphasized (*See* Fonts; Logical styles)
fonts for (*See* Fonts)
formatting of (*See* Formatting; Style sheets)
glyphs in, 110, 128
inside tables, 183–186, 186–193
justifying, 115
line breaks in (*See* Line break [**br**]; No line break [**nobr**])
in list items, 88
lists of plain, 82, 83–84
manipulation of, 219–221
multiline, 325–327
optional, in forms, 325–327
outside tables, 180–181
plain, 82, 83–84, 130, 456–457
for printer-friendly pages, 236
special characters in, 128–130
styles for quotations in, 125–126
with SVG images, 139
for when image unavailable, 146, 147, 161
text, 48
text-align, 115, 219, 220
text-decoration, 219, 220
Text-entry fields/boxes, 298, 309–312. *See also* Boxes
for changing background color, 421
color of, 307
default value for, 311–312
multiline, 325–327
optional text string for, 325–327
size of, 310–311
text-indent, 219, 220
Text module, 127–128
Text-only documents, 456–457
on Archie, 499
Web sites for, 472
Text-only/nongraphical browsers, 5, 8–9, 164, 476. *See also* Lynx
alt and, 144, 146, 147, 481–482
aural presentations on, 470–471
forms and, 307, 324, 335

image links and, 161
image maps and, 411, 417
previewing documents in, 17
title and, 307
text-shadow, 220
Text strings
concatenation (combination) of, 383, 396
XML and, 439
Text-to-HTML converter, 18, 20, 23, 470
text-transform, 220
textarea, 325–327
tfoot. *See* Table footer (**tfoot**)
th. *See* Table header (**th**)
thead, 199, 200
3Com, 500
Thumbnail images, 143, 148, 149, 476
".tif," 140
".tiff," 140
TIFF. *See* Tagged Image File Format (TIFF)
Tilde, 63
Time, 214, 250
audio and, 259
datetime and, 127
refreshing and, 360
"wait," 420
Time zone designator (TZD), 127
title, 32–33, 482
abbr and, 124
acronym and, 124
alt vs., 414
area and, 415
DTD and, 440
forms and, 307, 309, 310
frames and, 280–281
image maps and, 414
map and, 413–414
results of missing, 36
Titles
examples of good vs. bad, 33
headings vs., 33
style guidelines for, 479
TOC. *See* Table of contents (TOC)
Toggles, 44, 330
defer and, 378
ftp commands for, 486
Tomlinson, Ray, 498
Tool chain, 444
Tool tip message, 281, 307, 309–310, 482
Toolbars, 395
top, 152, 195, 226, 230–232
for table text, 184–185, 199
_top, 287
tr, 183, 184–186
Training, online, 464–465
Transitional DTC, 31
Translation systems, 124
Transmission Control Protocol/Internet Protocol (TCP/IP), 492, 498, 499, 500
transparent, 228, 230

Transparent border, 180, 225, 228, 230
Transparent GIF, 138
Travel advisories, 215–219
tt, 121
tty, 233
Tucows—The Ultimate Collection of Windows Software, 24
tv, 233
type, 245, 246
in forms, 309–310, 312–321, 324
JavaScript and, **377**
for list bullets, 93–94
in lists, 84, 85, 86, 87, 88–90
script and, 377
style sheets and, 113, 212
Type-valid, 439, 443
Typeface, 110. *See also* Fonts
cursive, 111, 114, 116
face and, 132, 133
fantasy, 111, 114, 116
font and, 132–133
monospace, 116
serif vs. sans serif, 111, 117
size of, 110, 111, 117–118, 120–121, 132
TZD. *See* Time zone designator (TZD)

u

u, 121
ul. *See* Unordered lists (**ul**)
Underline (**u**), 121
Underlined words, 2, 59, 71, 127, 163
Underscore, 285–287, 309
UNET, 500
Unicode, 129
Uniform Resource Identifier (URI), 15
Uniform Resource Locator (URL), 9–12
absolute vs. relative paths in, 63–66, 354–355, 362
audio and, 259
avoiding line break in, 164
background and, 45, 47–48, 222, 223
base and, 33, 354–355
CGI scripts and, 301, 302, 339, 347, 351
domain of, 11–12
examples of intersystem, 67
form of, 9
frames and, 269
href and, 61, 62, 66
in image links, 161–162
image maps and, 413, 415–416
intrapage targets and, 68, 71
JavaScript and, 377, 389, 397–398
links and, 62

notification of change of, 360–361
param and, 250, 251
path and filename in, 12
profile and, 32
protocol of, 10
in quotations, 126, 127
refreshing and, 359, 360, 362
server-side image maps and, 410
style guidelines regarding, 481
target (*See* Targets)
URI vs., 15
wireless data and, 467–468
United States Department of Defense, 500
United States Supreme Court, 357
University College London, 498
University of California, 498
University of Minnesota, 499
University of Sussex, 498
University of Utah, 498
University of Virginia's Electronic Text Center, 2, 5, 10, 457, 472
University of Wisconsin, 500
Unix, 326, 499
  audio plug-in for, 254
  Berkeley, 500
  CGI scripts on, 302, 353
  DocBook and, 442
  ftp and, 485, 495
  GUI of, 501
  and Internet history, 499, 500
  Lynx and, 8
  path names and, 63, 64
  scripts in, 374
  UNET and, 500
  uppercase *vs.* lowercase and, 63, 309
  vi editor of, 16
  videos and, 262
  vs. Windows, 495
Unix to Unix CoPy (UUCP), 485, 499
Unloading, 35
Unordered lists (**ul**), 82, 92–96
  bullets for, 92–94, 97, 113, 160–161
  directories replaced by, 103–104
  menus replaced by, 103–104
  nesting, 97–99
  within ordered lists, 96–99
  style sheets and, 113
Updating, 460
  with CGI, 347–348
  datetime for, 127
  del and, 126–127
  expires and, 357
  external style sheets and, 208
  of images, 146
  ins and, 126–127
  of logos, 146
  page footer and, 75
  refresh and, 358

server-side includes and, 77
style guidelines regarding, 476, 478, 481
Uploading, 485
URI. *See* Uniform Resource Identifier (URI)
URL. *See* Uniform Resource Locator (URL)
usemap, 411–413
USENET, 10, 499
"User agents," 15, 402
User ID, 487, 489. *See also* Login ID
User preferences, 421, 424, 428. *See also* Cookies
Username, telnet and, 10
Users
  communication from, 478
  complaints by, 482
  with limited mobility, 335
UTC. *See* Coordinated universal time (UTC)
Utilities, 252, 253, 263, 300
UUCP. *See* Unix to Unix CoPy (UUCP)
UUdecode, 499
UUencode, 499

V

Valid documents, 439, 443
Validation, 307, 311
  parsing and, 443
  recommended package for, 482
  XHTML and, 439
Validators, 357
  form and, 421, 423
  keywords and, 362
  parsers that are, 443
  recommended, 482
valign, 184–185, 188, 199
value
  for checkboxes, 314
  in forms, 308, 311–312, 314–321, 330–333
  in lists, 89–90
  with **param,** 250–251
  for radio buttons, 316
  for reset button, 319–320
  select and, 330
  for submit button, 320–321
Value checking, 307
Values, 379. *See also* Variables
  of cookies, 430–431
  in well-formed documents, 439
valuetype, 251
var, 122, 124, 128
Variable names, 250–251. *See also* Names
  defined, 379
  forms and, 299, 302, 308–309
  global, 423, 430
  meaningful, 308
  multiword, 309
Variable values (**var**), 122, 124

Variables
  defined, 379
  global, 423, 430
  local vs. global, 430
  subscripted, 403–405
Vector graphics, 139
version, 31
vertical-align, 219, 220
Vertical alignment, 146, 152–153
Vertical bar, 64
Vertical margins, 158
Vertical positioning, 223–224
Vertical table layout, 187, 188, 189
VfW. *See* Video for Windows (VfW)
vi editor, 16
Video for Windows (VfW), 263
Video games, 243, 244
Videos, 5, 261–263
  with applets, 243
  with audio, 256, 261, 262
  AVI, 263
  best-quality, 262
  links and, 56
  for manuals, 463
  MPEG, 256, 262
  QuickTime, 262
  sharing, 261
  standby and, 247
  streaming audio and, 262, 263
  wireless devices and, 466
View Code, 479
View menu options, 6
View Source, frames and, 269, 270
Virtual reality, 449
visibility, 226
visible, 226
Visual Basic, 33, 373
vlink, 48–49, 224, 476
  JavaScript and, 389, 421
".voc," 256
Voice families, 258, 471
voice-family, 260
Voices, 9, 254
  design and, 257
  and telephone-based browsing, 471
VoiceXML, 466, 468
void, 174
volume, 258, 260
vsides, 174
vspace, 158, 159

W

WAE. *See* Wireless application environment (WAE)
"Wait time," 420, 476
Wallpaper, 140
Walsh, Norman, 442
WANs. *See* Wide area networks (WANs)

WAP. *See* Wireless application protocol (WAP)
".wav," 255, 257
WAVany, 254
WAVE. *See* Resource Interchange File Format Waveform (RIFF WAVE)
W³C validator, 24
Web. *See* World Wide Web
Web administrator. *See* System/Web administrator
Web master, 16
Web pages. *See also* Pages
 creating (example of), 27–53
 elements of, 28–42, 128 (*See also* Elements)
 embedding HTML documents into other, 246–247
 frames for (*See* Frames)
 misconceptions about, 456
 moving around in, 56–58 (*See also* Navigation/moving)
 "one-shot," 23
 printer-friendly, 236, 469, 481
 searching for (*See* Search engines; Search sites)
 static, 55
 storyboards for, 56–58, 468, 469
 style manual for (*See* Style manual)
 testing links on, 21, 66, 67, 72, 476
 text-only, 456–469
 Web sites vs., 468–469
 XHTML Structure module for, 36
Web Publisher, 470
Web sites
 corporate, 201
 defined, 8
 designs for, 56–58, 201
 list of, 22–25
 notification of change in, 360–361
 searching for (*See* Search engines; Search sites)
 Web pages vs., 468–469
Web utilities, 252, 253, 263
Weblint validator, 21, 24
Well-formed documents, 438–439
White space
 browser display and, 2, 38, 41
 coding for margins of, 158–159
 in good design, 50
 paragraphs and, 40–41
 for readability, 100, 479
 in tables, 179, 181–183, 193 (*See also* Borders, for tables)
white-space, 226, 227–228
Wide area networks (WANs), 500
widow, 234
Widows, 234, 235–236
width

with applets, 243
 in boxes, 225, 228–230
 in forms, 321
 with frames, 287–289
 horizontal rule and, 44
 of images, 148–150
 object and, 246
 pre and, 131
 style guidelines regarding, 481
 with tables, 176–177, 191–192, 196, 198–199
Winamp plug-in, 254
Window object, 384, 385, 391–398
 closing, 396, 401
 dialog boxes and, 392–394
 existing vs. new, 391
 minimizing, 396
 new, 394, 395–398
 resizing, 396
window-target, 357
Windows. *See also* Window object
 access key in, 335
 audio files for, 255
 CuteFTP and, 489
 Mosaic and, 501
 path names in, 63, 64
 Perl for, 304
 vs. Unix, 495
 video files for, 263
 video plug-in for, 262
Windows Notepad, 16, 17
Windows XP, 309
WinHelp, 463
WinMX, 261
Wireless application environment (WAE), 466
Wireless application protocol (WAP), 466, 467–468
Wireless data, 467–468
Wireless devices, 465–468
 in Europe, 467
 HTML and, 466
 in Japan, 467
 knowledge advantage of, 467
 online manuals for, 463
 text-only documents and, 456
 videos for, 262
 XHTML and, 15, 466
 XML and, 466
Wireless Markup Language (WML), 466, 468
Wireless session protocol (WSP), 466
WML. *See* Wireless Markup Language (WML)
Word (Microsoft), 23, 449, 470
Word processing
 converting from, 470
 embedded codes in, 16
 HTML documents and, 16, 17, 18, 20, 23 (*See also* HTML editors)
word-spacing, 220

WordPerfect, 23, 470
Wordwrap, 327
Workaround, 389
Working draft (for W³C), 14
World Wide Web. *See also entries beginning* Web; Internet
 censorship on, 357
 education on, 464–465
 hyper documents and, 2
 images and, 137, 138
 international standards for, 14–16
 Internet history and, 497, 501
 Internet traffic and, 501
 pages on (*See* Documents; Pages; Web pages)
 private intranets vs., 456
 ratings scale for, 357
 searching (*See* Search engines; Search sites)
 as term, 501
 URLs and, 9 (*See also* Uniform Resource Locator [URL])
World Wide Web Consortium (W³C), 14–16, 25, 440
 char and, 185
 charoff and, 186
 DOCTYPE and, 31
 founding of, 501
 HTML validator from, 21, 24
 style sheets recommended by, 208 (*See also* Cascading style sheet [CSS])
 wireless devices and, 466
 XHTML and, 443
 XML and, 18, 22, 438, 442
wrap, 327
WSP. *See* Wireless session protocol (WSP)
WYSIWYG, 19, 416

X

x-high, 259
x-loud, 258, 260
x-low, 259
x-soft, 258, 260
X-windows, 501
Xanim, 262
Xbase, 444
XHTML. *See* Extensible HyperText Markup Language (XHTML)
XHTML modules
 Base, 355
 Client-side Image Map, 411
 Edit, 127
 Form, 336
 Hypertext, 59
 Image, 144
 Image Map, 411
 Link, 212
 List, 103

Metainformation, 356
Object, 252
Presentation, 122
Structure, 36
Style Attribute, 208
Table, 201
Text, 127–128
XHTMLMP. *See* Extensible
  HyperText Markup Language
  Mobile Profile (XHTMLMP)
Xinclude, 444
XLAN XT, 444
Xlink, 443, 444
XmetaL, 24
XML. *See* Extensible Markup
  Language (XML)
XML/EDI model, 441
XML editors, 18, 22
  sites for downloading, 24

XML Pro, 24
XML Schema, 449
XML Spy, 24
XML/XSLT, 445
Xpath, 443, 444
XPointer, 443, 444
Xquery, 444
XSL. *See* Extensible-style
  language (XSL)
XSL-FO, DTD and, 444
XSLT. *See* Extensible Stylesheet
  Language Transformer
  (XSLT)
XSLTproc, 444, 445–448, 449
XWML. *See* Extended Wireless
  Markup Language (XWML)
X,Y coordinates, 323, 324, 410,
  411–413

coords for, 415
server-side image maps
  and, 410
software packages and,
  416, 417

y

Yahoo, 25

z

ZDNet, 24
Ziff Davis Shareware
  Download, 24